"Elisabeth Griffith's *Formidable* is an essential history of the 100-year struggle between 1920 and 2020 by both Black and white women in America to achieve their equal rights. Griffith surveys the successes and setbacks that remained relevant and pressing across the century: voting rights, racial violence, health care, reproductive rights, working conditions, education, race and gender discrimination, electoral office. Through her comprehensive survey of the people, events and movements that marked this history, she highlights the women, and men, who were both pushing for change and those who resisted it. The final outcome of that struggle is not yet decided."

—Hillary Rodham Clinton, U.S. Senator,
Secretary of State, Presidential candidate

"In her new book *Formidable*, Elisabeth Griffith does a remarkable job bringing to life 'Act II' of American women's struggle for equal rights. And what an intriguing cast she pulls together to bring these stories to life. In the century following the passage of the Nineteenth Amendment, which expanded but did not complete the struggle, Dr. Griffith introduces us to American women of all racial, class and sexual identities who danced, frolicked, argued and trudged across the country in an intriguing, often-bitter, sometimes joyful, and never-ending parade. You'll read their stories and weep, gasp, applaud, and shout out 'right on, sisters!'"

—Adele Logan Alexander, PhD, author of *Princess of the Hither*
***Isles: A Black Suffragist's Story from the Jim Crow South* and other**
works of African American and women's history

"Just as fascinating as the struggle for women to vote is the fresh new focus on what the ensuing one hundred years has brought. Griffith's compelling narrative casts new light on victories but also persistent fault lines in the quest for equality across the social landscape. The portraits in *Formidable* pave the way for the inspiring work going forward. Based on her important scholarship of the last century, historian Elisabeth Griffith brings a fresh focus to what American women have done in the one hundred years since the Nineteenth Amendment passed. *Formidable* is a vibrant journey that leads authoritatively toward the challenges that still slow the road to equality."

—Ann Compton, ABC News White House
correspondent covering seven presidents

"Elisabeth Griffith is a consummate storyteller, combining research and riveting narrative to keep alive the political and social struggle for equal rights by American women front and center. Readers will be caught up in the heroism and resilience of this diverse cast of characters. Elisabeth magnificently covered the early campaign for suffrage, from Seneca Falls to 1920, in her first book, which helped to make our film about Elizabeth Cady Stanton and Susan B. Anthony—*Not for Ourselves Alone*. Now she carries that story forward to 2020, as Black and white women confront yet another set of obstacles and objectives."

—Ken Burns, documentary filmmaker

"Social change is slow and stumbling. For women, especially women of color, it's been a struggle to reach political equality. *Formidable* tells about those struggles—the players, the losses and the wins—that lead us to today. For those of us who demand political equality, it's important to understand where we've come from to appreciate where we're going. No defeat need be permanent. No victory is final. But change will come."

—Ellen Malcom, founder of EMILY's List

"Elisabeth Griffith offers an unprecedented survey of the women's suffrage movement that masterfully intertwines two parallel crusades for justice, those of Black and white women. Beginning with the certification of the Nineteenth Amendment and concluding with the 2020 presidential election, *Formidable* explains the complexities, nuances, and challenges of the fight for women's equality over the last century. Weaving together the separate and sometimes competing aspirations of Black and white women, Griffith provides the missing link in a crucial story of women's rights in contemporary America. Finally, we have one book that brings together American women in their many dimensions and complexities in one informative and compelling narrative."

—Lissa Muscatine, co-owner of Politics & Prose Bookstore, former chief speechwriter to Hillary Rodham Clinton

"As the author of *Freedom's Daughters*, the first history of women in the U.S. civil rights movement, I'm delighted to endorse Elisabeth Griffith's illuminating new examination of the seminal roles that Black women and white women have played in this country's never-ending struggles for equal rights. As Griffith notes, much has been written about the separate movements for women's equality and Black equality. But the interconnections between the two—and the complicated, often tortured relationships between the Black and white women involved in these battles—are topics that have not received the attention they deserve. The same is true of the close ties between misogyny and racism, meant to repress both women and Black people in defense of white male prerogatives—a particularly timely subject today."

—Lynne Olson, *New York Times* bestselling author of eight works of history, including *Freedom's Daughters: The Unsung Heroines of the Civil Rights Movement from 1830 to 1970*

"Taking the Nineteenth Amendment as a starting point instead of a finish line, *Formidable* explores the first hundred years of the struggle to complete the unfinished business of women's suffrage: women's equality. A keen and witty observer of American history and politics, Griffith seamlessly weaves together diverse stories of women both familiar and unheralded, and takes an unflinching look at the role of race, class, and religion. Epic in its scope and detail, *Formidable* tells the vital story of the last century of women's activism in all its messy, imperfect glory."

—**Rebecca Roberts, author of *The Suffragist Playbook:**
Your Guide to Changing the World

"In *Formidable*, Elisabeth Griffith offers a fascinating and necessary supplement to the standard history of the American Century—a narrow narrative usually centered solely upon on the actions of men. *Formidable* is the story of American women's political life—and strife—in the century following the adoption of the Nineteenth Amendment in 1920, giving us a panoramic view of women's role in the causes and conflicts of the twentieth and early twenty-first centuries. This colorful, character-driven tale features an extraordinary cast of women leaders and activists—some famous, some who need to be better known—working towards equality and empowerment, and promises to expand our understanding of not only history, but also the issues and forces confronting women today."

—**Elaine Weiss, author of *The Woman's Hour:**
The Great Fight to Win the Vote

"If there were ever a moment to look at where American women are, the hurdles we still face, and where American women have been, the challenges we've overcome, this moment of reckoning is it. In the aftermath of 'Me Too,' Breonna Taylor and the election of Vice President Kamala Harris, there is an urgent need to examine how we got here. Who were the women and what were the forces that brought us to this day? No one is better qualified than Elisabeth Griffith, expert and author of women's history, educator, and a political activist herself, to chronicle the fits and starts, the highs and lows, that led American women—all American women—to where we find ourselves in 2021. Her book is a gift to all of us who lived through any part of the past century or who want to understand it."

—**Judy Woodruff, anchor and managing editor,**
The PBS NewsHour

ALSO BY ELISABETH GRIFFITH

In Her Own Right: The Life of Elizabeth Cady Stanton
(Oxford, 1984)

FORMIDABLE

AMERICAN WOMEN AND
THE FIGHT FOR EQUALITY:
1920–2020

ELISABETH GRIFFITH

PEGASUS BOOKS
NEW YORK LONDON

FORMIDABLE

Pegasus Books, Ltd.
148 West 37th Street, 13th Floor
New York, NY 10018

Copyright © 2022 by Elisabeth Griffith

First Pegasus Books cloth edition August 2022

Interior design by Maria Fernandez

Library of Congress Cataloging-in-Publication Data is available.

ISBN: 978-1-63936-189-2

10 9 8 7 6 5 4 3 2 1

Printed in the United States of America
Distributed by Simon & Schuster
www.pegasusbooks.com

For all my teachers and students,
from whom I am still learning.

CONTENTS

Any great change must expect opposition, because
it shakes the very foundation of privilege.
—Lucretia Coffin Mott

———————————

We shall not be divided or defeated again.
—Coretta Scott King

———————————

You will not always be able to solve all of the world's problems
at once, but don't ever underestimate the importance you
can have, because history has shown us that courage can
be contagious and hope can take on a life of its own.
—Michelle Obama

———————————

We are in a time of both great peril and inspiration. If. We.
Organize! When we organize, we can change the world.
—Heather Booth

———————————

For all its excesses, feminism has been the most important
and the most salutary change in our lifetimes.
—David Brooks

———————————

Real change, enduring change, happens one step at a time.
—Ruth Bader Ginsburg

———————————

But while democracy can be periodically delayed
It can never be permanently defeated . . .
If only we are brave enough.
—Amanda Gorman

STORY LINES

There has always been more than one American story. The most popular account was about conquering a continent and creating a country, about democracy and manifest destiny. It was filled with explorers, exploiters, frontiersmen, military leaders, statesmen, inventors, and entrepreneurs. The story was revered, written down, and widely taught, but it wasn't the whole story.

Over time, the American story became more inclusive and accurate as more perspectives were included and more primary sources were uncovered. Some accounts had been lost with their original languages. Some narrators were purposely ignored or silenced, never taught to read or write. Others were too poor or overworked to leave a record. Some stories were never retold because no one valued the lives they recalled. If those stories were preserved, they ended up in attics rather than archives. Some women's lives were reduced to artifacts found by archeologists: needles, cooking pots, earrings, and children's toys.

Abigail Adams was an educated, prosperous wife, with a frequently absent husband. Had he not been notable, we might not have had her correspondence as a way to "remember the ladies," as she admonished her declaration-drafting spouse. We know, for example, that Abigail disapproved of Thomas Jefferson's relationship with Sally Hemings, who was both his enslaved concubine and his late wife's half-sister. We will never know what Sally thought. Her name appears only in a property inventory at Monticello.[1]

To recover lost Black voices, Carter Woodson's *Journal of Negro History* published articles about slavery in 1916 and professors from Fisk University collected stories from its survivors. Woodson established "Negro History Week" in 1926. Under the New Deal, the Federal Writers' Project hired unemployed white writers to conduct two thousand interviews of people who had been enslaved. The result reflected the bias of the practitioners, who transcribed the stories using an exaggerated "Negro dialect."[2]

American history was rewritten by veterans of World War II, who benefited from the Servicemen's Readjustment Act of 1944, known as the GI Bill. Passed by one vote, it covered tuition and books for college and graduate school. Frequently the first in their families to earn degrees, veterans filled campuses. These "social historians" wrote about soldiers, immigrants, factory workers, and farmers, still mostly men, but incorporated more ethnic and religious variation. Pollsters analyzed cohorts of voters. The civil rights movement increased attention to the history of slavery, reconstruction, Jim Crow laws, and racism. Eventually, we learned about Indigenous tribes as well as cowboys, and that some cowboys had been Black cavalrymen, known as Buffalo soldiers.

During the Vietnam War, when draft boards denied academic defer-ments, graduate programs admitted more women. If they pursued women's history, topics were at first limited by scarce or flawed sources, like the selective six-volume *History of Suffrage*, which omitted rivals and critics. They studied colonial midwives, Black and white female abolitionists, women on the frontier, female shoemakers in Philadelphia, and settle-ment house workers. They wrote biographies of women who did leave their mark, and their papers. As practitioners became more diverse, so did their topics. Historians of women learned how different the lives of women were. Women had been oppressors, progressives, enslaved, activists, adversaries, and allies. As women's history pioneer Gerda Lerner concluded, the majority finally found its past.[3]

This book recounts what American women did after the Nineteenth Amendment passed. It focuses on how white and Black women slowly accrued and used political power. Their struggles for equal rights had long been interwoven. White women had been complicit in slavery. Others had fought for emancipation. The abolition movement of the 1830s inspired the women's rights movement of the 1840s. The suffrage campaign engaged and excluded Black activists. The civil rights movement of the 1950s inspired the women's movement of the 1960s. Black and white women adapted each other's tactics: educating, organizing, demonstrating, boycotting, sitting in, filling jails, and keeping on. However disparate, the equal rights and civil rights movements were both part of the unfinished fight for "liberty and justice for all."

Women are a complex cohort. They differ by race, ethnicity, class, geography, religion, education, occupation, generation, marital and maternal status, sexual orientation, ability, politics, and experience. It's a risk to categorize or generalize because real people have multiple and individual identities. In addition to the diversity of its subjects and the scarcity of some sources, timelines and nomenclature present challenges for historians of women.

Fifty years ago, when women's history was struggling for legitimacy in academia, feminists divided American history into "blue" and "pink" timelines. Conference panels debated whether Zachary Taylor's presidency was more relevant to women's lives than the invention of the tin can or whether Jacksonian democracy deserved a chapter when the suffrage campaign did not. The standard "blue" timeline organized every textbook, defined by politics and economics: the colonial, revolutionary, federal, Jacksonian, etc. etc. eras.

Everyone experienced the events on that timeline, but differently, depending on their circumstances. For example, wars were deadly for men, but offered women wider job opportunities. A Black history timeline might begin with Juan Garrido, a free African and veteran conquistador who accompanied Ponce de Leon and Cortes before 1520.[4] It continues to 1619 and beyond, to emancipation, Tulsa, *Brown*, the election of Barack

Obama, and the murder of George Floyd. Milestones for women, on a "pink" timeline, included the invention of rubber nursing nipples and sewing machines, access to education and birth control, the Nineteen Amendment, Title VII, Title IX, and *Roe v. Wade*. I have used some of those "pink" events to divide chapters in this book. The goal is a multiracial, inclusive chronology.

Nomenclature, the words we use to name and describe people, is an essential tool. One example in women's history is the definition of working. All women work, but working commonly refers to paid labor, which has a cash value greater than how we value domestic or caregiving responsibilities. Similarly, power has traditionally been measured by physical strength, wealth, and political authority. By those terms, women have historically been powerless. Their influence, if any, relied on male relatives, the myth of motherhood, moral authority, and their race.

"Say Her Name!" was a demand by Black activists, that we acknowledge the Black women, as well as the men, who were victims of police violence. Historians of women want women to be visible, remembered, incorporated into the canon, and included in the curriculum. Women's changing names present a problem which biographers of men do not have to address. George Washington advanced from young George to Lieutenant Washington, to General and Mr. President. In comparison, his wife was born Martha Dandridge, took her first husband's name, became the Widow Custis, and then the General's Lady. After her husband's election, she was frequently called Lady Washington. When the term "First Lady" appeared in 1838, it referred to Martha Washington.[5]

I've named as many women as possible, both major and minor characters, to put them in the story. I use their full names, their name at birth, and their married names, if any: Martha Dandridge Custis Washington. My use of first names alone is not intended to be disrespectful or dismissive; it acknowledges the public recognition of Abigail, Eleanor, Betty, Gloria, Phyllis, Oprah, Anita, Hillary, and Kamala. Icons like RBG need only initials.

In other word choices, I have followed style guides and common practice: male, female, cisgender, gay, lesbian, transgender, and female-identifying.

For simplicity, the initials LGBTQ are intended to include LGBTQIA (lesbian, gay, bisexual, transgender, queer/questioning, intersexual, asexual) or LGBTQ+. In common usage, Asian American, referring to the fastest growing demographic group in the US, replaced Oriental years ago, but it lingered in federal law. In 2016, President Obama signed legislation to change "Negroes, Spanish-speaking, Orientals, Indians, Eskimos, and Aleuts" to "Asian American, Native Hawaiian, Pacific Islanders, African American, Hispanic, Native American, or Alaska Natives."[6] The use of Hispanic (referring to natives or descendants of Spanish-speaking countries), Chicana (a native of Mexico or a descendant living in the US), Latina (coming from a Latin American country), and Latinx (a gender-neutral term for a Latina/Latino) is individual and regional in the US.[7] Native American and Indigenous are capitalized and Black is used only as an adjective, because a person is not a color.

Following the *New York Times*, I haven't capitalized white or brown; the *Washington Post* capitalizes White and puts "Brown" in quotation marks.[8] I avoid "minority" because our country is too diverse to identify a numerical majority, other than women. "People of color" seems problematic. What makes a person "of color" is reminiscent of the racist "one drop" rule. To the discomfort of some, our national DNA increasingly mixes racial and ethnic markers. Harvard historian Henry Louis Gates Jr. states that average African Americans are 24% European, the result of centuries of sexual exploitation and complicated interracial relationships. No matter what they were called, there is no question that those Negros, African Americans, Black, brown, and people of color have been treated differently than the white population.

The history of Black ethnonyms tracks our American experience. The first enslaved people were called negro by their captors, reducing them to a color, the Spanish word for black. In response to the birth of Afro-European children, Virginia passed legislation in the 1620s redefining negro not as skin color but as ancestry. Those children were the property of their white fathers, but inherited their mothers' enslaved status, a radical departure from the common law. In 1787, founders of the Free African

Society, which established the African Methodist Episcopal (AME) Church, used African to acknowledge their heritage.

A century later, in 1887, the Afro-American League added a hyphen. Beginning in 1899, W. E. B. Du Bois campaigned to capitalize Negro: "I believe that eight million Americans are entitled to a capital letter." In 1930, the *New York Times* agreed. Du Bois was among the founders of the National Association for the Advancement of Colored People in 1909. "Colored" included people of mixed heritage and distanced Black people from negative stereotypes then associated with Africans. In the 1960s, "Black Pride" and "Black Power" were embraced as less subservient than Negro. As an alternative, Jesse Jackson proposed African-American, in 1988, to "put us in our proper historical context." He believed Black reduced the complexity of a race to skin pigment. The US Census added African American as an option in 2000. Today, Black, capitalized, as an adjective, is the norm to describe both lives and culture.[9]

I don't use slave as a noun; a person is not born a slave, a person has been enslaved. Readers will note my avoidance of "pro-life"; anti-abortion seems more accurate. I'm uncomfortable with "illegitimate" and "alien." I've used the spelling of antisemitism recommended by the International Holocaust Remembrance Alliance, without a hyphen or a capital S, and plural pronouns for transgender people.[10] My goal is to be linguistically correct and historically accurate. I don't describe Pauli Murray as they/them, because those terms were not used when she was alive.[11]

Because I'm writing American history about Black and white women, racism is part of this story. It cannot be whitewashed or deleted. Slavery sanctioned the violent sexual assault of Black women by white men, from slave ship crews to plantation owners, who enslaved and sold their Black children. Slave labor contributed enormously to the country's economic growth. Race, racism, and racial violence are part of our shared past, not theories or un-American propaganda. Because these topics make some people anxious, ashamed, or angry, writing about them can be fraught with peril. In June 2021, President Biden went to Tulsa to mark the centennial of the 1921 massacre of a prosperous Black community by a white mob, an event still not included in textbooks. "We should know the good, the bad, everything," he declared. "That's what great nations do. They come to terms with their dark sides. And we are a great nation."[12] We need to be mature enough to both confront and celebrate our history. Historians have a responsibility to be truthful witnesses and accurate recorders.

Part of my research for this book was a road trip to visit the sites of major events in the fight for civil rights, where students were tortured while sitting at lunch counters, where occupied buses and churches were bombed, where white mobs spat on school children, where activists were beaten, attacked by dogs, fire-hosed, and murdered. I came away horrified by so many examples of terror and trauma and in awe of the resilience and courage of those change agents. I feel equal admiration for the suffragists who endured prison and force-feeding.

This book recalls decades of tension between Black and white women, and the distrust caused by white racism. Given the ferocity of the current debate over how our nation addresses its past and present, there are critics who will charge me with appropriation, or misappropriation. My response is that we study history to learn, to be inspired, and perhaps chastised. Learning is our responsibility. Too many of us know too little about America's past. I'm a white, cisgender, feminist historian, writing about women who may or may not look like me. I have a doctorate in history, and I'm still learning. I'm also an optimist. I believe political and personal change is possible, as the past century demonstrates.

A final observation about writing women's history, or any history, has to do with our perspective on the past. Genocide was an unconscionable war crime. Slavery was evil. Internment was immoral. There are no excuses. Yet I'm uncomfortable with righteous judgments from later generations. We can condemn past actors and still consider their historical context. There have been eras in our history when religious leaders condoned burning women and enslaving people. We need to think historically and fact check. Rushing to judgment recently led the University of Wisconsin to remove alumnus and actor Fredric March's name from theaters on two campuses, over the objections of the NAACP, based on "social media rumor and grievously fact-free, mistaken conclusions."[13]

I believe in examining the context and allowing for nuance. People make mistakes, or huge errors in judgment, based on their experience, environment, and era. Individuals are more than one action or one choice. We can be honest about their failures and contradictions and still acknowledge their contributions. Some are deeply evil; others redeem themselves. Human beings are flawed. So is this author. In this chronicle of American women fighting for equal rights, I have aspired to be factual, inclusive, and respectful, telling a story worthy of its subjects.

CHAPTER ONE

"NOW WE CAN BEGIN"

S usan B. Anthony called the campaign to secure voting rights for American women "the long, hard fight." She died in 1906 and did not live to see the Anthony Amendment become the Nineteenth Amendment in 1920. After it passed, Carrie Chapman Catt, Anthony's anointed successor, recalled decades of state referendum campaigns, constitutional conventions, party platform fights, and congressional inaction. "It was a continuous, seemingly endless, chain of activity. Young suffragists who helped forge the links of that chain were not born when it began. Old suffragists who forged the first links were dead when it ended."[1] The amendment passed seventy-two years after the first formal women's rights convention in America, organized by Elizabeth Cady Stanton and Lucretia Mott in Seneca Falls, New York, in July 1848.

The drive for women's rights came from the abolition movement. Enslaved African Americans suffered, struggled, and sabotaged the system. A few other Americans sympathized and strategized to abolish it. White women were not exposed to the physical and sexual terror suffered by enslaved women, but their own physical vulnerability and legal subordination prompted comparisons. Male abolitionists, including Stanton's husband, a prominent anti-slavery agent, barred women from their organizations. Mott, a Quaker, founded the Philadelphia Female Anti-Slavery Society in 1833 with free Black women Sarah Mapps Douglass and Charlotte

Forten. Mott faced down mobs who burned her meeting house; she refused to use sugar or wear cotton. Stanton and Mott met at the 1840 World Anti-Slavery conference in London. Stanton had accompanied her husband; Mott was representing her organization but was not allowed to participate. The two friends vowed to organize a women's rights convention in America.

On the seventy-fifth anniversary of the Seneca Falls meeting, in July 1923, three years after the Nineteenth Amendment had passed, suffragist Alice Paul introduced the Lucretia Mott Amendment to ensure equal rights for women. A century later, the Equal Rights Amendment remained unratified. For many, the suffrage and ERA campaigns represent the first and second waves of the women's movement. In reality, there were many waves, shoals, breakers, and undertows. American women had long sought equal legal rights, education, and economic opportunities. White women wanted the same rights as white men. Black women wanted the same rights as white citizens; theirs was never a women-only movement. Civil rights advocates, social justice activists, and feminists pursued multiple goals, more often in competition than in coalition. Some ends could be achieved by legislative action, but actual equality for women and Black Americans proved elusive because racism and sexism were deeply entrenched.

VOTING RIGHTS FOR WOMEN

In 1848, Stanton demanded equal rights, suffrage, and personal autonomy for women. She did not specify which women, nor did she specifically include Black women. She drafted a Declaration of Rights and Sentiments, the same title as the 1833 charter of the American Anti-Slavery Society. She modeled hers on the Declaration of Independence. Her assertion, that "all men and women" were created equal, was shocking. Stanton called for the abolition of laws that "conflict, in any way, with the true and substantive happiness of women" or "place her in a position inferior to that of man."

One resolution encouraged women "to speak and teach in all religious assemblies." Another called for men to curtail "objections of indelicacy and impropriety . . . brought against woman when she addresses a public audience." Women who spoke in public meetings were deemed "promiscuous" if men were present. Yet, Stanton noted, men did not object to women performing on stage or at the circus. Stanton called for equal legal treatment and access to education, the "trades, professions and commerce." The document did not demand the abolition of slavery.[2]

"Resolved: That it is the duty of the women of this country to secure to themselves their sacred right to the elective franchise" was Stanton's most controversial proposal. Even with the endorsement of Frederick Douglass, the editor of Rochester's *North Star* newspaper, it was the only resolution that did not pass unanimously. The only African American present, Douglass had purchased his freedom. He was a compelling speaker and would become the most influential Black man in nineteenth century America. When news of the meeting sped across telegraph wires, editors and ministers condemned the idea of women voting as unseemly and outrageous.[3] Stanton's resolutions would become the agenda of the new women's movement.

On rare occasions, women had voted in America. Under British common law, property owners could vote, including the unusual circumstance of property-owning spinsters and widows. In 1648, Margaret Brent requested a vote in the Maryland provincial assembly. A single woman, she owned two thousand acres and acted as Lord Baltimore's attorney and executor. The governor refused, claiming the privilege was reserved for queens.[4] Lydia Chapin Taft, the widow of the highest taxpayer in Uxbridge, Massachusetts, was the first woman to cast a recorded vote in a 1756 town meeting.[5]

In 1776, New Jersey gave voting rights to all "inhabitants" with property worth fifty pounds. A 1797 statute explicitly referred to voters as "he or she." As one lawmaker reiterated, "Our Constitution gives this right to maids and widows, white and black." Scholars recently scoured surviving poll lists for women's names. In the state archives, they found 163 women voting in 1801. Only a few voters, all men, were identified as Negro. Charges of voter fraud, committed by men dressed as women, prompted the passage of a new law in 1807 explicitly limiting the franchise to white men and easing the property requirement.[6] In 1838, Kentucky allowed female heads of household to vote for school boards and bond issues.[7]

VOTING RIGHTS FOR BLACK AMERICANS

In the nineteenth century, white married women had no rights to their bodies, children, clothing, inherited property, or earnings. Enslaved Black women, considered property, had no rights at all and only limited means to resist. White women worked first for temperance to protect the vulnerable from drunken fathers and husbands. Privileged women like Stanton lobbied for married women's property rights and prioritized voting. Anthony campaigned for equal pay for teachers like herself. Factory women demanded shorter hours, higher pay, and safety measures. Some white women wanted to provide for widows and orphans, close brothels, and legalize divorce. Others proposed dress reform and modeled the "Turkish dress," trousers worn under shorter skirts, so women would not trip or catch fire.

Abolishing slavery was the most radical and urgent reform, attracting a liberal cohort of white and Black free men and women. Abolitionists preached against slavery, petitioned for emancipation, and helped the enslaved escape bondage. In 1865, this cohort cheered the passage of the Thirteenth Amendment ending slavery. The Fourteenth Amendment, making Black men citizens, was ratified in 1868. Some women objected to its definition of citizens as "male." Were women not citizens? Stanton abhorred that men had any rights women lacked:

> To have drunkards, idiots, horse-racing, rum-selling rowdies, ignorant foreigners, and silly boys fully recognized, while we ourselves are thrust out from all the rights that belong to citizens, it is too grossly insulting to the dignity of woman to be any longer submitted to.[8]

Abolitionists and suffragists had naively assumed that support for emancipation would be rewarded with universal suffrage for every adult. Only four Radical Republicans in Congress supported voting rights for any women, much less suffrage for Black women, European immigrants, Chinese laborers, or Native Americans.[9]

The Fifteenth Amendment stated that voting rights could not be denied to citizens, now specifically defined as male, on the basis of "race, color or previous condition of servitude." It enfranchised only Black men. Adding Black male voters but no women enraged Stanton. "Think of Patrick and Sambo and Hans and Yung Tung, who do not know the difference between a monarchy and a republic, [and have] never read the Declaration of Independence or Webster's Spelling Book, making laws." Anthony was less restrained, claiming she would "cut off this right arm of mine before I will ever work for or demand the ballot for [male] Negroes and not for women." Isolated in their outrage and intransigence, the duo offended former allies with their vehemently racial rhetoric. Tied to white extremists, they created a deep rift among reformers and between races. Former allies like Lucy Stone distanced themselves and later generations condemned them.[10]

Years later, in 1906, Black suffragist Mary Church Terrell expressed her disappointment in Anthony, but reminded her readers of the post-Civil War political climate. Republicans had rejected universal suffrage and betrayed all women:

> Having worked with such genuine, loving loyalty . . . to help free an oppressed race, it is no wonder that Miss Anthony was wounded to the heart's core, when men whom she had rendered such invaluable assistance in this cause, coolly advised her to wait . . . when she implored them to . . . secure justice and equality before the law for her own disenfranchised sex.[11]

Terrell saw Anthony as an occasional ally in enfranchising all women. Other Black women, like Adella Hunt Logan, distrusted her.

Liberal men believed that including any women would destroy the effort to enfranchise Black men. Douglass supported universal suffrage, but settled for half measures because the situation of Negro men was dire:

> When women, because they are women, are hunted down . . . dragged from their houses and hung upon lamp-posts; when their children are torn from their arms, and their brains dashed upon the pavement; when they are objects of insult and outrage at every turn; when they are in danger of having their homes burnt down over their heads, when their children are not allowed to enter schools; then [women] will have the urgency to obtain the ballot equal to our own.[12]

Stanton argued that he was ignoring the vulnerability of Black women: "Do you believe the African race is comprised entirely of males?"[13] Douglass responded, as white men would, that women had male relatives to protect and represent them. Black women themselves saw the amendment as a first step.

The fight over the Fifteenth Amendment caused a fundamental schism between Black and white activists, between rights for Blacks and rights for women.[14] Black women did not trust white women to protect their interests, but they did not allow racism to deter them. Speaking at the 1866 American Equal Rights Association meeting, African American author Frances Ellen Watkins Harper challenged attendees: "You white women speak here of rights. I speak of wrongs." After reciting a litany of the humiliations Black women faced, she concluded, "Are there no wrongs to be righted?" She called on suffragists to protect rights for Black Americans and to treat Black women as equals, rather than be "complicit in . . . oppression." Stanton omitted Harper's remarks from a record of the meeting.[15] African American distrust of white reformers was well deserved. Its current ran through the history of women's political action, a riptide of racism and white privilege.

In a profoundly segregated society, few white reformers acknowledged Black women as peers or saw their causes as complimentary. Anthony corresponded with Mary Church Terrell and Adella Hunt Logan, inviting them to attend suffrage meetings only when she did not expect Southern white women to attend. She remained embittered toward Douglass, while he and Stanton maintained friendly professional relations. Stanton defended Douglass's second marriage to a white woman, suffragist Helen Pitts, which caused a national outcry. Eventually reconciled, Douglass and Anthony appeared together at a National Council of Women meeting on the day he died in 1895. Generations later, Rochester, New York, named a bridge in honor of Anthony and Douglass and erected a statue of the two "Friends for Freedom" having tea.[16]

ANOTHER AMENDMENT

The Civil War amendments forced white suffragists to regroup. Challenging the definition of citizenship, they attempted to vote and run for office. Their primary goal was securing suffrage. Three generations of white leaders pursued two strategies. Stanton and Anthony's National Woman Suffrage Association sought a federal amendment, while Lucy Stone's American Woman Suffrage Association fought for local suffrage. Both suffered repetitive, expensive, and exhausting losses. Among the aging founders, only Anthony had a succession plan. With Stone's daughter, Alice Stone Blackwell, Anthony engineered a merger of the rival groups in 1890, establishing the National American Woman Suffrage Association (NAWSA).

Stanton and Stone, aging, former rivals, had titular roles, while Anthony elevated Anna Howard Shaw, a Methodist minister and medical doctor from Michigan, and Carrie Chapman Catt, a school principal and journalist from Iowa. More conservative and strategic, they forged broader alliances and appealed to the regional, racial, and religious biases of male legislators. To win support, they embraced white supremacy and nativism, arguing that allowing white women to vote would create a cohort large enough to outnumber Black and immigrant voters.[17] Supporting "educated suffrage" was another strategy to limit the vote to privileged whites.

The second generation was impatient with Stanton, who refused "to sing suffrage evermore," preferring "the rub-a-dub of agitation." She did not believe voting would be enough to overturn millennia of sexism, the insistence on female inferiority in patriarchal institutions, Judeo-Christian traditions, English common law, American statutes, and social customs. Women must be emancipated from "all forms of bondage, . . . custom, dependence and superstition," she declared to a congressional hearing.[18]

Stanton was a myopic visionary. She ignored Black women. For white women, she championed suffrage, coeducation, girls' sports, job training, equal wages, labor unions, "voluntary motherhood," cooperative nurseries and kitchens, reform of divorce laws, property rights for wives, and child custody for mothers. Every position alarmed NAWSA's new leaders. Catt considered Stanton "a selfish, foolish old woman" even before she challenged religious orthodoxy. Stanton did not believe that God intended women to be subservient to men.[19]

ATTACKING PATRIARCHY

Stanton did not publish *The Woman's Bible* until after NAWSA's lavish celebration of her eightieth birthday at the Metropolitan Opera House in November 1895. Her book dismissed the Adam's rib version of creation (Genesis, 2: 18, 21-23) in favor of the earlier verse (Genesis, 1: 26-27): "So God created man in his own image . . . male and female." She insisted it established the equality of the sexes and an androgynous God. Infuriated and embarrassed by Stanton's heresy, younger suffragists censured Stanton and canonized Anthony, creating a breach in their forty-five-year friendship.[20] Stanton was erased.

Stanton's attack on patriarchy was philosophical and theological. Other women tackled the topic scientifically. In 1885, the American Association of University Women (AAUW), an organization of white college graduates, funded research to refute claims by Harvard medical school professor Edward Clarke. In 1873, Clarke asserted that a college education would cause nervous collapse and infertility in women.[21] Antoinette Brown Black-well contested another white male conclusion, that female and Black brains were smaller and less intelligent. She was the first female minister ordained in a mainstream Protestant denomination and the sister-in-law of both suffragist Lucy Stone and Elizabeth Blackwell, the first formally trained female doctor in America. Having abandoned the ministry for scientific studies, in 1875 Brown Blackwell published *The Sexes Throughout Nature*, in which she found no examples of patriarchy in the animal kingdom.[22]

Author Charlotte Perkins Gilman made the case against patriarchy in her short story, "The Yellow Wallpaper" (1892); in her theoretical work, *Women and Economics* (1898); and in her novel, *Herland: A Feminist Utopian Novel* (1916). She described the patriarchal assumptions on which marriage and motherhood were based as risks to women's physical and mental health. Gilman saw her life as a choice between marital passion or an independent intellectual life. That tension prompted a breakdown. Treated for hysteria by a disciple of Dr. Clarke, Gilman was forbidden to read or write, like the heroine in her story. She recovered only after she abandoned her husband and child. In her utopian view, women could best manage their multiple roles in coopera-tive, female households, sharing domestic chores, kitchens, and nurseries.[23]

Also published in 1892 was Anna Julia Haywood Cooper's first book, *A Voice from the South*, considered the first expression of Black feminism. With Charlotte Forten Grimke, Ida Wells-Barnett, and Mary Church Terrell, Cooper was one of the "great race women" of the era. She and Terrell had been two of three Black women classmates at Oberlin and the first two to earn master's degrees there. Cooper would also earn a doctorate from the Sorbonne, translating an epic poem about the Crusades into modern French. A lifelong educator, she was principal of the M Street School, an elite Black high school in Washington, DC's segregated system. By insisting on a classical curriculum of Latin, Greek, history, literature, mathematics, and science, rather than an "industrial education," she sided with W. E. B. Du Bois against Booker T. Washington.[24]

Cooper's book was a collection of essays and speeches, including "Womanhood: A Vital Element in the Regeneration and Progress of a

Race." Cooper criticized Black men for claiming to represent their race but ignoring Black women. "Only the Black woman can say," Cooper asserted, "when and where I enter . . . Then the Negro race enters with me." Cooper, a widow who fostered and adopted children, believed that women's maternal roles could be used to empower them. As one scholar concluded, Cooper found in Black womanhood and domesticity the basis for "self-authority, self-interest, and self-development."[25]

These thinkers all rejected women's secondary status. According to Harvard historian Jill Lepore, suffragists believed, based on the findings of nineteenth century archeologists and anthropologists, that powerful women like the Amazons had once existed and that matriarchy predated patriarchy.[26] As feminist foremothers, Stanton, Brown Blackwell, Gilman, and Cooper wanted to undercut the roots of patriarchy, which sustained sexism and racism. They acknowledged that even if women secured equal legal rights and broader educational and employment opportunities, they would be held back by prejudice.

Anti-suffragists believed that voting was a white male activity. Women did not belong in the public arena any more than they belonged in barrooms or on battlefields. While women supposedly occupied an idealized "separate sphere," it did not protect vulnerable, poor, immigrant, or Black women from harsh working conditions or sexual violence. Women reformers slowly expanded their sphere, claiming the nation was their home and demanding better housekeeping. As one jingle proclaimed, "Mother mends my socks and shirts, Mother mends my coat; Maybe she could mend some laws, if she had the vote."[27] To achieve their ends, Black and white reformers, including those who did not have children, employed metaphors of virtuous motherhood, using the moral authority of motherhood to challenge the power of patriarchy.

WOMEN'S CLUB MOVEMENT

One vehicle for reform was the women's club movement. During the Progressive era, middle-class Protestant women organized into voluntary separate spheres, including literary societies. Some remained regional and parochial, while others grew into national organizations, promoting kindergartens, libraries, playgrounds, juvenile justice, and better sanitation. Recognizing that achieving their goals required political action, women's clubs formed suffrage departments. The Women's Christian Temperance Union (1873) wanted "home protection" from alcohol abuse; the American Association of University Women (1881) promoted academic engagement; the United Daughters of the Confederacy (1894) preserved the Lost Cause to promote white supremacy. Excluded by whites and Protestants, Black and Jewish women organized separately. The National Council of Jewish Women (1893) objected to immigration quotas and promoted assimilation.

For Black women, secular organizations provided more independent leadership roles than were available through church auxiliaries. While 90% of Black congregants were women, 90% of ministers were men, which gave them rare leadership roles under the emasculating authority of Jim Crow. Black women accepted that imbalance and embraced the women's club movement.[28] In 1896, Nannie Helen Burroughs, Frances Harper, Josephine St. Pierre Ruffin, Mary Church Terrell, Harriet Tubman, Margaret Murray Washington, and Ida Wells-Barnett founded the National Association of Colored Women (NACW), an alliance of fifty local clubs. It sought to end lynching, discrimination, disenfranchisement, and convict leasing. It proposed free daycare, kindergarten, and the admission of Black women into nursing and medical schools. Its motto was "Lifting as We Climb."[29]

Ida Bell Wells-Barnett was an anti-lynching crusader. Born enslaved in 1862, she became a teacher and an investigative journalist in Memphis. Seventy years before Rosa Parks, Wells bought a first-class train ticket and refused to move to a segregated car. Forcibly removed, she sued the railroad and won $500, until the Tennessee Supreme Court overturned the decision. In 1892, she published *Southern Horrors*, documenting that lynchings were prompted by economic envy disguised as trumped-up charges of sexual assault. *Her Red Record* (1895) included fourteen pages of statistics and attracted national attention. A white mob destroyed her press. Wells moved to Chicago, married attorney Ferdinand Barnett, became his partner in a publishing business, and lectured nationally, insisting her hosts provide childcare for her four children. She challenged racism everywhere, including boycotting the 1893 World's Columbian Exposition for excluding African Americans. Her courage was rarely rewarded with leadership roles.[30]

In contrast, Mary Church Terrell was elected president of NACW for three terms before being named honorary president for life. Terrell had two white grandfathers, slave owners who raped women they owned. Her enslaved parents were allowed to marry in one owner's home, where Mollie was born in 1863. After emancipation, her father became a wealthy Memphis real estate developer. She graduated from Oberlin College with two degrees, studied in Europe, and spoke five languages. In 1891, she married Robert Terrell, a graduate of Lawrence Academy, Harvard University, and Howard University law school. They lived in Washington, DC, teaching at the M Street School. In 1901, Theodore Roosevelt named Mr. Terrell the first Black Justice of the Peace, and in 1911, President Taft made him the first Black federal judge in the newly created DC municipal court. Such appointments depended on the patronage of Booker T. Washington and required Senate confirmation. In 1914, shortly after President Wilson segregated the federal government, Mississippi Senator James Vardeman (D) filibustered unsuccessfully to block Judge Terrell's reappointment.[31]

Despite being dependent on the founder of Tuskegee, the Terrells embodied the Black elite, Du Bois's "Talented Tenth." Mollie Terrell was the first Black woman to serve on the DC Board of Education, where she promoted Du Bois's classical curriculum rather than Washington's vocational model. Although she corresponded and visited with Anthony, Terrell maintained a "strategic distance" from white suffragists, many of whom endorsed lynching. Invited to speak at the 1898 NAWSA convention to mark the fiftieth anniversary of Seneca Falls, Terrell noted the thirtieth anniversary of the Fourteenth Amendment, calling it a "double jubilee." She titled her talk "The Justice of Woman Suffrage."[32]

Both Wells-Barnett and Terrell were founders of the National Association for the Advancement of Colored People (NAACP) in 1909, the centenary of Lincoln's birth. It was an outgrowth of the Niagara Movement, a

1905 gathering of Black activists organized by Du Bois and Mary Burnett Talbert on the Canadian side of the falls, since American hotels were segregated. The sixty NAACP organizers were a biracial group, including "white reformers . . . white philanthropists," three Black women, four Black men, and nine white women.[33]

THE SUFFRAGE CAMPAIGN

Terrell and Wells-Barnett were among dozens of Black women who marched in the 1913 suffrage parade on the day before Woodrow Wilson's inauguration. It was organized by Alice Paul, a Quaker who represented the militant third generation of suffrage leaders. A veteran of the violent British suffrage campaign, she had been arrested and force-fed seven times before returning to the US to complete her doctoral dissertation on the legal position of women in Pennsylvania. Introducing "outdoor tactics" to NAWSA, she produced a parade of five thousand women and a pageant on the steps of the Treasury Building.

Because NAWSA had pursued a "Southern strategy," it did not welcome Black suffragists. They were ordered to march in the rear behind white men in the colored section. Instead, they appeared throughout the ranks. The *Chicago Tribune* photographed Wells-Barnett, a member of the Illinois Equal Suffrage Association and founder of Chicago's Alpha Club, the first Black suffrage organization, marching with the Illinois delegation.[34] Terrell joined the Delta Sigma Theta sorority, newly formed at Howard University, in the contingent of college women, who were wearing their academic gowns. In 1917, Terrell and her daughter, Phyllis Wheatley Terrell, picketed the White House. She was still picketing in 1951, protesting segregated restaurants in Washington, DC.[35]

Paul's street theater, and the riot it engendered, made headlines for a federal suffrage amendment. In 1915, when Catt returned to NAWSA leadership, she banished Paul, who established the National Woman's Party (NWP). It adopted British tactics, picketing and holding the party in power, the Democrats, responsible for suffrage. By then, a messy coalition of self-interested suffragists had evolved. Clubwomen, progressives, settlement house workers, factory workers, and immigrant women allied under the purple, gold, and white suffrage banner. Divided by race, class, geography, and generation, they represented the different elements of the twentieth century's many women's movements. Their socially conservative, religiously traditional, nativist, and racist opponents represented a less diverse cohort.

Support for suffrage slowly took hold. By 1916, women were voting in twelve states, all west of the Mississippi River, except Illinois.[36] The first favorable congressional vote on the Anthony Amendment was on January 10, 1918. Jeannette Rankin, the first woman to serve in Congress, opened the debate. Elected in 1916 at age thirty-six, the Republican rancher, social worker, and NAWSA organizer from Montana was the only woman ever to vote for suffrage. Rankin was sworn in on April 2, 1917, the day President Wilson asked for a Declaration of War against Germany. Four days later, she cast her first vote, against the war.[37]

The *New York Times* described her as "weeping copiously" during the roll call, but witnesses found her composed. Joined by fifty-five men, forty-nine representatives, and six senators, only Rankin was condemned as cowardly and disloyal. Until then, her press coverage had been positive, if sexist, noting her red hair, "clinging gowns [and] French heels."[38] Catt, who was wooing Wilson's support for suffrage and had promised him NAWSA's full support for the war, was furious. When Catt endorsed her opponent in a 1918 Senate race, Rankin lost. During Rankin's second term in Congress (1941-43), she cast the only vote against entry into World War II. Always a pacifist, at age eighty-eight, she led a demonstration of fifteen hundred women against the Vietnam War. Asked how she might have lived her life differently, she retorted, "I would have been nastier."[39]

The 1918 House resolution on woman suffrage passed, 274–136, exactly the two-thirds needed for a constitutional amendment. Members came from sickbeds to vote, one with a broken shoulder, another on a stretcher. One came from his wife's deathbed and returned for her funeral. Out of 198 Republicans, 165 voted yes; those from major industrial states voted no. Democrats divided, 104–102; the majority of opponents were Southerners. Removed from the gallery for cheering, suffragists sang hymns in the foyer.[40]

The Senate stalled for nine months. It ignored a personal appeal from President Wilson delivered on October 1, 1918. In a speech he typed himself, Wilson declared woman suffrage an essential war measure.

> Democracy means that women shall play their parts in affairs alongside men and upon an equal footing with them. . . . We have made partners of women in this war, shall we admit them only to a partnership of suffering and sacrifice and not a partnership of privilege and right?[41]

The Senate defeated the Anthony Amendment, 62–34, two votes short.

During the debate, Senator Vardeman (D-MS) offered a substitute bill limiting suffrage to white women. The white supremacist had come to the Senate in 1913 promising to repeal the Fourteenth and Fifteenth Amendments. His voters were known as "red necks," for the neckerchiefs they wore to signal their support. To oppose Vardeman's ploy, Terrell mobilized the NAACP and six thousand members of the Northeastern Federation of Colored Women's Clubs to pressure NAWSA. Vardeman's motion lost. In July 2017, the University of Mississippi removed his name from a prominent building.[42]

In the 1918 midterm elections, Democrats lost their congressional majorities. Michigan, Oklahoma, and South Dakota granted women full suffrage. After the new Congress convened, with 117 new members, the House affirmed its pro-suffrage vote on May 21, 1919, by a larger margin, 304–89. Two weeks later, on June 4, 1919, the Senate passed the Anthony Amendment, 66–30, with two votes to spare.[43] As woman suffrage went to the states for ratification, Catt telegraphed her troops: "Our hour has come. Put on your armor!"[44]

RATIFICATION

Six states ratified the amendment in eight days. Seven Southern states rushed to reject it. By mid-1920, thirty-five of the thirty-six states needed had ratified the amendment, leaving only seven prospects. Florida, Louisiana, and North Carolina were unlikely. Republican governors in Connecticut and Vermont refused to convene their legislatures, and Republican infighting in Delaware defeated the amendment. That left Tennessee, which had recently passed partial suffrage for women.[45] "I had scarcely taken off my hat," Catt recalled, "before I was summoned to Tennessee."[46]

Catt arrived in Nashville in mid-July with an overnight bag and stayed for five weeks. She settled into the Hermitage Hotel, headquarters for both sides, and left the lobbying to Tennessee suffragists Anne Dallas Dudley, Catherine Kenny, Abby Crawford Milton, and Juno Frankie Pierce. Born during slavery and educated at Roger Williams University, one of four colleges founded in Nashville for freed slaves, Pierce had registered 2,500 Black women to vote in the 1919 municipal elections. She addressed the first meeting of the Tennessee League of Women Voters and established the Tennessee Vocational School for Colored Girls in 1923.[47] Sue Shelton White, a Tennessee native, represented the NWP, which had no money and few troops in the fight.[48]

In the hottest summer on record, one thousand pro- and anti-"suffs" poured into the city. Pro-suffrage legislators were threatened with primary challenges, business boycotts, and kidnapping. Opponents included brewers, party machines, Catholics, manufacturers, segregationists, and privileged white women, who claimed not to need the vote. Many people sincerely believed that women were emotionally unsuited for politics. Others thought female political involvement was abnormal: "The woman suffrage movement is an imitation-of-man movement and, as such, merits the condemnation of every normal man and woman."[49] The liquor lobby kept a hospitality suite at the Hermitage open around the clock.

The national Democratic Party, wary of being blamed for the amendment's failure in a presidential election year, pressured Governor Albert

Roberts to call a special session. Local Democrats urged him to resist because passing suffrage risked Black women voting and voting Republican. The night before the special session convened, Catt reported that legislators were "reeling through the halls . . . in a state of advanced intoxication!" On August 13, the Tennessee senate sobered up long enough to pass the amendment, 25–4. "We now have 35½ states," Catt reported.

> With all the political pressure, it ought to be easy, but the opposition of every sort is here fighting with no scruple . . . [Antis] are appealing to Negrophobia and every other cave man's prejudice. . . . It is hot, muggy, nasty . . . this last battle is desperate.[50]

The spotlight shifted to the lower house. Anti-suffrage ladies pinned red roses on opponents' lapels; supporters sported yellow boutonnieres.

When the bill reached the house floor, ninety-six members were present. Suffrage needed forty-nine votes to carry. A motion to table the amendment resulted in a 48–48 tie due to unexpected support from Democrat Banks Turner, who had been strong-armed by the governor. A tie vote on a motion to table required an immediate floor vote on ratification itself. If it ended in another tie, the amendment would fail. The seventh name in the roll call was Harry Burn, who sported a red rose. Twenty-four years old, a freshman Republican from rural East Tennessee, Burn voted yes. When Turner voted yes, the amendment carried 49–47. The "Sterling 49" made Tennessee "the Perfect 36."[51]

After the vote, the chamber erupted into chaos. Antis supposedly chased Burn out a window, across a ledge, and into the attic. Catt, who was not present, could hear the hullabaloo from her hotel. The next day, Burn admitted that he changed his vote because his mother asked him to. "I know that a mother's advice is always safest for a boy to follow and my mother wanted me to vote for ratification." In a letter Harry carried in his pocket, Phoebe Burn asked him to buy her some sheet music and to "vote for suffrage . . . don't keep them in doubt . . . be a good boy and help

Mrs. Catt."[52] On August 24, 1920, Governor Roberts sent Tennessee's notice of ratification to Washington on the mail train.

In 1899, Anthony had imagined the potential of a female voting bloc, telling the *London Times*, "when women get the ballot they will be on fighting ground . . . When men know that women can vote . . . then officials and office seekers will attend to women's wants."[53] Years later, after the 2016 and 2018 elections, women and their daughters plastered Anthony's grave with "I VOTED" stickers. Because the stickers were hard to remove, Rochester's Mount Hope cemetery enclosed her gravestone with Plexiglass. In 2020, women again covered her marker and those of other equal rights icons.[54]

In 1920, suffragists were jubilant and optimistic. White women believed voting would end discrimination based on sex and empower them to change America. Men worried they might be right. Wells-Barnett wished Anthony and Douglass "could have been here to see the day when a woman's ballot will count equally with a man's." NWP lobbyist Maud Younger predicted "the dawn of woman's political power in America." Crystal Eastman, a founder of the American Civil Liberties Union, stated simply, "Now we can begin."[55]

CHAPTER TWO

FLAPPERS & FEMINISTS, 1920–1928

S ecretary of State Bainbridge Colby left orders to be awakened the moment Tennessee's notice of ratification arrived at Union Station. The call came at 3:45 A.M. on Thursday, August 26, 1920. Secretary Colby signed a proclamation adding the Nineteenth Amendment to the United States Constitution at eight o'clock at his K Street home, without ceremony. There were no photographers and no suffrage leaders. The threat of an injunction prompted his haste and discretion. A petition brought by opponents was pending before the District of Columbia Court of Appeals, which opened at nine. If the injunction had been granted before Colby's certification, it would have derailed voting rights for American women. The wording of the amendment, named for Susan B. Anthony when it was introduced in 1878, had never changed: "The right of citizens of the United States to vote shall not be denied or abridged by the United States or by any state on account of sex."[1]

Later that morning, Carrie Chapman Catt, president of the National American Woman Suffrage Association (NAWSA), returned from Nashville. Expecting to witness the signing, she telephoned Secretary Colby. Assuring her the amendment had been safely signed, he invited her to his office to inspect the document. "So quietly as that, we learned that the last step in the enfranchisement of women in the United States had been taken," she recalled.[2] Alice Paul, head of the National Woman's Party (NWP), who had arranged for photographers and newsreel cameras, was not included. As the *New York Times* reported, Colby was aware of "frictions."

> [The] differences between the militant suffragists [Paul] and the mainstream suffragists [Catt] . . . could not be ironed out, so the Secretary of State had decided to issue the proclamation privately in order to avoid a clash.[3]

By including neither Catt nor Paul at an official signing, Colby diplomatically avoided crediting either with the amendment's success.

Everyone in Washington knew the two women detested each other. Catt considered Paul politically naïve and "stupendously stupid."[4] She criticized Paul's publicity stunts, the 1913 parade and pageant, and the White House pickets in 1917. A generation younger, Paul denigrated Catt for her alliance with Wilson and resented her success. A veteran of the radical branch of the British suffrage movement, Paul held the parliamentary view that Democrats, as the party in power, were responsible for suffrage, even though it needed bipartisan support to pass. They had supposedly not spoken to each other since April 1917, when they hosted a breakfast for two hundred women to welcome Jeannette Rankin to Washington.[5]

On that hot afternoon in August 1920, the rivals celebrated the amendment's victory on opposite sides of Pennsylvania Avenue. Catt had tea at the White House with President and Mrs. Wilson to salute the success of a campaign he had opposed for most of his two terms. Across the street, at her strategically located Lafayette Square headquarters, Paul toasted the NWP's purple and gold suffrage flag, to which she had added a star for each ratified state. Both events were captured on camera. That night, NAWSA held a victory rally in Washington. The next day, Catt continued her triumphal tour to New York City, where Governor Al Smith met her train and presented her with a huge bouquet of purple delphiniums and yellow mums. During a procession to the Astor Hotel, admirers "split their gloves" clapping.[6]

WHY SUFFRAGE WON

The Nineteenth Amendment passed because Catt had run a strategic, relentless, two-tiered campaign. To win state suffrage in New York in 1917, then the most populous and powerful state, she created a multi-generational, multiracial, cross-class coalition. That victory propelled the amendment toward its first favorable House vote in January 1918. As individual states passed suffrage, she directed local chapters to prepare for the ratification fight. Catt claimed that NAWSA had two million members and a presence in every congressional and state legislative district in the country.

The amendment passed because Paul's audacious street tactics generated headlines and influenced public opinion, which became more favorable after the picketers were treated harshly. Arrested for obstructing traffic, some were sentenced to seven months in the DC Jail or the Occoquan Work-house. In total, an estimated two thousand women picketed: 218 women from 26 states were arrested and 97 were imprisoned. Paul, Lucy Burns, Rose Winslow, and several others were brutally force-fed. In March 1918, the DC Court of Appeals invalidated every sentence.[7] While the NWP was never large or especially effective in garnering votes, Paul forced NAWSA, and the nation, to make federal suffrage the priority.

The amendment passed because women had contributed to the war effort in factories and fields, at home and on the European front, as nurses, ambulance drivers, and telephone operators, prompting President Wilson to declare suffrage a war measure. Specifically, the amendment passed because Harry Burn changed his vote. More significantly, the amendment passed because at least six million women were already voting. By 1919, women had full suffrage in fifteen states and "presidential only" suffrage in twelve. When suffrage passed, 64% of House members came from states where women voted. Nearly all of them supported the amendment.[8]

The amendment passed because strategists outmaneuvered their opponents. Manufacturers worried that progressive women would enact limits on child labor and insist on safety regulations. Brewers, distillers, and saloon keepers assumed women would enforce prohibition. The major parties believed women would be unpredictable voters. The Catholic Church believed suffrage threatened the authority of husbands and the sanctity of the home. Privileged white women disdained the amendment. Among the leaders of the National Association Opposed to Woman Suffrage were Eleanor Foster Lansing, the wife of Wilson's second Secretary of State, and Alice Hay Wadsworth, the daughter of former Secretary of State John Hay and the wife of Senator James Wadsworth (R-NY).[9] Segregationists abhorred the prospect of more African Americans voting and feared federal enforcement measures. When they failed to pass white-only suffrage, they found other means to suppress unwelcome voters. The threat of women actually voting unnerved opponents and motivated supporters in Congress and state legislatures.

While states could no longer discriminate on account of sex, state laws and party rules controlled elections. Women everywhere had to contend with complicated registration requirements, residency rules, mandated literacy tests, civics quizzes, and hostility from men. Poll taxes disproportionally burdened poor women.[10] The first challenge to the legitimacy of the Nineteenth Amendment came six weeks after it was certified. In October 1920, Cecilia Streett Waters and Mary D. Randolph registered to vote in Baltimore. Oscar Leser, representing the Maryland League for State Defense, sued to have their names stricken because Maryland had not ratified the amendment. Leser claimed that the Nineteenth Amendment was unconstitutional.

Leser v. Garnett was dismissed by a lower court and on appeal, but the Supreme Court granted a writ of certiorari in 1922. Catt asked Charles Evans Hughes, a former Supreme Court Justice, the Republican presidential candidate in 1916, and President Harding's Secretary of State, to file an amicus brief. In a unanimous decision written by Justice Louis Brandeis, the Court affirmed the Nineteenth Amendment's legitimacy. The Court emphasized that ratification was a federal function that transcended state constitutions and legislatures and that, by itself, the secretary of state's certification made the amendment valid.[11] The twelve unratified states eventually passed the amendment. Mississippi voted last, in 1984, after it had defeated the Equal Rights Amendment. According to historian Martha Jones, the long-delayed state ratifications of the Thirteenth, Fifteenth, and Nineteenth amendments reflected changing and more diverse electoral demographics. "It's deeply symbolic because . . . late ratifications are manifestations of the ways . . . political power has shifted [to] Black lawmakers, women lawmakers [and] Black women lawmakers."[12]

AN INCOMPLETE VICTORY

The Nineteenth Amendment enfranchised all Black women, but it did not protect their right to vote. When Black citizens attempted to register, local papers reported a near panic. Georgia and Mississippi claimed women had missed the registration deadline and refused to allow them to vote in 1920. States adopted white-only primaries, the equivalent of general elections in one-party states. In Florida, Black voting spurred Klan growth.[13] In addition to increased violence, economic pressure by employers and landlords proved effective. Black Americans were subject to blatantly discriminatory practices, including unfairly administered literacy tests and "grandfather clauses" that prevented descendants of enslaved people from voting while allowing illiterate whites to vote if their grandparents had. In 1944, in *Smith v. Allwright*, the Supreme Court outlawed white-only primaries. Lonnie E. Smith, a Black dentist, sued S. S. Allwright, an election official in Harris County, Texas, challenging a state Democratic Party rule barring Black voters from primaries. Thurgood Marshall represented Smith in his first Supreme Court appearance on behalf of the NAACP Legal Defense Fund.[14]

In the years that followed, it was clear that the Nineteenth Amendment was an incomplete victory. It enfranchised twenty-seven million women and doubled the number of eligible voters, but it did not enforce voting rights for Black women or cover American women married to foreigners, Asian immigrants, women living on reservations, in US territories, or in the District of Columbia. The first attempt to remedy its omissions was the 1922 Married Women's Independent Citizenship Act, known as the Cable Act. It reversed the 1907 Expatriation Act when Congress required American women to adopt the nationality of their husbands. If a husband were eligible for citizenship, his wife could also apply; if not, she could be detained or deported.[15]

Nativism prompted restrictions on Asian immigration and citizenship. In 1875, Congress passed the Page Act. It assumed Chinese women were all prostitutes, imported for "lewd and immoral purposes." Any Chinese woman entering the United States was subjected to humiliating interrogations, so many refused to come. Reducing the number of Asian women created a dramatic gender imbalance. The 1882 Chinese Exclusion Act declared Chinese immigrants "aliens ineligible for citizenship" and suspended further immigration due to fear of competition for jobs and concerns about "racial purity." Not until 1898 were children of Chinese immigrants born in the United States considered citizens. The restrictive 1924 Immigration Act, aimed at Jews, Italians, and "non-Nordics," barred Japanese and other "undesirables." In 1943, lobbied by Madame Chiang Kai-Shek, formerly Soon Mei-ling, who had graduated from Wellesley College in 1917, the Congress repealed the 1882 Exclusion Act, given America's wartime alliance with China. Japanese and other Asians were allowed entry after 1952, but patterns of discrimination continued. Until 1960, Asian women in New York City had to register annually at the police department, producing proof of literacy in English.[16]

To address Native American voting rights, Congress passed the Indian Citizenship Act in 1924. In recognition of the service of Native American soldiers, it granted full citizenship to all Native Americans, but did not enfranchise them.[17] Two Indigenous women played significant roles in passing the legislation. Marie Louise Bottineau Baldwin, a Turtle Mountain Chippewa, had come to Washington with her lawyer father to defend treaty rights. Early in her career in the Office of Indian Rights, she advocated assimilation, but in a photograph taken for her 1911 government personnel file, she wore Native dress. She worked with the Society of American Indians, testified before Congress on behalf of Indigenous women, and enrolled in the Washington College of Law, becoming its first graduate of color. In 1913, she marched with women lawyers in the suffrage parade.[18]

Working with Baldwin was Zitkala-Ša ("Red Bird"), born on the Yankton Sioux reservation in North Dakota in 1876. She was sent to a government boarding school in Indiana, where her braids were cut, her culture disparaged, and her name changed to Gertrude Simmons. She attended Earlham College, studied violin at the Boston Conservatory of Music, and performed for President McKinley. Working at another boarding school, she was fired for publishing exposés in the national press. In 1902 she married Raymond Bonnin, another boarding school survivor. Zitkala-Ša worked to preserve Native languages and stories. In 1913, she co-wrote *The Sun Dance*, the first Indigenous opera, based on Sioux rituals prohibited by the government. She joined Baldwin at the Society of American Indians in 1918 and was instrumental in the passage of the 1924 Indian Citizenship Act and the 1934 Indian Reorganization Act.[19]

Ever since *Cherokee Nation v. Georgia* (1831) allowed the government to seize Native lands, the US had treated Indigenous people as wards. States with large Indigenous populations in the Southwest, Northeast, and Upper Midwest restricted Native voting rights. Indigenous men, who had the highest rate of participation in the military, returned from World War II expecting to vote. In 1948, veteran Frank Harrison sued the county recorder to challenge Arizona's guardianship. In *Harrison v. Laveen*, the state Supreme Court found guardianship unconstitutional. "To deny the right to vote," Chief Justice Levi Stewart Udall concluded, "is to do violence to the principles of freedom and equality."[20]

In New Mexico in 1948, Marine veteran and Pueblo Indian Miguel Trujillo sued a county registrar who had denied his right to vote because Native people living on reservations paid no property taxes. In *Trujillo v.*

Garley, a three-judge panel found the New Mexico law unconstitutional because Indigenous people paid federal, gas, and sales taxes.[21] Utah was the last state to remove formal barriers in 1962, but hurdles remain. Because American Indians living on reservations do not use street addresses and some states do not recognize post office boxes or tribal identity cards, their voting rights are still contested. In 2019, Justice Udall's grandson, Senator Tom Udall (D-NM), introduced the Native American Voting Rights Act.[22]

The Nineteenth Amendment extended suffrage to women living in states but not territories. The Alaska Territory passed woman suffrage in 1913; Hawaii followed in 1920. Puerto Rico enfranchised literate women in 1929 and all women in 1935. Territory residents vote only in primaries. They have no voting representatives in the Congress and no votes in the Electoral College. Similarly, no resident of the District of Columbia could vote for President until the passage of the Twenty-third Amendment in 1961. It gave Washington three electoral votes, the same number as the smallest state, even though its population was larger. The District still does not have voting representatives in the Congress.[23]

THE 1920 ELECTION

In the autumn of 1920, Democrats and Republicans competed for white women voters. Democrats claimed that woman suffrage passed under a Democratic administration and a Democratic governor. Republicans took credit for the passage of the Nineteenth Amendment because they controlled twenty-nine of the thirty-six ratifying states. The GOP platform incorporated twelve of fifteen "women's planks" proposed by the League of Women Voters. Before the election, both parties established white and colored women's divisions, recruited female delegates, and paired men and women as national committee members.[24]

Mary Church Terrell played a significant role in the 1920 election. She formed the Women's Republican League, hoping it would be absorbed and financed by the Republican National Committee. Supported by prominent

Black Republicans, she was appointed Director of Work Among Colored Women of the East. Traveling her territory, she told Black women they had a responsibility to use the Nineteenth Amendment as "a weapon of defense," to uphold their constitutional rights, and to vote for politicians who would pass a federal anti-lynching bill. She urged women to track legislation, write their representatives, and vote. African Americans were alarmed by the GOP "seating . . . lily-white delegations." Terrell's husband declared, "I hate a lily white republican. Would rather vote for Vardeman than one of them." Harassed and threatened with arrest while campaigning, she resented "the insult not only to myself, but through me to the womanhood of the whole race."[25]

The election pitted Ohio Republican Senator Warren Harding and Massachusetts Governor Calvin Coolidge against Ohio Democratic Governor James Cox and former Assistant Secretary of the Navy Franklin Roosevelt. Harding, fifty-four, replaced his grass with gravel and campaigned from his front porch in Marion, Ohio. Every day, delegations arrived: business leaders, war veterans, Baptist ministers, "Negro Republicans," the Chicago Cubs. On August 26, he celebrated the ratification of the Nineteenth Amendment. In October, he hosted "Social Justice Day," specifying that it was "not Suffrage Day but rather Respectable Women's Day." He invited representatives of the League of Women Voters, the Women's Trade Union League, and the Business and Professional Women, as well as governors' wives and former President Roosevelt's daughter and sister. In his remarks, Harding went further than the GOP platform. He promised equal pay for equal work, an eight-hour day, expansion of the Children's Bureau, an end to child labor, enforcement of prohibition, prevention of lynching, protection of maternal and infant health, the appointment of women to federal posts, and the creation of a cabinet department of social welfare.[26]

The advent of woman suffrage introduced an unknown electoral factor. Polling places moved from barbershops and saloons to schools and fire stations. Smoking, spitting, swearing, and drinking were banned. "It ain't like it used to be," complained a New York City cop to a reporter. "Since women's been mixing in, politics ain't the same."[27] Girl Scouts volunteered to babysit. That November, Catt and her partner Mollie Hay voted in New York. Alice Paul sent an absentee ballot to New Jersey, as did President and Mrs. Wilson. The President had hoped to practice law with Bainbridge Colby but never recovered his health. He died in 1924 at his home in Washington, where Mrs. Wilson continued to live. As a DC resident, she never voted again. Another DC resident, Mary Church Terrell, only voted once, when she lived briefly in Chicago. Ida Wells-Barnett also voted in Chicago, where she had registered seven thousand Black voters. Harry Burn and his mother voted in Knoxville. He barely won a second term; Tennessee Governor Roberts lost his reelection.[28]

Harding won in a landslide, by twenty-six points, with 60% of the popular vote, the largest margin to date. Woman suffrage represented the largest expansion of the electorate in American history, but there was a national decline in voter turnout, down to 49.2% from 61.8% in 1916.[29] There were no exit polls and no systematic collection of voter data by gender at the national level until 1964. Analysts estimate that female turnout ranged from a high of 57% in Kentucky to a low of 6% in Virginia. Records indicate that few Southern or immigrant women registered, or were allowed to register, in the 1920s. In Massachusetts, more Republican than Democratic women registered.[30] Journalists claimed that the majority of female voters supported the silver-haired Harding because he was handsome. It's more likely women voted for the Republican ticket because their fathers, husbands, and the majority of the country did.

Only Illinois counted women's votes separately. To understand how women had voted in the 1923 Chicago mayoral race, researchers went door-to-door in several precincts. They found that three-quarters of eligible women had not registered: 33% claimed disinterest, ignorance, or timidity, and 11% believed women should not vote. Immigrants admitted to language barriers, and many women confessed that their husbands disapproved. Black women were encouraged by their communities to vote; white women were not. As a member of the Minnesota League of Women Voters reported, "Women, except for one or two hardy spirits, were too timid to participate in an election where men folks made it plain they were not wanted."[31]

During the 1920s, women were party volunteers, voters, lobbyists, and candidates, but the suffrage sisterhood splintered. Given competing priorities and racial tensions, the fragile coalition of Black and white middle-class clubwomen, settlement house volunteers, trade union organizers, pacifists, prohibitionists, politicos, and activists was unlikely to work together or vote as a bloc. Long before the amendment was ratified, suffrage allies had been planning ahead and falling back into self-interested silos. As Black and white women experienced individual and systematic discrimination, politically sophisticated suffrage veterans were already engaged.

Prior to ratification, in March 1919, Catt hosted a "Jubilee Convention," marking fifty years since the Wyoming Territory granted women the vote in 1869. She proposed converting NAWSA into a "League of Women Voters," as "the most appropriate and patriotic memorial . . . to 'Finish the Fight' and to aid in the reconstruction of the nation." Lacking unanimous support, her motion was tabled. Instead, Catt urged members to register, work with parties, draft legislation, and run for office. Jane Addams, the revered founder of Hull House, proposed instead that members should engage new voters in community organizing. The compromise in 1920 called for a nonpartisan league to educate women for citizenship.[32] Celebrating the success of a complex, strategic, multi-layered, and multi-year national campaign by creating a nonpartisan educational organization seemed anticlimactic.

SETTLEMENT HOUSES

Catt and Addams were widely and equally admired. Born a year apart, in 1859 and 1860, they had been allies in fighting for suffrage and promoting international peace. Both were college-educated Midwesterners. Addams was the daughter of an Illinois state politician; Catt's Iowa childhood was less privileged. While Catt struggled economically, Addams faced health issues, undergoing spinal surgery, which left her bedridden and depressed. When she recovered, she traveled to Europe for two years with her friend Ellen Starr. They visited Toynbee Hall, a "settlement house" in London's impoverished East End, where middle-class young people worked with local residents to address unemployment and disease.[33]

Returning to Chicago in 1889, Addams and Starr leased a neglected mansion on Halsted Street. They convinced daughters of the city's elite to volunteer in an immigrant neighborhood of factory workers. They offered English language classes; opened a daycare center and a kindergarten; provided a night school and a clinic; lobbied for public baths and garbage collection; taught cooking, art, and music; and added a library, an art gallery, a gym, and a playground. Volunteers investigated factory conditions and provided free legal counsel in juvenile court. By 1913, Hull House occupied fourteen buildings. Addams never lived anywhere else. In 1931, she was the first woman to win the Nobel Prize for Peace.[34]

Hull House attracted volunteers from across the country, especially among the first generation of college-educated middle-class women. As educational opportunities expanded for white and Black women, social work became a serious occupation. By 1920, there were almost five hundred settlement houses across the country committed to serving immigrants and the working class. Victoria Earle Matthews, born in slavery, chaired the executive board of the National Association of Colored Women and opened the White Rose Industrial Home for Working Class Negro Girls in New York City in 1897.[35] Mabel Ping-Hua Lee replaced her father as head of the Baptist Mission in Chinatown in 1924, eventually founding the American Baptist Home Mission Society. It provided English classes, a kindergarten, and a medical clinic. A Chinese immigrant, Lee rode a horse in the 1912 New York City suffrage parade when she was a teenager. With undergraduate and graduate degrees from Barnard College, she was the first woman to receive a PhD in economics from Columbia University in 1922. An active suffragist, Lee could not vote until 1943, when the Chinese Exclusion Act was repealed.[36]

In that same period, Lugenia Burns Hope created a model for African American community improvement and civil rights education in Atlanta, where her husband was president of Atlanta Baptist College, now Morehouse College. They came from Chicago, where she had studied at the

Art Institute and volunteered at Hull House. In 1908, she established the Neighborhood Union, the first woman-run social welfare agency in the South. It established daycare centers and kindergartens, lobbied for paved streets and sewers, and offered civics and sanitary education. When the segregated USO (United Service Organization) did not support Black or Jewish servicemen during the Great War, Hope worked through the Young Women's Christian Association. Secretary of Commerce Herbert Hoover appointed her to a board to respond to the Great Flood of 1927. A Vice President of the NAACP, Hope led the Board of Managers of the Neighborhood Union until her husband died in 1936, when she joined Mary McLeod Bethune to advance the New Deal.[37]

Hull House alumnae, a national network of change agents, were everywhere. Florence Kelley, daughter of Pennsylvania abolitionist and Republican Congressman William "Pig Iron" Kelley, was a Phi Beta Kappa graduate of Cornell University. She wrote her thesis on impoverished children. In 1891, she returned from graduate work in Zurich as a separated mother of three and a socialist. Based at Hull House, she conducted a slum survey, documenting sweatshops, child labor, and disease. She earned a law degree from Northwestern University and proposed reforms to the state legislature. Democratic Governor John Peter Altgeld named her Chief Factory Inspector for Illinois. In 1899, she moved to New York City and founded the National Consumer League, calling on shoppers to buy only products made under safe factory conditions.[38]

In 1902, Kelley's remarks at Mount Holyoke College inspired senior Frances Perkins to move to Chicago to volunteer at Hull House. Ellen Starr joined the Women's Trade Union League and organized strikes by women garment workers and waitresses. Addams's childhood friend Julia Lathrop taught the Sunday Plato class at Hull House, investigated child labor, and served as Illinois's first female Director of the Board of Charities. Grace Abbott founded the Immigrant Protective League. Lillian Wald established the Henry Street Settlement to serve immigrant Jews in New York's Lower East Side, coining the term "public health nurse." In that same slum, debutante Eleanor Roosevelt taught calisthenics to children as a member of the Junior League for the Promotion of Settlement Houses, founded by Mary Harriman, the railroad magnate's daughter.[39] Settlement houses became a new "separate sphere" for women, a sorority of social justice activists.

THE POST-SUFFRAGE AGENDA

After they won, suffragists returned to the causes they had sought the ballot to advance. NAWSA became the League of Women Voters, integrating some local chapters. Catt and Addams pursued international peace. As head of the National Consumers League, Kelley tried to eliminate sweatshops and establish a minimum wage. The General Federation of Women's Clubs, with 2.8 million members, focused on children. The Women's Trade Union League organized women workers. The YWCA protected their morals. The National Council of Jewish Women pressed for "Americanization education" and opposed quotas on Jewish immigrants and college applicants. The National Association of Colored Women worked to outlaw lynching, end segregation in the federal government, and improve their communities. In 1920, in response to the Sedition Act and the Red Scare, Jane Addams, Crystal Eastman, and Alice Stone Blackwell helped establish the American Civil Liberties Union to defend the Bill of Rights.[40] Over Kelley's objections, eight white organizations, claiming a combined membership of two million, founded the Women's Joint Congressional Committee in 1921. The *Ladies Home Journal* hailed it as "the most powerful and highly organized lobby in Washington." Its agenda included prohibition enforcement, public school improvement, physical education for girls, protection of women in industry, and world peace.[41] Its priority was infant health.

In 1920, with 111 deaths per 1,000 live births, the US ranked last among twenty industrial nations in infant survival rates. Eight years earlier, President Taft had established the Children's Bureau and appointed the first woman to head a major government agency, Hull House alumna Julia Lathrop, an expert on maternal and infant mortality. In 1918,

Congresswoman Rankin introduced the first "baby bill," when the US ranked eleventh. It failed. In 1919, Senator Morris Sheppard (D-TX) and Representative Horace Towner (R-IA) drafted the bipartisan "Promotion of the Welfare and Hygiene of Maternity and Infancy Act." It was the first government welfare bill, providing federal matching funds to train visiting nurses, license midwives, and establish clinics, primarily in rural areas.[42]

Sheppard–Towner did not pass until President Harding endorsed it in April 1921. Opponents called the bill socialism. The anti-suffrage Women Patriots, Daughters of the American Revolution (DAR), Women's Auxiliary of the American Legion, and the American Medical Association condemned it. Pediatricians seceded from the AMA, formed the American Academy of Pediatricians, and endorsed the bill. Among Senate opponents was Missouri Democrat James Reed. "It seems to be established doctrine of the [Children's] Bureau," sneered Reed, "that the only people capable of caring for babies and the mothers of babies are ladies who have not had babies." Another opponent wanted to rename Sheppard–Towner "A Bill to Organize a Delegation of Spinsters to Teach Mothers How to Raise Babies." An Iowa Senator cautioned his colleagues, "The old maids are voting now."[43]

Fear of women voters made the difference. As the *AMA Journal* concluded, "Women had just been given the vote. No one knew how they would use it. Nearly every congressman had a distinct sense of faintness at the thought of having all the women in his district against him." Rankin was in the gallery when Sheppard–Towner passed by a large margin. When female turnout proved elusive in 1924, the threat of a vengeful voting bloc evaporated. Senator Reed declared, "We would better reverse the proposition and provide for a committee of mothers to take charge of the old maids and teach them how to acquire a husband and have babies of their own." Funding was cut in 1927 before the bill was repealed in 1929. Under Sheppard–Towner, infant mortality had dropped to sixty-seven out of 1,000 live births, with greater improvement among non-white rural women.[44]

Victories for women's issues were rare. Reformers established the first federal prison for women, safeguarded appropriations for the Children's and Women's bureaus, and required gym classes for girls in public schools. Efforts to create a cabinet department of education failed because Southerners feared it would desegregate schools. In early 1924, social justice advocates introduced a constitutional amendment to regulate "the labor of persons under eighteen years of age." All three presidential candidates, Republican incumbent Calvin Coolidge, Democratic challenger John Davis, and Progressive Robert La Follette, endorsed the Child Labor Amendment. Parents, farmers, factory workers, manufacturers, and the Catholic Church opposed it. They did not want to regulate cheap labor, limit needed earners, or undermine parental authority. The proposed amendment was deemed an "unwanted intrusion . . . and interference with the traditions of families and farms." The intransigent Senator Reed concluded that the bill "would not receive a [single] vote in this body were there not so many individuals looking over their shoulders toward the ballot boxes in November."[45] Congress passed the proposed amendment before the 1924 election. It was never ratified.

The ability to enact change benefiting women and children peaked in 1924. Failure to ratify the Child Labor Amendment quickly marked the reversal of activists' political momentum because women voters did not materialize in 1924, when scarcely one-third of eligible women turned out. At 48.9%, it was the lowest election turnout on record. Incumbent Republican President Coolidge won with 54% of the vote. A 2016 analysis of women voting in 1924 drew several conclusions. Overall, women were labeled "peripheral voters," defined as less informed and engaged. Female turnout was higher where elections were competitive and legal barriers to voting were low.[46]

BLACK WOMEN'S PRIORITIES

While rural Black women benefited from Sheppard–Towner, such initiatives were not their priority. They wanted to end the legal terrorism of lynching, dismemberment, and burning in the Jim Crow South, where 90% of African Americans lived in 1920. To escape, 1.5 million African Americans migrated North and West from 1915 into the 1930s in search of safety and dignity. The Great Migration changed the social dynamic of race relations nationally. Black people found more job opportunities and higher wages, even in segregated, low-level jobs in meatpacking and auto plants, but they were still subject to racial violence, discrimination, and demeaning stereotypes.[47]

Black newspapers, like the *Chicago Defender* and the *California Eagle*, owned and operated by Charlotta Bass, fueled Black political machines. Chicago and Los Angeles elected the first Black aldermen and state legislators. In 1928, Oscar Stanton De Priest, a former Chicago housepainter and alderman, was courted by Republicans and elected the first Black member of Congress from outside the Reconstruction South. When First Lady Lou Hoover invited Mrs. De Priest to a White House tea for congressional wives, suggesting she was the social equal of the white guests, it caused an uproar. While the public censured Mrs. Hoover, Jessie De Priest praised the First Lady as "a most charming . . . cosmopolite [and] a wonderful hostess."[48]

Ending racial violence was imperative. The worst episode in American history took place in 1921 when a white mob destroyed the largest Black community in Oklahoma. As historian Scott Ellsworth has uncovered, Tulsa's Greenwood neighborhood, known as "the Negro Wall Street," had a hospital, two public schools, a post office, a library, fourteen churches, and 191 businesses, including fifteen groceries, four drug stores, two theaters, four hotels, thirty restaurants, two newspapers, and one gas station. The rampage began in late May after nineteen-year-old Dick Rowland, a Black shoe shiner, entered the Drexel Building to use the only "colored" toilet available downtown. He may have tripped. Seventeen-year-old Sarah Page, the white elevator operator, shrieked, and he ran.

Rowland was not arrested until the next day. The jail was on the top floor of the municipal building. When a mob gathered, the sheriff disabled the elevators, and a minister asked the crowd to disperse. When Black veterans arrived to offer their assistance, the white crowd was incensed. Shots were fired. The sheriff deputized the white mob, and enraged rioters rampaged through Greenwood until 2 A.M. The sheriff moved Rowland out of town. Sarah Page refused to press charges, and Rowland would eventually be exonerated, but the horror had just begun.[49]

The rampage lasted two more days. White vigilantes looted homes, pillaged businesses, and murdered Black citizens. Planes dropped kerosene bombs. A white National Guard unit strafed the brick Mount Zion Baptist Church with machine guns until it collapsed. The fire department failed to respond as thirty blocks burned, leaving only ashes and 10,000 homeless residents. There was no electricity, gas, or water. Survivors contested the body count, publicly estimated at eighty-five, with reports of three hundred bodies dumped into mass graves or the Arkansas River. Martial law was declared on June 1. A grand jury blamed the Black veterans. There were no prosecutions, no insurance payments, no reparations. The violence was covered by the *New York Times*, papers in England and India, and the *Tulsa Tribune* for one day. Neither white nor Black newspapers investigated further. Official records and photographs disappeared. The white community covered up the brutal attack.[50]

Its 2021 centenary prompted commissions, documentaries, and debates. Oklahoma called it the Tulsa Race Riot; Black citizens called it the Tulsa Massacre. The atrocities in Tulsa were part of a pattern of attacks on successful African American businesses and communities, including in Memphis in 1892; Atlanta in 1906; East Saint Louis, Illinois, and Chester, Pennsylvania, in 1917; and Chicago in 1919. In 1923, a white mob destroyed another Black community; Rosewood, Florida, was never rebuilt.[51] Evidence of Black prosperity generated hatred and challenged white supremacy.

Hoping facts would shame the public and stimulate Congress to act, the NAACP published lynching statistics, expanding on Wells-Barnett's 1892 groundbreaking investigation. Numbers peaked after the Great War and into the 1920s, declined in the 1930s and during World War II, only to rise again in the 1950s. From 1920 to 1938, the NAACP hung a flag outside its New York City headquarters to note every incident: "A Man Was Lynched Today."

Recently the Equal Justice Institute verified four thousand Black deaths by lynching between 1877 and 1950, still an incomplete count. The NAACP "History of Lynchings" counted 4,743 deaths of 3,446 Black men and women and 1,297 whites between 1882 and 1968. In the West, whites, Latinos, and Asians were killed. In the South, 79% of lynchings killed Blacks, including 581 in Mississippi, 531 in Georgia, and 493 in Texas.[52] The means varied, but not the intention: to intimidate, terrorize, and murder.

In 1916, white voters in St. Louis approved an ordinance to segregate the city geographically. To keep them from participating in the election, officials arrested three thousand Black residents.[53] Congressman Leonidas Dyer, a white Republican, represented a majority Black district. After race riots in 1917, he introduced a comprehensive anti-lynching bill in 1918, 1920, and 1922, when it passed the House with Harding's support. He was the first president to condemn lynching. Southerners threatened a filibuster and the Republican Senate majority retreated. Dyer worked closely with Mary Burnett Talbert, chair of the NAACP Anti-Lynching Committee. An Oberlin graduate, Talbert had secretly hosted the 1905 Niagara Movement meeting and was a rare Black Red Cross nurse on the Western Front.[54]

One month after defeating the anti-lynching bill, the Senate supported a proposal from the United Daughters of the Confederacy to dedicate a monument on the National Mall "to the Faithful Colored Mammies of the South." The mythical figure of a servant would cradle a white baby. The NAACP was silent, but Black women made themselves heard. Terrell refused to romanticize the symbol. "Colored women all over the United States stand aghast," given the helpless position of Black women caring for white children, "while her heart bled for her own." NACW head Hallie Quinn Brown was vehement: "Slave women were brutalized, the victims of white men's caprice and lust. Often the babe torn from her arms was the child of her oppressor." If Southern women were grateful, they could "make restitution" by working to "stop mob rule and lynching."[55] Blocking the monument was a demonstration of the moral authority and public engagement of Black women.

Anti-lynching efforts faltered until 1934, when the NAACP helped Democratic Senators Edward Costigan (CO) and Robert Wagner (NY) draft a new bill. It prosecuted sheriffs who did not protect their prisoners. President Roosevelt refused to endorse it because he depended on Southern Democrats in the Senate. In the 1930s, anti-lynching bills passed the House but repeatedly failed in the Senate. The Klan had attained widespread control of politics and law enforcement across the country, with an estimated six million members in forty-eight states. Several states elected Klan members governor and Senator, like Alabama's Hugo Black, whom Roosevelt named to the Supreme Court in 1937. Engaged in violence against Black Americans, immigrants, Catholics, and Jews, the Klan stood for white supremacy, white Protestantism, and equality between its male and female members.[56]

Black women had long been outraged by the slander that white women were chaste, while they were assumed to be promiscuous. Bethune called on Southern white women to take responsibility for halting racial violence. Jesse Daniel Ames, a white Atlantan, responded by founding the Association of Southern Women for the Prevention of Lynching in 1930. Ames was a college graduate, a suffragist, the founding president of the Texas LWV, and a delegate to Democratic conventions. Because "only white women could influence other white women," ASWPL members were white middle-class women. They signed a declaration asserting that the rapes which were "the supposed rationale for lynching," seldom occurred, and that the true motive was racial hatred:

> Lynching is an indefensible crime. Women dare no longer allow themselves to be the cloak behind which those bent on personal revenge and savagery commit acts of violence and lawlessness in the name of women. We repudiate this disgraceful claim for all time.

By 1940, the ASWPL had 109 chapters and four million members, but it did not endorse federal anti-lynching legislation.[57]

Lynching decreased during the Depression, so the ASWPL merged with the Commission on Interracial Cooperation in 1942. The CIC sought to end lynching, mob violence, and peonage or "debt servitude," but it did not question segregation. Together, Black and white clubwomen, many of them ministers' wives, created segregated day nurseries, clinics, and play-grounds. Like their white counterparts, the Black leaders were educated, middle-class, married women, but unlike white women, they were "double crossed" by race and gender.[58]

After decades of Republican allegiance, Black voters questioned their party loyalty. To sustain support for the party of Lincoln, in 1924 the Republican National Committee recruited Hallie Brown, a Republican state committee member in Delaware, to direct its Colored Women's Division. An educator and a magnetic "elocutionist," she had performed for Queen Victoria. As NACW president from 1920 to 1924, she and Mary Talbert launched an effort to preserve Frederick Douglass's home in Washington. She established a network of Black women's Republican clubs, spoke at the 1924 Republican convention, directed Colored Women's Activities for Coolidge, and supported Hoover. In return, President Hoover hosted a segregated inaugural ball.[59] Not to be outdone, in 1924 the Democrats named Alice Dunbar Nelson, a creole poet and essayist, to be Director of Colored Women. As a suffragist, Dunbar argued that voting would not interfere with the duties of wives and mothers any more than church activities did.[60] Black women were expanding their local and national networks.

THE EQUAL RIGHTS AMENDMENT

When it was proposed by Alice Paul, very few white or Black social justice activists supported the Equal Rights Amendment. It embodied many of the fissures in the women's movement that broke along class and racial lines. After the Nineteenth Amendment passed, Paul enrolled in the Washington College of Law, eventually earning three degrees. The law school, founded by women in 1896, was the first to have a woman dean and to graduate a class of all women. Like Stanton, Paul did not believe voting rights were equivalent to equality.

It is incredible to me that any woman should consider the fight
for full equality won. It is just beginning. There is hardly a field,
economic or political, in which the natural and accustomed
policy is not to ignore women. . . . Unless women are prepared to
fight politically, they must be content to be ignored politically.[61]

With an inner circle of advisors and millionaire benefactor Alva Belmont,
Paul explored ways to remove laws discriminating against women with
some form of blanket legislation. In February 1921, before Sheppard–
Towner had been reintroduced, Paul invited fifty women's organizations
to the National Woman's Party's national convention.[62]

The event began with a celebration of the founding mothers. Paul
wanted to install a statue of Stanton, Anthony, and Mott in the Capitol. In
the 1880s, Adelaide Johnson modeled individual busts of the Great Three
for an exhibit at the 1893 Chicago World's Fair. Paul commissioned a new
work. In Italy, Johnson chiseled the trio from a single piece of marble.
The 14,000-pound monument traveled by sled, railroad car, ocean liner,
and dray to the Capitol steps, where it remained in a crate while the Joint
Congressional Library Committee decided its fate. After negotiating with
Paul, the gentlemen agreed that the sculpture could be installed in the
Rotunda, for twenty-four hours.[63]

On February 15, 1921, the 101st anniversary of Anthony's birthday,
a parade of "banner-waving, wreath-bearing representatives" of seventy
women's organizations celebrated the passage of the Anthony Amendment
at the monument's unveiling. Among them was Hallie Brown, representing
NACW. Neither Catt nor the League of Women Voters participated.[64]
Edna St. Vincent Millay read her poem "To Inez Milholland," honoring
the woman who had led the 1913 suffrage parade on horseback. In 1916,
at age thirty, she died of pernicious anemia, exhausted from campaigning
against Wilson. The next day the statue was moved to the Capitol Crypt,
where it remained for seventy-five years.[65] In 1923, Millay won the Pulitzer
Prize for poetry and married Milholland's widower.

At the NWP convention, invited organizations presented their legislative priorities. Among them were initiatives for factory workers, immigrants, disarmament, divorce reform, children, and Black women. Crystal Eastman, who had been allied with Paul since 1913, reported that lynching was briefly discussed, but "all doubtful subjects, like birth control and the rights of Negro women, were hushed up, ruled out of order or postponed." Terrell and a delegation of sixty Black women from fourteen states demanded action to protect Black women attempting to register and vote. They asked Paul to endorse NACW's request for a congressional investigation into the disenfranchisement of Black women in the South. Paul dismissed it as a race issue, not a women's issue. Nor did she object when the convention venue refused to let Black women use the elevator.[66] Kelley believed the NWP had "welshed on the Negro question." Eastman damned Paul in an article in the *Liberator* and Freda Kirchwey, editor of *The Nation*, reported that "Miss Paul was indifferent" to the appeals of Black delegates. Nor was the LWV willing to address Black disenfranchisement.[67]

Ignoring every other issue, Paul declared that the NWP would have a single plank platform: ratification of an Equal Rights Amendment (ERA). Her first challenge was its wording. Earlier in 1921, Wisconsin passed a bill to grant women the same rights and privileges as men, exempting "the specific protection and privileges which they now enjoy for the general welfare."[68] Paul wanted no exceptions, even if the proposed amendment would endanger or eliminate provisions protecting women factory workers. She thought those protections should apply to both sexes, which had been the goal of reformers like Kelley before conservative courts struck them down.

The first breakthrough in securing protective labor legislation came in 1908, when the Supreme Court decided *Muller v. Oregon*. Oregon had passed the nation's first maximum ten-hour day law for women. Emma Gotcher, an employee in a Portland shirtwaist laundry, sued its owner, Curt Muller, for forcing her to work longer hours. Muller argued that the law violated the due process clause and infringed on his right to make a contract. After the Oregon Supreme Court upheld the law, Muller appealed to the Supreme Court. Kelley persuaded Boston lawyer Louis Brandeis to represent Oregon. Known as the "Robin Hood of the Law," he took the case pro bono.

Brandeis prepared two pages of legal arguments and 111 pages of expert evidence from physicians and investigators about the impact of working long hours on women's health, especially on their capacity to have children. The Court accepted the scientific evidence and ruled unanimously to uphold Oregon's law. *Muller* did not abrogate *Lochner v. New York* (1905), which refused to limit the hours of male and female bakers to sixty per week. Rather, it established the constitutionality of protective legislation for women. A woman was in "a class by herself" because "she is not an equal competitor with her brother." Women deserved protection of their "maternal functions."[69]

Was protection progress? By 1923, thirty-nine states limited women's hours, seventeen secured their minimum wages, and forty provided pensions for mothers and widows.[70] Limiting their hours made women ineligible for many jobs and for union membership. Rules protecting women from night work resulted in them being fired from jobs like streetcar conductor. Protection may have rescued women from harsh conditions in factories and mines, but it drove them into lower paying, sex-segregated occupations.

In 1923, the District of Columbia adopted a minimum wage law for women. Because her employer could not afford the new wage, hotel elevator operator Willie Lyons was fired. When a man not covered by the statute replaced her, she joined women working at a local hospital to contest the law. They sued Jesse Adkins, a member of the District Minimum Wage Board, for cutting their earnings. In *Adkins v. Children's Hospital of D.C.*, the Supreme Court held that minimum wage laws were an unconstitutional infringement on women's right to contract under the Fifth Amendment. Harvard law professor Felix Frankfurter defended the statute; Kelley and Paul entered opposing amicus briefs.[71]

Distinguishing between wages and hours, *Adkins* did not overturn *Muller*. The Court held that physical differences between the sexes could justify different hours but not different wages.

> [The] ancient inequality of the sexes, other than physical, as sug-
> gested in the *Muller* case, has continued with diminishing inten-
> sity. In view of the great—not to say revolutionary—changes
> which have taken place since that utterance, in the contractual,
> political and civil status of women, culminating in the Nine-
> teenth Amendment, it is not unreasonable to say that these dif-
> ferences now come almost, if not quite, to the vanishing point.

Writing for the majority, Justice George Sutherland asserted that woman suffrage nullified the need for protective legislation. Sutherland had been an ardent champion of suffrage when he served in the House and Senate (R-UT). The *Adkins* decision was 5–3. Justice Brandeis recused himself because his daughter worked for the Wage Board. (After he was nominated as the first Jewish justice, in 1916, the Senate convened the first ever confirmation hearings; without him present, his record was examined for four months.) Chief Justice William Howard Taft and Oliver Wendell Holmes wrote dissents, claiming that limiting "conditions leading to ill health, immorality or the deterioration of the race" was not unreasonable.[72] In 1925, Susan Brandeis became the first daughter of a justice to argue before the Court. The first Black woman admitted to the Supreme Court Bar was Violette Anderson, in 1926.[73]

Paul, whose slogan was "Equality Not Protection," endorsed political sameness. Convinced that sex-based laws inhibited women's advancement, Paul settled on her final wording for an Equal Rights Amendment: "No political, civil or legal disabilities or inequalities on account of sex or on account of marriage, unless applying equally to both sexes, shall exist within the United States or any territory subject to its jurisdiction thereof."[74] Social justice activists and labor leaders believed that a blanket amendment would damage working women. Kelley damned the proposed amendment as "miserable, monstrously stupid and deadly." She questioned how it would affect child support, illegitimacy, pensions, prenatal care, and penalties for rape or desertion.[75] Over the next fifty years, as protection became an impediment to equal treatment, Paul proved prescient.

Dismissing every objection, Paul alienated almost everybody. In July 1923, she introduced the pared-down Lucretia Mott Amendment in Seneca Falls: "Men and women shall have equal rights throughout the United States and every place subject to its jurisdiction." Paul again relied on a one-party legislative strategy. That December, two Kansas Republicans introduced the amendment. Representative Daniel Anthony was Susan's nephew. Senator Charles Curtis was the first politician with Indigenous roots elected to the Senate. The majority leader after 1924 and elected with Hoover in 1928, he was the first vice president of color. The ERA was reintroduced in every subsequent Congress, with occasional committee votes after 1938, but no floor vote until 1946.[76]

The amendment created yet another schism in the women's movement. For fifty years, organized labor and the League of Women Voters testified against it. The NWP endorsed Herbert Hoover in 1928 and 1932, annoying Democrats, the only time a feminist organization backed a major party candidate before 1984. Paul's disregard for working women isolated her from social justice activists. She excluded Black women from NWP membership and advocated rights that would primarily benefit privileged white women. Eastman, who wanted Paul to support birth control and "equal domesticity" between spouses, stuck with her, asserting optimistically, "This is a fight worth fighting, even if it [takes] ten years."[77] Although the BPW, made up of white office workers and accountants, endorsed the ERA in 1929, the NWP lost members, resources, and effectiveness. The Party was always reluctant to publish its membership, which peaked at six thousand in 1920. Paul claimed she preferred working with an elite group. As historian Nancy Cott concluded, Paul claimed to "stand for and speak for all women [but] the NWP would stand for and speak for fewer and fewer."[78]

WOMEN IN POLITICS

The small cohort of women who voted was too diverse to be a cohesive bloc. Women who had opposed suffrage fought the Joint Congressional

Committee's agenda. Nor did women make gains as candidates. Parties did not nominate women for seats that could be won. Five women ran for Senate in 1920, two on the Farm-Labor ticket, three as Prohibitionists. Two ran against each other. None won.[79] Seven women ran for Congress; one won. The Harding landslide swept Alice Robertson, age sixty-six, into the House. The Muskogee dairy farmer and cafeteria worker was president of the Oklahoma Anti-Suffrage Association. She supported Indigenous rights and lynching and opposed Sheppard–Towner and the Veterans' Bonus Bill. "I came to Congress to represent my district," Robertson declared, "not women." She retired after one term.[80]

Two women won special elections in 1922. Winnifred Sprague Huck (R-IL), the first wife and mother elected to Congress, replaced her father and served for fourteen weeks.[81] Mae Nolan (R-CA) was the first widow to succeed her husband, "because no one knows better than I do his legislative agenda." She served the remainder of his term and one of her own. Nolan supported minimum wages and the Child Labor Amendment. She refused to sit on the committee considering the ERA.[82] Ten women were nominated in 1924: four Democrats in GOP districts, one Republican in the South, four socialists, and a prohibitionist.[83] Only one won.

Mary Norton was the first Democratic and the first Catholic congresswoman. A working class high school graduate, whose only child died in infancy, "Battling Mary" worked with the Day Nursery Association in New Jersey. She demanded that Jersey City Democratic boss Frank Hague fund nursery schools; he made her his protégé. Elected to Congress in 1924, she declined being nominated for vice president in 1932, introduced the amendment to repeal prohibition, and, as chair of the Labor Committee, secured passage of the 1938 Fair Labor Standards Act. Norton served twenty-four years, until 1950.[84]

In total, eleven white women served in the House of Representatives in the 1920s, eight Republicans and three Democrats. Most of them came into politics through family ties, as most women would until 2001. Four were widows and two were daughters of politicians; one was both. Five women served only one term, including Robertson and Republican Ruth Hanna

McCormick, the daughter and widow of Senators, who left the House in 1930 to run for Senate from Illinois. Mollie Terrell moved to Chicago to campaign for McCormick. Using her daughter's residence, Terrell registered and voted for the first and only time.

> I have worked for suffrage all my life and the first vote I shall be
> able to cast will be for the first woman who has had the courage to
> run for the United States Senate. That certainly gives me a kick.[85]

McCormick came in first in a primary field of eight, but lost the general election. Three other women served just two terms in Congress, leaving three members with careers long enough to accrue some clout, including Norton.[86]

Republican Congresswoman Florence Kahn, from San Francisco, the first Jewish woman to serve, was elected in 1925 to fill the vacancy left by her husband. She refused an assignment to the Indian Affairs Committee ("The only Indians in my district are in front of cigar stores"), serving instead on the Military Affairs Committee. She argued for preparedness, honored Gold Star Mothers, and expanded the authority of the FBI. Kahn was the first woman to serve on the powerful Appropriations Committee. After six terms, she lost to a New Deal Democrat in 1936.[87]

Edith Nourse Rogers (R-MA) had been a Red Cross nurse during the Great War and worked with wounded veterans, earning the title "the Angel of Walter Reed." Succeeding her husband in a special election in 1925, Rogers polled more votes than he ever had. She served eighteen terms, the longest incumbency of any woman until Congresswoman Marcy Kaptur (D-OH), elected in 1982, surpassed Rogers' thirty-six-year tenure. She secured appropriations for veterans' hospitals, supported the GI Bill, created women's branches in the armed services, and advanced to chair the Veterans Affairs Committee in 1947. Her bipartisanship prompted Democratic House Speaker John McCormick, another member of the Massachusetts delegation, to protect her Republican seat from redistricting.[88]

Only one woman entered the Senate in the 1920s, holding office for one day, November 21, 1922, long enough for one vote and a photograph.

Democrat Rebecca Latimer Felton was the most prominent woman in Georgia, an antisemitic white supremacist who supported lynching and white-only suffrage. Born in 1835, the first woman senator was the oldest freshman to enter the Senate and the last member of Congress to have enslaved people. Newspapers described her as "dainty" and "poised." When Georgia's junior senator died, the governor appointed Felton. The appointment was symbolic because the Senate was not in session and Georgia elected a replacement.

Women pressured President Harding to call a special session. Besieged by letters, Harding demurred, until he needed to pass a ship subsidy bill. Senator Felton persuaded her successor to allow her to be sworn in, then answered the roll call to cheers from women packing the gallery and gave her only speech. She thanked her colleagues for their "chivalric" welcome and continued: "When the women of the country come and sit with you, though there may be few in the next few years, I pledge that you will get ability . . . integrity of purpose . . . exalted patriotism and . . . unstinted usefulness." The last item of business before adjournment was a resolution directing the Senate to pay Felton her $287.67 salary plus $280 for travel expenses.[89]

Even losing candidates were agents of change. Simply by running for office, women "re-gendered the landscape for both men and women."[90] The first two women governors succeeded their husbands. In another female first for Wyoming, Democrat Nellie Tayloe Ross won a special election in 1925, defeating the lieutenant governor. She narrowly lost her reelection bid because she supported prohibition and refused to campaign.[91] Miriam "Ma" Ferguson (D-TX) served one term, 1925–27, following her husband's impeachment and conviction, and a less controversial term, 1933–35. She assured voters she would follow her husband's advice and that Texas would get "two governors for the price of one." She supported a law forbidding Klan members to wear masks, which was overturned.[92] No other woman was elected governor until Lurleen Wallace (D-AL) filled in for her husband in 1967. In the 1920s, women won statewide races to be school superintendent, treasurer, auditor, and railroad commissioner. Many small towns and ten cities had women mayors. The largest, Seattle, elected Bertha Landes in 1928. Then as now, women won most often at the lowest levels of office.[93]

THE ROARING TWENTIES

Harding won because he promised a return to "normalcy" after a European war, a global pandemic, labor strikes, a Red Scare, and raging racial violence. What Americans got was the Roaring Twenties. The Jazz Age, a term coined by F. Scott Fitzgerald, described not only the rhythms of the era but also an attitude of improvisation. Rooted in African American culture, jazz and the blues were the downbeat of the Harlem Renaissance. There was a vibrant cacophony of white and Black creativity, including works by novelists Willa Cather, Jessie Fauset, Zora Neale Hurston, and Edith Wharton; by sculptors Augusta Savage and Meta Fuller; by abstract artist Georgia O'Keeffe and modern dancer Martha Graham.

Suffrage was not the only amendment added to the Constitution in 1920. The Eighteenth Amendment prohibited "the manufacture, transportation and sale of intoxicating beverages." It did not forbid drinking. The first amendment to have a seven-year ratification deadline, it passed in thirteen months, taking effect in January 1920. Supporters claimed that less drinking would result in less poverty, less crime, less immorality, less wife beating, fewer industrial accidents, and happier families. It would also clamp down on the boisterous drinking culture associated with immigrants, the urban working class, and Democratic machine politics. Originally a woman's issue, prohibition was appropriated by a coalition of "Drys": white progressives, Protestants, nativists, and racists. "Wets" also included progressives plus Catholics and city-dwellers. Prohibition was popular in the South and in small towns. Cities saw a surge of bootlegging and organized crime. In the 1920s, New York City had 32,000 mixed-sex, mixed-race speakeasies. Cocktail parties served new concoctions like Bloody Marys, sidecars, and Bee's Knees.[94]

Enforcement of prohibition was in the hands of Mabel Walker Willebrandt, the Assistant Attorney General, the highest-ranking woman in the federal government, appointed by Harding. She succeeded Wilson's appointee, Annette Abbott Adams, the first woman to hold the post. A divorcée, Willebrandt had been a Los Angeles public defender, advocating for fallen women and beaten wives. Over eight years under three presidents, she argued nearly eighty cases before the Supreme Court, recommended J. Edgar Hoover to lead the FBI, and charged mobsters with tax evasion. She claimed that government corruption and incompetence made enforcement of prohibition impossible. Ironically, without the tax revenue from alcohol sales, it was also unaffordable. When President Hoover did not name her Attorney General, she resigned. At age forty, she created a new career as an aviation and entertainment lawyer. When she died, noted lawyers declared, "If Mabel had worn trousers, she could have been President." Her nemesis was another Republican, Pauline Sabin. The New York socialite and political operative organized the repeal movement. In 1933, the Twenty-third Amendment ended prohibition and the White House resumed receiving beer deliveries.[95]

Prohibition fueled an inebriating mix of speakeasies, flappers, and Model-T Fords. One in three Americans owned a car, providing a sense of freedom and a place to indulge in backseat sex. Art deco influenced the design of skyscrapers, safety razors, wristwatches, and vacuum cleaners. Radio fostered a common culture and talking movies created celebrities. Aviators and baseball players replaced cowboys as symbols of masculinity. Flappers represented the changes in manners and morals of Cole Porter's lyric, "Anything Goes." With short hair and short skirts, these flat-chested, slim-hipped tomboys copied masculine behavior, drinking, smoking, dancing, and "makin' whoopee." In a 1927 romantic comedy, Clara Bow embodied the flapper's insouciance, becoming America's "It Girl." A year later, the boyish aviator Amelia Earhart became America's sweetheart, whereas Bessie Coleman, the first American woman to earn an international pilot's license, was refused admission to US aviation schools because she was African American.[96]

The iconic American flapper was Josephine Baker, a Black expatriate. Born Freda Josephine McDonald in St. Louis in 1906, she left after her home was burned in the 1917 race riots. In 1926, at age twenty, she appeared at the Folies Bergère in Paris, wearing only a skirt made of cloth bananas. Subverting stereotypes with humor, Baker danced the Charleston, the Black Bottom, and the Lindy Hop, named for Charles Lindbergh. Known as the Black Venus, she was the first international superstar, the world's highest paid entertainer, and the first Black woman to star in a major motion picture. Later she would join the French Resistance, earn the Croix de Guerre, and support the civil rights movement in the United States.[97] Even if only a fragment of the female population enjoyed such independence, the image of flappers may have advanced women's status more than voting rights.

In 1920, the US population passed 100 million. For the first time, more Americans lived in cities than on farms. The contrast between urban and rural life was stark. Nine out of ten farms were without electricity, which meant no running water, flush toilets, light bulbs, refrigerators, washing machines, or appliances like irons.[98] Rural women could not plug in or afford a KitchenAid electric mixer, introduced in 1922. To advise home bakers, General Mills also introduced the fictional Betty Crocker. Although her image did not appear until 1936, Betty starred in one of the most successful advertising campaigns in American history.[99]

Miss America, another symbol of idealized womanhood, also made her debut in 1921. To extend its tourist season, Atlantic City sponsored a "Golden Mermaid" competition. Local newspapers nominated nine contestants. Margaret Gorman was named "the most beautiful bathing girl in America." Despite a city law against women baring their knees, contestants were required to wear bathing suits. When she returned in 1922 to defend her title, the petite sixteen-year-old high school student was crowned "Miss America," the second-place title. The pageant grew in scope, adding a talent competition in 1938 and offering college scholarships instead of Hollywood contracts in 1944. The first went to Bess Myerson, the first and only Jewish Miss America. There were no Black contestants. After 1935, racial exclusion was formalized in Rule Seven: "Contestants must be of good health and of the white race."[100] Other girls in bathing suits also made news. In 1920, Aileen Riggin Soule, fourteen, won the first Olympic gold medal in three-meter diving. In 1926, New Yorker Gertrude Ederle, twenty, swam the English Channel. She wore a pair of aviator goggles sealed with candle wax. Her dad, a butcher, had promised her a red roadster if she succeeded.[101]

EMPLOYMENT AND EDUCATION

It was a decade of uneven opportunities for women. There were higher rates of college attendance, expanded employment opportunities, and more sexual freedom, but white women could serve on juries only in California, Colorado, Idaho, and Utah. Women were 44% of college students, though that number comprised less than 10% of all women ages eighteen to twenty-one. At historically Black colleges, women were in the majority. Three-fourths of Black and white female graduates got jobs as teachers, nurses, librarians, and social workers. One-third of doctorates went to women but only 4% of full professors were women.[102] Women were not admitted to the American Medical Association until 1915; African American doctors were barred until the late 1960s. Few hospitals accepted female residents. The percentage of women doctors fell further after medical schools imposed a 5% quota from 1925 to 1945.[103]

In 1924, Vassar College created an interdisciplinary course on the care of families. Other colleges offered home economics, not as a science but to prepare women for marriage and motherhood. The field was developed by chemist Ellen Swallow Richards at the Massachusetts Institute of Technology. She was MIT's first female graduate in 1873, and still its only one at the time of her death in 1911. Early in her career, Richards published *The Chemistry of Cooking and Cleaning: A Manual for Housekeeping* (1885) and analyzed sewer systems for the Massachusetts Board of Health. Her research convinced progressives to lobby for Pure Food and Drug laws.[104]

The marriage rate in 1920 was 92.3%, its historic high. Only one in seven marriages ended in divorce. Reformers addressed the age of consent, at which it was legal to marry or have sexual relations with young girls. In 1900, Delaware raised it from seven to ten years old, which was the standard in Georgia, Mississippi, and New York. In the 1920s, the age of consent rose to sixteen or eighteen in most states and fourteen in Georgia.[105] Most women stopped working when they married, but in low-income families, 25% of married women worked. Five times more Black women than white women worked outside their homes, primarily as servants and laundresses. The percentage of white married women in the workforce increased to 12%, including those with children. Some employers required a woman to have her husband's permission to work.[106] Working as domestic servants, farm laborers, teachers, typists, and clerks, women were a small percentage of the labor force in 1920. Jobs were segregated by race and ethnicity, with Black women getting the worst and lowest paid jobs. By 1930, more white women worked in the service sector than in domestic service. Only white women were hired to be telephone operators and sales clerks. As women became the majority of a field like "girl Fridays," wages dropped.[107]

Excitement about change and fear of change permeated the 1920s. Fear of science put fundamentalism on trial in Dayton, Tennessee, in July 1925, when high school teacher John Scopes was found guilty of teaching human evolution. The verdict was overthrown on a technicality, but publicity about the trial contributed to the decade's characterization of rural Americans as bumpkins and boobs. Fear of racial mixing contributed to huge growth in Klan membership, demonstrated by a thirty thousand-member march in Washington, DC, in August 1925. Fear of foreigners and Bolshevism was an element in the passage of the Johnson-Reed Immigration Act of 1924 and the execution of accused anarchists Nicola Sacco and Bartolomeo Vanzetti in 1927.[108] Despite rejecting the Versailles Treaty, it was hard to isolate the country from change.

BIRTH CONTROL

Sexual mores changed dramatically in the 1920s and represented a new kind of independence for women. Less chaperoned, young people had more opportunities to have sex. Birth control, a phrase coined by Margaret Sanger in 1913, remained contentious. Her campaign to provide contraceptive information and devices for women slowly gained legitimacy. Sanger was the sixth surviving child of Irish Catholic immigrants in Corning, New York. In thirty years of marriage, her mother had eighteen pregnancies, eleven live births, and seven miscarriages before dying at forty-nine. Sanger trained as a nurse, married an architect, and had three children. Working as a public health nurse in New York City, she treated tenement women so desperate to limit pregnancies that they attempted self-abortions with coat hangers and knitting needles. Sanger believed adequate, accessible contraception would negate the need for abortion or infanticide. From the beginning, birth control and abortion were linked.[109]

"Voluntary motherhood," or refusing a husband's conjugal rights, was not realistic. Some women knew about douches and vinegar sponge suppositories, but widespread education about limiting conception was non-existent. The Comstock Law, passed in 1873, outlawed distribution of any materials deemed "obscene, lewd or lascivious" through the US mail. The ban included information about contraception, abortion, venereal disease, even anatomy books. It was named for Anthony Comstock, a devout Christian appalled by prostitution and pornography. He founded the Society for the Suppression of Vice and served as a special agent for the Postal Service. Comstock died in 1915, but the federal government's interest in anti-obscenity laws continued.[110]

To educate women about contraception, Sanger wrote a newsletter, *The Woman Rebel*. Postal authorities suppressed five of seven issues. When she published *Family Limitation* in 1914, she was indicted under the Comstock Law. Rather than face a five-year sentence, Sanger fled to Europe. Estranged from her husband and damned for deserting her children, Sanger returned in 1915 to face the felony charge. While she awaited trial, her only daughter, age five, died of pneumonia. After several postponements, the government dropped its case. As the US Attorney for New York explained, he refused to make Margaret Sanger a martyr.[111]

Undeterred, Sanger and her sister Ethel Byrne opened the first birth control clinic in the United States, in Brooklyn, in October 1916. They advertised their services in English, Yiddish, and Italian.

> Mothers, Can you afford to have a large family?
> Do you want any more children?
> If not, why do you have them?
> Do not kill, do not take life but prevent [it].[112]

Nine days later, they were arrested for running a public nuisance. Found guilty, they were sentenced to thirty days in jail. After going on a hunger strike, Byrne became the first woman in America to be force-fed. She was released after ten days. Sanger served her sentence while contesting the verdict. The court refused her appeal, ruling that existing law allowed only doctors to prescribe birth control. The verdict suggested a new strategy.

To legitimize birth control, Sanger allied with the male medical community. In 1921, she founded the American Birth Control League (ABCL) and served as its president until 1928. Her 1922 book, *The Pivot of Civilization*, summarized her beliefs:

> . . . children should be (1) conceived in love; (2) born of the mother's conscious desire; and (3) only begotten under conditions which render possible the heritage of health. Therefore we hold that every woman must possess the power and freedom to prevent conception except when these conditions can be satisfied.[113]

With funding from the Rockefeller Foundation, Sanger established the first legal birth control clinic in New York City in 1923. Because it required supervision by a licensed physician, Sanger sought out women doctors as well as nurses and social workers.

In 1925, she hired Dr. Hannah Mayer Stone. With dual degrees in medicine and pharmacology, Stone served for sixteen years without pay and at great cost. After Stone was photographed being led to a paddy wagon following a wrongful raid on her clinic, the New York Medical Society tabled her application and she lost privileges at a maternity hospital. Stone may have been blackballed for being Jewish and female. A significant cohort of Jewish doctors staffed birth control clinics across the country.[114] Working with the Julius Rosenwald Fund, the Urban League, and the Reverend Adam Clayton Powell Sr., Sanger opened a clinic in Harlem in 1929, with a Black advisory board and staff.

Sanger resigned from the ABCL in 1928 but continued her research. When efforts to overturn restrictions on birth control failed, Sanger challenged the Tariff Act of 1930, which allowed the seizure of imported contraceptive devices. She asked Dr. Stone to order Japanese diaphragms for use in her private practice. The government confiscated the box and Stone sued. In *United States v. One Package of Japanese Pessaries* (1936), the US Court of Appeals for the Second Circuit held that physicians were exempt from such restrictions.[115]

Alarm about increasing rates of premarital sex, venereal disease, and divorce slowly made birth control more acceptable. It was eventually endorsed by the American Medical Association, added to medical school curricula, and encouraged by some Protestant churches, which argued that sex for reasons other than procreation would increase marital harmony. The Catholic Church remained opposed. "Birth control," intoned Boston's Cardinal William Henry O'Connell, is "a direct threat . . . towards increasing impurity and unchastity not only in our married life but . . . among our unmarried people."[116]

Sanger's charisma and causes made her a controversial celebrity. She moved to Tucson in 1938, lectured widely, and searched for better methods of birth control. Her second husband manufactured the first legal diaphragms in the United States. In 1942, the American Birth Control League changed its name to Planned Parenthood Federation of America, partly to separate itself from its founder. Sanger's association with eugenics in the 1920s made her a lightning rod. "More children from the fit, less from the unfit—that is the chief issue of birth control," Sanger proclaimed in 1919. She used "unfit" in reference to the mentally ill, a common expression then but abhorrent now.[117]

Eugenics was a "pseudoscience, promulgated in the early twentieth century, to improve human genetics." It was used to justify the forced sterilization of 64,000 Americans between 1907 and 1979 based on race, class, and perceived "feeblemindedness." Despite its inherent racism and immorality, many prominent Americans flirted with the idea, including Theodore Roosevelt, Booker T. Washington, and W. E. B. Du Bois. In 1924, Virginia passed a law authorizing compulsory sterilization of the intellectually disabled. Soon after, superintendents of the Virginia State Colony for Epileptics and the Feebleminded ordered the sterilization of Carrie Buck. The white seventeen-year-old had been raped by a relative, accused of promiscuity and feeblemindedness, and committed. Her mother had previously been institutionalized for prostitution and immorality. To create a test case, the institution hired a lawyer to sue on her behalf.

The case, *Buck v. Bell*, reached the Supreme Court on appeal. Writing for the 8–1 majority, Justice Oliver Wendell Holmes affirmed that Virginia had a compelling interest in curtailing Buck's ability to have children to prevent the nation from "being swamped with incompetence . . . Three generations of imbeciles is enough." The dissenting vote was cast by Justice Pierce Butler, the only Catholic on the Court. The ideal of a pure white race was a motivating factor. The *Buck* decision has been discredited but not overturned.[118] The 1990 Americans with Disabilities Act now protects both physically and intellectually disabled people. Some of those protections have been deemed restrictive by disabled activists.

It was not a leap for eugenicists to go from singling out the mentally disabled to discriminating against immigrants, African Americans, Jews, and the poor. Nazis used eugenics to rationalize the Holocaust. The sterilization of Black women who were not in institutions became so common in the South that it was called a "Mississippi appendectomy." Sanger tried to distinguish between birth control and eugenics, emphasizing that contraception was voluntary, but the link between eugenics and fascism damned her. Biographers cite her support from W. E. B. Du Bois and Mary McLeod Bethune, but acknowledge the stain of eugenics on her reputation. In 2015, the National Portrait Gallery refused a demand by Senator Ted Cruz (R-TX) to remove her bust because of Planned Parenthood's advocacy of abortion. In the historical reassessments of 2020, Planned Parenthood disavowed Sanger on account of eugenics, removing her name from an award and a New York City clinic.[119]

THE CRASH

There was no incumbent in the 1928 presidential race. Republican Secretary of Commerce Herbert Hoover ran against New York Democratic Governor Al Smith, a Catholic "wet." Women voted for "Hoover, Home and Happiness" and against "Rum and Romanism." He won 58% of the vote and carried forty states. While scientific polling did not exist, straw polls recorded a gender gap in turnout. For the first time, women voted at a higher rate than men. Smith won Southern and Catholic voters but lost New York, where Franklin Roosevelt won the governorship, one of few Democratic victories.[120] His wife Eleanor, by then the best known and most powerful Democratic woman in the country, became an unconventional First Lady in Albany. Unwilling to give up her public roles, she continued to organize, lobby, write, and teach at the Todhunter School, a K-12 girls' school she had purchased in 1927, in New York City. She served as associate principal and taught American history and current events. In 1939, Todhunter merged with the Dalton School.

The country's seemingly buoyant prosperity masked an economy out of balance. An orgy of speculation prompted an overheated stock market to crash in October 1929.[121] A decade of flash and dazzle collapsed into financial disaster. Similarly, as the end of the decade approached, journalists concluded that "the Nineteenth Amendment promised almost everything and accomplished almost nothing."[122] The Depression would reverse the few gains women had made, contributing to a sense of defeat. In a Republican decade, reform had failed. White women were occasional voters, while Black women were eager to vote but disenfranchised. Writing in *Redbook*, Eleanor Roosevelt assessed the situation: "Women have been voting for ten years. But have they achieved political equity with men? No. Politically, as a sex, women are generally 'frozen out' . . . The machinery of the party has always been in the hands of men and still is."[123]

Terrell and Roosevelt encouraged women to engage in politics, but gains were few. New Mexico elected Hispanic Soledad Chávez de Chacón, a Democrat, secretary of state in 1923. In 1925, Republican Cora Reynolds Anderson, an Ojibwa from the Upper Peninsula, won a seat in the Michigan house.[124] These small steps demonstrated historian Jo Freeman's thesis in *A Room at a Time: How Women Entered Party Politics*: "The myth that feminism failed after 1920 because feminists did not organize women into a major political force obscured what was really going on." She points to the women behind the scenes who were infiltrating party headquarters and back rooms, positioning themselves to exert influence. "Women went into politics the same way they got suffrage, slowly and persistently, with great effort, against much resistance."[125] Only Klanswomen were marching in the streets. Women who had struggled to secure suffrage contributed to the velocity of social change, but they had not yet accrued political or personal power.[126]

CHAPTER THREE

THE ELEANOR EFFECT, 1928–1945

leanor Roosevelt's biography is the story of one woman's transformation, and an example of the use of "soft power," of persuasion and moral authority. She was a neglected upper-class orphan, a well-educated debutante, a society bride, and an overwhelmed mother intimidated by her mother-in-law. Like many privileged women, her status derived from her relationship to powerful men: her uncle was President Theodore Roosevelt and her husband Franklin Roosevelt was Assistant Secretary of the Navy in the Wilson administration. A year older than Alice Paul, Eleanor lobbied for restrooms for women working in her husband's department, but she was not a suffragist. In 1918, when she was thirty-four, with five children ranging from two to twelve, she discovered her husband was having an affair with her social secretary. Their traditional marriage ended. It evolved into a unique political partnership as Eleanor acknowledged her own ambitions, priorities, and passions.[1]

In 1920, Franklin Roosevelt ran for vice president on the losing ticket. After he was stricken with polio in 1921, Eleanor convinced him to remain politically engaged. Initially acting as his surrogate, she became a robust politician in her own right. She allied herself with well-known

women leaders, including Catt, Addams, Kelley, and Alice Hamilton, a
Hull House alumna. Her discovery of the toxicity of lead paint and coal dust
prompted her appointment as the first female professor at Harvard medical
school. Roosevelt joined the League of Women Voters, the Women's Trade
Union League, international peace organizations, and the Women's City
Club in New York, a clubhouse for female activists. Members included Lillian Wald, Frances Perkins, and Molly Dewson. She invited Black educator
Mary McLeod Bethune to her home. These women became her political
and friendship network.[2]

"ER" volunteered with the Women's Division of the New York State
Democratic Party, registering women, organizing them into clubs, urging
them to purchase mimeograph machines and publish newsletters. She
toured every county in her blue roadster, speaking at crossroads and
reporting to her husband, who was recuperating in Warm Springs, Georgia.
She endorsed Sheppard–Towner and the Child Labor Amendment and
won a fight over who would choose New York's women delegates to the
1924 national convention, where she served as chair of a subcommittee on
women's issues. The Committee on Resolutions rebuffed her proposals. She
saw "for the first time where women stood when it came to the national
convention . . . outside the door of all important meetings."[3] Roosevelt
aspired to be an insider.

At the 1924 state Democratic convention, Franklin Roosevelt, supported
by his sons and iron leg braces, nominated Al Smith for his third term as
governor. Eleanor joined Smith's winning campaign against her cousin,
Theodore Roosevelt Jr. In 1926, she urged the Albany legislature to limit
the workweek to forty-eight hours over five days, rather than six ten-hour
days. She was charged with disorderly conduct for picketing a box-making
company to protest its working conditions.[4] In 1928, Franklin nominated
Smith for president and ran to replace him as governor. His wife campaigned for Smith rather than her husband. Smith lost, FDR won, and
Eleanor moved to Albany.

The 1929 stock market crash shattered financial markets but did not
cause an immediate catastrophe. At first, the economic downturn was

optimistically defined as a depression, part of the standard business cycle. By 1931, it had become the Great Depression. Farms foreclosed at a rate of 25,000 a week. Factories closed. Businesses and banks failed. Unemployment stood at 30%, almost fifteen million people, with another 10% of workers on short hours or reduced wages. Nine million families lost their homes and savings. "Hoovervilles" covered the landscape with tarpaper shacks.[5] The country faced unrelieved poverty, breadlines, and hopelessness. The most vulnerable, the elderly, the infirm, immigrants, women, and Black Americans, suffered most. Fear exacerbated racism.

Admired for two decades as a problem-solving engineer, President Hoover could not stop the disastrous downward economic spiral. Franklin Roosevelt's 1932 victory was less an enthusiastic endorsement than the repudiation of the incumbent. Despite the opposition of 60% of daily newspapers, FDR carried big cities and the South, winning forty-two states. Columnist Walter Lippmann dismissed the Democrat as "a highly impressionable person, without a firm grasp on public affairs and without very strong convictions." Others saw tremendous potential. On inauguration day, Roosevelt reassured the country that "this great nation will endure as it has endured," proclaiming famously, "the only thing we have to fear is fear itself."[6] There are more than eight hundred biographies and political histories of FDR and the New Deal. This book focuses on its impact on women, whose experiences differed based on race, class, geography, age, and marital and maternal status.

ELEANOR'S ROLE

The new First Lady was reluctant to move back to Washington, a city steeped in protocol and the scene of her husband's affair. After a decade of independent activity, she resisted traditional expectations and expanded her public roles. Eleanor challenged assumptions about how political wives should behave. She dressed as she wished, drove herself, and expressed her opinion. She became the voice of the underrepresented: women, the rural poor, young people, Jews, and African Americans. When the Bonus Army of Great War veterans returned to Washington in 1933, she visited their campsites. "Hoover sent the Army," one commented. "Roosevelt sent his wife."[7] It's more likely she went on her own.

During the contentious four-month transition (which would prompt a constitutional amendment moving the inauguration from March to January), Eleanor published a children's book, a memoir about her father, and a feminist call to arms. *It's Up to the Women* was part pep talk, part pragmatism. She reassured readers that the nation had survived earlier crises, thanks to women. She encouraged civic engagement and common sense, urging women to vote, get jobs, and exercise frugality. Her manifesto included maternal advice and recipes for inexpensive meals, provided by her cook. Eleanor's interest was not abstract equality but access and opportunities for women.[8]

Roosevelt produced articles and books for the rest of her life. From 1936 to 1962, she wrote a daily column syndicated in ninety newspapers, contributed a monthly column to *Woman's Home Companion*, hosted a weekly radio show, and spoke widely. Annoyed that she depended on an allowance from her husband, she was determined to match his salary, earning $75,000 during her first year in the White House. The first First Lady to earn an income, she ignored critics, paid her secretary's salary, underwrote pet projects, and donated her remaining income to charity.[9]

Both ER and her husband curried positive relationships with the press. She became so close to Lorena Hickok, who covered the presidential campaign, that the reporter's objectivity was questioned. "Hick" became a federal investigator, documenting poverty across the country, and moved into the White House, where their private relationship continued.[10] The First Lady hosted 348 press conferences in twelve years. She invited only female journalists, forcing news outlets to hire women correspondents. Because the Gridiron Club banned women reporters from its annual dinner, she hosted a Gridiron Widows dinner at the White House. Sensitive to criticism about her appearance and her children, she advised women in public "to develop skin as tough as a rhinoceros."[11]

Roosevelt used her role to advance women, beginning with appointments to government jobs. As soon as her husband was elected president, she and Molly Dewson compiled lists of women qualified for federal posts. Dewson was an 1897 graduate of Wellesley College, a suffragist and Kelley acolyte. She lobbied for a minimum wage law in Massachusetts and served as president of the New York branch of the National Consumers League. Eleanor recruited her to campaign for Al Smith in 1928. Recognizing her political skills, FDR put Dewson in charge of the Women's Division of the Democratic National Committee (DNC), making it a full-time post. Fifty of the sixty women she promoted were appointed. In 1937, Dewson was named to the Social Security Administration.[12]

FRANCES PERKINS AND SOCIAL SECURITY

In 1928, Dewson and Eleanor urged Governor Roosevelt to elevate Frances Perkins to lead the New York Industrial Commission. They pressed him again, in 1933, about naming her Secretary of Labor. When FDR formally offered Perkins the cabinet post, she listed her conditions: his support for "a forty-hour work week, a minimum wage, worker's compensation, unemployment compensation, a federal law banning child labor, direct federal aid for unemployment relief, social security, a revitalized public employment service and health insurance."[13] He agreed, and she proceeded to secure far-reaching social welfare legislation.

Perkins was the best-qualified person for the job. A 1902 graduate of Mount Holyoke College, with a degree in chemistry and physics, she had been inspired by Florence Kelley to work at Hull House. In 1910, she moved to New York to work for Kelley's Consumers League and pursue a master's in economics and sociology at Columbia University. By horrible happenstance, she was on the sidewalk near the Triangle Shirtwaist Factory when it caught fire on Saturday, March 25, 1911. It killed 146 workers, many the daughters of Jewish immigrants. Unable to escape, the teenagers jumped to their deaths. The owners responsible for the unsafe conditions were fined twenty dollars for locking the fire escape doors. They were acquitted of manslaughter. Perkins recalled the tragedy as "the day the New Deal was born."[14]

She became a fierce advocate of industrial safety, serving as the lead investigator of factory accidents in New York, allying with the Democratic machine for a fifty-four working hours per week bill and lobbying Franklin Roosevelt, then in the legislature, for his vote in 1913. Working in Albany prompted Perkins to don a disguise of dowdiness, with shapeless clothes and her trademark tricorn hat. She believed men would respond more positively to a woman who looked like their mothers.

> I tried to have as much of a mask as possible. I wanted to give the impression of being a quiet, orderly woman who didn't buzz-buzz all the time . . . I knew that a lady interposing an idea into men's conversation is very unwelcome. I just proceeded on the theory that this was a gentleman's conversation on the porch of a golf club . . . You can't butt in with bright ideas.[15]

She would not always conceal her opinions. Asked by a reporter if disrespectful men annoyed her, Perkins replied, "Not particularly, [because women] laugh . . . about the inadequacies . . . stupidity . . . [and] self-deceit of men."[16]

Perkins's work prompted Governor Smith to appoint her to the New York Industrial Commission, a post she held for his four terms. When FDR named her Chief Commissioner, she became the most prominent state labor official in the country. Despite being her family's breadwinner, Perkins was not an advocate for all working women. Married women faced legal and cultural prohibitions against working. Bans on married women teachers were common. By 1940, only 13% of school boards would hire wives and only 30% retained women after they married.[17] Perkins shared some of those negative attitudes, as she expressed in 1930:

> The woman "pin money" worker who competes with the neces-sity worker is a menace to society, a selfish . . . creature, who

ought to be ashamed of herself . . . Until we have every woman . . .
earning a living wage . . . I am not willing to encourage those
who are under no economic necessities to compete with their
charm and education, with their superior advantages, against
the working girl who has only two hands.[18]

The Depression would prove that even "pin money" was essential for
survival.

One of Hoover's efforts to reverse the Great Depression was the
Economy Act of 1932. Section 213 required the government to fire
one member of any married pair of federal workers. The bill did not
forbid federal jobs to other family duos, like fathers and sons. To avoid
fraud, the law required women to use their married names. The bill
was repealed in 1937, but attitudes did not change. In a 1936 poll commissioned by *Fortune*, only 15% of respondents agreed that married
women should have full-time jobs outside the home; three-fourths
of those opposed were women. Liberal journalist Norman Cousins,
learning in 1939 that the number of women in the workforce nearly
equaled unemployed men, offered a solution: "Simply fire the women
who shouldn't be working anyway. Presto! No unemployment. No relief
roles. No depression."[19]

Women's work was no joking matter. Patriarchal attitudes that men
should be heads of households drove unemployed husbands to desert
their families. In the Twenties, most white women could afford to quit
working when they had children. During the Depression, they worked to
support those children, who were cared for by Black women supporting
their children.[20] Few people knew that Secretary Perkins was a married
woman who kept her own name and worked to support her mentally
ill husband and fragile daughter, living in New York. Perkins shared
the Georgetown home of Mary Harriman Rumsey, who had organized the
Junior League in 1901. Supposedly the wealthiest woman in America,
Rumsey joined the New Deal as head of the Consumer Advisory Board
and recruited her younger brother Averell.[21]

As Secretary of Labor, Perkins accomplished everything on her list except universal health insurance, prompting *Forbes* magazine to herald her success as "the Perkins New Deal."[22] Her first proposal became the Civilian Conservation Corps (CCC). Beginning in April 1933, the government employed unmarried men, ages eighteen to twenty-five, to build trails and shelters and plant 3.5 billion trees in eight hundred state and national parks. Living in racially segregated camps, they earned thirty dollars a month and were required to send twenty-five dollars home. The CCC coordinated with the Emergency Educational Program to teach basic literacy.[23]

Both Perkins and ER wanted similar opportunities for women, but male administrators objected to white women working outdoors. Integrated Camps for Unemployed Women were set up for single women "without resources" ages eighteen to forty-five. Whereas CCC men got a wage of a dollar a day, the women got an allowance of fifty cents a week. The camps, which were modeled on the Bryn Mawr College Summer School for Women Working in Industry, began in 1921 to help factory workers attend classes in liberal arts. That summer school became a hotbed of labor leadership training and a model for the Highland Folk School in Tennessee and the Freedom Schools of the civil rights movement.[24]

One of the few Works Progress Administration (WPA) programs to hire Black women was a project to construct the Botanical Garden in Norfolk, Virginia. Over two hundred African American women built a levee, cleared paths, removed trees, and planted flowering shrubs. Before the Great Depression, many would have been members of Norfolk's numerous Black garden clubs.[25] Inspecting a camp in New York, Eleanor encountered Pauli Murray, a Black Hunter College graduate suffering from exhaustion, malnutrition, and pleurisy, who would play a leading role in the civil and women's rights movements.[26]

Perkins's signature accomplishment was the Social Security Act of 1935, intended to help the elderly and the unemployed. During the Great Depression, state pension plans served only 3% of the target population and poverty rates among the vulnerable old soared. Any relief initiative faced many challenges: the risk of uneven application, racial discrimination in state administered programs, and cost. Perkins's primary concern was conservative opposition. In a climate of increasing court hostility to New Deal programs, two Supreme Court Justices were secret allies. Over tea with Perkins, Harlan Stone whispered, "the taxing power, my dear." Louis Brandeis deputized his economist daughter Elizabeth and her husband, Paul Rauschenbush, director of Wisconsin's unemployment plan, to share his tax offset solution.[27]

While populist Louisiana Senator Huey Long harangued the administration for its inaction, Perkins's team finally came up with a solution: employee payroll contributions and payouts based on prior earnings. Because workers would not yet have contributed enough to support older retirees, Secretary of Treasury Henry Morgenthau proposed eliminating coverage of farmworkers, domestic servants, and employees of businesses with fewer than ten people, leaving 9.4 million workers, disproportionally Black and female, at risk. His changes made the bill palatable to the House Ways and Means and the Senate Finance committees, controlled by Southerners.[28]

Signing the Social Security Act in August 1935, the President declared:

> We can never insure one hundred percent of the population against one hundred percent of the hazards and vicissitudes of life, but we have tried to frame a law which will give some measure of protection to the average citizen and to his family against the loss of a job and against poverty-ridden old age.[29]

The final bill provided unemployment insurance, old age pensions, immediate grants to states for relief of the indigent elderly, Aid to Dependent Children (ADC), and minimal funding for public health programs. The ADC was imperative, according to Perkins, for "rearing fatherless families," when so many men had taken to the road to find work.[30] Incorporating elements of the Sheppard–Towner Act, Social Security became the cornerstone of the New Deal and the foundation of future federal welfare programs.

AFRICAN AMERICANS AND THE NEW DEAL

The experience of Black women in the Depression could not be separated from that of Black men. Both were threatened by institutional and customary racism, evident in the careless assumption of white supremacy: the peonage system of Southern sharecropping, poll taxes, literacy tests, the injustice of white juries, and the terror of lynch mobs. The seven-year saga of the Scotts-boro Boys, from their 1931 arrest, following a brawl with white hobos on a freight train, to their last trial in 1938, demonstrated the racism of Alabama's judicial system. Falsely accused of rape, eight of the nine teenagers were sentenced to death in 1932, but an appeal to the Supreme Court, *Powell v. Alabama*, determined that the defendants had been denied the right to counsel. In 1935, in *Norris v. Alabama*, the Court overturned the next verdict due to the systematic exclusion of Black jurors. After being incarcerated for years, charges were dropped, sentences reduced, and the defendants freed. In 2013, Alabama's Republican governor posthumously exonerated the defendants. The case reportedly inspired Harper Lee to write *To Kill a Mockingbird*.[31]

Eleanor and Molly Dewson worked hard to attract women and African Americans to the Democratic Party. Loyal to the party of Lincoln and unimpressed by FDR, African Americans voted for Hoover in 1932, despite a 38% Black unemployment rate. They despised Southern Democrats. After Roosevelt picked House Speaker John Nance Garner, a Texan, as his running mate, Republicans carried almost three-fourths of the Black vote. As a Black politician concluded:

> Colored voters . . . feel that by voting the Democratic ticket . . . they will be voting to give their endorsement . . . to every wrong of which they are victims, every right of which they are deprived and every injustice of which they suffer.[32]

The Democratic coalition expanded in the 1934 midterms, when the party gained seats, upsetting standard political predictions. Democrats secured two-thirds majorities in both chambers. In Chicago, Arthur Mitchell defeated the Black Republican incumbent, Oscar De Priest, to become the first Black Democrat elected to Congress.

The 1934 midterm results launched the "Second New Deal" and foreshadowed the President's landslide victory in 1936. Dewson secured new convention rules, requiring equal representation of men and women as delegates and removing the two-thirds vote requirement to nominate a candidate, curtailing the South's veto power. When a Black minister offered the invocation and a Black Congressman nominated the President, Southerners walked out. In November 1936, the nation voted overwhelmingly for FDR, giving him 523 Electoral College votes, the second largest victory in history. Kansas Governor Alf Landon won only two states and eight Electoral College votes, prompting the quip, "As Maine goes, so goes Vermont."[33] The largest Electoral College landslide came in 1820, when James Monroe won all but one vote, cast for John Quincy Adams.

Turnout rose nearly one-third in industrial cities. Like the country, Democrats were divided between rural and urban residents and values. The President used fireside chats to bypass the opposition of 85% of newspapers. Radio also fueled fundamentalism and populism. Voters rewarded FDR for Social Security and for appointing six times more Catholics to federal posts than Republicans had. Labor unions were enthusiastic. Registered African Americans changed parties, acknowledging efforts to integrate New Deal programs and Eleanor's attention.[34]

African Americans had at least one ally in the White House. ER was undeterred by the ferocity of racists opposed to relief programs for Black Americans. In January 1934, she invited notable Black men to dinner at the White House. College presidents, businessmen, and Walter White of the NAACP recalled an "unrestrained" discussion about lynching, inadequate schools, and the lack of jobs, housing, and running water in many communities. Eleanor promised to fight for better opportunities and more funding. Her guests stayed until midnight, when the President wheeled in to greet them. That same month, the field secretary for the Negro Press Association wrote ER suggesting that a "capable, intelligent Negro woman of fine training should be chosen to see to it that the Negro people [were] not ignored and left out."[35] The First Lady turned to Mary McLeod Bethune.

"From their first meeting [in the 1920s] . . . Eleanor was impressed by the vigor of Bethune's feminism, her race pride, and her compelling magnetism," concluded one biographer.[36] Born in South Carolina to parents who had been enslaved, the fifteenth of seventeen children, Bethune picked cotton and attended Presbyterian mission schools. Academic excellence led to a scholarship to the Moody Bible Institute in Chicago. She trained to be a missionary, but the board refused to send a Black woman to Africa. In 1904, she founded the Daytona Beach Literary and Industrial School for Training Negro Girls. The school grew from six students into a thriving enterprise of several institutions, including a Black hospital. In 1929, it merged with a men's college, becoming Bethune Cookman College, of which Bethune was president.[37] BCC survives today and made news in 2017 when seniors turned their backs on their graduation speaker, Trump's Secretary of Education, Betsy DeVos.[38]

In 1934, the First Lady arranged for Bethune to serve on an advisory committee for the National Youth Administration (NYA) and later as its Director of Negro Affairs, making her the first Black federal administrator. The NYA provided grants to students, ages sixteen to twenty-five, to stay in school.[39] It fell under the purview of Eleanor's friend Harry Hopkins at the Federal Emergency Relief Agency. He was among the cabinet members and agency heads she nagged with suggestions about including African Americans at every level. Some were more receptive than others. Perkins refused to add a Black woman to the Women's Bureau. ER's strongest ally was Secretary of Interior Harold Ickes, a progressive Republican and past president of the Chicago NAACP. He ended the Wilson administration's segregation in government cafeterias, restrooms, and national parks and oversaw the Public Works Administration. It had a quota system to increase Black employment.[40] Vocal in her support of civil rights, ER insisted that New Deal programs target 10% of welfare funds for African Americans, in proportion to the population, primarily through segregated programs in the National Youth and Works Project administrations.

To avoid any disrespect by White House guards, ER would walk to the gate to greet and be photographed with Bethune. Bethune organized the forty-five African Americans working in executive departments into an advisory group, known informally as the Black Brain Trust. Members included William Hastie and Robert Weaver. In 1937, FDR appointed Hastie to the District Court of the Virgin Islands, the second Black federal judge after Robert Terrell. In 1965, President Johnson made Weaver the first Black cabinet member.[41] After founding the National Council of Negro Women in 1935, Bethune asked ER to invite 450 NCNW members to the White House to discuss federal policies. Eleanor's support for Black Americans became a campaign issue, used both for and against FDR. As one Georgian sniped, "We didn't like her a bit; she ruined every maid we ever had."[42]

FAIR LABOR STANDARDS ACT

The President soared into 1937, only to crash after his attempt to pack the Supreme Court. The Court's conservatives, known as the "Four Horsemen," a reference to New Testament harbingers of apocalypse, had nullified many New Deal initiatives and seemed poised to declare Social Security and the National Labor Relations Act unconstitutional.[43] To change the balance on the bench, FDR proposed adding a justice for each member who did not retire at age seventy, citing a need for greater efficiency. His transparent "reform" infuriated his allies, enraged his enemies, and failed. The crisis was resolved when the Court announced its decision in *West Coast Hotel Co. v. Parrish.*

Elsie Parrish was a white chambermaid in a small hotel on the Columbia River. When she was discharged in 1935, she asked for her back pay of thirty cents an hour, an amount based on Washington State's women-only minimum wage law. When the hotel refused, she sued. In a 5–4 decision, the Court decided for Parrish, upholding the state law and reversing a series of precedents in which the court had invalidated legislation regulating business. According to commentators, it was the "greatest judicial somer-sault in history," the "switch in time that saved nine." In fact, the Court had voted to reverse it months earlier.[44] Chief Justice Charles Evans Hughes, appointed by Hoover in 1930, signaled the Court's willingness to defer to legislatures on economic matters.

The only significant New Deal initiative to pass after 1936 was the Fair Labor Standards Act of 1938 (FLSA). For industries engaged in interstate commerce with earnings of $500,000, it mandated an eight-hour day; a forty-hour week; a minimum wage of twenty-five cents an hour, keyed to inflation; overtime; and an end to "oppressive child labor" for those under sixteen. It would not have passed without Perkins, Dewson, former Director of the Children's Bureau Grace Abbott, and Congresswoman Mary Norton (D-NJ), who chaired the House Labor Committee. Perkins and FDR thought Norton was a "compromiser," but she reported the bill out of committee, pried it loose from the Rules Committee with a rare discharge petition, and secured passage without any changes.[45] For progressives, FLSA was a culmination of forty years of work.

FLSA applied to only 20% of the workforce and 14% of jobs held by women, including those in the garment and textile industries. To get Southern votes, it excluded most of the jobs held by Black workers and women in agriculture, domestic service, retail sales, laundries, hotels, food processing, and government, as well as independent contractors, part-time, and seasonal workers. Those exclusions had a negative financial impact on generations of people of color. FLSA was eventually expanded to cover workers in schools, hospitals, nursing homes, state and local government, and migrant and seasonal agricultural workers. In 2014, the Labor Department added domestic and home health care workers. FLSA does not provide overtime protections to farmworkers or live-in domestic workers. Tipped workers are not guaranteed the full federal minimum wage.[46]

No New Deal program reversed the devastation of the Depression. Conditions seemed to improve in 1937 but then declined into the "Roosevelt Recession." Corporate profits plunged, relief rolls surged, and unemployment stood at 19%. The Dust Bowl intensified the crushing impact of the Depression on farmers. During the Great War, demand for wheat and corn led to the over-plowing of grasslands. A postwar drop in crop prices prompted more plowing until there was little topsoil left. Beginning in 1931, a decade-long drought led to dust storms that blew particles from the prairie to the Statue of Liberty. It uprooted 2.4 million migrants known as "Okies."[47] Photographs like Dorothea Lange's "Migrant Mother" of Florence Owen Thompson captured their anguish. Woody Guthrie's lyrics told their story. Tom Joad, the migrant protagonist of John Steinbeck's *The Grapes of Wrath* (1939), replaced Jay Gatsby as the embodiment of an era.

WOMEN IN ELECTED POLITICS

A triumvirate of incumbents, Congresswomen Florence Kahn, Mary Norton, and Edith Rogers, were the only women serving in Congress when FDR was inaugurated. During his twelve-year tenure, twenty-three white women entered Congress. Most of the sixteen Democrats were defeated after a single term. The exception was New Yorker Caroline O'Day, who served four terms, 1935–43, defeating Republican women in every election. The 1938 midterm was a rebuke to the president. Republicans won seats in the House and Senate and twelve more governorships. As FDR's popularity declined, more Republican women won, including Jeannette Rankin in 1940. On the state level, in 1933, Republican Millie Craig became Leader of the North Dakota House, the first woman to hold a speakership.[48]

Arkansas Democrat Hattie Wyatt Caraway was the first woman elected to the US Senate. Initially appointed to succeed her husband in 1931, she won a special election without making a single campaign appearance. The front page of the *New York Times* declared that "women's clubs and party leaders sought to get out a large vote . . . Reports indicated probably more women than men voted" for Caraway. Assigned to Rebecca Felton's desk in the Senate chamber ("I guess they wanted as few of them contaminated as possible"), Caraway spent her time knitting. She had pledged not to run in the general election in 1932 but changed her mind, annoying but not alarming the six men in the race, including the governor. Her only support came from Senator Huey Long (D-LA), who campaigned with her across Arkansas, supplying volunteers and sound trucks. Caraway swept to victory, winning almost as many votes as the combined total for her opponents.[49]

Senator Caraway supported the ERA, farm relief, and flood control. She opposed anti-lynching bills and a ban on poll taxes. She was the first woman to preside over the Senate or chair a committee. While she seconded FDR's 1936 nomination and was effective in committees, "Silent Hattie" rarely spoke on the floor. In 1938, she easily defeated John McClellan's primary challenge. His slogan was "We need another man in the Senate." Due to limitations on rail travel, she was rarely in Arkansas during World War II and lost her primary in 1944. The winner was Representative J. William Fulbright, who had been a football star, Rhodes Scholar, and the youngest president of the University of Arkansas.[50]

WOMEN IN POPULAR CULTURE

After the 1929 stock market crash, the country retreated. Hemlines fell; even Betty Boop wore longer skirts. To escape the troubles of the real world, Americans went to the movies. The Thirties were Hollywood's Golden Age. In 1937, Walt Disney released *Snow White*, his first full-length animated film. While Fred Astaire and Ginger Rogers foxtrotted across the Great Depression, Shirley Temple tap-danced. Starting at age three, she was the most popular movie star from 1934 to 1938. Decades later, Republican presidents would appoint her Chief of Protocol and Ambassador to Ghana and Czechoslovakia. In 1940, Judy Garland, another child star, won an Academy Juvenile Award for her role in *The Wizard of Oz*.[51]

In the movies, career women eventually married. There was romance, but no sex. The Catholic League of Decency and fundamentalists thundered about chastity. Until 1937, beaches required tops for men, who were jailed for indecency if they bared their chests. In 1930, fearful of looming government censorship, movie producers adopted a voluntary morality code. Named for former Republican Postmaster General Will Hays, who was hired to polish the industry's image, the Hays Code set guidelines for depicting sex, drugs, violence, and crime. Enforcement tightened after 1934, banning interracial sex, revenge plots, disrespect for religion, and kidnapping, following the death of aviator Charles Lindbergh's son. Movies had to be approved in order to be released. The Code had the power to edit scenes. Before the release of *Casablanca* in 1942, its ending was changed. Instead of resuming her affair with Rick, Ilsa got on the plane with her husband. The Code remained in effect until 1968, when it was replaced by the Motion Picture Association rating system.[52]

Like American society, entertainment was segregated. In 1935 George Gershwin wrote *Porgy and Bess,* an opera about Black life set in Charleston, South Carolina. At the insistence of its Black cast, Washington's National Theater allowed the integrated seating.[53] From 1915 into the 1950s, Hollywood produced a genre called "race movies," with Black casts for Black audiences. In white films, Black actors played peripheral roles as entertainers or servants. In 1939, Hattie McDaniel was the first African American to win an Academy Award for Best Supporting Actress in *Gone with the Wind,* playing an enslaved maid. In 1954, Dorothy Dandridge was the first African American, male or female, nominated in the leading role category for *Carmen Jones,* about a woman punished for her independence. No Black woman would win a Best Actress Oscar until Halle Berry, in 2002, for her role in *Monster's Ball.*[54]

One could view the roles of women during the Depression as a black-and-white newsreel. Interspersed with coverage of the 1932 kidnapping of the Lindbergh baby, the capture of bank robbers Bonnie and Clyde, the Gloria Vanderbilt custody trial in 1934, the opening of the Golden Gate Bridge in 1937, H. G. Wells's "War of the Worlds" broadcast in 1938, and the rise of fascism, were flickers of women. Star athlete Mildred "Babe" Didrikson, nicknamed for the baseball slugger, won two gold medals in track and field at the 1932 Los Angeles Olympics. Baltimore divorcée

Wallace Simpson, for whom the King of England abdicated in 1936, was the first of five women, and the only American, ever named *Time* magazine's "Man of the Year." Wives of General Motors autoworkers in Flint, Michigan, armed with broomsticks, formed the Women's Emergency Brigade to support a forty-four-day sit-down strike in 1936–37. Amelia Earhart, who once took Eleanor Roosevelt flying, flew solo across the Atlantic in 1932 and disappeared in the Pacific in 1937. Throughout her career, the *New York Times* insisted on identifying Earhart as Mrs. George Putnam.[55]

In 1936, *Vogue* editor Marjorie Hillis published *Live Alone and Like It: A Guide for the Extra Woman*. Years ahead of Helen Gurley Brown's *Sex and the Single Girl*, the bestseller offered advice on gentlemen callers, hostess pajamas, and cocktail shakers. For six million single women, Hillis redefined spinsterhood as independence.[56] Some of those spinsters were likely lesbian or bisexual, words whispered in the 1930s. For the first time, love between women was assumed to be sexual, even when it was not. Fear of female homosexuality made it harder to organize women's groups and made female friendship networks like Eleanor's suspect. Jane Addams, Carrie Chapman Catt, and Molly Dewson had longtime partnerships that remained private. Lesbian communities thrived in Greenwich Village, Harlem, San Francisco, and Salt Lake City. Bessie Smith and Ma Rainey sang in Harlem's gay bars. According to Sigmund Freud, homosexuality was a disease. Unmarried women were considered neurotic and unfulfilled.[57] As Hollywood endings confirmed, women were incomplete without men.

Advertisers marketed products that would make women attractive to men. The curve-clinging evening dresses worn by movie stars in the Thirties were made possible by the invention of the tampon. While the Egyptians, Greeks, and Romans had used fiber-wrapped inserts, most women in America relied on rags or straw. One of the first reforms sought for factory women was adding restrooms where they could change menstrual dressings. After 1918, surplus high-absorption bandages, used in the war, were repurposed into sanitary napkins, sold as Kotex. In 1929, Dr. Earle Haas patented a telescoping "applicator tampon." Businesswoman Gertrude

Tendrich bought his invention, formed the Tampax Company, and began mass production. There was some competition from a "menstrual cup," but its manufacture was curtailed by wartime rubber shortages. Religious leaders called tampons immoral, claiming they destroyed physical evidence of virginity and encouraged masturbation.[58]

The Venereal Disease Control Act of 1939 promoted the use of contraception by men, but it remained controversial. In 1930, there were fifty-five birth control clinics in the country, mostly in cities. By 1938, there were three hundred. New York City had twenty-six, but most rural regions and some states had none. Unemployment had depressed marriage and birth rates. The 1930s had the highest rate of childlessness of any decade in American history, as couples delayed pregnancy. Black women had fewer babies than white women of similar income and status, but Southerners lived in fear of a Black population explosion. Unethical physicians continued to sterilize white and Black women without consent, for reasons related to eugenics and racism.[59]

MARIAN ANDERSON AND BILLIE HOLIDAY

Moviegoers would also have seen newsreels about world-renowned Black contralto Marian Anderson performing on the steps of the Lincoln Memorial in 1939, an event produced by the First Lady and Secretary of Interior Harold Ickes, when other venues refused Anderson access. Howard University, her host, tried to rent Constitution Hall, owned by the Daughters of the American Revolution. When the DAR barred Anderson, Eleanor publicly resigned as a member. The Interior Department proposed the Lincoln Memorial instead. Honorary sponsors included the cabinet, Chief Justice Hughes, Justice Hugo Black, and film stars Katharine Hepburn and Tallulah Bankhead. Bankhead's father was Speaker of the House and her uncle was a Senator, both staunch Alabama segregationists. Since District hotels and restaurants were segregated, Congresswoman Carolyn O'Day (D-NY) arranged private housing for Anderson and her party.[60]

The Freedom Concert began at 5:00 P.M. on Easter Sunday, April 9, before a live, integrated audience of 75,000 and five million listening on their radios. Secretary Ickes opened the program.

> In this great auditorium under the sky, all of us are free . . .
> When God gave us the sun and the moon and the stars, He
> made no distinction of race, creed or color . . . Genius, like
> Justice, is blind . . . Genius . . . has touched this woman, who,
> if it had not been for . . . the great heart of Lincoln, would not
> be able to stand among us today a free individual in a free land.
> Genius draws no color line. She has endowed Marian Anderson
> with such a voice . . . a matter of exultant pride to any race.[61]

Anderson, wearing a diva's mink coat, felt "a great wave of good-will." She opened with "My Country 'Tis of Thee," sang arias, classics, "America the Beautiful," and ended with spirituals. Two months later, Anderson sang at the White House for the King and Queen of England. It was the first visit by a British monarch to America. To spotlight American diversity, Eleanor invited Black performers, country musicians, cowboys, and square dancers to perform, and famously served the couple hot dogs at Hyde Park. In 1943, the DAR reversed its "white artists only" policy and invited Anderson to perform at a concert for war relief. She accepted on the condition that the audience be "de-segregated." She would perform there four more times.[62]

Anderson's thirty-minute appearance reclaimed the legacy of the Lincoln Memorial for civil rights. The Memorial was designed to be a symbol of sectional rather than racial reconciliation. Surrounded by thirty-six Doric columns, one for each of the reunited states, its walls were inscribed with the Gettysburg Address and the Second Inaugural, not the Emancipation Proclamation. Lincoln's surviving son, Robert, attended the segregated ceremony on Memorial Day, May 30, 1922. Black guests were herded into the colored section, behind choice seats assigned to Confederate veterans. The only Black speaker, Robert Moton, president of the Tuskegee Institute, was not permitted to sit on the speakers' platform. His remarks were censored, cutting his conclusion: "So long as any group within our nation is denied the full protection of the law, [Lincoln's] . . . work [remains] unfinished [and the Memorial] but a hollow mockery."[63]

Another Black singer, jazz vocalist Billie Holiday, was making news with her haunting song, "Strange Fruit." It was an indictment of racial violence. Written by Abel Meeropol (pen name David Lewis), a Jewish Communist teacher from the Bronx, it was inspired by a photograph of a lynching.

> Southern trees bear strange fruit
> Blood on the leaves and blood on the root
> Black bodies swinging in the southern breeze
> Strange fruit hanging from the poplar trees.
>
> Pastoral scene of the gallant south
> The bulging eyes and the twisted mouth
> Scent of magnolias, sweet and fresh,
> Then the sudden smell of burning flesh.[64]

"Strange Fruit" became Holiday's signature song, sung last under a single spotlight. Waiters would stop serving. Afraid of backlash from Southern retailers and radio stations, Columbia Records refused to produce it, but the label allowed her to record it elsewhere. The song sold one million copies in 1939, when she was twenty-four. It made Holiday a symbol of resistance to lynching and a civil rights icon, which led to government surveillance and harassment for the rest of her life.

Born Eleanora Fagan in 1915, the child of unmarried teenage parents, she was arrested with her mother for prostitution. She changed her name and began singing as Billie Holiday in 1931. Soon she was appearing at the Apollo Theater, making records, and headlining with Count Basie. In 1939, she joined Artie Shaw and his white band, the first time a Black woman had toured with a white band. She quit because of her treatment in Southern venues. Heroin addiction ravaged her volatile career. A sold-out

Carnegie Hall concert followed time in federal prison. As she lay dying of cirrhosis in 1959, she was arrested and handcuffed to her hospital bed for drug possession. In 1999, *Time* named "Strange Fruit" the Song of the Century and, in 2000, Holiday was inducted into the Rock and Roll Hall of Fame. In 2019, New York City announced plans to erect a statue of her in Queens.[65]

In January 1939, Eleanor Roosevelt, "speaking for myself, as an individual," publicly condemned lynching.[66] Between 1882 and 1933, sixty-one federal anti-lynching bills had been introduced and defeated. Between 1934 and 1940, there were 130 more bills, two of which passed the House, in 1937 and 1940. To placate the South and protect his legislative agenda, FDR did not endorse them. Among whites, Southern resistance and Northern indifference undermined decades of efforts to end racial terrorism with federal legislation.

In June 2018, Cory Booker (D-NJ), Kamala Harris (D-CA), and Tim Scott (R-SC), the three Black members of the Senate, introduced the Justice for Victims of Lynching Act. It defined lynching as "bodily injury on the basis of race, color, religion or nationality" and apologized for historic failures to prevent lynching in the past. It passed unanimously, but the session ended before the House could act. In February 2019, the House passed another version of the Senate bill, the Emmett Till Antilynching Act, by 410–4. In the Senate, Rand Paul (R-KY) blocked passage by objecting to unanimous consent.[67]

ELEANOR AND ANTISEMITISM

Ingrained isolationism undercut the country's ability to confront fascist aggression. It watched Mussolini occupy Ethiopia (1935), Franco destroy the republican government in Spain (1936), Japan savage Shanghai (1937), and Hitler seize national power (1933), reoccupy the Rhineland (1936), absorb Austria (1938), and take Czechoslovakia (1939). America wanted to avoid any economic or emotional causes for fighting another war.

Between 1935 and 1939, the Congress passed five neutrality laws forbidding arms sales to belligerents and disavowing responsibility for Americans traveling in war-torn waters, since American entrance into a European conflict in 1917 was provoked by ships attacked by German submarines.[68]

Nazi atrocities against Jews escalated from business boycotts, assaults, and segregation into the horrors of Kristallnacht and its aftermath. In November 1938, on the eve of the twentieth anniversary of the Armistice, German paramilitary and civilian mobs attacked Jewish homes and shops, leaving shards of glass in the streets. German authorities arrested twenty thousand Jews, confiscated their property, and ordered a nationwide pogrom of pillage and arson. Transportation to death camps followed. Americans could not comprehend such sanctioned hatred, dismissing press reports as exaggerations, while Hitler claimed to have based his suppression of Jews on America's racial segregation.[69]

American xenophobia, expressed in nativist immigration policies like the National Origins Act of 1924, intensified during the Depression, when newcomers were seen as adding more unemployed workers. After Germany seized their assets, Jews who could get visas were denied entry because they were indigents. Father Charles Coughlin spewed fascist invectives against Jews until the government pressured the Catholic Church to rein him in. Congress defeated proposals by Senator Robert Wagner (D-NY) and Representative Edith Rogers (R-MA) to allow 20,000 Jewish children to enter the country, and by Representative Emanuel Celler (D-NY) to exempt religious refugees from quotas. Senator Robert Reynolds (D-NC) thundered, "If I had my way I would . . . build a wall about the United States so high and so secure that not a single alien or foreign refugee from any country upon the face of the earth could possibly scale or ascend it." A 1939 poll asked if America should admit more refugees: 85% of Protestants, 84% of Catholics, and 26% of Jews said no.[70]

On Armistice Day 1938, Kate Smith sang "God Bless America," written by Jewish composer Irving Berlin. Antisemites and the Klan reviled Berlin for his presumption. Isolationists booed when the song was played and Woody Guthrie composed "This Land Is Your Land" as an alternative.

Berlin, who donated his proceeds to the Boy and Girl Scouts, was accused
of profiteering. Both FDR and Wendell Willkie used Berlin's song to
campaign in 1940. After 9/11, Congress sang it a cappella on the steps
of the Capitol. Because of racist lyrics in her repertoire, in 2019, the New
York Yankees banned Smith's iconic rendition of Berlin's classic, traditionally played during the seventh-inning stretch, and the Philadelphia Flyers
removed her statue from its arena.[71]

Events in Europe forced Eleanor Roosevelt to address antisemitism,
including her own. According to her principal biographer, she had the
"impersonal and casual . . . [biases] of her generation, class and culture."
She opposed bigotry but was oblivious to demeaning stereotypes expressed
by others. The First Lady did not socialize with Jewish allies in the Democratic Party and had few Jewish friends, with the exception of Treasury
Secretary Morgenthau and his wife, Elinor, the niece of Herbert Lehman,
New York governor and later US senator. When they were in Washington,
these upper-class women went riding in Rock Creek Park. Eleanor and
Secretary Morgenthau pressured the President to establish an Emergency
Visitor Visa Program to save "persons of exceptional merit." FDR did
not create a War Refugee Board until 1944. Eleanor hosted fundraising
concerts at the White House, showcasing Jewish musicians, and broadcast
appeals portraying refugee children as "temporary visitors, not immigrants."
She battled the "striped pants bigotry" of the State Department, whose
indifference and inaction condemned countless Jews to death.[72]

WARTIME DISLOCATION

As 1940 approached, the President was the lame duck leader of an economically weakened, diplomatically isolated, and unarmed nation. On
September 1, 1939, at 3:00 A.M., the President learned that Germany had
invaded Poland. The Nazis swept across Northern Europe, forcing the
surrender of every country in its path. The evacuation from Dunkirk in
June 1940 left England on its own. FDR believed only he could lead the

country in wartime. At the Democratic convention, a "spontaneous demonstration" clamored for the President's renomination. He was selected on the first ballot for an unprecedented third term. Mrs. Roosevelt accepted on his behalf, another first. Campaigning for preparedness and against war, Roosevelt won thirty-eight states, his narrowest margin to date. Voters had restored confidence in his leadership.[73]

The rest is history. After Japan attacked Pearl Harbor on December 7, 1941, "a day that will live in infamy," America declared war on Japan and Germany declared war on the United States. While her husband was focused on winning the war, Eleanor "insisted that the struggle would not be worth winning if the old order prevailed. Unless democracy was renewed at home, there was little merit in fighting for democracy abroad."[74] A global war transformed everyone, beginning with a population shift. Eight million Americans moved: men enlisted in the military; other men and many women took jobs in war industries; thousands of young women moved to Washington to work for the government, becoming "G-girls." While most Black women were already working and participating in their communities, the dislocation and separation caused by the war would challenge traditional views of all women's economic and social roles.[75]

Among the transients were the women who made up the All-American Girls Professional Baseball League, the subject of the 1992 movie *A League of Their Own*. Beginning in 1943, Philip Wrigley, who manufactured chewing gum and owned the Chicago Cubs, sought to attract fans with female athletes, playing a combined version of baseball and softball. These athletes were enormously popular, especially in small towns. The fact that women were taking on all kinds of new roles made acceptance easier. Mrs. Wrigley designed a short-skirted uniform with satin underpants, baseball socks, and caps. She hired Helena Rubenstein's salon to provide lessons in makeup and manners. Off the field, players were required to wear heels. During the national anthem, opposing teams formed a "V for Victory." Representing the "All-American girl next door," the League did not recruit Black players. Three women, including Toni Stone, played on professional Negro League teams. They refused to wear skirts. White women playing professional baseball were banned after 1952; Stone retired in 1954. All of them are included in the Baseball Hall of Fame.[76]

Twelve thousand Indigenous women left their reservations for war work, many in the aircraft industry as machinists, welders, and inspectors; eight hundred joined the armed forces. On reservations, they replaced men as teachers and administrators. In 1944, tribes formed the National Congress of American Indians to demand more rights. Ruth Muskrat Bronson, an Oklahoma Cherokee, Mount Holyoke College graduate, and modernist poet, served as executive director, the only woman on the leadership council.[77] Mexican American women undertook grueling seasonal manual labor as farm workers or moved into canneries, where 75% of the workforce was female. Sex segregation led to a sense of community. During the war, Luisa Moreno and Dorothy Rae Healey organized a female union at the California Sanitary Canning Company in Long Beach. They secured maternity leave, company-provided on-site childcare, and paid vacations for workers. Their union was broken after the war, charged with promoting communism.[78]

Not all migrations were voluntary. After Pearl Harbor, Hawaii put constraints on Japanese residents but did not remove them because they were half the population and indispensable to the economy. On the mainland, Japanese Americans were only 1% of the population. Many were socially isolated on self-sustaining vegetable farms and subjected to discrimination long before the war. In February 1942, President Roosevelt signed Executive Order 9066, authorizing the Secretary of War to remove people of Japanese descent from designated areas. Two-thirds of the 120,000 people removed were American citizens, born in the United States. The others were older Japanese people, earlier immigrants who were barred from citizenship by the 1882 and 1924 immigration acts. The same order put suspect Germans into camps. Restrictions on Italian citizens, who were required to register as enemy aliens at police stations, were removed on Columbus Day 1942, just ahead of the midterm elections.[79]

Given one week's notice, forced to abandon their homes and belong-ings, people of Japanese descent were transported to twenty-six hastily

constructed compounds with sentry towers and floodlights in less populated areas of the country like Arizona and Arkansas; eight camps were
in the desert.[80] Former Senator Alan Simpson (R-WY) and Representative Norman Mineta (D-CA) met as Boy Scouts on opposite sides of a
barbed wire fence near Cody, Wyoming. Conditions were humiliating,
eroding traditional practices of hygiene and arranged marriage. The disruption of family structure and gender roles gave women more autonomy
and authority. Young women filled a wide range of jobs in the camps and
asserted their right to date and marry whomever. Japanese American
men and women volunteered to serve in the military. The Navy and Air
Force refused to accept them, but the Army inducted 20,000 men into
segregated units in Europe. Women served in the Women's Army Corps
(WAC) and as Cadet Corps nurses.[81] Scholars later concluded that the
breakdown of traditional social norms contributed to postwar assimilation.

Another part of Executive Order 9066 dismissed all Japanese
American state employees, including Mitsuye Endo, a secretary with
California's Department of Employment. She was forced to move with her
parents to the Tule Lake Relocation Center, near the Oregon border.
Sixty-three fired employees hired lawyer James Purcell, who selected
Endo as an ideal plaintiff. She was a Methodist, had never visited
Japan, and her brother was serving in the military. To make the case
disappear, the government offered to release her. She refused and was
confined for months. In April 1944, in *Ex Parte Endo*, the Supreme
Court unanimously ruled in her favor: "The government cannot detain
a citizen without charge when the government itself concedes she is
loyal to the United States."[82]

Although the Supreme Court acknowledged "a melancholy resemblance
to the treatment . . . of the Jewish race in Germany," two decisions upheld
the validity of the executive order: *Hirabayashi v. United States* (1943) and
Fred Korematsu v. United States (1944). The government closed the camps
in 1944, but the Court's decisions have never been overturned. In 1988,
President Reagan signed the Civil Liberties Act. Admitting "race prejudice,
war hysteria and a failure of political leadership," it apologized to Japanese

detainees and provided reparations of $20,000 for each camp survivor. In 1998, President Clinton gave Fred Korematsu the Presidential Medal of Freedom.[83]

WASPS, WACS, WAVES, HEDY, AND ROSIE

For the duration, the war overturned many cultural norms. When men shipped out, women stepped in. The military actively recruited white women for every branch of service except combat. More than 25,000 women applied to be Women's Air Force Service Pilots (WASPs): 1,830 were accepted, 1,074 completed training, and thirty-eight died in service, without military death benefits. They ferried untried planes from factories to military installations and towed practice targets for anti-aircraft practice.

Life magazine reported that "girl pilots" were:

> very serious about their chance to fly . . . even when it means
> giving up nail polish, beauty parlors and dates for a regimented
> 22½ weeks . . . They each have on the GI coveralls . . . that
> are the regulation uniform . . . Though the suits are not very
> glamorous . . . the girls like their comfort and freedom.

In 1977, WASPs were granted full veteran status and benefits, but it took a bureaucratic battle before they were permitted burial at Arlington National Cemetery. In 2010, President Obama presented survivors with the Congressional Gold Medal.[84]

The original legislation for the Women's Auxiliary Army Corps (WAAC), drafted by Representative Edith Rogers (R-MA), did not give women equal standing. "Auxiliary" was removed in 1943 because the Army needed more women to serve as stenographers, drivers, mechanics, telegraphers, and telephone operators. Having WACs in the regular Army raised issues of authority. Female officers could not command men; instead they repeated orders coming from their male commanding officers. Around 150,000 WACs held ranks equivalent to men, for less pay and no benefits, including death benefits for women killed overseas. Florence Blanchfield supervised over 57,000 members of the Army Nurse Corps, who served on every battlefield. None received the pay or privileges of male officers of equivalent rank.[85]

After the war, the Army and Navy amended their policies, permitting women to hold full equivalent rank. General Eisenhower made Blanchfield a Lieutenant Colonel. More than 6,500 Black women served as WACs. Major Charity Adams, twenty-six, was the first African American WAC commanding officer. In January 1945, she led 855 Black women in the Postal Directory Battalion in bombed-out Birmingham, England. They sorted a backlog of seventeen million letters and packages intended for troops on the front line. Inspired by the motto, "No mail, no morale," and working around the clock, they completed their task in three months.[86]

WAC Director Oveta Culp Hobby reassured a public anxious about women serving in non-traditional roles: "This is a war that recognizes the distinctions between men and women." Service women were presented as "very feminine" in "smartly styled" uniforms. While men were issued condoms to prevent venereal disease, women were denied access to birth control. The rumor that they had been given diaphragms was so damaging that it had to be denied by the President, the First Lady, and the Secretary of War.[87] Every new opportunity was tempered by concerns about what were appropriate roles for women.

The Navy, historically receptive to women, made them members of the Reserves and the WAVES (Women Accepted for Voluntary Emergency Service), but did not allow them to serve on ships or overseas. In addition to administrative, clerical, and medical roles, they worked as control tower operators, aviation mechanics, and parachute riggers. They taught gunnery and aerial photography and tested planes in wind tunnels. White, middle-class, overwhelmingly Protestant, and educated, they had uniforms designed by American couturier Mainbocher.[88] In 1944, Secretary of the Navy James Forrestal admitted Black women to the WAVES. Two Chinese American women flew as WASPs, as did Native American Ola Mildred Rexroat. In total, 350,000 women served in the military. Lieutenant Annie

G. Fox of the Army Nurse Corps was the first woman to receive a Purple Heart, for wounds received at Pearl Harbor.[89]

Female code breakers, spies, and inventors worked in secret and remained invisible. Among them was the stunning actress Hedy Lamarr. Behind her silver screen image was a sharp scientific mind. Before she escaped to America, Hedwig Kiesler was a Viennese Jew married to a Nazi arms manufacturer. In Hollywood, in 1942, Lamarr developed a remote-controlled radio system using "frequency hopping." It allowed signals to be transmitted to torpedoes without risking detection or jamming. The War Department did not adopt the method but seized control of her patent application, since it had been submitted by a resident alien. Although not yet a citizen, Lamarr used her celebrity to encourage the sale of the equivalent of $343 million in war bonds. Years later, after the patent had expired, her invention was used as the basis for GPS, cell phones, Wi-Fi, Bluetooth, and military technology, including nuclear command and control. Only recently has Lamarr's pivotal role been acknowledged.[90]

Less glamourous than women in uniform or Hollywood were women working in war industries, who wore trousers, boots, safety helmets, and goggles. To recruit women workers, the government Manpower Commission wrote a jaunty jingle about a fictional riveter named Rosie:

> That little frail can do,
> More than a male can do,
> Rosie (brrrrr) the riveter.
> Rosie's got a boyfriend, Charlie;
> Charlie, he's a marine.
> Rosie is protecting Charlie,
> Working overtime on the riveting machine.[91]

It was more likely that Rosie was a low-skilled welder than a riveter, which required special training.

On the iconic 1942 "We Can Do It" poster, Rosie wore blue coveralls and a red polka dot bandana. On Norman Rockwell's 1943 *Saturday Evening*

Post cover, she was a strapping redhead with a powder puff in her pocket and a riveting gun across her lap. Rosie represented the changing role of women in the war, an image of "female masculinity," accessorizing work boots with lipstick.[92] Posed photographs of real Rosies competed with "Varga girls" and Betty Grable pin-ups. Marilyn Monroe, then Norma Jeane Dougherty, the eighteen-year-old wife of a merchant seaman, was pictured working at the Radioplane Munitions Factory in Burbank, California.[93]

There were news photographs but no posters of Black Rosies. Most war industry jobs were segregated, with African American women getting the toughest tasks at the lowest wages. Despite the upward mobility experienced by some Black women during the war, their relative position within the economy remained the same.[94] All the work was hard, hot, and dirty, but the war offered jobs never before available to any women. White women who had been working in department stores and restaurants for $24.50 per week could earn $40.35 making B-29 bombers, tanks, ships, and jeeps. The auto industry had been 90% male; when the plants were retooled for war production, 25% of the workforce was female. Half of women factory workers were in non-defense industries, "filling places in machine shops, steel mills, oil refineries . . . and lumber mills."[95] Women working with men in these occupations questioned the concept of "male jobs" and raised the issue of equal pay.

EQUAL PAY AND CHILDCARE

To pay women the same wage to do the same job as a man challenged ingrained attitudes about sex roles and work. To pay women less undercut the value of the task when men performed it. The government supported equal pay on account of "justice, sustaining men's wage rates, and increasing purchasing power," but mostly to protect male wages. In November 1942, the National War Labor Board issued General Order No. 16, permitting employers to "equalize the wage or salary rates paid to females with rates paid to males for comparable quality and quantity of work." It conceded that "there is no proof, scientific or otherwise," that women were innately less capable than men.[96]

"Comparable" did not prohibit wage differentials in sex-segregated occupations. Women protested that the same pay for the same work was a better standard than "comparable." During the war, women earned more in dollar terms than they had before the war, but the average full-time woman worker earned only fifty-five cents for every dollar her male coworker earned, compared to sixty-two cents in 1939. Some manufacturers with government contracts raised wages because they could pass the cost on. Others ignored the recommendation entirely. No one in authority questioned sex- or race-based job or wage discrimination.[97]

To protect the value of jobs, unions supported equal pay. Until veterans returned, unions advocated for women. Millie Jeffrey of the United Auto Workers asked women on assembly lines what they needed. The response was staggered shifts, on-site childcare, cafeterias with hot meals and take out service, extended hours at banks, asking butchers to reserve meat for war workers, and having grocers fill orders for pick up. Without such services, absenteeism soared and women gained a reputation for unreliability. In all, 36% of American women worked during the war, compared to 70% of British women, who benefited from many of those support systems.[98]

A decade after the government had tried to dismiss married women workers, it was now urging them into the workforce. The employment of white married women with children challenged traditional norms. The first federally sponsored childcare legislation, the Lanham Act, provided matching funds for states to establish 3,102 centers. Mothers employed in war industries paid fifty cents a day, half the cost. Due to inconvenient hours and locations, centers were under-enrolled. Mothers were reluctant to leave their children with strangers. Alternatives were makeshift, relying on relatives or leaving older children to fend for themselves and care for younger siblings. National ambivalence about women working resulted in inadequate support systems and fewer mothers in the workforce.[99]

By 1944, 37% of all adult women were employed, including one in ten married women and 12% of women with children under ten. Separated from husbands for long periods, married women were engaged in house-work and childcare; dealing with housing shortages near military bases; growing victory gardens; canning produce; volunteering as air wardens; and rationing food, tires, and gasoline. While the Depression had delayed marriage, the war rushed it. Early in the war, married men got draft defer-ments. The birthrate jumped by 5%, from 19.4 births per thousand in 1940 to 24.5 in 1943, the highest rate since 1927.[100] In the face of an uncertain future, couples raced to start families.

Widowhood, commonplace during war, also forced women into new roles. In politics, Republican Frances Bingham Bolton, from Cleveland, replaced her deceased husband in Congress in early 1940. One of the wealthiest women in America, she won a special election by a greater margin than her husband had earned in five terms. When her party wanted to replace her, she resisted: "The men so much wanted . . . me out that I determined that they would have to put up with me." She served until 1968, an advocate for equal rights and an expert on foreign policy. During the war, the Bolton Act created the Cadet Nurse Corps, which stipulated inclusion regardless of race or ethnicity. Three thousand Black women, forty Native American women, and many relocated Japanese American women participated. Although many men had followed their fathers or brothers into Congress, in 1952, Bolton and her son Oliver, representing another Ohio district, became the only mother and son to serve in Congress simultaneously. When Mr. Bolton voted against a measure his mother sup-ported, she muttered, "He's my adopted son."[101]

For years, Maine Republican Margaret Chase Smith had managed the office of her womanizing husband Clyde, an isolationist who died of advanced syphilis in 1940. She won both the special and general elections by sizeable margins, beginning a thirty-two-year congressional career. Her mother worked in a shoe factory and her father was a barber and a hotel clerk. She went to work at thirteen at a five-and-dime and never attended college. She was the first woman elected to both houses, the first female Republican Senator, and the first to have been elected without having been appointed to fill a vacancy. Representing a shipbuilding state, Smith strongly supported military preparedness, voting for the draft, lend-lease, and arming merchant ships. She served on the Naval Affairs Committee and introduced legislation to create the WAVES. "If she votes with us," Republicans complained, "it's a coincidence."[102]

VICTORY?

At the end of the war, women went from being comrades-in-arms to unseemly competition. Without war contracts, the industries employing the most women, aircraft and shipbuilding, reduced their workforces dramatically. There was a widespread conviction that women would willingly withdraw from the labor market. A Boeing supervisor believed women would "go back to their homes, and to their beauty parlors . . . and love the idea. They've done a grand job and learned a lot, but are they glad it's over!" One government pamphlet cautioned that "the war . . . has given women new status, new recognition . . . Yet it is essential that women avoid arrogance and retain their femininity."[103] Experts warned that veterans expected to be the breadwinners and that children would become delinquents without mothers at home. Women who had been motivated by patriotism and paychecks, who enjoyed the camaraderie and escaped from domesticity, were less eager to resume their former roles; 79% said they liked working. Women's labor force participation fell from 36% in 1944 to 28% in 1947, compared to 26% in 1940.[104]

Fighting for democracy united the country. It also demonstrated its flaws, in its refusal to admit refugees, its treatment of Japanese Americans, and its pernicious racism. African Americans hoped that their service would result in more rights and respect. They launched the "Double V" campaign: "victory against fascism abroad, victory against racism at home." In the military, segregated regiments were led by white officers because the War Department was "not to intermingle colored and white enlisted personnel in the same regimented organizations." The Air Corps and Marines refused to accept Black recruits. The regular Army had five Black officers, three of them chaplains. In the Navy, Black men worked as cooks, mess men, stewards, and stevedores, loading munitions in dangerous conditions. In July 1944, a ship exploded in Port Chicago, California, incinerating 320 sailors, including 202 African Americans. Refusing to load more ammunition in such conditions, fifty Black enlisted men were court-martialed for mutiny. An NAACP investigation pushed the Navy to change its policies and integrate three years before the other branches did.[105]

Similar cases drove up membership in the NAACP and the Congress of Racial Equality (CORE), established in 1942. Another force for change was A. Philip Randolph, a prominent civil rights and labor activist, who led the Brotherhood of Sleeping Car Porters, a primarily Black union. He was not a porter, so he could not be fired. Frustrated by going hat in hand to the White House to be charmed and dismissed by President Roosevelt, Randolph suggested a different tactic. In 1941, he threatened to lead a Negro March on Washington to protest the segregated army and the exclusion of Black Americans from roles in war industries. FDR called it extortion. Randolph didn't budge. Eventually, they reached a private bargain. The military was off the table, but the president issued Executive Order 8802: "There shall be no discrimination in the employment of workers in defense industries or government because of race, creed, color or national origin." The Fair Employment Practices Commission was created to investigate and enforce the measure. FDR's only civil rights initiative was a temporary measure. Having proved that militancy worked, Randolph called off the march.[106]

Lawsuits brought by the NAACP Legal Defense Fund were also effective. Established in the 1930s and led by Thurgood Marshall until 1961, the LDF challenged teacher salary differentials, convictions based on coerced confessions, segregation on interstate buses, real estate covenants, and the exclusion of Black voters from jury rolls and primaries in Southern states. It pushed to incorporate Black recruits into pilot training, resulting in the Tuskegee Airmen. By flying with the Red Tails, Eleanor Roosevelt demonstrated her support.[107] In 1945, Marshall hired Constance Baker as an intern. She was the first Black woman to graduate from Columbia law school.[108]

Marshall did not defend Pauli Murray's suit when she was denied admission to the segregated University of North Carolina law school. She had already made her case to the President, the First Lady, and the president of UNC. Marshall refused to take her case because it was not "airtight," based on the likelihood of winning and the background of the plaintiff. "We have to be very careful of the people we select." Her androgynous appearance and medical and family history were concerns.[109] The NAACP was known to be wary of taking on female plaintiffs, especially single women whose reputations might be vulnerable to attack. Murray and Marshall would eventually become allies.

During the Depression, the country counted on women to step aside and make do. During the war, the government expected women to step up and sacrifice, affording brief moments of equality in work and pay. Both events disrupted women's traditional roles, but net gains in rights or wages were negligible. Overwhelmed by economic and political realities, white feminist and social justice organizations floundered, splitting over race, class, and ideology.[110] Eleanor Roosevelt's role was significant because she inserted herself into national issues, but political women like Roosevelt, Perkins, Dewson, and Bethune still depended on men to implement change. Black women were discriminated against and, with regional exceptions, disenfranchised.[111] Women of color organized under the radar in church basements, canneries, and law offices, working as home demonstration agents, visiting nurses, church deacons, community organizers, teachers, and lawyers. They quietly educated and registered Black voters.[112] While "the Greatest Generation" was cheered, the women awaiting their return, who had also been toughened and transformed by the war, were not celebrated. After disproving many negative stereotypes, women were expected to retreat into their domestic spheres. Rosies were laid off to give male veterans preference. Laws requiring equal pay and childcare expired.

Only one woman seemed untouched by economic and international upheaval: a fictional amateur sleuth named Nancy Drew. She first appeared in print in 1930, following the success of the Hardy Boy series. Capable, confident, athletic, and feminine, the sixteen-year-old was the privileged daughter of a single dad attorney. In her blue roadster, the redhead (or blonde, depending on the decade) solved mysteries with two girlfriends and her hapless boyfriend, Ned Nickerson. Carolyn Keene was a pseudonym for the twenty-eight authors who continued the series until 2003. Mildred Wirt Benson wrote twenty-three of the first thirty volumes, imbuing the heroine with brains and spunk. Benson was the first person to earn a master's degree in journalism from the University of Iowa, in 1927. She earned $125 per book, but no royalties.[113] In the 1950s, Harriet Stratemeyer Adams, the publisher's daughter, rewrote earlier versions to remove ethnically offensive and feminist language. The girl detective became a cultural icon and the namesake for girls born in the Thirties and Forties, like Nancy Pelosi. Oprah Winfrey, First Lady Laura Bush, Secretary of State Hillary Clinton, and Supreme Court Justices Sandra Day O'Connor, Ruth Bader Ginsburg, and Sonia Sotomayor identified her as a role model.[114]

Drew joined the pantheon of imaginary white female icons created by men: the It Girl, Betty Crocker, Rosie the Riveter, and Wonder Woman. Insouciant, strong, brave, and smart, they combined characteristics of an ideal woman. Other than Betty Crocker, they rarely cooked. In 1945, Betty was the second-best known woman in America, after Mrs. Roosevelt.[115] Roosevelt, Constance Baker Motley, Pauli Murray, Margaret Chase Smith, Mary McLeod Bethune, Mary Church Terrell, and the alliance of reform leaders ER encouraged were real-life examples of political brokers and change agents. During her twelve-year tenure, Eleanor traveled to almost every state, drumming up support for the New Deal, advocating for the poor and disadvantaged, promoting civil rights, and demanding equal opportunities for women. When she attended the founding meeting of the Southern Conference on Human Welfare in 1938, in Birmingham, Alabama, she refused to participate in segregated seating and moved her chair into the center aisle. She joined the NAACP and, after the war, would serve on the board of both the NAACP and CORE. Married to one of the most consequential presidents in American history, she became and remained a force in her own right.[116]

CHAPTER FOUR

FROM ROSIE TO ROSA PARKS, 1945–1959

The day President Roosevelt died, April 12, 1945, he had been sitting for a portrait in Warm Springs, Georgia, in the company of his former mistress, Lucy Mercer. Mrs. Roosevelt was speaking at the Sulgrave Club in Washington. She returned to the White House to inform her children and the Vice President. Harry Truman, who was having a drink with House Speaker Sam Rayburn, blurted, "Jesus Christ and General Jackson!" That evening, the chief justice administered the oath of office. Truman had been vice president for eighty-two days. He had had two meetings with FDR, neither an intelligence briefing.[1]

FDR picked Truman because he was less liberal than his predecessor. In office, the new president exceeded expectations. Born in 1884, a Missouri farm boy with a high school education, Truman read voraciously. He served as a captain in World War I and failed at several occupations before running for local office. Despite having slave-owning grandparents and an unreconstructed mother, "the man from Independence" refused the Klan's endorsement. Rising in county and machine politics, Truman was elected US Senator in 1934 and again in 1940.[2]

The nation was still at war. Victory in Europe was declared on May 8. Three months later, after Truman ordered atomic bombs dropped on Hiroshima and Nagasaki, the Japanese surrendered. At a packed press conference on August 14, President Truman announced the end of the Second World War and declared a two-day national holiday.[3] The country spontaneously spilled into the streets to celebrate, where photographer Alfred Eisenstaedt snapped the iconic V–J Day picture of a sailor kissing a dental assistant in Times Square. The government ended gas rationing and lifted the thirty-five M.P.H. speed limit. Returning veterans were eager to make up for lost time, find jobs, and start families. America had become the strongest military and industrial power in the world, but its position was threatened. To achieve its goal of containing communism, America engaged in a forty-year-long Cold War. Geopolitics led to the establishment of the United Nations, the Marshall Plan, and membership in the North Atlantic Treaty Organization (NATO).

Truman respected smart women—his mother, his wife, and Eleanor Roosevelt. After the transition, he began a "robust correspondence" with the former First Lady. In November 1945, he appointed Eleanor Roosevelt to the first US delegation to the United Nations, meeting in London. He had already sent Mary McLeod Bethune to the organizing meeting in San Francisco, where she was the only woman of color in the world to have official status at the founding of the UN. In London, ER used her "shrill . . . strident and schoolmarmish" voice to promote equal rights. She was unanimously elected to chair the committee that established the UN Human Rights Commission, which drafted the Universal Declaration of Human Rights, issued in 1948. The Declaration listed thirty fundamental political, economic, social, and cultural rights to which everyone is entitled. "All human beings are born free and equal in dignity and rights . . . without distinction . . . such as race, color, sex, language, religion, political or other opinion, national or social origin, property, birth or other status." The Declaration lacked an enforcement mechanism and was not included in the binding international treaty that member nations signed.[4] Her global perspective did not change her view of the ERA, which she continued to oppose, although less publicly.

WOMEN CONTAINED

The United States sought to contain communism and defend the "American Way of Life." Security abroad depended on securing the home front—curbing racial disturbances, condemning homosexuality, and commending domesticity. As one historian summarized, "More than merely a metaphor for the Cold War on the home front, containment aptly describes the way in which public policy, personal behavior and even political values were focused on the home" and women.[5] After the war, white women were confined by a new suburban "cult of domesticity." Employers encouraged Rosies to return to traditional roles by laying them off from higher-paying war work. The military claimed it had fewer roles for women and denied benefits. Colleges promoted higher education as a way for women to become more interesting wives but discouraged them from pursuing degrees and limited admissions to make room for veterans.

While men had been at war, women had been at work as heads of households and wage earners. Now they were expected to welcome a return to dependence. Polls suggesting the majority of women wanted to continue working were ignored. Responding to a 1946 *Senior Scholastic* survey, 88% of girls wanted a career; 4% wanted to be homemakers. Yet magazines ran stories about women's eagerness to be home. As the *Atlantic Monthly* concluded, women were needed "to restore security in our insecure world."[6]

Even Wonder Woman was tempted to trade in her golden bracelets for a wedding ring. The comic book heroine, an advocate of peace, justice, and women's rights, was created in 1941 by a Harvard educated psychologist. William Marston lived with his wife Elizabeth and student Olive Byrne, Margaret Sanger's niece, fathering children with both women. Another woman he may have sexually exploited was Joye Hummel, who wrote the first three years of Wonder Woman scripts. Wonder Woman was an Amazonian princess, who disguised herself as Diana Prince to partner with US Army intelligence officer Steve Trevor, changing into a bustier to save the world. Since its heroine was "not sufficiently dressed," Catholic bishops banned the comic. In 1944, in a dream sequence, Diana agreed to marry Steve: "I'm ready to be your docile little wife." It turned out to be a nightmare. Diana divorced Steve and Wonder Woman went back to fighting Nazis. Although she had run for President in 1943, in the 1950s Diana was a babysitter, romance editor, model, and movie star. In 1972, she ran for president again, on the cover of the second issue of *Ms.* magazine.[7]

After the shortages and standards imposed by depression and war, women embraced the "New Look" created in 1947 by Christian Dior and translated into knockoffs in America. Fashion was confining. Cinched waists and pointed breasts emphasized femininity. Skirts were voluminous, supported by crinolines. Faille, shantung, taffeta, and pique fabrics were stiff and crisp. Accessories included hats, gloves, and charm bracelets, popularized by Mamie Eisenhower. "Mamie pink," the color of her inaugural gown, was copied in paint and bathroom tile. Girdles and long-line bras, called "Merry Widows," shaped and protected women with impregnable armor.[8] To suit the needs of suburban women, American designers adapted the shirtwaist, created sportswear and separates, and domesticated denim from work clothes to leisure wear. The French bikini, a skimpy two-piece bathing suit named for the atomic bomb test site in the Pacific, shocked Americans. Women brave enough to wear it were called "bombshells."[9] The dual identities of women as sexual and maternal were evident in tight sweaters topped with Peter Pan collars, and in the contrast between Hollywood stars like Elizabeth Taylor and Debbie Reynolds.

THE BABY BOOM AND THE 1950S CULT OF DOMESTICITY

In the midst of an arms race and anti-communist hysteria, experts declared the nuclear family "an antidote to the nuclear age."[10] Americans of every "racial, ethnic and religious group, of all socio-economic classes and educational levels" married younger and had more children than in any other period in the twentieth century.[11] After a spike to 43% in 1946, marking the end of hasty wartime marriages, the divorce rate remained low for the next twenty-five years.[12] Tax deductions for dependents encouraged marriage, and growing families created a postwar housing boom. Home loans benefited white buyers. Due to institutionalized racism in financial and government policies, not everyone could achieve the American Dream of a home in the suburbs, a breadwinning dad, a homemaking mom, and a station wagon full of kids.

In the Cold War against communism, affluent suburbs represented the triumph of capitalism. The idealized American home symbolized safety and abundance. "Levittowns" were communities of identical homes. The first 750-square-foot Cape Cod models had four-and-a-half rooms and an unfinished attic. Upscale ranch styles had 800 square feet for $7,990. They came with appliances and picket fences but without basements, garages, or driveways. The towns featured village greens, shopping centers, playgrounds, swimming pools, and sites for schools, churches, and fire stations.[13]

Levittowns were limited to whites, with restrictive covenants forbidding resale to Black buyers. The popularized term for white, "Caucasian," included immigrants, Jews, and Catholics, who might be unable to join restricted country clubs but could still join the middle class and advance in the suburbs. The end of immigration policies limiting the admission of Asian women changed the nature of bachelor-heavy Chinatowns. Japanese Americans, freed from the internment camps, also moved to the suburbs. Redlining and other forms of institutional racism excluded African Americans from the suburbs and deprived them of better housing, better public schools, opportunities for capital accumulation, and upward mobility.[14] The result was geographic segregation, leaving behind poor and middle-class Black families in cities or the South.

Developers sold homes but marketed happiness. Suburbs claimed to promote family togetherness, but actually separated commuting dads from stay-at-home moms. Advertising campaigns pictured families relaxing together, barbecuing, or watching television. The 1950s was "the Golden Age of Television." In 1956, Americans bought 20,000 televisions a day.[15] As the cost of producing TV sets fell and signals reached remote areas of the country, television reduced rural isolation and created a sense of shared national experience. In search of programming, networks broadcast the 1952 Republican and Democratic conventions and the 1953 coronation of Queen Elizabeth II.

Television reinforced cultural norms. Popular programs bolstered an image of domestic bliss in patriarchal white suburbs. On *Father Knows Best* (1954–1963), insurance salesman Jim Anderson and his wife Margaret had three children and easily resolved everyday problems. On *The Donna Reed Show* (1958–1966), the dad was a pediatrician. On *Leave It to Beaver* (1957–1963), Ward Cleaver was a trust officer. *The Adventures of Ozzie and Harriet* began on radio in 1944, with bandleader Ozzie Nelson and his singer wife Harriet. On television from 1952 to 1966, it was the longest-running series in television history until *NCIS*. The Nelsons employed their real sons in a benign family comedy led by an ad agency dad. All the moms wore aprons.[16]

I Love Lucy also evolved from a radio show. Unlike programs about white couples who lived in fictional suburbs, Lucille Ball and her real-life Cuban American husband, Desi Arnaz, lived on television in an apartment in New York City. CBS was initially reluctant to cast a leading man who played a nightclub owner and occasionally broke into rapid Spanish, but for four of its six seasons (1951–1957), *Lucy* was the most watched program on television. Unlike her counterparts, Lucy looked for paying jobs, which resulted in comic misadventures, reinforcing the message that women should stay home. The Ricardos slept in twin beds, but when Lucy was pregnant, the story was written into the script. Although the star was only filmed from the chest up, the decision to acknowledge her pregnancy was a ratings coup. More people watched the birth of the Ricardo baby than watched Eisenhower's 1953 inauguration. In reality, Lucille Ball was a working mother and the first actress to run a studio.[17]

Commercial sponsors, selling detergent, floor wax, and appliances, featured smiling white women in immaculate aprons, pearls, and high heels. As the 1950s progressed, the number of children appearing in the ads increased from one to four.[18] Television, magazines, and Sunday sermons reinforced domestic patriarchy. Religious observance grew from 49% in

1940 to 55% in 1950 and 69% in 1959. In 1955, 70% of Americans were Protestants. Billy Graham, a handsome evangelical preacher, attracted converts with huge revivals. In weekly telecasts and syndicated columns, Graham condemned drinking, smoking, swearing, card-playing, and dancing. After being dismissed by Truman, who believed firmly in the separation of church and state, Graham became an informal counselor to every president until his death in 2018.[19] Eisenhower, not a churchgoer before his election, attended Sunday services, opened cabinet meetings with a prayer, and supported adding "under God" to the Pledge of Allegiance in 1954.[20]

The ideal American family in the 1950s did not include grandparents. Postwar Americans were transient, pursuing job opportunities. Immigrant offspring were eager to escape native-speaking households with Old World rules, while Black families tended to migrate in sibling groups.[21] Without an older generation's wisdom, young families relied on experts like pediatrician Benjamin Spock, author of *The Common Sense Book of Baby and Child Care* (1946). Dr. Spock reassured mothers that "you know more than you think that you do" and encouraged them to respond to babies as individuals, to pick them up when they cried, and reject strict routines for feeding and sleeping. He urged dads to be involved so their sons would not become "sissies" or homosexuals, an unsettling prospect in that era. Although *Life* magazine worried about "the domestication of the American male," fatherhood was marketed as manliness. Father's Day, first proposed in 1957, became a permanent national holiday in 1972.[22]

SEX, EDUCATION, AND EMPLOYMENT

Attitudes about women's maternal roles were not all positive. In 1942, journalist and novelist Philip Wylie published a collection of essays, *Generation of Vipers,* which accused mothers of smothering and infantilizing their sons, creating juvenile delinquents. In *Modern Women: The Lost Sex* (1947), sociologist Ferdinand Lundberg and psychoanalyst Myrna Farnham denounced career women: "The independent woman is a contradiction in terms." Instead, women should be dependent, passive, and receptive to "the final goal of sexual life—impregnation, without resentment." Women who rejected traditional roles were "sick, unhappy [and] neurotic." In their opinion, feminists were frigid. Spinsters should be forbidden to teach and bachelors over thirty needed psychoanalysis.[23]

In contrast Alfred Kinsey's 1953 report, *Sexual Behavior in the Human Female*, shocked the country by portraying women as sexually active and actively interested. Trained as a zoologist, Kinsey had published parallel results about American men in 1948. All his subjects were white and middle class. With tables of statistics, he demonstrated that all men and 60% of women masturbated; that 90% of men and 50% of women engaged in premarital sex; that one-third of men had homosexual experience and one-quarter of women had extramarital affairs. Kinsey found "persons with homosexual history are to be found in every age group . . . social level . . . [and] conceivable occupation, in cities and on farms, and in the most remote areas of the country."[24]

Society expected women to be virgins at marriage. Scholars speculated that the urge for intercourse propelled young people from the courtship etiquette of going steady, necking, and heavy petting into early marriages. When white girls "got caught," they either married the father or were sent away to homes for unwed mothers. Their babies were put up for closed adoptions. Among African Americans, the babies were more likely to be kept in the family. The prevailing double standard maintained that sexuality was normal in men, but promiscuous in women. Since the Garden of Eden, men had been tempted by the daughters of Eve. Sex was the crime, pregnancy the punishment.[25]

To pace the "baby boom," the majority of middle-class couples used birth control. Except in Catholic-dominant Connecticut and Massachusetts, states allowed doctors to prescribe diaphragms, jellies, and intrauterine devices to married women.[26] Despite the emphasis on motherhood, breast-feeding was considered vulgar. Mothers gave babies formula. In 1956, Mary White, the mother of eleven children and a doctor's wife in suburban

Chicago, started an organization to encourage breastfeeding. Because the word "breast" was considered too sexual, she called it the La Leche League, referring to mother's milk. Contradicting male authorities, the League promoted breastfeeding as better for babies and mothers than formula.[27]

The seductive appeal of sex, marriage, and motherhood prompted white women to cut short their educations. Many married after high school. In 1920, women were 44% of all college students, but only 35% by 1958.[28] While white women were more likely than Black women to attend college, only 37% completed degrees, compared to 90% of Black women undergraduates. In 1956, one-quarter of white women got married in college, earning an "MRS" or a "PhT" ("putting hubby through"). Even with degrees, it was hard to find jobs in professions. As one woman recalled, "We married what we wanted to be."[29] In an unfavorable job market, Black women still pursued degrees. Due to discrimination and the pressure to work, Black men had fewer opportunities for higher education, resulting in a gap between more highly educated Black women and their spouses, the reverse of the white pattern of men with more education than their wives.

Wage-earning Black women were widely respected in their communities. *Ebony* magazine profiled professional women and two-career couples as role models.[30] For middle-class white women, working implied that their husbands were not sufficient earners. Fewer Black women had the option of staying home, because one Black income might not support a household or because they were single heads of households. Compared to 10% of white women, 25% of African American women were separated or divorced. Federal welfare benefits did not encourage poor couples to live together. By 1950, the number of Black women employed as domestic servants had declined, but 60% still worked as maids; only 5% held clerical posts.[31]

There were more white women working in the 1950s than the happy homemaker image suggested. The rate of women in the workforce began climbing again in 1947. For working-class women, "pink collar" service roles replaced better paid "blue collar" factory jobs. In 1950, fewer than 30% of women with children ages six to seventeen worked. That number rose to 34.7% in 1955 and almost 40% by 1960. Twice as many women were working in 1960 than in 1940. According to historian William Chafe, "female employment was increasing four times faster than that of men." White women worked until they married or until they had their first child, and again when their children went to school. Without childcare options, many worked part-time so they could be home after school. Middle-class women worked as teachers (where school boards allowed it), nurses, and real estate agents; 40% had clerical jobs. Postwar wages dropped 26% overall, which meant women were economically dependent, back to earning pin money. No matter the amount, a wife's income contributed to the family's standard of living and gave women more influence in purchasing decisions.[32] Disposable income triggered competitive consumerism and rising national prosperity.

Because white women were discouraged from pursuing careers, they became professional homemakers. One explanation for the increase in the birth rate was that if mothers could not find satisfying jobs, they would have more children. Research showed that women still spent fifty-five hours a week doing housework, the same as in 1920, before the invention of many labor-saving devices. Washing machines made the job much easier, but laundry was hung to dry. Before permanent press, it needed to be ironed. People who could afford a washer could also afford more clothes, so there was more laundry to do. To sell laundry soap, advertisers challenged women to have "whiter whites." Because they were expensive, only about 10% of Americans owned dryers or steam irons, new in 1955. In 1959 Bertha Berman, an African American, patented the fitted sheet.[33]

FEMINISM AND THE EQUAL RIGHT AMENDMENT

Also published in 1953 was the English translation of *The Second Sex* (1949) by Simone de Beauvoir. In a two-volume feminist manifesto, the French intellectual argued that the difference between the sexes was culturally created, not the result of biology. She rejected Freud and recognized that women were defined in relationship to men as "The Other." Because she asserted that women were enslaved by reproduction, the Vatican put her treatise on its List of Prohibited Books. Although Kinsey criticized de Beauvoir for a lack of scientific data, their books were seen as precursors of a new feminism.[34] Among some white women, increasing affluence, leisure, and an awareness of Black civil rights activism slowly began to generate greater political awareness and engagement.

Anne McCarty Braden, born in 1924, grew up in a traditional Southern family, but underwent a "racial conversion" and became a courageous white ally of the civil rights movement. As Braden said, "Either you find a way to oppose evil or the evil becomes part of you." She worked for the *Louisville Times* and married labor organizer Carl Braden. In 1954, they were approached by Black acquaintances, Andrew and Charlotte Wade, to help them buy a house in a white neighborhood. When the purchase was complete, white neighbors burned a cross on the lawn and shot out the windows before dynamiting the house. The actual bombers were not tried, the Wades moved into a Black area, and the Bradens were charged with sedition under Kentucky law. Carl was convicted and jailed, but released after the Supreme Court overthrew the state law. The couple continued to fight for Black rights, arguing that interracial organizations could better secure full social integration.[35]

Membership in civic organizations like the League of Women Voters declined among white women, while participation in the PTA and church auxiliaries increased. Groups like the John Birch Society, Moral Re-Armament, and White Citizens Councils appealed to conservative and racist women. Feminism fell from fashion. In 1940, Eleanor Roosevelt attended an event to mark the centennial of the 1840 World Anti-Slavery Convention, where Elizabeth Cady Stanton met Lucretia Mott and planned a women's rights assembly in America. The anniversary event addressed the challenge of diversifying American feminism to include Jewish, Black, working-class, and other marginalized women.[36] Anticipating the centennial of Seneca Falls in 1948, Gertrude Stein and Virgil Thomson wrote a witty opera, *The Mother of Us All*, about Susan B. Anthony, who had not attended the convention.[37] The opera was better attended than the centennial celebrations due to ongoing friction among rival leaders. A three-cent suffrage centennial stamp, featuring Stanton, Mott, and Catt, infuriated Catt's rival Alice Paul.

Throughout this period, Paul was still leading the National Woman's Party, still living at Belmont House, still lobbying for an Equal Rights Amendment. Republican sponsors still introduced the 1923 text of the ERA, while Democrats opposed it. After 1936, congressional subcommittees reported it out favorably almost every year. After the Supreme Court upheld the Fair Labor Standards Act, safeguarding protective legislation for women seemed less relevant. In response to objections to the amendment's wording, Paul changed it to "Equality of rights under the law shall not be denied or abridged by the United States, or by any State, on account of sex." In its 1940 platform, Republicans endorsed "submission" of the ERA, not ratification.[38]

In 1943, Senator Caraway (D-AR) and Representative Smith (R-ME) renewed the drive for the ERA. Given women's wider roles in the war, both House and Senate subcommittees approved the new language, as did the full Senate Judiciary Committee. Opposition arose from members with large Catholic constituencies. After twenty years, tempers had not cooled; the debate was "bitter and nasty." Eleanor Roosevelt, Frances Perkins, and Carrie Catt joined the antis. The Women's Trade Union League called the ERA "dangerous and vicious." Mary Anderson, a former shoe-stitcher and Director of the Labor Department's Women's Bureau since its inception in 1920, condemned the ERA as "impractical, dangerous, abstract, vague and legally unsound." The proposal was defeated in the House Judiciary Committee, 11–15.[39]

While President Truman dismissed the ERA as "a lot of hooey," it finally reached the Senate floor for its first vote in July 1946.[40] The ERA failed to get the two-thirds required for a constitutional amendment; the tally was 38–35, with twenty-three members not voting. It was opposed by progressives, organized labor, Catholics, Southerners, and the National Committee to Defeat the Un-Equal Rights Amendment. Signaling the shift from respecting women's war work to expecting them to resume traditional roles, the *New York Times* editorialized, "Motherhood cannot be amended, and we are glad the Senate didn't try."[41]

The NWP and its allies, the Business and Professional Women, the General Federation of Women's Clubs, and notables like Pearl Buck, Katharine Hepburn, Margaret Mead, Georgia O'Keeffe, and Margaret Sanger, tried again in 1950.[42] During the debate, proponents were surprised when Senator Carl Hayden (D-AZ) proposed additional gutting language: "The provisions of this article shall not be construed to impair any rights, benefits, or exemptions now or hereafter conferred by law upon persons of the female sex." The rider allowed Senators to be both for and against women's rights. Hayden, the former Sheriff of Maricopa County, had served in Congress since Arizona became a state in 1912. Elected to the Senate in 1926, he maneuvered in committees and cloakrooms. "No man in the Senate has wielded more influence with less oratory," concluded a colleague.[43] The Senate accepted the Hayden rider, 51–31, and voted on an eviscerated ERA, 63–19, only one vote short of two-thirds. In 1953, the Senate passed the Hayden rider, 58–25, and the amended ERA, 73–11, with more Republican than Democratic support. To halt the rider's momentum, sponsors withdrew the amendment from House consideration. In 1958, President Eisenhower asked a joint session of Congress to pass the ERA, but House Judiciary Committee Chairman Emanuel Celler (D-NY) refused to release it and the NWP retreated.[44]

WOMEN IN POLITICS

During the 1946 ERA vote, there were no women in the Senate. In 1950, Margaret Chase Smith voted for its passage with the Hayden rider, declaring: "It's time to quit thinking of women as second class citizens." Running for Senate in 1948, she defeated three men in the primary, thanks to women voters, and won the general election with 70% support, becoming the first woman Republican Senator. She was fifty-one. As the only woman Senator until 1961, she had to stand in line for the public restroom. She declined invitations to White House dinners until Jacqueline Kennedy suggested she bring an escort. As she told a BPW luncheon, she accepted "the responsibility of being senator-at-large for America's women."[45]

Her finest hour came in July 1950, when Smith stood to oppose the excesses of Senator Joseph McCarthy (R-WI). Without mentioning his name, the freshman Senator from Maine attacked his behavior and that of Congress. Political discourse, she observed, had been "debased to the level of . . . hate and character assassination."

> Those of us who shout the loudest about Americanism . . . are all too frequently those, who by our own words and acts, ignore some of the basic principles of Americanism—the right to criticize; the right to hold unpopular beliefs; the right to protest; the right of independent thought. [The Congress has been] debased to the level of a forum of hate and character assassination, sheltered by the shield of congressional immunity . . . I speak as a Republican. I speak as a woman. I speak as a United States Senator. I don't want to see the Republican Party ride to a political victory on the four horsemen of calumny—fear, ignorance, bigotry and smear.

She called her speech "A Declaration of Conscience." The reaction among McCarthyites was swift and harsh. She was ousted from a key committee and smeared at every opportunity.[46]

McCarthy was a bully. "Tail Gunner Joe," a former Marine, defeated his party's incumbent, Robert La Follette Jr., in the 1946 Republican primary and won Wisconsin's Senate seat. In a Lincoln Day speech in 1950, McCarthy claimed to have identified 205 communists in the State Department. The number increased in every subsequent speech.[47] McCarthyism became a synonym for witch hunting, prompting playwright Arthur Miller to write *The Crucible* (1953), metaphorically comparing McCarthyism to the Salem witch trials. Politicians were reluctant to condemn him and risk backlash from his base.

Supported by the Catholic Church and the Kennedy family, McCarthy launched a "Lavender Scare" against homosexuals, claiming a connection between so-called sexual perversion and communist depravity. The Senator and his legal counsels, Roy Cohn and Robert Kennedy, purged suspects from the State Department, Hollywood, unions, and universities. People were pressured to testify; many were blacklisted. More people lost their jobs charged with homosexuality than with communist sympathies. Finally, in 1954, when McCarthy attacked the Army in televised hearings, the Senate acted. In a rare measure, it condemned McCarthy for "inexcusable . . . reprehensible . . . vulgar and insulting" behavior, voting 67–22 to censure him. Senator John Kennedy (D-MA) was hospitalized and unable to vote. Because he never denounced McCarthyism, Eleanor Roosevelt refused to endorse JFK for vice president in 1956.[48]

With gender and sexuality seen as threats to postwar stability, few women entered national politics. The peak for women serving in Congress between 1946 and 1960 was the 1953–1955 session, when there were fifteen women, or 2.8%. Women would not reach 5% representation until the mid-1980s. There were too few to develop an agenda of common interests or accrue any leverage. Six widows of members served only single terms. The other nine had elected or party experience. Six had attended college; others claimed degrees earned in the League of Women Voters. Their median age was forty-nine, which was relevant if they were to serve long enough to gain seniority. Several were appointed to powerful "male" committees—Appropriations, Armed Services, Banking, Foreign Affairs, and Judiciary; others were given more stereotypical roles on the Education, Veterans Affairs, and Civil Service committees.[49]

Katherine St. George (R-NY), elected in 1946, coined the phrase "equal pay for equal work." In 1950, she failed to get enough signatures to discharge the ERA from the House Judiciary Committee. She would have greater success in the 1960s with the Equal Pay Act and with Title VII before losing her seat in the 1964 Goldwater debacle.[50] Edith Green (D-OR), the daughter of schoolteachers and head of the Portland PTA, arrived in 1955 and served on the Education and Labor Committee for eighteen years.

Known as "Mrs. Education," she was the architect of Title IX in 1973.[51] Florence Dwyer (R-NJ) began her eight-term career in 1956 with an upset victory. She helped create the Consumer Protection and the Environmental Protection agencies. While she supported equal pay and equal rights for women, she did not make gender an issue. Dwyer believed a congresswoman must "look like a girl, act like a lady, think like a man, speak . . . with authority, and most of all, work like a dog."[52]

Lenore Sullivan (D-MO) was the only woman not to vote for the ERA when it finally passed. After her husband died, the Democratic Party refused to nominate her to replace him. In 1952, running as Mrs. John Sullivan, she defeated seven men in the primary, including the incumbent, who had offered her a staff job had he won. She beat the Republican candidate two to one and served until 1977. Sullivan secured a childcare deduction for working mothers and proposed consumer protections like inspecting poultry and testing chemicals in food additives and cosmetics. Her 1959 Food Stamp initiative became part of Lyndon Johnson's War on Poverty.[53]

Martha Griffiths (D-MI), the first woman to serve on the House Ways and Means Committee, supported civil rights, tax reform, and the ERA. In the 1940s, Harvard law school did not accept women, so she and her husband attended the University of Michigan. When the Michigan Democratic Party recruited him to run for the legislature, he volunteered her. She served four years in the state house, lost a race for Congress in the 1952 Eisenhower landslide, and ran again in 1954. She campaigned in a mobile home and beat the incumbent 52% to 48%, without party or union support. She was never seriously challenged again. After retiring from Congress in 1974, Griffiths was elected Michigan's lieutenant governor.[54]

Cornelia "Coya" Knudsen's alcoholic husband sabotaged her career. A Minnesota high school teacher who had married her father's farmhand, she served in the state legislature before running for Congress in 1954, without the Democratic Farm-Labor Party, which found her too independent. Winning two terms, she worked to protect farm families and launched the first federal student loan program. Until it expired in 2017, Perkins Loans helped rural and low-income kids afford college. In 1958, the DFL conspired with her husband to subvert her career by suggesting that she was having an affair with her legislative aide, prompting a "Coya Come Home" campaign. The charges were false, but Mrs. Knudsen refused to discuss her private life. She won the primary but lost the general election by 1,390 votes to a Republican "family man." She was the only national Democratic incumbent to lose in 1958.[55]

While these women functioned in the political mainstream, the era also generated a more conservative cohort. Alarmed about the evils of communism and immorality, these women saw shifting populations, minority demands, and new theories in education and science as threats to traditional families. They laid the foundation for a pro-family conservatism, a form of housewife populism. Middle- and upper-class white women found allies among working-class men and women by concentrating on values rather than class. They were not yet winning elections. Republican Phyllis Schlafly lost a race for Congress in 1952 despite the Eisenhower landslide.[56] There was a through line from women opposed to suffrage to those who opposed Sheppard–Towner and anti-lynching legislation to supporters of McCarthy and segregation.

According to the *New York Times,* Harry Truman appointed more women to office than any of his predecessors. Credit went to India Edwards, a former women's page editor at the *Chicago Tribune,* who volunteered for the DNC Women's Division. "I'd read the obits and as soon as a man had died, I'd rush over to the White House and suggest a woman to replace him."[57] In 1949, Truman named Burnita Shelton Matthews to the US District Court for the District of Columbia, making her the first woman appointed to a federal trial court. Georgia Neese Clark served as US Treasurer and Anna Rosenberg as Assistant Secretary of Defense. Frieda Hennock became a Federal Communications Commissioner, where she reserved TV channels for educational programs. Truman named the first women ambassadors, sending Eugenia Anderson to Denmark and Perle Mesta to Luxembourg. He named former Congresswoman Clare Booth Luce Ambassador to Italy, the first woman to serve in a major diplomatic post. Eisenhower appointed former WAC director, Oveta Culp Hobby, to be Secretary of Health, Education, and Welfare, the second woman to serve in the cabinet. Ivy Baker Priest became US Treasurer and Mary Pillsbury Lord delegate to the UN Human Rights Commission.[58] Both Truman and Eisenhower relied more on appointments than on legislation to attract women voters.

In 1952, white women emerged as a significant electoral cohort. Women represented 51.2% of eligible voters. Between 1948 and 1952, turnout increased by 22% among women and 11% for men. Women preferred the Republican candidate, General Dwight Eisenhower, to Illinois Democratic Governor Adlai Stevenson by seventeen points. Male voters also gave Ike the majority. Pollster Lou Harris concluded that women "broke with the Democratic party . . . which they had taken to enthusiastically under Roosevelt" because of the Korean War, inflation, and alleged corruption in Washington. Some pundits suspected that white women changed parties because they were alarmed by Truman's civil rights agenda. Pollsters concluded that suburban white women were a "potent, more independent force in politics . . . less predictable . . . and apt to have standards for voting different from men." In a 1956 rematch, women again preferred the Republican, by twenty-three points.[59]

BLACK WOMEN LEADERS

The white press did not cover the activism of Black women. Many purposely avoided headlines. In the South, they worked through churches and organizations like the NAACP, the YWCA, the Home Demonstration Agency, and public health services to improve education, housing, sanitation, voter education, and registration.[60] In Northern cities they built more visible political networks. Juanita Jackson Mitchell, the first African American woman to graduate from the University of Maryland law school, was president of the Baltimore NAACP, succeeding her mother Lillian. She ran voter registration drives from the 1940s to the 1960s and pressed for the integration of restaurants, parks, and swimming pools. Her husband,

Clarence Mitchell Jr., was a national civil rights leader, and their sons became state senators.[61]

The Reverend Addie Wyatt was a renowned labor, civil rights, and religious leader in postwar Black Chicago. In 1930, at age six, she came from Mississippi in the Great Migration. When she applied to be a typist at the Armour meatpacking plant, she was sent to the factory floor. She joined the Amalgamated Meat Cutters and, in 1953, was elected the first African American vice president of a major union, recruiting members and fighting for equal pay for women. In 1955, she and her husband became ordained ministers and founded a Church of God as co-pastors. The church expanded from a garage to a storefront to a thousand-seat sanctuary. Wyatt joined civil rights protests with Dr. King and was a founding member of the National Organization for Women and CLUW, the Coalition of Labor Union Women.[62]

Dovey Johnson Roundtree was an AME minister and a criminal defense attorney in Washington, DC. She graduated from Spelman College, the "Black Vassar," in 1938, "a poor working student in a sea of Black privilege," and worked for Mary McLeod Bethune on the New Deal. A Women's Army Corps captain, she attended Howard University law school on the GI Bill. Roundtree's most historically significant case challenged segregated interstate bus travel. In 1952, WAC Private Sarah Keys was traveling to South Carolina in uniform. She refused to give up her seat to a white Marine and was jailed for disorderly conduct. Keys sued. Roundtree filed a complaint with the eleven-member Interstate Commerce Commission. The ICC was known as "the Supreme Court of the Confederacy" for its consistent support of segregation. Pressured by the *Brown* precedent and Harlem Congressman Adam Clayton Powell Jr. (D-NY), by the time the case was heard, in November 1955, the ICC agreed that "assignment of seats in interstate buses so designated as to imply the inferiority of the traveler solely because of race or color [was] unjust discrimination" and violated the Interstate Commerce Act. The dissenting chairman refused to order enforcement. Not until Freedom Riders were filmed being beaten and burned in Alabama in 1961 did Attorney General Robert Kennedy order the ICC to enforce the Keys decision.[63]

Roundtree's most controversial case involved defending Ray Crump, a Black day laborer, accused of the 1964 murder of Mary Pinchot Meyer, a white artist and socialite, the sister-in-law of journalist Ben Bradley, and an intimate of the Kennedys. That she was the president's mistress was not revealed during the trial. No forensic evidence linked Crump to the crime. Roundtree demonstrated that a Black lawyer could win an acquittal for a Black man before a white judge at a time when Black lawyers were banned from using the restrooms, library, and cafeteria at the District Courthouse. The Women's Bar Association of DC had a whites-only policy until Roundtree integrated it in 1962. Taking all kinds of cases, she worked "for eggs and collard greens" and represented generations of Black defendants. She called her autobiography *Justice Older Than the Law*. The Meyer murder has never been solved.[64]

Another Black attorney, Pauli Murray, added advanced degrees to her resume. Named a Rosenwald Fellow, she applied to Harvard but was refused on account of gender, not race. After attending law school in California, she published *States' Laws on Race and Color* (1951), which Thurgood Marshall called the Bible for civil rights lawyers. She believed she lost a post at Cornell University because the university considered her references too radical: Eleanor Roosevelt, Thurgood Marshall, and Philip Randolph. A founder of the Congress for Racial Equality (CORE), Murray adopted Gandhi's tactic of nonviolent civil disobedience.[65] In this period, she organized protests against segregated restaurants and department stores.

Joining Murray on the picket line outside Thompson's Restaurant in Washington, DC, in February 1950 was Mary Church Terrell, eighty-eight, a cane in one hand and a protest sign in the other. Terrell was chair of the Coordinating Committee for the Enforcement of DC Anti-Discrimination Laws. Called the "lost laws," they were passed in 1872 and 1873, never repealed, but not reprinted in the 1901 *DC Code*. Boycotts, picket lines, and sit-ins persuaded forty restaurants, including Hecht's and Kresge's lunch counters, to integrate. In *District of Columbia v. John R. Thompson Co.* (1953), the Supreme Court ruled, 8–0, that the "lost laws" were still valid.[66] Terrell, Bethune, and Murray linked generations of civil rights activists.

POSTWAR CIVIL RIGHTS

President Truman made equal rights for African Americans a personal priority.[67] The country he led was deeply segregated, with "whites only" restrooms, drinking fountains, restaurants, hotels, theaters, and transportation. Institutional racism was embedded in education, politics, banking, and the courts. The horrific treatment of returning Black servicemen angered Truman profoundly. In 1946, the police chief in Batesburg, South Carolina, forcibly removed US Army Sergeant Isaac Woodard Jr., a decorated veteran, from a bus. The chief beat Woodard and gouged his eyes with a blackjack, causing permanent blindness. President Truman ordered an unprecedented federal investigation. The sheriff was charged but acquitted by a white jury in twenty-eight minutes.[68]

Within a month of becoming President, Truman met with Walter White of the NAACP. Next he endorsed a permanent Fair Labor Practices Commission. In October 1945, Truman appointed Irvin Mollison to the US Customs Court, making him the third Black federal judge. In 1949, he elevated the second, William Hastie, to the US Court of Appeals for the Third Circuit, another first. Jane Brolin, the first Black female graduate of Yale Law School, had been appointed to the New York City Domestic Relations Court in 1939.[69] In December 1946, Truman used Executive Order 9808 to establish the first Presidential Committee on Civil Rights. Nicknamed the "Noah's Ark Committee," it had two women, two Southerners, two businessmen, two labor leaders, an Episcopal prelate, a Catholic bishop, a rabbi, and FDR Jr.[70]

The two Black members were Channing H. Tobias and Sadie Alexander. Tobias, a Methodist minister, college professor, National Secretary of the YMCA, and NAACP leader, was considered the "Booker T. Washington of his day."[71] Sadie Tanner Mossell Alexander was one of the first two Black women to receive doctorates in the United States; hers was in economics. Her dissertation was on the economic impact of the Great Migration on Black families in Philadelphia. She later earned a law degree from the University of Pennsylvania, served as solicitor for Philadelphia, and worked with Bethune and her protégé Dorothy Height. "Your creation of this committee," Alexander commended Truman, "is . . . the greatest venture in the protection of civil liberty officially undertaken by the government since reconstruction."[72]

African Americans were heartened when Truman addressed the annual meeting of the NAACP in June 1947, the first president to do so since Theodore Roosevelt. On a rainy Sunday afternoon, 10,000 people watched at the Lincoln Memorial. More listened on the radio. In a twelve-minute speech, President Truman committed the federal government to civil rights, calling it a moral imperative a generation before President Kennedy repeated that phrase in 1963.[73] Truman appointed four Supreme Court Justices, including Treasury Secretary Fred Vinson to be Chief Justice. The Vinson Court outlawed redlining (*Shelley v. Kraemer*, 1948), restrictive covenants in the District (*Hurd v. Hodge*, 1948), segregated interstate travel (*Henderson v. US*, 1949), and segregated law school (*Sweatt v. Painter*, 1950) and graduate school admissions (*McLauren v. Oklahoma*, 1950). Rulings that separate facilities were not equal began the assault on *Plessy v. Ferguson*. Thurgood Marshall called them "a serious blow to white supremacy."[74]

In April 1947, Jackie Robinson broke the color barrier in baseball, starting on first base for the Brooklyn Dodgers. Committed to the "Double V" campaign, Robinson had served as a lieutenant during the war. For refusing to move to the back of an Army bus, he was court-martialed and acquitted. Writing twenty-five years later, Robinson observed, "I cannot stand and sing the anthem. I cannot salute the flag; I know I am a Black man in a white world."[75] In December 1947, Truman's civil rights committee published its blueprint, *To Secure These Rights*. The NAACP called it "explosive"; the *Washington Post* declared it "social dynamite." Documenting widespread discrimination, it concluded that Black Americans lacked "the privileges of citizenship," including safety, security, and equal opportunity.[76]

In 1948, a presidential election year, Truman incorporated the recommendations into his State of the Union address, making "the essential human rights of all our citizens" the first of five goals. A month later he sent Congress "A Special Message" on civil rights, presenting a ten-point plan, including federal anti-lynching laws, measures to end discrimination in employment and transportation, and home rule and presidential suffrage for DC. Truman asserted that widespread racism was "the basis for the abridgment of constitutional rights" for Black Americans. In response, Congress threatened to filibuster the Marshall Plan. One Southerner called Truman's proposal "damnable, communistic, unconstitutional, anti-American [and] anti-Southern." Texas Congressman and Senate candidate Lyndon Johnson denounced Truman, while South Carolina Governor Strom Thurmond pledged to challenge him for the Democratic nomination.[77]

Democrats meeting in Philadelphia in July 1948 endorsed a liberal civil rights plank. Truman won the nomination despite 263 Southern delegates voting for Thurmond. Republicans nominated New York Governor Thomas Dewey. Henry Wallace, FDR's second vice president, ran as a Progressive. Thurmond announced his candidacy as a "Dixiecrat," hoping a four-way race would result in the House determining the outcome. Every candidate except Thurmond supported civil rights.[78] Undeterred by the Dixiecrat, Truman issued two history-making orders. Executive Order 9980 outlawed discrimination in all federal jobs and named a seven-member Fair Employment Board, with two Black members. Executive Order 9981 required the military to integrate all service branches as promptly as possible.[79] Its 1950 report, *Freedom to Serve*, documented the depth of discrimination in the military.

International affairs were urgent campaign issues, but Truman did not ignore his primary domestic concern. On the Saturday before the election, he held his last rally in Harlem, accompanied by Eleanor Roosevelt. A crowd of 60,000 African Americans applauded his repetition of the noun "we." Some were on their knees, praying for his victory.[80] The President won the Black vote and enough others to eke out an unexpected victory, captured in the famous photograph of him holding up a *Chicago Tribune* headline, "Dewey Defeats Truman!"

BROWN

The groundwork laid by Black leaders, the NAACP Legal Defense Fund, and Truman's initiatives led to the *Brown* decision. The case first came to the Supreme Court in 1952. It was named for the father of eight-year-old Linda Brown, who had to travel twenty-one blocks to a Black elementary school in Topeka, Kansas, although the family lived seven blocks from a white school. When the white principal refused to admit Brown's daughter, he sued. The Supreme Court had five school desegregation cases from different states on its docket, so the justices combined them into *Oliver Brown et al. v. The Board of Education of Topeka.* Because it came from the Midwest, the Court listed the Brown case first to emphasize that segregation was a national issue.[81]

Among the five cases, girls outnumbered boys as plaintiffs by two to one. Only one case was initiated by a student. In 1951, Barbara Rose Johns, sixteen, led a walkout of 450 students from a shabby, overcrowded, segregated school in Farmville, Virginia, named for Robert Moton, the Tuskegee president who had spoken at the dedication of the Lincoln Memorial. Johns's was the first public protest of the postwar civil rights era. When the superintendent threatened Black parents with repercussions, Johns contacted the NAACP. The case, *Davis v. Prince Edward Co.*, was incorporated into *Brown.* Feeling endangered, Johns finished high school in Alabama, attended Spelman College, graduated from Drexel University and worked as a librarian in Philadelphia schools. Rather than integrate, Prince Edward County closed all its schools for ten years, becoming a bastion of white resistance. In 2008, the Farmville library was renamed for Johns. In 2020, Virginia decided to replace its statue of Robert E. Lee in the US Capitol with one of Johns.[82]

The legal precedent for segregation was *Plessy v. Ferguson* (1896). Homer Plessy, thirty, was a mixed-race shoemaker, a creole de coleur who could pass for white but chose not to. He volunteered to challenge Louisiana's separate car rule, in cooperation with a citizens' committee and the railroad company. Transportation companies opposed segregation because it cost more money to run more cars. Plessy was arrested in the first-class car, tried by Judge John Ferguson, and appealed. The case established the principle of "separate but equal" accommodations for white and Black passengers on railroad cars and led to legally sanctioned segregation in America. Holding that the Fourteenth Amendment "could not have been intended to . . . enforce social, as distinguished from political, equality, or a commingling of the two races upon terms unsatisfactory to either of them," the 8–1 Supreme Court majority gave constitutional cover to white supremacy and Jim Crow apartheid. Justice John Marshall Harlan from Kentucky, "The Great Dissenter," who had been born into an enslaving family in 1861, objected: "Our Constitution is color-blind, and neither knows nor tolerates classes among citizens." In 2009, descendants of Plessy and Ferguson established a foundation to teach the history of civil rights.[83]

The NAACP had been preparing for a case like *Brown* since the 1930s. Rather than argue for equal funding or facilities for segregated schools, the Legal Defense Fund challenged the principle of segregation. Constance Baker Motley, LDF associate counsel, wrote the original complaint in *Brown*. In oral argument, Thurgood Marshall and his team employed a "Brandeis brief," providing evidence from four Black authorities, legal scholar Pauli Murray, historian John Hope Franklin, and psychologists Kenneth and Mamie Clark. Their famous doll test hypothesized that Black children chose to play with white dolls because they suffered low self-esteem due to learning in a segregated environment.[84]

When *Brown* reached the Court in 1952, only four justices were committed to overturning *Plessy*. The tide turned when Chief Justice Vinson died and President Eisenhower nominated Earl Warren in October 1953. The California governor regretted having overseen the internment of Japanese Americans during World War II and was now committed to civil rights. The new Chief Justice delayed voting on *Brown* in conference until he could guarantee a unanimous decision. Justice Stanley Reed of Kentucky, author of the *Allwright* decision banning white-only primaries, was the final holdout. The Chief Justice announced the decision on

May 17, 1954.[85] Between 2017 and 2020, the Republican Senate confirmed two hundred federal judges; more than thirty declined to endorse *Brown* as a precedent.[86]

The *Brown* decision caused an uproar. Ending school segregation threatened the foundation of white supremacy, the belief that Black people were by nature inferior. The backlash coalesced into a strategy of "massive resistance," including "white flight" academies. In 1956, Congressman Howard Smith (D-VA) introduced the "Southern Manifesto," a declaration of defiance signed by eighty-two representatives and nineteen senators from the former Confederacy. One outcome was the repeated refusal to admit Hawaii as a state because of its mixed-race population.[87] Both sides were fueled to fight. Racial terror increased and resistance mounted.

EMMETT TILL AND ROSA PARKS

Unlike most lynchings, the horrific murder and mutilation of fourteen-year-old Emmett Till on August 28, 1955 made national news. The Chicago teenager was visiting cousins in the Mississippi Delta. Carolyn Bryant, twenty-one, the white cashier at her family's market, told her husband and his half-brother that Till had grabbed her and whispered obscenities. That night the two men abducted and brutally beat the boy, shot him in the head, tied his body to a seventy-four-pound cotton gin fan with baling wire, and threw it into the Tallahatchie River. Fishermen found his grossly disfigured body. His mother, Mamie Till Bradley (now Mobley), insisted on an open casket funeral and allowed *Jet* magazine and the *Chicago Defender* to publish photographs of the corpse. The photographs sparked horror and outrage, but a white jury acquitted Till's suspected killers in sixty-seven minutes. Years later, they confessed but were not retried. Historian Timothy Tyson asserted that Bryant admitted to him in 2008 that she fabricated her testimony. The Justice Department reopened the case, but investigators found that the author could not corroborate his claim with tape recordings or transcripts.[88]

Rosa Parks recalled thinking about Emmett Till when she was arrested for refusing to change her seat on a segregated city bus in Montgomery, Alabama, on Friday, December 2, 1955. As secretary of the Montgomery NAACP, she knew local leaders had been looking for an opening to challenge segregated seating. Because she was forty-two, married, employed, and a respected and recognized community leader, Parks was the ideal plaintiff. Born in 1913, Rosa McCauley learned to sew from her grandmother. She attended a vocational school for girls, staffed by Northern teachers, and an experimental high school associated with Alabama State Teachers College. After breaks to care for family members, she graduated in 1933, when fewer than 7% of African Americans earned high school diplomas. She married barber Raymond Parks, worked as a domestic servant and a seamstress, and joined the League of Women Voters and the NAACP.[89]

Parks represented resistance to racism in the heart of the Confederacy. She had been fighting Jim Crow since the Scottsboro trial. She founded a Committee for Equal Justice, supported by W. E. B. Du Bois, Mary Church Terrell, and Langston Hughes. During the war, Parks worked at Maxwell Air Force base, an integrated federal facility, where she rode on an integrated trolley. In 1944, she investigated the gang rape of Recy Taylor, a twenty-four-year-old mother walking home from church, by six white men. No charges were brought. In 1949, Parks protested the rape of Gertrude Perkins by white police officers and demanded fair treatment for returning Black veterans.[90] After her arrest in 1955, R. D. Nixon, head of the local NAACP, bailed her out. He was accompanied by Clifford and Virginia Durr, her employers and friends. Parks and Mrs. Durr were members of an interracial women's group. Durr, whose sister was married to Justice Hugo Black, helped fund Parks's past attendance at the Highlander Folk School for training in nonviolent action, where Parks met Septima Clark.[91]

At least four other Black women had previously been arrested for refusing to sit in the segregated section: Aurelia Browder, Claudette Colvin, Susie McDonald, and Mary Louise Smith. Their cases were not pursued. Another Black woman, Jo Ann Robinson, a professor at Alabama State

College, had organized the Women's Political Council in 1946 to protest the mistreatment of Black women by bus drivers. After Parks' arrest, she secretly mimeographed 35,000 leaflets, calling for a one-day bus boycott on the following Monday, December 5.[92] That night, a community meeting was held in the basement of the Dexter Avenue Baptist Church, built on the site of a slave market across from the state capitol. Nixon and Robinson proposed extending the boycott, negotiating with the city, and establishing the Montgomery Improvement Association (MIA) to help arrange alternative transportation, using carpools and Black-owned taxis and hearses. The group chose Dexter's new pastor, Martin Luther King Jr., twenty-six, as their initially reluctant spokesperson. Their terms were modest: first-come-first-served seating, courteous treatment, and more Black drivers. It was not a sure strategy. In 1904, a two-year boycott of streetcars in Richmond had failed.

After the King and Nixon homes and several churches were bombed in early 1956, the MIA took legal action, represented by Fred Gray and the NAACP. Because Parks's case was in criminal court, he brought a suit on behalf of the four other women. They sued the city, charging that segregation by the bus company violated the equal protection clause. When the NAACP won at the state level, the city appealed *Browder v. Gayle* (Montgomery's mayor) to the Supreme Court, asking for an injunction to end the boycott. On November 13, 1956, the Supreme Court ruled unanimously that segregation on public transportation was unconstitutional. The city asked for reconsideration and the boycott continued. On December 17, 1956, the Supreme Court again ruled to end the segregation of city buses.[93] Three days later, the boycott ended. It was a triumph for the 40,000 harassed, heroic Black women and men who had walked, carpooled, and biked to work for 381 days.

In the aftermath, Aurelia Browder and the other litigants were less celebrated and less condemned than Parks. She and her husband lost their jobs and left Montgomery. The couple joined family in Detroit and struggled to find work. Eleven years after Parks's arrest, Black Congressman John Conyers (D-MI) hired her for his district office. When Parks died in

October 2005, her casket was placed in the Capitol Rotunda, an honor given to only four other private citizens and no other woman. Congress authorized the installation of her statue in the Capitol, which was unveiled by President Obama in 2013. The first full-size statue of an African American joined busts of Martin Luther King and Sojourner Truth. In 2019, a monument to Parks and the Browder plaintiffs was dedicated in Montgomery. Fred Gray, eighty-nine, sat in the second row.[94]

Gray continued to represent civil rights clients and causes, even after Alabama banned the NAACP from practicing law in the state for eight years. In 1970, he was elected to the state legislature, the first Black man to serve since Reconstruction. In 1972, he brought a class action suit against the Tuskegee Syphilis Study, *Pollard v. U.S. Public Health Services*, winning a $10 million settlement and medical treatment for its seventy-two survivors, who had been studied but never treated since the 1930s.[95] Dr. King had also intended to build his career in Montgomery, but the churchwomen urged him to do more. In April 1957, he invited Black ministers to his father's Ebenezer Baptist Church in Atlanta. They formed the Southern Christian Leadership Conference (SCLC), an umbrella organization of affiliates like the MIA. It intended to "redeem the soul of America" through nonviolent resistance.[96]

ELLA BAKER, DAISY BATES, AND AUTHERINE LUCY

Leadership of the civil rights movement by a cadre of charismatic ministers overshadowed the significant contributions of Black women.[97] Women remained behind the scenes, a remnant of the patriarchal hierarchy of Black (and Christian) churches and a strategic decision on their part to put Black men in the spotlight. In addition to his wife, Coretta Scott King, a graduate of Antioch College and the New England Conservatory of Music, Dr. King was supported by strong women leaders. Pivotal among them was Ella Baker, who ran the SCLC operation from its Atlanta headquarters as its first employee. Born in Virginia, she graduated from Shaw University as valedictorian in 1927. She moved to New York City during the Harlem Renaissance, worked as a journalist, organized New Deal programs, served as an NAACP field secretary, and traveled throughout the South, where she met Rosa Parks in the 1940s. She became head of the New York City chapter in 1952, the first woman in that role.

From there, Baker raised money for the Montgomery boycott and urged Dr. King to form the SCLC. She moved to Atlanta in 1958 to coordinate SCLC's Crusade for Citizenship, a voter registration campaign. Rather than rallying around a personality, Baker believed in servant leadership. She advised Student Nonviolent Coordinating Committee (SNCC) organizers to remain independent of the ministers. Described as a "whirlwind," the strategist was aware that the men with whom she worked devalued her advice. One of her many protégés, Marian Wright Edelman of the Children's Defense Fund, called Baker "a transforming . . . and overpowering justice warrior."[98]

Daisy Gatson Bates was the force behind the integration of Central High School in Little Rock, Arkansas, in 1957. She was a journalist, co-publisher of the *State Press* newspaper, and president of the state NAACP.[99] After the *Brown* decision, the Court left it up to states to integrate schools; many refused. Under increasing pressure from parents, the press, and the NAACP, the superintendent of Little Rock schools announced a plan to integrate Central High School. Bates recruited and vetted seventeen of the brightest teenagers in the city. Eight changed their minds, so six girls and three boys became the Little Rock Nine. She coached them, providing strategies to deal with the hostility and hatred they would face. Governor Orval Faubus ordered the Arkansas National Guard to block the doors. On September 4, 1957, Bates drove eight of the students to school. Elizabeth Eckford, whose family did not have a telephone, missed the carpool. She approached the school on her own before retreating in the face of snarling white parents and students. The crowd beat four Black journalists, assuming they were students.[100]

The second attempt to enter school was captured by television cameras, so the country saw a mob of racist adults and Arkansas Guardsmen denying the students entrance. The effort was abandoned for three weeks while NAACP attorneys sought an injunction and a solution. Finally, at the mayor's request, made "in the name of humanity, law, and order," President Eisenhower ordered the 101st Airborne Division to take charge. On September 25, they escorted the teenagers up the front steps and into their classrooms. It was the first time federal intervention was used to enforce *Brown*. The military stayed for a year. So did Daisy Bates, who took the Nine to and from school every day, supervising homework and offering moral support, while the Klan threw rocks through her windows and burned crosses on her lawn.[101]

Whites taunted and threatened the students daily. One Black girl said she never went to the bathroom because the soldiers could not protect her there. One had acid thrown in her face; one was cut with broken glass; another was kicked down the stairs. In February 1958, Minnijean Brown was expelled for retaliating. Gloria Ray's mother was fired. Ernest Green, the only senior, graduated in a ceremony attended by Dr. King. The following year, rather than desegregate, Governor Faubus closed all Little Rock high schools. The remaining eight students took correspondence classes or left the state. They all graduated. Bates left Little Rock. In 1998, President Clinton, a former Arkansas governor, gave each of the nine students a Congressional Medal of Honor. Arkansas plans to replace its current statues in the US Capitol with likenesses of Daisy Bates and country singer Johnny Cash.[102]

Another school integration milestone is marked by a different monument. In 1956, Autherine Lucy was admitted to the University of Alabama for a second college degree to advance her teaching career. The University accepted her and Pollie Myers without knowing they were Black applicants. Their arrival on campus was met with white violence. The University rescinded their admission and the women sued, represented by Thurgood Marshall. Because she had conceived a child before her marriage, the school barred Myers on the grounds that she was morally unfit. Lucy won her case, but when she returned to campus, hecklers followed her everywhere. Sorority girls staged a skit in blackface.[103] After three days, the University suspended Lucy, "for her own protection." She sued again, won again, and was expelled again, this time for maligning the University in her legal briefs.[104]

Less than a decade later, in 1963, two Black students enrolled successfully, despite Alabama Governor George Wallace standing blocking an entrance. In 1988, the University rescinded Lucy's expulsion. She returned and earned a master's degree in 1992, graduating on the same day as her daughter. In September 2017, the University invited Dr. Autherine Lucy Foster to unveil a plaque and clock tower marking her struggle to be admitted. Lucy's initial enrollment attempt prompted a forty-thousand-member spike in Alabama's White Citizenship Council. By 1959, only 6% of Black students in the South went to integrated schools.[105]

CULTURAL CHANGE AND BARBIE DOLLS

The pace of social change in the 1950s could not be contained. Science was literally skyrocketing. The Russians sent *Sputnik 1* into orbit on October 4, 1957, launching the space age and the space race. The news was met with apprehension, awe, and a new emphasis on improving American public education. Scientific innovations, like the Salk vaccine to combat polio, saved lives. To reduce infant mortality, obstetrical anesthesiologist Virginia Apgar, MD, the first female full professor at Columbia medical school, developed a test for newborns to assess risk factors. The "Apgar score" is still used.[106] In 1952, Grace Hopper, a naval officer and computer scientist, developed a new computer language that used common English words instead of numbers, the basis of COBOL (common business-oriented language). A Vassar graduate with a doctorate in math from Yale, Hopper served in the Navy during World War II as a WAVE, where she worked on designing a machine to calculate the trajectory of bombs and rockets. Known as "Amazing Grace," she became a US Navy Rear Admiral.[107]

In 1950, in a forerunner to the US Open, Harlem-raised Althea Gibson was winning a match against a white Wimbledon champion over jeers of

"Beat the n———!" Gibson lost but went on to desegregate tournament tennis, becoming the first Black player to be ranked number one in the world, the first to win at Wimbledon, in 1957, and the first Black woman to appear on the covers of *Sports Illustrated* and *Time*. Gibson, born on a South Carolina cotton farm, migrated North and dropped out of school at thirteen to devote herself to basketball. Although she dismissed tennis as a sport for weak people, she joined the Black American Tennis Association, which lobbied for Black players to compete in the USTA. "I have never regarded myself as a crusader," she wrote in 1958. "I don't consciously beat the drums for any cause, not even the negro in the United States." Her life in retirement was isolated and impoverished until a former doubles partner, Englishwoman Angela Buxton, raised funds to support Gibson until she died in 2003.[108]

Popular culture challenged conservative attitudes about sex. Rebellious white teenagers held adults in contempt. They had money for movies, blue jeans, fast food, and rock and roll records, rhythms appropriated from Black artists whose music was not played on white radio. Racy foreign films subverted the Hays Code, as did a 1957 Hollywood movie, *Peyton Place*. It featured three white women from different classes dealing with incest, adultery, and abortion.[109] Sex symbols James Dean and Elvis Presley stole the hearts of girl groupies and alarmed their parents, while a cool blonde Hollywood princess, Grace Kelly, married royalty. Heterosexuality was the norm. Homosexuals created two organizations: the Mattachine Society, named for French medieval masques, founded in 1950, and the Daughters of Bilitis, an organization for lesbians, begun in 1955.[110]

Sex even permeated the toy market. In 1959, Ruth Handler, vice president of Mattel, the third largest toy company, marketed a curvy doll named Barbie.[111] Parents responded so negatively that Sears refused to sell the doll. Barbies appealed to the instinct for role-playing, so Mattel provided a wardrobe for stewardesses, nurses, secretaries, and, sixty years later, pilots, astronauts, doctors, executives, and political candidates. In its first iteration, Barbies were white. Modern Barbies come in eight skin tones, twenty-three hair colors, twenty hairstyles, eighteen eye colors, and several body types, some with thicker waists and wider feet. In 2018, Barbie launched two new lines. "Sheros" included Ibtihaj Muhammad, a hijab-wearing American Olympic fencer. "Inspiring Women" honored notables like Black NASA mathematician Katherine Johnson. In 2019, Mattel released gender-neutral dolls with no assigned sex and a variety of wigs and clothes.[112]

It took almost half a century for Barbie to change; change for real women also came slowly. Campaigning for President, Illinois Governor Adlai Stevenson addressed Smith College graduates in 1955. The first divorced candidate urged them to embrace "the humble role of housewife." He extolled their "primary task," to use the "subtle arts" to influence their husbands. They might feel frustrated, but their role was essential. "Once they wrote poetry. Now it's a laundry list . . . Once they read Baudelaire. Now it is the Consumer's Guide."[113] Stevenson lost and several Smith alumnae failed to follow his advice, including poet Sylvia Plath, class of 1955, and activist Gloria Steinem, class of 1956.

In 1960, Mary Ingraham Bunting, a microbiologist, young widow, and mother of four, became president of Radcliffe College. To combat the "climate of unexpectation" that thwarted women in mid-century America, she recruited "intellectually displaced" white women, whose careers had been interrupted by marriage and motherhood, to be Radcliffe Fellows. Among the inaugural class were poets Anne Sexton and Maxine Kumin, friends and literary collaborators literally connected by a dedicated telephone line. Kumin had trained for the Olympics as a swimmer before attending Radcliffe. When she showed her work to instructor Wallace Stegner, still an unknown novelist, he dismissed it with a red-penciled note: "Say it with flowers, but, for God's sake, don't try to write poems."[114]

Kumin married, moved to the Boston suburbs, and had two children. During her third pregnancy, she started writing again and published four lines in the *Christian Science Monitor*. The *Saturday Evening Post* required her husband to send a letter from his employer certifying that her work was original. "Women," Kumin believed, "along with people of color, were still thought to be intellectually inferior, mere appendages in the world of *belles lettres*." Over time she published longer poems, taught, moved to New Hampshire, and won a Pulitzer Prize in 1973. "Until the Women's

Movement," she recalled, "it was commonplace to be told by an editor that . . . he'd already published one [poem] by a woman that month." Sexton was equally brilliant and better known, winning a Pulitzer in 1967. Frequently compared to Plath, Sexton died by suicide in 1974, at age forty-five.[115]

Nothing daunted Black playwright Lorraine Hansberry. Her life epitomized the progress of African Americans in the first half of the twentieth century. Her grandparents had been enslaved in Mississippi. Her parents migrated to Chicago and thrived as a real estate broker and a teacher. Part of an activist, literary elite, they belonged to the Urban League, contributed to the NAACP, voted Republican, and sent four children to college. Prospering from selling homes in segregated areas, in 1937 Mr. Hansberry moved his family to a white neighborhood covered by restrictive racial covenants. Hostile neighbors sued. Due to a precedent, the Illinois Supreme Court voided the sale and ordered the Hansberrys to move. The subsequent Supreme Court case, *Hansberry v. Lee* (1940), determined that the precedent did not apply, but the Court did not outlaw covenants. Despite winning their suit, the Hansberrys returned to South Side.[116]

Lorraine Hansberry chose the University of Wisconsin-Madison rather than a historically Black college. She integrated a dormitory and participated in student theater and political protests. She dropped out during her sophomore year and moved to New York City. Working for a leftist newspaper published by Paul Robeson, she covered a Washington march by Black women, the Sojourners for Truth and Freedom; the 1951 electrocution of Willie McGee, convicted of rape in Mississippi; colonialism; and discrimination. Hansberry married Jewish producer and songwriter Robert Neimeroff in 1953 and lived in Greenwich Village amid jazz clubs, beat poets, and liberal causes. His success allowed her to write full-time. A feminist, communist, and closeted lesbian, Hansberry divorced her husband in 1962; he remained her literary executor. As she told Studs Terkel in 1959, sounding like Anna Cooper and Mollie Terrell, Black women were "twice oppressed," so they should be "twice militant."[117]

Hansberry's *A Raisin in the Sun,* about a Black family confronted by restrictive covenants in Chicago, was the first play produced on Broadway written by a Black woman. An earlier effort failed. *Trouble in Mind*, a 1955 drama by Alice Childress, portrayed a company of Black actors putting on an anti-lynching play. When white producers insisted on an upbeat ending, Childress refused and the play never opened. Hansberry's title came from Langston Hughes's poem "Harlem": "What happens to a dream deferred? Does it dry up like a raisin in the sun?" At twenty-nine, Hansberry was the youngest person and first Black playwright to win the New York Film Critics' Drama Award. The film version of *Raisin* won at Cannes.

In the early 1960s, Hansberry protested in the South and joined James Baldwin in his 1963 meeting with Attorney General Robert Kennedy. Her second produced play, *The Sign in Sidney Brustein's Window*, about Village bohemians and mixed-race relationships, closed the night she died of pancreatic cancer in 1965. Robeson and James Forman spoke at her funeral; Baldwin and Dr. King sent messages. Her autobiography, *To Be Young, Gifted and Black*, was adapted for theater and inspired Nina Simone's song of the same name. *Raisin*, produced as a musical and revived as a play, continued to win accolades. Hansberry left four other plays. "Marrow," an unpublished script about lynching, was uncovered in 2020.[118]

The conformity of the 1950s could not contain the moral imperative of civil rights activism, the energy of the youth rebellion, or the creativity of the arts. Jazz and abstract art were American forms. Artists Helen Frankenthaler, Joan Mitchell, and Elaine de Kooning were rising stars in another male dominated field. Lesser known was African American abstract artist Alma Thomas, part of the Washington Color School. The first graduate of Howard's art department and a teacher in DC's segregated schools, she was eighty before her work was exhibited at the Whitney and the Corcoran museums. Between 1932 and 1972, the Museum of Modern Art mounted one thousand solo shows by male artists and five by women.[119] Idealization of the 1950s ignores its racial violence, nuclear threats, unhappy housewives taking tranquilizers, and men in grey flannel suits indulging in martini lunches, setting the scene for *Mad Men*. Domestic containment proved impossible.[120] Pressure was building. In the coming decade, the country would explode into political, social, and sexual revolutions.

CHAPTER FIVE

PILLBOXES & PROTESTS, 1960–1972

T he 1960s opened with two events that would signal major changes in American history: the election of the first president born in the twentieth century and the introduction of oral contraception. As Massachusetts Senator John F. Kennedy, forty-three, declared when he accepted the Democratic nomination for president, it was time for "a new generation of leadership." With his cosmopolitan wife Jacqueline, the first Catholic president changed the image of the office from stuffy to stylish. The new president inspired the country with soaring rhetoric but struggled to enact his legislative initiatives. In contrast, when the Federal Drug Administration approved "the Pill," a new form of birth control, it changed women's lives and revolutionized American society.

KENNEDY AND WOMEN

During the 1960 presidential campaign, the candidates debated the Cold War rather than civil rights. Few people noted the fortieth anniversary of the Nineteenth Amendment in August 1960 or another defeat of the Equal

Rights Amendment by Senator Hayden.[1] In a country unsettled by foreign threats and increasing domestic unrest, women were not newsworthy. The 1960 Republican and Democratic platforms both addressed the Equal Rights Amendment without enthusiasm. Vice President Nixon endorsed it obliquely: "I believe the Congress should make certain that women are not denied equal rights with men."[2] At the Democratic convention, labor operative and Kennedy supporter Esther Peterson testified against the ERA on behalf of twenty-four national organizations. Pressured by the ACLU, the AFL–CIO, nurses, and teachers, Democrats weakened their platform language, substituting "equal treatment" for equal rights.

When the National Woman's Party complained, Kennedy finessed:

> I have long been convinced that discrimination in any form
> is contrary to the American philosophy of government. It is a
> basic tenet of democracy to grant equal rights to all, regardless
> of race, creed, color or sex . . . You have my assurance that I will
> interpret the Democratic platform, as I know it is intended, to
> bring about . . . the full equality of women which advocates of
> the equal rights amendment have always sought.[3]

National Woman's Party President Emma Guffey Miller, the oldest member of the Democratic National Committee, was not appeased. Resorting to campaign sabotage, she amended Kennedy's statement, had it typed on campaign letterhead, and signed by an autopen. She avoided the required approval by Peterson of any campaign communication relating to women. The new letter read:

> Thank you for providing me with the opportunity to make a
> statement regarding the equal rights amendment . . . You have
> my assurance that I will interpret the Democratic platform . . .
> [to include] adoption of the Equal Rights Amendment.[4]

Peterson counseled Kennedy to ignore it.

After the election, Democratic women criticized Kennedy for appointing only ten women to Senate-confirmed policy-making and judicial posts. He did name Dr. Janet Travel the first female White House physician. Truman had named fifteen women, Eisenhower fourteen, for a combined average of 2.4% of all appointees in three administrations.[5] Only Roosevelt and Eisenhower put a woman in the cabinet. Unlike his predecessors, JFK had not depended on women volunteers to win and was estranged from Eleanor Roosevelt, who distrusted him, detested his father, and supported Adlai Stevenson in 1960.

Peterson became the most influential woman in the Kennedy administration. She was Director of the Women's Bureau and later served, simultaneously, as Assistant Secretary of Labor. Her appointment alarmed feminists like Guffey Miller, who did not find Peterson one of the "women who are for women."[6] The daughter of Danish immigrants, Esther Eggersten had grown up a Mormon in Provo, Utah. After graduating from Brigham Young University in 1927, she earned an MA in teaching from Columbia and married Oliver Peterson, with whom she had four children. In the 1930s, she taught at a private girls' school, a YWCA night school, and the Bryn Mawr Summer School, joining her factory worker students on picket lines. As a union lobbyist, Peterson met first-term Congressman John Kennedy in 1947.[7]

As they had since 1923, unions opposed the ERA. When World War II revived interest in the amendment, Representative Emanuel Celler (D-NY) proposed a Congressional Commission on the Status of Women as a stalling tactic. The 1947 proposal made compromise with ERA advocates impossible, stating:

> It is the declared policy of the United States that in law and its administration no distinctions on the basis of sex shall be made except such as are reasonably justified by differences in physical structure, biological or social function.[8]

Recognizing that women were no longer dependable Democratic voters, Peterson proposed another commission to help the President "do something for women" and still circumvent the ERA. While she assured Secretary of Labor Arthur Goldberg it "would substitute constructive recommendations for the present troublesome and futile agitation about the 'equal rights amendment,'" in public she avoided alienating ERA supporters.

The legal status of women in 1960 was static. Many states still had "head and master" laws, affirming that a wife was subject to her husband. In many states, women had no right to their husband's property or earnings, aside from the right to be supported. At least five states required women to get court approval before opening a business in their own names. Married or single, women had difficulty getting credit. All states restricted jury service for women; Alabama, Mississippi, and South Carolina did not allow it. Laws about adultery, spousal abuse, divorce, employment, and age at marriage discriminated against women.[9]

The number of women earning undergraduate degrees dropped from 41.3% in 1939–40 to 35.3% in 1959–60, and from 38.2% to 31.6% for master's degrees. The number of female college faculty also decreased. Professional schools had admission quotas. Women were 6% of doctors, 39% of lawyers, 1% of engineers, and 1.4% of the top four pay grades for federal workers.[10] Male-only bars, clubs, golf courses, gyms, and executive flights were common. Female labor force participation had risen from 27.9% in 1940 to 36% in 1960. The greatest increase was among married women. Women worked in sex-segregated, low-paid, hourly jobs, and could rarely support themselves or their children on their wages. Few women had careers.[11]

Male experts discounted women's discontent. "When women are encouraged to be competitive, too many become disagreeable," declared Benjamin Spock.[12] In March 1960, the science editor of *Newsweek* blamed female behavior on hormones:

> The educated American woman has her brains, her good looks, her car, her freedom . . . freedom to choose a straight-from-Paris dress . . . or to attend a class in ceramics or calculus . . . to determine the timing of her next baby or who shall be the next

President . . . [Yet she] is dissatisfied . . . Her discontent is deep, pervasive and impervious to . . . superficial remedies . . . From the beginning of time, the female cycle has defined and confined women's role. As Freud is credited with saying: "Anatomy is destiny." Though no group of women has ever pushed these natural restrictions as far as the American wife, it seems that she still cannot accept them with good grace.[13]

That leaders and scientists voiced opinions which reduced white women to their hormones and ignored Black women suggests that women might indeed have asked for more.

Similarly, male experts dismissed marine biologist Rachel Carson, whose groundbreaking 1962 bestseller launched the environmental movement. *Silent Spring* was a jeremiad against the "wholesale drenching of the landscape with chemicals," like the insecticide DDT. The success of earlier books about climate change allowed her to retire from the US Fish and Wildlife Service. Chemical companies smeared Carson, calling her "hysterical" and a communist. A former Secretary of Agriculture wondered why a childless spinster cared about the next generation. Hers was a legacy that future generations would revere. The Clean Air Act (1963) passed before Carson died of breast cancer in 1964. It was followed by the Occupational Safety and Health Act (OSHA, 1970), the Clean Water Act (1972), and the creation of the Environmental Protection Agency (1970).[14]

THE PRESIDENT'S COMMISSION ON THE STATUS OF WOMEN AND THE EQUAL PAY ACT

On December 14, 1961, Executive Order 10980 created the President's Commission on the Status of Women (PCSW) "to review progress and make recommendations as needed for constructive action."[15] Kennedy persuaded Eleanor Roosevelt, seventy-seven, to chair the Commission. As a progressive Democrat, she had opposed the ERA. In 1944, Democrats put equivocating language acceptable to labor into their platform. On the UN Human Rights Commission, the former First Lady embraced equal rights more globally than domestically.

As vice chair, Peterson vetted its twenty-six members, a group "not so diverse that it would be hopelessly divided in discussion."[16] There were fifteen women and eleven men: four cabinet secretaries, including Attorney General Robert Kennedy; two senators and two representatives; one designee each from Jewish, Catholic, and Protestant organizations; two members of organized labor; one homemaker, and no one from the NWP. Dorothy Height, head of the National Council of Negro Women, was the only Black commissioner. For credibility, Peterson included one ERA supporter, Texan Marguerite Rawalt, the first female president of the Federal Bar Association. She was the former head of the Business and Professional Women, long allied with the NWP. "Magnetic and winning," Rawalt was admired for her legal acumen and "the art of correct dressing."[17]

Peterson selected executive director Katherine (Kitty) Ellickson from the AFL–CIO and approved the public members and staff of seven committees. These included Catherine East, a Labor Department researcher, and Mary Eastwood, a Justice Department lawyer, both quietly pro-ERA, and Mrs. Roosevelt's protégé, Pauli Murray, then the first Black candidate for a JSD, a doctorate in the science of law, Yale law school's most advanced degree.[18] Each committee addressed elements of the Commission's investigation: education, home and community, employment, labor standards, income security, political rights, and continuing leadership. There were four additional "consultive bodies" to cover some issues in depth. The "Consultation of Negro Women" was the first time the executive branch had paid specific attention to Black women. When Mrs. Roosevelt died in November 1962, the President left her seat vacant: "It is my judgment that there can be no adequate replacement."[19]

According to the NWP, the new commission was "loaded . . . against equality."[20] Murray called the commission the "first high-level consciousness-raising group."[21] On the political rights committee, led by Congresswoman Edith Green (D-OR), Murray noted the parallels between race and sex discrimination. She argued that the equal protection language in the Fifth and Fourteenth Amendments should safeguard women's rights, if the courts would apply it.[22] After holding two hearings and gathering "divergent viewpoints," the Commission adopted this statement:

> Equality of rights under law for all persons, male and female, is so basic to democracy. . . that it must be reflected in the law of the land. The Commission believes that this principle of equality is embodied in the 5th and 14th amendments of the Constitution . . . [so a] constitutional amendment need not *now* [italics added] be sought in order to establish this principle.[23]

Rawalt insisted on inserting "now" as a workable compromise. "What they term a compromise," raged the NWP, "is really what [UAW leader Walter] Reuther and Peterson wanted."[24]

The PCSW presented its sixty-page report, *American Women,* on October 11, 1963, Mrs. Roosevelt's posthumous seventy-ninth birthday. It unanimously recommended improving women's access to education, childcare, and equal and part-time employment opportunities. It reassured the public that "widening the choices for women beyond their doorstep does not imply neglect of their . . . responsibilities in the home." The Commission was reluctant to take on discrimination in social security regulations or the military. Nor did it endorse adding "sex" to Executive Order 10925, which barred discrimination by federal contractors on the basis of race, creed, color, or national origin.[25]

In November 1963, President Kennedy established an interdepartmental committee and a citizens' advisory council to evaluate progress and propose further action on the status of women, especially in appointing women to government jobs. The President had already signed the Equal Pay Act, increased coverage of the Fair Labor Standards Act to include retail workers, established the Consumer Advisory Council, reduced quotas on women officers in the military, added childcare provisions for welfare recipients, and issued new rules enforcing nondiscrimination in the federal civil service. One wonders if JFK's actual attitude matched that of his brother Robert, expressed in a scribble on a February 1964 memo about "Employment Opportunities for Women." Addressed to division heads in the Justice Department, the Attorney General had written, "Women should stay home and have babies." He scratched that out, adding "Censored," "Oh Hell," and his initials.[26]

The final PCSW report documented extensive discrimination against women, dismissed the ERA as a solution, and proposed legislative responses to advance women's rights. The commission had earlier endorsed the Equal Pay Act. That measure banned discrimination on the basis of sex in jobs requiring the "same skill, effort and responsibility and which were performed under similar conditions" by employers engaged in interstate commerce. It allowed for seniority, merit, and other differentials. It exempted domestic workers and "persons employed in executive, administrative or professional" capacities, including secretaries, bookkeepers, and women working for the government, basically the majority of working women.[27] Corresponding with Ellickson, retired Congresswoman Green remembered,

> vividly the fight for Equal Pay for Equal Work . . . We had to accept an amendment exempting women in administrative, executive or professional positions from coverage. Otherwise we could not get enough votes to get it out of Frank Thompson's [D-NJ] sub-committee. And I believe you—or someone on the Commission—told me of Frank's filing system for Equal Pay legislation—"B" for Broads![28]

The Equal Pay Act was the first federal legislation since the Nineteenth Amendment to ban discrimination solely on the basis of sex.

THE PILL

More dramatic than government reports and legislation was the success of research into a new contraceptive pursued by Margaret Sanger. With a small grant from Planned Parenthood and full funding from Katharine Dexter McCormick, the MIT-educated, International Harvester heiress, Sanger had sought an easy, safe, affordable, effective, and discreet contraceptive. She recruited Gregory Pincus, a biochemist who had been dismissed by Harvard for creating test-tube rabbits; biologist Min-Chueh Chang; and Catholic gynecologist John Rock. Sanger's team cracked the chemical code to stop ovulation. combining estrogen and progestin to prevent ovaries from releasing an egg every month.[29]

Clinical trials on 897 Puerto Rican and Haitian women, conducted without informed consent, did not test for cancer or heart disease. In 1960, the Federal Drug Administration approved an application from G.D. Searle, Inc., to market the Pill as Envoid-10. It was available only to married women and only in some states. The FDA attempted to limit its use to two years, but overwhelming demand made enforcement impossible. By 1964, four million women, one out of every four married women under age forty-five, were "on the pill." Concerned about side effects, the FDA required prescriptions to have warning labels and informational materials, bypassing doctors to educate women directly.[30]

Some scholars consider the Pill a more important scientific advance than the atomic bomb or the Internet. It transformed sexual and social relations, empowering women to defer pregnancy, limit family size, finish school, or enter the workforce. It separated making love from making babies. Public disapproval of premarital sex fell from 68% in 1969 to 48% in 1973. According to critics, the Pill encouraged promiscuity, destroyed the sanctity of marriage, and prompted an increase in adultery, divorce, and marriage counseling. So did publication of *Human Sexual Response* (1966) by William Masters and Virginia Johnson, in part because the researchers had observed thousands of couples engaged in intercourse and concluded that women were capable of multiple orgasms.[31]

Conservatives blamed the Pill for a resurgence of rule breaking. Pope Paul VI called birth control "intrinsically wrong." Due to the power of the Catholic lobby, it was illegal in thirty states.[32] Estelle Griswold, head of Planned Parenthood of Connecticut, collaborated with a Yale gynecologist to open a birth control clinic in New Haven. Nearly fifty years after Sanger's arrest for opening her clinic in Brooklyn, they were arrested and convicted. On appeal, the doctor claimed that Connecticut denied his right to practice medicine. In *Griswold v. Connecticut* (1965), the Supreme Court struck down prohibitions on contraception, voting 7–2 that Connecticut violated a married couple's right to privacy. Although not specifically enumerated in the Constitution, Justice William Douglas found privacy rights in the "penumbra" (shadow) of the Ninth Amendment. Douglas heard from Sanger's niece, Olive Byrne: "I am sure Mrs. Sanger, who is very ill, would rejoice in this pronouncement, which crowns her 50 years of dedication to the liberation of women." Sanger died in 1966.[33]

In 1970, Congressman George H. W. Bush (R-TX) declared "family planning . . . a public health matter" and urged the federal government to fund birth control for poor women. Title X passed the House, 298–32, and carried the Senate unanimously.[34] In *Eisenstadt v. Baird* (1972), the Supreme Court overturned a Massachusetts "Crimes Against Chastity" law, which barred the distribution of birth control to unmarried women or by anyone except doctors or pharmacists. Sheriff Eisenstadt had arrested sex educator William Baird for giving a sample of vaginal foam to a female student at a Boston University lecture. In an 8–1 decision, the Court found the law violated the equal protection clause of the Fourteenth Amendment and the right to free speech. In extending the *Griswold* ruling to cover unmarried people, Justice Brennan wrote: "If the right of privacy means anything, it is the right of the individual, married or single, to be free from unwarranted governmental intrusion into matters so fundamentally affecting a person as the decision whether to bear or beget a child."[35] No longer dependent on doctors, clinics and college health centers began distributing contraceptives.

Availability of the Pill was the first of many pistons that would power the social revolution of the 1960s. *Sex and the Single Girl*, published in 1962, symbolized the shift from a Fifties mindset, in which an unmarried woman was an old maid at twenty-three, to an era of greater independence, when many women delayed marriage. Author Helen Gurley Brown grew up in Arkansas. She could not afford college, held seventeen secretarial jobs, rose to become an advertising executive, and married producer David Brown. As she described it, she became a "Geisha wife," referring to Japanese performance artists trained in the traditional arts of conversation and entertainment. Brown believed women could have it all: love, sex, and money.[36]

By 1965, Brown was editor-in-chief of *Cosmopolitan* and her book became a movie starring Natalie Wood. With breathless prose and covers that verged on pornographic, she created a magazine for single career women. It represented her credo, needlepointed on a pillow in her pink chintz office: "Good girls go to Heaven. Bad girls go everywhere." Today her advice seems quaint; at the time, it was scandalous. Feminists castigated her. Others celebrated her as "a pioneer in Prada, a revolutionary in stilettos." Brown outlived her relevance and her husband. Childless, she left $15 million each to Columbia University, the New York Public Library, and Stanford University.[37]

BETTY FRIEDAN AND THE FEMININE MYSTIQUE

According to novelist John Updike, "the Fifties didn't truly end until November of 1963, when John F. Kennedy was shot."[38] Some historians date "the second women's movement" from 1963 due to the PCSW report, the Equal Pay Act, and the publication of *The Feminine Mystique* by Betty Friedan. She debunked the myth of the happy housewife, basing her conclusion on survey results and the content and advertising in women's magazines.

> The problem lay buried, unspoken, for many years in the minds of American women. It was a strange stirring, a sense of dissatisfaction, a yearning that women suffered in the middle of the twentieth century in the United States. Each suburban wife struggled with it alone. As she made the beds, shopped for groceries, matched slipcover material, ate peanut butter sandwiches with her children, chauffeured Cub Scouts and Brownies, lay

beside her husband at night—she was afraid to ask even of herself the silent question: "Is this all?"[39]

Although critics called it "nonsense" and "rubbish," thousands of white
women claimed the book "changed my life." They remembered when and
where they read it. Reader responses fill 134 linear feet of shelf space at
the Schlesinger Library.[40]

It certainly changed Friedan's life, making her a feminist force for
forty years. Born in 1921 in Peoria, Illinois, Bettye Goldstein was the
daughter of first-generation Jewish immigrants. Her father owned a
jewelry store, "the Tiffany of Peoria." She recalled being too Jewish,
too smart, too unattractive: "I was just an ugly little girl." At Smith, a
women's college her maternal grandparents had forbidden her mother
to attend, Betty shortened her name. She majored in psychology, edited
the college newspaper, was elected to Phi Beta Kappa as a junior, and
graduated summa cum laude. Her editorials were combatively progressive. When she circulated a petition urging President Roosevelt to lift
quotas on Jewish refugees, none of her four Jewish classmates signed it.
She went to graduate school at the University of California Berkeley,
but turned down a doctoral fellowship to keep a boyfriend. In 1947, she
married another man, advertising executive Carl Friedan. She worked
part-time and recalled being fired from a communications job with an
electrical union during her second pregnancy.[41]

Freidan was not a happy homemaker. The suburban mother of three,
freelance writer, and community volunteer compared her home to
"a comfortable concentration camp," an offensive exaggeration.[42] To identify
the cause of her discontent, Friedan evaluated the results of an "intensive
questionnaire" she sent to two hundred members of her Smith College class
of 1942. Some respondents considered it "of inappropriate and unnecessary
depth." Friedan found the majority of those privileged white alumnae were
dissatisfied with domestic bliss. Similarly, twenty-four thousand readers
responded when *Redbook* magazine asked "Why Do Young Mothers Feel
Trapped?"[43]

Friedan's freelance pieces led to a book contract. Originally titled *The Educated American Woman, Her Problems and Prospects*, her book did not address the lives of all American women. There was no effort to expand the sample to include Black women, who were excluded from suburban prosperity; working class and immigrant women, who aspired to have the choice to stay home; or women whose sexuality was not deemed normal. Friedan's solution was for women to hire help, go back to school, get a part-time job, or find a creative hobby. Written when women still lacked many legal rights, the book did not call for political action.[44]

Overnight, Friedan became an expert on American women. She would write five more books and cofound the National Organization for Women (NOW), the National Women's Political Caucus, and a woman's bank. Celebrity did not improve her temperament. Her famous abrasiveness contributed to the long-standing caricature of feminists as unlikeable and humorless. Friedan was notoriously thin-skinned and impervious. "I've always been a bad-tempered bitch," she conceded. "Some people say I've mellowed." Her 2006 *New York Times* obituary noted "screaming fits of temper."[45] After her death, her ex-husband concluded: "She changed the course of history almost single-handedly. It took a driven, super aggressive, egocentric, almost lunatic dynamo to rock the world the way she did. Unfortunately she was that same person at home."[46]

THE SOUTHERN CHRISTIAN LEADERSHIP COUNCIL (SCLC)

The women's movement did not initially address the concerns of Black women. In addition to the assassination of President Kennedy, the most shocking events of 1963 dramatically demonstrated the status of Black Americans: Dr. King's Birmingham jail sentence in April, the murder of Medgar Evers in June, the March on Washington in August, and a church bombing in September. President Kennedy's successor, Lyndon Johnson, would seize the moment of national grief and raise awareness to press for legislative action on civil rights. A century after the Civil War, civil rights advocates were still fighting for justice.

The *Brown* decision and the Montgomery bus boycott had been met with "Massive Resistance." Southern politicians and white citizens vowed to resist court orders requiring integration. When six-year-old Ruby Bridges became the first Black child to integrate a New Orleans elementary school in 1960, angry white parents withdrew their children. Only Barbara Henry, a teacher from Boston, was willing to teach Ruby, in a class of one. Ruby's father lost his job, her mother was refused service at shops, and her grandparents were evicted. Ruby remained. Norman Rockwell portrayed her courage in his iconic painting, which President Obama hung in the White House.[47]

From 1957 to 1960, during what one historian called its "fallow period," the Southern Christian Leadership Conference (SCLC) floundered. There were disputes over tenets and tactics. Difficulties stemmed from Dr. King's political naiveté, management inexperience, and the reluctance of many Black Americans to pursue direct action. Although SCLC pledged to "seek justice" by engaging in nonviolent civil disobedience, the ministers were caught off guard by the student sit-in movement in early 1960. Resentment of Ella Baker's leadership style and her role in creating the Student Non-Violent Coordinated Committee (SNCC) prompted her replacement.[48]

In a new initiative, SCLC absorbed the citizenship literacy program of the Highlander Folk School. Established in Tennessee during the Depression as an integrated adult education center to help farm and factory workers, Highlander taught labor organizing and community building. In 1946, Zilphia Horton, wife of the founding director, adapted "We Shall Overcome" from a gospel lyric into a protest song.[49] Singing to cement bonds and rally courage was one of Highlander's lessons. In 1954, Highlander added civil rights to its mission, hiring Septima Clark. At fifty-six, she had lost her job and pension for demanding pay equity between Black and white teachers and for refusing to resign from the NAACP, as South Carolina law required. Despite multiple degrees, she was assigned segregated classrooms in impoverished districts, where she taught children by day and adults at night.[50] Her Highlander curriculum included reading, writing, African American history, the US Constitution, and how to take a driver's test, organize a credit union, sign a check, complete a mail order, register to vote, and lead a protest.

Claiming Highlander was a communist front, Tennessee revoked its charter in 1961 and seized its property. SCLC hired Clark and adopted her citizenship education curriculum. In charge of teacher training, Clark recruited 2,600 volunteers, who taught 23,000 students, resulting in as many as 700,000 registered voters over ten years. Citizenship schools empowered poor Black people, giving them the agency and tools to build a grassroots civil rights movement. After Clark retired in 1970, she returned to Charleston, served two terms on the school board, and won a suit to reinstate her salary and pension.[51]

Clark worked with Dorothy Foreman Cotton, the only other woman in SCLC leadership. Cotton was hired by Ella Baker's successor, the Reverend Wyatt Tee Walker, her minister in Petersburg, Virginia. Growing up in a home without books, Cotton worked as a housekeeper to cover her college tuition. After earning degrees in English and library science and an MA in speech therapy from Boston University, she volunteered for SCLC. "Our work . . . was not just a job," she recalled. "It was a life commitment." Cotton advanced from a clerical role to oversee the Citizenship Education Program, traveling with Clark and the Reverend Andrew Young. She convened meetings and rallied volunteers by singing. According to a King biographer, she was indispensable, but the highest ranking and most essential SCLC women in the 1960s were ignored. "Cotton and . . . Clark, were accorded doubly junior status . . . [The] men, the ministers, the direct action specialists . . . dominated the discussion."[52]

SIT-INS AND THE STUDENT NONVIOLENT COORDINATING COMMITTEE (SNCC)

Initially a cautious leader, Dr. King hoped to contain the student sit-ins. On Monday, February 1, 1960, four Black men, students at North Carolina Agricultural and Technical College in Greensboro, ordered lunch at the local

Woolworths. Denied service at the whites-only counter, they did not give up their seats. Waitresses called the police and a white ally called the press. The well-mannered, well-dressed men, who stayed until close of business, were not arrested. The next day, more students and more press showed up. By February 5, there were three hundred students, men and women. Their presence paralyzed Woolworths and surrounding shops. News coverage prompted students in fifty-five cities in thirteen states to stage similar sit-ins, among them Fisk students Marion Barry, John Lewis, and Diane Nash. The sit-ins lasted until late July, when Woolworths changed its policy.[53]

Angry white mobs tested the students' commitment to non-violence. They were pulled off their stools, beaten, kicked, and stomped. They were struck on the head with brass knuckles and broken glass sugar shakers. Cigarettes were stubbed out on the backs of their necks. Cuts were filled with salt. Ketchup, mustard, and sugar were poured on their heads while they were assaulted with verbal abuse. Many thought they were going to die. Police did not intervene until white assailants started looting.[54]

Proud of the students' passion and courage, Baker invited them to meet in Raleigh in April. With $800 from SCLC, she helped 126 delegates from twelve southern states and nineteen northern colleges organize the Student Non-Violent Coordinating Committee (SNCC). Among them were Marion Barry, Julian Bond, Stokely Carmichael, James Forman, John Lewis, Bob Moses, Diane Nash, and Marian Wright. Rather than become the youth arm of SCLC or the NAACP, Baker urged them to remain independent and work for broad social change, using non-violence as a tactic. "Strong people do not need strong leaders," she declared. According to Carmichael, "The most powerful person in the struggle of the sixties was Miss Ella Baker, not Martin Luther King."[55]

FREEDOM RIDERS

Inspired by the 1947 "Journey of Reconciliation," in 1961 Freedom Riders intended to travel from Washington, DC, to New Orleans, to challenge ongoing segregation on interstate buses, six years after the Interstate Commerce Commission had outlawed it in the *Keys* case. The original thirteen travelers (seven Black riders, six whites, three women) wrote wills. Interracial pairs sat together; one Black volunteer sat in the front of the bus; others sat in the back, ready to arrange bail. Southern sheriffs also had a plan. At each bus station, they allowed mobs to terrorize the riders before arresting them for provoking a riot. Seriously injured riders, reporters, and Justice Department agents were refused ambulance transport and hospital care.[56]

Raised in Chicago, Diane Nash had not been exposed to Jim Crow segregation until she enrolled at Howard University and then transferred to Fisk, in Nashville, where she attended civil disobedience workshops and organized sit-ins at local lunch counters. In May 1961, when the Freedom Riders were repeatedly beaten and their buses bombed in Anniston, Alabama, and when their Greyhound drivers refused to continue, Nash sent more buses and volunteers. As violence met every bus, Nash proposed a "jail no bail" strategy to clog the cells, the same strategy suffrage picketers had used in 1917. New recruits replaced the arrested riders. In jails, penitentiaries, and prison farms, the riders sang freedom songs. Some guards requested favorites, but Birmingham sheriff Bull Connor "couldn't stand their singing."[57]

Nash persuaded Dr. King to support the riders and Robert Kennedy to press Alabama's governor to protect the buses. Their heroic odyssey made for terrifying television news. The Attorney General sent John Siegenthaler, his Justice Department assistant, to Birmingham, where he was beaten and left in the street. As negative news coverage became international, the Kennedys considered the riders an embarrassment. They called for a cooling-off period. "We have been cooling off for 350 years," SNCC leader James Forman replied, "if we cooled off any more we'd be in the deep freeze."[58] By August 1961, there were sixty different Freedom buses crossing the South, as well as boycotts of restaurant and hotel chains. Larger companies changed their policies to avoid backlash in the North.

The violence shocked the nation, intensified resistance on both sides, and increased financial support for civil rights organizations. The ICC finally agreed to enforce the *Keys* decision, requiring open seating on buses and trains and removing signs segregating water fountains, toilets, waiting rooms, and restaurants in interstate facilities. In 1963, JFK added Nash, twenty-five, to the committee drafting the civil rights bill. On the fiftieth anniversary of the Anniston bus bombing, in May 2011, public television aired a documentary and Oprah Winfrey invited the surviving Freedom Riders to appear on her program. In his last week in office, President Obama declared the Anniston Greyhound station and bombing site the Freedom Riders National Monument.[59]

BLACK WOMEN'S LEADERSHIP

Women remained the backbone and sinew of the civil rights movement. Years later, when Andrew Young, then US Ambassador to the United Nations, eulogized Fannie Lou Hamer, he declared:

> Women were the spine of our movement. It was women going door to door, speaking with their neighbors, meeting in voter-registration classes together, organizing through their churches, that gave the vital momentum and energy to the movement, that made it a mass movement . . . Hundreds of women spoke up and took leadership.[60]

Black women were no longer behind the scenes.

In 1961, Constance Baker Motley and NAACP Legal Defense Fund lawyers, including Vernon Jordan, secured the admission of Charlayne Hunter (now Hunter-Gault) and Hamilton Holmes to the University of Georgia. A year later, after winning a challenge in the US District Court, Motley walked Air Force veteran James Meredith onto the University of Mississippi campus.[61] In 1962, Velvalea Rodgers Phillips, the first Black woman to graduate from the University of Wisconsin law school, introduced open housing bills on the Milwaukee City Council. Her advocacy led to the passage of the Fair Housing Act in 1968, six days after Dr. King's assassination.[62] Bernice Johnson Reagon and her husband Cordell (named for Cordell Hull, FDR's Secretary of State) founded the SNCC Freedom Singers to raise money and morale. After their divorce, Johnson Reagon led Sweet Honey and the Rock, a professional a cappella group.[63]

Anticipating arrest, Black women carried toothbrushes and toilet paper in their purses. In 1963, SNCC activist Fannie Lou Hamer was sexually assaulted and beaten so brutally in a Mississippi jail that she barely recovered. In 1961, she had been sterilized by a white doctor while seeking treatment for a tumor. The youngest of twenty children in a deeply religious and profoundly impoverished family, she had grown up in the Mississippi Delta picking cotton. With little schooling, she risked her life and livelihood to register her neighbors. She joined Unita Blackwell to lead the Mississippi Freedom Democratic Party. It unsuccessfully challenged the credentials of the state's white delegation at the 1964 Democratic National Convention.[64] When Blackwell first attempted to register, she was tested on the state tax code and fired from her job. As a community organizer, she was arrested dozens of times. In 1976, Blackwell was elected the first Black woman mayor in Mississippi.[65] Hamer understood that protesting racial, gender, and class discrimination intensified opposition. Her expression of frustration, "I am sick and tired of being sick and tired," would be repeated by civil rights activists for the next sixty years.

On June 11, 1963, the day after he signed the Equal Pay Act, President Kennedy finally addressed civil rights. He was forced to act by the persistent violence against Black Americans—bombings, clubbings, dog and water cannon attacks on demonstrators—and the intransigence of elected Southern leaders. That morning, Governor George Wallace had stood "in the schoolhouse door" at the University of Alabama to block the admission of Vivian Malone and James Hood. After the National Guard peacefully resolved the issue, President Kennedy addressed the nation to announce that he would call for comprehensive civil rights legislation. "This is not a sectional issue . . . Nor is it a partisan issue . . . We are confronted primarily with a moral issue. It is as old as the scriptures and is as clear as the

American Constitution."[66] That night in Massachusetts, NAACP leaders faced off with Louise Day Hicks, chairwoman of the Boston School Committee, who opposed busing to integrate schools, a struggle that would become spectacularly violent. Shortly after midnight, in Jackson, Mississippi, a white Klansman murdered NAACP field secretary Medgar Evers in his driveway. Dr. King would call the subsequent civil rights legislation "the child of a storm."[67]

THE MARCH ON WASHINGTON

In August 1963, Dr. King and A. Philip Randolph organized a March on Washington for Jobs and Freedom to focus the nation's attention on the goals of the civil rights movement. In 1941, Randolph had threatened FDR with a Washington march to get war jobs for African Americans. Twenty years later, John Lewis, the youngest speaker at twenty-three, told a crowd of 250,000, "We are tired. We are tired of being beaten by policemen." Because he was gay, organizers did not let James Baldwin speak. Roy Wilkins announced the death, the night before, of W. E. B. Du Bois. Then Dr. King presented his dream for America:

> . . . when all God's children, Black men and white men, Jews and Gentiles, Protestants and Catholics, will be able to join hands and sing in the words of the old Negro spiritual, "Free at last! Free at last! Thank God Almighty, we are free at last!"[68]

King's cadence did not include Black women and white women.

Up until the week before, no women other than performers were on the program. Marian Anderson appeared again on the steps of the Lincoln Memorial, in a hat and white gloves, to sing "He's Got the Whole World in His Hands." Joan Baez, Mahalia Jackson, Odetta, and Peter, Paul, and Mary all sang. Josephine Baker was not on the program, but the former showgirl, fifty-seven, wearing her French resistance uniform and medals, spoke for twenty minutes about the freedom she enjoyed in France but was denied in her homeland.[69]

Activist women asked to speak. Instead, organizers decided that Randolph would note their contributions and ask some to stand. The women countered, suggesting that Daisy Bates, Myrlie Evers, Dorothy Height, Diane Nash, or Rosa Parks offer the tribute. Bates was selected. At the microphone, she declared:

> The women of this country, Mr. Randolph, pledge to you, to Martin Luther King, Roy Wilkins and all of you fighting for civil liberties, that we will join hands with you . . . We will kneel-in, we will sit-in, until we can eat at any counter in the United States . . . until every Negro in America can vote. This we pledge.

Randolph bumped Bates from the podium and fumbled the introductions of the other women. No women joined the post-March meeting with President Kennedy. That delegation included more Black guests than had ever before visited the White House. Anna Arnold Hedgeman, who had worked with Randolph since 1943, recalled, "We recognized anew that Negro women are second-class citizens in the same way that white women are in our culture."[70]

Murder followed the peaceful march and powerful speech. On Sunday, September 15, four Klansmen bombed the Sixteenth Street Baptist Church in Birmingham, Alabama. They killed four girls: Addie Mae Collins, Carole Denise McNair, Carole Robertson, and Cynthia Wesley, and injured others. The FBI identified the murderers, but Director J. Edgar Hoover sealed the files because one was an undercover informer. No one prosecuted the crime for fourteen years, when overwhelming circumstantial evidence led to the conviction of one killer. Attending that trial was Doug Jones, then a law student. After President Clinton appointed Jones US Attorney for Alabama and the FBI files had been declassified, he won convictions of the remaining felons. In 2017, Jones won a special election to the US Senate.[71]

THE CIVIL RIGHTS ACT OF 1964

Civil rights and women's rights would converge in the 1964 Civil Rights
Act. Impelled by the Birmingham bombing in September and President
Kennedy's assassination on November 22, Lyndon Johnson seized the
initiative. On Wednesday, November 27, the new president addressed
the nation and a joint session of Congress.

> Let us put an end to the teaching and preaching of hate and evil
> and violence . . . Let us turn away from the fanatics of the far
> left and the far right, from the apostles of bitterness and bigotry
> . . . and those who pour venom into our nation's bloodstream. I
> profoundly hope that the tragedy and torment of these terrible
> days will bind us together in a new fellowship, making us one
> people in our hour of sorrow.[72]

Sitting in the gallery with Lady Bird Johnson was Zephyr Wright, a college
graduate and the Johnson family's cook for twenty-one years. Her travels
by car to and from Texas had demonstrated the legacy of Jim Crow, even
on an employee of the Senate Majority Leader and the Vice President of
the United States.

The Kennedy administration's draft bill had been strengthened in
the House Judiciary Committee, chaired by Emanuel Celler (D-NY).
Eleven sections, or "titles," addressed discrimination in voter registration,
jury selection, employment, and the ongoing segregation of schools and
public accommodations. The Judiciary Committee affirmed H.R. 7152 in
October 1963 and sent it to the Rules Committee, which set the timing
and terms for any bill reaching the floor. Its chairman, Howard Smith
(D-VA), had no intention of advancing the bill. One way to get Smith to act
was a discharge petition, a rare and risky maneuver because it undercut the
authority of chairmen. Celler started collecting the required 218 signatures
from 435 House members. At that time, in the history of the House, 825
discharge petitions had been filed. Thirty-two had gotten the required

number of signatures, fourteen had reached the House floor, and two had resulted in laws passed. In this case, the threat alone worked. Clarence Brown, a conservative Ohio Republican with two historic Black colleges in his district, signaled Smith that the petition had enough signers to embarrass him.[73]

The eighty-year-old Smith stalled, but his committee approved the bill, 11–4. Floor debate began on January 31, 1964, managed by Congressmen Celler and Bill McCullough (R-OH), closely watched by President Johnson, Robert Kennedy, and Dr. King. For a week, the pro side defeated every attempt to derail the bill, including adding "sex" to several sections. Then on Saturday, February 8, Judge Smith offered an amendment to Title VII, which barred discrimination in employment on the basis of race, creed, religion, or color. In a courtly drawl, Smith proposed inserting the word "sex" after religion. According to the *Congressional Record*, the chamber laughed.[74]

For decades, journalists and historians have examined Smith's motives. Was he trying to support women, embarrass Northerners, foil unions, overload and defeat the bill, or all of the above? An Alabama representative claimed, "Smith didn't give a damn about women's rights . . . [He] was trying to knock off votes . . . because there was always a hard core of men who didn't favor women's rights."[75] Yet Smith and Alice Paul were friends. Because he opposed protection for women textile workers in Virginia, he cosponsored the ERA. Furious that the PCSW had failed to endorse the ERA, Paul saw the civil rights bill as a logical and available alternative. In an echo of Elizabeth Cady Stanton in 1870, the National Woman's Party condemned the bill for failing to protect "a *White Woman*, a *Woman of the Christian Religion*, or a *Woman of United States Origin* [original italics]." Probed about his intentions on *Meet the Press* by veteran reporter May Craig, an NWP member, Smith responded, "I'm always strong for women." He volunteered that he was sincere in wanting to make sure white women had the same protections as Black women, but when he introduced the new language, his light-hearted tone alerted both his colleagues and his critics that he was not serious.[76]

Independently, Katherine St. George (R-NY) and Martha Griffiths (D-MI) had planned to insert "sex" into Title VII. When Griffiths learned

Smith's plan, she let him take the lead because he would bring Southern votes with him. She recalled Smith telling her later that his "amendment was a joke."[77] Whether it was a prank, a poison pill, or purposeful, it alarmed the bill's sponsors. Celler attacked the new language as a harbinger of the ERA, calling it "illogical, ill-timed, ill-paced and improper." Smith played his motion for laughs, claiming to champion spinsters. Lenore Sullivan warned Griffiths, "If you can't stop that laughter, you've lost." Griffiths took the floor.

> I presume that if there had been any necessity to have pointed out that women were a second-class sex, the laughter would have proved it . . . I rise in support of the amendment, primarily because I feel as a white woman when this bill has passed . . . that white women will be last at the hiring gate . . . She will continue to work in the greasy spoon, drive the school bus and do the other underpaid jobs.[78]

Without "sex" inserted, Title VII gave Black women legal recourse denied to white women. Griffith's motives were both civic and self-interested.

The twelve women serving in the House in 1964 were divided equally by party and split over adding "sex." St. George, Frances Bolton (R-OH), Edna Kelly (D-NY), Catherine May (R-WA), and Griffiths, the only lawyer, spoke in favor. St. George declared:

> I can think of nothing more logical than this amendment . . . We outlast you. We outlive you, we nag you to death . . . We are entitled to this little crumb of equality. The addition of the little, terrifying word "s-e-x" will not hurt this legislation in any way.[79]

Edith Green (D-OR) disagreed. Author of the Equal Pay Act and a member of the PCSW, she supported equal rights but believed the added word could kill the bill. Less eloquently than Frederick Douglass, she proclaimed, "For every discrimination that has been made against a woman in this country, there [have] been 10 times as [many] against the Negro."[80] A history of the House claims that Green was the only woman to vote against the addition of "sex," but there was no roll call. Smith's rewording passed, 168–133, on a head count. The final bill passed the House, 290–130, and moved to the Senate.[81] Griffiths warned the President that if the Senate or the conference committee removed "sex," she would write the female constituents of every opponent.[82] Title VII's wording was not changed.

To avoid Mississippi Senator James Eastland's Judiciary Committee, Majority Leader Mike Mansfield (D-MT) steered the bill directly to the floor. Introducing it, Hubert Humphrey (D-MN), who had come to national attention in 1948 for opposing Dixiecrats, spoke for three hours. He read aloud from two travel guides, *The Negro Motorist's Green Book* and one for families with dogs, noting that Augusta, Georgia, had five accommodations that allowed dogs and only one for Black travelers.[83] Eighteen Southern Democrats filibustered for 534 hours over 75 calendar days and 57 "working days," including Saturdays, while Humphrey and Tom Kuchel (R-CA) searched for votes for cloture. South Carolina's Strom Thurmond stormed that the bill was "unconstitutional, unnecessary and unwise." Georgia Senator Richard Russell declared war: "We will resist to the bitter end any measure or any movement which would have a tendency to bring about social equality and intermingling and amalgamation of the races in our [Southern] states."[84] In 2018, Russell's record of resistance prompted some Senators to propose renaming the Russell Senate Office Building.[85]

To woo Minority Leader Everett Dirksen (R-IL), President Johnson compared him to Lincoln and Humphrey schmoozed him nightly over drinks in Dirksen's private office. By agreeing to a slightly modified bill, supporters garnered the sixty-seven votes needed to end the filibuster. On June 10, the Senate voted for cloture, 71–29. It was the first time ever the Senate had ended a filibuster on a civil rights bill and the first successful cloture vote on any measure since 1927. On June 19, exactly a year after JFK had submitted the bill, the Dirksen substitute passed, 76–18, and was approved by the conference committee. Both Senators

Margaret Chase Smith (R-ME) and Maurine Brown Neuberger (D-OR) voted for it.[86]

The President and his allies had worked closely, sometimes tensely, with a grieving Robert Kennedy and impatient civil rights leaders to build public support and keep pressure on any wavering members. While LBJ, RFK, and MLK vied for credit, less attention was paid to Republicans McCullough and Dirksen, without whom the bill would not have passed. Offspring of the Great Migration were voting in districts represented by Northern Republicans. Congressional support was bipartisan, but Republicans provided more yes votes than Democrats: 80% of Republicans in the House and 82% in the Senate voted yes, compared to 63% and 69% of Democrats.[87] President Johnson signed the act on July 2, 1964.

FREEDOM SUMMER

Sex and race would collide again that summer in Mississippi, during a voter registration drive known as Freedom Summer. Hundreds of white college students moved South to join SNCC and CORE volunteers. Judge Smith rang the alarm:

> Already a second invasion of carpetbaggers . . . has begun. Hordes of beatniks, misfits, and agitators from the North, with the admitted aid of the Communists, are streaming into the Southland on mischief bent, backed and defended by other hordes of Federal marshals, Federal agents, and Federal power.[88]

The "hordes" were met with violence. On June 21, 1964, two days after the Civil Rights Act passed the Senate, three civil rights workers, Michael Schwerner, Andrew Goodman, and James Chaney, two Jews and a Black man, were murdered near Philadelphia, Mississippi. Their bodies were not found for six weeks. Over the course of ten weeks, 1,062 activists were arrested, eighty volunteers were beaten, and thirty-seven churches were bombed or burned. In total, three white civil rights workers and three Black activists were killed in Mississippi. Alabama had fifty-six unsolved bombings. Volunteers set up thirty-one Freedom Schools, but registered only 1,200 voters.[89]

As they faced this assault, three issues divided SNCC: growing impatience with nonviolent resistance, ever-larger numbers of volunteers stressing the organization, and growing resentment and ambivalence about the role of white reporters, volunteers, and sexual partners. Violence against whites generated more news coverage, sympathy, and contributions than had decades of terror against Black Americans. White women from the North did not anticipate community reaction to interracial sex, which endangered Black men and angered Black women. Some Black men interacted with white women for the first time. For centuries, the punishment for interracial sex, actual or alleged, consensual or not, had been lynching. People were tempted to break the taboo. SNCC staff knew the unwritten rules, but Northern volunteers were clueless, dividing recent recruits from veterans.[90] Multiple tensions would split the civil rights movement and divide Black and white women.

In 1960, twenty-four states banned interracial marriage. A poll that year concluded that 99% of Southerners and 92% of Northerners approved of laws banning racially mixed marriages.[91] In October 1964, in *McLaughlin v. Florida*, the Supreme Court ruled unanimously that banning interracial relationships was unconstitutional. The case did not address interracial marriage. When police raided the bedroom of newly-weds Richard Loving and Mildred Jeter, in 1958, they were arrested under Virginia's 1924 Act to Preserve Racial Integrity. Jailed briefly, the Lovings were barred from Virginia for twenty-five years. In 1963, Mildred appealed to Attorney General Kennedy, who referred her to the ACLU. Her suit triggered the Supreme Court's unanimous 1967 decision in *Loving v. Virginia*, outlawing such laws, four months before Thurgood Marshall became the first African American Justice.[92] As recently as 2019, Virginia marriage licenses required applicants to list their race. When couples sued, a federal judge struck down the practice as an unconstitutional "vestige of the nation's and Virginia's history of codified racialization."[93]

Related to sex were complicated attitudes about beauty and skin tone. Lighter skin among Black Americans signaled generations of sexual exploitation of enslaved women, as well as rare and forbidden interracial partnerships. Mixed-race offspring who chose to "pass" could avoid Jim Crow restrictions, prompting Southern states to define blackness as "one drop" of Negro blood. In a predominantly white culture, "white features," like light skin and straight hair, were deemed more attractive. Rejecting such stereotypes, many Black women and men adopted natural hairstyles called Afros and wore African fabrics as symbols of Black Pride.

White women's magazines and their advertisers had never put Black women in articles, advertisements, or on the cover. The first Black "Breck Girl," Donna Alexander, sporting a cropped Afro, appeared in a full-page shampoo ad in 1974, the same year Beverly Johnson was photographed for the cover of *Vogue*. Barbara Smith appeared on *Essence* and *Ebony* covers before securing a *Mademoiselle* cover in 1976. Like former model Martha Stewart, B. Smith would create a lifestyle empire. In September 2018, it was newsworthy that twelve mainstream fashion magazines put Black women on their covers. Bigger news was *Vogue* putting Black women on its cover two months in a row and *Vanity Fair* hiring a Black photographer for a cover shoot.[94] Black underrepresentation in the fashion industry remains an issue. To ban discrimination based on hair texture or style, in 2020, the House passed the C.R.O.W.N. Act ("Create a Respectful and Open World for Natural Hair").[95] The Senate has not acted.

Caught in the tension over roles for whites in the Black civil rights movement were two "golden girls," Mary King and Sandra Cason "Casey" Hayden. Ella Baker had recruited King, a white minister's daughter and Ohio Wesleyan graduate, to conduct workshops on racism for white institutions. On weekends, King volunteered for SNCC and ended up on staff in Mississippi.[96] Hayden was a Texan from a feisty multigenerational matriarchy. At the University of Texas, she joined lunch counter sit-ins and participated in a National Student Association Congress, where she met her husband, Tom Hayden, a founder of Students for a Democratic Society (SDS). She joined SNCC and trained as an organizer under Baker. "As a white Southerner, I considered the southern freedom movement against segregation mine as much as anyone else's," she wrote. Joining a pilot voter registration project in 1963, she chose not to do field work. "Being a white woman meant wherever I was, the Movement was visible, and where there was visibility there was danger."[97] Instead, she recruited students for the summer of '64.

Freedom Summer was exhilarating and terrifying. The FBI murder investigation moved slowly and President Johnson purposely pre-empted Mrs. Hamer's Democratic National Convention testimony with a tele-vised address. Discouraged, SNCC paid staff, those earning $10 a week, gathered in November 1964 for a "reassessment retreat." They met in Waveland, Mississippi, on the water between New Orleans and Biloxi, one of the few places where it was possible to convene an interracial group.[98] Staff wrote position papers. With Hayden, Mary King was the principal author of a paper on the role of women within SNCC, prepared secretly and presented anonymously.

It was a critique of male leadership. Item One read: "Staff was involved in crucial constitutional revisions . . . The committee was all men." It asked why "competent, qualified, experienced" women were assigned only "typing, desk work, telephone work, filing, library work, cooking . . . but rarely executive [roles]?" King compared the treatment of women by men to white supremacy:

> The average white person . . . *assumes he is superior* . . . [He] doesn't understand the problem of paternalism . . . [The] average SNCC worker finds it difficult to discuss the woman problem because of the assumption of male superiority. Assumptions of male superiority are as widespread and deep-rooted and every [bit as] . . . crippling to the woman as the assumptions of white supremacy are to the Negro.[99]

King and Hayden anticipated pushback. They did not expect "crushing criticism," recalling that they were "'buked." Black women repudiated the paper, condemning it as disruptive.[100]

One evening, a group was partying on the pier. Among them was Stokely Carmichael, twenty-four, a graduate of the Bronx High School of Science and Howard, known as "Starmichael" for his charisma and comic monologues. He began to riff on women, poking fun at himself, asking, "What is the position of women in SNCC?" and answering, "The only position of women in this movement is prone."[101] Intended as funny or not, his remarks were offensive. A year later, King and Hayden wrote another paper, "Sex and Caste: A Kind of Memo." No longer anonymous, they mailed it to forty women activists across the country. "We want to try to open up a dialogue to . . . talk more openly . . . and create a community of support for each other." An anti-war newspaper published it in April 1966.[102] The manifesto became a catalyst for white "consciousness raising" groups and grassroots feminism.

THE VOTING RIGHTS ACT OF 1965

Promising "We Shall Overcome," President Johnson pushed through the Voting Rights Act, signed in August 1965, to correct "a clear and simple wrong" and to enforce the Fifteenth Amendment. Three Black women were present at the signing: Zephyr Wright was the President's informal advisor and employee; Patricia Roberts Harris was a Howard law school dean, Pauli Murray's mentor, and the first Black ambassador; Vivian Malone had integrated the University of Alabama and worked for the Justice Department's voter education project. Dorothy Height, longtime leader of the National Council of Negro Women, concluded, "Fifty years ago, women got the vote; lynching, bombing, civil rights and the Voting Rights Act got it for Black women." By 1968, Black registration in the South had increased to 62% of eligible voters. The act was a fundamental affirmation of democratic values. It was repeatedly reauthorized by large margins for forty years.[103]

But the decade devolved into turbulence, at home and abroad. The ballot box did not stop the bullets or violence that ricocheted through 1965: the murder of Malcolm X; the "Bloody Sunday" massacre on Selma's Edmund Pettus Bridge; the Klan killing of Viola Liuzzo, a white woman who was shuttling Black demonstrators between Selma and Montgomery; and the Watts riots in August. In 1966, by a vote of 19–18, SNCC senior staff expelled their twenty-four white colleagues, who abstained.[104] Replacing John Lewis, Stokely Carmichael committed SNCC to Black Power and aligned it with SDS in the anti-war movement. The organization changed its name and purpose, from Nonviolent to National. Members of the Black Panther Party for Self Defense were photographed in leather jackets and berets, holding guns. They declared, "Violence is as American as cherry pie," provided breakfast for poor children, and protected their Berkeley community.[105]

Black Panther Angela Davis, with her cloudlike Afro, came to represent both Black Power and Black beauty. Growing up in Birmingham, Davis had been a Girl Scout. She was one of three Black students in her class at Brandeis, where she majored in French and spent junior year abroad, graduating Phi Beta Kappa and magna cum laude in 1965. As a graduate student and teaching assistant in California, she joined the Che-Lumumba Club, a Black branch of the Communist Party. That association prompted Governor Ronald Reagan to urge state university regents to fire her. She sued and was reinstated, but left when her contract expired. In 1970, Davis was charged as an accessory to murder when three felons attempted to escape during their trial. They used weapons registered to Davis to kill the judge, prosecutor, and two jurors. Charged with three capital crimes and jailed for eighteen months, she was acquitted by a white jury. Davis remained a civil rights, anti-war, pro-farm worker, feminist activist. She retired from the University of California Santa Cruz as professor emeritus. Decades later, her revision of the serenity prayer would appear on T-shirts: "I am no longer accepting the things I cannot change. I am changing the things I cannot accept."[106]

America was splintering among races, regions, generations, hawks, pacifists, patriots, flag burners, hippies, druggies, street fighters, liberals, conservatives, men, and women. There were forty-three race riots in 1966 and fifty-three in 1967. The Kerner Report, charged with examining race relations in America, concluded in 1968 that the issue was not Black riots but white racism: the country was "moving toward two societies, one Black, one white, separate and unequal."[107] Anger and activism fueled broader social change. Within the women's movement, three factions were developing. One was white, political, bipartisan, older, and middle-class. One was younger, more radical, diverse, urban, and underground. One was the outraged opposition, conservative, religious, middle-American, and increasingly Republican.

THE EQUAL EMPLOYMENT OPPORTUNITY COMMISSION (EEOC)

In 1965, Mary Eastwood and Pauli Murray published a landmark law review article, "Jane Crow and the Law: Sex Discrimination and Title VII," linking racism and sexism.[108] Title VII had established the five-member Equal Employment Opportunity Commission (EEOC) to induce compliance without enforcement powers. LBJ appointed FDR Jr. as chairman. Asked "What about sex?" Roosevelt responded, "I'm all for it." He maintained that banning sex discrimination was an inadvertent error. His successor claimed it was "conceived out of wedlock." The attitude of the four male commissioners about sex discrimination was "boredom or virulent hostility." The only female commissioner, Aileen Clarke Hernandez, was a magna cum laude Howard University graduate and union organizer.[109]

White women brought two of the first wave of complaints. One objected to the practice of designating "Help Wanted" ads as "Male" or "Female." In 1965, the EEOC voted, 3–2, that sex segregation in job advertising was permissible. Pressured by protests, it reversed itself in 1968. The ruling was confirmed, 5–4, by the Supreme Court in *Pittsburgh Press Co. v. Human Relations Commission* (1973). The *Washington Star* found the new regulation "a nuisance . . . [and a] nonsensical outrage."[110]

Cases brought by female flight attendants were more complicated. To avoid women accruing seniority, higher pay, and larger pensions, airlines wanted the jobs to be short-term. Stewardesses were fired on account of age, weight, height, marriage, and maternity. Boeing had hired the first "air hostesses" in 1930, replacing cabin boys. The first, Ellen Church, a registered nurse and private pilot, was told women were too emotional for the flight deck. Because most passengers were male, airlines used attractive white women to market air travel. The 1971, National Airlines' suggestive ad campaign featured headshots of pretty women: "I'm Cheryl. Fly Me." Continental's tag line was "We Move Our Tails for You." Braniff announced an end to the "plain plane" and introduced a high fashion "air strip," during which hostesses changed outfits designed by Pucci, turning aisles into mid-flight catwalks.[111]

The EEOC denied a cascade of claims. On behalf of the 6% of Black attendants, the NAACP won a case challenging the airlines' white beauty standards, which forbade Afros. Lawsuits struck down the marriage, pregnancy, and age requirements, but cases about weight dragged on. Uniforms became more professional and practical and many of the litigants became leaders in their unions. The reluctance of the EEOC to act on behalf of women brought Martha Griffiths to the House floor, attacking its attitude as "negative and arrogant." On the airline practice of hiring only single, attractive women, she warned, "If you are trying to run a whore-house in the sky, get a license."[112]

THE NATIONAL ORGANIZATION FOR WOMEN (NOW)

Copies of Griffiths's EEOC critique were handouts at the third annual meeting of State Commissions on the Status of Women in June 1966, where the EEOC defended its approach. Conference participants, among them Betty Friedan, were not impressed. A small group of women gathered in her hotel room to complain. Catherine East, a Labor Department researcher, proposed creating "an NAACP Legal Defense Fund for women." When discussion got heated, Friedan shouted, "Get out! Get out!" and locked herself in the bathroom.[113] The next day at lunch, Friedan scribbled the initials "N O W" on a napkin. That act became the creation myth of the National Organization for Women. Its purpose was "to bring women into full participation into the American mainstream *now*, . . . in truly equal partnership with men."[114]

At an organizing meeting in October 1966, the group "debated every comma" of NOW's charter. Three dozen women and men claimed to be founding members, including Shirley Chisholm, Kay Clarenbach, Catherine East, Mary Eastwood, Dorothy Haener, and Pauli Murray. Despite demurring, accurately, that she was "not good at organizations," Friedan became NOW's first president. Aileen Hernandez resigned from the EEOC to be vice president. Clarenbach, a political scientist and member of Wisconsin's Status of Women Commission, served as board chair and Marguerite Rawalt was legal counsel, with East and Eastwood on the legal committee.[115] Everyone contributed five dollars to open a bank account and the UAW provided a mailing address. When the NWP proposed that NOW endorse the ERA, the response was neither immediate nor unanimous, due to labor's long-standing opposition. Union support for protective legislation finally shifted in 1968, when a federal district court ruled that state labor laws protecting women only were unconstitutional.[116]

UNION WOMEN

In 1961, fifty years after the Triangle Shirtwaist Factory Fire, there were 3.5 million dues-paying women in the AFL–CIO, but not one on its executive council.[117] Addie Wyatt was a leader among Meatpackers. Millie Jeffrey, originally an organizer for the Amalgamated Clothing Workers, never wore anything without a union label. During World War II, Walter Reuther recruited Jeffrey to establish the UAW Women's Bureau.[118] Dorothy Haener and Olga Madar joined the UAW, building bombers at Ford's Willow Run plant. After the war, Haener was demoted to a lower-paid clerical job, but advanced in the union. Addressing pay inequity, Haener pushed for comparable rather than equal wages. She connected with Pauli Murray, co-founding NOW and serving on its first board.[119] Madar ended discrimination in the UAW's recreational activities, fighting for seven years to integrate its bowling leagues. In 1966, she was the first woman on the UAW board and, in 1970, the first elected vice president. As women became a larger segment of labor unions, they pressed for their concerns. Working with Addie Wyatt, Madar was the founding president of the Coalition of Labor Union Women (CLUW) in 1974. Through Madar's efforts, the UAW became the first union to endorse the ERA before its congressional approval; the AFL–CIO resisted until after March 1972.[120]

Thousands of working women were not in unions, including migrant agricultural workers. During the Depression, whole families followed the harvest to pick crops. To fill shortages of farm workers during World War II, the government created the bracero program in 1942, allowing Mexican men to enter the country to work the fields. Employers promised fair wages, housing, food, transportation, and health care, but conditions were horrible. Because farmers profited, the agreement was extended until 1964. Some workers were legal, some were not; most were men but women also came. All were essential.[121]

In the early 1960s, Dolores Huerta started organizing migrant farm workers. Born in New Mexico, she grew up in Stockton, California. Her father was a farmer and state assemblyman; her mother ran a hotel for low-wage workers. Huerta was an elementary school teacher, whose low-income students inspired her to create the Agricultural Workers Association. It lobbied for migrants to get public assistance, Spanish language ballots, and drivers' licenses. In 1962, she met Cesar Chavez, founded the United Farm Workers, and organized the Delano grape boycott. She successfully pressed for the 1975 California Agricultural Labor Relations Act, which granted farm workers collective bargaining rights. Huerta was with Bobby Kennedy when he won the California primary on June 4, 1968, the night he was shot. Her sixty-year commitment to social justice had a negative impact on her relationships and eleven children. In 2008, candidate Obama adopted

Huerta's motto, "*Si se puede*—yes we can!" In 2012, President Obama gave her the Presidential Medal of Freedom.[122]

From Indigenous tribes crossing a land bridge to European colonists searching for freedom, some of whom imported and enslaved Africans, voluntary and involuntary immigrants had populated America. When President Johnson signed the Immigration and Naturalization Act of 1965, only 5% of the US population was foreign born. At the base of the Statue of Liberty, a week before Columbus Day, LBJ reassured the country that it was "not a revolutionary bill . . . It will not reshape our daily lives." It abolished the national origin quotas, established in 1924; prioritized family members and professionals; banned homosexuals; and set rules for refugees and asylum seekers. Migrants who had arrived legally could sponsor family members. An unanticipated global economic upheaval and a population explosion prompted a surge in legal and illegal immigration and altered the demographics of America. In the last third of the twentieth century, the legal immigrant population tripled. By the new century, America was accepting foreign-born people at higher rates than any time since the 1850s.[123]

COMING APART: 1968

President Johnson's "Great Society" collapsed under the weight of the Vietnam War. By 1968, the country was imploding. Even before the Tet offensive or the Mỹ Lai massacre, protests surged. Dr. King's April assassination in Memphis was met with riots. Bobby Kennedy was killed. Students occupied campuses, and violence between police and demonstrators disrupted the Democratic convention. Flags and cities burned in anger and grief. Two Black sprinters and medal winners, Tommie Smith and John Carlos, were suspended from the US Olympic team for raising their fists in a Black Power salute while the national anthem played. They wore black gloves to symbolize Black Power and black socks to symbolize Black poverty.[124]

In September 1968, radical feminists protested the Miss America pageant. They attempted to burn bras, girdles, curlers, stenography pads, floor wax, and copies of *Cosmopolitan* in a "freedom trash can," but they couldn't get a fire permit. White protestors objected to the contest's sexism, while Black women fought its racism. The NAACP had abandoned efforts to integrate Miss America and created their own pageant. Three weeks earlier, the National Association of Colored Women's Clubs and the local NAACP crowned Saundra Williams the first Miss Black America. "With my title, I can show black women that they too are beautiful," declared the winner. Black women had won local crowns beginning in 1959, but no state sent a Black contestant to the Miss America contest until Cheryl Browne, Miss Iowa 1970. Oprah Winfrey participated as Miss Black Tennessee in 1971.[125]

1968 ended with the election of Richard Nixon. Also elected was Shirley Chisholm, the first "Black and proud" congresswoman. She served seven terms, working for expanded food stamp programs, childcare, and women and children's health care. A native of Barbados, Brooklyn teacher, and state legislator, she hired an all-female staff. "Unbought and unbossed" and wearing suffrage white, she ran for President in 1972, opposed by the entire Congressional Black Caucus and much of the Democratic Party. She was the first woman to participate in a presidential debate. "Racism is so universal in this country, so widespread and deep-seated," declared Chisholm, "that it is invisible because it is so normal." White Texas legislator Frances (Sissy) Farenthold, nominated for vice president at 1972 convention, won 407 delegate votes.[126]

The number of women in Congress had declined from twenty in 1961 to eleven in 1969. Senator Smith, the popular and principled Maine Republican, ran for President in 1964. Her independence, gender, and age, sixty-seven, defeated her. To protest Goldwater's selection, she refused to release her delegates, so his nomination was not unanimous.[127] From 1948 to 1960, more women than men voted for Republican presidential candidates. In 1964, more women than men turned out, 39.2 million women to 37.5 million men; they voted Democratic.[128] LBJ's prediction that civil rights legislation would drive Southerners from the Democratic

Party proved true. Five Southern states went for Goldwater; in 1968, five supported segregationist George Wallace.[129]

Nixon's law and order campaign had little effect in the era of *Easy Rider* and Woodstock. For three days in August 1969, an estimated 450,000 young people overran an alfalfa farm in Bethel, New York. News stories highlighted the traffic, the deluge, the mud, the long hair, and the marijuana. The festival included thirty bands. It ended with Jimi Hendrix's screeching national anthem. The performance by a pregnant Joan Baez, whose husband was in prison for draft evasion, was the most poignant and political. Participants were peaceful, cooperative, good-humored, and mostly stoned. Abbie Hoffman's "Woodstock Nation" and Charles Schultz's cartoon character, a small bird who couldn't fly straight, defined a counterculture.[130]

The turmoil of the Sixties was recorded on soundtracks. From "Mississippi Goddam," "We Shall Overcome," and "Give Peace a Chance" to songs by Bob Dylan, Johnny Cash, the Supremes, and the Beach Boys, lyrics addressed current events. In 1966, in "Don't Come Home A Drinkin' (With Lovin' on Your Mind)," country singer Loretta Lynn addressed alcoholism and spousal abuse. Conservative radio stations refused to air another Lynn song, "The Pill." Tammy Wynette paired her track "D-I-V-O-R-C-E" with "Stand By Your Man." Aretha Franklin's 1967 "R-E-S-P-E-C-T" became a feminist anthem, as did Helen Reddy's "I Am Woman, Hear Me Roar."[131]

THE EQUAL RIGHTS AMENDMENT: ROUND ONE

In the 1960s, competing causes threatened the tentative rapprochement among feminists, union women, civil rights organizers, and politicians begun with Title VII. At NOW's 1967 convention, UAW women withdrew their support when the ERA was included in its "Bill of Rights." Other women walked out over abortion.[132] While Haener and Madar tried to convert union leaders, Martha Griffiths (D-MI), representing a strong labor state, continued to sponsor the ERA, as she had "unequivocally" since 1954. She knew it would be exhausting to remedy discrimination in employment, credit, criminal justice, jury duty, and pensions statute by statute and state by state. Griffiths had no faith that the Supreme Court, "nine sleeping Rip Van Winkles," would apply the equal protection clause on behalf of women.[133]

In 1970, the country commemorated the fiftieth anniversary of the Nineteenth Amendment. Nixon ran on a pro-ERA platform and established a Task Force of Women's Rights and Responsibilities, "to improve the participation of women in American life." Its report, *A Matter of Simple Justice,* had twenty-two recommendations, including passage of the ERA; changes in childcare provisions, tax policy, and employment benefits; more women appointees; and a White House Office of Women's Rights.[134] Nixon named 105 women to policy-making posts in his first term. Among them were Anne Armstrong, the first female Counselor to a President, and Ramona Acosta Banuelos, the first Latina Treasurer of the US. Libby Koontz, an African American, led the Women's Bureau and reversed the Labor Department's fifty-year opposition to the ERA.[135]

Emma Guffey Miller, now ninety-six, asked Griffiths to revive the ERA, claiming that the NWP had commitments from seventy-one Senators and two hundred House members. With the support of Nixon and NOW, Griffiths made her move in 1970. The first obstacle was Emanuel Celler, who had blocked House Judiciary Committee hearings on the ERA since 1943. When Celler stonewalled, Griffiths filed a discharge petition. She buttonholed members and swapped favors. Majority Whip Hale Boggs (D-LA), doubtful she would succeed, told her to come back if she got two hundred signatures. She did and he signed. Her Michigan colleague, Minority Leader Gerald Ford, lined up Republicans. Griffiths garnered 218 names from 154 Democrats, 64 Republicans, 22 out of 33 committee chairs, and every woman except Lenore Sullivan (D-MO).[136]

A discharged bill went directly to the floor for one hour of debate, forty-five minutes pro, with no amendments. Neither side presented a well-argued case. Celler insisted that the "delectable and dedicated gentlewoman from Michigan" could not change women's weaker nature. Gerry Ford responded that he was looking forward to "conferring the full privileges of citizenship on his wife." On August 10, 1970, the House cast its first vote on the Equal Rights Amendment. It passed overwhelmingly, 350–15, with sixty-four not voting.[137] That evening, Griffiths dined with Marguerite Rawalt at the National Lawyers Club. When they entered, they turned the bust of William Blackstone, the eighteenth-century jurist who codified the common law concept of feme covert, to the wall.[138] Two days later, in an editorial titled "The Hen-Pecked House," the *New York Times* called for more careful analysis by the Senate. Later, the *Times* described the House vote as either "an irregular fit of conscience or [a] regular fit of opportunism."[139]

Likely unaware of Griffiths's ERA strategy, Friedan called for a Women's Strike for Equality in New York City to mark the fiftieth anniversary of suffrage on August 26, 1970. It was organized without NOW's backing or a parade permit. At a noon rally, speakers included Friedan, who was late coming from the hairdresser; Consumer Affairs Commissioner Bess Myerson, a former Miss America; polemicist Kate Millett; Eleanor Holmes Norton, chair of the city's Human Rights Commission; Bella Abzug, a candidate for Congress; and Gloria Steinem, a recent recruit. Police cleared a sidewalk, but marchers filled every lane of Fifth Avenue. It was the largest women's march to date. Reporters estimated 10,000 participants; Friedan claimed 50,000. Bedsheet banners read "DON'T IRON WHILE THE STRIKE IS HOT," "I LOVE YOU SUSAN B. ANTHONY," "FREE ABORTION ON DEMAND," and "HARD HATS FOR SOFT BROADS." One protester, seventy-nine, had marched for suffrage. There were sister events across the country. News anchors questioned the validity of the protest, citing a poll that found two-thirds of American women did not feel oppressed. Senator Jennings Randolph (D-WV) dismissed the marchers as "a band of braless bubbleheads."[140]

No one considered the march's impact on Senate passage of the ERA. Eighty-two Senators had cosponsored the ERA, never expecting to have to vote on it. The amendment's lead sponsor was Senator Birch Bayh (D-IN), a farmer, lawyer, and chair of the Subcommittee on Constitutional

Amendments. He had led the fight for the Twenty-fifth (presidential succession) and Twenty-sixth (eighteen-year-old vote) amendments. His attempt to abolish the Electoral College failed. Bayh credited his feminism to his wife Marvella, another lawyer. They met at an American Farm Bureau national collegiate debate competition. She won first prize and his fraternity pin.[141] Bayh asked Brenda Feigen Fasteau, a recent graduate of Harvard law school and NOW's legislative vice president, to coordinate ERA testimony for the September hearing. She wrote Steinem's remarks. Two years later, she joined the ACLU to co-direct its Women's Rights Project with Ruth Bader Ginsburg.[142]

Endorsed by Bayh's subcommittee, the ERA still met stiff opposition in the full Judiciary committee. At the request of Chairman James Eastland (D-MS), Senator Sam Ervin (D-NC) temporarily chaired the hearing. Ervin was a decorated war veteran, a former state supreme court justice, segregationist, congressman, and three-term senator. He began his career censuring Joe McCarthy and ended it chairing the Watergate hearings. He opposed the ERA because, in his opinion, God never intended men and women to be equal: "Unless Senators and Representatives believe God made a mistake by creating two sexes," there was no need for the ERA. It was a conspiracy by "professional harpies."[143] Ervin cleared the ERA for Senate consideration after adding two amendments. One exempted women from the draft; the other permitted prayer in public schools. Bayh proposed substitute language to safeguard protective legislation. Because Senator Smith had broken her hip, the ERA had no female floor manager for the three-day debate in October 1970. ERA advocates opposed both Ervin's and Bayh's changes. On November 19, 1970, by unanimous consent, the Senate "laid aside" the ERA.[144]

Griffiths and her allies met to assess their strategy going forward. The bipartisan group included Elly Peterson, a Republican National Committee member from Michigan; Virginia Allen from the White House; Gladys O'Donnell, head of the National Federation of Republican Women; NOW representative Flora Crater; Alice Paul; and Marguerite Rawalt. They discussed whether to pause for five years until they could generate broader public support or to press ahead while they had momentum and attention. They determined to proceed. Griffiths's wish, that there were more women in the Congress, led to the creation of the National Women's Political Caucus.[145]

Speaking to the Gridiron Club that November, the first woman to do so, Griffiths compared the ERA debate to "how Eve must have felt in the Garden of Eden, surrounded by serpents." In the Senate, she joked, the ERA "got as much support as our braless liberationists."[146] Women reporters did not become Gridiron members until 1975, three years after the first Black man was admitted. Veteran journalist Helen Thomas was the Gridiron's first female member. When the National Press Club admitted women, they were relegated to the balcony and not allowed to question speakers. Women were members of the White House Correspondents' Association, but its annual dinner was closed to them until 1962, when Thomas asked President Kennedy not to attend unless the ban was lifted.[147]

THE ERA: ROUND TWO

Both sides were better prepared for the second round of the ERA fight in 1971. Celler's position had not changed. His House Judiciary Committee approved riders offered by Charles Wiggins (R-CA) barring women from the draft and preserving state protections, including exemptions from jury duty and estate administration.

> This article shall not impair, however, the United States or any
> state which exempts women from compulsory military service
> or which is reasonably designed to promote the health, safety,
> privacy, education or economic welfare of women, or to enable
> them to perform their duties as homemakers or mothers.[148]

Wiggins had once suggested that the ERA would "require the same license fee for a bitch as for a dog." Robert McClory (R-IL) was the only

Republican to vote against the changes. Gladys O'Donnell, President of the Federation of Republican Women, was so alarmed that she called on House Republican leadership, warning that identifying the party as anti-ERA would be political suicide.[149]

On the House floor, proponents defeated the Wiggins' prohibition on drafting women, 265–87. On October 12, 1971, the House adopted an unamended ERA, by 354–23, more than two-thirds, with fifty-two members not voting.[150] Griffiths and Rawalt had modified the ERA's "enabling clauses," delaying implementation for two years, ensuring federal rather than state enforcement, and adding a seven-year ratification deadline, which had been common since 1945. Lenore Sullivan (D-MO) was the only woman to vote against it, asserting, "The ERA says you are my equal, but I think I'm a whole lot better." Edith Green (D-OR) was absent.[151]

On February 15, 1972, Anthony's birthday, Griffiths urged the Senate to act. She directed a letter-writing campaign to swamp Senate offices. The BPW made an unambiguous threat: "If this amendment is defeated, we [will] . . . get rid of those . . . who fought us." At the end of the month, without hearings, the Senate Judiciary Committee reported the ERA to the floor, where it survived ten amendments proposed by Senator Ervin. They addressed homosexuality, same-sex marriage, the draft, protective legislation, bathroom privacy (what Griffiths called "the potty argument"), sexual offenses, and paternal responsibilities.

As a courtesy, Griffiths, Bella Abzug (D-NY), and Margaret Heckler (R-MA) were invited to the Senate floor for the vote on March 22, 1972. Griffiths sat in the back row, tallying votes. Because of her misgivings about the ratification deadline, ERA author Alice Paul, eighty-seven, refused to appear in the gallery. Nearly fifty years after it had been introduced in Seneca Falls in 1923, the Equal Rights Amendment passed the Senate, 84–8.[152] The ERA had passed in both houses by more votes than either the Nineteenth Amendment or the Civil Rights Act. After the vote, one spectator claimed to see Senator Ervin fall to his knees in the well of the Senate to ask God's forgiveness.[153]

Gerry Ford called the ERA "a monument to Martha."[154] Griffiths deserved the credit. Without a cohesive organizational base, broad public support, or much media attention, she had managed a bipartisan power play and defeated two powerful chairmen. Within two hours of Senate passage, Hawaii ratified the ERA. Also competing to be first were Delaware, New Hampshire, and Nebraska, which acted the next day. In Arizona, State Senator Sandra Day O'Connor introduced the ERA, urging passage. In Texas, Delegate Sissy Farenthold and State Senator Barbara Jordan cosponsored ratification; both were the only women in their chambers.[155] Supporters predicted it would pass in less than two years. No one anticipated the fight to come.

CHAPTER SIX
BATTLE LINES,
1972–1980

I n June 1919, when Congress passed the woman suffrage amendment, Carrie Chapman Catt had launched ratification campaigns in every state. The fight lasted fifteen months. In March 1972, when Congress passed the Equal Rights Amendment, states vied to be first to ratify; after a decade, it had not passed. In 1972, twenty-three states considered the ERA and twenty-one ratified it. None conducted additional hearings. Support was bipartisan, floor debates brief. Kansas ratified in ten minutes. Colorado, Nebraska, and West Virginia voted unanimously. Momentum slowed in 1973 when thirty states considered the ERA, but only nine ratified and the Nebraska legislature rescinded its vote. In 1974, three states passed the ERA, and Tennessee rescinded.[1]

The downward trend continued: sixteen states introduced the ERA in 1975 and one ratified. Four states voted in 1976, but none ratified. Fourteen states considered the ERA in 1977. Only Indiana acted, ratifying the ERA by one vote, after First Lady Rosalynn Carter promised to campaign for the wavering legislator.[2] Idaho rescinded. There were close, crucial defeats by one or two votes in Florida, Nevada, North Carolina, and Virginia.[3]

Approval of a constitutional amendment required thirty-eight of fifty states. The ERA stalled at thirty-five, not counting the reversals.

One reason the ERA failed was political geography. The amendment passed more easily in the East, Midwest, and Far West, where proponents were concentrated. It lost in the South. People with college degrees, careers, two or fewer children, and infrequent church attendance supported it. People who had high school diplomas, hourly jobs, more than two children, went to church one or more times a week, and believed that God intended men to head households opposed it.[4] One group was comfortable with change, the other embraced tradition. Mormons mobilized to block ratification, despite a 1974 *Deseret News* poll indicating that 64% of Mormons supported the ERA.[5] A rule requiring a three-fifths vote, rather than a majority, kept Illinois in the unratified column. Control of the Florida Senate by panhandle conservatives stopped passage there. The demographics were daunting.

Catt had confronted a similar map. The Nineteenth Amendment needed thirty-six of forty-eight states. It had the support of Mormons and western states, but lost in eight southern states, controlled by Democrats, and in Connecticut, Delaware, Maryland, and Vermont, controlled by Republicans. But the ERA had no leader comparable to Catt. Martha Griffiths was a brilliant tactician, but there was no one with similar savvy to carry the fight beyond Congress. Her Thursday lunch group expanded into the National ERA Ratification Council, an informal coalition of more than one hundred organizations, from the American Association of University Women to Zonta. Whereas Catt had NAWSA troops already in place, state ERA campaigns were initially makeshift operations. There was no national strategy, no budget, and too many spokeswomen.

Over the objections of Alice Paul, NWP president Elizabeth Chittick joined the coalition.[6] Paul died in 1977, but her animosities lived on. After testifying against the ERA for almost fifty years, the League of Women Voters reversed itself after the amendment passed and joined the alliance, expecting a leadership role because it had national chapters. That attitude infuriated the NWP and irritated the Business and Professional Women, which had endorsed the ERA in 1929 and taxed its members for forty years to fund a war chest. Loyalty, money, and membership gave it authority. Political women, Black activists, labor unions, and associations of teachers, nurses, and social workers all participated in unruly meetings with large circles of folding chairs.[7]

NOW, still building its organization in 1972, was a part-time participant. Its administrative, legislative, and press offices were located in different cities, making national coordination difficult. State level organizations barely existed. Leadership was in disarray. Aileen Hernandez replaced Friedan as president in 1970. A Howard University graduate, she had worked for the ILGWU and was the only woman among the five original EEOC members named by LBJ. In 1977, NOW elected Pittsburgh housewife Eleanor Cutri Smeal president. For the first time, it united behind a single issue, passage of the ERA, starting with Indiana.[8] Among its tactics was a national boycott of unratified states, which backfired in Florida and Louisiana, making pro-ERA legislators in Miami and New Orleans vulnerable.

NATIONAL WOMEN'S POLITICAL CAUCUS

NOW members were among the 230 women from 26 states who organized the National Women's Political Caucus (NWPC) in July 1971. Participants were bipartisan and multiracial: Congresswomen Bella Abzug and Shirley Chisholm; Liz Carpenter, Lady Bird Johnson's former press secretary; Catherine East; Betty Friedan; Fannie Lou Hamer; La Donna Harris, a Comanche activist and wife of Senator Fred Harris (D-OK); Dorothy Height; Aileen Hernandez; Ann Lewis, political director of the Democratic National Committee; Eleanor Holmes Norton, a Yale Law School graduate and SNCC veteran, then at the ACLU; Elly Peterson, former vice chair of the Republican National Committee; Jill Ruckelshaus, a cabinet wife soon to join Nixon's staff; and Gloria Steinem, a New York journalist. "It was a spontaneous combustion of people from every state," recalled Steinem. "It was unruly and in need of someone [who] knew Robert's Rules of Order."[9]

Early NWPC record keeping was haphazard. Documents ended up in attics more often than archives. Its first executive director, Doris Meissner, was hired after its founding. There are competing recollections about where and when the Caucus was established. Not surprisingly, Friedan, no longer NOW president, claimed that the bipartisan political organization was her idea. Abzug, a fiercely Democratic partisan, hosted meetings for Democrats only, in her congressional office and at the Statler Hotel. Republican women met separately to decide whether to participate. Some credit NOW's Hernandez with chairing a committee that created the Caucus. In another creation myth, the group convened in the chapel of Mount Vernon College, an echo of the Methodist Chapel in Seneca Falls in 1848, history no one recalled.[10]

Its purpose was "to work in a nonpartisan way for greater representation of women in positions of power," reported Eileen Shanahan in the *New York Times*. The Caucus made a "public and irrevocable commitment" to oppose racism. Using separate partisan task forces and a national network of state and local caucuses, it would recruit and elect feminist women candidates, lobby for legislation beneficial to women, reform party rules, and ratify the ERA.[11] In an increasingly partisan era, the Caucus was scrupulously bipartisan. At both national conventions, in 1972 and 1976, it organized women delegates to press for women's issues in their platforms and for rule changes that would make the nominating process more accessible.

In January 1973, the NWPC held its own convention in Houston, where the Rice Hotel refused to allow women to be paged in the lobby, a practice deemed unladylike. Delegates elected Sissy Farenthold national chair. A former Texas state legislator, she had been a token Democratic nominee for vice president in 1972, earning 407 delegate votes.[12] The next Caucus chair was Audrey Rowe Colom, a Black Republican. A teacher, she had worked as a SNCC organizer in Mississippi and on behalf of poor children, incarcerated women, and welfare rights.[13]

ELECTED WOMEN

Before 1971, no one had bothered to measure women's political engagement. To collect that data, the Ford Foundation funded the Center for American Women and Politics (CAWP) at Rutgers University. At the time, there were two women in the Senate, Margaret Chase Smith (R-ME) and Elaine Edwards (D-LA), a widow who served three months. Thirteen women served in the House (10D, 3R). There were no women governors. In 1972, Nixon defeated Senator George McGovern (D-SD) in every state except Massachusetts, and Senator Smith lost. From 1960–1980, a period in which both parties supported women's and civil rights, the CAWP identified a racial voting gap: white women voted mostly Republican and Black women voted Democratic.[14]

After Smith's defeat, the Senate was without women until 1978, when two widows were appointed and Nancy Landon Kassebaum (R-KS) was elected. Her father, Governor Alf Landon, had run against FDR in 1936. In 1980, Florida elected Republican Paula Hawkins. When Ronald Reagan was inaugurated in January 1981, there were two Republican women Senators and twenty-one women in the House (11D, 10R), for a gain of eight women in a decade.[15]

Women improved the diversity of the House. Patsy Matsu Takemoto Mink (D-HI), elected in 1964, was the first Asian American Pacific Islander woman to serve. Of Japanese descent, she was the first woman of color in Congress. In 1972, three Black women joined Chisholm: Democrats Yvonne Brathwaite Burke (CA), Cardiss Collins (IL), and Barbara Jordan (TX). Burke was the first woman to have a baby while serving. In a stunning upset, Elizabeth Holtzman, an attorney and political unknown, defeated Emanuel Celler in a Democratic primary. Celler had served since 1922, the year before the ERA was introduced. In 1976, Ohio elected Mary Rose Oakar (D), the first Arab American to serve.[16]

By 1977, congresswomen felt they finally had enough members to form a bipartisan caucus. Their first conversation was about criminalizing spousal abuse. According to one scholar, the "gentlewoman amateur," who had come to Congress as a widow before WWII, had been succeeded by the "neutral professional" of the 1950s and then by the "feminist colleague" of the 1960s. Ninety-five women served in the House and Senate between 1917 and 1976; thirty-four were widows and almost half had some family connection. Widows generally served shorter terms. The exceptions were Florence Kahn (D-CA), 1925–37; Frances Bolton (R-OH), 1940–69; Margaret Chase Smith (R-ME), 1940–73; and Lindy Boggs (D-LA), 1973–91.[17]

A record number of women won major state offices in 1978. There were two women governors, Democrats Ella Grasso of Connecticut and Dixie Lee Ray of Washington. Lieutenant governors doubled, from three to six. Six treasurers, ten secretaries of state, and six judicial officers won statewide office. The total number of women state legislators jumped by 10%, from 703 to 761.[18] Having women in the pipeline should have led to more congressional candidates, but parties did not recruit women and many were reluctant to uproot their families or incur the cost of competing for higher office. They continued to serve in the highest numbers at the lowest levels. Women entering Congress were on average twenty years older than their male counterparts and less likely to rise to committee leadership or run for the Senate.

TITLE IX AND THE EQUAL CREDIT ACT

Even before their numbers increased, congresswomen engineered two major reforms, addressing sex discrimination in education and access to credit. Title VII of the Civil Rights Act exempted educational institutions, but in 1967 President Johnson signed Executive Order 11375, barring sex discrimination by federal contractors. Bernice Resnick Sandler, a lecturer at the University of Maryland with a PhD in psychology, investigated bias in hiring. Dismissed as "just a housewife who went back to school," she joined the Women's Equity Action League. As the sole member of its contract compliance committee, Sandler brought a class action discrimination suit on behalf of staff and students against 250 educational institutions that had federal research contracts.[19]

Because an executive order could be reversed, Sandler joined the staff of the House Committee on Education and worked with Democrats Edith Green and Patsy Mink to pass formal legislation. Title IX of the Education Amendments Act of 1972 prohibited sex discrimination in any federally funded educational program at any school, public or private, from pre-K to PhD. Sandler did not want opponents to think too deeply about its impact, so she discouraged feminists from testifying. Asked if the bill would allow women to play football, sponsors claimed that would never happen. Once it passed, it became clear that Title IX would apply to discrimination in athletics, evident in the unequal resources, coaching, training facilities, locker rooms, and equipment for women's teams. After Title IX, girls' participation in high school sports surged by 900%.[20] Girls playing on Little League and varsity teams produced professional sports teams, Olympic medalists, and World Cup champions.

"Before and after Title IX" became a generational marker. Before Title IX, competitiveness was seen as a male trait, unseemly in women, for whom playing full court basketball was deemed too strenuous. Some states prohibited any athletic competition among women.[21] After Title IX, scholars wrote papers about how sports made women more successful, especially in business and math-related fields. Heralded as the "godmother of Title IX," Sandler worked for twenty years overseeing the status of women for the Association of American Colleges. Because Title IX prohibited sex discrimination in educational institutions, it has recently been used to address uneven disciplinary responses to sexual violence on campus and to protect the rights of transgender athletes.[22]

Female competitiveness was demonstrated in 1973, when tennis star Billie Jean King defeated Bobby Riggs in the "Battle of the Sexes." King had won five Wimbledon singles championships and several Grand Slams. In 1972, she was the first woman featured as *Sports Illustrated*'s "Sportswoman of the Year." When she learned that the women's purse at the

US Open was less than the men's, she threatened a boycott. The Open became the first tournament to offer equal prize money.[23] King was the first female athlete to earn over $100,000, but she could not get a credit card in her own name. As a vestige of the common law, women were not eligible for credit. Loans were based on a husband's earnings. If a woman was over thirty, half of her income counted as an asset; her entire salary counted only if she was over forty or had been sterilized. Divorced and single women were considered poor credit risks. Women with absent, abusive, hospitalized, or imprisoned husbands still needed their signatures to rent apartments.[24]

The Equal Credit Opportunity Act, signed in October 1974, outlawed discrimination against credit applicants on account of race, color, religion, national origin, sex, marital status, age, veteran status, or source of income. Representative Corinne Claiborne (Lindy) Boggs (D-LA) added "sex" and "marital status" to the bill during its markup in the House Banking and Currency Committee. The widow of House Majority Leader Hale Boggs, she had won a special election in March 1973, garnered 80% of the vote in the 1974 general election, and served eighteen years. A colleague declared her "the only widow I know who is really qualified—damn qualified—to take over," a compliment that insulted dozens of capable congresswomen. Mrs. Boggs admitted that her only reservation about running was doing it "without a wife."[25]

Boggs believed "almost all women's issues are economic issues. . . . Women vote their pocketbooks." When the original bill failed to include protections for women, Boggs inserted the necessary words, took her draft to the copier, and returned with amended pages. As she handed them out, she declared, "Knowing the members of this Committee as well as I do, I'm sure it was just an oversight that we didn't have 'sex' or 'marital status' included. I've taken care of that and I trust it meets with the Committee's approval." Her male colleagues unanimously endorsed her wording.[26] Boggs also pushed for equal pay for women in government jobs and equal access for women competing for government contracts.

WOMEN'S MOVEMENT VARIATIONS

Economic issues and the ERA were two topics on which feminists could agree. At that time, the white women's movement was divided, simplistically, between political feminists working for political equality and "women's libbers" seeking personal liberation. They employed street tactics to protest patriarchy and gender stereotyping. Middle-aged, middle-class, college-educated white women were the majority of congressional, commission, and NOW members. Their daughters were more likely libbers. Some were veterans of Freedom Summer or the anti-war movement, where they had again been treated as sex objects and told that protesting war was men's work.

Both cohorts of mostly white women used consciousness-raising to organize. In small towns and big cities, they shared stories and secrets, identified common concerns, and complained about the unfairness of housework, childcare, wages, and orgasms. They got angry and organized. Unaware of Paul's precedent, some produced street theater, conducting a funeral for "Traditional Womanhood," burying a blond mannequin in curlers.[27] Libbers railed against oppression and embraced lesbian rights and abortion reform. For some white women, feminist coalitions were their first introduction to Black women, union members, lesbians, women on welfare, and women who didn't wear bras or shave their legs.

Betty Friedan was no longer the only feminist celebrity. Kate Millett, an academic and sculptor from an Irish Catholic family in Minnesota, was among the first women to earn first-class honors from St. Hilda's, Oxford. Her 1970 Columbia doctoral dissertation, "Sexual Politics," provided an intellectual underpinning for radicals. Millett claimed that "every avenue of power . . . is entirely in male hands," echoing Eleanor Roosevelt's assessment in 1930. The book was seen as a "blowtorch" so intense it would destroy "all vestiges of male chauvinism." She traced the power of patriarchy from Judeo-Christian traditions to Freud. *Time* magazine put her portrait, by Alice Neel, on its August 31, 1970, cover and the *New York Times* declared her "the high priestess of the current feminist wave." Millett ended her book hoping that "the new women's movement" would "ally itself on an equal basis with Blacks and students in a growing radical coalition."[28]

Another feminist philosopher was Shulamith Firestone, author of *The Dialectic of Sex: The Case for a Feminist Revolution* (1970). Firestone compared childbearing to Marxist theories of class oppression. Celebrity prompted both Millett and Firestone to withdraw from public view; Millett was institutionalized and Firestone died in obscurity.[29] *Sisterhood Is Powerful*, an anthology edited by Robin Morgan, also appeared in 1970, followed by Germaine Greer's *The Female Eunuch* (1971), Phyllis Chesler's *Women and Madness* (1972), Andrea Dworkin's *Woman Hating* (1974), and Susan Brownmiller's *Against Our Will: Men, Women and Rape* (1975).

Feminists adopted the tactics of civil rights activists. Millett was among the women who sat-in at the editorial offices of *Cosmopolitan*, demanding that Helen Gurley Brown attend a consciousness-raising meeting.[30] In March 1970, one hundred women occupied the offices of *Ladies Home Journal* editor John Mack Carter. For eleven hours, Media Women, NOW, New York Radical Women, and the Redstockings demanded that the fourteen-million-circulation magazine employ non-white women, hire women writers, raise salaries, provide childcare, refuse degrading advertisements, and end its "Can This Marriage Be Saved?" column. Reminded that the magazine's motto was "Never Underestimate the Power of a Woman," Carter added articles like "Advice to Draft Age Sons," "How Detergents Harm Our Rivers," and "Should This Marriage Be Saved?" to the August issue.[31]

On March 23, 1970, women at *Newsweek* held a press conference announcing they were suing the magazine for sex discrimination. Mail girls, clippers, researchers, and the few female reporters had plotted for months, meeting in the ladies' room. Their timing coincided with a *Newsweek* cover featuring a red-silhouetted, naked woman, her fist raised, breaking through the symbol for female. The forty-six women won their suit. In 2012, Lynn Povich, who had been *Newsweek*'s only woman junior writer, published the story *Good Girls Revolt*, which became an Amazon series.[32] Equal opportunity, equal pay, and childcare were common denominator demands of working women.

Redstocking was a play on the expression "blue stocking," applied to intellectual women who hosted literary salons and participated in political discourse in the early eighteenth century. It was a slur, a synonym for frumpy, brainy spinsters. In New York City in 1969, the Redstockings included Firestone, Kathie Sarachild (who invented her surname), Rita Mae Brown, and Alix Kates Schulman. The group stormed a New York legislative hearing on abortion. Lined up as expert witnesses were fourteen men and a nun. Insisting that sexually active women were the only experts, the Redstockings demanded repeal rather than reform of abortion laws. A month later, in March 1969, they hosted a "speak out" in New York City, at which twelve women described their abortions.[33] Attending was reporter Gloria Steinem.

GLORIA STEINEM

Steinem later said her "life as an active feminist" began that day. Born in 1934, Steinem survived a Toledo childhood defined by an absent father, a mentally ill mother, and poverty. Because it was "a way out of a not too great life in a pretty poor neighborhood," she competed in a teen beauty pageant. She graduated from Smith with a fellowship to study in India. Finding herself pregnant, she had an abortion in London at age twenty-two. Steinem dedicated her memoir, *My Life on the Road* (2015), to the physician who helped her. In the 1960s, she worked as a freelance writer in New York, covering civil rights, anti-war politics, labor unions, lesbians, and abortion. Researching an article on Playboy Bunnies in 1963, she was famously photographed working undercover, making her "the liberals' pin-up girl."[34]

According to Nora Ephron, Steinem became "the only remotely chic thing connected to the movement."[35] In August 1970, Steinem marched in the Women's Strike. That September she testified before the Senate Judiciary Committee on behalf of the ERA. She cofounded the Women's Action Alliance, the NWPC, the Coalition of Labor Union Women, and

Ms. magazine, proposing an honorific for women unrelated to their marital status. Initially hesitant to speak in public, Steinem teamed up with other feminists, among them child-welfare pioneer Dorothy Pittman Hughes and attorneys Flo Kennedy and Eleanor Holmes Norton, all Black activists. She was comfortable among radical, lesbian, African American, and political feminists.[36] Her long hair, long legs, short skirts, aviator glasses, and heterosexuality attracted media attention to the cause, an outcome most feminists accepted and Friedan abhorred.

Friedan was jealous. She was cast as the Wicked Witch while Gloria was Glinda.[37] Friedan was not comfortable among younger, diverse activists who did not revere her. She referred to lesbian participation in NOW as a "lavender menace" and expelled lesbians from the New York chapter. The mother superior of the women's movement since 1963, Friedan was replaced as NOW president in 1970. The next year, NOW passed a resolution declaring that "a woman's right to her own person includes the right to define and express her own sexuality and to choose her own lifestyle."[38] Steinem, assorted younger activists, and congresswomen challenged Friedan's authority. Between them, Abzug and Friedan raised the noise level of any meeting.

Friedan expected the prime place in increasingly crowded march vanguards and press conferences. Stunned to lose an election to the bipartisan Caucus steering committee in 1973, she threatened to sue.[39] According to Australian feminist Germaine Greer, Friedan was "disconcerted by lesbianism, leery of abortion, and ultimately concerned for the men whose ancient privileges she feared were being eroded. Betty was actually very feminine, very keen on pretty clothes and very responsive to male attention."[40] Friedan worried that gay rights and abortion advocacy would endanger ERA ratification. She was right.

BLACK FEMINISTS

There were many Black feminist leaders, but there was no lasting national organization. For many women of color, there was no liberation in a sisterhood that did not address racism and structural oppression. The white women's movement seemed anti-family and anti-religion. Where white women saw hairdressers as oppressive, Black women saw salons as gathering places. The overalls worn by libbers were reminders of sharecropping.[41] A 1973 meeting to discuss "Black women and their relationship to the women's movement" resulted in creation of the National Black Feminist Organization (NBFO). Five hundred women gathered in New York's Cathedral of St. John the Divine to form local chapters. Their agenda included discrimination, criminal justice, welfare, household workers' rights, and poverty. The organization sought to include lesbian and incarcerated women. Its first and only president was Margaret Sloan-Hunter, a Black lesbian, early editor of *Ms.*, and author of *Black and Lavender,* a collection of her poetry. The NFBO broke up after four years, "bogged down in . . . ideological disputes."[42]

An organizing challenge for Black feminists was the need to confront "interlocking oppressions," related to race, gender, class, and sexual orientation. The Combahee River Collective (CRC) grew out of the Boston chapter of the NBFO in 1974. The name honored the only Civil War combat operation planned and led by a woman. In 1863, Harriet Tubman, leading Black union soldiers, fought to free 750 slaves near the Combahee River in South Carolina. In its 1977 statement of purpose and philosophy, the Collective addressed identity politics and focused on local Boston issues. It disbanded after four years. The CRC established the Kitchen Table: Women of Color Press in 1980, run by two lesbians, academic activist Barbara Smith and poet activist Audre Lorde. It reprinted classic Black fiction and published work by feminist and lesbian writers of color. Florence Howe, a white architect of women's history, had founded the Feminist Press in 1970, to reprint classics and publish new research.[43]

Many Black women frequently felt disrespected and discounted. "We exist as women who are Black, who are feminists, each stranded for the moment, working independently because there is not yet an environment in this society remotely congenial to our struggle," wrote one.[44] A 1972 poll of four thousand women and men conducted by Harris and Associates found that 67% of Black women expressed sympathy for women's liberation, compared to 35% of white women. Figures for Black and white men were similar, with 50% of Black men and 41% of white men indicating support.[45] Such statistics demonstrated that Black women had been valued leaders in their community for generations.

New research into the lives of Black feminists confirms that they were essential to radical change in the 1960s and '70s, linking the civil rights, Black Power, anti-war, New Left, and feminist movements.[46] Among them was Florynce (Flo) Kennedy, described as "the biggest, loudest and, indisputably, the rudest mouth on the battleground where feminist activists and radical politics join in mostly common cause." Often photographed in a cowboy hat, fake eyelashes, and pink sunglasses, with her manicured middle finger raised, Kennedy was born in Kansas City in 1916, the daughter of a Pullman porter. Before enrolling at Columbia University as an undergraduate at twenty-eight, she worked as an elevator operator and owned a hat shop. She threatened a lawsuit to enter Columbia law school, becoming the only Black student and eighth woman in the class of 1951. In private practice, she represented Billie Holiday and was among the lawyers to challenge New York abortion laws. Kennedy was a member of NOW and cofounder of the Caucus, the NBFO, and the Feminist Party, which nominated Shirley Chisholm for President. "My main message," Kennedy declared, "is we have a pathologically, institutionally racist, sexist, classist society."[47]

Another Black feminist was independent scholar Barbara Smith, an early NBFO member and change agent in publishing, academia, and politics, as she recounted in *Ain't Gonna Let Nobody Turn Me Around: Forty Years of Movement Building* (2014). Any feminism that did not "account for the concerns of Black women, poor women, disabled women, lesbians and others was not really feminism," Smith declared in 1979; it was "merely female self-aggrandizement."[48]

LGBTQ RIGHTS

Flamboyant women like Flo Kennedy were assumed to be lesbians. Since the 1969 Stonewall Riot, homosexuality was still illegal but no longer in the closet. When President Obama alluded alliteratively to "Seneca Falls . . . Selma and . . . Stonewall" in his second inaugural address, he acknowledged advances made for women, Black Americans, and homosexuals, but abbreviated the history of those movements. None of them actually began in those locations. World War II was a milestone for homosexuals, when young men and women joined the sex-segregated armed services or moved to big cities, where they found privacy and partners.

Joe McCarthy's red hunt for communists became a lavender purge of homosexuals. In 1953, President Eisenhower issued Executive Order 10450, which allowed federal employees to be fired for "sexual perversion." More than five thousand men and women resigned rather than be exposed as "moral misfits." Franklin Kameny, an astronomer with a Harvard doctorate working for the Federal Map Service, fought his 1957 dismissal until the Supreme Court denied his last appeal. Kameny organized the gay rights movement in Washington, picketing the White House with signs demanding "CITIZENSHIP FOR HOMOSEXUALS."[49]

Kameny's greatest contribution was his pivotal role in persuading the American Psychiatric Association to remove homosexuality from its list of mental disorders. In 1973, the APA board declared that homosexuality "by itself does not necessarily constitute a psychiatric disorder." Conservative members demanded a referendum. The decision was affirmed, 5,854 to 3,810.[50] Based on its supposed pathology, homosexuality was illegal in every state except Illinois, which decriminalized sodomy in 1961. Gays were regularly bullied by police and barred from jobs, housing, dancing together, and wearing clothes that were not gender specific. At the time, less attention was paid to lesbians and trans women, who were banned from gay bars. Protesting violent police harassment, lesbians, drag queens, and trans people started the Compton Cafeteria Riot in San Francisco in 1966, predating Stonewall.[51]

On Saturday, June 28, 1969, at 1:20 A.M., eight members of the Public Morals Squad raided the Stonewall Inn in Greenwich Village. It was "our Rosa Parks moment," recalled one man, who compared gay bars to sanctuary churches. Stormé DeLarverie, a mixed-race singer and drag performer, threw the first punch during her arrest. As the cop swung his billy club again, protestors attacked him. When they threw bricks, bottles, and punches, the cops barricaded themselves inside the bar. The clash lasted until reinforcements arrived, but rioting continued for four days.[52] Media coverage of the New York confrontation triggered an explosion of activism, leading to the Gay Liberation Front. The Christopher Street Liberation Day March on the first anniversary of Stonewall morphed into annual Gay Pride parades across the country.

Scholars of Stonewall debate the connection between the riot and grief among gays following the death of actress Judy Garland. Her funeral in New York City, attended by 20,000 people, was June 27, the day before the Stonewall raid. A "disproportionate part of her nightly claque seems to be . . . the boys in tight pants," wrote *Time* in 1967.[53] To be a "friend of Dorothy," referring to Garland's role in *The Wizard of Oz*, was code for gay, because Dorothy befriended the Cowardly Lion, who called himself a sissy. When gay bar patrons were required to sign in, Dorothy Gale and Judy Garland were popular pseudonyms. Fans believe her song, "Over the Rainbow," inspired the rainbow flag.

Later in 1969, in *Norton v. Macy*, the US Court of Appeals for DC declared that homosexual civil servants could not be fired unless their behavior harmed "the efficiency of the service." In 1975, the Pentagon issued its first security clearance to a known homosexual. The Stonewall Inn is now the only National Park Service site devoted to LGBTQ history. From 1996 to 2020, gay cops in uniform marched in pride parades.[54] Fifty years after Stonewall, the police commissioner apologized. When President Obama signed a 2009 order granting benefits to same-sex partners of federal employees, he gave the first pen to Dr. Kameny.[55]

ABORTION

Gay and straight feminists shared concerns about women's health and sexuality. When the Boston Women's Health Collective published *Our Bodies, Ourselves* on stapled newsprint in 1970, it became a bible of self-help health care.[56] In consciousness-raising groups, women used magnifying mirrors to locate their cervixes. In 1965, University of Chicago student Heather Tobis helped a friend's sister find a doctor willing to do an abortion. Soon she was deluged by requests. She organized the Jane Collective, a network of women who posted signs inside bathroom stalls and advertised in underground newspapers, offering abortions, counseling, safe houses, and aftercare, all at anonymous locations.

When the Janes discovered that a provider was unlicensed, they learned to do the procedure themselves, administering anesthesia, inducing miscarriages, and performing twelve thousand abortions between 1969 and 1972.[57] That year, police raided an apartment where Janes operated and arrested the "Abortion Seven." The Supreme Court legalized abortion before their case went to trial. A veteran of Freedom Summer, Tobis married SDS activist Paul Booth and founded The Midwest Academy to train community organizers. A feminist and progressive, she is still protesting. Before she ran for office, when Elizabeth Warren (D-MA) asked how to organize a consumer rights movement, "I was told two words: Heather Booth."[58]

For centuries, women of all classes, races, and faiths have ended pregnancies with abortions, which had long been both commonplace and legal. The common law allowed abortion until "quickening," the feeling of the fetus moving, around twenty weeks or five months of pregnancy. Performing an abortion after that point was considered a misdemeanor. Women controlled the process: only pregnant women felt fetal movement and only midwives provided remedies. Abortions were usually induced with herbs like pennyroyal. As medical care supposedly became more scientific around the time of the American Revolution, male doctors lobbied for laws requiring training and licensing, from which they could bar midwives. Nonetheless, women continued to be treated primarily by women.[59]

The country's first anti-abortion regulations were poison control statutes. In 1821, Connecticut banned the use of poisonous herbs to induce an abortion after quickening; the punishment was a life sentence. "Abortifacients" were widely advertised. It was Susan B. Anthony's refusal to run these ads in *The Revolution* that prompted an anti-abortion group to claim her name. Anthony did not condemn abortion or infanticide among desperate women. She opposed quack remedies, which put women's lives at risk.[60] In 1845, Massachusetts made any form of abortion or attempted abortion illegal, a law it eventually modified but failed to repeal until 2018.[61] In 1857, the newly formed American Medical Association coordinated a national drive to outlaw abortion and midwifery, both to ensure women's safety and to eliminate competition for obstetrical patients. By 1900, every state had laws forbidding abortion by drugs or surgery. Almost all also had therapeutic exceptions, allowing physicians to use their discretion, putting a woman's decision whether or not to be pregnant in the hands of men.[62]

Even celibate men: in 1869, Pope Pius IX issued a dictum forbidding abortion at any stage of pregnancy. Previously, Catholics had allowed abortion until "ensoulment," similar to quickening. Protestant churches, worried that Catholics would out-propagate them, joined the opposition. None of these pronouncements actually ended abortion. One of the reasons Sanger was so adamant about the need for birth control and sex education was that self-induced abortions were killing hopeless mothers, but the Catholic Church continued to rail against birth control. In 1951, Pope Pius XII used the phrase "right to life" for the first time in a papal encyclical, directing midwives globally not to interfere with pregnancies. Catholic doctors, nurses, lawyers, and housewives launched the modern anti-abortion movement.[63] In 1967, the National Council of Catholic Bishops provided funding to form the National Right to Life Committee. To avoid charges of papal interference, NRLC sought allies among conservative Protestants. Small and geographically dispersed, local branches focused on state laws.

Restrictions created an abortion black market. The 1953 *Kinsey Report* asserted that 90% of premarital and 24% of married pregnancies were aborted.[64] There were always ways to circumvent the law: back-alley quacks, bribed professionals, an abortion ring, or DIY procedures involving coat hangers and bleach. Privileged women could get a "D&C," dilation and curettage of the cervix, a procedure usually performed following a miscarriage. Others went abroad. Doctors used their judgment in cases of rape or risk to the mental or physical health of the mother. If two psychiatrists and one physician agreed, a woman could have a therapeutic abortion.

Actual numbers of abortions and deaths from attempts were impossible to tabulate accurately. Unless they were botched, with women ending up in emergency rooms, illegal abortions were not reported. The National Center for Health Statistics listed 235 deaths from abortion in 1965. The Centers for Disease Control did not tabulate abortion-related mortality until 1972, counting twenty-four deaths from legal abortions and thirty-nine from illegal procedures. With improved antibiotics and safer procedures, mortality declined.[65]

Demand for abortions increased in the 1960s. Thalidomide, a sleeping pill, caused thousands of birth defects and an outbreak of German measles produced stillbirths and babies born with abnormalities.[66] Calls for a woman's right to safe and legal elective abortions increased. In 1962, Patricia Maginnis, considered the first American abortion rights activist, organized a symposium for doctors and lawyers. She founded the Association to Repeal Abortion Laws (ARAL), the predecessor of NARAL Pro-Choice America (since 1973, the National Abortion Rights Action League). The American Law Institute drafted a "Model Penal Code for Abortion," legalizing abortion under several circumstances.[67]

In 1967, Colorado decriminalized abortion in cases of rape, incest, or the disability of the mother. California followed, an act signed by then-Governor Ronald Reagan. Twelve states, including Alabama, Mississippi, and New Mexico, liberalized their laws between 1967 and 1970. Hawaii was the first state to legalize abortion in 1970. New York and Alaska decriminalized abortion. By 1973, abortion was legal in some circumstances in seventeen states.[68] It was not yet a national issue.

ROE V. WADE

In December 1971, the Supreme Court heard oral arguments in two cases challenging restrictive state abortion laws. In *Roe v. Wade*, "Jane Roe," an unmarried woman, sued the Dallas County District Attorney, seeking to overturn an 1857 Texas law. It prohibited abortions not needed to save the life of the woman and punished participants with two to five years in prison. In *Doe v. Bolton*, "Mary Doe" sued Georgia's Attorney General over a law requiring abortions be performed in hospitals after an examination by three doctors and approval by a committee. In both cases, lower federal courts declared the statutes unconstitutional.[69]

The Supreme Court recognized that the cases would be controversial and consequential. It scheduled a second round of arguments in October 1972, after Justices Lewis Powell and William Rehnquist filled vacancies. In the interim, Justice Harry Blackmun researched abortion at the Mayo Clinic, where he had been legal counsel, and the Court decided *Baird v. Eisenstadt*, granting unmarried couples access to birth control.[70] *Ms.* magazine's preview issue, released in March 1972, published a pro-abortion petition signed by fifty-three prominent women who had had abortions, including Steinem, Nora Ephron, Anais Nin, Susan Sontag, and Billie Jean King. At the Republican National Convention in August, Lenore Romney, a US Senate candidate, wife of Michigan's governor, mother of a future presidential candidate, and a Mormon, called for a plank making abortion legal.[71]

The decision was announced on January 22, 1973, the day Lyndon Johnson died, so it did not lead the news. Voting 7–2, the Supreme Court concluded that the Constitution protected a woman's right to abortion. Writing for the majority, Justice Blackmun acknowledged the "sensitive and emotional nature" of the issue between sides with "deep and seemingly absolute convictions." Rather than use the equal protection clause against sex discrimination, Blackmun relied on the *Griswold* right of privacy. "We do not need to resolve the difficult question of when life begins," he added, "[if] those trained in . . . medicine, philosophy and theology [cannot]."[72]

The fifty-page decision reviewed the history of abortion from ancient times to the current opinions of the American medical and bar associations.

Blackmun concluded in *Roe* that access to abortion was a "fundamental right." Only "a compelling state interest" could justify restrictive state regulations. The decision balanced a woman's interest with the state's, a balance that shifted as pregnancy advanced. In the first trimester, the state could not regulate or prohibit abortion; that decision was left to the woman. In the second trimester, until the fetus could survive outside the womb, the state could regulate abortion "in ways that are reasonably related to maternal health." In the third trimester, given its interest in the "potentiality of human life," the state could justify regulating or banning abortion, "except for the preservation of life or health of the mother."[73] Instead of applying the traditional timing of quickening, around twenty weeks, the Court created new gestational dividers, three-month increments, and a three-tiered legal framework. *Roe* made viability, when a fetus could survive outside the womb, key to abortion law.

Justices William Brennan, Warren Burger, William Douglas, Thurgood Marshall, Lewis Powell, and Potter Stewart joined the majority, four of them Nixon appointees. Brennan, a Democrat appointed by Eisenhower and the only Catholic on the Court, opposed abortion, but believed in separation of church and state between personal belief and public policy.[74] Chief Justice Burger wrote a separate concurrence, emphasizing that the decision did not permit "abortion on demand." The dissenters were Justices Byron White, who did not approve of abortion for "convenience, whim or caprice," and William Rehnquist, who challenged a constitutional right to privacy and thought abortion policy should be a "legislative judgment" rather than judicial decision.[75]

The decision came too late for Jane Roe, a.k.a. Norma Nelson McCorvey, who remained anonymous for sixteen years. She put her baby girl up for adoption. McCorvey had sought advice to get an abortion. Her attorneys, Sarah Weddington and Linda Coffee, took her case to challenge Texas law. Both were in their twenties, ambitious, and inexperienced. Weddington presented the case. It was so unusual for female attorneys to argue before the Court that the lawyers' lounge only had a men's room. McCorvey did not appear. She was an unsympathetic protagonist, a runaway with a ninth-grade education and a juvenile record. She had her first child at eighteen. Her mother raised that child; her second was put in foster care when she became pregnant a third time. McCorvey claimed she had been raped but later recanted. An alcoholic and drug addict, she subsisted on the margins, working as a bartender, a maid, a roller-skating carhop, and a house painter. She had some stability in a long-term lesbian relationship. In 1995, McCorvey had a conversion experience and was baptized in a swimming pool by an evangelical minister connected to Operation Rescue, an anti-abortion group. Before her death in 2017, she admitted, "It was all an act. . . . If a young woman wants to have an abortion, fine. It's no skin off my ass."[76]

Justice Blackmun issued a separate opinion for each case, but other justices wrote opinions that applied to both, so the cases were consolidated. In *Doe*, the Court decided that the right to an abortion was not absolute, but that Georgia's onerous requirements did not provide Doe with equal protection and due process.[77] Mary Doe was Sandra Cano, twenty-two, a homeless, indigent, abused mother of three, pregnant with her fourth child. She had sought legal help for a divorce, not an abortion. She did not get an abortion. All her children were put into foster care. Cano ultimately became an anti-abortion speaker.[78] Both sides exploited their white plantiffs. Their lives represented how messy the abortion issue was, and remains.

THE REACTION TO ROE

As *New York Times* Supreme Court reporter Linda Greenhouse summarized, "Abortion was not a partisan issue at the time. It was a medical problem [and] a social problem."[79] It became a political problem. Although *Roe* appalled Catholics and social conservatives, abortion was not a campaign issue in 1974. In 1975, the Council of Catholic Bishops issued a

"Pastoral Plan for Pro-Life Activities." Party platforms equivocated on abortion in 1976, as did the nominees. Pressed to take a position, President Ford and Governor Carter admitted they were personally opposed to abortion, but would uphold *Roe* and support the Hyde Amendment.[80]

The Hyde Amendment, attached to a budget bill funding what is now the Department of Health and Human Services, prohibited federal funding of abortion "except in cases where the life of the mother would be endangered." Proposed by Representative Henry Hyde (R-IL), it passed with bipartisan support in September 1976. The language could be removed or revised during each congressional budget cycle, adding or subtracting exceptions. The measure restricted the use of federal funds for abortions for women enrolled in Medicare and Medicaid and eventually women on reservations, US service women and veterans, women in the Peace Corps, female federal employees, and women in federal prison or immigration detention facilities.[81]

In *Maher v. Roe* (1977), the Supreme Court upheld a Connecticut law barring state funding for abortion. Writing for the 6–3 majority, Justice Powell asserted that *Roe* did not prevent the government from "favoring childbirth over abortion." Dissenting, Justice Brennan condemned the decision's "distressing insensitivity to the plight of impoverished pregnant women."[82] In *Harris v. McRae* (1980), the Court upheld Hyde, without exceptions. Justice Rehnquist wrote the decision, assisted by his clerk, John Roberts. In 2016, the Democratic platform called explicitly for repeal of the Hyde Amendment.[83]

While both sides had political action committees by 1978, there is no evidence that abortion was a significant factor in the midterms. With the election of Ronald Reagan in 1980, abortion opponents scored a stunning success, defeating twelve liberal Senators and electing a Republican Senate majority. According to journalist Anthony Lewis, abortion had become significant in its appeal to single-issue voters. Comparing it to gun control, busing, and capital punishment, he predicted that abortion was "likely to have the largest impact on American politics for the longest time."[84] Unlike *Brown*, *Roe* was not accepted as "settled law."

PHYLLIS SCHLAFLY

By the mid-1970s, social conservatives were trying to put the brakes on the speed of change. They were fed up with libbers, hippies, Panthers, druggies, gays, farm workers, and Native Americans occupying Alcatraz for eighteen months, to reclaim it as Native land. Among women, disrespect for house-wives had become a hurtful issue. Barbara Bush, the mother of six and the traditional political wife of the first US Liaison to China and later Director of the CIA, George H. W. Bush, admitted that she felt depressed by the women's movement. "It made me feel inadequate . . . [and] demeaned."[85] Many women felt the same way, as they fulfilled roles for which they had been raised and previously respected. The media fed the schism, pitting Betty Friedan against Betty Crocker.

Feminists believed that homemakers and housework were undervalued. They objected to the imbalance of power in conventional marriages and the assumption that women would do all the work. They argued that the contributions of stay-at-home wives should be respected and reimbursed. In 1969, Alix Kates Schulman, an encyclopedia editor, Redstocking, and mother of two, published an iconoclastic "Marriage Agreement." It outlined how she and her husband would equitably divide housework and childcare. "Husband does all house cleaning in exchange for wife's extra childcare and sick care." Meal preparation, dish washing, wake-up, and bedtime supervision alternated. Wife did home laundry; husband took dry cleaning. The agreement was widely debated, reprinted, and included in a Harvard law textbook on contracts. Soon divorced, Schulman negotiated a new contract for the first of twelve books, *Memoirs of a Prom Queen* (1972).[86]

Traditional women found a self-appointed leader in Phyllis Schlafly, who had been a Republican, Catholic, anti-communist dynamo long before the ERA or *Roe*. Although the anti-ERA fight was her first successful campaign, Schlafly was a brilliant political strategist, a conservative Catt. She defeated the ERA and divided the women's movement, contributing to the rise of the Republican Right and the election of Ronald Reagan. Born in St. Louis in 1924, Phyllis Stewart attended Catholic schools.

During the Depression, her mother supported the family as a librarian. Smart and ambitious, Phyllis won a scholarship to Maryville College of the Sacred Heart, then transferred to Washington University, earning her tuition during World War II by testing machine guns on the night shift at a munitions factory. She graduated in three years, Phi Beta Kappa, and secured a fellowship to Radcliffe in 1945 for an MA in political science. She worked at the conservative American Enterprise Institute, for a conservative Republican candidate, and at a bank where she met conservative Fred Schlafly, a wealthy corporate lawyer. Fifteen years older and President of the World Anti-Communist League, he supported Joe McCarthy.[87]

The Schlaflys married in 1949 and moved to Alton, Illinois. Phyllis had six children in eighteen years, breastfed each for six months, and homeschooled them until second grade. She was a delegate or alternate to Republican national conventions for forty years, beginning in 1952, when she supported Ohio Senator Robert Taft over Eisenhower. When her husband declined to run for Congress that year, Phyllis volunteered. She was twenty-six; her first child was eighteen months old. The morning after winning the primary against a heavily favored lawyer, she was photographed in a polka dot apron, making breakfast for her husband.[88] Despite a Republican landslide, Schlafly lost the race. From 1956 to 1964, she was President of the Illinois Federation of Republican Women. She lost another congressional primary in 1960.

Her 1964 manifesto, *A Choice Not An Echo*, sold 3.5 million copies. It propelled Arizona Senator Barry Goldwater to the Republican presidential nomination, after which he distanced himself. LBJ's landslide prompted Republicans to purge ultraconservatives like Schlafly, who had risen to first vice president of the 500,000-member General Federation of Republican Women. The GOP depended on the Federation to rally women volunteers and get out the vote. Members organized "Kitchen Kabinets . . . to share political recipes." A monthly bulletin asked, "What's Cookin' in Washington?"[89] By 1967, Schlafly was next in line to be GFRW president, but she was bypassed. The official slate nominated Gladys O'Donnell, a California grandmother who described herself as a "garden variety Republican."

Schlafly launched a floor fight. After a nasty battle, with charges of voter fraud and ballot rigging, she lost by 416 votes, out of 3,404 cast, and contested the result. Police had to be called to restore order at the Sheraton Park hotel ballroom. The two rivals refused to stand side by side at a press conference. Ronald Reagan's daughter Maureen, a Schlafly supporter, urged the delegates not to split the organization.[90] Four months later, Schlafly created the Eagle Trust Fund and invited Federation members to subscribe to "The Phyllis Schlafly Report," a four-page newsletter, diverting both members and dues.[91] Schlafly lost a third bid for Congress in 1970, while Maureen Reagan joined Gladys O'Donnell in supporting the ERA.

Schlafly was a natural leader in search of a cause and a constituency. She combined her formidable energy and intelligence with perfect posture, pearls, a DAR pedigree, and a blond updo. She claimed not to have paid much attention to the ERA until 1972. After it had been ratified by twenty-plus states, she founded STOP-ERA: "Stop Taking Our Privileges." Most ERA scholars agree that Schlafly did stop the ERA, harnessing socially conservative opponents under a banner of traditional family and religious values. She held training workshops and launched legions of carefully coiffed, well-rehearsed ladies, with STOP-ERA banners and homemade bread, to ask state legislators to oppose ratification or support rescission.[92] Schlafly outmaneuvered and exhausted ERA forces, who had to fight for every ratification and defend against reversals.

Like Catt, Schlafly was an autocrat. There was no coalition and no competition for the spotlight. She directed a national network of state coordinators and volunteers. In a 1988 interview, Schlafly asserted that her role was not easy, complaining that she had no national funding sources and had to manage a difficult alliance among distrusting religious denominations.[93] She outraged and intimidated proponents and reporters with misleading and inaccurate claims: that the ERA was an attack on wives and homemakers, that it would result in rampant abortion, coed bathrooms, same-sex marriage, and the end of alimony and maternal custody of children. Drafting women was the most alarming prospect, given the Vietnam body count. According to Schlafly, women preferred the privilege and protection of their pedestals to liberation. She demolished debate opponents, reducing Friedan to screeching. For years Steinem refused to engage. Betty Ford dismissed the opportunity: "I wouldn't waste my time."[94]

Only Martha Griffiths routed her: "I wish you were a lawyer or elected so you could be held accountable for your falsehoods." That taunt may have prompted Schlafly to enroll in law school at Washington University in 1975, at age fifty-one. While conducting the anti-ERA campaign, lecturing widely, producing a weekly radio program, and writing books, columns, and a monthly newsletter, she graduated in the top third of her class.[95] Insisting that she was "just a housewife," Schlafly began speeches by thanking "my husband Fred for letting me come . . . I like to say that because I know it irritates [the] libbers."[96] Schlafly claimed that motherhood was her primary career, but from the time her first child was still in diapers, she had traveled frequently. She had been liberated by marrying money, employing the same housekeeper for twenty-six years, having her mother live with her, and occasionally boarding her children with her sister in St. Louis.[97]

Schlafly's impact was immediate and immense. Ratification came to a standstill. Rescissions and court challenges mounted. She was no longer a pariah in her party. The 1976 Republican convention was held in Kansas City, Missouri, an unratified state, so the Caucus stayed in Kansas City, Kansas, home of the 1923 Republican sponsors of the ERA. Support for the ERA became a proxy war between incumbent President Ford and his conservative challenger, Ronald Reagan, who were nearly tied in delegates. By an 8–7 vote, Reagan supporters excised the party's historic endorsement of the ERA from a platform subcommittee draft. Ford delegates and feminists, organized by Pam Curtis, Patricia Goldman, and Alice Tetelman of the NWPC's Republican Task Force, fought to restore the language in the full committee. Championed by Mary Louise Smith of Iowa, the first woman to chair the Republican National Committee, Congresswomen Millicent Fenwick (NJ), and Margaret Heckler (MA), the ERA won by four votes, 51–47. Meanwhile, conservatives secured a plank opposing abortion, defeating moderates in a floor fight led by Fenwick.[98]

INTERNATIONAL WOMEN'S YEAR

Responding to STOP-ERA would require discipline, cooperation, and money. In 1975, the commission established by Congress to celebrate International Women's Year (IWY) set up a committee to study the ERA, headed by Representative Heckler and actor Alan Alda. It created a new ERA coalition. Like its predecessors, ERAmerica had a long letterhead of member organizations. It also had a budget, seven paid staff, office space, and an executive committee made up of the principal proponents: the American Association of University Women, American Civil Liberties Union, Business and Professional Women, Coalition of Labor Union Women, League of Women Voters, National Education Association, NOW, National Woman's Party, and the National Women's Political Caucus.

Pressured to present a united front, ERAmerica fractured. The same disputes arose over strategy, finances, partisan politics, past relationships, whether men could participate, who would call the shots, and who would get the credit. Power depended on troops on the ground, cash contributed, media attention, and reputation. NOW brought an ardent national membership of uneven political experience, given to dramatic gestures. The NWP was well endowed but unwilling to share its resources. The Caucus provided bipartisan contacts and an intelligence network. The AAUW, BPW, and the League had national chapters but were not used to partisan scrapping. The NEA housed the operation. Every meeting required a round table; every press conference had multiple microphones. Not much had changed. NOW quit.[99]

ERAmerica was relentlessly bipartisan, with paired co-chairs, beginning with former Democratic Congresswoman Martha Griffiths and attorney Jill Ruckelshaus, known as "the Gloria Steinem of the GOP." LBJ Democrat Liz Carpenter and former Republican Party vice chair Elly Peterson succeeded them. White-haired and good-humored, they joked that grandmothers supported the ERA. Governors' spouses Sharon Percy Rockefeller (D-WV) and Helen Milliken (R-MI) were the final duo. Perhaps most significant was the cooperation of First Ladies Betty Ford and Rosalynn Carter. Schlafly charged ill use of taxpayer dollars and picketed the White House.[100]

Schlafly was indignant about the November 1977 National Women's Conference in Houston, what Steinem called "the most important event nobody knows about."[101] Historian Marjorie Spruill has corrected that omission with a compelling chronicle. The Conference was the culmination of celebrations of the United Nations International Women's Year. President Ford named the original IWY Commission. President Carter expanded it, packing it with Democrats and appointing Bella Abzug presiding officer. His wife and many others objected that Abzug was too partisan and divisive. After three terms in the Congress, she resigned in 1976 to run for the Senate, but lost the primary by less than 2%. Carter had no Office of Women's Affairs, but his Assistant for Public Liaison, Midge Costanza, a former Abzug staffer, persuaded the President that only Abzug's huge ego could control rival feminist factions.[102] Attacks on Abzug as too loud, too brash, too abrasive, too "New York," verged on antisemitism. Jewish women had been in the forefront of social justice advocacy for generations.

The conference opened with a torch carried 2,600 miles, from Seneca Falls to Houston, by a relay of 2,000 runners in turquoise IWY T-shirts. Maya Angelou presented a new Declaration of Sentiments: "We promise to accept nothing less than justice for every woman." The president of the Girls Scouts, who made up the honor guard, called the conference to order with a gavel used by Susan B. Anthony, borrowed from the Smithsonian. With Abzug presiding, Congresswoman Barbara Jordan (D-TX), the first Black woman elected from the South, whose voice resonated from the Watergate hearings, delivered the keynote address. First Ladies Rosalynn Carter, Betty Ford, and Lady Bird Johnson joined hands on stage. Coretta Scott King declared, "We will not be divided or defeated again." The conference adopted twenty-six policy statements, including endorsements of the ERA, abortion, and gay rights.[103]

State conferences elected delegates to participate in the conference. Incensed that the government was underwriting a liberal boondoggle,

Schlafly rallied her troops to run as pro-family, anti-abortion delegates. Outnumbered four to one, her two hundred delegates turned their backs to the podium and bowed their heads in prayer when objectionable planks passed. Schlafly sold STOP-ERA merchandise in the IWY exhibit hall and organized a massive counter-rally at a football field across town. The 15,000 women and men in attendance were overwhelmingly white. Under a huge American flag, speakers included Nellie Grey, a Catholic lawyer who organized the first March for Life, and Texan Lottie Beth Hobbs, who led Women Who Want To Be Women. She asserted that the barriers feminists wanted to remove were really safeguards; removing them would result in "social and moral destruction."[104]

The 1977 Houston meetings boosted morale on both sides. Feminists were energized, ready to recharge the fight for the ERA and advance their agenda. Conservative women were electrified, ready to save the country from Bella, abortion, and lesbians. Over the cheers in both venues, what the nation heard were howls of division. When Abzug presented the conference's "National Plan for Action," Carter was circumspect. He replaced the commission with a National Advisory Committee for Women, with no budget or investigative authority. In an attempt to balance her belligerence, he paired Abzug with Carmen Delgado Votaw of the National Conference of Puerto Rican Women. He added new members, including Unita Blackwell from the Mississippi Freedom Party, Republicans Mary Dent Crisp and Jill Ruckelshaus, and two Democratic rising stars, Dallas County Commissioner Ann Richards and Black California legislator Maxine Waters.[105]

Carter replaced Costanza with Sarah Weddington, the attorney for Jane Roe. He had earlier appointed two Black women firsts, Juanita Kreps as Secretary of Commerce and Eleanor Holmes Norton as chair of the EEOC. Worried about reelection, Carter distanced himself from his IWY Commission and fired Abzug in November 1978. When she was not allowed to resign gracefully, Steinem proposed that the entire commission resign. Twenty-four of forty members did, including Ruckelshaus and cochair Votaw. Richards and Blackwell remained, arguing pragmatically that

women needed a pipeline to the President. Lynda Johnson Robb led the
newly renamed President's Advisory Committee on Women.[106]

ERA EXTENSION AND DEFEAT

For all its political and emotional impact, the Houston conference did not
advance the ERA. When it stalled in 1977, at thirty-five states, proponents
gambled on an untested ploy, an extension of the looming March 1979
deadline. It meant channeling limited resources into federal lobbying rather
than state ratification. Proponents risked losing either way, according to
Sheila Greenwald, executive director of ERAmerica. Plans included an
enormous march in Washington on July 9, 1978, the first anniversary of
Paul's death. On a humid Sunday, forty thousand women and men in suffrage white surged up Constitution Avenue.[107]

In Congress, roles had been recast. Martha Griffiths had returned to
Michigan. Celler's replacement, Elizabeth Holtzman, was not a committee
chair. Retired Senator Ervin made a cameo appearance to castigate the
whole proceeding. Republicans, its original sponsors, were reluctant to support the ERA. On the House Judiciary Committee, only William Cohen
(ME) and Hamilton Fish (NY) voted for extension. The critical vote was
17–16, for a three-year, three-month extension. In the Rules Committee,
only an 8–8 tie saved proponents from a requirement for a two-thirds vote
on any change to the ERA's original language, including the deadline.
The pro side no longer had that many votes in either chamber. The House
passed the extension, 233–189, in August 1978. After defeating amendments that would have legitimized rescission, extension passed the Senate
that December, 60–36.[108]

Schlafly called foul, accusing proponents of moving the goal posts in
the middle of the game. She vowed to lead rescission campaigns in every
ratified state. Seventeen states introduced such bills, but only South
Dakota reversed. Kentucky passed a rescission resolution in 1979, but
Democratic Lieutenant Governor Thelma Stovall vetoed it while the

governor was on vacation.[109] During the thirty-nine-month extension, no state ratified the ERA.

Faced with conservative control of the remaining legislatures, and lacking effective allies in either party, proponents were unable to rescue the ERA. ERAmerica lobbied legislators, defeated opponents and double-crossers, recruited and elected proponents, created state coalitions, and earned support from nuns, men, celebrities, and "Homemakers for the ERA." It raised millions for an advertising blitz. It reiterated that equal rights generally—and the ERA specifically—had majority support from almost everybody, except conservatives and communists, including 61% of lay Catholics.[110] The antis did not budge. In the last six months, delays and setbacks ended in heartbreaking defeats. As the deadline approached, proponents could not get the measure to the floor in critical states. ERA crusaders did not concede until midnight on June 30, 1982.

The cause of death of the ERA was complex. Demographics, geography, state legislative idiosyncrasies, the lack of local troops on the ground, the amendment's association with abortion, and the specter of drafting daughters all contributed. Schlafly's ability to articulate the visceral alarm of social and religious conservatives cannot be underestimated. Enough voters were disconcerted or threatened by changes to women's status to defeat the measure. The wording of the amendment, "based on sex," stirred debate over definitions of sex as biology, gender, or identity.[111] America is still addressing those topics.

The repudiation of the ERA by the Republican Party in 1980 signaled the end of a bipartisan women's movement. Opponents became enemies. The Detroit convention was a rout of ERA proponents, supporters of former President Ford, Republican moderates, and feminists by Reagan Republicans and Schlafly. On the 106-member platform committee, there were sixteen delegates who wanted to preserve support for the ERA in the platform, among them Congresswoman Heckler. By 90 to 9, the words Equal Rights Amendment were excised. They were replaced by a "commitment to [lower case] equal rights and equality for women." Conservatives acknowledged "the legitimate efforts of those who oppose or support ratification." The ERA did not have the twenty-seven signatures needed to bring a minority report to the convention floor. When RNC cochair Mary Dent Crisp of Arizona objected, "We are . . . about to bury the rights of over one hundred million American women under a heap of platitudes," Reagan fired her. Heckler demanded a meeting with Reagan, where she won a concession that he would name a woman to the Supreme Court.[112]

Defeating the ERA was a ploy to attract "family values" voters to the nominee. It symbolized support for a broad conservative agenda, an extension of a "Southern strategy." It attracted Southern Democrats and the religious right to the Republican Party. Schlafly was the convention's prom queen. She had decided not to challenge Senator Charles Percy (R-IL) in 1978. Instead, she set her sights on becoming Reagan's Secretary of Defense, only to be disappointed. She remained a polemicist, writing twenty-seven books on topics ranging from foreign affairs to phonics. She lectured widely, remaining outrageously quotable. "The solution to unwanted pregnancy is a shotgun marriage." "Sex education classes are like in-home sales parties for abortions." "A woman who keeps her marital vows cannot be raped." "Sexual harassment on the job is not a problem for a virtuous woman," she told a Senate Labor Committee hearing in 1981.[113]

The Eagle Forum absorbed STOP-ERA. In March 2016, when Schlafly endorsed Donald Trump, six of the eleven-member Forum board, including her daughter Ann, demanded her removal. They supported Ted Cruz. Schlafly countersued. The case was still being litigated when she died that September, at ninety-two. Her last book, *The Conservative Case for Trump*, was published the next day. Candidate and Mrs. Trump attended her funeral.[114] For fifty years, Schlafly had been an ardent anti-communist and a fierce anti-feminist. A 2020 Hulu series, *Mrs. America*, starring Cate Blanchett, dramatized her anti-ERA fight.

RUTH BADER GINSBURG AND THE SUPREME COURT

While the ERA was winning and losing, feminists fought other battles. Some shifted the fight to the courts, relying on Title VII and the

Fourteenth Amendment to advance women's rights. In 1972, the ACLU chose Ruth Bader Ginsburg and Brenda Feigen to lead a new initiative, the Women's Rights Project. Founded in 1920 by social justice activists, the ACLU played a role in the Scopes, Sacco and Vanzetti, and Scottsboro trials. Because of its progressive roots, the ACLU opposed the ERA until 1970, when its board endorsed the amendment, 52–1. In the 1960s, two board members, Pauli Murray and Dorothy Kenyon, the first woman to graduate from New York University law school, urged the ACLU to address sex discrimination, beginning with jury service. Most states did not require or allow women to serve on juries.[115]

In 1957, Gwendolyn Hoyt killed her emotionally abusive husband with a baseball bat and was convicted of second-degree murder. Florida forbade women to serve on juries until 1949, when the first woman elected to its legislature introduced an equal jury service bill. Opponents did not want "their wives and sisters exposed to the embarrassment of hearing filthy evidence." The compromise was that women could signal their willingness to serve by registering at a courthouse. Only 218 Tampa area women had registered; none was empaneled for Hoyt's trial. When *Hoyt v. Florida* (1961) reached the Supreme Court, Kenyon wrote the ACLU's amicus brief, arguing that Hoyt had not been tried by a jury of her peers. The Court was not persuaded and ruled unanimously that Florida could offer "the privilege of exemption," because "woman is the center of home and family life."[116]

In the 1960s, after white male juries in Alabama acquitted the alleged murderers of civil rights workers Viola Liuzzo and Jonathan Daniels, the ACLU and the Justice Department brought a class action suit to challenge racist customs and sexist statutes barring Black and women jurors. In *White v. Crook* (1966), Kenyon and Murray won the case before the US Court of Appeals for the Fifth Circuit. Striking down the arbitrary exclusion of women from jury pools, it was the first time that a federal court held that women were protected by the equal protection clause. In 1970, Kenyon, eighty-two, linked arms with Betty Friedan at the Women's Strike and Ruth Bader Ginsburg, thirty-seven, joined the ACLU.[117]

Ginsburg, petite, brainy, and quietly intense, ranked second in her class at Cornell. One of nine women in her Harvard class of 552, she served on the law review there and at Columbia, from which she graduated in 1959, tied for valedictorian. As a woman, a Jew, and a mother, she could not find a job with a New York City firm, so she taught law at Rutgers University. Responding to pressure to hire women, Columbia University made Ginsburg its first female, tenured, full professor in 1972 and converted a men's bathroom, leaving the urinals in place. In 1967, the top twenty-five national law firms had no women partners and only a dozen women taught at any law school. At the ACLU, Ginsburg brought six cases to the Supreme Court, argued four, and won five.[118]

Reed v. Reed (1971) was her first victory. After their adopted son died by suicide, Cecil and Sally Reed, divorced parents, separately sought to administer his modest estate. Cecil said Sally was "too dumb" for the task. Idaho law gave a preference to men, admitting discrimination but arguing administrative convenience. On appeal, the ACLU offered to assist Sally, as an opportunity to educate the Supreme Court about commonplace sex discrimination. Ginsburg's goal was to subject sex discrimination to "strict scrutiny," a standard established in *Korematsu* and *Brown*. It would require courts to examine cases of sex discrimination carefully, "to ensure that lawmakers had not relied on outdated stereotypes and assumptions" about women's subordinate legal status.[119]

Sally Reed insisted that her original attorney argue the case, despite his inexperience. Observers agreed his was the worst possible oral argument, but Ginsburg's brief was brilliant. The Court voted unanimously that there was no reasonable basis to bar women from estate administration. For the first time, the Supreme Court held that a sex-based classification was a violation of the equal protection clause of the Fourteenth Amendment. To acknowledge "those brave women," Ginsburg added Kenyon and Murray's names to her brief.[120]

One of Ginsburg's strategies was to defend men who were discriminated against on account of sex. In *Frontiero v. Richardson* (1973), she convinced the Court to overturn a military policy that provided housing allowances and medical benefits for the wives of officers, but not for the husbands of officers. In an 8–1 decision, Air Force Lieutenant Sharon Frontiero won her suit against Secretary of Defense Elliot Richardson. Justice Brennan challenged the "romantic paternalism which . . . put women not on a pedestal but in a cage." He could not persuade his colleagues to adopt strict scrutiny, to address "America's long and unfortunate history of sex discrimination." *Frontiero* was the first case Ginsburg argued before the Court.[121]

In *Taylor v. Louisiana* (1975), a male jury convicted Billy Taylor of kidnapping, rape, and robbery. Given the death penalty, he claimed his trial had been unfair. The ACLU took the case as an opportunity to overturn *Hoyt* and other states' exclusions of women from juries. Ginsburg quoted an earlier federal precedent: "the two sexes are not fungible; . . . the absence of either may make the jury even less representative of the community." She pointed out that the rationale for protecting homemakers and mothers excluded working and childless women but not single fathers. The Court held, 8–1, that Taylor's rights had been violated. The case was remanded to Louisiana for reconsideration.[122]

After Stephen Wiesenfeld's wife died in childbirth, he sued the Secretary of Health, Education, and Welfare to extend Social Security survivor benefits to widowers. In *Weinberger v. Wiesenfeld* (1975), Ginsburg contended that his dead wife was being discriminated against, since her Social Security contributions as a teacher were not being treated the same as those of salaried men. The Court voted, 8–0, without Justice Douglas, that a section of the Social Security Act was unconstitutional and violated the due process clause of the Fifth Amendment. The decision challenged the traditional male breadwinner/female homemaker model: "such a gender-based generalization cannot suffice to justify the denigration of the efforts of women who work and whose earnings contribute significantly to the families' support," wrote Justice Brennan. Ginsburg remained close to Wiesenfeld and his son, officiating at both their weddings.[123]

The "frat brothers case," *Craig v. Boren* (1976), was about beer. Curtis Craig sued Oklahoma's governor because he could not buy beer until he was twenty-one, whereas women could purchase it at age eighteen. Ginsburg submitted an amicus brief and was present at the counsel table. The Supreme Court decided, 7–2, that the gender classification was unconstitutional because the research on which the law was based was insufficient. The decision instituted a new standard of "intermediate scrutiny," applied to discrimination on the basis of gender, marital, or parental status, whereas strict scrutiny was restricted to the "suspect classes" of race, national origin, or religion.[124]

Like Kenyon and Murray, Ginsburg linked racism and sexism long before it was called intersectionality. Like Thurgood Marshall, she believed in minimalism and incremental progress. In 1980, in the waning months of his administration, President Carter appointed Ginsburg to the US Court of Appeals for the DC Circuit, after passing over her three times. The first woman he appointed to that court was Patricia Wald, another pioneer for women's rights. The DC Circuit was considered the second most powerful court in the country and the most liberal, until Ronald Reagan appointed Robert Bork, Kenneth Starr, and Antonin Scalia.[125]

"YOU'VE COME A LONG WAY, BABY"

Beginning in 1969, Ivy League universities admitted women or incorporated their sister colleges: Princeton (1969), Yale (1969), Brown (Pembroke, 1971), Dartmouth (1972), and Harvard (Radcliffe, 1977). In 1970, Laura X, who like Malcolm X would not use "her owner's name," established the Women's History Research Center to collect archival materials and establish women's history as an academic field. She is credited with coining the term "herstory," launching Women's History Month, and defining marital and date rape a crime.[126] In 1972, Juanita Kreps was the first female director of the New York Stock Exchange and two women joined the FBI, the first since three had been agents in the 1920s. Congress had its first female page in 1973. Women joined the corps of cadets at West Point in 1976 and twenty-four female Rhodes Scholars, thirteen from the US, arrived in Oxford in 1977. Rosalyn Sussman Yalow, a medical physicist, won a

Nobel Prize in Medicine in 1977. The San Francisco Museum of Modern Art installed Judy Chicago's "Dinner Party" in 1979. Her triangular table held thirty-nine multi-media place settings, each honoring a mythological or historical woman.[127]

Representative of the transformations individual women were undergoing was Katharine Graham, who made history in 1972 as the first woman to run a Fortune 500 company. After her husband died by suicide, she inherited the *Washington Post*, which her father had owned. Raised to be an ornament rather than an executive, the publisher and the mother of four overcame her shyness to help end the Vietnam War and bring down President Nixon. Dismayed by the disrespectful manners of some feminists, she nonetheless provided seed money for *Ms.* magazine.[128] In 1974, ABC journalist Ann Compton was the first woman assigned to cover the White House for network news. Cokie Roberts, Nina Totenberg, Linda Wertheimer, and Susan Stamberg became the founding mothers of National Public Radio in 1978. Phyllis George, a former Miss America, joined CBS Sports as a commentator. June Bacon-Bercey, an African American and the first scientifically trained TV meteorologist, as opposed to a "weather girl," broadcast from NBC's Buffalo affiliate in 1972. Beginning in 1978, hurricanes were named for men as well as women.[129]

In 1976, after decades of debate, Hebrew Union College ordained Sally Priesand, the first American woman reform rabbi and the second in Judaism. Conservative and orthodox Jews moved more slowly. The fifty women rabbis trained by 1982 had difficulty finding congregations. The first female Episcopal priest was ordained in 1976, although Alison Cheek, one of the "Philadelphia 11," defied church authority by celebrating the Eucharist in 1974. Pauli Murray, the civil rights icon, lawyer, professor, poet, and closeted lesbian, was ordained the first Black woman Episcopal priest in 1977, at age sixty-six. The descendant of enslaved people and friend of Eleanor Roosevelt, with degrees from Hunter, Howard, Yale, Berkeley, and the General Theological Seminary, Murray "was like a pixie, petite and energetic . . . afraid of nothing." When there was a vacancy on the Supreme Court, she submitted her resume. In 2012, Murray was sainted. The first female Episcopal bishop was Barbara Harris, a Black public relations executive who had marched for civil rights before a midlife calling to the ministry.[130]

Few of those women had the first name fame of Betty, Bella, Gloria, and Phyllis. However, the most popular woman in America was Farrah Fawcett, the golden-haired television star of *Charlie's Angels*. She appeared only in its first season, 1976–77, but a poster of her in a red tank suit sold twenty million copies. Television created many iconic leading women. Beginning in 1966, Nichelle Nichols played Nyota Uhura in the *Star Trek* series; she used her role to lobby NASA to hire female and Black astronauts. Diahann Carroll was the first Black woman to have a leading role on television, as *Julia* (1968-71), a nurse whose husband had been killed in Vietnam. Cicely Tyson played award-winning roles in *The Autobiography of Miss Jane Pittman* (1974) and in Alex Haley's *Roots* (1977), a twelve-hour mini-series watched by 130 million people. Carol Burnett was the first woman to host a variety show (1967–78). Mary Tyler Moore portrayed a spunky, single newswoman (1970–77). Lynda Carter was Wonder Woman (1976–79) and Jean Stapleton's Edith Bunker represented put upon wives in *All in the Family* (1971–79).[131]

In 1978, Melissa Rich, a nine-year-old baseball card collector, asked why there weren't any pictures of girls. Her mom agreed that women needed their own cards. With grant funding, they wrote five hundred prominent women, asking for photographs, biographical facts, and quotations, for a set of "Supersister" trading cards. Helen Hayes, Margaret Mead, Rosa Parks, Margaret Chase Smith, and Gloria Steinem responded. So did *Today* host Jane Pauley, songwriter Helen Reddy, puppeteer Shari Lewis, Rabbi Priesand, playwright Ntozake Shange, poet Maxine Kumin, skier Suzy "Chapstick" Chaffee, and flutist Doriot Anthony Dwyer, the great-grandniece of Susan B. Anthony. NOW president Ellie Smeal asked that her age not be listed. There were nineteen athletes, including Katherine Switzer, the first woman to compete in the Boston Marathon in 1967, and surfer Laura Lee Ching. The second set of seventy-two cards was equally inclusive and impressive. The cards came with a teacher's guide, suggesting that the Supersisters be used to increase awareness of women's contributions to society, counteract sex role stereotyping, and introduce career alternatives. The sets became collectors' items. One is safeguarded by the Metropolitan Museum of Art.[132]

The women's movement had enormous impact, positive and negative, on individual women, marriages, families, and American society. State governments, including those that had not ratified the ERA, passed laws to eliminate discriminatory statutes and practices. The Supreme Court expanded access to birth control, made abortion a constitutional right, and barred discrimination based on sex in other fields. Higher numbers of women were working, mostly still in sex-segregated jobs that paid less than those held by white and Black men with less education. Marital status created another division. Married women had safety nets that single women lacked. But as divorce rates and life expectancy rose, mothers could live forty years without children at home, and possibly without husbands.[133] Many women were finding liberation more challenging than empowering.

"You've Come a Long Way, Baby," the tagline of a cigarette advertising campaign, became a Seventies catchphrase. Long before its health risks were identified, smoking was deemed inappropriate behavior for women, especially in public. In 1967, the Federal Trade Commission recommended that the warning label on cigarettes, first required in 1965, be specific: "Warning: Cigarette Smoking Is Dangerous to Health and May Cause Death from Cancer and Other Diseases."[134] Concerned about losing market share, Philip Morris designed a cigarette especially for women. Virginia Slims were long, slender, and came in a gold-trimmed box.

A series of print and TV ads juxtaposed images of oppressed and liberated women. Sepia-toned photographs of women, wearing cumbersome corsets and dresses, secretly smoking while feeding livestock or hanging laundry, were paired with color shots of chic modern women smoking in public. Placed in women's magazines, frequently opposite ads for Pyrex casserole dishes or laundry detergent, the award-winning Virginia Slims ads signaled empowerment. They were applauded for acknowledging the women's movement and attacked for using the sexist diminutive "Baby."[135]

In 1984, the American Federation of State, County and Municipal Employees (AFSCME) sent thousands of its members a pamphlet with a red cover, depicting two nineteenth-century women, titled *You've Come a Long Way—Maybe*. Its contents emphasized the grim reality of women in the workforce. Despite the growing visibility of women in professional fields, 80% were confined to 5% of the country's low-wage jobs. The percentage of families in poverty was rising. AFSCME's goal was "equal pay for work of comparable value." The glossy pamphlet taught women how to investigate pay discrimination in their jobs.[136] In the 1980s, women would struggle for more than abstract equal rights. Women may have "come a long way," but how far, and which women, was still to be determined.

CHAPTER SEVEN

FACTIONS & FIRSTS, 1980–1992

T he transition from the modest manners of the Carter years to the glitz of the Reagan era was swift. The President-elect and his glamorous wife swept into Washington in a swirl of fur and flashbulbs, like a movie premiere. These old Hollywood stars would symbolize the optimism and excesses of the 1980s. Fashion featured *Dynasty*'s sequined shoulder pads, *Wall Street*'s suspenders, Madonna's lingerie, and Jane Fonda's leg warmers.[1] Sandra Day O'Connor rose to the Supreme Court and Sally Ride rocketed into space. On television, African American talk show host Oprah Winfrey became a first name phenomenon and fictional journalist Murphy Brown represented white working women and single mothers.

In 1980, the former Republican governor of California won forty-four states and 50.7% of the vote. His victory confirmed a realignment of the major parties into ideological camps. Republicans now included white, rural, evangelical, blue-collar, and conservative voters in the South and Southwest, many of whom had been the core of the New Deal coalition and Southern resistance to integration. Democrats appealed to liberals, people of color, working women, feminists, big cities, and both coasts. Parties no longer encompassed liberal, moderate, and conservative wings, and rarely both urban and rural constituents.

Conservative women, angry over the ERA and abortion, energized Republican politics. To distance themselves from the far-right extremism of white supremacists, the Klan, and the John Birch Society, they claimed to be the "New Right" and moved social issues to center stage. Phyllis Schlafly, the National Right to Life Committee, and evangelical ministers Jerry Falwell and Pat Robertson formed the Religious Round Table and the "Moral Majority." Because Reagan supported "family values," this unholy alliance overlooked his divorce. Litmus test issues were abortion, busing, "gays and guns," which became a campaign slogan. To counter the bias of the liberal media, conservatives used telemarketing, direct mail, radio, and cable networks "to segment the electorate and Balkanize the public."[2]

THE GENDER GAP AND GERALDINE FERRARO

In every presidential election since 1964, women turned out in larger numbers than men, based on proportions of eligible voters, but 1980 marked a significant "gender gap" between male and female party preferences. The term defines the difference between the percentage of women and men voting for a party or a candidate. The data lumped all women together. "Women," observed the *New York Times*, "whose political attitudes used to be barely distinguishable from those of men, are beginning to take positions . . . that differ sharply."[3] Both sexes favored Reagan in 1980, but women split narrowly, 47% voting Republican, 46% Democratic, while men voted Republican 55% to 36%. During the Reagan-Bush years, women continued to favor Republicans, but more men than women voted for Reagan and his successor. Similarly, polling did not separate the votes of Black men and women, but 86% of rural and urban African Americans voted overwhelmingly for Carter in 1980.[4]

Dotty Lynch, one of the few female pollsters and the first woman to be chief pollster for a presidential campaign, could not convince the

Democratic National Committee that the gender gap was real and that the party should appeal differently to women voters. She identified a wide disparity between men and women over foreign affairs, the economy, and social issues. Old school operatives assumed women voted like their fathers and husbands. The DNC fired Lynch. After she died, it issued a resolution honoring her as "one of the first pollsters to realize the importance of the women's vote to the Democratic Party."[5] Democrats would eventually appeal specifically to younger, college-educated, employed, and liberal women.

After the ERA failed in June 1982, its proponents were exhausted; they were not ready to try again. The amendment would never again have the bipartisan leadership or support to secure two-thirds of the Congress and three-quarters of the states. As one insider concluded, "We'll get the ERA when we no longer need it."[6] Yet, to woo women to the party, Democratic House Speaker Tip O'Neill (MA) and Judiciary Chairman Peter Rodino (NJ) made the amendment a legislative priority in January 1983.

In 1984, Democrats made history by nominating a woman for vice president. With no Democratic women governors or senators, contenders included Representative Patricia Schroeder of Colorado, former Texas Congresswoman Barbara Jordan, and San Francisco Mayor Dianne Feinstein. Three-term New York Congresswoman Geraldine Ferraro, an Italian American, former grade-school teacher and assistant district attorney, mother of three, and pro-choice Catholic, fit the bill. Delegations flew to Minnesota to lobby the presumptive nominee, Senator Walter Mondale. NOW threatened a floor fight if he did not act. Speaker O'Neill endorsed Ferraro, Gloria Steinem added her imprimatur, and the UAW's Millie Jeffrey acted as her political godmother. Wearing suffrage white and described as a bride, Ferraro accepted the nomination. "By choosing [a woman] to run for our nation's second highest office," Ferraro declared, "you send a powerful message to all Americans. There are no doors we cannot unlock . . . If we can do this, we can do anything."[7]

A torrent of applause, cheers, laughter, and tears filled the San Francisco coliseum. It was so unusual to have a dual gender ticket that advisors were unsure about how the running mates should interact. Even the term "mate" was suspect. They were told not to hold hands. They wanted to be seen as peers, a "TV anchor team, not a suburban couple," although Ferraro was posed carrying laundry detergent. Ferraro's nomination unleashed a burst of energy and enthusiasm. On the campaign trail, crowds were huge; parents brought their daughters. Due to the "Ferraro factor," the Democratic ticket surged eighteen points, to within two points of Reagan, but the bump didn't last. Questions about her husband's finances weakened Ferraro's candidacy, but political reality made it all but impossible for Democrats to win. Reagan was an immensely popular incumbent, the country was at peace, inflation and interest rates were down, and the economy was up. In a landslide, the President carried all but Minnesota and Washington, DC. Women again favored Reagan, with 58% of the vote, compared to 42% for Mondale, a sixteen-point difference; 91% of African Americans and 66% of Hispanics voted Democratic.[8]

1984 also marked the second time a Black candidate had mounted a presidential campaign. Jesse Jackson, a Baptist minister and civil rights leader, had been the quarterback and student body president at North Carolina A&T College before earning a divinity degree. He participated in sit-ins, joined Dr. King in the SCLC, and was present in Memphis when King was murdered. Headquartered in Chicago, Jackson led Operation Breadbasket, SCLC's economic arm, and founded the Rainbow Coalition. He paired his campaigns with voter registration drives to increase the Black vote. In 1984, he won five primaries and 18% of votes cast before the convention. In 1988, he won eleven primaries, 20% of primary votes, and more delegates than Senators Joe Biden, Dick Gephardt, or Al Gore, coming in second to the eventual nominee.[9]

Ferraro was not the first woman vice presidential nominee. In 1884, Belva Lockwood chose Californian Marietta Stow as her running mate on the Equal Rights Party ticket and Black publisher Charlotta Bass ran on the Progressive ticket in 1952.[10] In her autobiography, Ferraro admitted being surprised by "the fury, . . . bigotry and . . . sexism" she encountered. She never won another election, losing Senate primaries in 1992 and 1998, but her 1984 candidacy inspired other Democratic women to run for office.[11] For a decade, the National Women's Political Caucus, the Women's Education Fund, and the Women's Campaign Fund had recruited, trained, and funded women candidates from both parties. As partisan politics divided women in the 1980s, the GOP nominated fewer women and feminists supported fewer Republicans.

EMILY'S LIST

When Reagan was inaugurated in 1981, there were two women Senators, Republicans Nancy Kassebaum (KS) and Paula Hawkins (FL), and twenty-one women Representatives (11D, 10R). Three were women of color: Shirley Chisholm (D-NY), Cardiss Collins (D-IL), and Mary Rose Oakar (D-OH).[12] Electing a Democratic woman to the Senate was the goal of a small band of astute women operatives, including Marie Bass, Betsy Crone, and Joanne Howes, all Caucus veterans. They knew how hard it was to raise money for or from women. Not many women earned enough to make large, independent, discretionary contributions to political or charitable causes. It was the difference between back rooms and bake sales. Emily's List would change that. EMILY was an acronym: "Early Money Is Like Yeast (it raises the dough)," feminist word play and a throwback to the suffragists' political housekeeping.

Funding initially came from Ellen Malcolm, whose great-grandfather founded IBM. She had grown up in New Jersey and graduated from Hollins College in 1969, before coming to Washington to work at Common Cause and the Caucus. Acting anonymously, she sent four- and five-figure checks to causes and candidates she cared about. Eventually Malcolm shared her secret with Lael Stegall, a former Peace Corps volunteer and Caucus activist. They founded the Windom Fund, hanging a portrait of its fictional founder, Henrietta Windom, claiming she had invented Tampax. Stegall was executive director and Malcolm the silent CEO and anonymous donor. From 1980 to 1985, while earning an MBA, the progressive fairy godmother funneled more than $1 million toward women's issues and voter registration.[13]

In 1982, Malcolm decided to back the Senate candidacy of Harriet Woods to become the first female Democratic Senator who was not a politician's widow. Woods was a pro-choice Missouri state senator with a background in journalism. She defeated ten primary opponents to challenge the well-regarded Republican incumbent, Jack Danforth. Politicians and journalists wrote her off until money raised by Malcolm began to pour in. "Give 'Em Hell Harriet" could finally afford TV advertising. Earning newspaper endorsements and rising in the polls, by mid-October she was tied with Danforth at 47%. Then she ran out of money. Convinced a woman could not win, the Democratic National Committee refused to help. Woods lost by 26,200 votes out of 1.5 million cast. The only other woman running for Senate that year, pro-choice Congresswoman Millicent Fenwick (R-NJ), also lost.[14]

In 1984, seventeen Democratic women, including four Senate candidates, challenged congressional incumbents. Even with Ferraro on the ticket, only one won. In Missouri Harriet Woods was elected lieutenant governor, the only Democrat and the first woman to win statewide.[15] Malcolm sought counsel from Judith Lichtman of the Women's Legal Defense Fund and registered Emily's List as a political action committee. PACs like the Women's Campaign Fund were limited to giving $5,000 per candidate per election cycle. To raise unlimited amounts of money for pro-choice Democrats, Emily would operate as a donor network, "bundling" contributions, an innovative fundraising model. Donors solicited by direct mail became members of Emily's List and committed to giving $100 to recommended candidates. The goal was to raise $100,000 for each endorsed candidate.[16]

In 1986, Malcolm's attention returned to Harriet Woods and another Senate challenger, Barbara Mikulski. The daughter of a Polish grocer, Mikulski was a Catholic community organizer and social worker in Baltimore. She joked she didn't become a nun because she couldn't vow obedience: "Inside me beats the heart of a protestor." She gained national attention in 1970, declaring at a Catholic University conference that ethnic, working-class Americans, "forgotten and forlorn," were overlooked by elites and branded as racists. America was not a melting pot, she declared, but "a sizzling cauldron." Mikulski won a seat on the Baltimore City Council in 1971. At four feet, eleven inches she was a feisty, tough-talking populist.[17]

Mikulski first ran for the Senate in 1974, challenging Charles Mathias, a popular, progressive Republican incumbent, who won. It was the only election she ever lost. In 1976, she won a seven-way primary for an open House seat and easily won the general election. She served five terms. When Mathias announced his retirement in 1986, she ran against a sitting governor and an admired congressman in the primary. Leading in the polls, Mikulski fell behind in fundraising. Emily's organizers appealed to everyone in their rolodexes. By the March reporting deadline, Emily's members had given $60,000. Contributions to Mikulski totaled over $300,000, outdistancing her opponents. She won the primary and sailed to victory in the general, with 61% of the vote. Her opponent was Linda Chavez, Reagan's Assistant for Public Liaison. It was the second time two women had competed in a Senate race; a woman challenged Margaret Chase Smith in 1960. Chavez called Mikulski a "fascist feminist" and implied that she was a man-hating lesbian. "That would be a real shock to my dad, my nephews and the guys at Bethlehem Steel," responded Mikulski.[18]

As lieutenant governor, Woods did not have a primary challenge in 1986. Given her narrow loss in 1982, Republicans did not underestimate her. Her opponent for the open seat was former governor Kit Bond. Both were appealing candidates. Woods raised almost as much money as Bond, but one of her campaign ads, featuring a farmer in tears, backfired. Woods fell in the polls and lost, with 47% of the vote. She remained lieutenant governor until 1989 and then served as head of the NWPC.[19]

WOMEN IN OFFICE

The *Washington Post* predicted Mikulski would be another Bella Abzug, a "brassy, bomb-throwing feminist." Instead she became "one of the boys," effective and funny.[20] By her retirement in 2017, Senator Mikulski, eighty, was the longest-serving woman member of Congress, at forty years, counting her ten years in the House and thirty in the Senate, exceeding Margaret Chase Smith's thirty-three years. Yet progress for elected women still lagged. Between 1973 and 1986, Republican women in the House increased from two to eleven members; Democratic women dropped from fourteen to twelve. In 1987, those twenty-three women made up 4.9% of House membership. Women were 15.6% of state legislators. No Democratic woman ran for Senate in 1988 and two Republican women lost. The House gained six women for a total of twenty-nine (16D, 13R), bringing the House and Senate total to thirty-one. Cardiss Collins (D-IL), Mary Rose Oakar (D-OH), Patricia Fukuda Saiki (R-HI), and Ileana Ros-Lehtinen (R-FL) were the only women of color.[21]

Emily's criteria included viability, which eliminated many candidates of color. It sought candidates for open seats in Democratic-leaning districts. In 1988, its third election cycle, Emily raised almost one million dollars and reversed the decline of Democratic women in the House by supporting Nita Lowey (NY) and Jolene Unsoeld (WA). Among other winners was a short-term incumbent from San Francisco, who had won a special election in April 1987, following the death of Sala Burton. Burton handpicked Nancy Pelosi, forty-seven, the mother of five and chair of the California Democratic Party, a rare leadership role for a woman. She was smart, chic, wealthy, and connected. Her father, Tommy D'Alesandro, had served four terms in Congress and twelve years as mayor of Baltimore, a post her brother also held. They were all tough, shrewd, "devoutly Catholic, deeply patriotic [and] staunchly Democratic."[22]

Malcolm understood that to elect more women to Congress, Emily would need to develop a state-level pipeline. She was not the only person impressed by two-term Texas treasurer Ann Richards, the first woman elected statewide since Sissy Farenthold. "Silver-haired and silver-tongued," Richards was acerbic and attractive. When Democrats featured her during prime time at their 1988 convention, she dazzled. She compared women in politics to Ginger Rogers and Fred Astaire: "She had to do everything he did, backwards and in high heels." She disparaged Republican candidate George H. W. Bush: "He was born with a silver foot in his mouth." Democrats nominated Massachusetts Governor Michael Dukakis and Texas Senator Lloyd Bentsen. Their campaign was the first managed by a woman, Susan Estrich, a Harvard law professor and the first woman elected editor-in-chief of the *Harvard Law Review,* in 1976. The ticket lost by eight points.[23]

In 1990, Richards, a divorced single mother, charismatic grandmother, and recovering alcoholic, won the Texas governor's race. She defeated the incumbent in the Democratic primary and beat the attorney general in a run-off. Emily's List had been her single largest contributor, with $200,000, but she emerged from the primary battered, broke, and behind by twenty-six points. Despite being outspent two-to-one in the general, Richards won, with a coalition of female, Hispanic, and Black voters.[24] In 1994, she lost her reelection bid to George W. Bush, whom she called "Shrub." Before she died in 2006, she declared, "I do not want my tombstone to read, 'She kept a really clean house.' [I'd prefer,] 'She opened government to everyone.'"[25] That year Cecile Richards, one of her four surviving children, took over Planned Parenthood.

Before 1980, there had been five women governors, all Democrats. The first three succeeded husbands: Nellie Ross (WY) and Ma Ferguson (TX) in the 1920s, and Lurleen Wallace (AL) in 1967. Ella Grasso (CT) was the first elected in her own right, in 1974, followed by Dixie Lee Ray (D-WA) in 1976. Four more served in the 1980s: Martha Collins (D-KY), Madeline Kunin (D-VT), Rose Mofford (D-AZ), and Kay Orr (NE), the first Republican. Two more Democrats won in 1990: Joan Finney (KS), who opposed abortion, and Barbara Roberts (OR). Dianne Feinstein (D-CA) and Evelyn Murphy (D-MA) lost. Few Black women have run for governor and none has yet won. Every female gubernatorial candidate was subjected to rumors about extramarital affairs, divorces, drinking, drug use, or homosexuality.[26] Polling indicated that voters did not like ambitious women and were less likely to support a woman who tried to advance from a legislative to an executive role.[27]

SANDRA DAY O'CONNOR

President Reagan's claim to have appointed more women to high-ranking positions than Carter was disputed because many were not in full-time, policy-making posts. The exceptions were United Nations Ambassador Jeanne Kirkpatrick and Secretary of Transportation Elizabeth Dole, both outstanding firsts. Out of Reagan's sixty-five initial federal judicial appointments, only three were women; one was historic.[28] In July 1981, President Reagan kept a campaign promise and appointed a woman to the Supreme Court. Sandra Day O'Connor had grown up on a ranch. She graduated at the top of her Stanford law school class, served as the first female majority leader of a state senate, and was a judge on the Arizona Court of Appeals. She was fifty-one, married, and the mother of three sons.[29] Overruling his Justice Department's recommendation of Robert Bork, Reagan did not ask her about *Roe*.

More press credentials were issued for her confirmation hearings, the first to be broadcast live, than during Watergate. O'Connor's photograph was on every magazine cover. The outcome, reported the *New York Times*, was "such a foregone conclusion that the Senate chamber was nearly deserted" for the debate, which ended with a 99–0 vote.[30] Three days later, Chief Justice Burger escorted Justice O'Connor down the steps of the Supreme Court to face a scrum of photographers, proclaiming, "You've never seen me with a better-looking Justice!"[31] In order to present a dignified image, O'Connor ignored such remarks. "Sandy" became Sandra.

The new Justice was more popular with the press than with her Court brethren. Even William Rehnquist, her law school classmate and former beau, who had privately lobbied for her appointment, kept his distance. Neither disclosed that she had refused his marriage proposal, instead marrying John O'Connor, another classmate.[32] The Court voted to change their titles, from Mr. Justice to Justice, but installed no convenient women's restroom. On the first Monday in October, her inaugural appearance on the bench, a lawyer talked over her question. "I feel put down," she wrote in her journal. Smart and tough, O'Connor was on her own at the Court, although she and John cut a social swath on dance floors and tennis courts. "She will make a large place for herself on the Washington scene," Justice Powell predicted.[33]

Presidents since FDR had been lobbied to appoint a woman to the Court. Nixon put California Judge Mildred Lillie on his short list, but the American Bar Association deemed her "unqualified."[34] In 1979, nine hundred constitutional lawyers endorsed Shirley Hufstedler. As senior judge on the US Court of Appeals for the Ninth Circuit, she was the highest-ranking woman in the federal judiciary, but Carter was the only twentieth-century president with no Supreme Court vacancies to fill. Instead, he named Hufstedler Secretary of the new Department of Education.[35] Historically, the law had been a male domain. Law schools barred women or imposed quotas. A few women studied law independently in states that required only residency and white skin.

The first woman to argue a case before the Supreme Court was Belva Lockwood in 1880. It took five years to persuade Congress to admit women to the Supreme Court bar. A widow, single mother, suffragist, and schoolteacher, Lockwood attended Columbian law school, now George Washington University. It admitted women, although recitations were sex-segregated and degrees were withheld because male students refused to appear with women at graduation. Without a diploma, Lockwood could not join the DC bar, so she appealed to President Grant. Two weeks later, she had her diploma, becoming the second woman licensed to practice law in DC. When Virginia refused to let her practice, she sued. The Supreme Court denied her appeal and determined, *In re Lockwood* (1894), that states could exclude women from those defined as "persons" under the law.[36]

The first woman to earn a law degree was African American Charlotte Ray, in 1872. Confronted by racism and sexism, the Howard University graduate abandoned her profession. Constance Baker Motley was the first Black woman to argue before the Supreme Court. She won nine of her ten cases; the tenth was eventually overturned. Her work desegrated Memphis restaurants, Alabama lunch counters, transportation, and Southern universities. She was serving as the first Black woman in the New York state senate when President Johnson appointed her to be the first Black female federal judge in 1966. Senate Judiciary chairman James Eastland (D-MS) called her a communist and held up her confirmation for seven months. On the bench she ruled that women reporters could enter the Yankees's locker room.[37]

The first Indigenous woman to argue before the Supreme Court was Lyda Burton Conley, who demanded that the United States honor a tribal treaty in 1910.[38] During World War II, Justice William Douglas hired the first female clerk, Lucile Lomen. The second was appointed in 1966. The number increased modestly until O'Connor's appointment. Justice Brett Kavanaugh employed only female clerks in his first term but did not continue that practice. The percentage of clerks of color remains low; of clerks appointed between 2005–2017, 85% were white. In the court term that ended in June 2020, only 13% of arguments had been presented by women. In the last decade, the average ranged from 12% to 15%.[39]

SALLY RIDE

Another barrier was broken in June 1983, when astronaut Sally Ride spent six days in space aboard the *Challenger*. The first corps of American astronauts had been military test pilots, who symbolized a masculine mystique. At that time, thirteen women pilots had qualified independently. The youngest was Wally Funk. In 2021, at age eighty-two, she accompanied Amazon's Jeff Bezos on an eleven-minute private space flight.[40] Geraldyn "Jerrie" Cobb, twenty-eight, passed seventy-five qualifying tests in 1959. NASA's refusal to accept any women led to congressional hearings in 1963. "We women pilots . . . are not trying to join a battle of the sexes," Cobb testified. "We [want] a place in our nation's space future without discrimination." John Glenn testified the next day. "Men go off and fight the wars and fly the airplanes and come back and help design and build and test them. The fact that women are not in this field is a fact of our social order," he declared, ignoring the role of women pilots in World War II.[41] That view prevailed despite specialists in aerospace medicine, who testified that women would make excellent astronauts. "They generally weighed less than men and were shorter, so they would need less oxygen and less food and water . . . they were more resistant to radiation, less prone to heart attacks and better suited to handling pain, heat, cold and loneliness."[42]

After a 1972 amendment to the Civil Rights Act prevented discrimination by federal agencies, NASA could no longer exclude women or applicants of color. Over eight thousand people responded to an open call, including 1,251 women; 208 were tested. In 1978, NASA named thirty-five new astronaut candidates, fifteen pilots and twenty mission specialists. Three were Black men. Six were white women: two physicians, a biochemist, a geophysicist, an engineer, and a physicist, Dr. Sally Ride. The women underwent the same training and testing as men. Few gender accommodations were made: seats were adjusted for shorter legs, a privacy curtain was installed around the toilet, and tampons, moisturizer, and "hair restraints" were allowed on board. Male engineers estimated Ride would need one hundred tampons for a seven-day trip.[43]

Ride had dreamed of being an astronaut. An exceptional student and talented athlete, she transferred to Stanford as a junior and joined the rugby and tennis teams. Billie Jean King urged her to compete professionally. Years later, when a girl asked her why she chose science over tennis, Ride replied, "a bad forehand." She earned dual degrees in English and physics and a PhD in astrophysics. Selected to be the first woman because the crew needed her specific skill set, operating the space arm to retrieve a satellite, Ride emphasized that she was a team member and a scientist, not a female scientist. Nonetheless, she endured sexist questions: "Would she wear a bra or makeup in space?" "Did she cry on the job?" "How would she deal with menstruation?" At thirty-two, she was the youngest American to go into orbit. Despite Ride's modesty, America was mesmerized. Veterans of the Women's Air Force Service Pilots (WASPs) were in a crowd, estimated at 250,000, to watch the launch. Many wore "Ride, Sally Ride" T-shirts, a riff on Wilson Pickett's 1966 song, "Mustang Sally." When she landed, her mother exclaimed, possibly apocryphally, "Thank God for Gloria Steinem!" Exiting the cockpit, Ride refused to accept a bouquet.[44]

Ride's second flight, in October 1984, included her classmate, geophysicist Kathryn Sullivan, who became the first woman to walk in space. Ride's third flight was cancelled after the 1986 *Challenger* explosion killed another classmate, engineer Judith Resnik, and Christa McAuliffe, a New Hampshire junior high school teacher, chosen from 10,463 applicants to be the first private citizen to go into space. NASA halted recruitment and suspended flights for three years and Ride retired.[45] She served in academic and defense advisory roles and wrote six children's books. In one she explained how to make a sandwich in space. Notably reserved, Ride guarded her private life. She married and divorced a fellow astronaut and had no children. When she died in 2012, her company identified Tam O'Shaughnessy, her partner of twenty-seven years, as a survivor, the first public indication that Ride was gay. *New York Times* editors debated whether to out Ride in her obituary, setting off a debate about posthumous privacy.[46]

Mae Jemison was the first of six Black women astronauts to date. Born in 1956, she entered Stanford at sixteen and earned dual degrees in chemical engineering and African American studies. After graduating from Cornell medical school, she worked as a general practitioner and volunteered for the Peace Corps. Inspired by Ride, Jemison applied to NASA. In 1992, she joined the *Endeavor* crew, conducting forty-three experiments on 126 earth orbits. She subsequently taught at Dartmouth, founded a technology company, and established an international science camp for high school students.[47] Ellen Ochoa was the first female Hispanic astronaut and the second woman to lead NASA. As of 2019, 12% of astronauts have been women. They piloted shuttles, commanded missions, and undertook spacewalks. In October 2019, Cynthia Koch and Jessie Meir made history on the first spacewalk conducted by women only.[48]

AFFIRMATIVE ACTION

Ferraro, O'Connor, Ride, and other high achieving women benefited from the women's movement, Title VII, and affirmative action. That term was first used in the 1935 National Labor Relations Act, which required employers who committed unfair labor practices "to take . . . affirmative action." In 1961, Executive Order 10925 urged federal contractors to "take affirmative action" not to discriminate.[49] The policy pressed employers and institutions to diversify their white, male organizations. Quotas had long been used to limit the admission of women, Jews, and applicants of color to universities and professional schools, while preferences were given to male athletes in college admissions and veterans in hiring. Previously advantaged white men now felt discriminated against if seats or jobs were reserved for others. The results of affirmative action were soon evident in many workplaces, from police departments to news bureaus.

In 1973, twelve medical schools rejected Allan Bakke, thirty-three, citing his age. His GPA, GMAT scores, and credentials as a former Marine, Vietnam veteran, and NASA engineer were impressive. The University of California-Davis medical school said he applied too late. One interviewer gave him a negative review. In an effort to redress long-standing minority exclusion, UC-Davis had reserved sixteen out of one hundred slots in each class for traditionally underrepresented students. With scores higher than the sixteen admitted students, Bakke sued, asserting discrimination on the basis of race.[50] Amid widespread publicity, the case reached the Supreme Court.

In *Regents of the University of California v. Bakke* (1978), the Court issued six opinions, which split on the question of whether affirmative action violated the Fourteenth Amendment's equal protection clause. Four Justices held that any racial quota system violated the Civil Rights Act of 1964. Justice Lewis Powell agreed, ordering UC-Davis to admit Bakke. Four other Justices held that the use of race as an admissions criterion was constitutional. Justice Powell joined that opinion too, contending that race was a permissible standard. The Court found for Bakke and for an institution's right to consider race in admissions.[51] Both sides claimed victory. Bakke enrolled, graduated at age forty-two, and worked as an anesthesiologist at the Mayo Clinic.

Public opinion was as divided as the Court. The issue of historic race and sex discrimination continues to be debated, litigated, and defended.

Proponents believed that talent was evenly distributed but opportunity was not. Institutions trying to reflect local demographics, their customers, or audience were denounced as "politically correct." Women and people of color, assumed to have been advanced on account of affirmative action, felt labeled as less qualified. Confronted with the question, O'Connor was practical rather than ideological. She did not like affirmative action, but supported it. "How do you think I got my job?" she asked opposing Justice Antonin Scalia.[52]

Resentment fueled more racism. Congress had secured legal and voting rights for people of color but states resisted enactment and enforcement. Laws did not change minds or erase bias among Americans divided by years of custom, ignorance, and hate. An agreement to honor Martin Luther King Jr. with a federal holiday took fifteen years. President Reagan signed the bill in 1983 after it passed both houses by veto-proof majorities. It took effect in 1986, but not every state chose to observe it; Utah and South Carolina finally complied in 2000.[53] Court-ordered school desegregation failed in Charlotte, Detroit, and Boston, defeated by white fear, white flight, white suburbs, and parental anxiety on both sides.[54] As populations shifted, Black politicians won elections as big city mayors, state legislators, and members of Congress. Television modeled racial harmony on *Sesame Street*, which premiered in 1969, and *The Cosby Show* (1984–1992), but the reality of racism and inequality persisted.

THE IMPACT OF REAGAN POLICIES

Black and poor women were especially vulnerable to Republican policies. Reagan's call for a balanced budget became an assault on women. In 1981, one-third of major tax cuts and budget restrictions gutted programs helping poor women and children: Medicaid, food stamps, child nutrition, school lunches, childcare, fuel assistance, and housing.[55] "Welfare queens" were demonized as cheaters. Underfunded social services, rising divorce rates, and increasing numbers of children born to single mothers drove women into poverty. Between 1970 and 1990, "illegitimacy" rose from 38% to 67% among Black mothers and from 6% to 17% among white women.[56] The majority of homeless women were victims of domestic violence; others were runaway teens, addicts, impoverished, or mentally ill. "Bag lady" was added to the dictionary.

The first divorced president, Reagan signed a no fault divorce law in 1969, as governor of California. Because of its unintended consequences, he later considered it "one of the biggest mistakes of his political life." Nationally, no fault divorce was embraced as a reform. It allowed couples to end marriages without blaming either party. Previous grounds had been cruelty, adultery, and desertion. After a postwar spike, the divorce rate slowed during the 1950s. It shot up between 1960 and 1980, when 50% of first marriages ended in divorce.[57] One result of an increase in female-headed households was the "feminization of poverty."

Many judges deplored what they saw as an unfair outcome. In 1977, when Judge Robert Gardner sat on the Orange County, California, Superior Court, he ruled that a woman who had been a homemaker was unlikely to find employment and handed down a scathing indictment of no fault divorce.

> The husband simply has to face up to the fact that his support
> responsibilities are going to be of extended duration, perhaps
> for life. [It has] nothing to do with feminism, sexism, male
> chauvinism, or any other trendy ideology. It is ordinary common
> sense, basic human decency. [No fault divorce] may not be used as
> a handy vehicle for the summary disposal of old and used wives.
> A woman is not a breeding cow to be nurtured during the years
> of her fecundity, then conveniently and economically converted
> to cheap steaks when past her prime.[58]

Only 10% of women got alimony. Because they could not support a family in poorly paid, sex-segregated jobs, two-thirds of female-headed households depended on Aid to Families with Dependent Children, part of the original Social Security Act. Most Black and white women still worked in the lowest paid occupations, in clerical and service roles, sales, garment making, data entry, and childcare. One-quarter of female heads of households with children had incomes under the poverty rate. Childcare was inadequate or nonexistent. In 1972, President Nixon vetoed the Comprehensive Child Development Act, which would have supported childcare regardless of ability to pay, on the grounds that it would destroy the nuclear family and "Sovietize American children."[59]

Reagan's additional Supreme Court nominees moved the Court to the right. In 1986, he elevated William Rehnquist to be Chief Justice and appointed Antonin Scalia. Anthony Kennedy followed in 1988, after Robert Bork's nomination was blocked in the Senate.[60] During this period, the Court both advanced and obstructed women's rights. It found "head and master" laws, a remnant of the common law that gave husbands sole control of marital property, unconstitutional.[61] It avoided the concept of comparable work in addressing the lower wages paid to female prison guards.[62] It did not require women to register for the draft, since they were not allowed in combat.[63] It found the exclusion of women from the Rotary, a business association as opposed to a private club, discriminatory.[64] It allowed colleges to avoid Title IX if only some departments received federal aid.[65] In a case in which a man was denied admission to the Mississippi University for Women's School of Nursing, it held that the state did not provide "persuasive justification" for the gender based distinction. If anything, Justice O'Connor argued, Mississippi "tends to perpetuate the stereotyped view of nursing as an exclusively women's job."[66]

In 1988, George Herbert Walker Bush succeeded President Reagan and advanced Republican policies. Bush was the first sitting vice president to be elected president since Martin Van Buren in 1836. His election was the first since 1948 to return the same party to office after two previous terms. His popular vote of 53.4% and Electoral College tally of 426, while lower than those for FDR, LBJ, or Reagan, set records not broken since. The scion of the Eastern elite, Bush was the son of a US senator. With his grosgrain watchbands and courtly manners, including handwritten correspondence, he was caricatured as an aging preppy, a class satirized in

The Official Preppy Handbook (1980). More significantly, he was the last president from the "greatest generation," a Navy pilot and war hero who epitomized duty, honor, and service.[67]

While Bush had supported women's rights and family planning early in his career, his record as president was poor. Although he campaigned on the issue, Bush twice vetoed the Family and Medical Leave Act, which would have required employers of more than fifty workers to grant time off, without pay, for births, adoptions, or family emergencies. He appointed Elizabeth Dole Secretary of Labor, Barbara Franklin Secretary of Commerce, and Antonia Novello the first woman and first Latina Surgeon General.[68] His most controversial nomination was Clarence Thomas to the Supreme Court.

One major legislative initiative was passage of the Americans with Disabilities Act (ADA) in 1990. Modeled on the Civil Rights Act of 1964, it remains a comprehensive piece of civil rights legislation, prohibiting discrimination against people with physical or mental impairments and guaranteeing them equal opportunities in employment and access to services, transportation, accommodations, and more.[69] The movement for rights for individuals with disabilities began in the 1970s. Judith Heumann, who had suffered from polio as an infant, organized demonstrations in ten cities to pressure Joseph Califano, Carter's Secretary of Health, Education, and Welfare, to authorize Section 504 of the Rehabilitation Act of 1973, the first federal protection for people with disabilities. One sit-in by 150 people in San Francisco lasted twenty-eight days, the longest time a federal building has been occupied. Heumann worked in the Clinton and Obama administrations and at the World Bank and the Ford Foundation as an advocate of disability rights.[70]

ABORTION CASES

In the decades following *Roe*, the Court addressed an array of abortion-related cases regarding spousal consent, parental consent, informed consent, waiting periods, and access. These challenges signaled that *Roe* was not accepted as "settled law." In *Planned Parenthood of Central Missouri v. Danforth* (1976), the Court overturned a law requiring a married woman to have her husband's consent, 6–3, because, Justice Blackmun concluded, "the woman bears the child." In *Belotti v. Baird* (1979), the Court struck down a strict Massachusetts parental consent law which allowed a minor to seek a "judicial bypass." In *Planned Parenthood Association of Kansas City v. Ashcroft* (1983), the Court overruled a two parent consent rule and upheld the bypass, because it imposed "no undue burden." *Akron v. Akron Center for Reproductive Health* (1983) related to informed consent. Ohio doctors were required to tell women seeking abortions about "physical and emotional complications." Voting 6–3, the Court found that the information was designed not to educate but to dissuade. It also invalidated a twenty-four-hour waiting period and a requirement that abortions be performed in hospitals.[71]

The Bush Justice Department filed amicus briefs urging the overturn of *Roe*.[72] *Webster v. Reproductive Health Services* (1989) addressed a Missouri law stating that life began at conception, requiring viability tests before the third trimester, forbidding state employees from performing abortions, and banning the procedure from public hospitals. In a fractured 5–4 decision, the Court upheld each provision. Because the conception language appeared in a preamble to the statute, it was allowed. Chief Justice Rehnquist dismissed *Roe*'s three-tier framework as "a web of legal rules" and found no reason to be rigid about viability testing. Four justices, led by Scalia, called for an overturn of *Roe*. O'Connor, the fifth vote, found each provision valid under the "no undue burden" test, but saw "no necessity" to reconsider *Roe*. Justice Blackmun's blistering dissent charged Rehnquist with "stealth tactics." He described the opinion as "filled with winks . . . nods, and knowing glances to those who would do away with *Roe* explicitly." *Roe* survived but, Blackmun warned, "The signs [were] ominous" for its future.[73]

Webster demonstrated that the Court was willing to uphold state restrictions on abortion. Three years later, when the next challenge came, two new justices had joined the Court, David Souter and Clarence Thomas.

Neither revealed his position on abortion during confirmation hearings. *Planned Parenthood of Southwestern Pennsylvania v. Casey* (1992) involved informed consent, parental and spousal consent, and a twenty-four-hour waiting period, all provisions previously invalidated by the Court. The Court rendered another splintered opinion. The three centrists, Justices O'Connor, Kennedy, and Souter, joined conservative Justices Rehnquist, Scalia, Thomas, and White, 7–2, to uphold the Pennsylvania law, except for spousal notification. They significantly changed the trimester framework. States could now regulate abortion throughout a pregnancy and require pre-abortion counseling and waiting periods, as long as they did not create an "undue burden" or a "substantial obstacle." The Court replaced the stricter standard of "compelling state interest" with the less rigorous "undue burden" norm, which had been O'Connor's long-held position.[74]

The centrists joined the two liberals, Justices Blackmun and Stevens, 5–4, to affirm *Roe*'s "central holding" that the state may not prevent pre-viability abortions. They rejected arguments for overthrowing *Roe*, focusing on the importance of reproductive choice for women. They argued that the right to terminate a pregnancy had less to do with privacy than sex discrimination. O'Connor, Kennedy, and Souter were emphatic: "The ability of women to participate equally in the economic and social life of the Nation has been facilitated by their ability to control their reproductive lives." Women had relied on *Roe* for two decades, the decision continued. The cost of overturning it could not be dismissed, so the Court sustained *Roe*, strengthening it as a precedent.[75]

Harry Blackmun and John Paul Stevens were steadfast defenders of reproductive rights in an increasingly hostile climate. Blackmun was the only justice voting on *Casey* who had voted for *Roe*. The father of three daughters, the Minnesotan had served as legal counsel at the Mayo Clinic, where he developed his interest in medical law. He regularly received hate mail and death threats for his pro-choice opinions. Blackmun distrusted O'Connor.[76] Justice Stevens argued that state laws incorporating the view that life began at conception were theological and amounted to an unconstitutional establishment of religion. In *Hodgson v. Minnesota* (1990), Stevens found the state law requiring women under eighteen to notify both parents and wait forty-eight hours, unless it was a medical emergency or in cases of parental abuse, unconstitutional and the judicial bypass inadequate. O'Connor wrote a separate opinion, striking down dual notice as unreasonable but upholding the bypass. It was the first time O'Connor had ever voted to invalidate a state abortion restriction.[77]

WOMEN AT WORK

By 1990, 57.5% of American women were in the paid workplace, where they confronted sexual harassment and discrimination. For the first time, in *Meritor Savings Bank v. Vinson* (1986), the Supreme Court held that sexual harassment was a form of sex discrimination under Title VII. After being fired, Black bank employee Mechelle Vinson claimed that she had been subjected to years of sexual harassment, including rape. It was defined as "quid pro quo" harassment, in which supervisors demoted or fired employees who did not agree to sexual demands. Vinson suffered extreme physical and emotional distress, including hair loss. According to bank policy, her only remedy was to complain to her supervisor, who was her abuser, so she sued the bank for monetary damages. In a 6–3 decision, written by Justice Rehnquist, the Court supported Vinson, asserting that the manager had created a "hostile work environment," defined as "sufficiently severe and pervasive to alter the conditions of the victim's employment and create an abusive working environment."[78] The Vinson case was a preview of the #MeToo Movement.

In *Price Waterhouse v. Hopkins* (1989), a senior accountant, deemed not feminine enough to be named partner, challenged that decision. One of the largest accounting firms in the country, Price Waterhouse had seven female partners out of 622. Ann Hopkins, a white woman, was the only woman among eighty-eight candidates being considered for partner. She had secured the firm's most lucrative contract and billed more hours than any other applicant, but was seen as "aggressive" and "abrasive."

Hopkins smoked, drank beer, and rode a motorcycle. She was advised by her male mentor to "walk more femininely, talk more femininely, dress more femininely; wear makeup and jewelry; have your hair styled." Hopkins was thirty-nine, the mother of three young children with no time and an allergy to makeup. She bought a pink skirt suit. She did not make partner.[79]

Hopkins's lawsuit addressed how gender norms influence women's success in the workplace. The firm claimed the issue was not femininity but likeability. Hopkins's counsel produced an expert witness on gender stereotyping, the first time such evidence had been offered. The Court ruled, 6–3, that when employees were demoted or fired, the employer had to prove that they would have made the same decision if gender were not an issue. "We are beyond the day when an employer could evaluate employees by assuming or insisting that they matched the stereotype of their group," wrote Justice William Brennan. Even though the firm made clear she was unwelcome, Hopkins returned as a partner in 1991, with $370,000 in back pay, and stayed until she retired in 2002.[80]

Wherever women of any race worked or walked past a construction site or attended a convention, casual sexual harassment was commonplace. When Navy and Marine "Top Gun" aviators convened in Las Vegas in September 1991, drunken debauchery resulted in assaults on eighty-three women and seven men, who were grabbed, groped, stripped, or raped. Much of the sexual activity was consensual, but unwilling participants were purposely swept into a gauntlet. Such obscene behavior had become a Tailhook "tradition," assumed to be condoned by the US Navy. Navy Lieutenant Paula Coughlin, a helicopter pilot, complained to her superior officer, who cautioned against filing a complaint. She ignored his advice. No man brought a complaint. Eventually, 119 Navy and 21 Marine officers were cited for "indecent assault, indecent exposure [and] conduct unbecoming." Officers were censured, fines were levied, but no one was tried. Coughlin and the Navy Secretary resigned. The Defense Department issued a zero tolerance policy that has not been consistently enforced.[81]

CLARENCE THOMAS AND ANITA HILL

In July 1991, President Bush nominated Clarence Thomas to replace Thurgood Marshall as the second Black justice on the Supreme Court. The grandson of a Georgia sharecropper, Thomas had earned a scholarship to a Catholic boarding school before attending seminary. Following Dr. King's assassination, he abandoned his ambition to become a priest to work for civil rights. He graduated from Holy Cross and entered Yale law school, benefiting from affirmative action. Thomas had worked for Senator John Danforth (R-MO); in the Department of Education Office for Civil Rights; as chair of the EEOC, where he vehemently opposed affirmative action; and briefly as a US Court of Appeals judge. Because of his judicial inexperience, the fourteen-man Senate Judiciary Committee focused on his origin story. After the brouhaha around the unexpected defeat of Robert Bork's nomination, the committee anticipated an easy confirmation with bipartisan support.[82]

Thomas's nomination alarmed law professor Anita Hill, who had worked for him at the Education Department and the EEOC from 1981 to 1983. She quit because of his persistent sexual harassment. To avoid endangering her career prospects, she did not complain. For professional reasons, she maintained occasional contact with Thomas, behavior not uncommon among victims of workplace harassment. Hill had remained silent but was now ambivalent, given the prospect of Thomas's lifetime appointment. She had sworn friends who knew about his behavior to secrecy, but by September, rumors of her experience had reached Senate staff, who called her. Hill did not volunteer information until asked.[83] She was the youngest of thirteen children of African American farmers in Lone Tree, Oklahoma. The high school valedictorian graduated from Oklahoma State University and Yale law school. After working in DC, she returned to Oklahoma to teach contract and commercial law. She was a reserved woman, who saw speaking up as "an unpleasant civic duty."

After delays and miscommunication, Hill agreed to be interviewed by the FBI. She hoped to trigger an investigation, believing that the facts would prompt Thomas to withdraw. She expected the FBI report to be circulated to committee members before they voted. It was not. The ranking member, Senator Strom Thurmond (R-SC), eighty-nine, still an unrepentant fanny-patter, did not brief Republicans on the committee. Senator Ted Kennedy's philandering paralyzed him. Senator Howard Metzenbaum (D-OH) admitted, "If that's sexual harassment, half the Senators on Capitol Hill could be accused." Chairman Joe Biden (D-DE) did not delay the committee's September 27 vote, which resulted in a 7–7 tie and no recommendation. A floor vote was set for October 8.[84]

The tie vote triggered press curiosity. NPR's Nina Totenberg heard that the FBI had reopened its background investigation into possible personal misconduct. On October 5, she identified and contacted Hill and ran the story on October 6.[85] It was explosive. Hill was unprepared for the barrage of phone calls, the invasion of reporters, the need for personal security, or the possibility of collateral damage. *New York Times* journalists Jane Mayer and Jill Abramson, who have written a definitive account, found "working women of all ages and in all kinds of jobs identified . . . with the issue of sexual harassment."[86] Black Americans were divided. Many blamed Hill for attacking a respected man. Some called Hill a Black Jezebel. On Hill's behalf, 1,600 Black women paid for a full-page ad in the *New York Times*, signed "African American women in defense of themselves."[87]

The Senate did not see sexual harassment as disqualifying. To delay the vote would suggest an error in the proceedings. On Tuesday, October 8, Senator Mikulski demanded a delay: "What disturbs me as much as the allegations themselves is that the Senate appears not to take the charge of sexual harassment seriously." While Senate Democrats caucused, seven Democratic congresswomen marched across the Capitol and banged on the door, demanding new hearings. As the day progressed, the whip count fluctuated; Republicans were no longer confident of confirmation. Biden decided to reopen committee hearings and reschedule the vote.[88]

Hill assembled a team of attorneys and allies, among them Judy Lichtman of the Women's Legal Defense Fund, to draft her statement and prepare for her appearance. Seeing Thomas's confirmation as inevitable, the NAACP and the Black Caucus stood down. Hill felt she "had a duty to report." She expected indifference or dismissal, but not disbelief: 60% of Americans thought she was lying.[89] Hill's team turned to Lloyd Cutler, President Carter's former White House counsel, a white-haired, wise, white man. Uncomfortable with the sexual details presented in Hill's opening statement, Cutler withdrew. Until two hours before the hearing, Hill did not have an attorney. Charles Ogletree, a Black Harvard law professor up for tenure, reluctantly agreed to appear.[90]

The hallway in the Russell Building was lined with hundreds of Black women wearing T-shirts supporting Thomas, "TAKING A STAND FOR RIGHTEOUSNESS." Chairman Biden allowed Thomas to testify first and to rebut Hill after she had finished. Outraged by the accusations and the attack on his reputation, Thomas denied her claims. He warned that he would not tolerate questions about "what goes on in the most intimate parts of my private life," refusing to "provide the rope for my own lynching." Thomas's strategy was to make himself the victim and to destroy Hill, depicting her as a spurned woman, an incompetent staffer, and a psychologically unstable liar.[91]

After an hour, the Committee rushed Hill to the hearing. There was no time to seat her parents; the trip to DC was her father's first airplane ride. A trim Black woman in a tailored turquoise suit, Hill read her statement, detailing Thomas's prurient behavior and references to pubic hair, breasts, and penis size. Listeners were stunned by its content and candor. For seven hours she answered questions, grilled by former prosecutor Arlen Specter (R-PA). Poised and sincere, she managed to create an atmosphere of doubt. Rumors flew that President Bush would withdraw the nomination. Biden did not call experts on sexual harassment or the four witnesses who could confirm Hill's charges. Nor did he reprimand colleagues for treating Hill with disrespect. One Republican characterized her as "nutty and . . . slutty." While Republicans coordinated their questions with Thomas's legal team, Democrats abandoned Hill.[92]

Hill ended her testimony at 7:40 P.M. on Friday, October 11. Thomas returned to a prime-time audience. He was furious. Advised by Senator

Orrin Hatch (R-UT), Thomas played the race card against Hill, claiming that her characterization of him was an example of negative stereotypes of Black men as sexual predators. Previously evasive, wooden, and carefully coached, Thomas was passionate in his defense, blasting the proceeding as a "high-tech lynching for uppity Blacks."[93] He made a committee of privileged white men squirm. Hill's reputation was trashed, an effort organized by Thomas's sponsor, Senator Danforth (R-MO). She refused to reappear. Without calling Hill's corroborating witnesses, Biden gaveled the hearings to a close at 2:03 A.M. on Monday, October 14.[94]

Hill returned to Oklahoma, facing hecklers in the airport. At a rally in the University of Oklahoma student union, she made one statement and took no questions:

> Words simply cannot express the kind of anguish I have experienced over the past several days. I have been deeply hurt and offended by the nature of the attacks on my character. I had nothing to gain by subjecting myself to the process. In fact, I had more to gain by remaining silent. The personal attacks on me without one iota of evidence were particularly reprehensible, and I felt it necessary to come forward to address those attacks. It was suggested that I had fantasies, that I was a spurned woman, and that I had a martyr complex. I will not dignify those theories except to assure everyone that I am not imagining the conduct to which I testified.[95]

A group of Minnesota women launched a campaign to endow a chair at the law school in Hill's honor. The Oklahoma legislature responded by demanding her resignation, introducing a bill to prohibit out-of-state donations, and another to close the law school. Officials attempted to revoke her tenure. After five years, Hill resigned and the University defunded her chair.[96] She became a professor of women's studies and social policy at Brandeis and, later, head of the Hollywood Commission on Eliminating Sexual Harassment and Advancing Equality, part of the #MeToo

Movement. In his 2007 autobiography, Justice Thomas called Hill's testimony "traitorous." His wife continued to excoriate Hill.[97]

On Tuesday, October 15, the Senate confirmed Thomas by 52–48, the narrowest margin in history until 2018.[98] Senator Biden voted against confirmation. Three days later, worried that information about Thomas's interest in pornography might leak, the White House staged a fake swearing in on the South Lawn. A week later, Thomas was officially sworn in by the Chief Justice in an unusual private ceremony at the White House. No other justices attended.[99] When Thomas appeared on the cover of *People*, featuring a first-person story by his white wife that castigated Hill, Justice O'Connor was "aghast." But when he arrived at the Court, seemingly isolated and overwhelmed, she encouraged him to join the other Justices at their weekly luncheons.[100] At forty-three, Thomas was the youngest member of the court; by 2020, he was the longest serving.

A month later, President Bush dropped his opposition to the Civil Rights Act of 1991, signing a bill that would compensate victims of sexual harassment. In the aftermath of the Thomas hearings, Senators were booed by constituents and faced challenges at the polls. Senators Danforth and Metzenbaum retired. Kennedy confessed that his past behavior had compromised him.[101] Biden later admitted that he acted "in fairness to Thomas, which in retrospect he didn't deserve." In 2019, running for President a third time, Biden was prodded to apologize to Hill. He said he was "sorry for the way she was treated." He did not say he was sorry for how he treated her. Trying again, Biden took "responsibility that she did not get treated well." His private call to Hill "left her feeling deeply unsatisfied," but after he won the nomination, she endorsed him for president.[102]

THE WOMEN'S MOVEMENT REVIVED

For women who believed Hill, the Thomas hearings were motivating. NOW membership rose by nine thousand new members a month. Twenty-five years after its founding, NOW had floundered over issues of pornography, lesbian rights, and sexual violence. In *The Second Stage*, Betty Friedan had declared the "end of the beginning" of the women's movement.[103] "It would be a mistake to think the women's movement is dead," declared Caucus chair Kathy Wilson, "just because we're not behind a microphone bellowing about abortion and the ERA."[104] Meanwhile, domestic terrorists bombed abortion clinics and murdered providers.

NOW president Patricia Ireland, a bisexual former flight attendant, insisted NOW would always be "cutting edge [and] controversial." In April 1992, she led the largest protest march in Washington's history to date, a 750,000-participant March for Women's Lives, demanding full reproductive freedom for women.[105] Conservative preacher Pat Robertson described feminism as a movement that "encourages women to leave their husbands, kill their children, practice witchcraft, destroy capitalism and become lesbians." Almost 80% of women supported the women's movement, but only 34% called themselves feminists.[106]

Race, ethnicity, and class remained obstacles to sisterhood. Black women founded separate organizations. Working-class women perceived the women's movement as interested in individual rights for the privileged rather than collective rights for all women. According to one critic, "Feminists wanted to integrate the Metropolitan Club, not the Elks."[107] Smaller organizations attempted to address specific needs like childcare, housing, health care, pensions, and personal safety. The Women's Economic Justice Center targeted local issues affecting women earning less than $13,000 annually, who were two-thirds of the female work force.[108] Progress was incremental and uneven. Activists moved from picket lines into politics.

WHERE ARE THE WOMEN?

The image of fourteen white men confronting Hill raised the question, "Where are the women?" Polling indicated that women were angry that Congress seemed clueless about sexual harassment. According to Ellen Malcolm, "Anita Hill's courage . . . unleashed years of pent-up rage."[109]

The first proof of that fury was the Illinois Senate primary in March 1992. An impressive but unknown Black state representative, Carol Moseley Braun, challenged the Democratic incumbent, who had won twenty-nine consecutive elections, and a wealthy trial lawyer. Moseley Braun did not meet Emily's viability criterion. She had no organization, no money, and no media. During a televised debate in which the men ignored her and attacked each other, her poll numbers rose by twenty points. Jesse Jackson jumped in with radio endorsements. Gloria Steinem spoke at a Chicago fundraiser and then called Malcolm, pressing her to reconsider. Emily sent $5,000. Moseley Braun won the primary with a coalition of urban Blacks and suburban white women, as did other women on the ticket, including legislative candidates, judges, and three women candidates for the Metropolitan Sanitary Commission.[110]

The Thomas hearings and redistricting following the 1990 census created new seats, fueling "The Year of the Woman." Thirteen women won Senate nominations.[111] In Pennsylvania, Republican Senator Specter, who had accused Hill of "flat-out perjury," barely defeated first-time candidate Lynn Yeakel.[112] Four Democrats vying for open Senate seats won. After her nail-biter primary, Moseley Braun's general election campaign looked "like a celebrity road tour."[113] Patty Murray (WA), an environmental activist, had been dismissed by her male state senator: "You're just a mom in tennis shoes. Go home." Murray won school board and state senate seats and handed out shoelaces in her winning US Senate race.[114] Due to an early retirement, California had two open Senate seats and elected two women, Representative Barbara Boxer and former San Francisco Mayor Dianne Feinstein. The duo became a phenomenon. Impatiently, Malcolm declared, "If one more reporter asks me if California is ready to elect two Bay Area, Jewish, liberal, right-handed, dark-haired, lipstick-wearing women, the answer is, 'HELL YES!'"[115] California became the first state to be represented by two women Senators.

The number of women serving in the House increased from 30 to 47 (35 D, 12R). There had been 106 female candidates, 38 open seats, and 24 new members. Democratic women called themselves "Anita's class."[116] Women Senators increased from two to six. Incumbents Barbara Mikulski (D-MD) and Nancy Kassebaum (R-KS) were joined by Democrats Boxer, Feinstein, Moseley Braun, and Murray. Moseley Braun was the first Black woman Senator, the first Black Democratic Senator, and one of only two Black Senators elected in the twentieth century. There had been two Black Senators, Hiram Rhodes and Blanche Bruce, elected during Reconstruction by Black Republicans in the Mississippi senate.[117] Following a special election in June 1993, Texas Republican Kay Bailey Hutchison made the total seven (5D, 2R). In 1992, Emily's List contributed six million dollars to Democratic women candidates, making it the nation's largest funder of federal candidates.[118]

To counter the impact of Emily's List, pro-choice Republican women, increasingly an oxymoron, created the WISH (Women In the Senate and House) List in 1992. Among its founders was investment banker Candace Straight. WISH recruited and funded federal and state candidates. It supported Olympia Snowe (ME) and Kay Bailey Hutchinson (TX) for Senate seats and Susan Collins (ME) and Christine Todd Whitman (NJ) for governor. After polling the pro-choice contributors to Emily and the WISH List, the *Political Research Quarterly* concluded that Democratic women donors were liberal feminists, while Republicans were moderate libertarians.[119] The WISH List and the Republican Majority for Choice, another PAC, declined in influence after 2000.

Senator Mikulski was delighted to have new colleagues but annoyed by the hype. "Calling 1992 the Year of the Woman makes it sound like the Year of the Caribou or the Year of the Asparagus. We are not a fad, a fancy or a year."[120] When Mikulski was elected in 1986, she was surprised to learn that her Republican counterpart, Senator Kassebaum, stood in line to use a public restroom. Mikulski appealed to Senate wives to give up their reserved lounge on another floor. With seven women in the Senate, the Capitol architect built a two-stall restroom closer to the chamber. Over the next decades, the number of women and toilets would increase.[121]

BILL AND HILLARY

1992 was a presidential election year. Democrats narrowed a broad field
to nominate Arkansas Governor Bill Clinton and Tennessee Senator Al
Gore. Colorado Representative Patricia Schroeder won five convention
votes. Conservative Pat Buchanan challenged President Bush in the GOP
primary and populist Ross Perot ran as an independent. A businessman,
Perot accused Bush of "voodoo economics," blamed free trade for job losses,
and rang alarms about the deficit.[122] The Clinton-Gore ticket represented
a triumph of Democratic centrism and a generational change. Clinton won
43% of the popular vote, the lowest total since Woodrow Wilson in 1912,
with 37.4% for Bush and 18.9% for Perot. For the first time, the gender
gap swung toward Democrats. According to exit polls, Clinton won 45%
of women.[123] "Reagan Democrats," ethnic, blue-collar voters, came back
to the party.

During the Republican convention, Buchanan seconded Bush's nomination and declared that the election would be a "war for the soul of America,"
the culmination of a culture war that began in the 1960s. "The agenda that
Clinton & Clinton would impose on America [is] abortion on demand,
a litmus test for the Supreme Court, homosexual rights, discrimination
against religious schools, women in combat units . . . [and] radical feminism."[124] In contrast, Republicans would defend family values. A civil war
over permissiveness raged. The press was less willing to overlook immoral
behavior, extramarital sex, or drug use by candidates and office holders. It
focused on character, even as the country seemed more tolerant.[125] Voters
veered from how the country should be governed to who should govern it.

Clinton's candidacy was weakened by his reputation as a player who
cheated on his wife. Over the course of his career, Paula Jones, Kathleen
Wiley, Gennifer Flowers, and Juanita Broaddrick had accused him of
sexual harassment, including rape. In 1988, allegations of adultery had
forced Senator Gary Hart (D-CO) out of the presidential primary, but
Clinton, defended by his wife, survived. In a *Sixty Minutes* interview, she
claimed that she was not "Tammy Wynette, standing by her man." Rather,

she believed in his plans for the country. She would defend him again, in 1998, when the President denied "having sexual relations with that woman," White House intern Monica Lewinsky, then twenty-two.[126]

During the presidential campaign, candidate Clinton bragged that voters would get "two for the price of one," acknowledging the assets his wife would bring to the White House. Hillary Rodham Clinton was a whip-smart, politically savvy attorney. A product of the Midwest, a "Goldwater Girl," she was president of the Wellesley College Young Republicans. As student government president, Hillary pushed to end restrictive curfews. Her classmates lobbied the college president to allow a student to speak at graduation and chose Hillary to represent them.[127] The tumult of the Sixties had proved a conversion experience.

The official speaker was Edward Brooke (R-MA), the only Black member in the US Senate in 1969. He acknowledged that the "country has profound and pressing social problems" and "needs the best energies of all its citizens, especially its gifted young people, to remedy these ills." He did not mention civil rights or Vietnam, events that had galvanized Hillary's class. Provoked by an advance copy of his remarks, she defended "the indispensable task of critic[al] and constructive protest." She ended with a pledge: "to practice politics as the art of making what appears to be impossible, possible." Four hundred classmates stood to applaud, while their parents sat, stunned by what many thought was ill-mannered behavior. Hillary's parents were not there.[128]

As Hillary recalled, "accolades and attacks" followed. *Life* magazine photographed her wearing big glasses and striped bell-bottoms. She spent the summer after her graduation gutting salmon in Alaska. When she visited Alaska as First Lady, Hillary joked that "sliming fish was pretty good preparation for life in Washington." A biography of achievement followed: Yale law school, where she met a Rhodes Scholar named Bill Clinton; work with Marian Wright Edelman at the Children's Defense Fund (CDF); registering Texas voters for George McGovern in 1972; joining the staff of the committee investigating impeachment charges against Richard Nixon; moving to Arkansas, where Bill was running for Congress in 1974.

Childhood friends and Wellesley chums urged her instead to launch her own political career in Illinois, but Hillary was in love.[129]

Adapting to Arkansas was a challenge for a Northerner who lived in jeans, rarely wore makeup, and cut her own hair. Bill lost the election and she taught law at the University of Arkansas-Fayetteville, one of two female faculty members. After they married in October 1975, Hillary kept her name. When Bill was elected Attorney General in 1976, they moved to Little Rock. She joined the prestigious Rose Law Firm, became its first woman partner, earned more than her husband, and pursued her interest in children's rights. Bill won the governorship in 1978 but lost his reelection bid. Analysts blamed his arrogance and her feminism. Chastened, both changed tack. Although critical press attention made her more defensive, she began to refer to herself as Hillary Rodham Clinton, got contact lenses, and dyed her hair.[130]

Bill was reelected governor in 1982 and served ten years. As Arkansas's First Lady, Hillary practiced law and advised Bill about educational policy and judicial appointments. She was the first woman on the Wal-Mart board and chaired CDF's national board. Their only child, Chelsea, was born in 1980. Arriving in Washington, Hillary was the first First Lady with a graduate degree. Twice named to the list of 100 Top Lawyers in the country by the *National Law Review,* she became the administration's defense attorney. Famously, she did not bake cookies. For the first time in their partnership, she was unemployed, taking on a role defined by protocol. No wonder Eleanor Roosevelt was her role model.[131]

DECADE OF CHANGE

There was no winner in the culture war and no going back. The pace of change continued to challenge social norms, especially regarding women's roles. Although its infamous Rule Seven had been abolished in 1950, no states had sent Black contestants to the Miss America contest until 1970. In 1983, four Black women competed and Vanessa Williams won. The movies *Nine to Five* (1980) and *Working Girl* (1988) raised issues of equal pay, sexual harassment, and unions for office workers. The dress code for businesswomen was a power suit with padded shoulders and a pussy bow blouse. Donna Karan offered more sophisticated separates and Diane von Furstenberg designed an iconic wrap dress.[132] In 1986, the *New York Times* adopted "Ms.," a term coined by Gloria Steinem in 1972. Judy Woodruff, Cokie Roberts, and Elizabeth Drew formed the first all-female news team, covering the 1987 Iran-Contra hearings for PBS. Martha Stewart became a first name domestic diva. Thelma and Louise were an unexpected power couple.[133]

In 1984, the Metropolitan Museum of Art presented "An International Survey of Painting and Sculpture." Fewer than 10% of the 169 artists represented were women. That was an improvement over 1969, when Helen Frankenthaler was the only female artist in an enormous Met exhibit, "New York Painting and Sculpture, 1940–1970." In protest, a group of women researched and published the small numbers of women who were included in textbooks, exhibited in galleries and museums, or served as curators or museum directors, few of whom were women of color. They paid for an ad that appeared on New York City buses: "Do women have to be naked to get into the Met?" While women created 5% of the Met's collection, 85% of its nudes were female. These guerilla fighters wore gorilla masks, a visual pun.[134]

Museum representation and public monuments marking women's achievements became another measure of their slow progress. In Washington, DC, Wilhelmina Cole Holladay opened the National Museum of Women in the Arts in 1987.[135] As a 2019 investigation found, works by women represented just 11% of acquisitions and 14% of exhibitions at twenty-six American cultural institutions between 2008 and 2018. During the centennial of the Nineteenth Amendment and after the cultural reconsideration prompted by Black Lives Matter protests, many museums addressed the lack of diversity in their holdings and staff.[136]

"Firsts" are symbolic. They demonstrate not only individual achievement but also progress for a cohort. They break through barriers, challenge stereotypes, become role models, and carry the burden of representation, until there are seconds, thirds, and multiples.[137] Female firsts in the 1980s did not offset the realities of race and sex discrimination, violence, and poverty women had to endure and overcome. Feminists recognized that women's legal and social advances could be overturned. Conservative women were equally motivated and more unified in opposition than were proponents. Other than Emily's List, feminist organizations lacked focus and lost momentum. Partisan division over issues like abortion and civil rights deepened the gender and racial gap in voting patterns, and fueled the election of more Democratic women. Women were advancing in terms of legal rights and economic opportunities, but not across the board or at the same pace. Nothing came without a fight, against opponents, among allies, between races and classes. Women had never been a unified cohort. By the 1990s, their divisions seemed sharper.

CHAPTER EIGHT
ISOLATION & INTERSECTIONALITY, 1993–2008

T he dates defining this chapter track the arc of Hillary Rodham Clinton's career from presidential spouse to presidential contender, which parallel and chronicle changes in the women's movement. It was no longer a single issue, pro-ERA, or pro-reproductive rights movement, if it ever had been. Its attention was spread among many causes and campaigns for women's rights, civil rights, and social change. It was younger, more inclusive, more diffuse, more isolated, and less visible. Some women continued to accrue power and advance in politics and other leadership roles. Others resisted being part of a traditional hierarchy. The question remained, what would it take to ensure equal treatment, equal opportunity, and equal rights for all women?

Women opened rape crisis centers and shelters for abused women, created gender studies courses, established think tanks and foundations, and developed caucuses within their professions, from chemistry to Congress. The Center for American Women in Politics, Catalyst, and The Feminist Majority Foundation conducted research and collated data to promote women in sundry settings. The Ms. Foundation for Education and Communication funded groups working on behalf of women and girls. In 1993, it launched "Take Your Daughter to Work Day"; sons were included after 2003. The Foundation's attempts to bring newer, smaller groups under its aegis were firmly resisted.

By the 1990s, the organized women's movement had expanded and fragmented. There were over one hundred national, specifically feminist organizations, not counting older, more traditional women's groups that functioned as allies, and thousands of smaller, niche nonprofits and working groups addressing multiple women's issues. NOW remained the dominant mainstream group, its membership primarily white and middle class. It was described as "the McDonald's of the women's movement, recognizable and accessible."[1] No one organization could address the lengthy list of women's needs.

Some focused more narrowly on an issue or an identity. Organizations formed around causes like childcare, domestic violence, economic inequality, environmental toxins, food deserts, health care, incarceration, labor conditions, maternal mortality, police accountability, and women with disabilities, among many other concerns. Groups formed around shared identities—lesbians, Latinas, librarians, women on welfare, women in physics, Native Americans, and so many others. Overlapping interests and identities defined intersectionality.

Intersectionality was originally the connection between race and gender. Kimberlé Williams Crenshaw, a Black feminist legal scholar, coined the word in 1989. She has spent her career studying civil rights and race. The concept had been expressed in the 1890s by scholar Anna Julia Cooper and activist Mary Church Terrell, both prominent "race women." It described the many ways Black women are disadvantaged and discriminated against by racism and sexism. Clearly other elements of identity, like class, education, religion, sexual orientation, marital and maternal status, ability, geography, and age, could be factors in how one is treated legally and socially.[2] In the current political climate, intersectionality is condemned as identity politics, rather than reality.

One individual identity is age, clearly an element in the evolution of the women's movement. Activists who grew up in the Fifties and rebelled in the Sixties secured greater access to birth control, abortion, equal pay, equal credit, equal educational opportunities, political office, and job opportunities, which their daughters take for granted. White women benefited more, because they were white in a country still confronting its racism and white supremacy, but all women remain underrepresented, underpaid, and undervalued. Too many women of color are severely disadvantaged by ingrained sexism and racism. Younger feminists were less interested in the past than the future.

In 1995, the seventy-fifth anniversary of the Nineteenth Amendment passed without hoopla. Congresswoman Pat Schroeder (D-CO) asked the Postal Service to commemorate the event with an anniversary stamp, as it had in 1970. The USPS refused, but reconsidered when Schroeder joined the House Post Office and Civil Service Committee. The 32-cent stamp overlaid an image of the 1913 suffrage parade with a picture of an ERA march. Schroeder felt it was essential to illustrate women's ongoing struggle for equality; critics called it "blatantly political."[3]

The suffrage anniversary reminded older activists that the "Portrait Monument to Suffrage Pioneers," presented to the Congress in 1921 by the National Women's Party, was still buried in the Capitol Crypt. Originally intended for George Washington's remains and sometimes used as a broom closet, the crypt became a public space in 1963, populated with leftover statues, including the Stanton-Anthony-Mott monument. Congress ignored petitions to return it to the Rotunda, claiming it was too heavy, too cumbersome, and too ugly. Congresswoman Carolyn Maloney (D-NY) organized a bipartisan campaign to resurrect it. The Army Corps of Engineers determined that the seven-ton sculpture was not too weighty, but Speaker Newt Gingrich, chair of the Capitol Preservation Committee, refused to release funds to pay for the move. The public fundraising campaign was the first project of the National Women's History Museum, which existed only on paper.

Black women leaders, led by C. Delores Tucker, a veteran civil rights activist and former Secretary of State of Pennsylvania, protested that the monument did not accurately represent the suffrage movement. She wanted

Sojourner Truth added or a new statue commissioned. Those views did not prevail.[4] Three years later, to mark the 150th anniversary of the first women's rights convention, Hillary Clinton spoke to a huge crowd in Seneca Falls in July 1998.[5] At the initiative of its founding Superintendent, Judy Hart, Seneca Falls had become the National Park Service's first regional park, encompassing several locations, including Stanton's home and the site of the former Methodist Chapel, which had been converted into a car dealership and a laundromat before being torn down.

Younger women redefined the women's movement. According to a 2005 CBS poll, 69% of women believed the women's movement had improved their lives, compared to 43% in 1997, but only 24% called themselves feminists. Almost 80% of the respondents did not know who Gloria Steinem was.[6] Friedan died in 2006. Younger activists grew up in a more diverse if still deeply divided America. They saw feminism as the freedom to be sexually independent. Interracial and LGBTQ relationships were becoming commonplace. They used technology to build online communities, publish blogs like feministing.com, which ran from 2004–2019, founded by sisters Vanessa and Jessica Valenti, and magazines like *BUST,* founded in 1993 "for women with something to get off their chest," or *Bitch,* established in 1996.[7]

THE CLINTON ADMINISTRATION

Clinton appointed more women to his cabinet than any previous president, added a second woman justice to the Supreme Court, and signed significant legislation, but he was impeached for lying about having sex with an intern. The first Democrat to win two terms since FDR, Clinton was a centrist. He enjoyed a one-party government until the 1994 "Republican Revolution" made Newt Gingrich Speaker. The Georgian enforced strict party-line voting and a three-day work week. The schedule undercut socializing among members' families, which had enhanced bipartisanship. Due to a veto-proof Republican Congress, many of Clinton's initiatives failed.

President Clinton appointed the most diverse cabinet and staff to that point. Alexis Herman served as the first Black Secretary of Labor, Hazel O'Leary as Secretary of Energy, and Donna Shalala as Secretary of Health and Human Services. He named Madeline Albright the first female Secretary of State. An immigrant from Czechoslovakia and a Wellesley graduate with a PhD in international affairs, she had worked on Carter's National Security Council. Before becoming the highest-ranking woman in the government, Albright served as Clinton's Ambassador to the United Nations (1993–1997).[8] Janet Reno, the first female Attorney General, was Clinton's third nominee. Corporate lawyer Zoe Baird and Judge Kimba Wood were disqualified for employing undocumented nannies. The childless Reno, a six-foot-one Harvard law school graduate and state's attorney from Miami, served eight years.[9]

Reno confronted rampant domestic terrorism. Between 1977 and 2001, protestors invaded 371 abortion clinics, burned 166, bombed 41, and killed 7 people. Conspiracy theorists formed private militias and stockpiled munitions. Reno inherited the fifty-one-day FBI siege of a religious sect's compound near Waco, Texas, in 1993, that ended in eighty-six deaths, including twenty-five children and four ATF agents. Waco was a catalyst for the 1995 Oklahoma City bombing, according to the perpetrator; 168 people died, including 15 infants. Reno's department also caught and convicted the 1993 World Trade Center terrorists and Unabomber Ted Kaczynski.[10]

Clinton's nomination of Ruth Bader Ginsburg to the Supreme Court, in June 1993, was his most consequential appointment. She was not his first choice. For three months, the White House sorted through forty-two nominees, publicly embarrassing the runners-up. New York Governor Mario Cuomo had been Clinton's first choice. Stephen Breyer, Chief Judge of the US Court of Appeals in Boston, had been told to prepare acceptance remarks while waiting in a Washington hotel room. Then the President changed his mind, choosing Ginsburg two days later. Asked about the "zigzag quality" of his decision-making, Clinton abruptly left a press briefing.[11]

Ginsburg, sixty, was the first justice picked by a Democrat in twenty-six years, since LBJ named Thurgood Marshall in 1967. She was the first Jew to serve on the Court since Abe Fortas retired in 1969. She was one of the few justices, besides Marshall, to have argued cases before the Court. In 1960, Ginsburg had applied to clerk for Felix Frankfurter, but he refused to hire a mother.[12] Governor Ann Richards was an enthusiastic supporter. Other feminists were ambivalent, because Ginsburg had criticized *Roe* as "too broad, too far, too fast."[13] Since Robert Bork's 1987 confirmation hearing, when his outspoken opposition to abortion raised a red flag, Court nominees had been "cagey about . . . *Roe.*" Ginsburg was the exception, linking "abortion rights to women's full citizenship." Abortion, she testified, was:

> central to a woman's life, to her dignity. It's a decision she must make for herself. And when government controls that decision for her, she's being treated as less than a fully adult human, responsible for her own choices.[14]

The Senate confirmed Ginsburg, 96–3.

Senator Jesse Helms (R-NC) was one of three Southerners who voted no, because of her "unreserved" support for abortion and the likelihood she would "uphold the homosexual agenda." Appointed to be a consensus builder and an "instrument of . . . common unity," Ginsburg became famous for her dissents on an increasingly conservative bench.[15] Court watchers could identify her "dissent collar," a jabot that resembled medieval armor. The Justice did not become the "Notorious RBG" until after her dissent in the 2013 *Shelby* case. A law student posted the name on her Tumblr account, referring to the rapper, the Notorious B.I.G.[16] Ginsburg's popularity prompted action figures, biopics, board games, children's books, T-shirts, a workout routine, and standing ovations wherever she went.

On the Court, Justice Ginsburg advanced "equality feminism."[17] In *Harris v. Forklift Systems* (1993), the Court ruled that the manager of a Tennessee truck leasing company had systematically harassed Teresa

Harris, even though his behavior did not "seriously affect her psychological well-being." Justice O'Connor, writing the unanimous opinion, found any "hostile and abusive" behavior illegal.[18] *J.E.B. v. Alabama* (1994) related to jury selection in a suit over support for an illegitimate child. The mother's attorney tried to exclude men from the jury. The Court ruled, 6–3, that potential jurors could not be excluded on account of sex, just as one could not exclude Black jurors. Wrote Justice Blackmun, "gender simply may not serve as a proxy for bias."[19]

CLINTON POLICIES

Clinton's first legislative success on behalf of women, the Family and Medical Leave Act (FMLA), signed in February 1993, had been in the works before he was elected. It required companies with more than fifty employees to provide twelve weeks of unpaid leave and to protect the jobs of employees absent on account of childbirth, adoption, foster care placement, family illness, or military duty. Family was narrowly defined as a parent, spouse, and child until 2008, when next of kin and adult children were added. In 2010, new language included children "regardless of the legal or biological relationship" and same-sex relationships. Individual states expanded the definition of family to include parents-in-law and stepparents.[20] But without paid leave and adequate childcare, these efforts were not enough. In contrast to other countries, by 2014, the rate of women employed in the United States declined, even as private employers expanded paid family leave.[21]

The Violence Against Women Act (VAWA), signed in 1994, was the first federal legislation to acknowledge domestic violence and sexual assault as crimes. Under common law, marital rape had not been illegal, since a wife's unconditional sexual consent was legally required. Nebraska was the first state to declare marital rape criminal, in 1976, but almost a dozen states still have loopholes to shield spouses.[22] To protect women from domestic violence, sexual assault, and stalking, Senator Biden (D-DE) worked with

NOW's Legal Defense and Education Fund. The bill included provisions on rape and battery, funding for victim services, a requirement that states respect injunctions issued in other jurisdictions, and the right of women to sue for civil damages under the commerce clause. VAWA was attached to the Violent Crime and Law Enforcement Act of 1994.[23]

The Crime Act was contentious. Its minimum sentencing guidelines and "three strikes rule" turned drug laws "into a new Jim Crow" and incarcerated a generation of young men of color.[24] Senator Biden and Black Representative James Clyburn (D-SC) voted for it, but the Black Caucus was divided. The National Rifle Association objected to its ban on select assault weapons and threatened to punish lawmakers who supported it. Sixty House Democrats defeated a motion to bring the Crime Bill to the floor. Unable to win over enough Democrats, Clinton compromised with Republicans representing suburban districts. They demanded concessions, including limiting the weapons ban to ten years. Clinton signed the bill and Democrats lost their majorities in the 1994 midterms. It was the first time Republicans had controlled the House since 1952.[25]

VAWA was not secure. House Republicans attempted to cut its funding. In 2000, in *United States v. Morrison*, by 5–4, the Supreme Court struck down the provision allowing women to use the commerce clause to sue their attackers. The suit originated in 1994, when two Virginia Tech football players allegedly raped Christy Bronkala. One went unpunished and the other had his suspension set aside. The victim dropped out and sued for civil damages in federal district court, which dismissed her complaint. When the case reached the Supreme Court, O'Connor voted with the majority; Ginsburg with the minority.[26] Without the option of civil damages, a weaker VAWA was reauthorized in 2000 and 2005 with virtually unanimous support. A pattern of expiration and renewal followed. Conservatives opposed extending protections to same-sex couples, strengthening Indigenous courts, and allowing battered undocumented immigrants to claim temporary visas.[27]

Clinton promised to end the exclusion of homosexuals from military service. Conservatives wanted to ban their participation, claiming that gays undermined unit cohesion. Military leaders wanted to respect those who had been serving honorably or who might volunteer. General Colin Powell, Chairman of the Joint Chiefs of Staff, proposed Clinton's "Don't Ask, Don't Tell" compromise in 1993, ending prosecution of closeted LGBTQ service members, while banning military personnel who were out. It was the military's official policy until conservatives overrode the directive, writing a more restrictive law into a defense authorization bill.[28] All prohibitions ended in July 2011, when a federal appeals court barred enforcement of any ban on openly gay service members.

The specter of gays anywhere alarmed conservatives. The idea that gays might marry was especially offensive. Marriage had not been an LGBTQ priority until the AIDS epidemic raised questions about who was allowed into hospital rooms or was eligible for survivor benefits. In 1990, the Hawaii state health department denied marriage licenses to three gay couples. They sued under the Fourteenth Amendment and Hawaii's ERA. Hawaii's Supreme Court held that the state had failed to show a compelling interest in prohibiting same-sex marriage.[29] Had Hawaii legalized gay marriage, the US Constitution required other states to recognize the decision, making gay couples eligible for a range of benefits.

The Hawaii legislature stayed the court decision. A commission created to study the matter recommended that the legislature allow same-sex marriage and pass a comprehensive domestic partnership act. Rejecting that suggestion, a new state health director brought another suit, *Baehr v. Miike* (1996), demonstrating compelling cause to ban gay marriage. It failed, making Hawaii the first state to legalize same-sex marriage. Two years later, a referendum amended the state constitution, to "reserve marriage to opposite sex couples."[30]

The threat of same-sex marriage energized Republicans in Congress, who drafted the Defense of Marriage Act (DOMA) in 1996. It expressed "moral disapproval of homosexuality" and affirmed that "marriage is the legal union of a man and a woman." It allowed states to pass their own laws but removed the requirement that same-sex unions be recognized in other states or by the federal government. DOMA passed by veto-proof margins, 342 votes in the House and 84 in the Senate. It had the support of a majority of Democrats and every Republican in both houses, except Steve Gunderson (R-WI), one of three openly gay members. President Clinton signed DOMA after midnight, on September 21, 1996, without photographers. He regarded marriage as a union between a man and a woman but considered the bill unnecessarily divisive. His press secretary called it "gay baiting."[31]

By 1990, the religious right had introduced ballot measures limiting LGBTQ rights in state after state. Lesbians and gay men were presumptive felons in twenty-five states and Washington, DC.[32] Voters in Colorado added a provision to the state constitution that nullified existing civil rights protections for "homosexual, lesbian, or bisexual orientation, conduct, practices or relationships." By a 6–3 vote, in *Romer v. Evans* (1996), the Supreme Court struck down that rule as a violation of the equal protection clause and "a bare desire to harm a politically unpopular group."[33] In October 1998, the battered body of Matthew Sheppard, a gay student, was found strung on a fence near Laramie, Wyoming. The case prompted a call for national hate crime legislation protecting the LGBTQ community.[34]

Acceptance of gays advanced, due in part to television programs like *Ellen* (1994–98), a popular sitcom starring comedian Ellen DeGeneres, and *Will and Grace* (1998–2006), the highest-rated sitcom among viewers eighteen to forty-five. In May 1997, DeGeneres came out as a lesbian to Oprah Winfrey. Academics underscored the significance of her declaration: "This is important, especially in the Midwest, because Ellen is such a mainstream character. Television is . . . where . . . people get their ideas about other people." Her show won ninety-six daytime Emmys. Jerry Falwell called her Ellen Degenerate.[35]

Women in the military were another source of anxiety for conservatives. In 1994, President Clinton signed a defense authorization bill that repealed the combat exclusion for women fighter pilots. The Defense Department still forbade women from serving in units "whose chief mission is to engage in direct ground combat," a ban that remained until 2013.[36] As individuals, women had participated in every American war since the Revolution, often in disguise, sometimes in combat or as nurses and spies. By signing the Women's Armed Services Integration Act in 1948, President Truman gave them permanent (rather than auxiliary) status and veterans benefits. The Act put a 2% cap on the total number of women in each branch, restricted promotions, and banned them from combat roles. JFK eliminated quotas on women officers.

In the 1970s, the military academies and college ROTC programs admitted women; in 1978, the Coast Guard assigned women to ships. The all-volunteer army increased the number of women on active duty, reaching 8.5% by 1990. They operated construction equipment, directed air traffic, flew helicopters, worked as chaplains and military police, protected embassies, and guarded the Tomb of the Unknown Soldier. As the nature of warfare and weapons changed and front lines disappeared in the sand, combat got harder to define. In the 1991 Persian Gulf War, women were 7% of American forces. In addition to medical roles, women drove trucks, crewed planes, directed artillery, served in myriad non-combat roles, and came under enemy fire. Five women were killed in action and two were prisoners of war.[37]

As he had when he was governor, Clinton asked his wife to lead a major policy initiative, to draft an affordable health care plan. The group worked in secret, without involving Congress, opening the Clintons to more criticism. Its 1,342-page proposal was complicated and vulnerable to attack. By the summer of 1994, health care reform was doomed; it never came up for a vote.[38] Another Clinton campaign promise was "to end welfare as we know it." Federal welfare programs were the legacy of the New Deal, FDR, and Frances Perkins. The 1935 Social Security Act intended to protect the most vulnerable victims of the Great Depression. It provided unemployment insurance, old age pensions, and Aid to Families with Dependent Children (AFDC). It did not relieve race-based poverty. In the 1980s, despite low rates of fraud, Reagan stigmatized "welfare queens," single mothers who were supposedly manipulating the system. After the 1994 midterms, any reform Clinton might propose was at the mercy of a Republican Congress.

The Personal Responsibility and Work Opportunity Reconciliation Act of 1996 ended federal control of welfare programs, scrapped the AFDC, gave states block grants, and introduced Temporary Assistance for Needy Families (TANF). The bill imposed deadlines to find work, cut food stamps to people without children, and stripped benefits from legal immigrants. Some elements seemed sensible but proved disastrous. According to several studies, TANF "barely [reached] even the poorest Americans and [had] all but ceased doing the work of lifting people out of poverty." The number of women and children of color living in poverty increased.[39] It had a negative impact on marriage and family patterns. Longtime Clinton allies were appalled. Four senior HHS administrators resigned in protest, including Peter Edelman. His wife, Marian Wright Edelman, Hillary's mentor and friend, raged: "President Clinton's signature on this pernicious bill makes a mockery of his pledge not to hurt children."[40]

MONICA LEWINSKY

Clinton's legislative program was overshadowed by his affair with Monica Lewinsky, which resulted in impeachment charges and negative repercussions for everyone involved. It was a blatant case of workplace sexual harassment. In contrast to their outrage over the treatment of Anita Hill, many feminists savaged Lewinsky's reputation, calling her a bimbo and a "consenting adult," ignoring the age difference and power imbalance. In another contrast, conservative Christian leaders who had pilloried Anita Hill defended Lewinsky. It took twenty years and the #MeToo movement to shift public sympathy to Lewinsky.[41] The sex scandal was discovered by independent counsel Kenneth Starr, who was investigating a series of alleged Clinton improprieties. Concluding that the President had lied about the affair to a grand jury, Starr submitted his 445-page report to Congress in 1998. It contained no other charges.[42]

Because the President was unwelcome on the campaign trail, Hillary crisscrossed the country, in demand among Democrats. Confronted with

constant impeachment coverage, voters recoiled. While Republicans maintained control of Congress, they made no gains in the Senate and lost five
seats in the House. It was the first time since 1934 that a president's party
gained seats in a midterm election. Narrow GOP majorities, of 55–45
in the Senate and 223–211 in the House, made impeachment less likely.
In December, the President's approval rating reached its all-time high of
73%.[43] "I totally underestimated the degree to which people would just
get sick of 24-hour-a-day talk television and talk radio and . . . [how] this
whole scandal became just sort of disgusting by sheer repetition," Speaker
Gingrich admitted. Republicans hurled recrimination at each other. Four
days after the election, Gingrich announced he would quit as Speaker and
resign from office. A Democrat called it "the aftershock from Tuesday's
earthquake." Gingrich's replacement as Speaker also resigned, charged
with marital infidelity.[44]

In December, the House approved two articles of impeachment. The
Senate trial began in January, during the lame duck session. Chief Justice
William Rehnquist, who had written a book about the impeachments of
Justice Samuel Chase in 1804 and President Andrew Johnson in 1868,
presided, wearing a robe trimmed with four bars of gold braid. Conviction
required sixty-seven votes. A motion to dismiss the articles for lack of
merit lost. On February 12, 1999, the Senate denied the perjury charge,
55–45. The obstruction charge failed in a 50–50 tie. Five Republicans,
including Maine Senators Susan Collins and Olympia Snowe, joined
the forty-five Democrats to vote for acquittal.[45] In retrospect, historians,
journalists, and lawyers agreed that Clinton's personal behavior did not
merit impeachment.

NEW MEDIA

Every salacious scene of every Clinton melodrama had been broadcast
and amplified by tabloids, talk radio, and cable television. It was hard to
distinguish journalism from gossip. Satellite technology, cable television,

personal computers, the Internet, and cell phones reshaped the experience of all Americans and made possible the further realignment of the political parties. The revolution in communication technology drove the nation further apart. People moved from a shared public square into opposing corners, into silos and sects of growing political, economic, and cultural division. "Narrowcasting" replaced broadcasting. Customized cable channels like ESPN (1979) and MTV (1981) appealed to specific viewers; news outlets quickly followed suit.[46]

Partisan coverage and commentary were legal after 1987, when the Federal Communications Commission revoked its "fairness doctrine," which required network neutrality and a balance of views. It left the "equal time rule" in place for political candidates. That change led to an explosion in conservative talk radio, which reached twenty million Americans on 659 stations. Conservatives accounted for 70% of listeners.[47] *The Rush Limbaugh Show*, first aired in 1988, was a combination of political commentary and caller input. It became the most popular program in the country, with fourteen million listeners.[48] Among his admirers was Mike Pence, who hosted an Indianapolis talk radio show. Calling himself "Rush Limbaugh on decaf," Pence used his daily program as a springboard for his political career.[49] In 1994, the incoming Republican congressional class made Limbaugh an honorary member. Clarence Thomas officiated at his wedding. The combative host ridiculed liberals as "commie-libs" and "environmental wackos." He damned the Democratic "raw new deal." His favorite epithet was "feminazi," for women who wanted to ensure "that as many abortions as possible occur."[50]

Among Limbaugh's primary targets was Hillary Clinton, who suffered both self-inflicted wounds and collateral damage from political shrapnel. Despite incoming fire over health care policy, sundry scandals, and her husband's infidelity, Hillary never surrendered. Rather, she armored herself in a carapace of reserve. She dismissed accusations of being anti-homemaker: "I don't think being a feminist . . . implies the rejection of maternal values, nurturing children or caring about the men in your life. That is just nonsense."[51]

BEIJING, 1995

It was Eleanor Roosevelt who first pressed the fledgling United Nations to consider women's rights in its charter documents. Fifty years later, another first lady would reiterate the claim, in a memorable speech to the United Nations Fourth World Conference on Women in Beijing. On September 5, 1995, wearing a pink suit, Hillary listed the abuses and injustices women suffered globally as violations of human rights. She enumerated babies starved or suffocated because they were born girls; women and girls sold into "the slavery of prostitution"; incinerated because their "dowries are deemed too small"; raped as "a tactic or prize of war"; subjected to violence in their own homes; "brutalized by . . . genital mutilation"; and "denied the right to plan their own families . . . forced to have abortions or sterilized." She had not cleared her conclusion with the White House or the State Department. "Human rights are women's rights and women's rights are human rights." The *New York Times* called it "her finest hour in public life." Delegates from 189 countries unanimously adopted a global agenda for gender equality.[52]

The next day, she drove forty miles north to speak in the small, muddy town of Huairou. Thirty-thousand representatives of global NGOs (non-government organizations), including eight thousand from America, had been penned in a hundred-acre campus by the Chinese government. For twelve days, an enormous and diverse gathering of women, representing "nearly every conceivable feminist issue and identity group," met in tents to connect and rethink the women's movement, both domestically and globally. According to an analysis by history professor Lisa Levenstein, by the 1990s, the achievement of feminist goals was in the hands of older organizations, frequently run in a top-down manner by white women. Younger feminists, interested in gender equity and sexual expression, were multiracial and more loosely allied in grassroots groups. These women, especially women of color, had come to feminism on "separate roads."[53]

Americans meeting in China were "electrified." They acknowledged their differences, expanded their networks, reworked coalitions, recognized the reality of intersectionality, and bonded in discomfort. Essential in making connections was the Internet. Email, listservs, electronic bulletin boards, and databases "jump-started the growth of online feminism," independent of older organizations. Not that older feminists were retiring. Bella Abzug was among the unofficial participants, in a wheelchair and a big hat. Learning that lesbians had been arrested for unfurling a "Lesbian Rights Are Human Rights" banner, Abzug yelled, "Give me my lipstick!" before negotiating their release.[54]

WOMEN IN THE HEADLINES

Women's issues were more normal than newsworthy in the 1990s. There were fewer firsts, and not many seconds. Mona Van Duyn was the first woman Poet Laureate in 1992, followed in 1993 by Rita Dove, the youngest Poet Laureate and first African American. Toni Morrison won the Nobel Prize in Literature in 1993. She was the first Black and only the eighth woman selected in ninety years. Poet Gwendolyn Brooks had been the first Black writer to win a Pulitzer Prize in any category in 1950.[55] Another Black woman, tennis ace Venus Williams, made her professional debut in 1994 at age fourteen.[56] The colorful quilts being made by Black women in Gee's Bend, Alabama, discovered in 1998, were considered art, admired by contemporary collectors and curators. The designs looked geometric and abstract because they were made from clothing scraps.[57]

The 292 American women competing in the 1996 Olympics in Atlanta were more than half of the US team. Nicknamed "the girls of summer," they won gold medals in gymnastics, basketball, softball, and soccer, the last two sports added for the first time. They restored the reputation of women athletes after the Nancy Kerrigan-Tonya Harding skating scandal at the 1994 Winter Olympics.[58] The first generation of women athletes raised after Title IX attracted huge crowds and commercial endorsements. Nike seized the opportunity to sell more athletic gear to a new market, with a series of award-winning ads. In one, the voice over declared: "There is a girl being born in America. Someone will give her a doll. Someone will give her a ball. Someone will give her a chance."[59]

TOP LEFT: Frances Ellen Watkins Harper. *Library of Congress: LC-USZ62-1180946.* TOP RIGHT: Julia Anna Haywood Cooper. *Library of Congress: LC-b5-50626.* BOTTOM LEFT: Ida B. Wells-Barnett. *Library of Congress, Print and Photograph Division, Visual Materials from the NAACP records: LC-DIG-ppmsca-23822.* BOTTOM RIGHT: Mary Church Terrell. *Library of Congress: LC-USZ62-54722.*

ABOVE LEFT: Jeannette Rankin, the first woman elected to Congress, in 1916, was the only woman to vote for the Nineteenth Amendment, in January 1918. *Library of Congress: LC-USZ62-8422*. ABOVE RIGHT: The suffrage amendment was ratified when Tennessee legislator Harry Burn changed his vote, because his mother Phoebe asked him to. *Photograph of Burn statue in Knoxville, TN, taken by the author*. BELOW: After the 2016 and 2020 presidential elections, women in Rochester, NY, plastered Susan B. Anthony's grave with "I VOTED" stickers. *Daniel Penfield, CC BY-SA 4.0, via Wikimedia Commons*.

VICTORY CELEBRATIONS, AUGUST 1920

Alice Paul toasts the suffrage flag at the National Woman's Party headquarters, across from the White House on Lafayette Square. *Library of Congress: LC-USZ62-20176.*

Carrie Chapman Catt's triumphal tour took her from Washington, DC, to New York City. Women clapped so hard they split their gloves. *Library of Congress: LC-USZ62-49122.*

INDIGENOUS WOMEN LOBBIED FOR NATIVE AMERICAN CITIZENSHIP

Marie Louise Bottineau Baldwin. *Library of Congress: LC-B2-3194-10.*

Zitkála-Šá (Gertrude Simmons Bonnin). *Library of Congress: LC-USZ62-119349.*

Inviting Jessie De Priest, wife of the only Black congressman, to tea at the White House caused a scandal in 1929. *History.house.gov/exhibitions-and-publications/BAIC/Jessie De Priest.*

FLAPPERS & FEMINISTS

Josephine Baker, ex-patriate show girl in Paris. She later became a resistance fighter and civil rights activist. *Library of Congress: LC-USZ6-1301.*

Margaret Sanger, birth control pioneer. *Library of Congress: LC-USZ62-29808.*

Soledad Chávez de Chacón, the first Hispanic and first woman secretary of state of New Mexico, elected 1922. *www.sos.state.nm.us, file: Soledad Chacon.*

Secretary of Labor Frances Perkins, honored as America's Outstanding Woman by Chi Omega Sorority in 1934, receives a medal from Eleanor Roosevelt at the White House. *Alamy: CSU 2015 9 1073 or F280JK.*

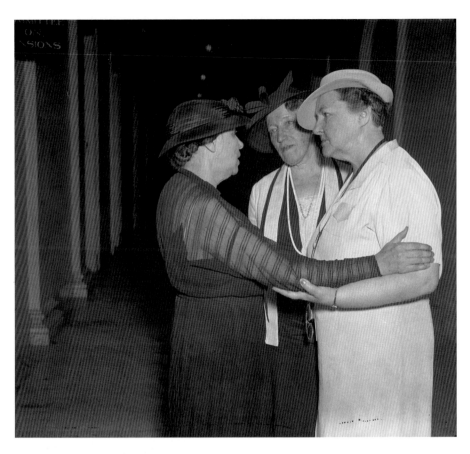

ABOVE: "Lady Lawmakers": Senator Hattie Caraway (D-AR) greets Congresswomen Caroline O'Day (D-NY) and Mary Norton (D-NJ). The three were the only women chairs of congressional committees in 1937. *Library of Congress: LC-DIG-hec-23080.* LEFT: "Outwardly female, inwardly male," Pauli Murray won a Mademoiselle magazine merit award in 1946 for achievement in the law. *Library of Congress: LC-USZ62-109644.*

In 1942, celebrated contralto Marian Anderson and Mary McLeod Bethune, National Youth Administration Director of Negro Affairs, launched the SS *Booker T. Washington*, the first Liberty ship named for a Black man. *Library of Congress: LC-USE6-D-007654.*

Republican Margaret Chase Smith, the first woman to serve in the House (1940–48) and the Senate (1949–72), was sworn in by House Speaker William Bankhead (R-AL) and Representative James Oliver (R-ME) in 1940. *Library of Congress: LC-DIG-hec-28784.*

Lathe operator Annie Tabor was one of thousands of Black Rosies contributing to the war effort. *Library of Congress: LC-DIG-fsa-8b07728.*

In 1944, before she became Marilyn Monroe, Norma Jeane Dougherty worked as a Rosie at the Radioplane Company in California. *David Conover, US Army, Wikimedia Commons.*

ABOVE: Working closely with Thurgood Marshall at the NAACP Legal Defense Fund, Constance Baker Motley was the first Black woman federal judge, appointed by President Johnson in 1966. *@Dr. Ernest C. Withers, Sr. courtesy of the Withers Family Trust.* BELOW: Mary Louise Smith, standing next to a statue of Rosa Parks in Montgomery, Alabama, joined Aurelia Browder, Susie McDonald, and Claudette Colvin as plaintiffs in the Supreme Court suit, *Browder v. Gayle* (1956), that resolved the bus boycott. *@Mickey Walsh, USA TODAY NETWORK.*

CHANGE AGENTS

LEFT: Working with Dr. King at the Southern Christian Leadership Conference, Ella Baker was the conscience and backbone of the civil rights movement. *Library of Congress, Print and Photograph Division, Visual Materials from the NAACP records: LC-USZ62-118852.* BELOW: Daisy Gatson Bates, head of the Arkansas NAACP, shepherded the Little Rock Nine to integrate public schools in 1957. Bates is standing, second from right. *Library of Congress, Print and Photograph Division, Visual Materials from the NAACP records: LC-USZ62-119154.*

Lorraine Hansberry was the first woman, first Black person, and youngest playwright to win sundry awards for "Raisin in the Sun" in 1959. *Library of Congress: LC-USZ62-113271, from the New York World-Telegram & Sun Collection.*

Ruby Bridges and President Obama inspect Norman Rockwell's painting of Bridges integrating a New Orleans elementary school in 1960. *Courtesy Barack Obama Presidential Library.*

Esther Peterson presents the report of the President's Commission on the Status of Women to President Kennedy, October 1963. Dorothy Height, of the National Association of Negro Women, is in the flowered hat at left; Mary Bunting, president of Radcliffe College, is to the right of Peterson. *Cecil Stoughton, White House Photographs, John F. Kennedy Presidential Library and Museum, Boston.*

Patsy Takemoto Mink, the first woman of color in Congress, joined her colleagues in 1965. Standing: Florence Dwyer (R-NJ), Martha Griffiths (D-MI), Edith Green (D-WA), Mink (D-HI), Lenore Sullivan (D-MO), Julia Hansen (D-WA), Catherine May (R-WA), Edna Kelly (D-NY), Charlotte Reid (R-IL). Seated: Senator Maurine Neuberger (D-OR), Frances Bolton (R-OH), Senator Margaret Chase Smith (R-ME). *Courtesy of the National Archives and Records Administration.*

Betty Friedan, author of *The Feminine Mystique*, joins NOW co-founder Marguerite Rawalt outside the White House. *Schlesinger Library, Harvard Radcliffe Institute: W723794_1.*

Fannie Lou Hamer, representing the Mississippi Freedom Party, testified at the Democratic National Convention, August 1964. *Library of Congress: LC-DIG-ds-7134.*

College professor and Black Panther Angela Davis was acquitted of murder and kidnapping conspiracy charges in 1972. *Library of Congress: LC-DIG-yan-1a38470.*

Dolores Huerta co-founded the United Farm Workers Union in 1962. *Walter P. Reuther Library, Archives of Labor and Urban Affairs, Wayne State University.*

ABOVE: Feminist activists Ti-Grace Atkinson, Flo Kennedy, Gloria Steinem, and Kate Millett in 1977. *Harvard University, Schlesinger Library of the History of Women.* BELOW: Demographics, geography, religion, and politics played a role in the defeat of the ERA, a campaign led by Phyllis Schlafly. *Library of Congress: LC-DIG-ds-00757.*

ABOVE: 1972, Ruth Bader Ginsburg co-founded the ACLU Women's Rights Project. *Lynn Gilbert, 1977, CC BY-SA 4.0, Wikimedia Commons.* BELOW: Congresswoman Nancy Mace (R-SC) was the first female graduate of The Citadel. Cadet photo courtesy of *The Citadel, ocm@citadel.edu; Mace.house.gov/about/headshot.*

Year of the Woman: An increase in the number of women in the Senate in the 1990s created a demand for a designated restroom. Senators Susan Collins (R-ME), Patty Murray (D-WA), Olympia Snowe (R-ME), Carole Moseley-Braun (D-IL), Kay Bailey Hutchison (R-TX), Barbara Mikulski (D-MD), Diane Feinstein (D-CA), and Mary Landrieu (D-LA) celebrate its opening in 1997. *AP Images/Joe Marquette.*

ABOVE LEFT: Ellen Malcolm created and chaired Emily's List, which is still funding pro-choice Democratic women candidates. *US Department of Labor: 4E8A0147.* ABOVE RIGHT: Geraldine Ferraro's 1984 vice presidential nomination energized women candidates in both parties. *National Air and Space Museum, Collection of Sally Ride, Gift of Tam O'Shaughnessy, NASAM2016-02424.* BELOW: The treatment of Anita Hill during the Clarence Thomas Supreme Court confirmation hearings in 1991 prompted many women to run for political office. *Library of Congress: LC-DIG-ppmsca-65032.*

Jenny Beth Martin, founder of the Tea Party, spoke at C-PAC in 2016. Gage Skidmore, CC BY-*SA 2.0, Wikimedia Commons.*

After her son was murdered by a white man, Lucy Mcbath (D-GA) won a Congressional seat in 2018. *Mcbath.house. gov/about/headshot.*

BLM leaders Alicia Garcia, Patrisse Cullors, and Opal Tometi. *Ben Baker/ Redux Pictures.*

RIGHT: Nancy Pelosi (D-CA) was the first (2007–11) and second (2019–present) woman to serve as Speaker of House. *US Department of Labor, www.flickr.com /people/52862363@N07.* BELOW: The Supremes: Sandra Day O'connor joins justices Sonia Sotomayor and Ruth Bader Ginsburg for Elena Kagan's investiture, October 1, 2010. *Steve Petteway, Collection of the Supreme Court of the United States.*

ABOVE: Hillary Rodham Clinton, wearing suffrage white, accepts the Democratic Party nomination for President, July 28, 2016, in Philadelphia, ninety-six years after women passed the Nineteenth Amendment. *Mark Pazniokas, CT Mirror.* BELOW: 2017 Women's March leaders Tamika Malloy, Carmen Perez, Linda Sarsour, and Bob Bland. *Will Kirk, Johns Hopkins University.*

In 1921, to celebrate passage of the Nineteenth Amendment, the National Woman's Party donated Adelaide Johnson's "Portrait Monument" of Elizabeth Cady Stanton, Susan B. Anthony, and Lucretia Mott to the US Capitol. *Library of Congress, LC-DIG-hec-30740.*

SOJOURNER SUSAN B. ELIZABETH CADY
TRUTH ANTHONY STANTON

WOMEN'S RIGHTS PIONEERS

To mark the centennial of the Nineteenth Amendment, in August 2020, New York City added a monument by Meredith Bergmann to Central Park. "Women's Rights Pioneers," Sojourner Truth, Anthony, and Stanton, is the first statue of real women in Central Park. *Photograph by the author.*

Women's soccer became a professional sport in 1991 and its stars exploded. The highpoint was the July 1999 Women's World Cup final, when the US defeated China. An audience of 90,000 filled the Rose Bowl, setting an attendance record for any women's sport. After ninety minutes of regulation play, thirty minutes of sudden death and no goals, Brandi Chastain scored a game-winning penalty kick. She celebrated by whipping off her jersey, falling to her knees, and raising her fists, wearing a black sports bra. What the *New York Times* described as the "most iconic photograph ever taken of a female athlete" appeared everywhere. In 2019, a statue of Chastain in that pose was installed at the Rose Bowl. It was a moment of celebration and liberation that kicked off decades of discussions about women athletes, sex appeal, power, and professionalism. Taking off a jersey was common in men's games, but the next year, the international soccer association made it a yellow card violation for both sexes. Now a varsity college coach, Chastain titled her autobiography, *It's Not About the Bra*.[60]

In the absence of enough girls for a team, both Chastain and teammate Mia Hamm had played on boys' teams growing up. As a soccer superstar, Hamm scored a career 158 international goals, a record for men or women, only surpassed by Abby Wambach in 2013. As of 2022, Megan Rapinoe has scored sixty-two goals. In 2012, ESPN named Hamm "the greatest female athlete." She was also the most marketable female athlete of her generation, with multiple endorsements, a Wheaties box, a Barbie doll, and a video game. Hamm appeared in Nike's "If You Let Me Play" advertisements.[61] The Women's National Basketball Association, playing its first games in 1997, also got a Barbie, accessorized with a doll-sized ball, hoop, and water bottle.[62]

Women were also changing the game in the entertainment industry. Journalists and academics debate whether *Sex and the City* (1998–2004) advanced feminism or set it back. According to one source, the HBO series about four white, privileged, thirty-something single women, set in New York City, portrayed four stereotypes: "the Slut, the Prude, the Career Woman and the Heroine." It also depicted the endurance of female friendship, lots of sex, and fabulous clothes, a combination of couture and street fashion. In the *New Yorker*, Emily Nussbaum concluded that the show described the complexity of women's lives, whether they were "second wave" or "post feminists." Its controversial ending, a wedding to the wrong man, is still dissected.[63] Another reiteration of a sexy sisterhood was *The L Word*, from Showtime (2005–2009). It was the first television series devoted exclusively to the social lives of lesbians, a cohort of Los Angeles fashionistas. "Before *The L Word*, lesbian characters barely existed on television," concluded one critic.[64]

EDUCATION

In 1992, the American Association of University Women released *How Schools Shortchange Girls*, a study of another gender gap. It presented "compelling evidence that girls are not receiving the same quality, or even quantity, of education as their brothers." Despite the fact that girls got better grades and were more likely to graduate than boys, the report claimed that even women teachers treated girls "as though their desks were in the hallway." Boys needed more attention because they were often less prepared, less socialized to sit still, and more disruptive. It concluded that ignoring girls resulted in young women feeling inadequate and suffering from eating disorders, higher rates of depression, and suicide.[65]

The AAUW report corresponded to a 1989 analysis of gender and racial discrimination in the SAT, the college admissions exam. It aligned with Harvard sociologist Carol Gilligan's study, *In a Different Voice* (1982), about how girls and women make ethical decisions, and anticipated *Reviving Ophelia: Saving the Selves of Adolescent Girls* (2005) by Mary Pipher.[66] The important outcomes were more attention to the role of gender and race in the education of all students and an understanding that inequality persisted. In 1993, Congress passed the Gender Equity in Education Act, sponsored by Pat Schroeder (D-CO), to provide additional teacher training and encourage girls in math and science.[67]

In 1993, the Citadel, a military college in Charleston, admitted Shannon Richey Faulkner, assuming the applicant was male. When it learned she was not, the Citadel withdrew its offer, and she launched a two-year legal battle. The court fight provoked a heated public response, including vandalism of her home, rude T-shirts, and bumper stickers: "SAVE THE MALES" and "1,952 BULLDOGS AND ONE BITCH." Threatened with the loss of state funding, the Citadel admitted Faulkner, nineteen, in August 1995. After grueling training in intense heat, subjected to death threats and sexist slurs, and under protection from federal marshals, she retreated to the infirmary, citing physical and mental exhaustion. After six days, she withdrew.[68]

Against that background, Justice Ginsburg announced the Supreme Court's decision in *United States v. Virginia* (1996), ordering the Virginia Military Institute to admit women or refuse public money.[69] VMI had been the last public college in Virginia to desegregate, in 1968. A lower court favored VMI's assertion that to admit women would undermine its mission. The US Court of Appeals for the Ninth Circuit was also sympathetic, but said women deserved a parallel experience. VMI had three options: admit woman, establish a sister school, or forego taxpayer support. VMI proposed a Virginia Women's Institute for Leadership at Mary Baldwin College.

After delays and appeals, the case reached the Supreme Court amid an avalanche of amicus briefs. The Court held that VMI's response did not satisfy the equal protection clause. Justice Scalia dissented and Justice Thomas recused himself because his son attended VMI. Writing for the 7–1 majority, Justice Ginsburg declared invalid any "law or official policy that denies to women, simply because they are women, equal opportunity to aspire, achieve, participate in, and contribute to society, based upon what they can do." The law required "all gender based classifications" to be evaluated with "heightened scrutiny." VMI surrendered and admitted women.[70] When Justice Ginsburg visited VMI to mark the decision's twentieth anniversary, she was greeted like a rock star. By 2020, 602 women had graduated, an annual average of twelve per class. After the VMI decision, the Citadel reversed its male-only policy. Between 1996 and 2020, 180 women enrolled. The first, Nancy Mace, graduated in 1999. A Republican, she won a state delegate seat, representing Charleston, and was elected to Congress in 2020. In May 2019, Sarah Zorn was named regimental commander, the first female top cadet in the Citadel's 175-year history.[71]

WORK, WAGES, AND THE MOMMY WARS

Employment patterns had shifted dramatically since the 1960s. The number of men in well-paid manufacturing jobs declined, while low-paid service economy jobs held by women increased. Due to decades of economic discrimination, Black women in every class had always worked. White women, lacking role models, struggled. They abandoned family meals, church attendance, and volunteer work. Many relied on fast food, frozen meals, slice-and-bake cookies, and latch keys. The reality was the exhausted, harassed supermom. Deindustrialization led to the feminization of work; divorce had led to the feminization of poverty. By the 1990s, nearly 60% of all children, including preschoolers, had moms working outside their homes. Women had always worked; now more were paid. As employed mothers moved to the center of the nation's economic life, family patterns and community attitudes changed. If they were single parents, they worked because their income was essential to survival; if they were married, their income was necessary for financial stability.[72]

The percentage of women in the workforce in 2000 reached a high of 46.5%. Women were the major breadwinners in 40% of families and co-earners in another 30%.[73] Working women had been filing more complaints and bringing more suits charging discrimination. A database, www.wageproject.org, tracked cases in which women had prevailed. Liquor store clerks, university professors, airline ramp agents, stockbrokers, waitresses, and state troopers won suits because their bosses said they couldn't do the job if they were pregnant or should be home with their kids. It was easier to sue male managers who broadcast their bias.

The majority of working women were mothers. Bearing and raising children meant that women's participation in the workforce was interrupted and would rarely match that of men, creating a "biological gap,"

which contributed to the wage gap.[74] Catalyst, founded in 1962 "to accel-
erate progress for women through workplace inclusion," had studied that
gap for decades. It compared the median hourly wage earned by women,
working full-time, year-round, to every dollar earned by men and identified several contributing factors. The calculation controlled for education,
college majors, grades, age, experience, parental status, location, region,
occupation, and industry. It documented that women majored in the liberal
arts and education, the "softer fields," rather than economics or science;
the exception was graduates of women's colleges. Many women sought
jobs with more flexible hours that would be compatible with motherhood,
even if they paid less. They took maternity leave, usually unpaid, and interrupted their careers to care for their families, especially after a second child,
which reduced their lifetime earnings. Nor did women regularly negotiate
for salary increases. In 2007, the wage differential was 77 cents earned by
women, compared to a male dollar, up from 64 cents in 1983. The gap was
greater for Black and brown women.[75]

According to Catalyst, accounting for those elements brought the differential up to 94 cents. Persistent sex discrimination and institutional
racism cost women at least six cents of every dollar earned. Studies found
that women who acted in ways consistent with gender stereotypes, such as
focusing on creating connections in the workforce or expressing empathy
or interest in other perspectives, were considered less competent by male
bosses. If they acted with assertion and ambition, they were "too tough" or
"unfeminine," which was another reason they did not get raises when they
did negotiate. Women were frequently sidelined into human relations or
communications, jobs less likely to lead to executive roles. Even as women
entered the workforce in larger numbers, the public's image of leadership
remained male.[76] Sex role stereotyping endured.

When Lisa Belkin profiled female Ivy League graduates who were
leaving high-power, high-paying jobs to stay home, the response was outrage, because those women had the potential to advance. In *Get to Work*
(2006), Linda Hirshman chastised women for wasting their degrees, having
more than one child, and retreating from the adult world of work. The idea

that working was a choice fueled the "mommy wars," an emotional battle zone among white women, a renewal of the skirmishes first fought in the 1960s. Only privileged women had choices, because they could afford a variety of childcare options. Many felt guilty for leaving their children with someone else.[77]

Most women had to balance the cost of childcare with their salaries; many stayed home because it was less expensive. Poor women and many single moms had no option but lousy wages and inadequate childcare. No one criticized men for leaving their children in the care of their wives or nannies, but dads were shamed when they took extended paternal leave or opted to stay home. The culture supposedly worried about the welfare of children and claimed to value motherhood, but gave more status to jobs with paychecks. Every mother knew that caring for children was hard, isolating, exhausting, discounted, and vital. Feminist Katha Pollitt doubted there would be a conflict if there were safe, affordable, widely accessible childcare.[78]

The expression "choice feminism" gained currency in 2006. It encompassed the idea that the goal of the women's movement, of feminism, was for women to be free to make independent choices, to work or not, to marry or not, to have children or not.[79] "Choice" also referenced reproductive rights. Women favoring access to abortion framed their position as "pro-choice." Women could choose to end a pregnancy or not, but should not limit the choices of other women. "Choice feminism" ignored how difficult achieving economic and emotional independence was for most women. In reality, few women earned enough to support themselves or their children. Without equal pay and opportunity, without paid family leave and adequate childcare, in a tighter labor market and an economic downturn, the participation of American women in the workforce began to decline. Internationally, in 1990, the US had the sixth highest female labor force participation; by 2010, it had fallen to seventeenth.[80] Choice was an illusion.

Two categories of working women were especially vulnerable: immigrant, mostly Asian women, working in nail salons, massage parlors, and restaurants, and the two million housecleaners, health aides, and nannies,

Black and brown women, immigrant and US born, working in private homes. Their cultural and physical isolation made them hard to organize and protect. In the 1960s, Dorothy Bolden, a Black domestic worker in Atlanta, used buses for de facto organizing. In 1968, she helped establish the National Domestic Workers Union of America as an advocacy group. She required all members to register to vote.[81]

Forty years later, Ai-jen Poo, executive director of the National Domestic Workers Alliance, organized household workers by visiting bus stops and playgrounds. Her first goal was a Domestic Workers' Bill of Rights, covering minimum wages, overtime pay, days off, and human rights protections. It took six years for that legislation to pass in New York, in 2010.[82] The daughter of a neuroscientist and an oncologist, immigrants from Taiwan, Poo attended high school at Phillips Academy Andover and graduated from Columbia University. Her work organizing domestic workers and creating coalitions to address long-term elder care led to a MacArthur Genius Award and recognition as a "world influencer" by both *Time* and *Newsweek*.[83] One hundred years after *Muller* and the Triangle Fire, women workers, especially immigrants, were still at risk. By 2000, 29% of the population, twenty-eight million Americans, were foreign born. That number included a higher proportion of women due to more families migrating together and the kinds of jobs available in the US.[84]

WOMEN AND TECHNOLOGY

The ubiquity of computers in the workforce diminished the number of jobs on factory floors and in offices, laying off secretaries, bank tellers, grocery clerks, and retail workers. New jobs frequently came with variable, unpredictable schedules, which made childcare arrangements even more difficult. With the disappearance of manufacturing and the growth of service jobs, women's participation in labor unions increased. Flight attendants, clerical workers, teachers, and nurses challenged the assumption that women could not be organized. Women union members lobbied for comparable pay, maternity leave, childcare, flextime, and affirmative action. With nearly 50% female members, the AFL–CIO established a women's department. The Service Employees International Union (SEIU) organized hospital staff, home care aides, nursing home workers, local and state government employees, janitors, security officers, and food services workers. Las Vegas became a base of labor feminism when multiethnic hotel maids turned the city's Hotel and Culinary Workers into the largest union local in the country.[85]

Feminism and technology collided as women confronted bias in science and Silicon Valley. When Mark Zuckerberg launched Facebook in 2007, he symbolized the hoodie-wearing, garage band, male dominance of tech entrepreneurs. The AAUW reported that the number of female programmers declined from 35% in 1990 to 26% in 2013. The irony was that women had been the original human computers. In the 1840s, British mathematician Ada King, the Countess of Lovelace and Lord Byron's daughter, helped engineer the first mechanical computer. Beginning in the eighteenth century, mathematically minded women were hired for computation, because they worked for less than men and tolerated the tedium of rigorous, repetitive calculations. In the nineteenth century, to economize, the Harvard Observatory employed only female computers, frequently their wives, daughters, and housemaids. Women calculated algorithms in astronomy, navigation, and surveying. During both world wars, they calculated artillery trajectories. Because the work was considered low status, African Americans, Jews, and polio survivors were also employed.[86]

Coding became another pink-collar, sex-segregated ghetto. Only recently has attention been paid to women like Katherine Johnson and Mary Jackson, among eighty Black women employed by NASA in the 1950s, the "Hidden Figures" of Margot Lee Shetterly's book and a feature film. These mathematicians transferred their skills from computing with pencils to programming computers. The first general purpose computer, the ENIAC (Electronic Numerical Integrator and Computer), was programmed entirely by women working for the Army. Not one received credit.[87] Women were not encouraged to pursue math and science. Those who made it to graduate schools in physics, astronomy, engineering, or technology found themselves in a small minority, rarely mentored, invited to co-author papers, or selected for fellowships.[88]

THE 2000 ELECTION

In 2000, Hillary Clinton ran for the Senate from New York and Elizabeth Dole ran for President, as her husband had in 1996. Dole had served in cabinet posts in two Republican administrations and led the American Red Cross. She dropped out of the primary for lack of funding, but sexism played a role. The White House project analyzed 462 news articles about the four Republican primary contenders: George W. Bush, Steve Forbes, John McCain, and Dole. More than a third of the articles were about Dole's hair, her handbag, or her husband. The former Duke sorority sweetheart was slammed as a "ballbuster" and a "bitch."[89] As the new century opened, the idea of a woman president was no longer unimaginable, but sexism remained implacable.

The Supreme Court decided the outcome of the 2000 Presidential election between Texas Governor George W. Bush, son of former President Bush, and Vice President Al Gore. The Republican was dismissed as a "likeable lightweight"; the Democrat was mocked as stuffy and stuck up. It was an election of personality versus policy. Nationally, Gore beat Bush by more than 540,000 popular votes. In the Electoral College, it was Gore 267, Bush 246, before counting Florida's twenty-five contested votes. Bush's narrow five-hundred-vote Florida margin prompted a recount. Amid "hanging chads" and "butterfly ballots," the process uncovered many irregularities.[90] Led by James Baker, former Secretary of State and his father's consigliore, Bush's legal team included Ted Cruz, Brent Kavanaugh, John Roberts, and an associate named Amy Coney. Gore's equally distinguished team challenged the decision of Florida's Republican Secretary of State to ignore the recount option available under the state's election code.

The Florida Supreme Court required a recount and extended the certification deadline. Bush appealed that decision to the Supreme Court. After sundry maneuvers, it voted, 7–2, that a recount was unconstitutional, and then decided, 5–4, that no constitutional recount could be concluded in a timely manner. There were four dissenters: Justices Breyer, Souter, Ginsburg, and Stevens.[91] On December 12, 2000, Vice President Gore conceded. In April 2001, the *Miami Herald* and *USA Today* published a comprehensive review of the Florida recount effort and concluded that Bush would have won by 1,665 votes. Nationally, women favored Gore over Bush, 54% to 44%, while men went for Bush, 54% to 34%.[92]

President Bush appointed six women to his cabinet: Ann Veneman (Agriculture), Gale Norton (Interior), and Elaine Chao (Labor) in his first term, and Condoleezza Rice (State), Margaret Spellings (Education), and Mary Peters (Transportation) in his second.[93] Rice, like Angela Davis a decade earlier, grew up in segregated Birmingham, Alabama. Born in 1954, she was the daughter of a minister and a teacher. With a PhD in international studies, she joined the Stanford University faculty in 1981, rising to provost in 1993. An expert in Soviet and Eastern European affairs, she served with the Joint Chiefs under Reagan and with the National Security Council under the senior Bush. She was the first Black woman to serve as National Security Advisor (2001-2005) and Secretary of State (2005-2009), under his son. She followed Colin Powell, the first Black Secretary of State. A classical pianist and athlete, in 2012 Rice was one of two women invited to join the Augusta National Golf Club, which had long banned women members and WPGA tournaments.[94]

Elaine Chao was the first Asian American to hold a cabinet post. Born in Taiwan in 1953, she knew no English when she came to America at age eight. Her father became an international shipping magnate. A graduate of Mount Holyoke College and Harvard Business School, she pursued a career in finance. Chair of the Federal Maritime Commission under Reagan and Deputy Secretary of Transportation under George H. W. Bush, she married Senator Mitch McConnell (R-KY) in 1993.[95] Bush's first choice was Linda Chavez, a Latina and the highest-ranking woman in the Reagan administration. She withdrew following charges of sheltering illegal immigrants, blaming the era's "search and destroy . . . politics."[96] In 2017, President Trump made Chao Secretary of Transportation.

After the attacks on September 11, 2001, the Bush administration was consumed by counter-terrorism, war in the Middle East, Katrina disaster relief, and the 2008 financial crisis. First Lady Laura Bush, the second with a professional degree and a former school librarian, supported her husband's "No Child Left Behind" education reform. She emphasized early childhood reading programs and launched the National Book Festival. Internationally, she spoke out against the Taliban's treatment of women and human rights abuses in Burma. In Africa and Asia, she promoted global health initiatives to fight malaria and AIDS.[97] But women's issues were not a priority for her husband.

REPRODUCTIVE JUSTICE AND THE ROBERTS COURT

On the day after his inauguration, George W. Bush reinstated the "gag rule," a ban on aid to international groups that offered information about abortion as part of family planning programs. Reagan initiated the ban; Clinton did not enforce it. After Republicans retook the Senate in 2002, Bush signed the Partial-Birth Abortion Ban Act. "Partial birth" was a term coined by the National Right to Life Committee. The medical term is "D&X," dilation and extraction, a procedure used in 0.2% of the 1.3 million abortions performed in 2000, according to the Guttmacher Institute. Spearheaded by Representative (now Senator) Marsha Blackwell (R-TN), it was the first law to put a federal ban on abortion. It overturned *Stenburg v. Carhart* (2000), which struck down a Nebraska ban on the procedure, and invalidated thirty other state laws.[98]

A new voice in the conversation about abortion came from the Sister-Song Women of Color Reproductive Justice Collective, founded in 1997 in Atlanta. In contrast to the focus on the needs of middle-class white women, it sought to serve the most marginalized: young mothers, sex workers, LGBTQ people, the incarcerated, disabled, or poor. It broadened the conversation to reproduction, forced sterilization, maternal mortality, inequities in health care, racially biased immigration, incarceration, and police practices. In April 2004, SisterSong pressed NOW to rename its March for Choice to the March for Women's Lives.[99] It was heralded as the largest march of any kind to date, drawing one million people to Washington. The police estimated 750,000. SisterSong's Loretta Ross joined Gloria Steinem, Dorothy Height, Madeline Albright, and Hillary Clinton on stage. "If all we do is march . . ." Clinton cautioned, "[We] will not change the direction of this country, unless women vote."[100] Democrats did not win in 2004, but would retake the Congress in 2006.

President Bush's appointments of John Roberts, to replace Chief Justice Rehnquist in 2005, and Samuel Alito, to replace Justice O'Connor in 2006, maintained a conservative majority on the Supreme Court. In *Gonzales v. Planned Parenthood* (2007), the Roberts Court denied a challenge to the Partial-Birth Abortion Ban. Whereas O'Connor had been an essential swing vote in *Casey* in 1992, Justice Alito joined the conservative 5–4 majority. The *Gonzales* ruling departed from past decisions, which had made an exception to protect a woman's health.[101]

Two other high court cases had a negative impact on women's lives. In Castle Rock, Colorado, Jessica Lenahan-Gonzales had a permanent restraining order against her husband. When he seized their three daughters in violation of the order, she called the police four times and visited the station in person to demand their help. The police took no action until her husband showed up at the station and was killed in a shoot-out. The children were found murdered in his car. Their mother sued the police department. In *Town of Castle Rock v. Gonzales* (2005), the Court ruled, 7–2, that the town and the police had not violated her right to due process and could not be sued. Justice Scalia's opinion found that state law did not entitle the holder of a restraining order to any specific action by the police, who had the right to act at their discretion. Justices Ginsburg and Stevens dissented.[102] The outcome seemed to encourage police inaction and sanction violence against women and children.

Another Ginsburg dissent came in *Ledbetter v. Goodyear Tire & Rubber Company* (2007), a case about equal pay. After Lilly Ledbetter discovered that she had been paid less than her male coworkers for nineteen years, she sued her employer under Title VII. Goodyear countered that Title VII required her to bring claims within 180 days. The Court upheld the rule, voting 5–4 in favor of Goodyear. Ginsburg's dissent pointed out that Ledbetter could not have filed sooner since she only discovered the pay discrepancy years later. "The Court's insistence on immediate contest overlooks common characteristics of pay discrimination," she wrote. "Comparative pay information, moreover, is often hidden from the employee's view." Rather than file her dissent with a clerk, Ginsburg insisted on reading a summary from the bench, a rare public rebuke. She called on Congress to override "a cramped interpretation of Title VII."[103]

WOMEN IN POLITICS

Election by election, the number of women in Congress from both parties slowly increased. After the "Year of the Woman," there were fifty-four women in office (40 D, 14 R) in 1993. By 2003, there were seventy-four (48 D, 26 R), including the Sanchez sisters, Loretta and Linda, Democrats from California, who served simultaneously. Olympia Snowe (R-ME) won a Senate seat in 1994. When Susan Collins was elected in 1998, Maine became the second state represented by two women. Sheila Frahm (R-KS) was appointed to fill Bob Dole's seat when he ran for President in 1996. Carol Moseley Braun lost her seat in a primary challenge in 1998, leaving the Senate without a Black member until Barack Obama's arrival in 2005.[104]

In the 1990s, women overturned the long-standing dress code for members of Congress. The rules required suits for men and skirts for women. Bella Abzug had never been allowed to wear her hat on the floor. The dress code represented more than protocol. Wearing trousers had long been a metaphor for women's empowerment. "Who wore the pants?" asked who wielded authority. In 1990, Susan Molinari (R-NY) wore pants on the House floor and no one objected. Barbara Mikulski instigated the change in the Senate. The Senate Sergeant of Arms, Martha Pope, amended the skirts for women rule in 1993, but required jackets for all. Individual members can still require skirts and hose for female staff.[105]

When Senator Tammy Duckworth (D-IL), a combat veteran who lost both legs serving in Iraq, brought her ten-day-old daughter to the floor for a vote in April 2019, both mother and child wore jackets and the baby was allowed to wear a cap. The baby's appearance was the result of months of negotiation to change the Senate rules forbidding children in the chamber. After assuaging concerns about breastfeeding and diaper changing, Amy Klobuchar (MN), the senior Democrat on the Rules Committee, drafted language that passed unanimously. The new rule allowed both male and female Senators to bring infants up to age one into the chamber during votes.[106]

The return of Democrats to power after the 2006 midterms renewed interest in the ERA, renamed the Women's Equality Amendment, but not reworded. It had been introduced in every Congress since its defeat in 1982, but neither of its chief sponsors, Senator Ted Kennedy (D-MA) nor Representative Carolyn Maloney (D-NY), could compel their respective judiciary committees to schedule hearings. The ERA lacked bipartisan support in the Congress and the country. As Maloney concluded, "Rumors of our progress are greatly exaggerated."[107]

The Democratic majority elected Nancy Pelosi Speaker of the House of Representatives in January 2007. She took the gavel surrounded by the children of members.

> This is a historic moment—for the Congress and the women of this country. It is a moment for which we have waited more than 200 years . . . [Women] weren't just waiting; women were working . . . to redeem the promise of America, that all men and all women are created equal. For our daughters and grand-daughters . . . we have broken the marble ceiling . . . I accept

this gavel in the spirit of partnership, not partisanship. In this House, we may belong to different parties but we serve one country.[108]

First elected in 1987, from one of the safest Democratic districts in the country, Pelosi had served as minority whip and minority leader when Republicans held the majority. At sixty-six, she became the most powerful woman in the country, next in line for the presidency after the vice president. She was the first woman, the first Californian, and the first Italian American to become Speaker.[109] Although *Time* magazine did not mark the milestone with a cover story, the Smithsonian asked her to donate her ceremonial gavel and the burgundy skirt suit she wore. It would be displayed with the dress Marian Anderson wore at the Lincoln Memorial in 1939, Sally Ride's spacesuit, and Justice O'Connor's robe.[110]

Pelosi's elevation signaled the rising presence and power of women in politics. The Smithsonian owns the gown Hillary Clinton wore to the inaugural ball in 1992, but it has not yet acquired one of her iconic pantsuits. In 2006, Senator Clinton won a second term. She was one of eighty-eight women members of Congress, sixteen Senators (11 D, 5 R) and seventy-two Representatives (52D, 20R). Women were governors of nine states: Alaska, Arizona, Connecticut, Delaware, Hawaii, Kansas, Louisiana, Michigan, and Washington.[111] When Arizona Senator John McCain won the Republican nomination for president in 2008, he picked one of them, Sarah Palin of Alaska, a self-described "hockey mom," to be his vice president.

2008 PRESIDENTIAL PRIMARY

Gender, generation, and race were elements in the Democratic presidential primary. Senator Clinton, the presumed front runner, narrowly lost to a younger, less experienced and very appealing candidate, the junior Senator from Illinois. She would have been the first woman nominated for president; Barack Obama was the first African American nominee. By June 2008, the contenders were nearly tied. Clinton won more delegates in primaries; Obama won more in caucuses and secured the majority of Democratic Party "superdelegates," the first time they had played a determining role.[112] On June 7, 2008, Clinton conceded.

> Although we weren't able to shatter that highest, hardest glass ceiling this time, thanks to you it's got about 18 million cracks in it. And the light is shining through like never before, filling us all with the hope and the sure knowledge that the path will be a little easier next time.

The expression "glass ceiling" was coined in 1984, the same year as "date rape."[113]

Sexism played a part in Clinton's loss. Journalists rarely wrote about it, although some of them perpetuated it. Newspapers commented on Hillary's thick ankles and changing hairstyles. On television, Tucker Carlson called her "castrating." Chris Matthews commented on her "cackle" and compared her to Nurse Ratched. Mike Barnacle joked that she looked like "everyone's first wife standing outside probate court." Nora Ephron accused Clinton of having the "authenticity of Naugahyde." Yet a decade earlier, when Clinton was First Lady, Ephron, herself a Wellesley alumna, had told graduates: "Understand: every attack on Hillary Clinton for not knowing her place is an attack on you."[114] On the night before the New Hampshire primary, the first in the nation in January 2008, rowdies interrupted Clinton's speech, shouting, "Iron my shirt!" After they were removed, she laughed, "Oh, the remnants of sexism—alive and well!" "IRON MY SHIRT" became one of many nasty T-shirts. Merchandise proclaiming "LIFE'S A BITCH, DON'T VOTE FOR ONE," "F--- HILLARY: GOD KNOWS SHE NEEDS IT," and "KFC HILLARY MEAL DEAL: TWO FAT THIGHS, TWO SMALL BREASTS AND A BUNCH OF LEFT WINGS" appeared wherever she went.[115]

Navigating the thicket of stereotypes and double standards was a challenge. On the day of the New Hampshire primary, Hillary had teared up, overcome by fatigue and frustration. Five days before, she had come in third in the Iowa caucuses, after Obama and North Carolina Senator John Edwards. The candidate crying scene was replayed all day. Many credited that moment of vulnerability with her New Hampshire victory, winning the popular vote, splitting delegates with Obama, and becoming the first woman in American history to win a fully contested presidential primary. (Chisholm won a nonbinding preferential primary in New Jersey, in 1972, but few other contenders were on the ballot.)[116] Was crying a sign of humanity or weakness? Could women leaders be both powerful and popular? If likeability was an issue, she was "likeable enough," as Obama conceded gracelessly. "Well, that hurts my feelings," she responded.[117]

Clinton had made a decision not to emphasize her gender: "I am not running because I am a woman. I'm running because I think I'm the most qualified and experienced person to do the job that has to be done."[118] Hillary was a feminist, damned as a "radical feminist." Despite her devotion to her family, it was hard for Hillary the candidate to take on the mantle of traditional womanhood. Voters remembered her dismissal of staying home and baking cookies. Some voters recoiled at the idea of having her husband back in the White House and the possibility of more domestic drama.[119] Disguising her femininity in pantsuits, Hillary wanted to win on a gender-neutral playing field. She demonstrated she could take a punch and throw one. "When you're attacked, you have to deck your opponent." According to one observer, "she consistently made passing the masculinity test her top priority."[120]

In contrast, Sarah Palin played up her gender. Feminine and flirty, McCain's running mate blew kisses at rallies. She campaigned in red high heels and pencil skirts, surrounded by her brood of children. Male voters dubbed her a MILF ("Mother I'd Like to F---"). Portraying herself as a frontierswoman, a gun-toting "grizzly mama," Palin symbolized the myth of the Western woman, one of the few images of tough women in American culture. Woman had first won suffrage in the West. Kansas elected the first woman mayor in 1887; Colorado elected women state representatives in 1894; Utah elected the first female state senator in 1896. Jeannette Rankin had been a rancher. The first women governors were elected in Wyoming and Texas. Sandra Day O'Connor castrated bulls and shot coyotes. Ann Richards and Nancy Pelosi were flinty women. Before she was shot in 2011, Congresswoman Gabrielle Giffords (D-AZ) was a markswoman.[121]

Both Clinton and Palin, directly or unconsciously, addressed the "masculine mystique," the dominance of men in American politics. Political scientists have concluded that when female candidates "violate social norms" and act like ambitious men, voters dislike them.

> Politics, so long dominated by men, has a masculine ethos; women and men alike perceive political success as being linked to masculine traits such as self-promotion and fighting . . . more aggressive than nurturing.[122]

To appear both qualified and likeable, women have to navigate between masculine and feminine qualities. Gallup first asked voters if they would vote for a woman for President in 1937; 33% said yes. By 2003, that number rose to 87%.[123] The question was, "Which woman?"

Belittling coverage of both Clinton and Palin was consciousness-raising for younger women, who thought the fight for equal rights and respect was over. Stereotypes of Clinton as the brainiac and Palin as the bimbo annoyed and angered their supporters. Chris Matthews, who made a career out of bashing Hillary on MSNBC, disdained her as the "know-it-all girl" nobody asked to high school dance. Palin was the prom queen. In the primaries, Clinton won almost eighteen million votes. In the presidential contest, the Republican ticket won about fifty-eight million votes. In total, roughly seventy-six million people voted for a woman to be president or vice president in 2008.[124] Women were in the arena. They counted as voters and candidates, but had yet to break the cultural barriers between them and the presidency, a symbol of patriarchal power. By proving themselves capable of meeting any challenge, women across the political and social spectrum drew attention to women who had less access to personal or political autonomy. The fight for equality wasn't over. It would be fought on many fronts, by a more divided women's movement confronted by white conservatives.

CHAPTER NINE

LEANING IN & LOSING, 2009–2016

Barack Obama caught the country's attention when he delivered a keynote address at the 2004 Democratic National Convention. The Illinois state senator and US Senate candidate introduced himself as the son of a Black father from Kenya and a white mother from Kansas, explaining that Barack meant "blessed." He called for Americans to unify around common values and shared behaviors, worshipping "an awesome God," and coaching Little League. He continued in the cadence of a Black preacher:

> . . . there is not a liberal America and a conservative America, there is the United States of America. There is not a Black America and a White America and Latino America and Asian America, there's the United States of America . . . Pundits [divide] our country into . . . Red States for Republicans, Blue States for Democrats . . . [but] We are one people, all of us pledging allegiance to the stars and stripes.[1]

Dividing America into red and blue states was the work of television news mapmakers. The colors changed over time and networks. Since 2000, the red/Republican, blue/Democrat scheme has been standard. Toss-up states are purple.[2]

In 2008, presidential candidate Obama campaigned for "hope and change." The economic crisis overshadowed global events, undermined faith in Republican leadership, and defeated John McCain. The electorate was the most diverse in American history. One in four votes was cast by a person of color. Turnout among Black, Latino, Asian, young, and Southern voters increased. At 68.8%, Black women had the highest turnout rate. Obama won with 53% of the popular vote and 365 Electoral College votes. He won 95% of Black voters, 67% of Hispanics, and 43% of whites. Among all women, Obama won 56%, compared to 49% of men, a seven-point gender gap; white women split 46% for Obama, 53% for McCain.[3] The majority of white women had not voted Democratic since 1964. Since then, married, rural, and suburban white women trended Republican, while single, highly educated, and urban white women were reliably Democratic. Women of color turned out in historically high numbers and voted overwhelmingly Democratic, a crucial factor for Obama and Democrats running for Congress.[4]

Sexism and racism had an impact on the campaign. Sarah Palin's inexperience and ignorance made it easy for news outlets and late-night comics to characterize her as a dunce. Michelle Obama was a more formidable and vulnerable target. Raised in South Side Chicago, educated at Princeton University and Harvard law school, she had held high-powered jobs in a law firm, city government, and a university hospital. She outranked and out-earned her husband, but she was a reluctant political spouse. This accomplished attorney was depicted as an "angry Black woman" and denigrated as a "baby mama" rather than the married mother of two daughters.[5] A *New Yorker* cover presented her as a terrorist, with an AK-47 and combat boots, fist-bumping her husband, a turbaned Muslim, while an American flag burned. The magazine defended the caricature as satire. Both campaigns called it "tasteless and offensive." Others found it incendiary.[6] When she wasn't being compared to Angela Davis, "Michelle O" was called the "Black Jackie O," a reference to Jacqueline Kennedy Onassis. After eight years as First Lady, Michelle Obama had become a commanding figure, with a best-selling autobiography and a rock star book tour. She was "the most admired woman in America," according to Gallup, ending Hillary Clinton's seventeen-year run.[7]

Democrats maintained their majority in both chambers in the 2008 election, adding eight Senate seats and twenty-one House seats, the largest party majority since the 1994 Gingrich takeover, but gains for women were minimal. There were ninety women in Congress, including seventeen in the Senate (13D, 4R), a decline of one. Kirsten Gillibrand (D-NY) replaced Hillary Clinton, who resigned to join the cabinet. Kay Hagan defeated incumbent Elizabeth Dole in North Carolina, reducing the number of Republicans. The House added only one woman, for a total of seventy-three (56D, 17R). Nancy Pelosi remained Speaker. New Hampshire elected a majority of women to its state senate, a low-paying, part-time job.[8]

There were seven women governors at the start of 2009. Sarah Palin resigned. Obama appointed Kansas Governor Kathleen Sibelius to be Secretary of Health and Human Services (HHS) and Arizona Governor Janet Napolitano to lead Homeland Security. The President's most unexpected cabinet appointment was Hillary Clinton to be Secretary of State. His cabinet was a model of expertise and diversity, including two Republicans, Roy Lahood (Transportation) and Robert Gates (Defense). In Obama's first term, Latina Hilda Solis served as Secretary of Labor and Susan Rice, an African American, as Ambassador to the United Nations. Later appointments included Loretta Lynch (Attorney General), Sally Jewell (Interior), Penny Pritzker (Commerce), Sylvia Mathews Burwell (HHS), and Samantha Power (UN).[9]

OBAMA'S RECORD ON WOMEN'S ISSUES

A week after his inauguration, President Obama chose the Lilly Ledbetter Fair Pay Act for his first signing ceremony, surrounded by beaming women lawmakers, including Republican Senators Collins and Snowe of Maine and Patty Murray (D-WA). Senator Mikulski (D-MD), who had sponsored the bill with then-Senator Obama, patted the President's shoulder. She had pushed the bill since 2007, but President Bush threatened a veto. The law was named for the unassuming Alabama woman who had sued Goodyear Tire for wage discrimination, having been paid less than her male counterparts for nineteen years. When Ledbetter lost her Supreme Court appeal in 2007, Justice Ginsburg's dissent called on Congress "to correct this Court's parsimonious reading of Title VII." The bill reset the clock for filing paycheck discrimination claims, but Ledbetter was never compensated for lost pay.[10]

In 2009, for the first time in history, close to a majority of American workers were women, due to layoffs of men. Almost 40% of those were the primary breadwinners in their households. At the same time, women's earnings had fallen by 2%. Women were more likely to hold sub-prime mortgages, making them more vulnerable in the housing crisis. Many professions remained sex segregated. Women were 10% of civil engineers, one-third of physicians and surgeons, and 98% of dental assistants and kindergarten teachers. The wage gap for all women had improved from 58 to 77 cents for every dollar men earned, but with a greater disparity for Black and brown women.[11]

Fifty years after passage of the Equal Pay Act, wage discrimination persisted. Everyday experience and two major studies proved that gender-based discrimination persisted. The Institute for Women's Policy Research examined earnings data. In the twenty most common occupations for women and nineteen of the twenty most common occupations for men, women earned less than men. The exception was stock clerks. The American Association of University Women analyzed the wages of college graduates with one year of experience in their fields and found a 5% wage gap between men and women. Senator Mikulski introduced a Paycheck Fairness Act again and again, but it failed due to Republican filibusters. The bill would have amended the 1938 Fair Labor Standards Act to provide more effective remedies for victims of pay discrimination.[12]

Over eight years, Obama asked for an Equal Paycheck Act, an expansion of paid leave, reauthorization of the Violence Against Women Act, laws to combat human trafficking, and increased access to science, technology, engineering, and math (STEM) education for girls. He designated Alice Paul's National Woman's Party headquarters the Belmont-Paul Women's Equality National Monument and established a White House Council on Women and Girls, led by Valerie Jarrett and Tina Tchen, to ensure that the needs of women and girls were taken into account in federal programs.

Obama's second Secretary of Defense, Leon Panetta, removed the military's ban on women serving in combat. In November 2013, three women completed the Marine Corps' Infantry Training course, ready to serve as a rifleman, machine gunner, and mortar Marine. Two other women failed to pass the Marine Infantry Officer Corps "gender integrated curriculum." Army Ranger and Navy SEAL units opened positions to women. Captain Kristen Griest and 1st Lieutenant Shaye Haver were the first women to graduate from Ranger School. Griest transferred to the regular Army and became its first female infantry officer, 233 years after Deborah Sampson disguised herself as a man to fight in the Continental Army during the Revolutionary War. In 2016, Defense Secretary Ash Carter opened all combat jobs to women, ordering the integration of female combat soldiers "right away."[13]

In 2005, an Army sergeant was the first woman since World War II to earn a Silver Star and the first ever to win it for combat valor. Sergeant Leigh Ann Hester, twenty-three, was guarding a supply convoy when it was ambushed outside Baghdad. Her team outflanked and eliminated the attackers. She shot three enemies in close quarters. The body count was twenty-seven insurgents dead, six wounded, one captured. Every member of Hester's unit survived. After Iraq, she served as a police officer before joining the National Guard and spending eighteen months in Afghanistan in 2014. "She's the type of soldier you want next to you in combat," declared one of her male comrades.[14]

The controversial Patient Protection and Affordable Care Act (ACA), called Obamacare, included many elements beneficial to women. It prohibited them from being billed more than men for health insurance or charged for pre-existing conditions like C-sections or cancer. It required health plans to cover care for newborns, mental health, and substance abuse.[15] With an estimated forty-five million people without medical insurance, health care had been a major campaign issue. Senate Republicans filibustered the ACA until December 24, 2009, the first time the Senate had been in session on Christmas Eve since 1865. Every Democrat plus two independents outnumbered every Republican for a cloture vote, 60-39. The same tally passed the actual bill. Massachusetts Senator Ted Kennedy, a champion of health care since 1970, had died that August. In January, Republican Scott Brown won a special election to fill his seat. With Brown in the Senate, Democrats could not stop a future filibuster if its version of the ACA did not pass the House.[16]

To appease those opposed to any abortion funding under the ACA, Obama issued Executive Order 13535, reaffirming the Hyde Amendment. Unable to amend the Senate bill and unwilling to risk starting over, the House passed an imperfect bill, 219–212, in a rare Sunday session. Every yes vote was cast by a Democrat; all 178 Republicans and 34 Democrats voted against it.[17] Because Leader Pelosi's ability to discipline her caucus was vital, she received one of the twenty-two pens the President used to sign the ACA, on March 22, 2010. Another pen went to Victoria Reggie Kennedy, the Senator's widow. Guests at the East Room signing ceremony cheered the most expansive social legislation passed in decades, while Republicans vowed to repeal it.[18]

THE TEA PARTY

National pride and optimism over the election of a Black president were met with massive resistance among white conservatives. Republicans were intractable. House Minority Whip Eric Cantor (VA) pledged to defy him. Senate Minority Leader Mitch McConnell (KY) declared that making Obama a "one term president [was] the single most important thing we want to achieve." His purpose in the minority "was to become the majority." McConnell would stall cabinet and judicial confirmations and filibuster "without remorse or restraint."[19] Congressional Republicans were abetted by an unexpected grassroots movement called the Tea Party.

In February 2009, Rick Santelli, a CNBC business reporter based in Chicago, declared that "America needed a new Tea Party" to protest government spending on bailouts. That night Rush Limbaugh amplified Santelli's anger, tapping populist resentment. Referring to the colonial patriot protest in 1773, the Tea Party fused Constitutional idealism and economic libertarianism. White, evangelical, and conservative, it supported Second Amendment gun rights and prayer in schools. It opposed federal debt, corporate bailouts, abortion, and marriage equality. One critic called it "a hysterical grassroots tantrum about the fact that a Black guy was president." Covered enthusiastically by Fox News, the Tea Party accused Obama of running a "gangsta government," a racist reference to criminal street gangs.[20]

Although the Tea Party felt alienated from the GOP establishment, it helped Republicans take the House and net six more Senate seats in the 2010 midterms. The President conceded that his party had been "shellacked." Pelosi surrendered her gavel to John Boehner (R-OH), who found it hard to control the hard-right GOP Freedom Caucus. He did convert the former office of the parliamentarian into a women's restroom. It had a chandelier, a fireplace, four stalls, two sinks, and, anticipating the future, a baby changing station. Senate women had had their own restroom since 1993.[21] The female total in both houses fell from ninety to eighty-eight members, the first decline in forty years. In the representation of women, the United States tied with Turkmenistan for seventy-eighth place.[22]

Women were well represented in the Tea Party. Jenny Beth Martin was driving to a housecleaning job in Georgia when she heard Santelli's call to arms. Due to tax debts, she and her husband had lost their home to foreclosure, sold their second car, held a garage sale, and filed for bankruptcy. They were the only employees of their cleaning service. Responding to the call for action, the mother of twins used Facebook and Twitter to organize a protest in Atlanta a week later. Five hundred people showed up in driving rain. She called for a National April 15 Tax Day Tea Party. With a lawyer she met online, she created the Tea Party Patriots. In 2010, *Time* listed Martin as one of the "100 Most Influential Leaders in the World."[23]

The Tea Party attracted conservative women like Sarah Palin, Congresswoman Michele Bachmann (R-MN), and Penny Nance, head of Concerned Women for America, an anti-abortion organization. They called themselves feminists. "Not the kind who loaf around in the faculty lounge of some East Coast women's college," Palin explained, but "a gun toting, self-reliant, pro-life Christian woman who credits her gender as the source of her power."[24] They were not feminists. In 2010, Steve Bannon wrote and directed a documentary about fifteen Tea Party women for Citizens United Productions, part of a political action committee that made television ads and documentaries for conservative candidates and causes. *Fire From the Heartland: The Awakening of the Conservative Woman* depicted resilient, strong-willed, conservative, and passionate Christian women. Many came from poor backgrounds and struggled to succeed. Among them was Bachmann, a tax attorney, who credited her professional success to her submission to Jesus and her husband. She described herself as "fiscally conservative, pro-life, [a] butt-kicker in public, [a] cooperative helpmate at home, and a Christian wife and mother."[25]

Palin and Bachmann responded to sexism in different ways. The press viewed Palin as a "calendar model for a local body shop." When David Letterman compared Palin's look to a "slutty flight attendant," she punched back. In contrast, Bachmann forgave men who demeaned her. Chris Wallace called her a "flake" on Fox News. Senator Arlen Specter (D-PA) chastised her: "Act like a lady. Do not interrupt me." When a congressman denigrated her "sex appeal," she accepted it as flattery: "If someone wants to compliment me on my appearance at 55 . . . I welcome that."[26]

Their embrace of motherhood as a source of authority had wide appeal. No one asked conservative women, from Schlafly to Bachmann, "Who's taking care of your children?" Palin campaigned in 2008 with her five children, including a newborn with Down syndrome and her unwed pregnant teenager. Bachmann had five biological children, whom she homeschooled. In the 1990s, she worked with a private foster care agency to house twenty-three girls for six years. Her political career derived from her campaign to include an explicitly Christian curriculum in public schools. The first Republican woman elected to the House from Minnesota, in 2006, Bachman was a founding member of the Tea Party Caucus and ran for President in 2012.[27]

The Huffington Post declared that "evangelical feminism" was an oxymoron. In the 1970s, when the term first appeared, it was based on the belief that Christian principles and the ideals of equality were compatible. The alternative was "complementarianism," the view that God designed men and women not to be equal, but complementary, with men as leaders and women as lieutenants. So-called evangelical feminism recalled the revivalism of the 1820s, which inspired women to save their souls with good works. Would-be reformers expanded their domestic spheres into wider roles, as Palin and Bachmann had. Like nineteenth-century reformers, they made the case that motherhood motivated their political engagement and politics enhanced their roles as dutiful wives, devoted mothers, and faithful churchgoers.[28]

THE POLITICS OF MOTHERHOOD

Mothers across the political spectrum understood what it meant to be a "grizzly mama," fiercely protective of their children. How best to parent led to new skirmishes in the mommy wars. Michelle Obama was criticized for abandoning her career. In her speech at the 2008 Democratic convention, she introduced herself as "a sister, daughter, wife, and mother." Choosing to put her children first, she described her role as "mom in chief" and grew vegetables at the White House.[29] She gracefully navigated the challenges of being a Black woman and First Lady, in the same way that her wardrobe incorporated edgy designers and J. Crew sweater sets.

In July 2012, Anne-Marie Slaughter, the State Department's Director of Policy Planning under Secretary Clinton, explained her resignation in a cover story for the *Atlantic*. "Why Women Still Can't Have It All" became the most read article in the history of the magazine and refueled the debate over whether domestic roles were obstacles to women's equality. The author admitted that she could not juggle the demands of her job in Washington and her family in Princeton, concluding that women could not have children and executive positions without better childcare and flexible schedules. She took incoming fire for her entitlement and her insensitivity to all the women who did manage, without her white privilege. Within two years, Slaughter had returned to DC as the CEO of a think tank.[30]

Even the essay's title was provocative, evoking *Cosmo* editor Helen Gurley Brown's 1982 autobiography, *Having It All: Love, Success, Sex, Money*. The childless Brown did not include motherhood among her goals. That women could have it all had been an unrealistic aspiration of the women's movement. Its roots were in marketing pitches made to "liberated" consumers in the 1970s. Working women were advised to multitask, but for most, the answer to having it all was "not all at once" or not without lots of help. The debate over "having it all" distracted from needed reforms like equal pay, parental leave, and affordable day care. By 2015, the percentage of women in the workforce fell; 61% of non-working women cited family responsibilities as the reason.[31]

The next salvos came from Silicon Valley. The same month Slaughter's article appeared, Marissa Mayer, thirty-seven, became Yahoo's CEO. A Stanford University graduate, she dismissed the challenges working mothers faced. Mayer took two weeks maternity leave with her first child, built a nursery adjacent to her office, and hired a nanny. After the birth of twins in 2015, she took five days off. Admiration for her work ethic and ability to "balance a Blackberry and a breast pump" was undercut by criticism of her management style, her refusal to let employees work from home, and her rigidity about flexible hours. Mayer claimed she was "blind to gender" and "not a feminist."[32]

The chief operating officer of Facebook, Sheryl Sandberg, advised women to "lean in." A Phi Beta Kappa graduate of Harvard, Sandberg, forty-three, was a self-identified feminist whose goal was equality at work and at home. Published in 2013, fifty years after *The Feminine Mystique*, her book grew out of a Ted Talk about the paucity of women leaders. *Lean In: Women, Work and the Will to Lead* put her on the cover of *Time*, *Fortune*, and *CosmoCareers*. Using her privilege as a platform, she urged readers to "embrace ambition," "sit at the table," "negotiate," "make your partner a real partner," and "not . . . leave before you leave," meaning do not pass on opportunities because you may take maternity leave in future. She supported structural corporate changes, paid maternity leave, and affordable childcare.[33]

The backlash hit her for being naïve, wealthy, and white; for assuming partners were male; and focusing on middle-class married women with children. "Leaning in" left corporate male culture intact and depended on underpaid female domestic workers to support women "leaning in." One critic advised women to "RECLINE! . . . Leaning In Is Killing Us!" Suddenly widowed in 2015, Sandberg faced the challenges of single parenthood. "Before I did not get it. I did not really get how hard it is to succeed at work when you are overwhelmed at home."[34] In November 2018, Sandberg and Facebook were investigated for #MeToo scandals and their role in Russian efforts to use Facebook to influence the 2016 presidential election. Michelle Obama bluntly dismissed leaning in, telling women on her blockbuster book tour: "that whole 'you can have it all'—nope, not at the same time; that's a lie. It's not enough to lean in, because that s--- doesn't work all the time."[35]

POPULAR CULTURE

The daily tedium of most women's lives was not depicted in popular culture. The combination of women working outside of their homes and cable news coverage of murder trials, car chases, and royal divorces killed soap operas. Those daytime dramas, which began on the radio in the 1930s and drew huge audiences, had long connected women across the country. In the Sixties, they introduced topics like interracial marriage, anti-war protests, and abortion. They were replaced by the fake "reality" of boardrooms and McMansions. Scripted and unscripted programs about contemporary women, like *Desperate Housewives* (2004–2012), *Real Housewives* (2006–2020), and *Keeping Up with the Kardashians* (2007–2020), emphasized sexual femininity, nouveau riche values, and conspicuous lifestyles. Whether Black or white, other than being "spenders and trenders," most of the characters did not have jobs. Gloria Steinem skewered the programs as "minstrel shows," about women who are "all dressed up . . . inflated . . . plastic surgeried . . . false bosomed . . . fighting with each other."[36]

Women in more traditionally powerful roles were rare on television. Those portraying female presidents had short terms, on *Commander in Chief* (2005–06), *24* (2008–2010), *State of Affairs* (2014–2015), and at the end of *House of Cards* (2018). *Veep* (2012–2019), about a female vice president, lasted longest. On *Madame Secretary* (2014–2019), a female Secretary of State was elected president in its last season. In the final episode, she endorsed the ERA. The most powerful fictional politician on television was a political fixer and the president's mistress, depicted by Kerry Washington on *Scandal* (2012–2018). It was the first major network program starring a Black actress since *Julia* in 1968.[37]

2012 ELECTION

In November 2012, President Obama won reelection, defeating Mitt Romney and Paul Ryan. Republicans still controlled the House and Democrats held the Senate. The Republican platform reflected the influence of the Tea Party. Since the 1970s, the alliance of Southerners, social conservatives, and evangelicals had pushed the party right, from its centrist, fiscally cautious but socially and environmentally progressive positions of the 1960s. In 1976, Republicans added anti-abortion language to their platform. In 1980 they removed the ERA and in the 1990s included a pro-life litmus test for judges, prayer in public schools, and posting the Ten Commandments in public spaces. "Family values" insisted on traditional marriage.[38] Democrats claimed Republicans had waged "a war against women," pledging to defund Planned Parenthood, voting against reauthorization of the Violence Against Women Act, and condoning offensive remarks about "legitimate rape."

One of the driving issues in the presidential campaign was the economy. It prompted women to turn out in record numbers. Obama attracted the support of 55% of all women voters, compared to 45% of men. Among unmarried women, many of them heads of households, the gap was thirty-eight points. According to Democratic pollster Celinda Lake, "It proves that you don't make women angry." Obama's 51% popular vote and 332 Electoral College total were lower than his 2008 results, an outcome not seen for a two-term president since Woodrow Wilson's reelection in 1916. The President earned support from 93% of Black voters, 73% of Asians, 71% of Hispanics, 39% of whites, 64% of people who had not finished high school, and 55% of people who had attended graduate school.[39]

Once again, women of color, especially Black women, were key to Obama's victory. In 2012, for the first time in history, the turnout rate of Black voters surpassed that of whites, 66.2% compared to 64.1% of eligible non-Hispanic whites. All women voted at higher rates than men: by 4% among white women and 9% among Black women. Black women voted at a higher rate than any other group, across gender, race, and ethnicity. While fewer whites went to the polls in 2012 than in 2008, Black turnout increased.[40] Republicans conducted an autopsy of the 2012 results, but could not agree on whether to be more broadly inclusive or more narrowly focused. Thirty GOP-controlled state legislatures responded with new voting laws, restricting early voting, eliminating same day registration, limiting voting hours, and increasing identification requirements.[41]

The 2012 election increased female representation in the House to eighty (61D, 19R). Post-census redistricting had created opportunities. Thirteen women won open House seats. Tulsi Gabbard (D-HW) was the first Hindu and Tammy Duckworth (D-IL), born in Thailand, was the first disabled congresswoman. Both were war veterans. New Hampshire sent an entirely female delegation to Congress, two Senators and two Representatives, and elected Governor Maggie Hassan. As chair of the Republican Conference, Cathy McMasters Rodgers (R-WA) held the fourth-highest post in GOP leadership. Candace Miller (R-MI) was the only Republican woman serving as a committee chair, assigned to House Administration, which dealt with housekeeping tasks like office space.[42] Women increased the diversity of the Congress. Twenty-eight women of color were elected: thirteen Black, nine Latina, and six Asian American Pacific Islander representatives. Counting all the women and members of color, white men were no longer the majority of the Democratic Caucus.[43] Further down the ballot, with the election of Republican Katrina Shealy to the South Carolina senate, there were no more male-only state legislatures.[44]

The 1992 Year of the Woman tripled the number of women in the Senate, from two to six. Only forty-four women had ever served in that body. The 2012 cycle resulted in twenty women Senators (16D, 4R), five of them newcomers. In Massachusetts, Elizabeth Warren defeated Scott Brown. Running for an open seat in Wisconsin, Democrat Tammy Baldwin became the first openly lesbian US Senator. Mazie Hirono (D-HI) was the first female Japanese American Senator, the first Buddhist, and only the second woman of color in the Senate. (In 1964, Patsy Mink, another Hawaiian Democrat, was the first woman of color and the first Japanese American in the House.) Nebraska Republican Deb Fischer handily defeated former Democratic governor and incumbent Senator Bob Kerrey and Democrat Heidi Heitkamp won in North Dakota.[45]

A record number of Democratic women chaired Senate committees. The most senior, Barbara Mikulski (MD), led the powerful Appropriations Committee, its first female chair. Patty Murray (WA) chaired the Budget Committee; Dianne Feinstein (CA), the Intelligence Committee; Debbie Stabenow (MI), Agriculture; Barbara Boxer (CA), Environment and Public Works; and Mary Landrieu (LA), Small Business.[46] In a tradition begun by Mikulski, every few months Senate women met for dinner in the Capitol's Strom Thurmond Room, named for the former Dixiecrat, who was a notorious womanizer. "I know, the irony," commented Olympia Snowe (R-ME). They talked about families, books, and vacations and hosted a bridal shower for Senator Collins, age sixty. They built a network of rare bipartisan respect, evident in cooperation on legislation related to financial security for women, family health care, children's issues, developmental disabilities, and sexual assault in the military.[47]

A LITANY OF LOSS

There were no solutions to gun violence by criminals and police. A tragically growing cohort of Black women were the wives and mothers of men and boys killed by white men, many of them police officers. The 2012 murders of two Black teenagers in separate incidents in Florida drew national attention. In February, Trayvon Martin, seventeen, was walking home through a gated community in Sanford, near Orlando, wearing a grey hoodie and eating Skittles. Deemed suspicious by a neighborhood watch volunteer, the unarmed boy was accosted. After a fight, he was shot and killed. The case provoked anger and attention to racial stereotyping. President Obama observed, "If I had a son, he'd look like Trayvon." The shooter claimed that he acted in self-defense, under Florida's "stand your ground" laws. In July 2014, a jury found the assailant not guilty of second-degree murder or manslaughter. All six jurors were women, five white women and one of mixed Black and Mestizo heritage. Two men and two women, all white, served as alternates. Outside the courthouse, hoodie-wearing protestors chanted, "No justice, no peace!"[48]

On the day after Thanksgiving, 2012, Jordan David, seventeen, was killed at a gas station near Jacksonville after an argument with a white man who complained about loud rap music. The software engineer fired ten shots into the young man's car and drove away. Convicted two years later, the trial judge handed down the maximum sentence for first-degree murder: life without parole; three consecutive thirty-year sentences for the attempted murder of the teenager's friends, who were in the car; and fifteen years for shooting from a moving vehicle. David's divorced parents had asked the prosecution not to pursue the death penalty. His mother, Lucy McBath, broke down in the courtroom. "I choose to forgive you . . . for taking my son's life. I choose to release the seeds of bitterness and anger and honor my son's love . . . knowing God's justice has been served."[49]

McBath became a spokesperson for Moms Demand Action for Gun Sense and Mothers of the Movement, a group of Black mothers whose children had been killed by gun violence. Six years after her son's murder, she entered politics in Georgia, where she had been based for thirty years as a Delta flight attendant. She had intended to run for the state senate, but the 2018 shootings of seventeen students at Marjory Stoneman Douglas High School prompted her to run for Congress instead. McBath beat the Republican incumbent, winning 50.5% of the vote in a suburban Atlanta district with 13% Black residents, once represented by Newt Gingrich.[50]

GUN CONTROL

The demand for sensible gun control, background checks, a ban on assault weapons, and other reforms empowered women across the country to organize and oppose the NRA. The death of twenty kindergartners and first graders and six adults at Sandy Hook Elementary School in Newtown, Connecticut, on December 14, 2012, horrified the country. Before entering the school at 9:30 A.M., the twenty-year-old white shooter killed his mother. Armed with several guns, including an AR-15 assault rifle, he blasted through a locked door. Police arrived in less than three minutes, at which point the gunman shot himself. President Obama teared up when he spoke to the nation that afternoon. "We have endured too many of these tragedies . . . I know there's not a parent in America who doesn't feel the same overwhelming grief I do."[51]

A month later, the President announced a plan to reduce gun violence, having solicited suggestions from 229 organizations. He recommended closing background check loopholes, banning assault weapons and high capacity magazines, securing schools, and increasing mental health services. He immediately signed twenty-three executive orders and sent twelve proposals to Congress. On April 17, 2013, the Senate held nine gun control votes in a row. To avoid a filibuster, each bill needed sixty votes to pass. Senator Dianne Feinstein (CA) implored her colleagues to "show some guts." Every bill failed.[52]

A ban on assault weapons lost, 40–60. A bill to limit the size of magazines lost, 46–54. An amendment to impose stiff penalties on gun trafficking, supported by the NRA, lost, 58–42. The reform most likely to pass was a bipartisan bill, introduced by Senators Joe Manchin (D-WV) and Pat Toomey (R-PA), both gun owners. It expanded background checks to include purchases made at gun shows and on the Internet. The NRA called the proposal "misguided." It blamed shootings on mental illness and violent video games. In the gallery, former Congresswoman Gabrielle Giffords (D-AZ), still recovering from a 2011 assassination attempt in a grocery store parking lot, joined the parents of dead Black boys and of the children who had died at Sandy Hook, Virginia Tech, and Aurora, Colorado. Four Republicans crossed party lines to support the measure: Susan Collins (ME), Mark Kirk (IL), John McCain (AZ), and Toomey. Supporter Frank Lautenberg (D-NJ) came to the floor in a wheelchair. The bill failed, 54–46. Forty-one Republicans and five Democrats from red states with high gun ownership, including Max Baucus (MT), Mark Begich (AK), and Heidi Heitkamp (ND), rejected it. "Shame on you!" shouted the moms.[53]

President Obama echoed that sentiment. Speaking to families and supporters in the Rose Garden, he called it a "shameful day for Washington." He excoriated the NRA for "willfully" lying and called out Senators who had "caved to pressure." He cited the 90% of Americans who supported universal background checks, to keep convicted felons, perpetrators of domestic violence, and the severely mentally ill from buying guns. "No single piece of legislation can stop every act of violence and evil," Obama conceded, "[but] we had an obligation to try." The effort would require continued "passion [and] persistence."[54] Congress had failed and the violence escalated.

BLACK LIVES MATTER

Three months later, in July 2013, the acquittal of Trayvon Martin's killer launched the Black Lives Matter movement. It began with a Facebook hashtag, #BlackLivesMatter, and exploded into national protests. Beginning with a slogan, three Black women formed a coalition, the Movement for Black Lives. Patrisse Khan-Cullors, from Los Angeles, was an artist, author, Fulbright Scholar, and chair of Reform LA Jails. Alicia Garza, from Oakland, was a writer, organizer for the National Domestic Workers Alliance, and advocate for trans and gender-nonconforming women of color. Opal Tometi, from Brooklyn, a Nigerian-American writer who led the Black Alliance for Just Immigration, was inspired by Ella Baker. They met through a leadership training program for community organizers.[55]

#BLM gained national attention in the summer of 2014 following the deaths of Eric Garner on Staten Island in July and Michael Brown in Ferguson, Missouri, in August. Both died at the hands of white police officers charged with using excessive force. Garner was arrested for selling single cigarettes from packs without tax stamps. He was filmed being held in an illegal chokehold by a police officer, with others pressing on his back. Garner gasped, "I can't breathe," and subsequently died of suffocation. His words became a rallying cry for demonstrations against harsh police practices across the country. The officers, who claimed they were carrying out orders, were not indicted. A Justice Department debate over whether to bring federal civil rights charges ended five years later, after Trump's Attorney General William Barr ordered the case dropped.[56]

In Ferguson, Michael Brown, eighteen, and a friend were walking in the middle of Canfield Drive. A policeman in a patrol car asked them to move to the sidewalk. The exchange led to a scuffle and ended with the officer shooting Brown, who was unarmed. After his body was left in the street for four hours, neighbors lashed out. A candlelight vigil ended in a riot, with buildings looted and burned. Protestors carrying BLM signs chanted, "Don't shoot," holding their arms up. Cori Bush, a Black pastor and registered nurse, became an activist that night. In 2020, she was elected to

Congress. The governor declared a state of emergency and involved the National Guard, the FBI, and the Justice Department. A November grand jury decision not to indict the officer turned protests violent.[57]

In March 2015, the Justice Department announced that it would not prosecute violations of Brown's civil rights. Instead, it released a scathing report, finding racial bias among the police and courts involved. Eight days later, during a demonstration in Ferguson, two St. Louis police officers were shot. The perpetrator was charged with first-degree assault. In 2016, Ferguson and the Justice Department agreed to sweeping reforms and in 2017, a federal judge in St. Louis approved a wrongful death settlement, awarding Brown's parents $1.5 million. President Obama issued an executive order to curtail Pentagon programs that transferred military surplus and tactical weapons to local law enforcement.[58]

Unimaginable violence against Black Americans had become an undeniable, daily reality. In June 2015, a twenty-one-year-old Confederate sympathizer killed nine Black parishioners attending Bible study at the historic "Mother Emanuel" AME Church in Charleston, South Carolina. The country mourned with President Obama when he delivered the eulogy for Clementa Pinckney, the senior pastor and a state senator. The killer assumed he "would deepen divisions that trace back to our nation's original sin," Obama said. "God had different ideas . . . He has given us a chance, where we've been lost, to find our best selves." He ended by singing "Amazing Grace."[59] Months later, a unanimous decision found the accused guilty on thirty-three counts. The jury was made up of two Black women, eight white women, one Black man, and one white man. The murderer was sentenced to death by lethal injection, the first time a death penalty verdict was rendered in a federal hate crime case. The confessed killer appealed.[60]

Throughout this period of grief and unrest, the country debated the role of guns, Confederate symbols, and Black Lives Matter. People took sides based on race, geography, and experience. BLM was accused of reverse racism. Signs proclaiming "All Lives Matter" misunderstood the meaning of BLM. Older civil rights activists expressed concerns about tactics. Following the shooting of the Ferguson policemen, "Blue Lives Matter" appeared on bumper stickers. In 2014, only 43% of people surveyed thought there was a broad problem about inequitable police treatment of Blacks. By the summer of 2020, after another death by police chokehold, that number increased to 74%. Thousands of multiracial demonstrators carrying BLM signs would demand racial justice, chanting, "I Can't Breathe!"[61]

The "Say Her Name" campaign was an initiative begun in 2014 by Kimberlé Crenshaw to include women in the conversation about race and policing. While Black men make up the majority of people shot by police, Black women are 17% more likely to be stopped by police and almost twice as likely to be killed than their white counterparts. Crenshaw, the legal scholar who coined intersectionality, established the African American Policy Forum, to make sure female victims were not overlooked, that Natasha McKenna, Tanisha Anderson, Michelle Cusseaux, Aura Rosser, Maya Hall, and Breonna Taylor, among too many others, would be remembered.[62]

THE SUPREME COURT AND WOMEN

During the 2012 presidential campaign, Democrats urged the reelection of Obama in order to safeguard the Supreme Court. Ginsburg had been the sole female justice after O'Connor resigned in 2006. Sixty when President Clinton appointed her, she was seventy-five at the beginning of Obama's first term. In August 2009, she was diagnosed with pancreatic cancer, but it was Justice David Souter who retired. President Obama named the first Hispanic and third woman to the high court. Sonia Sotomayor had ideal credentials. Born in 1954, the daughter of Puerto Ricans who had moved to the Bronx, she was valedictorian of her Catholic high school. After graduating summa cum laude and Phi Beta Kappa from Princeton, she advanced to Yale law school. George H. W. Bush nominated her to the US District Court for the Southern District of New York, where she was mentored by Constance Baker Motley. Bill Clinton named her to the US Court of Appeals for the Second Circuit. She was confirmed by a bipartisan Senate vote, 68–31.[63]

The first case Justice Sotomayor heard was *Citizens United v. Federal Election Commission* (2010). Citizens United, a political action committee, had produced *Hillary: The Movie*, which questioned Senator Clinton's fitness to be president. Based on the Bipartisan Campaign Reform Act, the Court determined that the movie was an "electioneering communication." Even if a candidate had not authorized a project, it fell under the requirement to disclose donors. In a complicated decision, the Supreme Court ruled, 5–4, that corporate funding of independent political broadcasts was protected as free speech, under the First Amendment. Justice Sotomayor dissented.[64]

Elena Kagan, the first female Solicitor General, argued for the government against *Citizens United*. In 2010, she was Obama's second Supreme Court appointment. Her career was a mix of law and politics. Born in 1960 in New York City, she excelled academically, graduating summa cum laude from Princeton and magna cum laude from Harvard law school. She clerked for Thurgood Marshall, worked in private practice, and served in the Clinton White House. In 1999, Clinton nominated her for the US Court of Appeals in Washington, DC, but Senate Judiciary Chair Orrin Hatch (R-UT) refused to hold hearings. She returned to Harvard as dean of the law school before Obama appointed her to the Justice Department.[65]

During the Obama administration, the Supreme Court addressed employment, pregnancy, birth control, abortion, and LGBTQ rights. At the beginning of the twentieth century, social justice activists and the courts sought to protect women workers from harsh and dangerous conditions in mines and factories. One of those protections involved restrictions on lifting heavy objects. What began as a safeguard became an impediment. Women made the case that they regularly hoisted children weighing more than most of the limits, but restrictions remained, especially for pregnant workers like Peggy Young, a United Parcel Service driver in Maryland. Her doctor recommended not lifting more than twenty pounds. The UPS standard was seventy pounds, although most deliveries weighed less than twenty. The company put her on unpaid leave, even though drivers charged with drunk driving could remain on paid light duty. Because Young needed a job, she drove a florist's van, lifting bulky items, and sued UPS.[66]

The suit recalled an earlier, lower court case, *Weeks v. Southern Bell Telephone & Telegraph*. In 1969, a Georgia telephone company clerk, Lorena Weeks, applied for a better-paying job as a switchman. She was told she was ineligible because it was illegal, under Georgia law, for women to lift a thirty-pound piece of equipment. The company did not acknowledge that she lifted her thirty-four-pound typewriter on and off her desk daily. Weeks's attorneys, Marguerite Rawalt and Sylvia Roberts, persuaded the US Court of Appeals for the Fifth District that the rule was arbitrary and paternalistic. While arguing the case, Roberts lifted sundry objects in the courtroom, including a bench. Because the equipment in question was usually transported on a dolly, Georgia Bell could not prove that the job was "strenuous."[67]

It had been common policy for public school boards to dismiss pregnant teachers five months before their due dates, with no guarantee of being rehired. In 1974, *Cleveland Board of Education v. LaFleur* (1974) found that practice overly restrictive and arbitrary. In 1978, the Pregnancy Discrimination Act amended Title VII to declare that discrimination based on pregnancy was sex discrimination. The law covered every area of employment. Some employers were reluctant to comply.[68]

In *Young v. United Parcel Service, Inc.* (2015), the company argued that it treated all pregnant workers equally. Justice Scalia described Young as expecting "most favored nation," a misleading phrase meaning equal treatment among parties; Justice Ginsburg accused the company of seeking "least favored nation status." Justice Kagan asserted that UPS was stereotyping pregnant women as marginal workers. Young's attorneys claimed that Young was not treated the same as non-pregnant workers with temporary disabilities. The Court concurred, 6–3.[69] Despite that decision, two-thirds of women asking for accommodations at work have been denied in court. Twenty-seven states passed laws that required employers to offer pregnant women the same accommodations they would offer employees with disabilities. Meanwhile, advocates hoped to enact a Pregnant Workers Fairness Act.[70]

LANDMARK CASES: CONTRACEPTION, ABORTION, MARRIAGE EQUALITY, AND VOTING RIGHTS

Avoiding pregnancy was the topic of a series of Supreme Court cases. Birth control, whether prescribed to avoid pregnancy or treat other female conditions, is the most frequently taken drug among women ages fifteen to sixty. As of 2020, the Pill costs about $30 a month; an IUD (intrauterine device), which can last from three to ten years, costs as much as $1,000. Obamacare covered contraception as a preventative health measure and required all employers and educational institutions to include contraception in their health care plans. There was an exception for churches but not for religious hospitals, charities, or universities. A Senate amendment allowing those organizations to refuse coverage if it "violated their religious or moral beliefs" was narrowly defeated. The Obama administration proposed an "opt-out." By notifying the government of their objections, religious entities could trigger an insurer to provide the coverage directly. The US Conference of Bishops opposed the new rule because it required Catholics in the insurance industry to violate their consciences.[71]

Private employers joined the fray. In 2012, Hobby Lobby, a nationwide arts and crafts retailer, sued the Secretary of Health and Human Services for violating its First Amendment rights by requiring contraception coverage. The evangelical Green family, based in Oklahoma City, with a net worth estimated at $5 billion, owned Hobby Lobby. It underwrote the Museum of the Bible, which opened in 2017 near the National Mall.[72] After serial hearings and appeals, the US Court of Appeals for the Tenth Circuit allowed that corporations were "persons" with First Amendment rights.

When *Burwell v. Hobby Lobby Stores* (2014) reached the Supreme Court, the question was whether the Constitution and the 1993 Religious Freedom Restoration Act (RFRA) allowed a for-profit, privately held company to deny health insurance coverage for contraception, based on its owner's religious beliefs. The RFRA required the government to have a compelling reason for laws that "substantially burden religious beliefs." A 5–4 majority found that requiring contraception imposed a significant burden on Hobby Lobby's religious freedom. Justices Breyer, Kagan, and Sotomayor joined Justice Ginsburg in the minority, reiterating that for-profit corporations cannot be considered religious entities and that contraception coverage was vital to women's health and reproductive freedom.[73] The ruling, that the government cannot force certain employers to pay for birth control through their insurance plans, was "more than a rebuke to President Obama," wrote the *New York Times*. "It was vindication of the conservative movement."[74]

A second challenge to the Affordable Care Act's contraception mandate came after the death of Justice Scalia left an eight-member court. Seven religious nonprofits from around the country, ranging from universities to small service organizations, objected to the mandate because it required them to "facilitate" the provision of insurance to cover contraception. Among them were the Little Sisters of the Poor, Catholic nuns who ran a home for the indigent elderly in Washington, DC. The cases were consolidated into *Zubik v. Burwell* (2016). David Zubik was the Bishop of the Diocese of Pittsburgh; Sylvia Mathews Burwell had succeeded Kathleen Sibelius as Secretary of Health and Human Services. Having determined that insurance companies could provide coverage, the Court remanded the case to the lower courts with an unprecedented 345-word order. It basically told the parties to work it out and outlined the compromise it expected. Institutions would bypass notification, without signing anything, and their insurance companies would step in. That solution unraveled.[75]

A century after Sanger's pioneering initiatives, women's reproductive rights remained insecure. In *Whole Woman's Health v. Hellerstedt* (2016), a group of abortion providers sued John Hellerstedt, the Texas Commissioner of Health Services. The case originated in 2013, when the Texas legislature passed an omnibus abortion bill. It required abortion providers to have admitting privileges at hospitals within thirty miles of an abortion clinic and clinics to comply with standards for ambulatory surgical centers. Neither standard would have been easy to meet. Three-quarters of Texas clinics would close, placing a "substantial burden" on women seeking abortions. The emphasis on women's health, concluded Court reporter Linda

Greenhouse, reflected the evolution of the anti-abortion movement from its original focus on the fetus.[76]

It was the first major abortion case since *Planned Parenthood v. Casey* (1992), when Justice O'Connor was the only woman on the Court. There were now three women Justices, whose questions from the bench indicated their indignation. Chief Justice Roberts could not enforce time limits. Justice Sotomayor pointed out that most abortions required taking two pills. Justice Kagan probed the consequences of clinics closing. Justice Ginsburg asserted that modern abortions were safer than childbirth and many other medical procedures conducted in doctor's offices. She reiterated the position of the American Medical Association, that there was no medical justification for these rules. Based on the data presented, Justice Breyer and a 5–3 majority held that Texas imposed an unnecessary and unconstitutional "undue burden on the right to abortion," the standard since *Casey.* Justices Alito, Roberts, and Thomas, all Catholics, dissented.[77]

Gay rights were another legal battleground. The 1996 Defense of Marriage Act (DOMA) stated that, in federal law, "marriage" referred to unions between men and women. Several states, including New York, authorized same-sex marriage. When Thea Spyer died in 2009, she left her estate to her wife and sole executor, Edith Windsor. The couple had married in Canada but lived in New York. Because the federal government did not recognize their marriage, Windsor did not qualify for a marital exemption and paid estate taxes of $363,000. She sued. President Obama and Attorney General Eric Holder announced that they would not defend DOMA, so House conservatives created a legal team to protect it. Windsor's lawyer asserted that DOMA denied equal protection under the Fifth Amendment. In *United States v. Windsor* (2013), the Court held, 5–4, that DOMA imposed "a disadvantage, a separate status, and so a stigma" on same-sex couples, in violation of the Constitution.[78] Windsor got a tax refund.

As traditionalists feared, *Windsor* was a precursor of federal marriage equality. Massachusetts was the first state to issue same-sex marriage licenses. In 2015, a case brought by fourteen same-sex couples and two widowers suing four midwestern state agencies reached the Supreme Court. The claims were consolidated into *Obergefell v. Hodges*. Because James Obergefell's suit had the lowest case number, the cases were presented under his name. He was a Cincinnati real estate broker whose twenty-year partnership and three-month marriage to John Arthur ended when his husband died. Because same-sex marriage was illegal in Ohio, the couple chartered a medical plane, funded by friends. Accompanied by a nurse and Arthur's aunt, who had been ordained for the occasion, they flew to Maryland and were married on the tarmac of Thurgood Marshall Airport outside Baltimore. Because Obergefell wanted to be identified as the surviving spouse on Arthur's death certificate, issued by Ohio, he sued Richard Hodges, Director of the Ohio Department of Health. A federal judge ruled in the widower's favor, prompting a Republican state lawmaker to demand the judge's impeachment.[79]

When the case reached the Supreme Court, it narrowed the questions to two. Did the Fourteenth Amendment require states to license same-sex marriage and to recognize marriage rights across state lines? Justice Kennedy delivered the 5–4 opinion affirming that the due process clause guaranteed the right to marry. Denying a "fundamental liberty" would abrogate equal protection of the law. "It is demeaning to lock same-sex couples out of a central institution of . . . society." Practically, the decision extended social security, survivor, and health care benefits to same-sex spouses. In dissenting, Justice Roberts wrote that while same-sex marriage might be legitimate, the Constitution did not address it; the Court had exceeded its authority. Justices Alito, Scalia, and Thomas believed states should define marriage.[80]

Another key Court decision addressed voting rights. As women had argued since 1848, voting rights were a women's issue. The decision in *Shelby County v. Holder* (2013) was germane because it weakened key provisions of the 1965 Voting Rights Act. An Alabama jurisdiction sued Attorney General Holder over the Justice Department's ongoing over-sight of its elections. The Court held, 5–4, that one section of the law was unconstitutional. The majority believed it was no longer necessary to monitor election practices previously suspected of bias, because bla-tant discrimination was no longer evident. Justice Ginsburg dissented, asserting that the Fourteenth and Fifteenth Amendment's enforcement powers encompassed the Voting Rights Act and that there was still a need for some states to justify their practices.[81] The decision meant that voters would have to bring suits retroactively, after their rights had been abridged. According to an analysis conducted in 2018, in jurisdictions formerly under "preclearance," based on past patterns of discrimination, voter identification laws became more cumbersome and voting more difficult for poor and elderly Black and brown citizens, many of them women.[82]

THE 2014 MIDTERMS

Fury over Obamacare, the rise of the Tea Party, and the expansion of LGBTQ rights fired up Republican voters. After the 2010 midterms, Democrats lost sixty-three seats and the House. In 2014 they lost the Senate. In 2015, the number of women in Congress edged up to 105, twenty in the Senate (14D, 6R) and eighty-five in the House (63 D, 22R). As non-voting delegates, women also represented American Samoa, Guam, the Virgin Islands, and DC.[83] Senate Democratic women lost their chairmanships and Republican women gained two. Lisa Murkowski (AK) took over the Energy Committee and Susan Collins (ME) led the Committee on Aging.[84]

Of the fifteen women who ran for the Senate in 2014, four won, including incumbents Collins (R-ME) and Jeanne Shaheen (D-NH). Newcomer Shelley Moore Capito (R-WV), a governor's daughter and former college administrator, had served seven terms in the House. Joni Ernst (R-IO) was the first female combat veteran elected to the Senate, following a twenty-three-year military career. Campaigning as a mother, a soldier, and a farm girl who could castrate pigs, she vowed to "cut the pork" in Washington. Utah sent Ludmya (Mia) Love to the House, the first Black Republican congresswoman. The daughter of Haitian immigrants, a Mormon convert, former flight attendant, and small-town mayor, Love won an open seat.[85]

Twice as many Democratic as Republican women ran for Senate and House seats. Even with the backing of Emily's List, 2014 was a disappointing year for Democrats and women in general. Academics debated why women were still hard to recruit and reluctant to run. The Brookings Institute asserted that women had "an ambition gap." Democrat Celinda Lake and Republican Kellyanne Conway, pollsters, strategists, and coauthors of *What Women Really Want* (2005), believed gender mattered. Conway critiqued media coverage of women that focused on cleavage and hairdos, demanding, "Where are the comparable stories about paunchy beer-bellies and bad comb-overs?" She did not then anticipate working for Donald Trump. Lake claimed that being a woman was an advantage with Democrats, but not with Republicans.[86]

For years, one argument used to elect women was their assumed ability to work together. Women were supposedly more collaborative and cooperative. "[It's] much less about ego and more about problem solving," claimed Senator Debbie Stabenow (D-MI). In 2013, women members negotiated a budget deal to reopen the government and put sexual assault in the military on the Senate's agenda. Cooperation ended in 2015. Joni Ernst promised to "unload" on Obamacare. Mia Love intended to be "a nightmare for [Democrats]." Newly elected Democrat Gwen Graham (FL) pledged to oppose Leader Pelosi. As Politico summarized, "Say goodbye to your illusions of a kinder, gentler sisterhood in government."[87]

There was little incentive for anyone, male or female, Republican or Democrat, to reach across the aisle. With both houses in Republican control, President Obama had no room to maneuver. The Congress did not engage in problem solving; its public approval ratings plummeted. Leader McConnell refused to schedule hearings for Obama's Supreme Court nominee, Judge Merrick Garland, to replace Justice Scalia, who died in February 2016. Hyper-partisanship was evident not only between the parties but also within them, between conservative and Tea Party Republicans and between moderate and left-leaning Democrats. That dynamic would play out in the presidential election.

2016 PRESIDENTIAL POLITICS

Without an incumbent in 2016, there were almost two dozen aspirants. Among them were senators, governors, a Black male neurosurgeon, a female CEO, a sitting vice president, a former First Lady, and a reality TV star. Republican Donald Trump, a self-proclaimed billionaire and real estate developer, was best known from television, talk radio, and tabloid press headlines about his two divorces, three marriages, five children, and six bankruptcies. He repeated the false Obama "birther" claim that the President was born in Kenya, which would have disqualified him from office. Lacking any government or military service, Trump was the least prepared candidate in history. He declared his candidacy in June 2015, vowing to "Make America Great Again." Within a year, he had vanquished and humiliated a large field of more qualified Republicans, among them "Low Energy Jeb" Bush, "Lyin' Ted" Cruz, and "Little Marco" Rubio. He was ready to take on "Nasty Hillary."

Secretary Clinton left the State Department at the end of Obama's first term. In January 2014, *Time* ran a cover story, "Can Anyone Stop Hillary?" The cover art portrayed a tiny man, dangling from a giant high heel, worn by a pantsuited leg.[88] After "years of speculation and coy denials," she announced her second try for the presidency in April 2015. Her endorsements, deep pockets, and 81% support among Democratic voters scared off challengers, including Vice President Biden, New York Governor Andrew Cuomo, and Senator Elizabeth Warren.[89] Clinton easily outdistanced all comers.

Then independent Vermont Senator Bernie Sanders declared his candidacy. He condemned Hillary's alleged ties to Wall Street and foreign donors to the Clinton Foundation. Under the banner of "democratic socialism," he represented the impatient left wing of the party. Free college tuition, universal childcare, a higher minimum wage, single-payer health care, a carbon tax, relief from student debt, and higher taxes for billionaires and corporations appealed to a broad base, especially younger voters.[90] Sanders's supporters saw him as an affable, avuncular agitator. His opponents considered him a churlish, grumpy grandpa.

Sanders's persistence turned the Iowa caucuses into a squeaker, 49.9% for Clinton and 49.6% for him. Going into New Hampshire, Hillary was eighteen points behind and lost by twenty-two.[91] She recovered after wins in Nevada and South Carolina and on Super Tuesday. The assumed frontrunner had to fight for every delegate. By June, Clinton had won thirty-four contests and more pledged delegates than Sanders, but she needed the votes of superdelegates to clinch the nomination. Superdelegates were unpledged party loyalists, mostly current and former office holders. Sanders seized on the narrative that elites would pick the nominee. With or without superdelegates, he did not have enough votes to secure the nomination. The drama bred resentment in his ranks. He stalled until two weeks before the Democratic convention in Philadelphia, before endorsing Hillary.[92]

On July 28, 2016, Hillary Rodham Clinton became the first woman to accept the presidential nomination of a major political party. She wore a suffragist white pantsuit. "Standing here as my mother's daughter, as my daughter's mother, I'm so happy this day has come. When any barrier falls in America, for anyone, it clears the way for everyone."[93] Her husband cried. A letter to the *New York Times,* from Sara Jane Witkin Berman of East Williston, New York, captured the feelings of many women:

> This is for you, Susan B. Anthony. You were arrested for casting your vote. That was for you, "iron-jawed angels." You were force-fed in jail. That was for you, young seam-stresses. You lost your lives in the 1911 fire at the Triangle Shirtwaist Factory. That was for you, battered wives. Most of all, that was for my 8-year-old granddaughter, to whom I can now say, "When you grow up, you may well become president of the United States."[94]

This time, Hillary did not play down her gender. She ran under her first name, identified herself as a grandmother, and called on voters to make history by electing a woman president. She "was running because she would be the best president," but she was "proud to be running as a woman."[95] Her forty-year record as an advocate for children, co-star in the Clinton presidency, respected Senator, globetrotting diplomat, and America's "most admired woman" was both an asset and an indictment. Few voters doubted her credentials, experience, or ability to govern. Instead, they questioned her ethics. Every act, every statement by her, or her husband, was scrutinized and weaponized. BLM activists criticized her support of her husband's 1994 anti-crime bill, when she described Black street gangs as "superpredators."[96]

Ever since the 1830s "Cult of True Womanhood" defined women as pious and pure, they had benefited from a "virtue advantage." Suffragists exploited it, promising to clean up government. The cost of an ethical infraction was higher for women. Men are excused for misdeeds ("boys will be boys") while women are blamed for their mistakes, and those of their spouses and children. Female ambition was a character flaw. Clinton's use of a private email server and her donor relationships raised questions about her integrity. Her resistance to criticism, her refusal to respond, her self-righteousness, and her stoic reserve prompted the public and pundits to see her as disingenuous if not dishonest. In truth, PolitiFact found that 60% of Trump's campaign claims were false, compared to 13% of Clinton's, but the public found them almost equally dishonest, 61% to 59%.[97]

Coverage and condemnation of her email account were constant. Even if most voters did not understand the details, it was the most reported story of the entire campaign. Hillary accused the *New York Times* of covering her emails "like Pearl Harbor." According to Harvard's Shorenstein Center on Media, Hillary's emails received four times more attention than Trump's treatment of women and sixteen times more than any policy proposal. In contrast, Trump's daily gaffes and blunders were one-day stories.[98]

This list of phrases and quotations provides an abbreviated account of the 2016 campaign.[99]

- Hillary's emails (March 2015)
- Bernie, Wall Street speeches
- "Mexicans are rapists." (Trump, June 2015)
- "The American people are sick and tired of your damn emails."(Bernie, September 2015)
- Eleven hours of Benghazi testimony
- "Crooked Hillary"
- "Muslim ban"
- Iowa caucus
- "There's a special place in hell for women who don't help each other." (M. Albright)

- New Hampshire primary (February 2016)
- "She's playing the woman card." (Trump)
- "Extremely careless" emails but no charges (FBI Director Jim Comey, July 2016)
- "Lock Her Up!"
- Gold Star parents
- Emails, Anthony Weiner sexting
- "Superpredators"
- "Deplorables"
- HRC pneumonia
- Debate I: watched by 80 million people, the most in history (September 26)
- *Access Hollywood* tape: "I just grab them by the pussy." (Trump, October 7)
- Podesta emails hacked, included excerpts of Wall Street speeches (October 8)
- Debate II: Trump invites Bill's accusers, stalks HRC, no handshakes (October 9)
- Debate III: "bad hombres," "nasty woman" (Trump, October 19)
- Emails, Comey reopens investigation based on Weiner laptop (October 28)
- Emails, Comey finds "no evidence of wrongdoing in Clinton emails." (November 6)
- Election Day (November 8, 2016)

After an exhausting campaign full of barbs and braggadocio, many voters saw the election as an unprecedented and unpalatable choice between a bitch and a bully, between Lady Macbeth and a male chauvinist pig. Never had nominees had higher disapproval ratings. The candidates were equally disliked and distrusted.

Nonetheless, everybody expected women to carry Hillary to the White House. Pantsuit Nation, a Facebook group of four million members, encouraged Hillary's supporters to wear pantsuits to the polls.[100] On

Sunday, October 2, a #Pantsuitpower flash mob appeared in Union Square in New York City. Almost two hundred dance enthusiasts, professionals, pregnant moms, dentists, soccer players, men, women, and kids put on a four-minute performance. The soundtrack was Justin Timberlake's contagiously upbeat "Can't Stop the Feeling." The choreography combined hip-hop, ballet, Broadway, and break-dancing. Raised fists signified #BlackLivesMatter; circling hips represented reproductive rights; kneeling evoked quarterback Colin Kaepernick's protest against police brutality. Everybody, even toddlers, wore colorful pantsuits. They provided a rare bright spot in a grim campaign. The video ended with this statement:

WE DANCE
    Because Love is Love
    Because Black Lives Matter
    Because climate change is real
    Because women's rights are human rights
    Because immigrants make America great
    Because every vote matters
    We dance for Hillary
    Because she fights for us.

In two days, the video had two million views on Facebook.[101]

UPSET

In 2016, women were 50.8% of the population and 52% of the voting age population. Among eligible women voters, ten million more turned out than men, 63.3% to 59%. Clinton won 54% of all women; Trump won 42%, a twelve-point gap. The gap was reversed among men, who voted 53% for Trump, 41% for Clinton.[102] Exit polls, conducted by Edison Research for a consortium of news organizations, suggested that 52% of white women voted for Trump, compared to 43% for Clinton. In August 2018, the Pew

Research Center published a more in-depth analysis, concluding that 39% of all women voted for Trump, while 54% voted for Clinton. White women split narrowly: 47% for Trump to 45% for Clinton. Non-white women voted for Clinton by a huge margin, 82% to 16%. She won 94% of Black women and 68% of Hispanic and Latina women voters. Younger Black women were less supportive. Trump won 35% of college-educated white women and 56% of white women without college degrees.[103] One observer concluded:

> White working-class women saw [her] as another privileged white woman wanting to break the glass ceiling. That metaphor makes sense if your central goal is to gain jobs that privileged men have. Hillary's feminism was not about them.[104]

Women voters under thirty voted for Clinton over Trump, 63% to 31%. Trump won older voters.[105]

No Democrat had succeeded a two-term Democratic President since 1836, when Martin Van Buren followed Andrew Jackson.[106] Convinced Clinton would win, some supporters stayed home. She won the popular vote by a margin of 2,858,686, but lost the Electoral College, 304 to 227. Trump joined four other presidents in history who won despite losing the popular vote: John Quincy Adams, Rutherford B. Hayes, Benjamin Harrison, and George W. Bush.[107] In Michigan, Trump beat Hillary by 10,704 votes, while the Green Party candidate, Jill Stein, drew 51,463 votes, presumably away from Clinton. Trump victories by less than 1% in Michigan, Pennsylvania, and Wisconsin totaled 79,646 votes, fewer people than fit into the Ohio State University football stadium.[108]

Everybody had an explanation for why Hillary lost, including the candidate. "I was running a traditional presidential campaign with carefully thought-out policies and painstakingly built coalitions, while Trump was running a reality TV show that expertly and relentlessly stoked Americans' anger and resentment."[109] There was also the media's obsession with Trump, emails, and Comey. To that list Clinton would add misogyny. Ever since Arkansas, Hillary had been attacked for being herself, for her hair, body shape, clothes, voice, laugh, career, marriage, and keeping her own name. The GOP had warned male candidates to avoid another "war on women," so slurs were slyer. No one expected Trump's gleeful gutting of every woman in his path.[110] The constant onslaught made Clinton more defensive, protecting herself behind a public persona people found inauthentic, with a cohort of close friends and advisors, whom outsiders saw as a cabal, if not a coven.

Others added insensitivity and elitism to the reasons Hillary lost. The Democrats did not seem to understand the deep resentment of whole segments of the country, who felt flown over and left out. More than one-fifth of American men, ages twenty to sixty-five, had not worked for a year. Economic downturns left them unemployed, unskilled, and at risk of opioid addiction and suicide. These white voters responded to Trump's hypermasculinity, sexual swagger, brash promises, and appeals to grievance. The most potent sentiment among them was resentment of Black people and immigrants.[111] Hillary's disastrous "basket of deplorables" remarks, about "racist, sexist, homophobic, xenophobic, Islamophobic" voters supporting Trump, were despicable, even if sometimes true.[112] She seemed to disdain everyday Americans who lived between the coastal elites and had not been protected by the so-called social safety net. Their populist anger inflamed America and ignited Trump.

Attempting to explain the outcome, the candidates, also-rans, strategists, journalists, and historians have written dozens of books. Their titles offer another summary of the campaign: *Chasing Hillary*; *The Apprentice*; *Defying the Odds*; *Hacks*; *Russian Roulette*; *Angry White Male*; *Unbelievable*; *An Unprecedented Election*; *Trumped*; *What Happened*; *What the Hell Happened?*; and *Shattered*.[113] On election night, the country was shell-shocked. The press was stunned. Global markets stumbled. Hillary was stoic. She called Trump to congratulate him, and then called Obama to apologize. He was "glacial." Trump was astonished; he had told his private pilot to fuel up for a flight to Scotland.[114] Editors had to scrap "First Woman Elected President" headlines. Neither candidate had prepared for this outcome. Nobody had a contingency plan.

Clinton did not formally concede until the next day. The campaign's lease on the Javits Center had expired at 2 A.M., so staff scrambled to book a hotel ballroom. A hastily constructed stage was lined with American flags. The space was full of friends, staff, and pool reporters, many of them "the girls on the bus." Hillary and Bill, Chelsea and her husband Mark, Virginia Senator Tim Kaine, the vice presidential nominee, and his wife took the stage. Looking grim and red-eyed, Bill wore a purple tie. It matched the purple collar of the grey pantsuit Hillary wore. She had packed a white suit for her victory speech and intended this outfit for her first trip to Washington as president-elect. Purple signaled bipartisanship or, as one reporter suggested, penance, the color of Catholic vestments during Lent.[115]

Hillary spoke for twelve minutes:

> This is not the outcome we wanted or that we worked so hard for. I'm sorry that we did not win . . . for the values and vision we share . . . for this hopeful, inclusive, big-hearted country. Donald Trump is going to be our President. We owe him an open mind and the chance to lead. I know how disappointed you feel, because I feel it too and so do tens of millions of Americans who invested their hopes and dreams in this effort. This is painful and it will be for a long time . . . Never stop believing that fighting for what's right is worth it. It is always worth it. We haven't yet shattered that glass ceiling . . . Someday, someone will, and hopefully sooner than we might think right now. To all the little girls who are watching this, never doubt that you are valuable and powerful and deserving of every chance and opportunity in the world to pursue and achieve your dreams.

She ended with a New Testament reference, paraphrasing Galatians 6:9: "Let us not grow weary in doing good. In due season, we shall reap, if we do not lose heart." The verse ends, "for there are more seasons to come and there is more work to do."[116]

CHAPTER TEN
ENRAGED & EMPOWERED,
2017–2020

A mong her supporters, the response to Hillary's loss was "soul-crushing and gut-wrenching." Democratic women were "appalled [and] afraid." Their stages of grief were denial, despair, division, and defiance. There would be no acceptance, only recriminations. Black women blamed white women, who blamed other white women. America had rejected "the most qualified presidential candidate in history," reminding women that "it's not even enough to be twice as good." Electing a man accused of sexual assault created a nationally hostile environment for women. Trump's election was a "stunning affirmation of white male privilege."[1]

THE 2017 WOMEN'S MARCH

Just hours after the polls closed, Teresa Shook, a retired lawyer and grandmother in Hawaii, posted on Facebook, "What if women marched on Washington around Inauguration Day?" Overnight, there were 10,000 responses. Mari Lynn Bland, known as Bob, a self-described "fashion incubator" in New York City, had a similar idea. Having sold "NASTY

WOMAN" T-shirts during the campaign, she had a modest Internet following. Lacking organizing experience and politically aware, the two white women were reluctant to be the sole faces of protest.[2] Vanessa Wruble, a white woman who had cofounded OkayAfrica, a media platform dedicated to African culture, intervened. She introduced Bland to three seasoned activists, Tamika Mallory, Carmen Perez, and Linda Sarsour. They identified not as Democrats or feminists but as community organizers.[3]

Including Bland, thirty-six, the four New Yorkers became the multicultural image of the Women's March. Mallory, thirty-eight, an African American social justice activist, gun control advocate, and Obama advisor, was executive director of the Reverend Al Sharpton's National Action Network. Perez, forty-one, a Mexican American, led Harry Belafonte's Gathering for Justice, which focused on juvenile justice and education. Sarsour, thirty-eight, a Brooklyn-born Palestinian-American Muslim, led the Arab American Association of New York. Wruble served as director of operations.[4] It was not a protest organized by the aging doyennes of the women's movement.

Planning evolved from an awkward start into a seemingly nimble organization, capable of raising money and securing permits, sponsors, and speakers, if not an adequate sound system. Gloria Steinem, eighty-three, and Harry Belafonte, eighty-nine, served as honorary co-chairs. NOW, NARAL Pro-Choice America, and Planned Parenthood were key partners. An anti-abortion sponsor was uninvited. Difficult conversations raged online about abortion, inclusion, race, white privilege, and the definition of feminism. The organizers stumbled into the same conflicts over race and class that had plagued every generation of the women's movement.[5] Calling it the Million Woman March offended Black women, who had marched under that banner in 1997, but the Women's March on Washington, evoking Dr. King's mythic Lincoln Memorial gathering in 1963, was blessed by his daughter Bernice.[6]

"Women" turned out to be a big tent, "large enough to contain almost every major strain of protest against Trump."[7] The March's platform was as diffuse as its organizers were diverse, a laundry list rather than a legislative agenda. It was anti-Trump and pro-equal rights for everybody, except pro-lifers. Eight "Unity Principles" supported reproductive rights, LGBTQIA rights, worker's rights, civil rights, disability rights, immigrant rights, environmental justice, and ending violence. It addressed the right to a living minimum wage; affirmed that all domestic and caregiving work is work, even if unpaid; asked for "solidarity with the sex worker's rights movement;" and endorsed the Equal Rights Amendment.[8] The leadership quartet emphasized and epitomized "intersectionality."

In contrast to the 1913 suffrage parade, the 2017 Women's March was a national and international phenomenon. More than 500,000 people gathered on the National Mall on Saturday, January 21, the day after President Trump's inauguration. There were sister marches in 670 cities and towns in all fifty states. Ten thousand people showed up in Seneca Falls. People marched in 400 foreign cities and on every continent, including Antarctica. In total, an estimated 3.5 million participants worldwide marched for women's equality. Cartoonist Tom Toles drew the statues of Liberty and blindfolded Justice joining the March, with the caption "Impressive Turnout."[9] Taken altogether, the Women's March was the largest political demonstration in American history.

For participants, the numbers were uplifting. Jammed into subway cars, people could barely step off onto crammed platforms. Before it opened the turnstiles and stopped counting, the Metro system recorded 1,001,613 trips, exceeded only by President Obama's inauguration.[10] At street level, it was a crush of people and a sea of pink hats. Critiqued in advance for being unabashedly girlie, the "pussy" caps were a catty response to a candidate who had bragged about grabbing women's genitals.[11] Like the red "MAKE AMERICA GREAT AGAIN" trucker caps worn the day before, pussyhats identified one's tribe and telegraphed defiance. After the March, an illustration by Abigail Gray Schwartz of a brown-skinned Rosie wearing a pink pussyhat graced a *New Yorker* cover. In addition to hats in every shade of pink, women wore Rosie the Riveter bandanas, American flag hijabs, rainbow flag cloaks, and purple and gold suffrage sashes. Girls came as GI Jane, Wonder Woman, and Princess Leia. Abigail Adams's seven-times-great-granddaughter Quincy, age eight, wore a "Future President" T-shirt.[12]

The multigenerational multiracial crowd was jubilant. There were no arrests. Homemade signs were pro-women and anti-Trump. BABES AGAINST BULLSHIT. #BLM. DEPORT TRUMP NOT IMMIGRANTS. DISSENT IS PATRIOTISM. FEMINISM IS FREEDOM. FIGHT LIKE A GIRL. HATE DOESN'T MAKE AMERICA GREAT. INAUGURATE THE RESISTANCE. MAKE AMERICA KIND AGAIN. MAKE AMERICA SANE AGAIN. NASTY WOMEN UNITE. OMG GOP WTF. RESIST.[13]

The plan was to rally near the Capitol. Beginning at 10:00 A.M., dozens of speakers addressed the crowd, in alphabetical order by first name: Angela Davis, now a retired university professor, followed Ai-Jen Poo of the National Domestic Workers Alliance. Alicia Keys sang "Girl on Fire." Actor America Ferrera declared, "We march . . . for the moral core of the nation." Hillary Clinton, who had attended the inauguration with the former president, tweeted "gratitude and good vibes."[14] Without jumbotrons or amplifiers, most of the crowd could not hear anything except rumbling waves of cheers. People carrying anti-abortion signs were met with shouts of "My Body, My Business!" Images streamed across social media. By afternoon, people slowly swarmed toward the White House, marching until after dark. Many left their signs outside the barriers protecting the Trump hotel.

President Trump was as dismissive of the marchers as President Wilson had been of suffragists. Wilson was annoyed that the 1913 procession was larger than his inaugural crowd. Trump insisted that his crowd was massive. Early the next morning, he tweeted, "Watched protests yesterday . . . Why didn't these people vote? Celebs hurt cause badly." By midmorning, the message was more politic: "Peaceful protests are the hallmark of our democracy. Even if I don't always agree, I recognize the rights of people to express their views."[15] The President was not the only critic of the March. Reporters found women indifferent or antagonistic in rural communities, the Rust Belt, and some affluent suburbs.[16]

The Women's March drew women who had marched for decades and others who had never been politically engaged. A group of former congressional staffers, calling themselves the Indivisible Project, urged the newcomers to replicate the Tea Party's tactics, hosting house parties, educating themselves, and organizing.[17] After the March, Indivisible posted an "Action Checklist for Americans of Conscience," starting with "Gear up for the next 652 days to the midterm elections."[18] Membership in the League of Women Voters soared. Donations of $29 million poured into the ACLU. Almost 34,000 women requested information about running for office from Emily's List. A National Education Association campaign, opposing Trump's nominee for Secretary of Education, yielded more than one million emails to Senators.[19]

TRUMP

Trump's cabinet was whiter and more male than Reagan's. Out of twenty-four posts, six went to women and non-whites: Alex Acosta (Labor), Ben Carson (Housing), Elaine Chao (Transportation), Betsy DeVos (Education), Nikki Haley (UN), and Linda McMahon (Small Business). The first nominee for Labor withdrew, due to questionable treatment of female employees. Among White House aides, men outnumbered women two to one. Female staffers were required to "dress like women." Trump addressed even senior women as "honey," "sweetie," and "darling."[20] One of few high-ranking women was Kellyanne Conway. The first woman to run a successful presidential campaign was named Counselor to the President. Separate from criticism of her "alternative facts," she endured sexist attacks. "Hillary is called castrating or shrewish, Conway is . . . called a slut," concluded one reporter.[21] Discomfort with smart, assertive women was bipartisan. At the first black tie White House dinner, the President welcomed the nation's governors and "your wives and daughters." Six governors were women.[22]

Within a week, the President's actions fired up more protests. On Monday, he reinstated the "global gag rule," banning aid to groups that counseled women overseas about abortion. On Friday, he suspended immigration from seven majority Muslim countries and sent a supportive message to the March for Life.[23] For forty-four years, it had rallied on the January 23 anniversary of *Roe v. Wade* to mark its resistance, sometimes in snow and sleet. Reported as "massive," it was much smaller than the inaugural crowd or the Women's March. "Bikers for Life" and five hundred Catholic school students from Alabama, sporting orange knit caps, marched to the Supreme Court. Conway and Vice President Pence reassured them that Trump would appoint pro-life judges, make the Hyde Amendment permanent, defund Planned Parenthood, and limit all abortions after twenty weeks. It was the first time a vice president had personally appeared at the rally.[24] In 2020, Trump was the first president to address March for Life participants in person.[25]

When President Trump announced the Muslim ban, protestors spontaneously showed up at the White House, Trump Tower, and major airports, signs in hand. Between January and June 2017, the National Park Service processed 388 permits for demonstrations in Washington, a 30% increase over 2016. Polls found that one in five Americans had joined a protest; 70% of them disapproved of Trump. By July 2018, there had been over ten thousand marches in the previous 547 days, in every state. Concern about march fatigue grew, as protest became the "new Sunday brunch," a privileged pastime.[26]

MARCH INC.

Differences over what resistance entailed split Women's March organizers. The New York quartet incorporated.[27] On International Women's Day, March 8, 2017, Women's March Inc. called for a "Day Without Women," urging women to stay home from work, ignore all obligations, and buy nothing. Intended to draw attention to the vital role women play in the economy and to issues of unequal pay and family leave, it demonstrated the chasm created by class and race within the women's movement. Women who were primary or sole breadwinners did not have the option to take an unpaid day off and risk losing their wages or jobs.[28]

In October 2017, March Inc. hosted a three-day convention in Detroit. For the four thousand participants, it was a raucous reunion, with a long list of grievances and causes: the treatment of immigrants, mass incarceration, reproductive rights, sexual assault, the Affordable Care Act, and threats to the environment, issues already addressed by other organizations and interest groups. March Inc. was faulted for inviting Bernie Sanders but not Hillary. They rescinded his invitation because theirs was "a woman led movement."[29] Its leaders were plagued by problems. Sarsour, a Muslim, was condemned as a "sharia-loving, terrorist embracing, Jew-hating, ticking time bomb of progressive horror." For links to Louis Farrakhan, head of the Nation of Islam, the quartet faced charges of antisemitism. After two years of controversy, March Inc. replaced Bland, Mallory, and Sarsour, citing concerns about "antisemitism, infighting and financial mismanagement."[30] Despite overhauling its mission, structure, and leadership, "the organization once considered the beating heart of the anti-Trump movement seem[ed] to be on life support."[31]

In the exhilaration that followed the Women's March, few expected it to become an annual event. On its first anniversary, in 2018, "thousands" gathered in half as many cities. At the Lincoln Memorial, House Minority Leader Nancy Pelosi (D-CA) and Senator Kirsten Gillibrand (D-NY) urged participants to support women candidates. Remarks about #MeToo resonated.[32] The March's second anniversary, in 2019, was Day 29 of the longest government shutdown to date. To avoid association with antisemitism, many chose not to participate. Disappointed by the tension and the turnout, one DC participant was defiant: "Apathy is not an option."[33]

In 2020, March Inc. downsized expectations. It hoped to re-energize its base with a story slam, a brunch with drag queens, and briefings about reproductive rights, immigration, and climate change. About 4,500 intrepid protestors showed up on a wintry MLK weekend. A drumline of Piscataway Nation women and a Chilean feminist collective performed. Martin Luther King III spoke about voting rights. No Washington or Hollywood A-listers appeared.[34] "Nobody needs another pink hat," concluded Dana Fisher, an academic who had studied protests.[35] "This is the last women's march we're going to need," declared one marcher, "because Trump is going to be gone." In 2021, COVID cancelled both the Women's March and March for Life.[36]

Trump's presidency was punctuated by people protesting in the streets. A protest has power because it amplifies issues and signals the passion and capacity of the forces it represents, if those forces can be harnessed. Columbia professor Todd Gitlin, a founder of Students for a Democratic Society in 1960 and a student of protests, concluded that marches fail unless they trigger political action.[37] The 1913 parade reignited the campaign for a federal suffrage amendment. It succeeded because NAWSA had the necessary national organization, financial resources, and political skills to secure passage. Trump's election drove progressive women into greater political activism, but it was more individual than organizational. Women challenged their representatives, registered voters, canvassed neighborhoods, operated phone banks, wrote postcards, enlisted in campaign bootcamps, and ran for office.[38]

When the President spoke to a joint session of Congress in February 2017, House Democratic women wore suffrage white, looking like a choir. Republicans controlled both houses, in which 110 women served. There were eighty-seven female House members (64D, 23R) and twenty-three women Senators (17D, 6R), including the first Latina, Catherine Cortez Masto (D-NV).[39] Republican women were barely 10% of their caucus, "so underrepresented," concluded the director of the Center for American Women and Politics, "they don't register in [the] power hierarchy."[40]

Women made more progress on the state level. In November 2017, a surge of women candidates ran in three off-year elections, beating incumbents in Georgia, New Jersey, and Virginia.[41] Women in Nevada's legislature, almost 40% of the body, introduced bills to ratify the ERA, close the wage gap, rank companies by how they treated women, remove "pink taxes" on tampons and diapers, eliminate copays on birth control, and provide office breaks to pump breastmilk.[42] In a special election, Black women and some suburban white women elected Democrat Doug Jones to Alabama's open Senate seat, defeating an alleged sexual predator endorsed by Trump.[43]

Despite admonishments to keep quiet, women spoke out. In February 2017, when Senator Elizabeth Warren read a letter from Coretta Scott King, criticizing Attorney General nominee Jeff Sessions, Majority Leader McConnell (KY) reprimanded her. His sarcastic dismissal, "Nevertheless, she persisted," became a rallying cry for feminists. In July, committee chairman Richard Burr twice ordered Kamala Harris to be quiet, lecturing the former prosecutor about "courtesy" when questioning witnesses. Another representative called Pramila Jayapal (D-WA), fifty-one, a "young lady . . . who doesn't know a damned thing," when she objected to an amendment. In September, when Hillary Clinton published her campaign memoir, many reviewers suggested that she should "shut the f--- up."[44]

#METOO

The #MeToo movement urged women to speak out about sexual harassment and assault. Tarana Burke, a Black activist from the Bronx, created the "Me Too" mantra in 2006: "To help survivors of sexual violence [and] . . . reframe and expand the global conversation."[45] The #MeToo founder was one of thirty-five diverse "silence breakers" named as *Time*'s 2017 "Person of the Year." They included singer Taylor Swift, three actresses, an engineer, a lobbyist, a state senator, a dishwasher, entrepreneurs, professors, a food blogger, a strawberry picker, journalists, hotel housekeepers, and two men. To represent women who hadn't yet come forward, one face was obscured and unnamed.[46]

As victims exposed one predator after another, #MeToo exploded. In July 2016, Fox News removed Roger Ailes, following charges made by Gretchen Carlson and nineteen other newswomen. In September 2016, the *Indianapolis Star* investigated complaints against Larry Nassar, the USA Gymnastics physician. After his conviction for sex crimes, 156 women gave victim statements.[47] Fox host Bill O'Reilly was fired in April 2017. Comedian Bill Cosby, "America's Black dad," was tried for drugging and assaulting one of sixty accusers.[48] The Harvey Weinstein case was the big white whale. The Hollywood producer and Democratic donor was known for making movies with strong female roles. In October 2017, the *New York Times* and the *New Yorker* documented his creepy criminal behavior: importuning, pawing, assaulting, and raping actresses and assistants.[49] Eventually, more than eighty women came forward. In February 2020, Weinstein was convicted in New York; additional charges awaited in California.[50]

The "Weinstein effect" led to firings, lawsuits, financial settlements, and new laws. States banned nondisclosure agreements covering sexual harassment. Congress reformed procedures for staff reporting sexual misconduct. Legislation was introduced to extend the statute of limitations for rape and to raise hourly wages for tipped workers, who were vulnerable to predatory customers.[51] Women prominent in Hollywood founded Time's Up, an advocacy organization and legal defense fund for lower-wage survivors. Attorney Tina Tchen, Michelle Obama's former chief of staff, became its CEO, and Anita Hill led its Commission on Sexual Harassment in the Entertainment Industry. To highlight the issue, actors wore black and invited activists to be their guests at the 2018 Golden Globes. Michelle Williams was paired with Tarana Burke and Meryl Streep hosted Ain-jen Poo.[52]

BRETT KAVANAUGH NOMINATION

Trump had acted promptly on his promise to nominate conservative judges. To fill the Scalia vacancy, he immediately named Neil Gorsuch, who had clerked for Justice Anthony Kennedy. Fourteen months later, in September 2018, Kennedy retired and Trump chose Brett Kavanaugh, another former clerk.[53] Until an unassuming Palo Alto professor of psychology confidentially contacted Senator Feinstein, the White House had not expected Kavanaugh's nomination to be contentious. Christine Blasey Ford's testimony and Kavanaugh's defense recalled the hard-drinking, adolescent, white boy "bro-culture" of the 1980s. The nominee admitted that he "sometimes . . . had too many beers."[54]

After allegations surfaced that Kavanaugh had assaulted Ford in 1982, Women's March activists and #MeToo survivors objected fiercely to his nomination. His confirmation process recalled the Thomas hearings twenty-seven years earlier. Octogenarian Republican Senators Charles Grassley (IO) and Orrin Hatch (UT) were still members of the Judiciary Committee, which had added four Democratic women. Like Hill, Dr. Ford was a reluctant and sober witness. Like Thomas, Kavanaugh responded with red-faced indignation. Unlike 1992, however, the charge was not sexual harassment but sexual assault.[55]

Public opinion broke down by gender. Women believed Ford by 55% to 37%. Men supported Kavanaugh, 49% to 40%. Sneering Senators ripped Ford's testimony apart because, like many victims, she could not recall every detail of the assault. The hashtag #WhyIDidntReport spread on social media. The mantra "Believe Women" recalled "I Believe Anita."[56] "Incandescent with rage," women flocked to Capitol Hill. They were arrested for blocking hallways. They "bird-dogged" Senators, tracking them to restrooms and into restricted elevators, where Ana Maria Archila and Maria Gallagher chastised Jeff Flake (R-AZ) for endorsing an alleged rapist. Mormon Women for Ethical Government pressed Flake and the three other Mormons on the committee to reconsider.[57] Within hours, Flake announced that he would support Kavanaugh only if there were a further FBI investigation. After an abbreviated probe, the FBI delivered one copy of its forty-five-page report to the Senate SCIF (Sensitive Compartmented Information Facility), where only members could read it.

Republicans had a narrow margin in the Senate, 51R to 49D. Joe Manchin (D-WV), up for reelection, said he would vote for Kavanaugh, shifting the count to 52-48. A tie would defeat the nomination so attention focused on two pro-choice Republican women, Senators Collins (ME) and Murkowski (AK). After privately grilling Kavanaugh, Collins accepted his statement that *Roe* was "settled law." Protestors dressed in red *Handmaid's Tale* costumes demonstrated outside her home.[58] Murkowski hesitated. Appointed to the Senate in 2002 to fill her father's seat, she won a full term in 2004 by three points. When she lost the 2010 primary to a Tea Party challenger, she launched a write-in campaign, which required teaching voters how to spell Murkowski. With the backing of women and Native tribes, she was the first write-in candidate to win a Senate seat since Strom Thurmond (D-SC) in 1954. After 2016, she was impervious to challengers.[59] Murkowski was more alarmed by Kavanaugh's record on Indigenous rights than on abortion. In the end, she decided his behavior during the hearings did not meet the standard of judicial conduct. Collins and Murkowski sat next to each other in the Senate. Collins's speech explaining her vote was met with a standing ovation among Republicans; Murkowski's was met with silence. Paired with a Democratic colleague who was attending his daughter's wedding, she voted "present." The final vote, on Saturday, October 6, was 50-48-2 (present), the closest margin for a Supreme Court justice since 1881.[60]

PELOSI AND THE PINK WAVE

The 2018 midterms were five weeks later. Already driven by "enormous frustration," 516 women had filed for Congress, compared to 312 in 2016. Post primaries, 251 women candidates ran for the House and twenty-six for the Senate; 75% were Democrats. In 2018, there were six women governors. Sixty-one women filed for governor in thirty-six states; eighteen ran in the general election.[61] Donations to women from women increased, what the Women's Philanthropy Institute called "rage giving."[62]

Women candidates ripped up the playbook, ignoring old rules about hemlines and hairstyles. They wore skinny jeans and T-shirts and talked personally about abuse, addiction, debt, and gender identity. Moms took their kids everywhere. Congressional candidate Liuba Grechen Shirley (D-NY) convinced the Federal Election Commission to allow the use of campaign contributions to pay for childcare.[63] Motherhood was no longer a disadvantage, disproving a 2016 study that found voters had deep misgivings about electing mothers of young children. Women listed motherhood as a credential. As a "Navy pilot, federal prosecutor, mother of four," congressional candidate Mikie Sherrill (D-NJ) won. Two gubernatorial candidates were filmed breastfeeding.[64]

Childless candidates like Stacey Abrams, the Black attorney and minority leader of the Georgia assembly running for governor, surrounded herself with nieces and nephews. Abrams lost her race to Georgia's Secretary of State, who was in charge of elections, leading to claims of discrepancies. Instead of conceding, Abrams launched Fair Fight to advance voter education, conduct registration drives, and challenge obstacles to voting. Groups like the New Georgia Project, the Black Voters Matter Fund, Higher Heights for America, She the People, and Power Rising worked to transform the electoral landscape. These organizations extended the work of Black women agricultural agents in the 1930s, of Ella Baker, Septima Clark, Fannie Lou Hamer, and Freedom Summer activists in the 1960s.[65]

The 2018 election attracted the highest midterm turnout in fifty years. Democrats won the national vote by the largest margin in history. They won the women's vote by nineteen points; in 2014 the gap had been four points. Polling found that voters trusted Democrats to advance women's rights more than Republicans, by twenty-six points. Among women, the margin was thirty-six points, 62% to 26%. The country elected 101 women to the House (88D, 13R), including 22 Black women and 39 newcomers, all but one a Democrat.[66]

"Younger, bluer, and more diverse" women won across the board.[67] Alexandria Ocasio-Cortez (NY), twenty-nine, was the youngest woman ever elected. Donna Shalala (FL), seventy-seven, former cabinet secretary and university president, was the oldest. The first two Muslim women, Ilhan Omar (MN) and Rashida Tlaib (MI), joined the first two Native American women, Sharice Davids (KS), a lesbian, and Deb Haaland (NM). Five women had military or intelligence backgrounds: Mikie Sherrill (NJ) and Chrissy Houlihan (PA) had been fighter pilots; Elaine Luria (VA) commanded a warship; Elissa Slotkin (MI) served three tours in Iraq as a CIA analyst; Abigail Spanberger (VA) had been a covert CIA operative. Other rookies were Kendra Horn (OK), an aerospace engineer; Jahana Hayes (CT), a once-homeless Teacher of the Year; and Katie Hill

(CA), the first openly bisexual House member. For the first time, Texas elected two Hispanic women, Sylvia Garcia and Veronica Escobar. The only new Republican woman was Carol Miller (WV), a bison farmer and NRA supporter.[68]

The number of Republican women in Congress declined from 29 to 20, and from 705 to 660 in state legislatures, the pipeline to higher office. Liz Cheney (WY) was the only woman on the GOP leadership team. Wrongly assumed to be more moderate than male candidates, Republican women lost primaries. They had no funding source equivalent to Emily's List; it raised $110 million in 2018. Exit polls indicated that only 17% of Republican voters thought it was important to elect women, compared to 82% of Democrats. Retiring Indiana Republican Congresswoman Susan Brooks decided to reverse that trend. She actively recruited ninety-four women candidates for 2020, nearly double the number who ran in 2018.[69]

Marsha Blackburn (KY), who had served in the House, and Cindi Hyde-Smith (MS), who had been appointed to fill a vacancy, were the only non-incumbent Republican women to join the Senate, along with Democrats Jacklyn Rosen (NV) and Kyrsten Sinema (AZ). Sinema, the first openly bisexual Senator, had narrowly defeated Martha McSally, the first woman combat pilot. Arizona's governor appointed McSally to finish John McCain's term. Five Senate races had pitted women against each other. Female duos represented six states: Arizona, California, Minnesota, Nevada, New Hampshire, and Washington. The one Black woman in the Senate, Kamala Harris (D-CA), was the second after Carol Moseley Braun.[70] Women were 23.7% of the entire Congress, making the US seventy-fourth, between Bulgaria and Cabo Verde, in the Inter-Parliamentary Union rankings of female representation. When Nancy Pelosi returned to power, the US became one of very few nations with a woman leading its legislature.[71]

Democrats took back the House and reelected Speaker Pelosi. Many new Democrats, running in red districts, had campaigned against her. To defeat Republican incumbents and secure the Democratic majority, Pelosi's response was "just win." Among the newcomers was "the Squad": Alexandria Ocasio-Cortez (NY), Ilhan Omar (MN), Ayanna Pressley (MA), and Rashida Tlaib

(MI) represented a diverse sisterhood and a generational rebellion. When tensions with the Speaker surfaced, Pelosi dismissed them. "All these people have their public whatever and their Twitter world . . . They're four people and that's how many votes they [have]."[72] Measuring power in votes, she seemed disrespectful of their youth, ethnicity, passionate political engagement, and influence. On opening day, Pelosi, seventy-eight, surrounded by members' children, including her nine grandchildren, paid tribute to woman suffrage. "I am particularly proud to be a woman speaker of the House of this Congress, which marks 100 years of women winning the right to vote."[73]

The "pink wave" sweeping women into office was a tsunami. Women won 30% of state legislative seats, five times as many as in 1971, when CAWP started counting, and the largest gain for Black women since 1994. Nevada and Colorado elected majority female legislatures. West Virginia had the lowest representation, at 13.4%. Almost every state legislature was controlled by one party: thirty by Republicans; eighteen by Democrats. Minnesota was divided and unicameral Nebraska was nonpartisan.[74] Women held ninety-one statewide offices. Michigan Democrats elected a woman governor, US Senator, attorney general, and secretary of state.[75] Nine women were governors (6D, 3R). Black women were mayors of seven major cities. In the country's third largest county, encompassing Houston, nineteen Black women ran against incumbent Republican judges. Seventeen won terms in civil, criminal, family, and probate courts.[76] Women objected to describing their wins with a pastel color. Pink was "exactly the opposite of the red-hot rage fueling many women in this election cycle," declared one analyst. They also disliked Year of the Woman. "It makes us look like outliers," objected Debbie Walsh, CAWP director.[77] Women wanted to be the norm, not a novelty.

2020 PRESIDENTIAL PRIMARY

Hillary Clinton had been both a trailblazing and a transitional figure. After her defeat, observers wondered whether a woman would or should run for president again. Six Democratic women tried, joining a primary field that began with twenty-six contenders. Representative Tulsi Gabbard (HI), thirty-eight, a Hindu and a veteran, wore white on the debate stage. Senator Kirsten Gillibrand (NY), fifty-three, fiercely feminist, was the first to drop out. Senator Kamala Harris (CA), fifty-four, a Black Asian American, had been state attorney general. Senator Amy Klobuchar (MN), fifty-nine, a former prosecutor, brought Midwestern humor and common sense to the fray. Senator Elizabeth Warren (MA), seventy, a liberal firebrand, was a former law professor. Author Marianne Williamson, sixty-seven, identified herself as "Oprah's spiritual advisor." One observer naively predicted that "more women meant less attention to pantsuits and more on policies."[78]

Last names were no longer a woman's first asset. None of the candidates had come into politics as someone's wife, widow, or daughter. Only Gillibrand used her husband's name.[79] Every female candidate dealt with sexism, and some dealt with racism. Warren was "schoolmarmish." Gillibrand was "too nice." Reporters scrutinized Harris's dating history, insinuating that she had slept her way to success. Klobuchar was a "mean boss." Based on a survey of congressional staff, seven women were among the top ten worst bosses. As a female journalist commented, "Please . . . [bad bosses] are a dime a dozen on Capitol Hill and they're usually called men."[80] With "conspicuous irritation," Klobuchar noted that any woman with Pete Buttigieg's resume, a "38-year-old former mayor of the fourth largest city in Indiana," would not be taken seriously, as Williamson was not. Harris, Klobuchar, and Warren faced more attacks from right-wing and fake news sites than any other candidates. Warren and Klobuchar earned the endorsement of the *New York Times*.[81]

Research consistently found that voters regarded "power seeking women with contempt and anger but saw power seeking men as strong and competent." Because the "norm" was male, white, and straight, executive offices remained the hardest for women to win. The further off the norm—female, non-white, LGBTQ—the more obstacles a candidate faced. Among women voters, beating Trump mattered more than electing a woman. Polling showed that 71% of Americans would personally vote for a woman, but 33% did not think their neighbor would.[82] Queried about whether a woman could beat Trump, Klobuchar responded, "Nancy Pelosi does it every day."[83]

During primary season, Pelosi tried to fend off a House vote to impeach Trump. She thought it would divide the country and fail in the Senate. Worried about a general election challenge from former Vice President Biden, Trump attempted to sully his reputation, based on his son Hunter's business dealings in Ukraine. Impeached by the House for that scheme, Trump was cleared by the Senate in January 2020. In February, the Democratic primaries came down to a race between two white septuagenarians, Joe Biden and Bernie Sanders, before Black voters in South Carolina resurrected Biden's candidacy. By March, the politics of impeachment and the primaries had been overtaken by a pandemic. The country was in lockdown.

PANDEMIC

COVID-19, or coronavirus, caught the Trump administration unprepared. Before it organized a response, hot spots arose in Seattle and New York City. Given the size of the country and differences in population density, the virus spread with varied intensity. Not everyone took it seriously, including the President, who sent inconsistent signals, spread misinformation, and contradicted scientists appointed to a White House Task Force. His labeling COVID the "Chinese virus" or "Kung-flu" led to a rash of anti-Asian harassment. Governors scrambled to find PPE (personal protective equipment) for essential health care workers and respirators for ICUs. Emergency rooms and morgues were overwhelmed. Although the United States was 4% of the world's population, it had 25% of COVID cases and five times the average global death rate.[84]

Erratic leadership and reckless re-openings delayed recovery. Travel was limited; schools were unsure about opening. People lost their jobs and their lives. They were worn out from working from home, homeschooling children, and dealing with shortages of toilet paper and flour. Trump's refusal to wear a mask made the best means of preventing contagion a political statement rather than a public health measure. Anti-maskers claimed wearing one infringed on their personal liberty. According to an Associated Press poll, three-quarters of Americans favored mask wearing in public, 89% of Democrats and 59% of Republicans.[85]

The pandemic revealed stark inequities in health care, employment, public education, and domestic life, many of them long-standing. Most vulnerable to infection were the elderly, incarcerated, urban residents, Native Americans, the poor, and people with pre-existing conditions, many of whom were people of color or immigrants. Black, brown, and immigrant women were also the majority of essential workers, putting themselves at risk as nurses, respiratory therapists, pharmacists, cleaners, and grocery clerks. One in three jobs held by women was deemed essential. Men held only 28% of essential jobs, most in law enforcement, transit, and utilities. There were four times more nurses than police officers on duty.[86]

Economic consequences were severe. Large factories, small businesses, and restaurants closed. Schools and daycare centers shuttered. Transportation systems shut down. Evictions and foreclosures loomed. Congressional relief packages could not meet the need. Unemployment and uncertainty inflamed partisan division. Mobs protesting state shutdowns wore Trump paraphernalia and carried Confederate flags and assault weapons. Conservatives fought to close abortion clinics and keep gun shops and mega churches open.

Before the pandemic, nearly 20% of white, prime age men were not working full-time. Many lacked high school diplomas, technological savvy, and transportation. Available jobs were part-time, without predictable hours, steady wages, or job security. Working-class men and women endured lost wages, family dysfunction, anger, and anxiety. Men suffered higher suicide rates.[87] "More Americans die every two weeks from drugs, alcohol and suicide—'deaths of despair'—than died in 18 years of war in Afghanistan and Iraq," wrote Nicolas Kristof, author of *Tightrope*. He linked lower levels of education to lower incomes, poorer health care, more chronic pain, and greater drug abuse. Poor housing produced low property taxes and poor schools, which produced fewer graduates, more unemployed, and more poverty, in an ongoing downward spiral.[88] These problems were all connected, and made worse by institutional racism.

THE IMPACT ON WOMEN

Before the pandemic, women had reshaped the economy. In 2020, women were briefly more than half the national workforce, at 50.04%, for the second time in history. The first time was during the 2009 recession, when men lost manufacturing jobs. This time, it was caused by the high number of women employed as home and health care workers, the fastest growing segment of the economy. It was also the lowest paid, even as minimum wages rose to an average of $11.80/hour, without benefits.[89] Women of color held the majority of those jobs.

The pandemic wiped out the progress women had made. Waitresses, daycare workers, hairstylists, hotel maids, dental hygienists, retail clerks, cashiers, receptionists, and housecleaners were hard hit by job losses. Two-thirds of the 22.2 million workers in the forty lowest paid jobs were women; two-thirds of them were sole or primary breadwinners. Until April 2020, women had never experienced double-digit unemployment, when it reached 16.2%. The share of women working fell to its lowest level since 1988, wiping out decades of hard-won gains.[90]

Essential as they were in the war on COVID, women played equally vital roles on the home front. According to one authority, the 2020 pandemic unmasked the "grotesque" gender inequality in domestic roles.[91] It increased the demand for meals prepared at home and added homeschooling to the jobs most moms did, between Zoom meetings if they had adequate Internet access. Families had to function without grandparents or babysitters. With schools closed, parents left their jobs to be at home. "Based on what we know about the labor market and social norms, most of those people are . . . women," asserted an economist. "The childcare crisis could set women back for a generation." By September 2020, 865,000 women had dropped out of the workforce, four times as many as men.[92]

Traditional gender expectations, income inequality between spouses, and corporate culture accounted for that imbalance. Most institutions, including marriage, had not changed to embrace or accommodate women's wage-earning lives.[93] No matter how many hours women worked, even if they were primary breadwinners, they spent at least twice as much time as men on childcare and housework. Although the sample is small, same-sex couples have a more equitable distribution of labor.[94] Because so many women had essential jobs during the health crisis, dads became primary parents. Many were stunned by the constant demands parenting and housework required. The *New York Times* reported that half of 2,200 men surveyed said they did most of the homeschooling; 3% of their wives concurred; many women suspected the number had been rounded up.[95] Researchers debated whether the crisis cemented traditional gender roles or fast tracked "seesaw marriages," in which earning and domestic roles shift between spouses, a challenge in an economy that seemed to demand two incomes.[96]

Motherhood may have been revered, but it was not respected enough to be supported by useful public policies. The Economic Policy Institute valued women's work, at a minimum, at $24,000 per child per year, based on average childcare costs. The estimate did not include elder care. Lack of stable, affordable childcare had a huge impact on women's employment. It is one of the reasons women's workforce participation stalled and women's wages lag behind men's. Women are least likely to be employed in states with the highest childcare costs and the shortest school days.[97] To work for pay, women need affordable childcare, paid family leave, universal pre-K, kindergarten, after school and summer programs, telecommuting, and flextime.

Male and female employees in larger companies may take up to twelve weeks of unpaid leave, to deal with childbirth, adoption, foster care, illness, and other obligations. Only 16% of private sector workers get paid leave. In December 2019, President Trump signed the Federal Employee Paid Leave

Act, part of an extensive defense spending bill. Republicans voted for paid leave in exchange for Democratic support for Trump's Space Force. Due to a "technical and drafting error," the law did not cover postal, aviation, public health, veterans affairs, TSA, or financial regulatory employees, federal judges, or political appointees.[98]

GEORGE FLOYD

President Trump predicted that the virus would evaporate by Memorial Day. After two months of shutdowns, people were eager to resume normal life. Celebrating summer at crowded bars and beaches led to new hot spots in areas previously less infected. Without adequate testing, tracing, or a vaccine, COVID was out of control. Added to the national petri dish of pandemic and unemployment was another incident of racial violence. On Memorial Day, May 25, 2020, four white Minneapolis police officers murdered George Floyd, a Black man. One of them knelt on Floyd's neck for almost nine minutes. His victim pleaded "I can't breathe!" and called for his mother before he died. The excruciating scene was captured on cell phone video and viewed globally. As the Black actor Will Smith observed, "Racism isn't getting worse, it's getting filmed."[99] There had been video evidence since before the 1991 police beating of Rodney King, but this time, more white people were watching.

Black people have been victims of violence in America for four centuries. Deaths at the hands of whites had been met with anguish and anger in the Black community and, too often, by indifference and ignorance among whites. There had been no outrage over Klan rampages, race riots, the Tulsa Massacre or decades of deaths: Isaac Woodward, Emmett Till, Medgar Evers, James Chaney, Martin Luther King Jr., Malcolm X, Amadou Diallo, Ahmaud Arbery, Breonna Taylor, George Floyd, a litany known to the Black community and a lesson for whites.[100] As the country convulsed, crowds chanted, "Say his name!" There were too many names.

Black deaths at the hands of white police accelerated nationwide protests after Floyd's murder. In six weeks, there were 5,700 anti-racism marches, in every state, even in cities and tiny towns with few Black residents. Children marched, chanting, "Abolish the Police," a far cry from Mister Rogers and Officer Friendly. Protests in large cities continued for three months. Overseas, people marched, from Antwerp to Adelaide. What was different in 2020 was the increased engagement of whites, estimated at 53% in Los Angeles, 61% in New York City, and 65% in DC. Utah Republican Senator Mitt Romney marched in Washington, "because Black lives matter."[101]

Grief for George Floyd combined with mourning for the state of the country. Violence against Black victims resulted in lost partners, orphaned children, broken families, and disrupted communities. On a larger scale, it contradicted America's ideals and shaped national politics. Like Freedom Summer in 1964, Floyd's murder was a catalyst. Facts about disproportional arrests rates, mass incarceration, and police shootings of Blacks demonstrated stark racial disparities in the justice system, and support for BLM surged in June and July.[102] The words BLACK LIVES MATTER, all caps, were painted in bright yellow, 35-foot letters on Sixteenth Street in Washington, in front of Trump Tower in New York City, and in Tulsa, among other sites. Marchers shouted "I Can't Breathe" or stood silently for eight minutes and forty-six seconds.

An array of racist iconography was toppled. Aunt Jemima and Uncle Ben products, sports teams, and country singers changed their names. Mississippi redesigned its flag. Schools, streets, and bird species were renamed. The Defense Department proposed renaming bases. The Boy Scouts created a merit badge for diversity training. The *Scrabble Dictionary* eliminated 250 words. Sales of *White Fragility* by Robin DiAngelo soared. Major League Baseball stenciled BLM on pitchers' mounds. The National Football League reversed its opposition to players kneeling during the national anthem. Whites learned about Juneteenth. Historic perpetrators of genocide came under attack; statues of Christopher Columbus were beheaded. A statue of Lincoln, erected in Washington by freed slaves in 1876, was challenged because its design seemed demeaning.[103] Critics dismissed gestures like banners and book groups as too easy, too late, or too little. Others focused on reforming police practices, registering voters, and passing a new voting rights act to replace protections removed by *Shelby v. Holder*. Proponents suggested naming it for civil rights icon John Lewis (D-GA), who died in July 2020. His last public appearance was at BLM Plaza in Washington. He recalled that Emmett Till had been his George Floyd.[104]

THE COURT

George Floyd's death dominated the news. Two end-of-term Supreme Court decisions about women's reproductive rights got less attention. In June 2020, in *June Medical Services LLC v. Russo*, the Court invalidated a Louisiana law requiring abortion clinics to meet certain standards. It had found an identical Texas law unconstitutional in 2016 because it created an "undue burden" on women. Chief Justice Roberts, who had dissented in the Texas case, respected the precedent and joined the majority in the Louisiana case. His vote reassured abortion proponents, suggesting he might uphold *Roe* as a precedent.[105] According to legal expert Linda Greenhouse, should *Roe* be overturned, leaving abortion regulation up to the states would "create a new underground railroad."[106]

In July 2020, the Court decided a birth control case, *Little Sisters of the Poor v. Pennsylvania*. It was another challenge to the Obamacare requirement that employers cover the cost of contraception, with exemptions for some religious institutions. In 2014, in *Hobby Lobby*, the Court allowed privately held corporations, "with moral and religious objections," to refuse coverage. A related case, *Zubik v. Burwell* (2016), was remanded to the lower courts. After his election, in May 2017, Trump issued an executive order which allowed exemptions for more employers. That rule was struck down by a federal appeals court, prompting a challenge by the Little Sisters of the Poor and others.[107]

The Court voted, 7–2, to expand the exception and limit contraception coverage. In a separate concurrence, Justices Kagan and Breyer explained their vote. They followed the original Obama exemption as a precedent, but warned that the new rule's "overbreath causes serious harm." Justice Ginsburg, joined by Justice Sotomayor, dissented. "May the Court jettison an arrangement that promotes working women's well-being while accommodating employers' religious beliefs, although that course harms women who do not share those beliefs?" She predicted that the ruling would force women to use less effective methods of contraception. "Ready access to contraception," she concluded, "safeguards women's health and enables women to chart their own life's course."[108]

KAMALA HARRIS

August 12 was the third anniversary of a 2017 demonstration in Charlottesville, Virginia, demanding removal of a statue of Robert E. Lee. White supremacists, Klansmen, and neo-Nazis had also marched, carrying torches and chanting fascist, antisemitic, and racist slogans. When former Vice President Biden announced his 2020 candidacy, he credited President Trump's inadequate and insensitive response ("some very fine people on both sides"). It inspired Biden to run and engage "in a battle for the soul of America."[109] On August 12, 2020, Biden picked Kamala Harris to be his running mate.

Biden's choice signaled the ascendance of women. It elevated the visibility of the other prospects, an array of strong women governors, lawmakers, and senior officials, among them four Black women and two women of color. Harris, the junior Senator from California, was the first Black woman to be named vice president by a major party. Charlotta Bass, another Californian and a Black newspaper publisher, was the VP nominee on the Progressive party ticket in 1952.[110] Harris's pedigree as the mixed-race daughter of South Asian and Jamaican immigrants represented America's promise of opportunity and equality. She was raised by a single mom, bused to public school, attended Howard, an HBCU, joined Alpha Kappa Alpha, and graduated from a state law school. A "Converse-and-pearls-wearing"

Black Baptist married to a white Jew, she was a stepmother and part of a blended family. When asked to describe herself, Harris responded, "I am a proud American."[111]

Within hours, Harris's announcement was met with sexist and racist insults. Trump labeled her "the meanest," "the most horrible," a "mad woman," and "a phony." His son tweeted that she was a "whorendous pick," calumny followed by "JOE AND THE HOE" T-shirts. The President raised the racist trope of the angry Black woman ("so angry") and repeated false claims about her citizenship, recalling his birther attacks on Obama. He dismissed Harris as "nasty," "extraordinarily nasty," and "very, very nasty," the same insult he flung at Hillary Clinton ("such a nasty woman"), Elizabeth Warren ("nasty mouth"), and Nancy Pelosi ("a nasty vindicative horrible person").[112] A group called We Have Her Back, a coalition including Color of Change, Emily's List, Planned Parenthood, Time's Up, and UltraViolet, rallied to defend Harris and fight racism and sexism.[113]

COVID changed the format of the national party conventions. Instead of happening on-site in Wisconsin and North Carolina, Democrats and Republicans met unconventionally. The new virtual format was a tightly edited production, with recorded performances and satellite-linked speakers. It was the first makeover of the standard camp revival since 1948, when conventions were first widely televised. Conventions had not brokered a presidential selection since the 1976, when incumbent Gerry Ford narrowly defeated Ronald Reagan. They had become extended campaign commercials, intended to rally partisans. Now they were slicker and shorter, broadcast without the filter and interruption of commentators.[114]

The Democratic convention, in Wilmington, Delaware, opened with the national anthem sung by fifty-seven people in red, white, or blue T-shirts, representing each state and territory, appearing in zoom boxes. Delegates cast their ballots from their home states, reminding viewers of the vast geographic and demographic diversity of the country. Speeches were delivered into silent spaces without cheers or applause. Fireworks replaced balloon drops. Republicans broadcast their convention from Fort McHenry, outside Baltimore, and the White House, flaunting the Hatch Act, which barred political activity on federal property. Analyses of the television audience for each convention revealed viewing patterns as deeply divided as the country. Americans "head[ed] into a high stakes election relying on information sources that . . . affirm[ed] pre-existing points of view."[115]

In nominating Biden, the Democrats chose character, civility, and decency, to contrast with an incumbent many found coarse and divisive. It hoped to create an anti-Trump coalition around the pandemic, the economy, race, and climate change. Culminating with former President Obama's speech, the convention portrayed Trump as a danger to democracy. In response, Republicans claimed Biden would raise taxes, "abolish immigration enforcement, abolish the suburbs, abolish effective policing . . . and abolish the American way of life." "No one will be safe in our country," Trump declared, calling himself "the only thing standing between the American Dream and total anarchy, madness and chaos."[116]

Once again, the election was fought in battleground states: Michigan, Pennsylvania, Wisconsin, North Carolina, and Florida. The country was so divided that there were few undecided or independent voters to persuade. Both parties sought to turn out loyalists and register new voters. While Republican voters were increasingly "downscale," Democrats hoped to reunite the New Deal coalition of the white, working class, immigrant, rural, urban, and Black voters.[117] Black women remained steadfast Democrats. "When you fire up a Black woman, she doesn't go to the polls alone. She brings her house, her block, her church, her sorority, and her union," declared Glynda Carr, head of Higher Heights for America.[118] Both sides focused on women voters.

Attention turned to the cohort Trump called "suburban housewives," white, college-educated women, supposedly threatened by the integration of their neighborhoods. Statistically, only 4% of American women lived in traditional breadwinner/homemaker households. Stay-at-home moms were an artifact of an earlier era.[119] Since the gender gap had been identified in the 1980s, pollsters had tracked the inclinations of white "soccer moms," "security moms," and "hockey moms." In 2020, some women called themselves "rage moms [and] turned the gender gap into a 'canyon.'" Despite his disrespect and dismissal of women, Trump begged them to "please like me." In a *Washington Post*/ABC poll in August 2020, suburban women favored Biden over Trump by twenty-four points; among men, the gap was four points.[120]

MOTHERHOOD AND MORAL AUTHORITY

Women found common ground in the anxiety and exhaustion caused by the pandemic. There was a ceasefire in the mommy wars as women struggled to safeguard their families, educate their children, and keep their jobs in the midst of chaos. The instability of school systems, the uncertainty of the economy, the injustice of racial violence, and the failure of leadership fueled political action. According to a Kaiser Family Foundation poll, women were twice as likely as men to have participated in a protest since 2018. Since 2017, women had run for office in record numbers. "Women are mobilized on a bigger scale than we've seen in a generation," asserted historian Annelise Orleek. "Women are organizing across the spectrum."[121]

Greater political engagement intensified polarization between liberals and conservatives, and distrust between white and Black women. In the past, white women had been plantation mistresses, segregationists, Klan members, and leaders of movements that opposed equal rights, racial justice, reproductive freedom, marriage equality, and immigration. The conservative One Million Moms fought indecency, code for opposing LGBTQ rights.[122] According to Dani McClain, author of *We Live for the We: The Political Power of Black Motherhood* (2019), the wider white community had rarely protected children of color.[123] White women rarely understood the burden of terror and grief carried by Black mothers, that their children could be killed for the color of their skin. While many women protested locally, there had been no mass maternal outrage when Black children were shot or orphaned by gun violence or when immigrant children were separated from their mothers and caged at the US-Mexican border. Seyward Darby, author of *Sisters in Hate: American Women on the Front Lines of*

White Nationalism (2020), documented how white women have sustained white nationalism. "Frustrated by feminism," these women feel a deep "sense of dislocation" in a rapidly changing, no longer majority white or Christian country. The "hate movement" fed on "perceived victimization" and "social anxiety."[124]

Historically, motherhood had given women moral authority and motivated them to act.[139] After emancipation, Black and white women occasionally allied as reformers, suffragists, and neighbors to address concerns like sanitation, streetlights, and playgrounds. In 1967, to oppose the Vietnam War, women created Another Mother for Peace. Mothers Against Drunk Driving (MADD) organized in 1980. Moms Demand Action for Gun Sense responded to the Sandy Hook shooting. Mothers of the Movement had Black children who had been killed by police or gun violence. Black Moms Against Senseless Killing worked to prevent violence. Madre organized women internationally. Every Mother Counts tried to improve maternal health. Mothers Ought to Have Equal Rights, Dreamers' Moms, Moms Rising, Mothers Movement Online, and Vote Like a Mother were advocacy groups using motherhood as an organizing principle.[125]

In 2020, white suburban moms were marching under BLM banners, "organizing protests and reading groups, posting links to bail funds, discussing antidotes to tear gas." Their signs read "WHEN GEORGE FLOYD CALLED FOR HIS MAMA, HE SUMMONED ALL THE MAMAS."[126] In response to federal troops occupying Portland, Oregon, a Wall of Moms arose. Locking arms, wearing yellow T-shirts, bike helmets, and goggles, the predominantly white women stood between demonstrators and police. They chanted, "Feds Stay Clear, Moms Are Here." Vomiting from tear gas, one woman told a reporter, "We're trying to protect everyone's kids as if they were our own." Chapters spread across the country, from Maine to New Mexico.[127] Portland organizers directed participants to "dress like moms . . . like they were going to Target. Because who wants to shoot a mom?" Moms are stereotypes, "often associated with the word 'middle': middle class, middle aged, soft in the middle."[128] In 2020, there was no middle ground. Suburban moms were taking sides.

The elevation of maternal righteousness needed to be sensitive to the 20% of women who were not mothers, not always by choice. Entitled white women, even self-described "allies," needed to avoid appropriating the rage and grief of Black women.[129] Not all moms were sisters; not all moms were feminists; some moms were "Karens." The name described white women who embodied entitlement and white privilege. These women fabricated accusations against Black birdwatchers in Central Park, demanded to speak to the manager, brandished guns at protestors, refused to wear masks, and were invited to speak at the 2020 Republican convention.[130]

SEPTEMBER SURPRISES: RBG AND ACB

For the first time since 1992, the challenger had a lead over the incumbent in national polls. By Labor Day, Biden was ahead of Trump by seven points.[131] The pandemic raised questions about the health risks of in-person voting and Trump raised alarms about the security of mail-in ballots. Voters and journalists were anticipating the debates and wondering about an "October surprise," a last minute disruption, completely unexpected or strategically timed. It could alter the outcome of an election, as the Access Hollywood recording of Trump's crude remarks about women and FBI Director Comey's reopening of Clinton's email investigation had in 2016. Given how unpredictable 2020 had been, a rash of September upheavals should not have been a surprise. There had been 200,000-plus deaths from COVID. New hot spots ignited after Labor Day; wildfires burned over four million acres in the West; and so many hurricanes pounded the Southeast that forecasters had exhausted the English alphabet and begun using Greek letters to name them. The country felt it was suffering from plagues, fires, and floods of Biblical proportions. Then came death and what some voters saw as the apocalypse.

Supreme Court Justice Ruth Bader Ginsburg died from cancer on Friday, September 18. It was the Jewish New Year. Many Jews believe that those who die on Rosh Hashanah are "the righteous."[132] While her casket lay in state outside the Supreme Court, people lined up for blocks, from dawn to midnight, to pay their respects from the foot of the steps. Little girls wore lace collars or Wonder Woman costumes. One T-shirt declared, "NEVER MIND PRINCESS, CALL ME YOUR HONOR." Memorial services were held at the Court, where her clerks lined the steps, and at the Capitol, where women members stood at attention to bid her casket farewell. Rosa Parks had been the first woman to lie "in honor" in the Rotunda; Justice Ginsburg was the first woman and the first Jew to lie "in state."[133]

RBG was known for her brilliant mind, incisive opinions, her reserve, and her close friendship with the late Justice Scalia, her opponent on the bench. At eighty-seven, she was the senior member of the liberal bench, joined by Justices Kagan, Sotomayor, and Breyer. Women saw her as a model of "female influence, authenticity and dignity." Refraining from using the term "women's rights," Ginsburg believed in "the equal-citizenship stature of women and men as a fundamental constitutional principle." Often in the minority, she would don her dissent collar to deliver her opinions. She wore it the day after Trump was elected in 2016.[134] Recognizing the risk to her legacy, Ginsburg dictated her dying wish to her granddaughter: "My most fervent wish is that I will not be replaced until a new president is installed." When President and Mrs. Trump appeared at the Court to pay their respects, the crowd booed and shouted, "Honor Her Wish!" Fox News commentator Tucker Carlson cast doubt on its veracity, which had been confirmed by the attending doctor. Trump asserted that Ginsburg's last statement was a lie, dictated by Democrats.[135]

Majority Leader McConnell promised the Senate would act as soon as it had a nominee. Republicans who had blocked President Obama's nomination of Merrick Garland for nine months, because 2016 was an election year, scrambled to defend their actions five weeks before the 2020 election, after early voting had begun. Every Democrat along with Republican Senators Collins (ME) and Murkowski (AK) called for a delay. A *Washington Post/ ABC* poll showed that a vast majority of Americans preferred that the winner of the election select Ginsburg's successor.[136] A week after RBG's death, before she was buried at Arlington, the President announced his nominee at a crowded Rose Garden ceremony, where few guests wore masks.

Amy Coney Barrett was an accomplished academic. A judge for less than three years, she had never been a trial attorney. Born in 1972, the oldest of seven children, she had grown up in a close-knit faith community and attended Catholic schools in Louisiana. She graduated magna cum laude and Phi Beta Kappa from Rhodes College in Memphis and summa cum laude from Notre Dame law school, where she served on the law review. Clerkships at the US Court of Appeals for DC and the Supreme Court, under Justice Scalia, brought her to Washington. She worked as an associate in private practice and was part of the Bush 2000 legal team.[137] Trump appointed her to the US Court of Appeals for the Seventh Circuit in 2017. Judge Barrett commuted between Chicago, where the Court sat, and South Bend, Indiana, where she lived and her husband practiced law. Jesse Barrett, who had graduated two years after her from Notre Dame, had been a federal prosecutor and assistant US attorney in the Northern District of Indiana. They had seven children, ages five to sixteen. Two were adopted from Haiti; the youngest had Down syndrome. An aunt and special aides helped with childcare.[138]

According to extensive reporting by the *New York Times,* Barrett described herself as a Catholic and never spoke publicly about her association with a small, conservative Christian community called the People of Praise.[139] It had 1,650 adult members in twenty-two cities. South Bend was its national hub. People of Praise is not a church, but an ecumenical "covenant community," where people with "a wide variety of religious and political views can live together in harmony." Founded in 1971, it was rooted in charismatic Catholicism and communal practices. Members tithe 5% of their income and are deeply embedded in each other's lives, offering advice on marriage, family, and careers. Members undergo a "discernment process" and then sign a commitment document. All references to the Barretts have been scrubbed from its website.[140]

The group believes in traditional gender norms and hierarchical leadership, with men as heads of the faith community and individual households.

Female leaders were "handmaids," after Mary, "the handmaid of God," until Margaret Atwood's *Handmaid's Tale* gave the word a negative connotation. Women are fundamentally equal but designed for different roles. "Wives should take husbands' directives seriously"; husbands have "a responsibility to correct their wives." In a community in which most women stay home with their children, "Judge Barrett's career is an anomaly," according to observers. Barrett's commitment to faith and family made her an icon for conservative Christian women and for mothers of large families and adopted or disabled children. They admire "ACB" for her ability to be "unabashedly ambitious, . . . deeply religious, and pro-life."[141] Conservative women and anti-abortion, evangelical Christians were voters Trump needed to win reelection. Many in this cohort had ignored or forgiven his personal behavior because of his promise to overturn *Roe* by naming anti-abortion justices to the Supreme Court.

Judge Barrett's connection to an insular sect made her suspect among liberals. Her record in speeches, articles, and opinions was pro-life. In 2006, she signed a newspaper advertisement calling *Roe* a "barbaric legacy" and demanding a "right to life from fertilization to natural death."[142] Even before Senate hearings began, the Trump campaign and religious conservatives made the case, in television ads and opinion pieces, that to question Barrett about how her faith influenced her judicial decisions would be an example of anti-Catholic bias. They ignored attacks made by Republicans on Catholic candidate Biden: Biden will "hurt God"; Biden was "Catholic in name only"; Biden was "an existential threat" to the church.[143]

Equally alarming to legal scholars was her reputation as an "originalist" and a "textualist." Like her mentor Scalia, she relied on the specific meaning of the words in statutes and the Constitution, at the time they were written. According to one authority, that suggested a narrow view of the Court's role and skepticism about precedents. Barrett acknowledged that there are "super precedents" like *Brown*, but she did not count *Roe* among them. Critics questioned her views on race, the Affordable Care Act, Title IX, unions, and LGBTQ rights.[144] By nominating a forty-eight-year-old judicial conservative to replace Justice Ginsburg, Trump intended to shift the balance of the Supreme Court for decades.

CONEY BARRETT CONFIRMATION

On October 12, Senator Lindsay Graham (R-SC), chair of the Senate Judiciary Committee, opened confirmation hearings for Judge Barrett. Graham, who had run for President in 2016, was a Trump convert. Running for reelection in an unexpectedly competitive race, he used his opening statement as a campaign appeal. Progressives worried that ranking member Dianne Feinstein (D-CA), eighty-seven, the oldest member of the Senate, wasn't up to the challenge.[145] In contrast, Judge Barrett was poised and prepared.

With some chilling exceptions, the hearings were an "exercise in evasion." Barrett conceded that the *Brown* desegregation decision and the *Loving* case, allowing interracial marriage, had been decided correctly. She balked at *Griswold*, the 1965 case that found the right of married couples to use contraception. Based on a right to privacy, *Griswold* was the basis of *Roe*. Justices Roberts, Alito, and Thomas had all agreed that *Griswold* was a precedent. Trump's two other nominees, Gorsuch and Kavanaugh, had ducked. Despite acknowledging *Loving*, Barrett refused to say whether *Obergefell*, a marriage equality case, had been correctly decided. During twenty hours of testimony, Barrett declined to share her legal views on abortion, gun rights, health care, immigration, climate change, or presidential power, prompting Senator Richard Durbin (D-IL) to observe, "I'd be afraid to ask her about the presence of gravity."[146]

What was unusual was the emphasis on Barrett as a mother. "While I am a judge," she said the day she was nominated, "I'm better known back home as a room parent, carpool driver, and birthday party planner." During the hearings, her children were introduced individually. Republican Senators praised her as a "remarkable," "tireless," "legal titan who drives a minivan." Senator Josh Hawley (R-MO) asked for parenting advice; Senator John Cornyn (R-TX) asked who did the laundry. Annoying Democrats, Senator Feinstein asked if Barrett had a "magic formula." The GOP strategy was to reassure voters that Barrett could manage the demands of the job. No one had asked O'Connor about her three sons. Parenthood had not been seen as a qualification for Antonin Scalia, the father of nine, or Brett Kavanaugh, who coached his two daughters' basketball teams. Fathers are rarely asked how they would juggle their personal and professional lives, because most do not. Caregiving remains the cultural and actual responsibility of women.[147]

Barrett emerged unscathed. On a party-line vote, the Judiciary Committee recommended her to the Senate. Liberal activists were outraged when Senator Feinstein noted Chairman Graham's graceful conduct of the hearings. NARAL Pro-Choice America called for her removal from the committee.[148] On Monday, October 26, thirty-eight days after Ginsburg's death and eight days before the election, the Senate confirmed Amy Coney Barrett, 52 to 48. Republicans cast all the yes votes. Senator Collins (R-ME) voted with the Democrats, but stressed that her objection was not to Barrett, but to the timing of the confirmation process, during an election. With only Republicans supporting her nomination, Barrett was the first Supreme Court Justice confirmed without bipartisan support since 1869, when Reconstruction Republicans approved Lincoln's Secretary of War, Edwin Stanton.[149]

Democrats were powerless, but not silent. "The majority has trampled over norms, rules, standards, honor, values . . . in its monomaniacal pursuit to put someone on the court who will take away the rights of so many Americans," raged Minority Leader Charles Schumer (D-NY). The shift from Ginsburg to Barrett was tectonic. That evening, the President produced a prime time, unofficial swearing in ceremony, conducted by Justice Thomas, on the Blue Room balcony, complete with bunting, bands, and a crowd of guests. Barrett, wearing a plain black dress, used her remarks to assert her independence from Trump.[150]

CAMPAIGN COUNTDOWN

The Supreme Court was a topic at the first presidential debate, on September 29. The audience at the Cleveland Clinic was required to wear masks. Once seated, the Trump family took theirs off. Within minutes, it was clear that the event would not be a debate but a debacle. The President was belligerent. During the ninety-minute melee, he blustered and bullied, repeatedly interrupting both Joe Biden and moderator Chris Wallace of Fox News. Biden, whose campaign strategy was to appear presidential, in contrast to the incumbent, had difficulty restraining himself. He finally called the president a clown, a liar, a racist, and "the worst president America has ever had." Attempts to focus on the virus, the economy, and racial violence were thwarted by Trump's barrage. Two critical moments related to Trump's discomfort condemning white supremacists and his refusal to commit to abiding by the election results.[151]

People demonstrating for racial justice were again in the headlines, following a September 23 announcement, related to Breonna Taylor's death the previous March, in Lexington, Kentucky. During a botched narcotics raid, three white policemen had killed Taylor, twenty-six, a Black emergency medical technician, in her home. Daniel Cameron, the Black state attorney general who had spoken at the Republican convention, reported the grand jury's finding. None of the officers faced charges related to Taylor's death. One was charged with wanton endangerment for shooting into neighboring apartments. Because her boyfriend had fired one shot against what he believed were intruders, the police were "justified in their use of force," firing forty rounds. The case raised questions about "no knock warrants," the failure to use body cameras, and police training. Between 2015 and 2020, the *Washington Post* tracked 5,600 fatal shootings by police nationally. Of those victims, 247 were women; 48, or 20%, were Black women, 7 of whom were unarmed.[152]

In a seemingly endless cycle of headlines, bulletins, and Trump tweets, reporters and viewers barely had time to process these developments before news broke that White House insider Hope Hicks had tested positive for COVID, two days after the debate. Then, early on Friday, October 2, the President announced on Twitter that he and the First Lady had tested positive. Later that day he took a helicopter to Walter Reed National Military Medical Center, where he remained for three nights. Within a week, thirty-three others tested positive, including two members of the Senate Judiciary Committee and the president of Notre Dame. The Rose

Garden gathering and an indoor reception for Judge Barrett were identified as "super-spreader" events.[153] It had been two weeks since Ginsburg's death.

Timed to be covered on the evening news, the President returned to the White House at sunset, on Monday, October 5. He walked up the steps to the Blue Room balcony, took off his mask, and saluted his helicopter. On some footage it appeared that he was having trouble breathing. In subsequent days, he claimed to have recovered fully, due to excellent doctors and experimental drugs.[154] For the vice presidential debate on October 7, the nonpartisan Commission on Presidential Debates moved the candidates farther apart and installed Plexiglas panels between them. A notable element of their encounter was Senator Harris's crisp response to the Vice President's interruptions: "I'm speaking." Her rejoinder resonated with many women.[155] The commission also determined that the second presidential debate, a town hall planned for Miami, would move online. When the President refused to participate, the commission cancelled it.[156]

After the debate, Trump again attacked Kamala Harris as "totally unlikeable," "a communist," and twice, "this monster." His allies called her "condescending," "smirking," and an "insufferable lying bitch." Racist and sexist remarks had been rampant since Harris was nominated, underscoring the double standards and dual identities women, and women candidates of color, confront. Black women were libeled as "angry, mean, aggressive, disrespectful." Women were still expected to be feminine, polite, docile, and likeable, characteristics not commonly associated with leadership. The overlapping sexism and racism expressed against Harris demonstrated another form of intersectionality.[157]

The day after the Harris-Pence debate, federal and state law enforcement officers arrested thirteen men accused of plotting to kidnap Michigan Democratic Governor Gretchen Whitmer. The conspirators had bragged online about drilling for combat and building explosives.[158] When the governor enforced strict shutdown rules earlier in the pandemic, Trump encouraged armed protests against her. An analysis of a leaked membership list of a group called the Oath Keepers counted two-thirds of the 25,000 members as former or current members of the military or law enforcement.[159] The Whitmer incident alarmed people, who worried that the President would call on far-right paramilitary groups to "stand down and stand by," intimidate voters at the polls, and protest if he lost.

Friday, October 23, marked the highest daily number of new COVID cases, 82,600, surpassing records set during the summer surge. On the day of the Senate's confirmation vote, there were 74,497 new cases and 2,824 deaths. The total death rate approached 329,000. There was an up-tick in thirty-eight states. Five states had positive test rates above 20%. South Dakota's was 35.8%; Iowa's 48.4%. More than 170 counties, in 36 states, were designated hot spots. Rural hospitals had reached capacity. Forty times more Americans had died of COVID than on 9/11.[160]

The ferocity and fatality of the pandemic raised fears about the country's ability to conduct an election. The general election date, the first Tuesday after the first Monday in November, set by federal statute, was November 3, 2020. Thirty-nine states and the District of Columbia allowed early voting at traditional polling places, election offices, or by mail.[161] As of October 25, the Sunday before the Senate confirmed Judge Barrett, almost sixty million people had voted, representing 43% of all the votes cast in the 2016 election. Mail ballot return rates were multiples of 2016: 80% in Texas, 70% in Montana, 65% in North Carolina, 60% in Washington State. Lines at polling places were as long as lines at food banks.[162] Turnout was expected to reach record levels.

Voters were uneasy about their safety at the polls. In addition to the virus, people worried about violence and intimidation. There were no national laws about guns at polling places and different rules in every jurisdiction. Depending on the state, guns were banned in polling places in churches and schools. Six states and DC banned firearms at polling locations and four others banned concealed weapons. Michigan's secretary of state, Democrat Jocelyn Benson, issued a ban on openly carrying weapons inside or within one hundred feet of polling places. Claiming an infringement on their right to bear arms, opponents won an injunction. Benson appealed, but the state Supreme Court did not act before Election Day.[163]

Voters were also worried about the outcome. Both sides recognized the stakes. Biden held his lead by just below ten percentage points. Local polling margins were narrower.[164] Democrats swung between predicting an Electoral College landslide and being haunted by their 2016 loss. Republicans were confident in the President's predictions of an easy reelection. If Trump lost, it proved his claims of fraud in a rigged system. In 2020, the country marked the centennial of the Nineteenth Amendment and the fifty-fifth anniversary of the Voting Rights Act, the death of a feminist legal icon, the elevation of another woman to the Supreme Court, and the nomination of a Black woman for vice president. Voting rights, equal rights, civil rights, reproductive rights, and Black lives were on the ballot, and at risk.

NOT ENOUGH

T here were many parallels and contrasts between 1920 and 2020. Both were presidential election years. Both election seasons were fraught with racial violence. In both eras, a pandemic killed hundreds of thousands and infected the incumbent presidents. Turnout in 1920 was 49.2%, an all-time low. Turnout in 2020 was 66.7%, the highest since 1900. Ten million more women than men turned out.[1] In 1920, newly enfranchised white women were an unpredictable factor. Politicians worried about how many women would vote and for whom. Republicans half-heartedly courted Black women. No one in power protested, or protected them from the institutional racism that barred them from voting in the South. Racial discrimination was still a factor in the 2020 election, but Black women determined its outcome. Polling indicated that race played a stronger role in voting than gender. Black, Asian, and Latina women voted Democratic by large margins. Joe Biden won 91% of Black women and 43% of white women. White suburban women swung to Biden, as did 64% of college-educated women.[2] In 1920, almost no women ran for office; in 2020, there were too many women candidates to count, including the vice presidential nominee.

Following the Great War, the world was "knocked to pieces, leaky, red-hot, threatening to blow up." America was anxious about immigrants and alien ideas like Bolshevism.[3] In 2020, America was in turmoil, dealing with a pandemic, police violence, racial reckoning, immigration, and economic uncertainty. In both eras, Americans longed for a return to "normal," but many people, especially women and people of color, were no longer willing to settle for the customary inequities of sexism and racism. It was not enough.

EQUAL RIGHTS WITHOUT REPRODUCTIVE FREEDOM?

Since ratification of the Nineteenth Amendment and passage of the Voting Rights Act, there have been many positive advances for all women. They can make choices that had been denied them, "on account of sex," for centuries. Women can enroll in college, play sports, take a job, pursue professions, keep their wages, own property, open businesses, sign contracts, vote, serve on juries, join the military, and fly in space. They can marry whomever they want and get an uncontested divorce. They can wear trousers, run marathons, or run for office. No longer bound by confining undergarments, restrictive dress codes, and rigid social rules, women have much greater physical and personal freedom.

Within limits set by majority male legislatures and courts, women can limit their fertility. Three Trump Supreme Court appointees question *Griswold*, the landmark 1965 case allowing married couples to use birth control. Unavailable in Margaret Sanger's era, effective birth control was widely prescribed in 2020, but it was not uniformly covered by health insurance. Obamacare mandated employer-provided, cost-free birth control, but the Supreme Court expanded the list of exempted employers to include religiously affiliated institutions, privately held companies, and publicly traded corporations, basically all employers. Justice Ginsburg, who dissented in those cases, understood that a woman's ability to control conception was essential to her equal citizenship. Reproductive rights result in greater educational attainment, an increase in labor force participation and earnings for women, and a decrease in poverty for them and their families.[4]

Sanger's hypothesis that adequate birth control would lower the risk of ending unwanted pregnancies with abortion proved true. According to the Guttmacher Institute, contraception drove a long-term decline in pregnancy and a subsequent decline in abortion. In 2019, only 13.5 out of 1,000 women had abortions, the lowest recorded rate since before *Roe*. Yet, despite access to birth control, millions of American women have experienced an unintended pregnancy. Experts estimated that one in four American women will have an abortion before age forty-five. Among women who have had abortions, 55% had had their lives disrupted by a job loss, sexual assault, or another crisis; 58% were in their twenties; 61% already had at least one child; 75% were economically disadvantaged. Likely related to disproportionate levels of poverty and unequal access to medical attention, Black women are five times more likely to get abortions. The most common reasons women terminate a pregnancy are rape, incest, poverty, desperation, fatal fetal abnormalities, and risk to the mother of septic shock, stroke, or blood loss.[5]

Abortions are legal, voluntary procedures, but state laws control access. At last count, between 2011 and 2020, Republican states had passed 480 restrictions on reproductive freedom. They include spousal and parental notification and consent; mandatory waiting periods; counseling intended to discourage procedures; "fetal personhood" laws; banning abortion after the first signs of a fetal heartbeat at six to eight weeks, before an actual heart has developed; requiring ultrasounds, with the volume turned up; redefining of fetal viability; limiting public and private insurance coverage; requiring the remains of abortions to be buried or cremated; limiting admitting privileges for providers; setting stricter standards for clinics; and protecting protestors who harass patients.[6] One-third of abortions are medical, a prescription of two pills, which some states have also outlawed.

As a result, there are no clinics in 87% of US counties. Kentucky, Mississippi, Missouri, North Dakota, South Dakota, and West Virginia have one clinic for the entire state. Four states passed constitutional amendments declaring that they do not protect the right to abortion. An analysis of Google searches found that requests for information about self-induced abortion were highest from areas where legal abortion was unavailable.[7] During the pandemic, seven states classified abortion as an unnecessary medical procedure.[8] The intimately personal has become intensely political.

According to a 2019 Public Religion Research Institute poll, Americans find abortion an uncomfortable, complicated issue. The public supports "safe, legal and rare" abortion. Voters reject both total bans and "abortion on demand." A December 2019 *Washington Post/*ABC poll counted 60% of Americans in support; a Pew survey found 70% do not want to overturn *Roe*. Only 14% of respondents said abortion should be completely illegal. In 2020, support for legal abortion was the highest it had been in two decades. The gap between Democratic and Republican support for abortion was thirty-six points.[9] The Republican platform insisted on the appointment of anti-abortion judges. Democrats called for repeal of the Hyde Amendment.[10] When the Republicans controlled the Senate, they confirmed conservative judges who opposed abortion, including Supreme Court appointees committed to overturning *Roe*. For almost fifty years, social and religious conservatives have tried to reverse that decision. Both sides engaged in constitutional trench warfare. It was a battle between science and ideology.

MAJORITY RIGHTS?

Women are everywhere, except the Oval Office and several places of worship. They are on the Supreme Court, on submarines, in surgical theaters, c-suites, and coal mines. Women appear in advertising in all media, because women make more than 85% of all purchases.[11] At 50.8% of the population, women are the numerical majority, but many do not enjoy equal status.

- Women are underpaid. They are almost half of the workforce, but two-thirds work in the lowest paid segments of the economy, essential but unappreciated. A gender pay gap is evident across the board.[12]

- Women are undervalued in their unpaid domestic roles as partners, parents, and family caregivers, roles in which they are overrepresented. Wage-earning mothers lack adequate government support; the US is the only wealthy country that does not provide paid family leave.[13]
- Women are unbanked or underbanked: 28% of unmarried women do not have the minimum deposit required to open an account or have access to conveniently located banks.[14]
- Women are underrepresented in almost every profession, except in those fields traditionally associated with caregiving and education, such as childcare workers, elementary school teachers, librarians, nurses, and social workers.
- Women outnumber men among eligible voters and turn out at higher rates, but they are the minority of elected officials. They hold fewer than one-third of the seats in any governing body, from school boards to state legislatures to the US Senate.[15]
- Women die having children at an unacceptably high rate, due to inequitable medical treatment.
- Women are the vast majority of victims of domestic violence.

When you start at barely any and advance to more, the line on a graph tracking women's progress might suggest dramatic improvement. If you amortize those changes over a century, the pace is slower and the line is flatter.

HEALTH AND SAFETY: AT RISK

Sexual intimidation and violence against women were patriarchal prerogatives. That power was rooted in religious orthodoxy, white supremacy, territorial conquest, manifest destiny, frontier mythology, and masculine identity. Lawlessness was institutionalized as legal violence against Native Americans, Black men, ethnic minorities, immigrants, and all women. The country has still not passed federal anti-lynching legislation or common sense gun laws.[16] Before the pandemic, domestic violence had reached epidemic proportions. Fifty women a month were killed by their partners. One in three female murder victims was killed by a domestic partner. One in four women experienced severe, intimate partner physical violence, sexual violence, or stalking. One in five women had been raped during her lifetime. According to the National Coalition Against Domestic Violence, on any day, domestic violence hotlines received over twenty thousand calls. When the pandemic isolated families, the phones stopped ringing. Escaping domestic violence was the leading cause of homelessness among women. A 2018 survey found that 81% of women had experienced sexual harassment.[17]

The fourth reauthorization of the 1993 Violence Against Women Act, in 2019, closed the infamous "boyfriend loophole." It barred non-spousal partners previously convicted of domestic abuse from purchasing firearms. The bill passed the House with bipartisan support, but Senate sponsors Dianne Feinstein (D-CA) and Joni Ernst (R-IO) could not garner enough votes. During the hearings, Ernst recounted being raped in college. Proponents wanted the new bill to cover genital mutilation, honor killings, sex trafficking, and women in living in federal prisons or on reservations. Reauthorization failed.[18]

In the 1920s, reformers prioritized women's healthcare. Then and now, conditions related to childbirth were among women's principal health concerns. The 1921 Sheppard–Towner Act passed in response to a maternal death rate that was the highest among twenty major nations.[19] Maternal deaths were notoriously underreported until 2018, when every state adopted a maternal mortality check box on death certificates. That year, the US mortality rate was 17.4 deaths out of 1,000. There were stark racial and ethnic disparities. Black and Native American/Alaska Native women were three times more likely than white women to die of pregnancy-related causes, 37.1 out of 1,000, compared to 14.7 among white and 11.8 among Hispanic women. In 2019, the most recent year with available data, Black infants were twice as likely as white children to die before their first birthdays.[20] Experts believed 60% of maternal and infant deaths could have been prevented with proper medical intervention. In recent years, maternal mortality has fallen by almost half in all developed countries; it has doubled in the United States. Among developed nations, the US has the highest rate of pregnancy-related deaths. Globally, the US ranks forty-sixth.[21] Despite America's scientific and financial resources, women's well-being remains vulnerable to male violence, gender and racial discrimination, disparities in health care, class differences, and conservative courts.

EDUCATION

In 1920, access to education was a priority for women. Today girls and women are 70% of high school valedictorians and the majority of students in college and graduate schools. They earn more undergraduate and advanced degrees than men, who were now the "second sex" in higher education. Men outnumber women in only four of eleven graduate fields measured: engineering (76.6% male), math and computer science (75.2%), physical and earth sciences (64.8%), and business (53.2%). Women earn 51.4% of graduate biology degrees and 71% in health and medical sciences.[22]

Many are accruing crushing tuition debt. While women of color and poorer women continue to confront structural impediments to educational access, the percentage of Black women earning college degrees has outpaced all other racial and gender cohorts. Black women are consistently more than half of Black graduate students. The Brookings Institute concluded that the benefit of higher education is undercut by other forms of historic discrimination, in employment, wages, and housing.[23] Black women have high levels of education, civic engagement, and business ownership, but they are underrepresented in elected office, earn less than white women, and are twice as likely to be incarcerated, live in poverty, and suffer higher rates of major illness and domestic violence, according to a 2017 report by the National Domestic Workers Alliance.[24]

PROFESSIONS

Educational achievement opened more occupations to women. In 2019, women were:

- 38% of lawyers and 22% of law partners[25]
- 36% of doctors, 50.5% of medical school students, and 63% of pharmacists[26]
- 13% of all engineers and 26% of computer scientists[27]
- 76% of public school K-12 faculty, including 98% of kindergarten teachers[28]
- 31% of full-time college faculty, an increase of only 5% in seventy-five years[29]
- 30% of college presidents, primarily at public universities; half of the Ivy League has had at least one woman president[30]
- 41.8% of college varsity coaches [31]
- 14% of farm owners[32]
- 6.5% of commercial pilots[33]
- 4% of firefighters[34]
- 3% of plumbers[35]

Despite programs encouraging young women to enter STEM fields, progress has been negligible and turnover is high. A 2018 report by the National Academies of Sciences, Engineering, and Medicine found that sexual harassment pushed talented women out of scientific fields. As of 2017, half of current astronauts was female.[36] In 2020, NASA named its Washington headquarters for Mary Jackson, the agency's first Black engineer, one of its "hidden figures." It renamed its space telescope in honor of NASA's first chief astronomer, Nancy Grace Roman, the "Mother of Hubble."[37] Since Nobel Prizes for chemistry and physics were first awarded in 1901, eleven women have been honored. The first two prizes went to Marie Curie, for physics in 1903 and for chemistry in 1911; the third went to her daughter. Four American women have been among the honorees, including, in 2020, biochemist Jennifer Doudna, who shared the Nobel in chemistry with Frenchwoman Emmanuelle Charpentier, and Andrea Ghez, who shared one for physics.[38]

BUSINESS

In business, "gender parity moved at a glacial pace." Until 1972, when Katharine Graham became CEO of the *Washington Post*, there were no women CEOs of Fortune 500 companies. In early 2020, there were thirty-seven, an all-time high. Three were women of color; none was a Black executive. Only five Fortune 500 CEOs are Black men. The first Black woman on the list was Ursula Burns, CEO of Xerox (2010-2016). The announcement that Jane Fraser would take over as CEO of Citigroup, one of the ten largest banks in the US, in 2021, was seismic.[39] By 2020, women, frequently the same women, held one-fifth of the board seats of the 3,000 largest publicly traded companies. Amazon, Best Buy, CBS, General Motors, and Tupperware were among only twenty-six companies whose boards are half female. More diverse boards hire more diverse CEOs. The research also demonstrated that mixed teams outperform homogeneous ones. Burns now advocates quotas to improve diversity, using a "hatchet [rather than] a paring knife," an approach she "loathes."[40]

To demonstrate the paucity of "Black, Hispanic, Asian, Native American, multiracial or otherwise [people] of color," in September 2020, the *New York Times* published a three-page, color spread of headshots of the leaders of major institutions. It did not highlight women. It pictured governors, senators, judges, CEOs of the highest valued companies, owners of professional sports teams, music producers, university presidents, and Trump cabinet members. In every category the number of diverse leaders was small. Women were half of the commanders of the largest police forces and of prosecutors in the largest police districts; one-third of editors of the most read magazines and of people who run television networks or Hollywood studios; and one-fourth of board members of major newspapers and broadcast networks.[41] The highest paid showrunner and producer in television is Shonda Rhimes. The Black creator of *Grey's Anatomy* and *Scandal* is known for casting roles without adhering to traditional notions of skin color, body shape, ethnicity, or gender.[42]

THE MILITARY

Progress for women in the military was an obstacle course. By 2020, when all military jobs were open to women, they represented 16.5% of active-duty troops, including infantry, cavalry, and fire support roles; one-third are Black women.[43] There are few women leaders. General Ann Dunwoody, now retired, was the first woman to become a four-star general, in 2008. Of the forty-three four-star generals and admirals serving in 2020, Air Force General Jacqueline Van Ovost was the only woman. To avoid Trump's intervention, the Pentagon delayed promoting Army Lieutenant General Laura Richardson to four-star status until 2021.[44]

Women are 28% more likely than men to leave the military. One reason was their inability to pass physical fitness tests. An effort "to establish gender blind standards [to] improve soldier readiness" found that the new tests challenged already underrepresented women. They failed at significantly higher rates, 54% compared to 7% of men. There were different tests for different career fields, but they were still difficult for women, who on average weigh less, have less muscle mass, and less upper body strength. Acknowledging physical differences, the military is redesigning body armor to better protect female bodies, and adding maternity uniforms.[45] The other reason women left the military was sexual harassment. The Pentagon reported a 38% spike in "unwanted sexual conduct," ranging from groping to rape. During a 2019 hearing on sexual assault in the military, Senator Martha McSally (R-AZ), the first woman pilot to fly combat missions, revealed being raped while at the Air Force Academy.[46] The problem remains unresolved. The response was not enough.

SPORTS

In 1921, women activists secured legislation requiring physical education classes for girls in public schools. In this area, given the opportunities afforded by Title IX, women have leapt ahead. Champions in many sports, women athletes still fight for equal resources and, professionally, for equal pay. In May 2020, a federal judge rejected a suit over pay equity and working conditions brought by the US women's soccer team, four-time World Cup winners, against the US soccer federation. Frustrated, team captain Megan Rapinoe exclaimed, "One cannot simply outperform discrimination."[47] Another area of inequality is endorsement revenue. In twenty-five years, only ten players in the Women's National Basketball Association (WNBA) have had signature shoe deals. In 2020, there were none, compared to eighteen for current NBA players.[48] Women are slowly making gains as coaches and officials for teams at all levels, including the National Football League.[49] A new challenge relates to the rights of transgender athletes to play sports in school. Most states exclude them from participation.[50]

EMPLOYMENT

After the Rosies were laid off from war production jobs, women remained about one-third of American workers into the 1960s. By 2019, women were almost half of all workers. Among women age sixteen and over, 57.4% work for wages, compared to 69.2% of men. The pandemic erased progress it had taken women decades to achieve. According to the Department of Labor, there were fewer women in the workforce in October 2020 than a year before. The largest decline was among women with children. COVID created a childcare crisis for both providers and working mothers with children under eighteen, who are 32% of all employed women.[51]

"Men who are out of work are still presumed to be workers, but women aren't, because we frame work for women as a choice," observed sociologist

Sarah Dameske.[52] Working is not a choice. Two-thirds of women work in low-paying, hourly jobs. Under the Fair Labor Standards Act, employers meeting certain criteria must pay the federal minimum wage, or $7.25/hour in 2020. State minimum wages ranged from $5.15, in Georgia and Wyoming, to $14 in California. Wage discrimination is not limited to one sector or income level; it happens to every marginalized woman.[53]

In the 1920s, union activity declined due to low unemployment, judicial hostility, and its association with Bolshevism. Women were rarely union members. Decades later, the decline of American manufacturing made unions less effective. By 1980, they represented one in five workers. In 2020, the ratio was one in ten: 10.5% of female and 11.7% of male workers. Members were less likely to be autoworkers or coal miners and more likely to be government office workers, teachers, police officers, or school bus drivers.[54] When social justice advocates were fighting to protect women factory workers, one demand was for access to restrooms, a demand repeated in 2020 by warehouse workers. Unions do not protect domestic, childcare, and home health care workers, who are primarily Black, brown, Asian, and immigrant women. The exception is the Culinary Workers Union in Las Vegas. As the pandemic proved, women's jobs are essential and undervalued. Working women need affordable childcare, universal pre-K and kindergarten, before and after school care, paid family leave, transparent pay scales, comparable pay, increased child tax credits, and stiffer consequences for sexual harassment.

MOTHERHOOD

The fertility rate is the average number of children a woman will have during her lifetime. Historically, factors like access to hygiene, medical care, birth control, and education have reduced that number. The birthrate declined from 3.3 children in 1920 to 2.0 in 1940, after the Depression. It soared during the Baby Boom, to over 3.5 average children, from 1946 to 1964. Fertility reached its lowest rate, 1.7 children, in 1979.[55]

In 2020, 86% of American women were mothers by age forty-four. According to the Pew Research Center, average family size is 2.4 children. Among mothers in 2020, 41% have two children, 24% have three children, and 14% have four or more children. The proportion of mothers who have "onlies" doubled, from 11% in 1976 to 22% in 2015. Two cohorts of women have larger families: women without a high school diploma and those with multiple degrees.[56] Only 41% of Americans believe that children are important to marital happiness; more households own dogs than have children.[57]

Since 1988, for all racial and age groups, the birthrate has fallen steadily. Among adults, the decline is in part related to later marriage and a narrower window for fertility, possibly broadened by in vitro fertilization and surrogacy. Data for 2019, from the Centers for Disease Control, recorded a sharp decline among teenagers, to 17.4 births out of 1,000 girls age fifteen to nineteen. The pandemic accelerated the decline in the US birth rate by 4% overall for 2020, to 1.64. One demographer considered the birthrate "a barometer of despair," reflecting an economic downturn, job insecurity, and political turmoil.[58] Current data connects the decline to lack of support for mothers, including paid leave. A declining birthrate has lasting, negative consequences.[59]

MARRIAGE AND DIVORCE

Not all mothers were married. As social mores changed, so did patterns of marriage and divorce. In 1920, the marriage rate hit its historic high, 92.3 per 1,000 women. In 2017, it was 32.2.[60] In 2020, standard households included single parents (9%), married couples with children (19%), people living alone (28%), and unrelated roommates (35%). Since 1967, the number of interfaith and interracial couples has increased. Pew reported that 19% of new marriages involve different racial or ethnic couples, up from 11% in 2000. In 1920, the median age at marriage for women was twenty-one. It dropped to twenty during the 1950s. By 2018, it was twenty-nine. In 2020, thirty-four million women, nearly one in three, had never married.[61]

For a married woman to keep her "birth" or "maiden" name was once both illegal and an act of feminist rebellion. Neither Elizabeth Cady Stanton nor Lucy Stone vowed to obey their husbands. Stone refused to take Henry Blackwell's name when they married in 1855. When Massachusetts granted limited local suffrage to women in 1879, the state insisted that Stone register in her married name. She refused, and never voted. Frances Perkins was another member of the "Lucy Stone League" of women keeping their names. Today, 68.5% of women take their partner's name, including in 49% of LGTBQ marriages; 22% keep their birth names; and 8.9% use hyphens or create a new surname. The number of women keeping their names is increasing among highly educated and high earning women, those who marry later, celebrities, and women committed to their personal "brand."[62]

Later marriage also contributed to the lowest divorce rate in fifty years. According to census data, as of 2019, only 14.9 marriages out of 1,000 ended in divorce. Same-sex couples were as likely as straight couples to divorce. The last peak was 22.6, in 1980.[63] "Grey divorces," among older couples, doubled after 2000, whereas people born between 1981 and 1996 married later and stayed married. Among college-educated Americans in the top third income bracket, 64% are in intact marriages, in contrast to 24% of couples in the lower third income bracket. People who married young, who have less education and lower incomes, or whose parents divorced, were more likely to be divorced. Divorce became less taboo. Social media now reports the "evolution of dissolution" and "conscious uncoupling" among celebrities, rather than separation and divorce.[64] Although ordinary women filed for divorce twice as often as men, it still had harsher consequences for them, including poverty. Declines in birth and marriage rates meant many Americans lack the support offered by family structures. According to the US Census, by 2020, one in four children did not live with both biological parents.[65]

EQUAL RIGHTS

In the 1920s, the Equal Rights Amendment divided feminists. After its 1972 passage by Congress, the ERA divided the country. A ten-year ratification campaign failed, three states short. When it resurfaced after the 2017 Women's March, ERA proponents urged passage by three more states. Justice Ginsburg hoped "to see in the Constitution a statement that men and women are people of equal citizenship stature," but she urged ERA supporters to start over.[66] With thirty state legislatures controlled by Republicans, and less than two-thirds of the House or the Senate in favor of the ERA, starting again would be futile, as would efforts to challenge the 1982 deadline. Reintroduction of the ERA in every session since 1983 undercut the argument that the 1972 amendment was still in play, needing only three more states to act. Nonetheless, Nevada (2017), Illinois (2018), and Virginia (2020) finally ratified the amendment.

Those states sent their ratifications to the National Archivist for certification, no longer the purview of the Secretary of State. Ignoring a ruling by the Justice Department's legal counsel, that "Congress may not revive a proposed amendment after its deadline has expired," Representatives Carolyn Maloney (D-NY) and Jackie Speier (D-CA) introduced a bill to eliminate the deadline. It passed the House in February 2020, in a largely symbolic vote, because it would die in the Senate. More recently, Maloney has insisted that ratification by thirty-five states, over a forty-eight-year span, should automatically add the ERA to the Constitution.[67] A poll conducted by the Fund for Women's Equality found that 80% of Americans think the ERA has already passed.[68]

One reason to reintroduce the ERA would be to change its "on account of sex" wording. In 1923, sex referred to men and women and unchangeable body parts. Gender was a changeable social construct, defined by culture and community. Now body parts can be surgically changed and gender means a person's psychological identity, which may not correspond to an individual's biology at birth.[69] In 2019, the House passed the Equality Act, by 236–173, prohibiting discrimination based on sex, sexual orientation, and gender identity. Eight Republicans voted in favor. The bill died in the Senate Judiciary Committee.[70]

LGBTQ RIGHTS

In June 2020, in *Bostock v. Clayton County, Georgia*, the Supreme Court held that the word "sex," in Title VII, protected the employment rights of LGBTQ people. Gerald Bostock, a county employee, had been fired for "unbecoming conduct" because he played on a gay softball team. Another plaintiff, Aimee Stephens, a transgender Michigan woman fired for wearing a dress to work, died before the case was decided. Writing for the majority, Justice Gorsuch cautioned, "We do not purport to address bathrooms, locker rooms, or anything else of the kind."[71] The Court refused to review a Pennsylvania school district policy allowing trans students to use restrooms and locker rooms that matched their gender identities. It upheld Trump's ban on trans Americans enlisting in the military and reversed an Obama era rule prohibiting discrimination against trans people in health care.[72] The Trump administration packed federal courts with judges hostile to gay rights and several states passed laws targeting trans citizens.[73]

According to a 2020 Gallup poll, 5.6% of American adults identifies as LGBTQ, including one in six adults born between 1965–1980. While same-sex marriage is legal, sundry state laws allow LGBTQ people to be fired, evicted, or denied service. Twenty-seven states deny housing on account of sexual orientation and forty-one bar LGBTQ people from jury service. Other states have passed laws specifically prohibiting such discrimination. Eight out of ten Americans favor laws to protect LGBTQ people.[74]

WOMEN IN POLITICS

Before the 2020 election, American women were 29.2% of state legislators, 27% of mayors, and 18% of governors, including two Latinas and one Asian

American Pacific Islander (AAPI) woman, but no Black women to date. In the Congress, women were 26% of the Senate and 23.7% of the House. Women of color were 38.7% of congresswomen. There were 126 women in the House (105D, 21R) and twenty-five in the Senate (17D, 8R).[75] The nomination of Kamala Harris to be vice president improved the chances of women presidential nominees from either party in future.

In the 2020 election, Black and suburban white women elected the Biden-Harris ticket by more than seven million votes, 51.4% for the Democrats to 46.9 % for the Republican incumbent. It was the first presidential ticket to win by more than eighty million votes. The Electoral College confirmed Biden's victory, 306 to 232. It was the exact reverse of the 2016 result, which Trump had called a "massive landslide."[76] The Republican Party gained seats in the House, narrowing the Democratic majority to ten votes (221 D, 211 R), plus three vacancies. The new Congress had 140 women members: 117 in the House (89 D, 28 R) and 23 in the Senate (16 D, 7 R). Democrats lost one woman; Republicans gained fourteen and won nine out of the thirteen seats that flipped from blue to red. Among the new members was Nancy Mace (R-SC), the first woman graduate of the Citadel. There were fifty-one women of color (46 D, 5 R), up from forty-eight, including the first three Korean American women, five Native Americans, and one Hawaiian. The Senate had five Hispanics, three Black members, and two of Asian descent. There were eleven LGBTQ members in the whole Congress.[77]

Republicans controlled the majority of state legislatures, which would determine redistricting for the next decade. Party allegiance shifted. Among Republicans, female registration declined from 50% to 46%. The party had become more male (54%) and less educated. More women, 61%, up from 58%, identified as Democrats.[78] The Voting Rights Act of 1965 finally removed legal barriers to Black voting, but the Supreme Court undercut those safeguards in *Shelby v. Holder* (2013). Recently, Republican states passed laws restricting ballot access. The role of women, especially Black women, as activists and voters was undeniably significant in 2020, but it was not enough.

FEMINISM

Not all women are feminists. Before and after suffrage, many politically active white women opposed political involvement by women, as did Margaret Washington, widow of Booker T. Washinton."[79] Other women were anti-feminists, racists, nativists, and antisemites. Had feminism failed? The question recalled critiques of woman suffrage after its first decade. In 1932, Genevieve Parkhurst, former editor of *Pictorial Review,* assessed women's status in an article titled, "Is Feminism Dead?" Discrimination persisted, she contended, because [white] women's organizations lacked "ideological consensus or inspired leadership." Others believed that, in the 1920s, the women's movement was so entangled in fighting over the ERA, that it ignored more pressing issues.[80]

Journalists asked the question again at the end of 2020. When a *New York Times* columnist concluded that "feminism has failed women," readers objected.[81]

> Feminism has not failed women. Society has failed feminism. Blaming feminism is one more way to blame women for society's failures, and to divide women from one another. The lack of adequate child care and paid family leave, improved health care benefits, better social supports and income equity are all issues at the forefront of the feminist movement. Feminism isn't the problem; it's the only answer.

But it was not enough.

The dictionary defines feminism as the advocacy of political, economic, and social equality of men and women. In the wake of the 2017 Women's March, Merriam-Webster's dictionary dubbed feminism its "word of the year," the most researched word on its website. It credited the spike in interest to White House advisor Kellyanne Conway's denial that she was a feminist:

It's difficult for me to call myself a feminist in the classic sense because it seems to be very anti-male, and it certainly is very pro-abortion, and I'm neither . . . So there's an individual feminism . . . that you make your own choices . . . I look at myself as the product of my choices, not a victim of my circumstances.[82]

Can a woman who claims personal autonomy for herself but opposes it for other women be a feminist?

There are all kinds of self-described feminists: moderate, militant, Republican, radical, Black, conservative, frontier, choice, hashtag, pop, and difference feminists. In *Hood Feminism: Notes from the Women that a Movement Forgot* (2021), Mikki Kendall, a veteran and cultural critic, identified "hood" feminists, referring to a cohort of Black women: "[You] can't 'lean in' when you can't earn a legal living wage." Kendall contends that feminist issues are inadequate wages, food insecurity, unaffordable housing, poor healthcare, and mediocre public education.[83] Many white women, working in low-paid jobs, living in rural America or urban enclaves, lacking childcare and broadband, would agree. Very few women have a choice between staying home or working, unless they have their own money or partners willing to support them, even after a divorce. The majority could not support themselves or their children on the average female median salary of $47,299 in 2019. The average for Black women was $41,098.[84] The wealth gap, rooted in historic discrimination, institutional racism like redlining, and tax policy, has grown.

At its inception, the women's movement was not supposed to be about self-aggrandizement. It was supposed to lift and liberate every woman, but as it evolved, it left too many behind. In legislatures and the courts, political feminists fought for voting rights, legal equality, equal pay, access to education, and credit. Women's libbers fought, in the streets and the media, to end sexism, all the ways in which women were diminished and demeaned. Civil rights activists fought to secure and protect equal civil rights, voting rights, and equal economic opportunity for Black, brown, Indigenous, immigrant, indigent, and LGBTQ Americans. These activists had different priorities but similar goals and the same enemies. They showed up at the Women's March in 2017 and at BLM marches in 2020.

In a July 2020 Pew Research Center poll, seven in ten respondents believed feminism had done "at least a fair amount to advance women's rights." Among all women, four in ten said feminism "has helped them personally." Almost half of respondents (49%) believed women's suffrage was the most important milestone in advancing the position of American women; 29% cited the Equal Pay Act; 12% pointed to passage of the Family and Medical Leave Act; and 8% credited the availability of the Pill. A majority thought the country had not gone far enough in granting women equal rights. They identified discrimination in the workplace, sexual harassment, and unequal representation of women in business and political leadership as barriers to women's equality.[85] The activists of the 1920s would have saluted the ways contemporary women have protested, organized, canvassed, campaigned, lobbied, and voted to advance their causes. They would also have recognized the racial divisions, class differences, bias against immigrants, generational conflict, and partisan antagonism that impede progress.

BARBIES AND BEAUTY QUEENS

It's unlikely that suffragists, civil rights activists, and other social justice advocates would have anticipated measuring their success by Barbie dolls or beauty queens, but some cultural changes have had more immediate impact than legal action. In the aftermath of the failed ERA campaign, social norms imploded. Similarly, BLM summer prompted a widespread cultural reconsideration. It led to removal of Confederate iconography and the inclusion of more diversity in the programing and leadership of arts institutions. Another symbol of change was the evolution of actor Jane Fonda, from a sex symbol and anti-war pariah into an exercise guru, an advocate for working women, an icon for octogenarians, and a climate change activist, getting arrested every "Fire Drill Friday."[86] As Paul proclaimed a century ago, there was more to equal citizenship than voting. Suffrage was only a first step. It was not enough.

By 2020, Barbie dolls had run for president six times. The Daughters of the American Revolution, who refused Marian Anderson its stage in 1939, added its first Black board member in 2019, acknowledging the role African Americans played in the Revolutionary War. Walmart refused to display *Cosmopolitan* near checkout lines because its covers objectified women. Pressure grew on states, schools, and employers, including the US military, to end prohibitions on natural Black hairstyles, a form of racial discrimination. The Hallmark channel reversed its prohibition of advertising featuring LGBTQ couples and produced movies with more diverse characters and love stories. Its parent company, Hallmark Cards, markets gender-neutral wedding and baby cards.[87]

Eliminating bathing suits from the Miss America contest was a belated victory for the 1968 bra-burners. As early as 1942, contestants had objected to wearing bathing suits. Miss America 1950 refused to wear one during her reign, declaring, "I'm an opera singer, not a pin-up." In response, Catalina, a swimsuit manufacturer and pageant sponsor, started the rival Miss USA competition.[88] By 2020, neither pageant drew the two million viewers it had in 1970. To revive a culturally marginalized contest, Miss America's organizers recruited Gretchen Carlson in 2018. The Fox journalist, who had successfully sued Roger Ailes for sexual harassment, had been Miss America 1989, representing Minnesota. Carlson banned swimsuits.[89]

The 2020 pageant, "Miss America 2.0," introduced contestants by career category: arts, business, education, or science. The winner, Camille Schrier, was a Black doctoral candidate in pharmacology from Virginia. For the talent portion, she put on a lab coat and a chemistry demonstration, creating exploding goo.[90] Since 1983, there have been eight Black winners, two Asian Americans, and one lesbian. Recent winners of the five major beauty pageants have all been Black women. They believe the recognition sends a "powerful message that today's beauty standards are evolving beyond Barbie-lite, or an era when contestants were prized solely for smooth hair, light skin color and thin lips."[91] Miss Navajo Nation 2019, Shaandiin Parrish, who qualified by butchering a lamb, a traditional tribal skill, spent her reign distributing food and water on reservations during the pandemic.[92]

THE SUFFRAGE CENTENNIAL

The last week in August 2020 was full of newsworthy events. Another Black man was shot by police. President Trump accepted renomination. Civil rights activists returned to the Lincoln Memorial, fifty-seven years after Dr. King's "I Have a Dream" speech. On August 26, the country marked the centennial of the Nineteenth Amendment, in COVID-appropriate ways. Five hundred buildings across the country, including the Capitol and the White House, were illuminated in purple, gold, and white lights. The Air Force coordinated women-led flyovers. A 1,000-square-foot mosaic of Ida B. Wells was installed at Washington's Union Station.[93] New York City installed a statue of Susan B. Anthony, Elizabeth Cady Stanton, and Sojourner Truth in Central Park.

Acknowledging the role of white and Black women in American history, the centennial memorial was also an effort to correct the "bronze imbalance" in public monuments. Following the seventy-fifth anniversary of suffrage, the 1921 bust of Stanton, Anthony, and Mott had returned to the Capitol Rotunda. At that time, C. Delores Tucker, head of the National Congress of Black Women, suggested adding Sojourner Truth to the remaining space on the slab.[94] The Black abolitionist had also been left off the Central Park statue until white activists and Black historians like Martha Jones demanded a redesign. Although they were allies, it's unlikely the three women were ever at the same table, as they are depicted. Sculptor Meredith Bergmann added Truth, literally and figuratively, just as the history of suffrage has been corrected and expanded to incorporate the contributions of diverse activists as more facts are unearthed, more contributions acknowledged, and more stories shared.[95]

In 1921 and 2020, controversial statues celebrated passage of the Nineteenth Amendment. In the intervening century, there were dramatic advances for women. Resistance to those changes has been unabated among some elites and many social conservatives, who were not all white nationalists and racists. The country remains deeply divided by demographics and by debates over our democratic values. The quest for equal rights and social justice follows the long arc of American history. It is not finished. The march to equality, from the 1913 suffrage parade to the street protests of the 1960s, the 2017 Women's March, and the BLM demonstrations in 2020, is ongoing. Gendered and racial discrimination remains too deeply rooted. Sexism and racism overlap but are not equivalent. Two hundred and fifty years of slavery and another hundred years of Jim Crow established a legacy of racism that has been very hard to overcome. Until activist allies can increase their political power, secure racial justice, safeguard reproductive rights, insure equal economic opportunities, provide affordable childcare, and address historic inequities, the work of the women's movement is not only incomplete, but at risk.

JANUARY 2022

The inauguration of the new president took place on January 20, 2021. The ceremony was held outside, on the west front of the Capitol, where two weeks earlier, insurrectionists had broken through security barriers, trying to stop the peaceful transfer of power. The lineup of former presidents lacked only President Carter, ninety-six, and President Trump, who refused to attend. Seating was socially distanced; masks were required. Spotlights lined the Reflecting Pool to commemorate the more than 400,000 people who had died from COVID. An art installation of 200,000 flags covered the Mall, representing Americans who could not attend.[96] There was no inaugural crowd to count.

The program emphasized unity and diversity. It showcased women in prominent roles. A female firefighter spoke and signed the Pledge of Allegiance. Lady Gaga, combining pomp and camp in a dramatic red and navy ball gown, sang the national anthem. The first Hispanic Supreme Court Justice, Sonia Sotomayor, swore in the first female, Black, Asian American Vice President, using Thurgood Marshall's Bible. Kamala Harris wore her Black sorority's signature pearls. Her purple coat echoed Shirley Chisholm's campaign colors and the suffrage banner. Hillary Clinton also wore purple. Jennifer López sang Woody Guthrie's "This Land Is Your Land" and

"America the Beautiful," written in 1893 by Wellesley graduate Katharine Lee Bates. Wearing suffrage white, Lopez punctuated the medley with the final words of the Pledge of Allegiance, in Spanish: "*Una nacion bajo Dios con libertad y justicia para todos!*"[97]

President Biden, sworn in by the Chief Justice, referred to the suffragists who had marched the day before the 1913 inauguration. He promised a government that "looked like America" and selected a "cabinet of firsts," the most racially and ethnically diverse team ever assembled. More than half were non-white, including six African Americans, four Hispanics, and one Native American. Among senior administrators were openly gay and transgender leaders. Almost half of the nominees, the most ever, were women.[98] Jill Biden would continue her day job as a community college professor, the first First Lady to earn independent income since Eleanor Roosevelt.

At Dr. Biden's suggestion, the ceremony concluded with a poetry reading by Amanda Gorman, twenty-two, the first National Youth Poet Laureate. The young Black woman wore a yellow Prada coat and red headband, reinforcing the optimistic theme of her poem. Oprah had given her a ring featuring a caged bird as a tribute to Maya Angelou, Clinton's inaugural poet in 1993.[99] "The Hill We Climb" evoked a "shining city on a hill," a reference to Puritan Boston and Reagan's America, a beacon of hope. Acknowledging the challenges facing the country, Gorman asked, "Where can we find light/ In this never-ending shade?" She did not deny the reality of the riot:

We've seen a force that would shatter our nation rather than share it,
Would destroy our country if it meant delaying democracy.
And this effort very nearly succeeded.
But while democracy can be periodically delayed,
It can never be permanently defeated.

She concluded:

When day comes, we step out of the shade,
Aflame and unafraid.

The dawn blooms as we free it,
For there is always light,
If only we're brave enough to see it,
If only we're brave enough to be it.[100]

For feminists and social justice activists, the day was both uplifting and sobering. Symbolic gestures had not secured equity or equality for American women in the past. The newest women's movement's more inclusive, intersectional feminism confronted an equally committed opposition. Americans have long fought to make the ideals of our founding documents a reality, to make the country better. As the fierce conflicts of January 6 and the past century had demonstrated, there was more work to do, "if only we are brave enough." It was time to begin. Again.

ACKNOWLEDGMENTS

I inherited my love for history and storytelling from my mom, a teacher still remembered and revered by her students. During the Great Depression, when many married women were laid off, she lost her job. In the 1950s, when other moms stayed home, she earned advanced degrees and went back to work. From her, I learned about the excavation at Troy, Irish playwrights, and the Harlem Renaissance. My field is American women's history. The topic was not offered when I was in school, but my timing was fortuitous. I graduated on the cusp of the revived women's movement in the 1970s. While I was in graduate school, I attended Berkshire Women's History conferences, volunteered with the National Women's Political Caucus, marched for the Equal Rights Amendment, and designed one of the first women's history courses for high school students. On behalf of the Caucus, I searched for connections between the Nineteenth and the Equal Rights Amendments and met Edie Mayo, curator for political history and an expert on woman suffrage and Black women at the Smithsonian's National Museum of American History. She remains a mentor.

One outcome of my activism was my dissertation, a biography of Elizabeth Cady Stanton. I later abandoned writing a book about the Equal Rights Amendment and teaching at American University to lead an independent girls' high school, where I taught women's history. Thanks to owner Lissa Muscatine, I've continued to teach at Politics & Prose, an independent bookstore in Washington, DC, and to lecture for the Smithsonian Associates, courtesy of Rebecca Roberts. I learned how women's history engages and outrages students at every age, and how much I was still learning. Galvanized by the 2017 Women's March and the 2020 centennial of the Nineteenth Amendment, I wrote this book.

It relies on the work of stellar historians: Adele Alexander, William Chafe, Bettye Collier-Thomas, Nancy Cott, Ellen Carol DuBois, Paula Giddings, Liette Gidlow, Martha Jones, Linda Kerber, Lynne Olson, Alison Parker, Anne Firor Scott, Marjorie Spruill, Rosalyn Terborg-Penn, Susan Ware, and Eileen Weiss, among many others. I'm indebted to three historians and gifted storytellers, now dead. In her classic, *A Century of Struggle*, Eleanor Flexner provided an example of engaging scope, packing facts and personalities into a page-turner. Cokie Roberts valued the dual, public and private roles women played and the stories found in the common artifacts of women's lives, in cosmetic jars and cooking pots. Barbara Tuchman propelled her narratives with energetic verbs and telling anecdotes.

My investigation of primary sources, including interviews with activists, was undertaken when I was researching the ERA. My assistant then was Julie Goetz, who had been my student at American University. More recently, Susan Green, a lawyer who took one of my P&P classes, provided insights into Supreme Court cases. My sister, Jane Griffith Bryan, head of the reference departments at the University of Pennsylvania and Princeton University libraries, was always ready to answer questions, as have librarians at many other institutions: Kristi Finefield at the Library of Congress; Kate Long at the Smith College Special Collections; Michelle Strizever in the Office of the Clerk, US House of Representatives; Mary Wallace at Wayne State University Archives of Labor and Urban Affairs; and Jeff Dayton provided technical assistance with good humor and patience.

As an independent scholar no longer connected to a university, I rely on professional journals and the annual meetings of the Organization of American Historians to preview recent scholarship. Former OAH president

Alan Kraut, who served on my dissertation committee, is still advising me. Two historians provided significant critiques. John Milton Cooper was the first reader of my college thesis, my Stanton biography, and this book. Ours is an example of the friendships that develop between students and teachers. Krystle Merchant, a younger colleague and co-teacher, offered a crisp contemporary critique, catching factual and linguistic errors. Each draft was improved by feedback from early readers: Sophie Bryan, Kelly Herman, Louisa Swain, and especially from Nancy Rosebush. Any mistakes that remain are entirely my responsibility.

I'm grateful to my steadfast agent, Max Sinsheimer of Sinsheimer Literary, LLC, for his enthusiastic advocacy. He's been another teacher, guiding me through this process from proposal to publisher. Claiborne Hancock at Pegasus Books was keen about this project from the first. His talented team, including my editor Jessica Case, copy editor Victoria Flickinger, proofreader Mary O'Mara, publicist Meghan Jusczak, and designer Maria Fernandez, is A-plus.

I've been cheered on by many chums: Barbara Augenblick, Ann Compton, Leslie Fitch, and Doris Meissner. Judy Hart, Hanns Kuttner, Mary Morgan, and Gaines Post offered long distance support.

I've been sustained by family: my children, Megan and John David; my bonus daughters, Anne and Katie; and my extended family. We still tell stories about my late husband, John Deardourff, a feminist fellow who marched beside me, lobbied for the ERA, and believed in me wholeheartedly. I am enormously grateful to all the storytellers, mentors, role models, colleagues, students, friends, and my beloved family who have inspired this book.

ENDNOTES

Author's Note: Story Lines

1. Annette Gordon-Reed, *The Hemingses of Monticello: An American Family* (New York: W.W. Norton & Co., 2008), 200–01.
2. Annette Gordon-Reed, "Black America's Neglected Origin Stories," *The Atlantic*, June 2021, www.theatlantic.com/magazine/archive/2021/06/estebanico-first-africans-america/618714.
3. Gerda Lerner, *The Majority Finds Its Past: Placing Women in History* (Chapel Hill: University of North Carolina Press, 2005, 1979).
4. www.nps.gov/people/juangarrido.htm.
5. www.whitehouse.gov/about-the-white-house/first-families/martha-dandridge-custis-washington.
6. Yanan Wang, www.washingtonpost.com/news/morning-mix/wp/2016/05/13/the-long-history-and-slow-death-of-a-word-used-to-describe-everyone-from-turks-to-the-chinese.
7. "Latinx Used by Just 3% of US Hispanics," www.pewresearch.org/fact-tank/2021/09/23/who-is-hispanic.
8. Nancy Coleman, "Why We're Capitalizing Black," *New York Times*, July 5, 2020, www.nytimes.com/2020/07/05/insider/capitalized-black.html; www.washingtonpost.com/pr/2020/07/29/washington-post-announces-writing-style-changes-for-racial-and-ethnic-identifiers.
9. Angela Joy, "Bound Together by Name: A Timeline of Black Ethnonyms in America," *Black Is a Rainbow Color* (New York: Roaring Brook Press, 2020).
10. www.holocaustremembrance.com/sites/default/files/memo-on-spelling-of-antisemitism.
11. Melena Ryzik, "Pauli Murray Should Be a Household Name. This Film Shows Why," *New York Times*, September 15, 2021.

12. www.whitehouse.gov/briefing-room/speeches-remarks/2021/06/02/remarks-by
   -president-biden-commemorating-the-100th-anniversary-of-the-tulsa-race-massacre.

13. John McWhorter, "The University of Wisconsin Smears a Once Treasured Alum,"
   www.nytimes.com/2021/09/17/opinion/wisconsin-fredric-march.html.

Chapter One: "Now We Can Begin"

1. Eleanor Flexner, *Century of Struggle: The Woman's Rights Movement in the United States*, rev. ed. (Cambridge: Belknap Press of Harvard University Press, 1975), 176.

2. "Declaration of Sentiments and Resolutions," in *American Women's Suffrage: Voices from the Long Struggle for the Vote, 1776–1965*, ed. Susan Ware (New York: Literary Classics of the United States, 2020), 36–42.

3. Elisabeth Griffith, *In Her Own Right: The Life of Elizabeth Cady Stanton* (New York: Oxford University Press, 1984), 55–57.

4. Ann Baker, "Margaret Brent (ca. 1601–ca.1671)," Maryland State Archives, 1997, msa.maryland.gov/msa/speccol/html/brochure.

5. Casey Cep, "Finish the Fight!" *The New Yorker*, July 8 & 15, 2019, 64.

6. Jennifer Schuessler, "'The Jersey Exception,'" *New York Times*, February 25, 2020, C1.

7. Randolph Hollingsworth, "History of Kentucky Women's Suffrage: An Overview," February 3, 2018, networks.h-net.org/node/blog/history-kentucky-womens-suffrage.

8. Griffith, 56.

9. Jamelle Bouie, "Equality That Wasn't Enough," *New York Times*, February 16, 2020, SR3; Rebecca Zietlow, "150th Anniversary of the 14th and 15th Amendments in Retrospect," paper delivered at Organization of American Historians [OAH], Philadelphia, PA, April 6, 2019. Sen. Charles Sumner (MA) and Reps. James Ashley (NH), George Julian (IL), and William Kelley (PA) supported universal and woman's suffrage.

10. Griffith, 129, 133; Brent Staples, "How the Suffrage Movement Betrayed Black Women," *New York Times*, July 28, 2018, www.nytimes/2018/07/28/opinion/suffrage.

11. Alison M. Parker, *Unceasing Militant: The Life of Mary Church Terrell* (Chapel Hill: University of North Carolina Press, 2020), 124–25.

12. David W. Blight, *Frederick Douglass: Prophet of Freedom* (New York: Simon & Schuster, 2018), 490, 492.

13. Griffith, 123; Blight, 491–92.

14. Ellen Carol DuBois, "Interchange: Women's Suffrage, the Nineteenth Amendment, and the Right to Vote," *Journal of American History* 106, no. 3 (December 2019): 666; Susan Schulten, "The Crooked Path to Women's Suffrage," *New York Times*, June 4, 2019, www.nytimes.com/2019/06/06/opinion/the-crooked-path-to-womens
   -suffrage.

15. Brent Staples, "When the Suffrage Movement Sold Out," *New York Times*, February 3, 2019, SR1; Kerri Lee Alexander, "Frances Ellen Watkins Harper," National Museum of Women's History newsletter, vol. 34, summer 2020, 15–16.

16. Blight, 493; Michael Brown, "The Fifteenth Amendment," paper delivered at OAH, Philadelphia, PA, April 6, 2019.

17. Sarah Egge, "How Midwestern Suffragists Used Anti-Immigrant Fervor to Help Gain the Vote," September 17, 2018: zocalopublicsquare.org/2018/09/17/midwestern
   -suffragists-used.

18. Griffith, 182, xviii, 203–04.

19. Griffith, xiv, 211.

20. Noelle A. Baker, ed., *Stanton in Her Own Time* (Iowa City: University of Iowa Press, 2016), 172–74; Griffith, xv, 210–13.

21. www.newenglandhistoricalsociety.com/edward-hammond-clarke-chance-girls/; Sue Zschoche, "Dr. Clarke Revisited: Science, True Womanhood and Female Collegiate Education," *History of Education Quarterly* 29, no. 4 (January 1, 1989): 545–69.

22. Kimberly A. Hamlin, *From Eve to Evolution: Darwin, Science, and Women's Rights in Gilded Age America* (Chicago: University of Chicago Press, 2014), 73–80, 105–08.

23. Ann J. Lane, *To "Herland" and Beyond: The Life of Charlotte Perkins Gilman* (New York: Pantheon/Random House, 1990), 14, 60, 121, 135, 143.

24. Charles Lemert and Esme Bhan, eds., *The Voice of Anna Julia Cooper* (Lanham, MD: Rowman & Littlefield Publishers, Inc., 1998), 5–13.

25. Duchess Harris, "From the Kennedy Commission to the Combahee Collective: Black Feminist Organizing, 1960–80," in *Sisters in the Struggle: African American Women in the Civil Rights–Black Power Movement*, Bettye Collier-Thomas and V.P. Franklin, eds. (New York: New York University Press, 2001), 281; Lemert, 27.

26. Jill Lepore, "The Last Amazon: Wonder Woman Returns," *New Yorker*, September 22, 2014.

27. Amy Aronson, *Crystal Eastman: A Revolutionary Life* (New York: Oxford University Press, 2020), 107.

28. Henry Louis Gates, Jr., *The Black Church: This Is Our Story, This Is Our Song* (New York: Penguin Press, 2021), 63, 99–101.

29. Alison M. Parker, *Unceasing Militant: The Life of Mary Church Terrell* (Chapel Hill: University of North Carolina Press, 2020), 56, 58, 79.

30. Paula J. Giddings, *Ida: A Sword Among Lions: Ida B. Wells and the Campaign Against Lynching* (New York: Armistad/HarperCollins, 2008); Jones, 151–56; Blight, 717; Arlisha Norwood, "Ida B. Wells-Barnett, National Women's History Museum, 2017, www.womenshistory.org/education-resources/biographies/ida-wells-barnett.

31. Parker, 80, 91, 115-16.

32. Martha S. Jones, *Vanguard: How Black Women Broke Barriers, Won the Vote, and Insisted on Equality for All* (New York: Basic Books, 2020), 158–59; Parker, 79, 49.

33. Lynne Olson, *Freedom's Daughters: The Unsung Heroines of the Civil Rights Movement from 1830 to 1970* (New York: Scribner, 2001), 71–73; "Niagara Movement," History Channel online, February 5, 2021, www.history.com/topics/black-history/niagara -movement.

34. Susan Ware, *Why They Marched: Untold Stories of the Women Who Fought for the Right to Vote* (Cambridge: Harvard University Press, 2019), 101–03.

35. Parker, 126–27.

36. Flexner, 287.

37. Karen Foerstel and Herbert N. Foerstel, *Climbing the Hill: Gender Conflict in Congress* (Westport, CT: Praeger, 1996), 2–3.

38. David M. Kennedy, *Over There: The First World War and American Society* (New York: Oxford University Press, 1979, 2004), 23; Taylor Telford, "Retailer Offers Wardrobe Assist to Women Seeking Office," *Washington Post*, February 20, 2020, A17.

39. www.brainyquote.com/authors/jeannette_rankin.

40.   Flexner, 301–02, 19.

41.   John M. Cooper, Jr., *Woodrow Wilson: A Biography* (New York: Alfred A. Knopf, 209), 414.

42.   Elizabeth Cobbs, "How Race Affected Women's Right to Vote," *Washington Post*, June 3, 2019; Melissa Korn, "University of Mississippi Will Remove Name of White Supremacist from Building," *Wall Street Journal*, July 7, 2017.

43.   Flexner, 324.

44.   Flexner, 327–28.

45.   Carol Lynn Yellin and Janann Sherman, *The Perfect 36: Tennessee Delivers Woman Suffrage* (Oakridge, TN: The Iris Press, 1998), 77.

46.   Flexner, 328, 331–32.

47.   Marjorie Spruill Wheeler, *New Women of the New South: The Leaders of the Woman Suffrage Movement in the Southern States* (New York: Oxford University Press, 1993), 173; Janice Bliss, "New Nashville Park Named for Influential African American Women's Suffrage Leader Frankie Pierce," *The Tennessean*, November 13, 2019, www.tennessean.com/story/news/2019/11/13/frankie-pierce-park-nashville -suffrage-leader-honored/2534066001/.

48.   Yellin, 84–87.

49.   Yellin, 92–93.

50.   Flexner, 335–36.

51.   Yellin, 97, 107.

52.   Flexner, 336.

53.   Lynn Sherr, *Failure Is Impossible: Susan B. Anthony in Her Own Words* (New York: Random House/Times Books, 1995), 68.

54.   Sarah Lyall, "Moved by History's Ghosts, Women Pay Tribute at the Ballot Box," *New York Times*, November 9, 2016, P3; Cleve R. Wootson, Jr., "Women Have Started Putting 'I Voted' Stickers on Susan B. Anthony's Tombstone," *Washington Post*, November 6, 2018, www.washingtonpost.com/midterms/midterm-election -updates/women-have-started-putting-i-voted-stickers-on-susan-b-anthonys -tombstone/.

55.   Ellen Carol DuBois, "How Women's Suffrage Changed America Far Beyond the Ballot Box," *Wall Street Journal*, August 22–23, 2020, C1.

Chapter Two: Flappers & Feminists, 1920–1928

1.   "Colby Proclaims Woman Suffrage," *New York Times*, August 27, 1920; "Women Achieve the Right to Vote," in New York Times Editors, *The Roaring '20s: Flappers /Bootleggers/Gangsters/Suffragists*, single issue magazine, January 3, 2020 (New York: Meredith Corp., 2020), 18; Elaine Weiss, "The Fight to Nullify the Nineteenth Amendment," *New York Times*, August 30, 2020, SR1.

2.   Jacqueline Van Voris, *Carrie Chapman Catt: A Public Life* (New York: CUNY Feminist Press, 1987), 161; Angela P. Dodson, *"Remember the Ladies:" Celebrating Those Who Fought for Freedom at the Ballot Box* (New York: Center Street/Hachette Books, 2017), 321.

3.   Editorial, "With Neither Dear Charmer," *New York Times*, August 28, 1920, quoted by Van Voris, 255, n. 18.

4.   Van Voris, 139.

5.   Eleanor Flexner, *Century of Struggle: The Woman's Rights Movement in the United States*, rev. ed. (Cambridge: Belknap Press of Harvard University Press, 1975), 293; Van Voris, 161–62.

6.   *The Woman Citizen*, September 4, 1920, quoted in Van Voris, 161.

7.   Flexner, 295; Christine A. Lunardini, *From Equal Suffrage to Equal Rights: Alice Paul and the National Woman's Party, 1910–1928* (New York: New York University Press, 1986), 138; Doris Stevens, *Jailed for Freedom: American Women Win the Vote*, ed. Carol O'Hare, rev. ed. (Troutdale, OR: NewSage Press, 1995), 205–211, lists all the suffrage prisoners.

8.   Anne Firor Scott and Andrew MacKay Scott, *One Half the People: The Fight for Woman Suffrage* (Champaign: University of Illinois Press, 1982), 42, 132, 161–63, 166–68; Anne Valk, "Woman Suffrage, Civil Rights, and Prohibition," *Radcliffe Second Century*, June 1988.

9.   Ellen Carol DuBois, *Suffrage: Women's Long Battle for the Vote* (New York: Simon & Schuster, 2020), 211, 243; Flexner, 280, 306; Jone Johnson Lewis, "National Association Opposed to Woman Suffrage, NAOWS 1911–1920," ThoughtCo., January 31, 2019, https://www.thoughtco.com/national-association-opposed-to -woman-suffrage-3530508.

10.   Liette Gidlow, "Beyond 1920: The Legacies of Woman Suffrage," National Park Service, April 6, 2020, www.nps.gov/articles/beyond-1920-the-legacies-of-woman -suffrage.htm.

11.   "Leser v. Garnett (1922)," https://caselaw.findlaw/us-supreme-court/258/130.html.

12.   Martha Jones quoted by Suyin Haynes, "Mississippi Didn't Ratify the 19th Amendment Until 1984," *Time*, August 17, 2020, www.time.com/5876762 /19th-amendment-ratified/.

13.   Jessie Brannon-Wranosky, "The 19th Amendment Turns One Hundred: Its Impact and Legacy," OAH annual meeting, Philadelphia, PA, April 5, 2019; Liette Gidlow, "Interchange: Women's Suffrage, the Nineteenth Amendment, and the Right to Vote," *Journal of American History*, 31 (December 1919): 680; Liette Gidlow, "The Long Nineteenth Amendment" panel, OAH annual meeting, Chicago, April 17, 2021.

14.   *Smith v. Allwright*, Oyez, www.oyez.org/cases/1940-1955/321us649.

15.   Meg Hacker, "When Saying 'I Do' Meant Giving Up Your U.S. Citizenship," *Prologue*, Spring 2014, National Archives, www.archives.gov/files/publications /prologue/2014/spring/citizenship.pdf.

16.   "Chinese Exclusion Act," History Channel online, www.history.com/topics /immigration/chinese-exclusion-act-1182.

17.   "Native American Citizenship 1924 Act," Nebraska Studies, https://nebraskastudies .org/0700/stories/0701_0146.html.

18.   "Marie Louise Bottineau Baldwin.htm," National Park Service, April 18, 2019, www.nps.gov/people/marie-louise-bottineau-baldwin.htm; Cathleen D. Cahill, "An Ojibwe Woman in Washington, DC: Marie Louise Bottineau Baldwin," *Recasting the Vote: How Women of Color Transformed the Suffrage Movement* (Chapel Hill: University of North Carolina Press, 2020), 83–96.

19.   Patrice H. Kunesh, "Women's History Month: Remembering Zitkala-Ša (Red Bird), Cultural Bridge Builder as Accomplished Author, Musician, and Champion of Native American Rights," March 6, 2018, https://www.minneapolisfed.org

/article/2018/womens-history-month-remembering-zitkala-sa; Cahill, "To Help Indians Help Themselves: Gertrude Simmons Bonnin," *Recasting the Vote,* 243–61.

20. Dean Chavers, "A History of Indian Voting Rights and Why It's Important to Vote," *Indian Country Today,* October 29, 2012, www.indiancountrytoday.com/archive/a -history-of-indian-voting-rights-and-why-its-important-to-vote; Theresa Vargas, "Stories of Service Beyond Code Talkers," *Washington Post,* November 12, 2020, B1.

21. Sarah Rounsville, "Trujillo v. Garley: The Struggle for Native American Voting Rights," *Intermountain Histories,* https://www.intermountainhistories.org/items /show/251; https://www.history.com/topics/native-american-history.

22. Maggie Astor, "Voting Rights Victory for N. Dakota Tribes," *New York Times,* February 14, 2020.

23. Erik Sherman, "Millions of 'Citizens' in the US Have No Guaranteed Rights," *Forbes,* August 26, 2019, www.forbes.com/sites/eriksherman/2019/08/26/millions -of-citizens-in-the-us-have-no-guaranteed-rights..

24. Dorothy M. Brown, *Setting a Course: American Women in the 1920s* (Boston: G. K. Hall & Co., 1987), 67.

25. Alison M. Parker, *Unceasing Militant: The Life of Mary Church Terrell* (Chapel Hill: University of North Carolina Press, 2020), 149–51.

26. Brown, 51; Ronald G. Shafer, "The Candidate Who Stumped from His Front Porch," *Washington Post,* May 6, 2020, B3.

27. Lynn Sherr, "'Politics Ain't the Same'—How the 19th Amendment Changed American Elections," *Moyers & Company,* August 23, 2016, https://billmoyers.com /story/politics-aint-19th-amendment-changed-american-elections.

28. J. D. Zahniser and Amelia Fry, *Alice Paul: Claiming Power* (New York: Oxford University Press, 2014), 320; Susan Ware, *Why They Marched: Untold Stories of Women Who Fought for the Right to Vote* (Cambridge: Harvard University Press, 2019), 284; David M. Kennedy, *Over There: The First World War and American Society* (New York: Oxford University Press, 1979, 2004), 362.

29. Michael McDonald, "National General Election VEP Turnout Rates, 1789-Present," United States Election Project, www.electproject.org/national-1789 -present; Thomas Mallon, "The Normalcy Election," *New Yorker,* September 21, 2020, 26–30.

30. Sarah Jane Deutsch, *From Ballots to Breadlines: American Women 1920–1940, From the Roaring Twenties to the Great Depression.* Vol. 8 of *The Young Oxford History of Women in the United States,* Nancy F. Cott, ed. (New York: Oxford University Press, 1994), 26; David Pietrusza, *1920: The Year of Six Presidents* (New York: Basic Books, 2007), 415; J. Kevin Corder and Christina Wolbrecht, *Counting Women's Ballots: Female Voters from Suffrage Through the New Deal* (New York: Cambridge University Press, 2016), 3, 153–54.

31. William H. Chafe, *The American Woman: Her Changing Social, Economic, and Political Role, 1920–1970* (New York: Oxford University Press, 1972), 23, 31–32; Paula J. Giddings, *Ida: A Sword Among Lions: Ida B. Wells and the Campaign Against Lynching* (New York: Armistad/ HarperCollins, 2008), 523–46; Ware, *Why They Marched,* 99–110.

32. Angela P. Dodson, *"Remember the Ladies:" Celebrating Those Who Fought for Freedom at the Ballot Box* (New York: Center Street/Hachette Books, 2017), 318–19; Van Voris, 157–58; Flexner, 340.

33. Jean Bethke Elshtain, *Jane Addams and the Dream of American Democracy: A Life* (New York: Basic Books, 2002).

34. Elshtain, 91–101.

35. Steve Kramer, "Uplifting Our 'Downtrodden Sisterhood': Victoria Earle Matthews and New York City's White Rose Mission, 1897–1907," *Journal of African American History*, 91 (2006): 243–66; Rosalyn Terborg-Penn, *African American Women in the Struggle for the Vote, 1850–1920* (Bloomington: University of Indiana Press, 1998), 87.

36. "Dr. Mabel Ping-Hua Lee," National Park Service, www.nps.gov/people/mabel-lee .htm; Jia Lynn Yang, "Mabel Ping Lee, 1895–1966," *New York Times*, September 21, 2020, A22.

37. Juan Cardoza-Oquendo, "Lugenia Burns Hope (1871–1947)," *New Georgia Encyclopedia* (2010), https://www.georgiaencyclopedia.org/articles/history -archaeology/lugenia-burns-hope-1871-1947/.

38. Arlisha R. Norwood, "Florence Kelley (1859–1932)," National Women's History Museum, https://www.womenshistory.org/education-resources/biographies /florence-kelley.

39. Blanche Wiesen Cook, *Eleanor Roosevelt, 1884–1933*, vol. 1 (New York: Viking, 1992), 134–35; "The Women of Hull House," documentary video produced by Jane Addams' Hull House Museum.

40. Brown, 51; Melissa R. Klapper, *Ballots, Babies and Banners for Peace: American Jewish Activism, 1890–1940* (New York: New York University Press, 2013), 7–8.

41. Brown, 52.

42. J. Stanley Lemons, *The Woman Citizen: Social Feminism in the 1920s* (Urbana: University of Illinois Press, 1975), 155–57.

43. Jone Johnson Lewis, "Sheppard–Towner Act of 1921," ThoughtCo., July 23, 2018, https://www.thoughtco.com/sheppard-towner-act-of-1921-3529478.

44. Brown, 53.

45. Brown, 57.

46. Corder, 183–85.

47. Rhae Lynn Barnes, "Baseball, Apple Pie, Blackface," *Washington Post*, February 10, 2019, B1.

48. Martha S. Jones, *Vanguard: How Black Women Broke Barriers, Won the Vote, and Insisted on Equality for All* (New York: Basic Books, 2020), 207–08; Annette B. Dunlap, "Tea and Equality: The Hoover Administration and the DePriest Incident," *Prologue*, Spring 2015, National Archives, https://www.archives.gov /files/publications/prologue/2015/summer/ddepriest-pdf.

49. DeNeen L. Brown, "In Search of an Uncomfortable Truth," *Washington Post*, March 22, 2020, A20; Brent Staples, "The Burning of Black Wall Street, Revisited," *New York Times*, June 21, 2020, SR8.

50. DeNeen L. Brown, "The Mystery at a Massacre's Center," *Washington Post*, May 31, 2021, A1; Scott Ellsworth, *The Ground Breaking: An American City and Its Search for Justice* (New York: Dutton/Penguin Random House, 2021), 14–21, 26, 33–42.

51. Eugene Robinson, "It Was Much More than Tulsa," *Washington Post*, June 1, 2021, A19; Adelle M. Banks, "Amends for 1923 Violence Against Black Enclave May Be a Model for Others," *Washington Post*, December 26, 2020, B2.

52.   Danny Lewis, "This Map Shows Over a Century of Documented Lynchings in the United States," *Smithsonian Magazine,* January 24, 2017, https://www.smithsonian mag.com/smart-news/map-shows-over-a-century-of-documented-lynchings-in-the -united-states-180961877/; Simon Romero, "Latinos Were Lynched in West; Descendants Want It Known," *New York Times,* March 3, 2019, A13. Elizabeth Alexander, *The Trayvon Generation* (New York: Grand Central Publishing, 2022), 76.

53.   Martha S. Jones, "Tackling a Century-old Mystery: Did My Grandmother Vote?" *New York Times,* August 14, 2020, https://www.nytimes.com/2020/08/14/us /suffrage-segregation-voting-black-women-19th-amendment.html.

54.   Laquantae Davis, "Mary B. Talbert (1866–1923)," February 18, 2009, www. blackpast.org/african-american-history/talbert-mary-b-1866-1923/; Theodore R. Johnson, "Yes, Anti-lynching Laws are Mostly Symbolic. That's Why They Matter," *Washington Post,* October 29, 2021, B1.

55.   Alison Parker, "Mary Church Terrell: Unceasing Militant," OAH annual meeting, Philadelphia, PA, April 6, 2019; Jones, *Vanguard,* 195–96.

56.   Linda Gordon, *The Second Coming of the KKK: The Ku Klux Klan of the 1920s and the American Political Tradition* (New York: Liveright Publishing Corp., 2017); Terence McArdle, "The Day 30,000 White Supremacists in KKK Robes Marched in the Nation's Capital," *Washington Post,* August 11, 2018, https://www.washingtonpost .com/news/retropolis/wp/2017/08/17/the-day-30000-white-supremacists-in-kkk -robes-marched-in-the-nations-capital; Elizabeth Dias, "Extremism From Whites Has Strong Roots in U.S.," *New York Times,* February 8, 2021, A11.

57.   Jacquelyn Dowd Hall, *Revolt Against Chivalry: Jessie Daniel Ames and the Women's Campaign Against Lynching,* rev. ed. (New York: Columbia University Press, 1993), 159–64, 180–82, 107.

58.   Ann Ellis Pullen, "Commission on Interracial Cooperation," December 23, 2004, *New Georgia Encyclopedia,* www.georgiaencyclopedia.org/articles/history-archaeology /commission-on-interracial-cooperation.

59.   Marylou Tousignant, "How Three Brave Suffragists Helped Women Win the Right to Vote," *Washington Post,* June 4, 2019, C8; Vivian Njeri Fisher, "Brown, Hallie Quinn," *Black Women in America: An Historical Encyclopedia,* vol. 1, ed. Darlene Clark Hine et al., (Bloomington: Indiana University Press, 1993), 176–78.

60.   Gloria T. Hull, "Dunbar-Nelson, Alice Ruth Moore," in *Black Women in America: An Historical Encyclopedia,* vol. 1, ed., Darlene Clark Hine et al. (Bloomington: University of Indiana Press), 359–63.

61.   David Dismore, "September 10, 1920," https://www.smithsonianmag.com/history /suffragist-statue-trapped-broom-closet-75-years-180963274/.

62.   Nancy F. Cott, "Feminist Politics in the 1920s: The National Woman's Party," *Journal of American History* 71, no. 1 (June 1984): 47; Chafe, *American Woman,* 23; Susan D. Becker, *The Origins of the Equal Rights Amendment: American Feminism Between the Wars* (Westport, CT: Greenwood Press, 1981).

63.   "The Portrait Monument: A Symbol of Struggles and Triumphs," National Women's History Museum, https://www.smithsonianmag.com/history/suffragist-statue -trapped-broom-closet-75-years-180963274/.

64.   Cott, *JAH,* 48, 55.

65. Sandra Weber, *The Woman Suffrage Statue: A History of Adelaide Johnson's "Portrait Monument" at the United States Capitol* (Jefferson, NC: McFarland & Company, Inc., 2016).

66. Leila J. Rupp and Verta Taylor, *Survival in the Doldrums: The American Women's Rights Movement, 1945 to the 1960s* (New York: Oxford University Press, 1987), 154; Deutsch, 31; Parker, "Terrell," OAH; Janet Adamy, "Black Women's Long Struggle for Voting Rights," *Wall Street Journal*, August 1–2, 2020, C3.

67. Brown, 60; Cott, *JAH*, 54, 53; Gidlow, *JAH*, 681.

68. Cott, *JAH*, 58; Brown, 60.

69. Clare Cushman, ed., *Supreme Court Decisions and Women's Rights: Milestones to Equality* (Washington, DC: Supreme Court Historical Society), 16–18.

70. Jill Lepore, *These Truths: A History of the United States* (New York: W.W. Norton & C., 2018), 382; Cushman, 19.

71. Deutsch, 31; Cushman, 19–21.

72. Leslie Friedman Goldstein, *The Constitutional Rights of Women: Cases in Law and Social Change*, rev. ed. (Madison: University of Wisconsin Press, 1988), 24–36; Ronald G. Shafer, "First Jewish Supreme Court Justice Was First to Face Confirmation Hearings," *Washington Post*, March 5, 2022, B5.

73. Cushman, 23, 280.

74. Ellen Carol DuBois, "How Women's Suffrage Changed America," *Wall Street Journal*, August 1–2, 2020, C1; Jane J. Mansbridge, *Why We Lost the ERA* (Chicago: University of Chicago Press, 1986), 8.

75. Brown, 61–62.

76. Christine Hauser, "The Vice President Who Broke the Racial Barrier," *New York Times*, November 13, 2020, A20; Cook, 1:259.

77. Amy Aronson, *Crystal Eastman: A Revolutionary Life* (New York: Oxford University Press, 2020), 226–28; Jo Freeman, "Gender Gaps in Presidential Elections," published as a letter to the editor of *P.S.: Political Science and Politics* 32, no. 2, (June 1999): 191–92; Cook, 1:356.

78. Cott, *JAH*, 55.

79. Pietrusza, 416.

80. "Alice Robertson," Committee on House Administration of the U.S. House of Representatives, *Women in Congress* [hereafter *WIC*] (Washington, DC: U.S. Government Printing Office, 2006), 49–50; Foerstel, 6; Pietrusza, 417.

81. "Winnifred Sprague Huck," *WIC*, 49–50.

82. "Mae Nolan," *WIC*, 56–57.

83. "Women Pioneers on Capitol Hill, 1917–1934," *WIC*, 23–26.

84. "Mary Norton," *WIC*, 61–64, 32; Foerstel, 9.

85. Parker, *Militant*, 160.

86. Center for the American Woman and Politics, Rutgers University, database, cawp .rutgers.edu.

87. "Florence Kahn," *WIC*, 66–69; Foerstel, 9.

88. "Edith Nourse Rogers," *WIC*, 70–75.

89. "Rebecca Felton," *WIC*, 53–55; Foerstel, 8; Gillian Brockell, "The Last Enslaver to Join the Senate, in 1922, Was Its First Woman," *Washington Post*, January 16, 2022, A14.

90.   Linda Van Ingen, *Gendered Politics: Campaign Strategies of California Women Candidates, 1912–1970* (Lanham, MD: Rowman & Littlefield Publishers, Inc., 2017), xiii.

91.   David Mark, "Ross Elected First Female Governor, Nov. 4, 1924," *Politico*, November 4, 2009, http://www.politico.com/story/2009/11/ross-elected-first-female -governor-nov-4-1924-029077.

92.   John D. Huddelston, "Miriam A. Ferguson," The Texas Politics Project: Governors of Texas, texaspolitics.utexas.edu/archive/html/exec/governors15.html.

93.   cawp.rutgers.edu.

94.   Jennifer Harlan, "A Splashy Start to Prohibition," *New York Times*, January 3, 2020, A16; Lisa McGirr, "How Prohibition Fueled the Klan," *New York Times*, January 16, 2019, www.nytimes.com/2019/01/16/opinion/prohibition-immigration-klan.html; Casey Cep, "Fighting Mad: Reconsidering the Political Power of Women's Anger," *New Yorker*, October 15, 2018, 83.

95.   "Mabel Walker Willebrandt Dies," *New York Times*, April 9, 1963, A31; Elizabeth Winkler, "Alcohol Was A 'Women's Issue,'" review of *Liberated Spirits: Two Women Who Battled Over Prohibition* by Hugh Ambrose, *Wall Street Journal*, October 27–28, 2018.

96.   Linda Simon, "The Original 'It' Girl," *Smithsonian*, September 2017, 9–11; Linda Dyett, "Bye to 'Real Housewife' Hair: Why the Bob Has Been Relevant for Over a Century," *New York Times*, January 8, 2019, https://www.nytimes.com/2019/01/08 /style/should-I-cut-my-hair.html; Daniel E. Slotnik, "Bessie Coleman, 1892–1926," *New York Times*, December 16, 2019.

97.   "Josephine Baker Is Dead in Paris at 68," *New York Times*, April 13, 1975, https://www .nytimes.com/1975/04/13/archives/josephine-baker-is-dead-in-Paris-at-68.html.

98.   Harold D. Wallace, Jr., "Power from the People: Rural Electrification Brought More Than Lights," National Museum of American History, February 12, 2016, americanhistory.si.edu/blog/rural-electrification.

99.   "KitchenAid Celebrates Its Centennial," *New York Times*, July 17, 2019, F3; Tori Avey, "Who Was Betty Crocker?" February 15, 2013, www.pbs.org/food-home /the-history-kitchen.

100.   Angela Saulino Osborne, *Miss America: The Dream Lives On: A 75 Year Celebration* (Dallas: Taylor Publishing Co., 1995), 100; Roxane Gay, "Dethroning Miss America," *Looking for Miss America: A Pageant's 100-Year Quest to Define Womanhood* by Margot Mifflin, *The New Yorker*, September 7, 2020, 72–75; Amy Argetsinger, "The First Miss America Pageant Was as Messy as Today's," *Washington Post*, December 16, 2021, B5.

101.   Sally Jenkins, "The Power and the Passion: Gertrude Ederle's Goggles," *Smithsonian Magazine* (March 2019): 48–49.

102.   Brown, 146; Deutsch, 44, 68; J.R. Thorpe, "7 Things Women Couldn't Do in 1920," *Bustle*, August 26, 2016, https://www.bustle.com/articles/180664-7-things-women -couldn't-do-in-1920.

103.   Deutsch, 44; Klapper, 151.

104.   Deutsch, 68; "Ellen H. Swallow Richards (1842–1911)," American Chemistry Society, https://www.acs.org/; Petula Dvorak, "American Women Tried but Couldn't Do It—Yet," *Washington Post*, November 11, 2011, B1.

105. Julissa Cruz, "Marriage: More Than a Century of Change, 1890-2011," National Center for Family and Marriage Research, https://www.bgsu.edu/content/dam /BGSU/college-of-arts-and-sciences/NCFMR/documents/FP/FP-13-13.pdf; Doris Weatherford, *Victory for the Vote: The Fight for Women's Suffrage and the Century that Followed* (Coral Gables, FL: Mango Publishing, 2020), 274.

106. Deutsch, 47, 38–39; Pat Palmieri, "Office Politics," review of *Beyond the Typewriter: Gender, Class and the Origins of Modern American Office Work, 1900–1930*, by Sharon Hartman Strom, *The Women's Review of Books*, vol. X, no. 3 (May 1993): 29.

107. Kennedy, *Over There*, 285.

108. David M. Kennedy, *Freedom from Fear: The American People in Depression and War, 1929–1945* (New York: Oxford University Press, 1999), 413–14; Linda Gordon, "The Original Wall," review of *The Guarded Gate: Bigotry, Eugenics and the Law That Kept Two Generations of Jews, Italians and Other European Immigrants Out of America*, by Daniel Okrent, *New York Times Book Review*, July 7, 2019, 14; "Immigration Act of 1924: The Johnson-Reed Act," U.S. Department of State Office of the Historian, https://history.state.gov/milestones/1921-1936/immigration-act.

109. Jean H. Baker, *Margaret Sanger: A Life of Passion* (New York: Hill and Wang, 2011), 10. See also Ellen Chesler, *Woman of Valor: Margaret Sanger and the Birth Control Movement in America* (New York: Simon & Schuster, 1992).

110. David M. Kennedy, *Birth Control in America: The Career of Margaret Sanger* (New Haven: Yale University Press, 1970), 23–24, 45; Baker, 67–68.

111. Baker, 101–02, 108.

112. Klapper, 84; Kennedy, *Birth Control*, 83.

113. Margaret Sanger, *The Pivot of Civilization*, Appendix, nrs.harvard.edu/urn -3:FHCL:664616.

114. Klapper, 151; "Hannah Stone: The Madonna of the Clinic," *Margaret Sanger Papers Project Newsletter #9* (Winter 1994–1995), https://sanger.hosting.nyu.edu/articles /hannah_stone/; Marion Shulevitz, "Hannah Mayer Stone, 1893–1941," *Jewish Women's Archive*, https://jwa.org/encyclopedia/article/stone-hannah-meyer.

115. Lakshmeeramya Malladi, "United States v. One Package of Japanese Pessaries (1936)," The Embryo Project Encyclopedia, May 24, 2017, https://embryo.asu.edu /pages/united-states-v-one-package-japanese-pessaries-1936.

116. Deutsch, 66, 90.

117. John J. Conley, "Margaret Sanger Was a Eugenicist: Why Are We Still Celebrating Her?" www.americanmagazine.org/politics-society/2017/11/27/margaret-sanger -was-eugenicist-why-are-we-still-celebrating-her.

118. Kennedy, *Birth Control*, 115; Gillian Brockell, "Spears Saga Reflects History's Treatment of 'Unfit' Women," *Washington Post*, October 1, 2021, B8; *Buck v. Bell* (1927), Oyez, www.oyez.org/cases/1900-1940/274us200.

119. Amy Davidson Sorkin, "Ted Cruz vs. Margaret Sanger's Portrait," *New Yorker*, October 28, 2015, https://www.newyorker.com/news/amy-davidson/ted-cruz -vs-margaret-sangers-portrait; Nikita Stewart, "Planned Parenthood in New York Disavows a Founder," *New York Times*, July 22, 2020; Alexis McGill Johnson, "I'm the Head of Planned Parenthood. We're Done Making Excuses for Our Founder," April 17, 2021, www.nytimes.com/2021/04/17/opinion/planned-parenthood -margaret-sanger.html; Ellen Chesler, Letter to the Editor, "Defending Margaret

Sanger, Planned Parenthood's Founder," www.nytimes.com/2021/04/20/opinion /letters/margaret-sanger-planned-parenthood.html.

120.   H. B. Shaffer, "Women in Politics," *Editorial research reports 1956* vol. I, http://library .cqpress.com/cqresearcher/cqresrre1956022000.

121.   Brown, 23, 71, 24.

122.   Anna L. Harvey, *Votes Without Leverage: Women in American Electoral Politics, 1920–1970* (Cambridge, UK: Cambridge University Press, 1998), 209; Chafe, *American Woman*, 45; Deborah Cohen, "More Than the Vote," *The Atlantic*, January /February 2021, 86–89.

123.   www.dalton.org/about/mission-statement/past.

124.   Cook, 1:367.

125.   Liette Gidlow, "Beyond Suffrage: The Legacies of Woman Suffrage," National Park Service, April 6, 2020, www.nps.gov/articles/beyond-1920-the-legacies-of-woman -suffrage.htm; Barbara Winslow, "The Nineteenth Amendment Turns One Hundred: Its Impact and Legacy," paper, OAH, Philadelphia, PA, April 5, 2019.

126.   Jo Freeman, *A Room at a Time: How Women Entered Party Politics* (Lanham, MD: Rowman & Littlefield Publishers, Inc., 2002), 2.

Chapter Three: The Eleanor Effect, 1929–1945

1.   Blanche Wiesen Cook, *Eleanor Roosevelt, 1884–1933*, vol. 1 (New York: Viking, 1992), 367.

2.   Susan Ware, *Partner and I: Molly Dewson, Feminism, and New Deal Politics* (New Haven: Yale University Press, 1987), 144.

3.   Cook, 1:271, 350.

4.   Cook, 1:373, 363.

5.   David M. Kennedy, *Freedom from Fear: The American People in Depression and War, 1929–1945* (New York: Oxford University Press, 1999), 38, 93; John Steele Gordon, "Hard Times for Hoover, and FDR," review of *Winter War: Hoover, Roosevelt and the First Clash Over the New Deal* by Eric Rauchway, *Wall Street Journal*, December 12, 2018.

6.   Author's notes from Nancy Cott, Presidential Address, Organization of American Historians Annual Meeting, Philadelphia, April 8, 2017; Kennedy, *Freedom*, 101, 103, 134.

7.   Paul Dickson and Thomas B. Allen, "Marching on History," *Smithsonian Magazine*, February 2003, https://www.smithsonianmag.com/history/marching-on-history -75797769.

8.   Blanche Wiesen Cook, *Eleanor Roosevelt, 1933–1938*, vol. 2 (New York: Viking, 1991), 52–59, 46, 75; Eleanor Roosevelt, *It's Up to the Women*, rev. ed. (New York: Nation Books, 2017).

9.   Cook, 2:115, 141.

10.   Cook is credited with "outing" the romantic relationship between ER and Lorena Hickok, based on 3,300 letters found at the Roosevelt Library by Doris Faber, the basis of *The Life of Lorena Hickok: E.R.'s Friend* (New York: William Morrow & Co., 1980). Cook, 1:495–97.

11.   Cook, 2:47, 66.

12.   Susan Ware, *Beyond Suffrage: Women in the New Deal* (Cambridge: Harvard University Press, 1981), 8–10; Cook, 2:67–68; Ware, *Partner*, 167, 205–06, 184–85.

13. Kirstin Downey, *The Woman Behind the New Deal: The Life of Frances Perkins, FDR's Secretary of Labor and His Moral Conscience* (New York: Doubleday, 2009), 114–15, 1; Ware, *Partner*, 153.

14. David Von Drehle, *Triangle: The Fire That Changed America* (New York: Atlantic Monthly Press, 2003), 256; "Frances Perkins, 1880–1965: The Woman Behind the New Deal," pamphlet published by the Frances Perkins Center, Newcastle, ME.

15. Downey, 45, 160.

16. Downey, 16–17, 105, 118.

17. Sarah Jane Deutsch, *From Ballots to Breadlines: American Women 1920–1940, From the Roaring Twenties to the Great Depression*, vol. 8 of *The Young Oxford History of Women in the United States*, Nancy F. Cott, ed. (New York: Oxford University Press, 1994), 87.

18. Erin Blakemore, "Why Many Married Women Were Barred from Working During the Great Depression," History Channel online, March 5, 2019, https://www .history.com/news/great-depression-married-women-employment.

19. Blakemore; Elaine Tyler May, *Pushing the Limits: American Women 1940-1961, From Rosie the Riveter to the Baby Boom and Beyond*, vol. 9 of *The Young Oxford History of Women in the United States*, Nancy F. Cott, ed. (New York: Oxford University Press, 1994), 19.

20. Deutsch, 87.

21. Downey, 71–73, 250–52; Marjory Potts, "Averell Harriman Remembers Mary," *Junior League Review* (Fall 1983): 12.

22. Perkins Center pamphlet.

23. Cook, 2:89; "Civilian Conservation Corps," History Channel online, May 11, 2010, https://www.history.com/topics/great-depression/civilian-conservation-corps.

24. Cook, 2:88–90.

25. Stephanie J. Richmond, "Tending Our Gardens," *The Trillium* 1, no. 3 (Spring 2021), 3.

26. Patricia Scott-Bell, *The Firebrand and the First Lady: Portrait of a Friendship: Pauli Murray, Eleanor Roosevelt, and the Struggle for Social Justice* (New York: Alfred A. Knopf, 2016), 3.

27. Kennedy, *Freedom*, 261, 264–65; Downey, 232, 235–36; Michael S. Rosenwald, "The Progressive Love Story Behind the Nation's First Unemployment Check," *Washington Post*, April 19, 2020, B3.

28. Kennedy, *Freedom*, 267–69; Cook, 2:249.

29. Downey, 233.

30. Kennedy, *Freedom*, 271; Downey, 203; Ware, *Partner*, 144.

31. https://www.history.com/topics/geat-depression/scottsboro-boys; Katharine Seelye, "Sheila Washington, Who Fought to Exonerate the Scottsboro Boys, Dies at 61," *New York Times*, February 28, 2021, A27.

32. Martha S. Jones, *Vanguard: How Black Women Broke Barriers, Won the Vote, and Insisted on Equality for All* (New York: Basic Books, 2020), 204; "Party Realignment and the New Deal," History, Art & Archives, U.S. House of Representatives, Office of the Historian, Black Americans in Congress, 1870–2007. Washington, D.C.: U.S. Government Printing Office, 2008. "Party Realignment And The New Deal," https://history.house.gov/Exhibitions-and-Publications/BAIC/Historical-Essays /Keeping-the-Faith/Party-Realignment--New-Deal/.

33.   Kennedy, *Freedom,* 341, 286.

34.   Cott OAH address; Kennedy, *Freedom,* 284–86.

35.   Cook, 2:153, 158.

36.   Cook, 2:159–60.

37.   Martha S. Jones, "Beyond the Ballot," *Smithsonian,* July–August 2020, 16–21;
       Kim Warren, "Mary McLeod Bethune" paper, "Connecting Contemporary U.S.
       Elections with Historic Working Class Women Political Mobilization," OAH
       annual meeting, Philadelphia, PA, April 6, 2019.

38.   Erica L. Green, "Bethune-Cookman Graduates Greet Betsy DeVos with Turned
       Backs," May 10, 2017, https://www.nytimes.com/2017/05/10/us/politics/betsy
       -devos-bethune-cookman-commencement.html.

39.   https://www2.gwu.edu/~erpapers/abouterp/overview.cfm.

40.   Cook, 2:158–59.

41.   Bell-Scott, 7; Cook, 2:160; Jill Watts, *The Black Cabinet: The Untold Story of African
       Americans and Politics During the Age of Roosevelt* (New York: Grove Press, 2020).

42.   Jones, *Vanguard,* 218; Cook, 2:155.

43.   William E. Leuchtenburg, "When Franklin Roosevelt Clashed with the Supreme
       Court—and Lost," *Smithsonian Magazine,* May 2005; Kennedy, *Freedom,* 328–29,
       374.

44.   *West Coast Hotel Company v. Parrish,* Oyez, www.oyez.org/cases/1900-
       1940/300us379; Kennedy, *Freedom,* 334–35.

45.   Ware, *Beyond,* 102–04; Downey, 267–68.

46.   Caroline Fredrickson, *Under the Bus: How Working Women Are Being Run Over* (New
       York: New Press, 2015), 15, 120–27; Joe Davidson, "Democrats Push to Undo
       New Deal's Racist Aspects," *Washington Post,* June 14, 2021, A5.

47.   Kennedy, *Freedom,* 349–50; "Dust Bowl," History Channel online, October 27,
       2009, https://www.history.com/topics/great-depression/dust-bowl.

48.   Karen Foerstel and Herbert N. Foerstel, *Climbing the Hill: Gender Conflict in Congress*
       (Westport, CT: Praeger, 1996), 11–12; "On This Day in History: Woman Is Speaker
       of North Dakota House, January 4, 1933," *New York Times,* January 4, 2017, A2.

49.   Foerstel, 10–11; "Hattie Ophelia Wyatt Caraway, 1878–1950," www.encyclopediaof
       arkansas.net/encyclopedia/entry-detail.aspx?entryID=1278; "Hattie Caraway,
       Ex-Senator, Dies," *New York Times,* December 22, 1950, https://www.nytimes
       /1950/12/22/archives/hattie-carraway-exsenator-dies-first-woman-ever-elected-to
       -post-she.html.

50.   R. W. Apple, Jr., "J. William Fulbright, Senate Giant, Is Dead at 89," *New York
       Times,* February 10, 1995.

51.   Deutsch, 94–95.

52.   Petula Dvorak, "1930s Saw an Outbreak of People Baring Their Chests on the
       Beach—Men," *Washington Post,* January 8, 2019, B5; "Remembering Hollywood's
       Hays Code, 40 Years On," *All Things Considered,* August 8, 2008, https://www.npr
       .org/template/story/story.php?storyid=93301189.

53.   Anne Midgette, "It's Not About the Music but the Symbol," *Washington Post,* April 28,
       2019, E2.

54.   Nicole Herrington, "Telling Their Stories: Black Women in Film," *New York Times,*
       January 12, 2020, C12.

55.   Deborah G. Felder, *A Century of Women: The Most Influential Events in Twentieth Century Women's History* (Secaucus, NJ: Carol Publishing Co., 1999), 121–22, 146–50; Gillian Brockell, "A Girl Named Greta and the Seriously Sexist History of Time's Person of the Year," *Washington Post,* December 12, 2019, www.washington post.com/history/2019/12/11/greta-thunberg.

56.   Joanne Kaufman, "A Guide for the Single Girl," review of *The Extra Woman: How Marjorie Hillis Led a Generation of Women to Live Alone and Like It* by Joanna Scutts, *Wall Street Journal,* November 11–12, 2017, C6.

57.   Deutsch, 66–67, 78; Lillian Faderman, *To Believe in Women: What Lesbians Have Done for America* (Boston: Houghton Mifflin Co., 1999).

58.   Kat Eschner, "The Surprising Origins of Kotex Pads," *Smithsonian Magazine,* August 11, 2017, www.smithsonianmag.com/innovations/surprising-origins-kotex -pads-180964466/; Mary Bellis, "A Brief History of the Tampon," ThoughtCo., September 24, 2018, https://www.thoughtco/com/history-of-the-tampon-4018968.

59.   David M. Kennedy, *Birth Control in America: The Career of Margaret Sanger* (New Haven: Yale University Press), 260; Deutsch, 91; May, 18–19; Melissa R. Klapper, *Ballots, Babies and Banners for Peace: American Jewish Activism, 1890–1940* (New York: New York University Press, 2013), 139–40.

60.   Blanche Wiesen Cook, *Eleanor Roosevelt: The War Years and After, 1939–1962,* vol. 3 (New York: Viking, 2016), 32–36.

61.   Cook, 3:35.

62.   Cook, 3:66; Denise Doring VanBuren, "Embracing Our Enduring Bond with Marian Anderson," Daughters of the American Revolution, January 11, 2021, https://blog.dar.org/embracing-our-enduring-bond-marian-anderson.

63.   Harold Holzer, "An American Icon that Almost Wasn't," *Wall Street Journal,* February 16–17, 2019.

64.   "The Strange Story of the Man Behind 'Strange Fruit,'" NPR, September 5, 2012, https://www.npr.org/2012/12/30/168292529/the-strange-story-of-the-man-behind -strange-fruit.

65.   Susan C. Cook, "Holiday, Billie," in *Black Women in America,* Darlene Clark Hine et al. eds. (Bloomington: University of Indiana Press, 1993), 1:565–69; Gail Collins, "Where the Girls Aren't," *New York Times,* March 30, 2019, A29.

66.   Cook, 3:32.

67.   Louis Masur, "Why It Took a Century to Pass an Anti-Lynching Law," *Washington Post,* December 28, 2018, https://www.washingtonpost.com/outlook/2018/12/28 /why-it-took-century-pass-an-anti-lynching-law/; Li Zhou, "Rep. Bobby Rush on How His Bill Would Address the 'Modern Day Lynching' of Ahmaud Arbery," *Vox,* May 13, 2020, https://www.vox.com/2020/5/13/21254988/bobby-rush-anti -lynching-act-ahmaud-arbery.

68.   Kennedy, *Freedom,* 393.

69.   Kennedy, *Freedom,* 413, 411.

70.   Anna Altman, "Keeping Immigrants Out," review of *The Unwanted: America, Auschwitz, and a Village Caught in Between,* by Michael Dobbs, *New York Times Book Review,* May 5, 2019, 21; Kennedy, *Freedom,* 416–17.

71.   James Kaplan, "More Than Just a Song," *New York Times,* November 10, 2018; Willard Spiegelman, "Diverse Interpretations for a Diverse Nation," *Wall Street*

Journal, June 27–28, 2020, C14; Dan DeLuca, "What's the Story Behind Those Kate Smith Songs with Racist Lyrics?" *The Philadelphia Inquirer,* April 22, 2019, https://www.inquirer.com/entertainment/columnists/kate-smith-racist-songs-lyrics -got-bless-america-flyers-20190422.html.

72.   Cook, 1:390, 3:126.

73.   Kennedy, *Freedom,* 405, 458, 464; Cook, 3:287, 297–99.

74.   Doris Kearns Goodwin, *No Ordinary Time: Franklin and Eleanor Roosevelt: The Home Front in World War II* (New York: Simon & Schuster, 1994), 10.

75.   Jessica Wolfrom, "During War, She Served as a 'G-Girl,'" *Washington Post,* May 28, 2020; Kennedy, *Freedom,* 747; Jones, 217.

76.   "All-American Girls Professional Baseball Leagues," www.aagpbl.org; Martha Ackmann, *Curveball: The Remarkable Story of Toni Stone, the First Woman to Play Professional Ball in the Negro League* (Chicago: Lawrence Hill Books, 2017).

77.   May, 29–30; www.nytimes.com/1982/06/24/obituaries/ruth-muskrat-bronson-84-a -specialist-in-indian-affairs.html.

78.   Vicki L. Ruiz, *Cannery Women, Cannery Lives: Mexican Women, Unionization, and the California Food Processing Industries, 1930–1950* (Albuquerque: University of New Mexico Press, 1987), 12, 21, 46–47; May, 34.

79.   "Executive Order 9066: The President Authorizes Japanese Relocation," History Matters, historymatters.gmu.edu/d/5154.

80.   Kennedy, *Freedom,* 748–50.

81.   May, 48; https://dp.la/exhibitions/japanese-internment/home-family/women; https://www.jstor.org/stable/3346082.

82.   Michelle Konstantinovsky, "Mitsuye Endo: The Woman Who Took Down Executive Order 9066," How Stuff Works, May 14, 2019, https://people.howstuff works.com/mitsuye-endo-executive-order9066.htm; *Ex Parte Endo,* 23 US 283 (1944).

83.   Kennedy, *Freedom,* 749, 755, 759–60; "Hirabayashi v. United States," *Oyez,* www .oyez.org/cases/1940-1955/320us81; "Korematsu v. United States," *Oyez,* www.oyez .org/cases/1940-1955/323us214; Erick Trickey, "Fred Korematsu Fought Against Japanese Internment in the Supreme Court . . . and Lost," *Smithsonian Magazine,* January 30, 2017, www.smithsonianmag.com/history/fred-korematsu-fought-against -japanese-internment-supreme-court-and-lost-180961967/.

84.   June A. Willenz, *Women War Veterans: America's Forgotten Heroines* (New York: Continuum Publishing, 1983), 24; Paul L. Newman, "Remember These War Heroes Too," *Washington Post,* May 29, 2020.

85.   Goodwin, 415.

86.   "Florence Blanchfield," *Writer's Almanac,* NPR, July 9, 2021; Christina Brown Fisher, "The Battalion of Black Women Who Stood Up to a White Army," *New York Times,* September 6, 2020, F16.

87.   Willenz, 18–24.

88.   May, 27.

89.   Felder, 343; Katie Hafner, "Hazel Ying Lee and Maggie Gee," *New York Times,* May 25, 2020, A22; Emily Bobrow, "Mari Elder," *Wall Street Journal,* July 31– August 1, 2021, C6.

90.   Liza Mundy, *Code Girls: The Untold Story of the American Women Code Breakers of World War II* (New York: Hachette Books, 2017); Greg Myre, "'A Woman of No

Importance' Finally Gets Her Due," *Morning Edition,* April 18, 2019; Shivaune Field, *Forbes,* February 28, 2018, "Hedy Lamarr: The Incredible Mind Behind Secure Wi-Fi, GPS and Bluetooth," https://www.forbes.com/sites/shivaunefield /2018/02/28/hedy-lamarr-the-incredible-mind-behind-secure-wi-fi-gps-bluetooth/.

91. Redd Evans and John Jacob Loeb, "Rosie the Riveter," 1943, www.loc.gov/program /journey/rosie-transcript.html.

92. Nancy Baker Wise and Christy Wise, *A Mouthful of Rivets: Women at Work in World War II* (San Francisco: Jossey-Boss, 1994); Donna B. Knaff, *Beyond Rosie the Riveter: Women of World War II in American Popular Graphic Art* (Lawrence: University Press of Kansas, 2012).

93. Sandy Fitzgerald, "Marilyn Monroe Was a Real-Life Rosie the Riveter in WWII," *Newsmax,* June 5, 2014, https://www.newsmax.com/us/marilyn-monroe-rosie-the -riveter/2014/06/05/id/575399/.

94. Karen Anderson, *Wartime Women: Sex Roles, Family Relations, and the Status of Women During World War II* (Westport, CT: Greenwood Press, 1981), 39–41.

95. May, 35, 24–25.

96. Alice Kessler-Harris, *Out to Work: A History of Wage-Earning Women in the United States* (New York: Oxford University Press, 1982), 289.

97. Kessler-Harris, 290.

98. Kennedy, *Freedom,* 778.

99. Kessler-Harris, 294; "Child Care: The Federal Role During World War II," CRS Report for Congress, congressionalresearch.com/RS20615/document.php.

100. May, 46; Kennedy, *Freedom,* 781.

101. "Frances Bingham Bolton," Committee on House Administration of the US House of Representatives, *Women in Congress, 1917–2006* [hereafter *WIC*] (Washington, DC: Government Printing Office, 2006), 91–98; Foerstel, 12–13; Liz Eberlein, "Making a Difference: The US Cadet Nurse Corps," *National Women's History Museum,* April 18, 2019, www.womenshistory.org/articles/making-difference-us -cadet-nurse-corps; "On This Day In History: Mother and Son Elected to Congress, November 6, 1952," *New York Times,* November 6, 2018, A2.

102. "Margaret Chase Smith," *WIC,* 197–201; Foerstel, 13; Gail Collins, "Hillary on the March," *New York Times,* July 28, 2016; Peggy Noonan, "Who'll Be 2020's Margaret Chase Smith?" *Wall Street Journal,* December 5–6, 2020, A15.

103. Anderson, 162; Goodwin, 556; May, 37.

104. Kennedy, *Freedom,* 779; Goodwin, 555–57.

105. Michael Stolp-Smith, "Port Chicago Mutiny (1944)," Blackpast, March 27, 2011, https://www.blackpast.org/african-american-history/port-chicago-mutiny-0/; Kennedy, *Freedom,* 766.

106. Andrew E. Kersten and Clarence Lang, eds., *Reframing Randolph: Labor, Black Freedom, and the Legacies of A. Philip Randolph* (New York: New York University Press, 2015); Lucy G. Barber, *Marching on Washington: The Forging of An American Political Tradition* (Berkeley: University of California Press, 2002), 108–09.

107. "Eleanor Roosevelt and the Tuskegee Airmen," www.fdrlibrary.org/tuskegee.

108. Tamika Brown-Nagen, "The Civil Rights Queen: Constance Baker Motley," OAH annual meeting, Philadelphia, PA, April 6, 2019.

109. Bell-Scott, 37–38.

110.   Lois Scharf and Joan M. Jensen, eds., *Decades of Discontent: The Women's Movement, 1920–1940* (Westport, CT: Greenwood Press, 1983), 242.

111.   Kessler-Harris, 287.

112.   Cherisse Jones-Branch, "Connecting Contemporary U.S. Elections with Histories of Working Class Women's Political Mobilization," Organization of American Historians, Philadelphia, April 6, 2019.

113.   Douglas Martin, "Mildred Benson Is Dead at 96; Wrote 23 Nancy Drew Books," *New York Times,* May 30, 2002.

114.   Carolyn Stewart Dyer and Nancy Tillman Romalov, eds., *Rediscovering Nancy Drew* (Iowa City: University of Iowa Press, 1995).

115.   Deutsch, 93; https://kinginstitute.stanford.edu/encyclopedia/roosevelt-anna -eleanor.

116.   "Ladies First," *American Magazine,* Fall 2021, 37.

Chapter Four: From Rosie to Rosa Parks, 1946–1959

1.   Blanche Wiesen Cook, *Eleanor Roosevelt: The War Years and After, 1939–1962*, vol. 3 (New York: Viking, 2016), 539; Andrew Glass, "Truman Sworn in as 33rd President, April 12, 1945," *Politico,* April 12, 2018, https://www.politico.com/story/2018/04/12 /harry-truman-sworn-in-as-33rd-president-april-12-1945-511037.

2.   Michael R. Gardner, *Harry Truman and Civil Rights: Moral Courage and Political Risks* (Carbondale: Southern Illinois University Press, 2002), 8, 1.

3.   James T. Patterson, *Grand Expectations: The United Sates, 1945–1974* (New York: Oxford University Press, 1996), 3.

4.   Doris Weatherford, *Victory for the Vote: The Fight for Woman's Suffrage and the Century that Followed* (Coral Gables, FL: Mango Publishing, 2020), 316; Cook, 3:548–51, 558; James Loeffler, "How the Promise of Universal Human Rights Fell Short," *Washington Post,* December 23, 2018, B5.

5.   Elaine Tyler May, *Homeward Bound: American Families in the Cold War Era,* rev. ed. (New York: Basic Books, 2017); Brett Harvey, *The Fifties: A Women's Oral History* (New York: Harper Collins, 1993), xiv.

6.   Doris Kearns Goodwin, *No Ordinary Time: Franklin and Eleanor Roosevelt: The Home Front in World War II* (New York: Simon & Schuster, 1994), 556, 623; Alice Kessler-Harris, *Out to Work: A History of Wage-Earning Women in the United States* (New York: Oxford University Press, 1982), 296.

7.   Jill Lepore, *The Secret History of Wonder Woman* (New York: Alfred A. Knopf, 2014), 230; Neil Genzlinger, "Joye Hummel, 97, First Female Writer of Wonder Woman Comics, Dies," *New York Times,* April 19, 2021, B6.

8.   Hettie Judah, "The House That Built Dior," *Art Quarterly* (Winter 2018): 41–44; Kristen A. Hunter, "'The Mamie Look': The Americanness of First Lady Mamie Eisenhower's Off-the-Rack Fashion," *White House Quarterly: Journal of the White House Historical Association* 52 (2019): 18–29; Harvey, xi.

9.   "War Boots and Work Suits: American Style 1940–1950s," *CNN* documentary broadcast January 13 and 20, 2019.

10.   Elaine Tyler May, *Pushing the Limits: American Women 1940–1961, From Rosie the Riveter to the Baby Boom and Beyond,* vol. 9 of *The Young Oxford History of Women in the United States,* Nancy F. Cott, ed. (New York: Oxford University Press, 1994), 51–52.

11. May, *Homeward*, 1–3; Rachel Anderson Ryan, "The Changing Lives of Women in the 1960s: *Ladies Home Journal* and the Early Women's Movement," Master's thesis, Harvard University, 2004, 12.

12. Jennifer L. Betts, "Historical Divorce Rate Statistics," Love to Know, https://divorce.lovetoknow.com/Historical_Divorce_Rate_Statistics.

13. Patterson, 72; Margaret Lundrigan Ferrer and Tova Navarra, *Levittown: The First Fifty Years* (Charleston, SC: Arcadia Publishing, 1997); "House Builder Levitt: For Sale: A New Way of Life," *Time*, June 3, 1950.

14. May, *Homeward*, 27, 11.

15. Harvey, *The Fifties*, xv.

16. Stephanie Coontz, *The Way We Never Were: American Families and the Nostalgia Trip* (New York: Basic Books, 1992); Vincent Terrace, *Television Series of the 1950s: Essential Facts and Quirky Details* (Lanham, MD: Rowman & Littlefield, 2016), 54, 4, 47, 92.

17. Terrace, 80–82; Manohla Dargis, "Don't Let the Sitcom Fool You," *New York Times*, December 10, 2021, C6; Tom Gilbert, "Real-Life Reasons to Love Lucy," *New York Times*, January 16, 2022, AR24.

18. William H. Chafe, *Paradox of Change: American Women in the 20th Century* (New York: Oxford University Press, 1991), 186.

19. Patterson, 17, 330.

20. Sonia Rao, "Patriotism, Politics Play a Role in the Pledge's Past," *Washington Post*, May 5, 2017, C8.

21. May, *Homeward*, 84.

22. May, *Homeward*, 139; "Father's Day 2019," History Channel online, February 5, 2019, https://www.history.com/topics/holidays/fathers-day.

23. Chafe, *Paradox*, 176–80; Patterson, 36.

24. May, *Pushing*, 92, 95.

25. Flora Davis, "Female in the '50s," review of *The Fifties: A Women's Oral History* by Brett Harvey, *Washington Post*, April 5, 1993; Jane Marcellus, review of *Bad Girls: Young Women, Sex and Rebellion Before the Sixties* by Amanda H. Littauer, *The Journal of American History* (September 2016): 544, https://doi.org/10.1093/jahist/jaw305.

26. Harvey, *The Fifties*, xix.

27. James R. Hagerty, "Mary White, 1923–2016," *Wall Street Journal*, June 10, 1016.

28. Mary Ann Dzuback, review of *College Women in the Nuclear Age: Cultural Literacy and Female Identity, 1940–1960* by Babette Faehmel, *The Journal of American History* (March 2013): 1301–02. https://doi.org/10.1093/jahist/jas627.

29. May, *Pushing*, 61–2.

30. Bruce Glasrud, "Ebony Magazine," BlackPast, September 18, 2007, www.blackpast.org/african-american-history/ebony-magazine/.

31. May, *Pushing*, 85; Ryan, 14–15.

32. Chafe, *Paradox*, 192–93; May, *Pushing*, 54–57.

33. Ryan, 14–15; Margaret Morris, "The History of the Clothes Dryer," The Classroom, July 21, 2017, https://www.hunker.com/13410374/the-history-of-the-clothes-dryer; Andrea Hermitt, "About Fitted Sheets," ehow, https://www.ehow.com/about_4689834_fitted-sheets.html.

34.   Susan Stamberg, "Imagine What It Was Like to Sit Down at Simone De Beauvoir's Desk," *Morning Edition,* May 16, 2017.

35.   Margalit Fox, "Anne Braden, 81, Activist in Civil Rights and Other Causes, Dies," *New York Times,* March 17, 2006, www.nytimes.com/2006/03/17/us/anne-braden -81-activist-in-civil-rights-and-other-causes-dies.html; Anne Braden, *The Wall Between* (Knoxville: University of Tennessee Press, 1999); Catherine Fosl, *Subversive Southerner: Anne Braden and the Struggle for Racial Justice in the Cold War South* (Lexington: University of Kentucky Press, 2006).

36.   Melissa R. Klapper, *Ballots, Babies and Banner for Peace: American Jewish Activism, 1890–1940* (New York: New York University Press, 2013), 205.

37.   David J. Baker, "Thomson: *The Mother of Us All; "The Mother of Us All" Suite,"* *Opera News,* June 2015, https://www.operanews.com/Opera_News_Magazine/2015/6 /Recordings/THOMSON__The_Mother_of_Us_All.html.

38.   Jo Freeman, "What's in a Name? Does It Matter How the Equal Rights Amendment Is Worded?" June 1996, https://www.jofreeman.com/lawandpolicy/ername.htm.

39.   Committee on House Administration of the US House of Representatives, *Women in Congress, 1917–2006* (Washington, DC: US Government Printing Office, 2006), 148; Cynthia E. Harrison, *On Account of Sex: The Politics of Women's Issues, 1945–1968* (Berkeley: University of California Press, 1988), 22; Susan D. Becker, *The Origins of the Equal Rights Amendment: American Feminism Between the Wars* (Westport, CT: Greenwood Press, 1981), 214.

40.   David McCullough, *Truman* (New York: Simon & Schuster, 1992), 471.

41.   William H. Chafe, *The American Woman: Her Changing Social, Economic, and Political Role, 1920–1970* (New York: Oxford University Press, 1972), 187; Harrison, 19, 23.

42.   Patterson, 37.

43.   "Carl T. Hayden Is Dead at 94; Arizonan in Congress 56 Years," *New York Times,* January 26, 1972, https://www.nytimes.com/1972/01/26/archives/carl-t-hayden-is -dead-at-94-arizonan-in-congress-56-years-7term.html.

44.   Chafe, *American,* 187.

45.   Leila J. Rupp and Verta Taylor, *Survival in the Doldrums: The American Women's Rights Movement, 1945 to the 1960s* (New York: Oxford University Press, 1987), 65; Karen Foerstel and Herbert N. Foerstel, *Climbing the Hill: Gender Conflict in Congress* (Westport, CT: Praeger, 1996), 13; Rebecca Traister, review of *The Highest Glass Ceiling: Women's Quest for the American Presidency* by Ellen Fitzpatrick, *New York Times,* March 15, 2016, http://nyti.ms/22hVPig.

46.   *WIC,* 147; Foerstel, 14; David von Drehle, "Liz Cheney's McCarthy-era Kindred Spirit," *Washington Post,* February 8, 2022, www.washingtonpost.com/opinions /2022/02/08/liz-cheney-margaret-chase-smith-gop-smears.

47.   "Joseph McCarthy," History Channel online, October 29, 2009, https://www.history .com/topics/cold-war/joseph-mccarthy.

48.   May, *Homeward,* 13; Eleanor Roosevelt, "On My Own," *Saturday Evening Post,* March 8, 1958, https://www2.gwu.edu/~erpapers/mep/displaydoc.cfm?docid=jfk15.

49.   *WIC,* 138–39.

50.   "Katherine St. George," *WIC,* 258–61.

51.   "Edith Green," *WIC,* 353–57.

52.   "Florence Dwyer," *WIC,* 374–377; Foerstel, 23.

53.   "Lenore Sullivan," *WIC*, 307–08.

54.   "Martha Griffiths," *WIC*, 359–63.

55.   "Coya Knudsen," *WIC*, 365–69.

56.   Mary C. Brennan, review of *Mothers of Conservatism: Women and the Postwar Right* by Michelle M. Nickerson, *The Journal of American History* (March 2015): 1316–17, https://doi.org/10.1093/jahist/jas563.

57.   Joan Cook, "India Edwards Dies: Advocate of Women in Politics Was 94," *New York Times,* January 17, 1990, https://www.nytimes.com/1990/01/17/obituaries /india-edwards-dies-advocate-of-women-in-politics-was-94-html; India Edwards, *Pulling No Punches: Memoirs of a Woman in Politics* (New York: G.P. Putnam's Son, 1977).

58.   Susan Ware, *Beyond Suffrage: Women in the New Deal* (New Haven: Yale University Press, 1987), 133.

59.   Anna L. Harvey, *Votes Without Leverage: Women in American Electoral Politics, 1920–1970* (Cambridge, UK: Cambridge University Press, 1998), 211–12; Jo Freeman, "Gender Gaps in Presidential Elections," published as a letter to the editor of *P.S.: Political Science and Politics* 32, no. 2 (June 1999): 191–2, www.jofreeman .com/polhistory/gendergap.htm.

60.   Gail S. Murray, review of *Crossing the Line: Women's Interracial Activism in South Carolina During and After World War II* by Cherisse Jones-Branch, *The Journal of American History* (March 2015): 1323–24, https://doi.org/10.1093/jahist/jav110.

61.   Amy Brown, "Juanita Jackson Mitchell (1913–1992)," BlackPast, June 10, 2009, https://www.blackpast.org/aah/mitchell-juanita-jackson.

62.   Marcia Walker-McWilliams, *Reverend Addie Wyatt: Faith and the Fight for Labor, Gender, and Racial Equality* (Urbana: University of Illinois Press, 2016).

63.   Harrison Smith, "Defense Lawyer, Civil Rights Warrior Lived to 104: Dovey Johnson Roundtree, 1914–2018," *Washington Post*, May 23, 2018, A1.

64.   Alina Cohen, "The Forgotten Female Artist Who May Have Been Murdered by the CIA," Artsy, May 16, 2019, https://www.artsy.net/article/artsy-editorial-forgotten -female-artist-murdered-cia; Ben Bradlee, *A Good Life: Newspapering and Other Adventures* (New York: Simon & Schuster, 1996); Katie McCabe and Dovey Johnson Roundtree, *Justice Older Than the Law: The Life of Dovey Johnson Roundtree* (Jackson: University Press of Mississippi, 2009).

65.   https://www.paulimurraycenter.com/who-is-pauli?

66.   John Kelly, "The 'Lost Laws' and the Fight Against Racial Discrimination in D.C. Restaurants," *Washington Post*, February 12, 2018, B3.

67.   Gardner, 166.

68.   Audra D. Burch, "This Town Repressed the Memory of a Brutal Racial Attack, Until Now," *New York Times,* February 9, 2019, A17; David W. Blight, "Blind Justice," review of *Unexampled Courage: The Blinding of Sgt. Isaac Woodard and the Awakening of President Harry S. Truman and Judge J. Waites Waring* by Richard Gergel, *New York Times Book Review,* February 10, 2019, 10.

69.   Gardner, 10; Gilbert Ware, *William Hastie: Grace Under Pressure* (New York: Oxford University Press, 1984), 192ff; Douglas Martin, "Jane Bolin, the Country's First Black Woman to Become a Judge, Is Dead at 98," *New York Times,* January 10, 2007, www.nytimes.com/2007/01/10/obituaries/10bolin.html.

70.   Gardner, 23.

71.   H. Viscount Nelson, "Channing H. Tobias (1882–1961)," BlackPast, January 17, 2007, https://blackpast.org/african-american-history/tobias-channing-h-1882-1961/.

72.   V. P. Franklin, "Alexander, Sadie Tanner Mossell (1898–1989)," *BWA*, 1:17–19. Georgiana Simpson earned a PhD in German from the University of Chicago; Gardner, 25.

73.   Gardner, 28–32.

74.   Gardner, 193.

75.   Jon Meacham, "'I Am a Black Man in a White World,'" *New York Times Book Review*, August 2, 2020, 11; E. J. Dionne, Jr., "Patriotism and the Promise of Black Liberation," *Washington Post*, May 30, 2021, A17.

76.   Jill Lepore, *These Truths: A History of the United States* (New York: W.W. Norton & Co., 2018), 531–32.

77.   Gardner, 58, 51, 80.

78.   Patterson, 155–56.

79.   Gardner, 107, 112, 114.

80.   Gardner, 122, 138–39.

81.   LeRhonda S. Manigault-Bryant, review of *A Girl Stands at the Door: The Generation of Women Who Desegregated America's Schools* by Rachel Devlin, *New York Times Book Review*, August 5, 2018, 20; Harrison Smith and Ellie Silverman, "Girl at the Center of *Brown v. Board* Case: Linda Brown Thompson," *Washington Post*, March 27, 2018.

82.   Lance Booth, "Overlooked No More: Barbara Johns, Who Defied Segregation in Schools," *New York Times*, May 8, 2019, www.nytimes.com/2019/05/08/obituaries /barbara-johns-overlooked.html; Matthew Brown, "Statue of Barbara Johns, Virginia Civil Rights Icon, Expected to Replace Robert E. Lee in US Capitol," *USA Today*, December 17, 2020, www.usatoday.com/news/politics/2020/12/17/barbara-johns -statue-replace-virginias-robert-e-lee-us-capitol/3937916001/.

83.   "Plessy v. Ferguson," History Channel online, October 29, 2009, https://www .history.com/topics/black-history/plessy-v-ferguson; Gardner, 9–10; Ted Jackson, "Plessy and Ferguson Unveil Plaque Today Marking Their Ancestors' Actions," *New Orleans Times-Picayune*, February 11, 2009, https://www.nola.com/news /article_a11a310a-0f86-54f6-9a34-89372abf0c91.html.

84.   Sonya Ramsey, "The Troubled History of American Education After the *Brown* Decision," *The American Historian*, February 2017, 36.

85.   Ian Millhiser, "Brown v. Board of Education Came Very Close to Being a Dark Day in American History," Think Progress, https://archivethinkprogress.org/brown-v -board-of-education-came-very-close-to-being-a-dark-day-in-american-histpry -dd231ad0f2f2/; Richard Kluger, *Simple Justice: The History of Brown v. Board of Education and Black America's Struggle for Equality*, rev. ed. (New York: Random House, 2004); "May 17, 1954, *Brown v. Board*," *Writer's Almanac*, NPR, May 17, 2016.

86.   Sherrilyn Ifill, "Turning Their Backs on 'Brown,'" *Washington Post*, May 13, 2019.

87.   "The Southern Manifesto of 1956," History, Art & Archives, history.house.gov /Historical-Highlights/1951-2000/The-Southern-Manifesto-of-1956/; Patterson, 398; "On This Day in History: August 22, 1959: Hawaii Becomes the 50th State: New Flag Shown," *New York Times*, August 22, 2018, A2.

88. Devlin Barrett, "Justice Department Ends Emmett Till Investigation," *Washington Post*, December 7, 2021, A2; Timothy B. Tyson, *The Blood of Emmett Till* (New York: Simon & Schuster, 2016); Dave Tell, *Remembering Emmett Till* (Chicago: University of Chicago Press, 2019).

89. "Rosa Parks, 92, Founding Symbol of the Civil Rights Movement, Dies," *New York Times*, October 25, 2005, https://www.nytimes.com/2005/10/25/us/25parks.html.

90. "Recy Taylor, Rosa Parks, and the Struggle for Racial Justice," National Museum of African American History & Culture [hereafter NMAAHC], March 15, 2018, https ://nmaahc.si.edu/explore/stories/recy-taylor-rosa-parks-and-struggle-racial-justice.

91. Jeanne Theoharis, "Rosa Parks' Real Story," *New York Times*, February 7, 2021, SR8.

92. Jo Ann Gibson Robinson, *The Montgomery Bus Boycott and the Women Who Started It: The Memoir of Jo Ann Gibson Robinson* (Knoxville: University of Tennessee Press, 1987); "Montgomery Bus Boycott," History Channel online, February 2, 2010, https://www.history.com/topics/black-history/montgomery-bus-boycott.

93. Jonathan Gold, "Browder v. Gayle," *Teaching Tolerance* 53 (Summer 2016), https://www .tolerance.org/magazine/summer-2016/browder-v-gayle.

94. Martha S. Jones, *Vanguard: How Black Women Broke Barriers, Won the Vote, and Insisted on Equality for All* (New York: Basic Books, 2020), 250–56; Ashley Southall, "Statue of Rosa Parks Is Unveiled at the Capitol," February 27, 2013, www.nytimes .com/2013/02/28/us/politics/statue-of-rosa-parks-is-unveiled-at-the-capitol.html; "Rosa Parks Statue Unveiled in Alabama," *New York Times*, December 3, 2019, C3.

95. Fred D. Gray, *Bus Ride to Justice: The Life and Works of Fred D. Gray*, rev. ed. (Montgomery, AL: NewSouth Books, 2013).

96. Adam Fairclough, *To Redeem the Soul of America: The Southern Christian Leadership Council and Martin Luther King, Jr.* (Athens: University of Georgia Press, 2001); "Southern Christian Leadership Conference (SCLC)," The Martin Luther King Jr. Research and Education Institute, January 10, 1957, https://kinginstitute.stanford .edu/encyclopedia/southern-christian-leadership-conference-sclc.

97. Sara M. Evans, review of *Southern Black Women in the Modern Civil Rights Movement*, ed. by Bruce A. Glausrud and Merline Pitre, *Journal of American History* (September 2014): 646–47.

98. Barbara Ransby, *Ella Baker and the Black Freedom Movement: A Radical Democratic Vision* (Chapel Hill: North Carolina Press, 2003); Lynne Olson, *Freedom's Daughters: The Unsung Heroines of the Civil Right Movement from 1830 to 1970* (New York: Scribner, 2001), 139–40.

99. "Daisy Gatson Bates, 1912–1999," *The National Women's History Project: Honorees Tribute Program*, March 2016, 11; Olson, 135–38.

100. Paula Giddings, *When and Where I Enter: The Impact of Black Women on Race and Sex in America* (New York: Amistad/HarperCollins, 1984), 269–70; Lonnie Bunch, "Little Rock Nine," NMAAHC, April 1, 2017, https://nmaahc.si.edu/blog-post /little-rock-nine.

101. "Central High School, September 25, 1957," *Writer's Almanac*, NPR, September 25, 2007.

102. Colby Itkowitz, "A Capitol Statue for the Man in Black," *Washington Post*, April 19, 2019, C2.

103. Richard Fausset and Campbell Robertson, "A Cascade of Revelations Shows the Quiet Persistence of Blackface in Private," *New York Times*, February 8, 2019, A14.

104. Giddings, *Where*, 269.

105. Bob Greene, "The University of Alabama Earns a Victory Over an Ugly History," *Wall Street Journal*, January 6–7, 2018; Giddings, *Where*, 269.

106. "Dr. Virginia Apgar, Changing the Face of Medicine," National Library of Medicine, https://cfmedicine.nlm.nih.gov/physicians/biography_12.html.

107. "Grace Murray Hopper," Yale University, https://cpsc.yale.edu/grace-murray-hopper.

108. Sally H. Jacobs, "She Received Many Firsts. She's Getting Her Due At Last," *New York Times*, August 26, 2019, D1, D4; Matt Schudel, "Angela Buxton, who won Wimbledon Doubles Title with Althea Gibson Dies at 85," *Washington Post*, August 22, 2020, https://www.washingtonpost.com/local/obituaries/angela-buxton-who -won-wimbledon-doubles-title-with-althea-gibson-dies-at-85/2020/08/22/88ce2fe4 -e496-11ea-b69b-64f7b0477ed4_story.html.

109. Grace Metalious and Ardis Cameron, *Peyton Place*, rev. ed. (Lebanon, NH: Northeastern University Press, 1999); Roger Ebert, "Some Like It Hot," January 9, 2000, https://www.rogerebert.com/reviews/great-movie-some-like-it-hot-1959.

110. Jess McHugh, "'The Beginning of the Conversation': What It Was Like To Be an LGBTQ Activist Before Stonewall," *Time*, June 25, 2019, https://time.com /longform/mattachine-society/.

111. Robin Gerber, *Barbie and Ruth: The Story of the World's Most Famous Doll and the Woman Who Created Her* (New York: HarperCollins, 2009).

112. Amy Held, "Barbie Heads into New Ground with Hijab-Sporting Doll," *All Things Considered*, November 14, 2017; *People*, October 14, 2019, 4.

113. May, *Pushing*, 63.

114. Maggie Doherty, *The Equivalents: A Story of Art, Female Friendship and Liberation in the 1960s* (Cambridge: Harvard University Press, 2021).

115. Margalit Fox, "Maxine Kumin, Pulitzer-Winning Poet With a Naturalist's Precision, Dies at 88," *New York Times*, February 7, 2014, https://www.nytimes.com/2014/02/08 /books/maxine-kumin-pulitzer-winning-poet-dies-at-88.html; "Anne Sexton Dies, Pulitzer Poet, 45," *New York Times*, October 6, 1974, www.nytimes.com/1974/10/06 /archives/wnne-sexton-dies-pulitzer-prize-poet-45-bad-case-of-melancholy.html.

116. *Hansberry v. Lee Case Brief*, https://www.casebriefs.com/blog/law/civil-procedure /civil-procedure-keyed-to-marcus/establishing-the-structure-and-size-of-the -dispute/hansberry-v-lee-2/.

117. "Lorraine Hansberry, Playwright (1930–1965)," Biography.com, January 19, 2018, https://www.biography.com/writer/lorraine-hansberry; "Lorraine Hansberry Discusses Her Play," Studs Terkel Radio Archive, original air date May 12, 1959, https://studsterkel.wfmt.com/programs/lorraine-hansberry-discusses-her-play -raisin-sun; Margaret B. Wilkerson, "Generations of Struggle and Freedom Dreams: Lorraine Hansberry and Radical Protest from the 1930s to the Present," Organization of American Historians, Philadelphia, April 7, 2017; Jeff Lunden, "A Prescient Play About Race in America Has ITRs Long Overdue Broadway Premiere," *Morning Edition*, December 6, 2021.

118. Blair McClendon, "Radical Acts: The Many Lives of Lorraine Hansberry," *The New Yorker*, January 24, 2022, 65–69; Daniel Pollack-Pelzner, "A Pioneer's Unpublished Script," *New York Times*, June 7, 2020, AR4.

119. Nancy Gibbs, "What Women Want Now," *Time*, October 26, 2019, 26.

120. May, *Pushing*, 16–18.

Chapter Five: Pillboxes & Protests, 1960–1972

1. Marie Smith, "Suffrage Birthday Is Marked, Future Dark for Equal Rights," *Washington Post*, August 26, 1960, in Anna Kelton Wiley Papers, Box 16, Library of Congress, Washington, DC.

2. Richard Nixon, September 3, 1960, clipping, Wiley Papers, Box 19, LC.

3. John F. Kennedy statement, September 28, quoted in Letter to NWP members from Alma Lutz, October 18, 1960, in Wiley Papers, Box 16, LC.

4. Cynthia Harrison, *On Account of Sex: The Politics of Women's Issues, 1945–1968* (Berkeley: University of California Press, 1988), 117–19.

5. "This Day in History, January 27, 1961: Kennedy Doctor Prescribes Swim," *New York Times*, January 27, 2021, A2; Cynthia E. Harrison, "A 'New Frontier' for Women: The Public Policy of the Kennedy Administration," *Journal of American History* 67, no. 3 (December 1980): 635.

6. Harrison, *JAH*, 637.

7. Esther Peterson biographical note, undated, Petersen Papers, 84–M161, carton 1, Schlesinger Library, Radcliffe College, Cambridge, MA.

8. Harrison, *JAH*, 632.

9. Stephanie Coontz, *A Strange Stirring: The Feminine Mystique and American Women at the Dawn of the 1960s* (New York: Basic Books, 2011), 5–8.

10. Catherine East, *American Women: 1963, 1983, 2003* (Washington, DC: National Federation of Business and Professional Women's Clubs, Inc., 1983), 6–7; Gail Collins, *When Everything Changed: The Amazing Journey of American Women from 1960 to the Present* (New York: Little, Brown and Co., 2009), 20.

11. Harrison, *JAH*, 631; East, 7.

12. Collins, 11.

13. Edwin Diamond, "Young Women with Brains: Babies, Yes—But What Else?" *Newsweek*, March 7, 1960.

14. Linda Lear, "Rachel Louise Carson," rachelcarson.org/Bio.aspx; "Rachel Carson," January 24, 2017, https://www.pbs.org/video/american-experience-rachel-carson/.

15. Harrison, *JAH*, 638.

16. Katherine Pollak Ellickson, "The President's Commission on the Status of Women: Its Formation, Functioning, and Contribution," unpublished manuscript, January 1976, 4, provided to the author by Catherine East.

17. *American Women: Report of the President's Commission on the Status of Women* (Washington, DC: US Government Printing Office, 1963), 85; Collins, 73.

18. Harrison, *JAH*, 638–39.

19. Duchess Harris, "From the Kennedy Commission to the Combahee Collective: Black Feminist Organizing, 1960–80," in *Sisters in the Struggle: African American Women in the Civil Rights–Black Power Movement*, Bettye Collier-Thomas and V.P. Franklin, eds. (New York: New York University Press, 2001), 285; Sue Cronk, "Her Chairman's Seat Remains Vacant," *Washington Post*, November 15, 1962, Peterson Papers, Box 8, folder 211, Schlesinger Library.

20. Carl Brauer, "Women Activists, Southern Conservatives, and the Prohibition of Sex Discrimination in Title VII of the 1964 Civil Rights Act," *Journal of Southern History* (February 1983): 41.

21. Collins, 72.

22.   Rosalind Rosenberg, *Jane Crow: The Life of Pauli Murray* (New York: Oxford University Press, 2017), 250–52.

23.   Ellickson, "Formation," 14–15.

24.   Brauer, 41.

25.   Harrison, *JAH*, 644.

26.   Memo, Attorney General to Heads of All Divisions, February 18, 1964, Robert Kennedy Papers, Box 10, John F. Kennedy Library, Boston, MA.

27.   "Equal Pay Act," History Channel online, November 30, 2017, https://www.history .com/topics/womens-rights/equal-pay-act.

28.   Letter, Edith Green to Katherine Ellickson, August 2 [no year], Ellickson Papers, 77-M15, Schlesinger Library.

29.   Jonathan Eig, *The Birth of The Pill: How Four Crusaders Reinvented Sex and Launched a Revolution* (New York: W.W. Norton & Co., 2012); Robert D. McFadden, "George Rosenkranz, Part of Team That Developed Birth Control Pill, Dies at 102," *New York Times,* June 24, 2019, A21.

30.   Gardiner Harris, "It Started More Than One Revolution," *New York Times,* May 4, 2010.

31.   Elaine Tyler May, *Homeward Bound: American Families in the Cold War Era,* rev. ed. (New York: Basic Books, 2017), 211.

32.   May, *Homeward,* 143; Tom Gjelten, "50 Years Ago, The Pope Called Birth Control 'Intrinsically Wrong,'" *Morning Edition,* July 3, 2018.

33.   Leslie Friedman Goldstein, *The Constitutional Rights of Women: Cases in Law and Social Change,* rev. ed. (Madison: University of Wisconsin Press, 1988), 310–322; Jill Lepore, "The Last Amazon: Wonder Woman Returns," *New Yorker,* September 15, 2014, www.newyorker.com/magazine/2014/09/22/last-amazon.

34.   Ann Gerhart, "Pill Fight Pops Up Again," *Washington Post,* February 21, 2012, C1.

35.   Goldstein, 322–32; Ruth Marcus, "No, the Constitution Is Not 'Neutral' on Abortion," *Washington Post,* December 10, 2021, A19.

36.   Margalit Fox, "Helen Gurley Brown, Who Gave 'Single Girl' a Life in Full, Dies at 90," *New York Times,* August 14, 2012, https://www.nytimes.com/2012/08/14/business /media/elen-gurley-brown-who-gave-cosmopolitan-its-purr-is-dead-at-90.html.

37.   Moira Weigel, review of *Enter Helen: The Invention of Helen Gurley Brown and the Rise of the Modern Single Woman,* by Brooke Hauser, *New York Times Book Review,* July 17, 2016, 12.

38.   John Updike, quoted by Catherine Morley, *The Quest for Epic in Contemporary American Fiction: John Updike, Philip Roth and Don DeLillo* (New York: Routledge, 2009), 7.

39.   Betty Friedan, *The Feminine Mystique,* rev. ed. (New York: W.W. Norton & Co., 1963, 1997), 57.

40.   Sarah Larson, "What Friedan Changed," *The New Yorker,* March 8, 2013, https://new yorker.com/books/page-turner/what-friedan-changed; author's notes, Stephanie Coontz remarks at "Fifty Years After The Feminine Mystique: What's Changed at Home and at Work," November 19, 2013, Radcliffe Institute for Advanced Study, Harvard University; Maggie Doherty, *The Equivalents: A Story of Art, Female Friendship, and Liberation in the 1960s* (Cambridge: Harvard University Press, 2021), 177.

41.   Susan Oliver, *Betty Friedan: The Personal Is Political* (New York: Pearson Longman, 2008), 2–3, 7; Betty Friedan, *Life So Far: A Memoir* (New York: Simon & Schuster, 2000), 26–27.

42. William H. Chafe, *The American Woman: Her Changing Social, Economic and Political Role, 1920–1970* (New York: Oxford University Press, 1972), 277.

43. Collins, 56; Betty Friedan, *The Feminine Mystique* (New York: W.W. Norton & Co.,1963, 2001), 49.

44. May, *Homeward,* 199.

45. Margalit Fox, "Betty Friedan, Who Ignited Cause in 'Feminine Mystique,' Dies at 85," *New York Times,* February 5, 2006, https://www.nytimes.com/2006/02/05/us /betty-friedan-who-ignited-cause-in-feminine-mystique-dies-at-85.html/.

46. James Langton, "Feminist Writer Betty Friedan 'Brought Terror to Marriage,'" *Telegraph,* July 16, 2000, https://www.telegraph.co.uk/news/worldnews/northamerica /usa/1348841/Feminist-writer-Betty-Friedan-brought-terror-to-marriage.html.

47. Debra Micals, "Ruby Bridges," National Women's History Museum, https://www .womenshistory.org/education-resources/biographies/ruby-bridges; Ruby Bridges, *This Is Your Time* (New York: Penguin Random House, 2020).

48. Adam Fairclough, *To Redeem the Soul of America: The Southern Christian Leadership Conference & Martin Luther King, Jr.* (Athens: University of Georgia Press, 1987), 53, 66.

49. Thomas Bledsoe, *Or We'll All Hang Separately: The Highlander Idea* (Boston: Beacon Press, 1969); Jon Meacham and Tim McGraw, *Songs of America: Patriotism, Protest, and the Music That Made a Nation* (New York: Random House, 2019).

50. Lynne Olson, *Freedom's Daughters: The Unsung Heroines of the Civil Rights Movement from 1830 to 1970* (New York: Scribner, 2001), 215–19.

51. "Septima Clark, 89, Active in Civil Rights in South Since 1918," *New York Times,* December 17, 1987, https://www.nytimes.com/1987/12/17/obituaries/septima-clark -89-active-in-civil-rights-in-south-since-1918.html.

52. Dorothy Cotton, Vincent Harding et al., *If Your Back Is Not Bent: The Role of the Citizenship Education Program in the Civil Rights Movement* (New York: Simon & Schuster Atria Books, 2012); Fairclough, 169; Harrison Smith, "Dorothy Cotton, 88: Civil Rights Leader, Confidante to King," *Washington Post,* June 13, 2018.

53. Olson, 156–59; Janet Dewart Bell, *Lighting the Fires of Freedom: African American Women in the Civil Rights Movement* (New York: The New Press, 2018), 95–102.

54. Matt Schudel, "John Salter, Jr., 84: Helped Spur Movement at a Miss. Lunch Counter," *Washington Post,* January 13, 2019, C8.

55. Barbara Ransby, *Ella Baker & the Black Freedom Movement: A Radical Democratic Vision* (Chapel Hill: University of North Carolina Press, 2003), 240–46; Olson, 148–50; https://www.quotetab.com/quotes/by-ella-baker; Author conversation with Marian Wright Edelman, July 3, 2019.

56. Marian Smith Holmes, "The Freedom Riders, Then and Now," *Smithsonian Magazine* (February 2009); "Freedom Riders: Threatened, Attacked. Jailed," a film by Stanley Nelson, May 2011, www.pbs.org.wgbh/americanexperience/freedomriders.

57. Olson, 158.

58. Douglas Martin, "James Forman Dies at 76; Was Pioneer in Civil Rights," *New York Times,* January 12, 2005, https://www.nytimes.com/2005/01/12/obituaries/james -forman-dies-at-76-was-pioneer-in-civil-rights.html.

59. https://www.nps.gov/places/freedom-riders-national-monument.htm.

60. Mary King, *Freedom Song: A Personal Story of the 1960s Civil Rights Movement* (New York: William Morrow & Co., 1987), 469–70.

61.   Charlene Hunter-Gault, "I Made History, but It Didn't End There," *New York Times,* January 10, 2021, SR3; Denny Chin and Kathy Hirata Chin, "Constance Baker Motley, James Meredith, and the University of Mississippi," *Columbia Law Review* 117, no. 7 (no date), https://columbialawreview.org/content/constance -baker-motley-james-meredith-and-the-university-of-mississippi/.

62.   Richard Sandomir, "Vel Phillips, Housing Rights Champion in the 60s, Is Dead at 95," *New York Times,* April 25, 2018, https://www.nytimes.com/2018/04/25/obituaries /vel-phillips-housing-rights-champion-in-the-60s-dies-at-95.html.

63.   https://www.bernicejohnsonreagon.com; Meacham, 149; Lawrence Van Gelder, "Cordell Hull Reagon, Civil Rights Singer, Dies at 53," *New York Times,* November 19, 1996, https://www.nytimes.com/1996/11/19/us/cordell-hull-reagon-civil-rights -singer-dies-at-53.html.

64.   Martha S. Jones, *Vanguard: How Black Women Broke Barriers, Won the Vote, and Insisted on Equality for All* (New York: Basic Books, 2020), 256–61; Thomas A. Johnson, "Fannie Lou Hamer Dies, Left Farm To Lead Struggle for Civil Rights," *New York Times,* March 15, 1977, https://www.nytimes.com/1977/03/15/archives /fannie-lou-hamer-dies-left-farm-to-lead-struggle-for-civil-rights.html.

65.   Marian Wright Edelman, "Remembering Unita Blackwell," Child Watch Column, May 24, 2019, Children's Defense Fund, https://www.childrensdefense.org/child -watch-columns/health/2019/remembering-unita-blackwell/; Maggie Jones, "Unita Blackwell," *New York Times Magazine,* December 29, 2019, 18–19.

66.   Peniel E. Joseph, "Kennedy's Finest Moment," *New York Times,* June 11, 2013; full text at https://www.nytimes.com/2013/06/11/opinion/kennedys-civil-rights -triumph.html.

67.   Louis Menard, "The Sex Amendment," *The New Yorker,* July 21, 2014, 76.

68.   "March on Washington," History Channel online, October 29, 2009, www.history .com/topics/black-history/march-on-washington; "Dream Songs: The Music of the March on Washington," *New Yorker,* August 28, 2013, www.newyorker.com/culture /culture-desk/dream-songs-the-music-of-the-march-on-washington; Meacham, 158–59.

69.   Jessica Goldstein, "March on Washington Had One Female Speaker: Josephine Baker," *Washington Post,* August 23, 2011, https://www.washingtonpost.com /lifestyle/style/march-on-washington-had-one-female-speaker-josephine-baker /2011/08/08/gIQAHqhbaj_story_html.

70.   Jennifer Scanlon, "Where Were the Women in the March on Washington," *New Republic,* March 16, 2016, https://newrepublic.com/article/131587/women-march -washington; Krissah Thompson, "The Sisters Were Almost Forgotten," *Washington Post,* August 23, 2013, C1.

71.   Sydney Treant, "Birmingham's 'Fifth Girl' Wants Restitution," *Washington Post,* March 8, 2020, A1; Becky Little, "How Doug Jones Brought KKK Church Bombers to Justice," August 31, 2018, www.history.com/news/how-doug-jones-brought -kkk-church-bombers-to-justice; Giulia McDonnell Nieto Del Rio, "'Fifth Girl' in Church Bombing Gets Apology from Alabama's Governor," *New York Times,* October 4, 2020, A23.

72.   Todd S. Purdum, *An Idea Whose Time Has Come: Two Presidents, Two Parties, and the Battle for the Civil Rights Act of 1964* (New York: Henry Holt and Co., 2014), 154–55.

73.   Purdum, 168.

74. Brauer, 47–48; Purdum, 195.

75. Brauer, 41–42.

76. Charles W. Whalen, Jr., "Unlikely Hero," *Washington Post*, January 2, 1984, https://www.washingtonpost.com/archive/politics/1984/01/02/unlikely-hero /9f5d8288-e55e-4175-b87b-895152db6923/; Brauer, 43–44.

77. Emily George, *Martha W. Griffiths* (Lanham, MD: University Press of America, 1982), 149; Brauer, 45.

78. George, 150; Collins, 77; Brauer, 49.

79. Purdum, 197.

80. Brauer, 50.

81. Purdum, 198–99; "Delivering on a Dream: The House and the Civil Rights Act of 1964," History, Art & Archives, April 8, 2022, https://history.house.gov /exhibitions-and-publications/civil-rights/1964-essay.

82. George, 151.

83. Bruce Ackerman, "Dignity Is a Constitutional Principle," *New York Times*, March 30, 2014.

84. Robert D. Loevy, *To End All Segregation: The Politics of Passage of the Civil Rights Act of 1964* (Lanham, MD: University Press of America, 1990), 166, 158.

85. Catie Edmondson, "A Segregationist Legacy Back in the Conversation," *New York Times*, August 28, 2018.

86. Purdum, 303, 307.

87. https://www.archives.gov/legislative/features/civil-rights-1964/senate-roll-call.html.

88. Menard, 80.

89. "Freedom Riders" documentary; King, 438.

90. King, 465–66.

91. May, *Homeward*, 10–11.

92. *McLaughlin v. Florida*, Oyex, www.oyez.org/cases/1964/11; "Loving v. Virginia," History Channel online, November 17, 2017, https://www.history.com/topics/civil -rights-movement/loving-v-virginia.

93. Rachel Weiner, "Judge Strikes Down Virginia Race Requirement for Marriage License as Unconstitutional," *Washington Post*, October 11, 2019, C1.

94. William Grimes, "B. Smith, Model Turned Restaurateur and Lifestyle Guru, Dies at 70," *New York Times*, February 23, 2020, https://www.nytimes.com/2020/02/23 /obituaries/b-smith-dead.html; Anika Reed, "A Proud Moment: Black Women Command the Covers of 2018 September Issues," *USA Today*, August 9, 2018, https://www.usatoday.com/story/life/people/2018/08/09/beyonce-rihanna-black -women-command-covers-2018-september-issues/944560002/; Jessica Testa, "A Photographic Milestone at Conde Nast," *New York Times*, July 16, 2020, D1.

95. Emily Tannenbaum, "The Crown Act Was just Passed by the House of Representatives," *Glamour*, September 22, 2020, www.glamour.com/story/the-crown-act-banning -hair-discrimination; https://fortune.com/2022/03/21/crown-act-workplace-hair -discrimination-black-women/; "The Fashion World Promised More Diversity. Here's What We Found," *New York Times*, March 4, 2021, www.nytimes.com/2021/03/04 /style/Black-representation-fashion.html.

96. King, 44.

97. "Casey Hayden," Digital SNCC, https://snccdigital.org/people/casey-hayden.

98.   King, 449.

99.   "SNCC Position Paper, November 1964 (Name withheld by Request)," King, 567–69.

100.   King, 449–50, 453.

101.   King, 451–52.

102.   King, 456–57.

103.   Jim Rutenberg, "We Shall Overcome," *New York Times Magazine*, August 2, 2015, 32; Jones, 262.

104.   Holliman, Irene, "Student Nonviolent Coordinating Committee," *New Georgia Encyclopedia*, last modified July 15, 2020, https://www.georgiaencyclopedia.org /articles/history-archaeology/student-nonviolent-coordinating-committee-sncc/; Michael Witmer, Oliver Groeneveld, et al., "1965-1966: The SNCC Project: A Year by Year History, 1960-1970," Mapping American Social Movements, University of Washington, https://depts.washington.edu/moves/SNCC_map-events.shtml.

105.   H. Rap Brown, "Violence Is as American As Cherry Pie," https://blackthen.com /h-rap-brown-violence-is-as-american-as-cherry-pie/; "Black Panthers History," History Channel online, November 3, 2017, https://www.history.com/topics/civil -rights-movement/black-panthers.

106.   Lavanya Ramanathan, "Angela Davis, Caught Up in Controversy," *Washington Post*, February 27, 2019, C1; Nelson George, "Angela Davis," *New York Times Magazine*, January 3, 2021, 78–84.

107.   "Kerner Commission," History Matters, historymatters.gmu.edu/d/6545; Alice George, "The 1968 Kerner Commission Got It Right, But Nobody Listened," *Smithsonian Magazine*, March 1, 2018, https://www.smithsonianmag.com /smithsonian-institution/1968-kerner-commission-got-it-right-nobody -listened-180968318/.

108.   Pauli Murray and Mary O. Eastwood, "Jane Crow and the Law: Sex Discrimination and Title VII," *George Washington University Law Review* 34, no. 2 (December 1965).

109.   Collins, 82–83; Menard, 80; Richard Sandomir, "Aileen Hernandez, 90, Ex-NOW President and Feminist Trailblazer, Dies," *New York Times*, February 28, 2017, www .nytimes.com/2017/02/28/us/aileen-hernandez-dead-womens-rights-champion.html.

110.   Linda Tanenbaum and Mark Engler, "Help Wanted—Female," *New Republic*, August 30, 2017, newrepublic.com/article/144614/help-wanted-female; Wyndham Robertson, "50 Years of Unisex Classified Job Ads," *New York Times*, December 3, 2018; George, 154.

111.   Liza Weisstuch, "Getting on Board with Modern-day Flight Attendants," *Washington Post*, May 16, 2021, E25; Gillian A. Frank and Lauren Gutterman, "How Flight Attendants Organized Against Their Bosses to End 'Swinging Stewardesses' Stereotyping," November 19, 2018, https://pictorial.jezebel.com/how -flight-attendants-organized-against-their-bosses-1830282960.

112.   Menard, 80; George, 155.

113.   Liz Gilchrist, "In Memoriam: Dorothy Haener; 'Sometimes You Need to Rock the Boat,'" https://www.proquest.com/trade-journals/memoriam-dorothy-haener -sometimes-you-have-rock/docview/222047901/se-2.

114.   "Founding," https://now.org/faq/when-and-how-was-now-founded/; Rachel Shteir, "In Her Own Words: Betty Friedan," *New York Times*, February 3, 2021, https ://www.nytimes.com/2021/02/03/us/betty-friedan-feminism-legacy.html.

115.   "A New Civil Rights Organization Is Born," https://now.org/about/history/founding
        -2/; Betty Friedan, *Life So Far: A Memoir* (New York: Simon & Schuster Paperbacks,
        2000), 174–178.

116.   Menard, 81.

117.   Marie Smith, "Women Blame Own Labor Bosses," *Washington Post*, June 15, 1961,
        Wiley Papers, Box 16, LC.

118.   Steven Greenhouse, "Mildred Jeffrey, 93, Activist for Women, Labor and Liberties,"
        New York Times, April 5, 2004, https://www.nytimes.com/2004/04/05/us/mildred
        -jeffrey-93-activist-for-women-labor-and-liberties.html; Author's recollection.

119.   Gilchrist obituary; Tom Brokaw, *The Greatest Generation* (New York: Random
        House, 1998), 96–99.

120.   Wolfgang Saxon, "Olga Marie Madar, 80, Pioneer For Women in the Automotive Union,"
        New York Times, May 18, 1996; "Olga Marie Madar/UAW," https://uaw.org/women
        /biographies/olga-marie-madar/; Brigid O'Farrell and Joyce L. Kornbluh, eds., *Rocking the
        Boat: Union Women's Voices, 1915–1975* (New Brunswick, NJ: Rutgers University Press, 1996).

121.   Deborah Cohen, *Braceros: Migrant Citizens and Transnational Subjects in the Postwar
        United States and Mexico* (Chapel Hill: University of North Carolina Press, 2011).

122.   "Dolores Huerta: The Feminist Seed Is Planted," https://doloreshuerta.org
        /doloreshuerta; "Dolores: Portrait of a Labor and Feminist Icon: Dolores Huerta,"
        premiered March 27, 2018, directed by Peter Bratt, https://www.pbs.org
        /independentlens/films/dolores-huerta.

123.   Muzaffar Chishti, Faye Hipsman and Isabel Ball, "Fifty Years On, the 1965
        Immigration and Nationality Act Continues to Reshape the United States,"
        Migration Policy Institute, October 15, 2015, https://www.migrationpolicy.org
        /article/fifty-years-1965-immigration-and-nationality-act-continues-reshape
        -united-states; https://cis.org/Report/HartCeller-Immigration-Act-1965.

124.   Matthew Twombley, "1968: A Seismic Year," *Smithsonian Magazine*, January–
        February 2018, 52–55.

125.   Lauren Collins, "Contested," review of *Looking for Miss America: A Pageant's 100-Year
        Quest to Define Womanhood* by Margot Mifflin, *The New Yorker*, September 7, 2020,
        74; Roxane Gay, "Dethroning Miss America," *Smithsonian Magazine*, January–
        February 2018, 107.

126.   "Chisholm, Shirley Anita," History, Art & Archives, https://history.house.gov
        /people/detail/10918; Tera W. Hunter, "The Forgotten Legacy of Shirley Chisholm:
        Race versus Gender in the 2008 Democratic Primaries," in *Obama, Clinton, Palin:
        Making History in Election 2008*, ed. Liette Gidlow (Urbana: University of Illinois
        Press, 2011), 66–68; Joe Holley, "Prominent Feminist Was a Lodestar for Texas
        Liberals," *Washington Post*, September 28, 2021, B6.

127.   Barbara Winslow, review of *The Highest Glass Ceiling: Women's Quest for the American
        Presidency* by Ellen Fitzpatrick, in *Journal of American History* (March 2017): 1115;
        Jill Lepore, *These Truths: A History of the United States* (New York: W.W. Norton &
        Co., 2018), 615; www.cawp.rutgers.edu/women-us-congress.

128.   www.cawp.rutgers.edu/facts/voter/turnout; "The Rise of the Political Gender Gap,"
        Wall Street Journal, August 1–2, 2020, C2; Jo Freeman, "Gender Gaps in Presidential
        Elections," published as a letter to the editor of *P.S.: Political Science and Politics* 32,
        no. 2 (June 1999): 191–92, https://www.jofreeman.com/polhistory/gendergap.htm.

129. Purdum, 307; the states were Alabama, Georgia, Louisiana, Mississippi, and South Carolina, "Presidential Election Interactive Maps," www.270towin.com/1964 _election. In 1968, South Carolina went for Nixon and Arkansas voted for Wallace.

130. Hua Hsu, "Surviving Woodstock," *New Yorker*, August 5 & 12, 2019: 72–73; "Woodstock: Three Days That Defined a Generation," for PBS *American Experience*, August 6, 2019, www.pbs.org/wgbh/americanexperience/films/woodstock; Michael Cavna, "A Bird of Peace Among the Dogs of War," *Washington Post*, August 17, 2019, C1.

131. Ken Burns and Dayton Duncan, "Country Isn't Just Good Old Boys," *New York Times*, September 14, 2019; www.pbs.org/show/country-music; "8 Awesome Feminist Anthems in Honor of Women's History Month," Goodnet, March 11, 2019, www.goodnet.org/articles/8-awesome-feminist-anthems.

132. "Minutes from the Second National Convention of NOW," November 18–19, 1967, Washington, DC, https://350fem.blogs.brynmawr.edu/1967/11/19/national -conference-of-now-minutes/.

133. George, 168, 170.

134. "Citizens Advisory Council: New 20 Member Panel Named," *New York Times*, August 17, 1969, 41.

135. "Advancing the Cause of Women," January 19, 2017, Richard Nixon Foundation, https://www.nixonfoundation.org/home/exhibit/advancing-women/.

136. George, 168, 136; Robert Sherrill, "That Equal-Rights-Amendment—What, Exactly, Does It Mean?" *New York Times Magazine*, September 20, 1970, section 6, 101, in Women's Rights, Box 1, Sophia Smith Collection, Smith College, Northampton, MA.

137. *Congressional Record*, House, 91st Congress, 2d Session (August 10, 1970): 28005.

138. Sherrill; George, 171–72.

139. "The Hen-Pecked House," *New York Times*, August 12, 1970; Sherrill.

140. Linda Charlton, "Women March Down Fifth Avenue in Equality Drive," *New York Times*, August 27, 1970, A1; Sasha Cohen, "The Day Women Went on Strike," *Time*, August 26, 2015, www.time.com//4008060/women-strike-equality-1970/.

141. "Birch Bayh, 91: Senator Championed Title IX, ERA," *Washington Post*, March 15, 2019, B6; "Birch Bayh, Senator Who Drove Title IX and 2 Amendments, Dies at 91," *New York Times*, March 15, 2019, A28.

142. Brenda Feigen, *Not One of the Boys: Living Life as a Feminist* (New York: Alfred A. Knopf, 2000), 29–30, 33, 72–73.

143. Sam J. Ervin, Jr., *Preserving the Constitution: The Autobiography of Senator Sam J. Ervin, Jr.* (Charlottesville: The Michie Co., 1984), 270; George, 173.

144. Leslie W. Gladstone, "The Proposed Equal Rights Amendment," Congressional Research Service Report No. 82-51 GOV, HQ 1428, U.S.D., March 25, 1982, https://digital.library.unt.edu/ark:/67531/metacrs8412/.

145. Author interview with Flora Crater, June 15, 1987.

146. George, 176.

147. Patricia Sullivan, "Helen Thomas Dies at 92; Journalist Was the Feisty Scourge of Presidents," *Washington Post*, July 20, 2013, www.washingtonpost.com/local /obituaries/helen-thomas-feisty-scourge-of-presidents-dies-at-92/2013/07/20 /82285f4e-f145-11e2-a1f9-ea873b7e0424_story.html.

148. Jo Freeman, "What's in a Name? Does It Matter How the ERA is Written?" June 1996, https://www.jofreeman.com/lawandpolicy/eraname.htm.

149. George, 178.

150. Eileen Shanahan, "Equal Rights Amendment Passed by House, 354-23," *New York Times,* October 13, 1971, A1; Anna L. Harvey, *Votes Without Leverage: Women in American Electoral Politics, 1920–1970* (Cambridge, UK: Cambridge University Press, 1998), 214–25.

151. *Women in Congress,* 308.

152. George, 180–81; Gladstone.

153. Author interview with Carol Burris, NOW lobbyist, who lived with Alice Paul at NWP Headquarters, March 1977.

154. George, 168.

155. Evan Thomas, *FIRST: Sandra Day O'Connor* (New York: Random House, 2019), 79–81; Holley, Farenthold obit.

Chapter Six: Battle Lines, 1972–1980

1. Jill Lepore, *These Truths: A History of the United States* (New York: W.W. Norton & Co., 2018), 652; Marjorie J. Spruill, *Divided We Stand: The Battle of Women's Rights and Family Values That Polarized American Politics* (New York: Bloomsbury, 2017), 14, 29–33, 126–27.

2. Hilary Mills, "Writing and the Role of the Washington Wife," *Washington Star,* October 28, 1979, H6.

3. Data collected by the author.

4. Jane J. Mansbridge, *Why We Lost the ERA* (Chicago: University of Chicago Press, 1986), 212–213; Donald G. Matthews and Jane Sherron DeHart, *Sex, Gender, and the Politics of ERA: A State and a Nation* (New York: Oxford University Press, 1990), ix.

5. Jon Krakauer, *Under the Banner of Heaven: A Story of Violent Faith* (New York: First Anchor Books/Random House, 2004), 25.

6. Maria Karagianis, "Alice Paul Still Wait for Equal Rights: A Battler for 90 Years," *Boston Globe,* February 1, 1976, C1, 7.

7. Author's recollection.

8. Mary Thornton, "NOW Put Aside Feuds to Push for ERA," *Boston Globe,* April 25, 1977.

9. "Early History," National Women's Political Caucus, https://www.nwpc.org/history/; Richard Sandomir, "Aileen Hernandez, Ex-NOW President and Feminist Trailblazer, Dies at 90," *New York Times,* March 1, 2017, A24.

10. Spruill, 25–29; Author conversation with Pat Goldman, via Zoom, February 4, 2021.

11. Eileen Shanahan, "Women Organize for Political Power," *New York Times,* July 11, 1971, A1, www.nytimes.com/1971/07/11/archives/women-organize-for-political-power-200-women-organize-for-political.html.

12. Author's recollection; *The Hand That Rocks the Ballot Box,* documentary about the NWPC produced by ABC News correspondent Marlene Sanders, July 26, 1972, https://vimeo.com/337042560.

13. "Women's Caucus Leader," *New York Times,* June 3, 1975, www.nytimes.com/1975/06/03/archives/womens-caucus-leader-audrey-rowe-colom.html/.

14. Conor Friedersdorf, "Why Have White Women So Often Voted for Republicans," *The Atlantic*, November 26, 2016, www.theatlantic.com/ideas/archive/2018/11/white-women-gop/576586/.

15. https://www.cawp.rutgers.edu.

16. Maurice Carroll, "Emanuel Celler, Former Brooklyn Congressman, Dies at 92," *New York Times*, January 16, 1981, https://nyti.ms/29z0R9R.

17. Committee on House Administration of the US House of Representatives, *Women in Congress, 1916–2006* (Washington, DC: US Government Printing Office, 2006), 1–6.

18. Spencer Rich, "Women Candidates Achieve Office in Record Number: The Political Success Stories for Women in 1978 Are the State and Local Races," *Washington Post*, November 10, 1978.

19. Emily Langer, "Bernice Sandler, 'Godmother of Title IX,' Who Championed Women's Rights on Campus, Dies at 90," *Washington Post*, January 7, 2019, https://www.washingtonpost.com/local/obituaries/bernice-sandler-godmother-of-title-ix-who-championed-womens-rights-on-campus-dies-at-90/2019/01/07/9633e7b4-1297-11e9-90a8-136fa44b80ba_story.html.

20. "Bernice (Bunny) Sandler," *The National Women's History Project*, March 2016, 29; "Title IX," *The Writer's Almanac*, June 23, 2019, https://www.garrisonkeillor.com/radio/; Kevin M. Kruse and Julian E. Zelizer, *Fault Lines: A History of the United States Since 1974* (New York: W.W. Norton & Co., 2019), 73.

21. Catherine East, *American Women: 1963, 1983, 2003* (Washington, DC: The National Federation of Business and Professional Women's Clubs, 1983), 6.

22. Samantha Pell, "Transgender Policy Violates Title IX, Connecticut Girls Say," *Washington Post*, June 20, 2019, D1.

23. Kruse, 74; Emily Bobrow, "Billie Jean King," *Wall Street Journal*, August 14–15, 2021, C6.

24. Gail Collins, *When Everything Changed* (New York: Little, Brown and Co., 2009), 250–51, 22–23.

25. "Boggs, Corinne Claiborne (Lindy)," History, Art & Archives, https://history.house.gov/People/Listing/B/BOGGS,-Corinne-Claiborne-(lindy)-(B000592)/.

26. Lindy Boggs with Katherine Hatch, *Washington Through A Purple Veil: Memoirs of a Southern Woman* (New York: Harcourt Brace & Co., 1994), 276–78; Douglas Martin, "Lindy Boggs, Longtime Representative and Champion of Women, Is Dead at 97," *New York Times*, July 27, 2013, https://nytimes.com/2013/07/28/us/politics/lindy-boggs-longtime-representative-from-louisiana-dies-at-97.html.

27. Lepore, *Truths*, 651; Roxane Gay, "Fifty Years Ago, Protestors Took on the Miss America Pageant and Electrified the Feminist Movement," *Smithsonian Magazine*, January 2018, https://www.smithsonianmag.com/history/fifty-years-ago-protestors-took-on-miss-america-pageant-electrified-feminist-movement-180967504/.

28. Emily Langer, "Kate Millett, 82: Writer and 'High Priestess' of Second-Wave Feminism," *Washington Post*, September 8, 2017; Carol J. Adams, "The Book That Made Us Feminists," *New York Times*, September 10, 2017.

29. Susan Faludi, "Death of a Revolutionary: Shulamith Firestone," *The New Yorker*, April 15, 2013, 52–61; Margalit Fox, "Shulamith Firestone, 67, Feminist Writer, Is Dead," *New York Times*, August 31, 2012, B14.

30.   Margalit Fox, "Helen Gurley Brown, Who Gave 'Single Girl' a Full Life, Dies at 90," *New York Times,* August 13, 2012, www.nytimes.com/2012/08/14/business /media/helen-gurley-brown-who-gave-cosmopolitan-its-purr-is-dead-at-90.html; Madeleine Schwartz, "Notes From Many Years," *The Nation,* September 1, 2016, https://www.thenation.com/article/archive/notes-from-many-years/.

31.   Rachel A. Ryan, "The Changing Lives of Women in the 1960s: The *Ladies' Home Journal* and the Early Women's Movement" (master's thesis, Harvard University, 2004), author's copy; Linda Napikoski, "*Ladies' Home Journal* Sit-In: Feminists Take Over a 'Women's,' Magazine," ThoughtCo., March 16, 2019, thoughtco.com /ladies-home-journal-sit-in-3528969.

32.   Lynn Povich, *Good Girls Revolt: How the Women of 'Newsweek' Sued Their Bosses and Changed the Workplace* (New York: PublicAffairs, 2012); Eleanor Clift, "When Women Said 'No,'" *Newsweek,* December 31, 2012, 44–50.

33.   https://www.redstockings.org.

34.   Carolyn G. Heilbrun, *The Education of a Woman: The Life of Gloria Steinem* (New York: Dial Press, 1995); Gloria Steinem, *My Life on the Road* (New York: Random House, 2016); Lauren Collins, "Contested," review of *Looking for Miss America: A Pageant's 100-Year Quest to Define Womanhood* by Margot Mifflin, *The New Yorker,* September 7, 2020, 75.

35.   Nora Ephron, "Miami," *Crazy Salad: Some Things About Women* (New York: Alfred A. Knopf, 1975).

36.   Jane Kramer, "Road Warrior: After Fifty Years, Gloria Steinem Is Still at the Forefront of the Feminist Cause," *The New Yorker,* October 19, 2015, 46–57.

37.   Ephron.

38.   "Timeline of NOW's Work on Lesbian Rights: 1971," https://now.org/resource /now-leading-the-fight/.

39.   Author was the winning candidate. Stephanie Harrington, "Betty Friedan," review of *It Changed My Life: Writings on the Women's Movement* by Betty Friedan, July 4, 1976, https://archive.nytimes.com/www.nytimes.com/books/99/05/09/specials /friedan-changed.html.

40.   Germaine Greer, "The Betty Friedan I knew," *The Guardian,* February 7, 2006, www.theguardian.com/world/2006/feb/07/gender.bookscomment.

41.   Michele Wallace, "A Black Feminist's Search for Sisterhood," in *All the Women Are White, All the Blacks Are Men, But Some of Us Are Brave,* edited by Gloria T. Hall, Patricia Bell-Scott, and Barbara Smith (New York: The Feminist Press at CUNY, 1981), 5–12; Ashley D. Farmer, *Remaking Black Power: How Black Women Transformed an Era* (Chapel Hill: University of North Carolina Press, 2017); Bonnie J. Morris and D-M Withers, *The Feminist Revolution* (Washington, DC: Smithsonian Books, 2018), 60.

42.   Anne M. Valk, *Radical Sisters: Second-Wave Feminism and Black Liberation in Washington, DC* (Urbana: University of Illinois Press, 2008); Charles Burress, "Margaret Sloan-Hunter," SFGate, October 13, 2004, www.sfgate.com/bayarea /article/Margaret-Sloan-Hunter-united-black-feminist-2687932.php; Duchess Harris, "From the Kennedy Commission to the Combahee Collective," in *Sisters in the Struggle: African American Women in the Civil Rights–Black Power Movement,*

Bettye Collier-Thomas and V.P. Franklin, eds. (New York: New York University Press, 2001), 288–92.

43. Harris, "From the Kennedy Commission," 294, 294, 300; Alethia Jones and Virginia Eubanks, eds., *Ain't Gonna Let Nobody Turn Me Around: Forty Years of Movement Building with Barbara Smith* (Albany: SUNY Press, 2014); Bonnie Wertheim, "Florence Howe, 'Mother of Women's Studies', Dies at 91," *New York Times*, September 13, 2020, www.nytimes.com/2020/09/13/us/onaldt-howe-dead.html.

44. Wallace, 12.

45. Renee Ferguson, "Women's Liberation Has a Different Meaning for Blacks," *Washington Post*, October 3, 1970, C1, C3; J. V. Reistrup, "Women Still Cool to Lib but Want Better Status," *Washington Post*, March 24, 1972, A1, A10.

46. Martha S. Jones, *Vanguard: How Black Women Broke Barriers, Won the Vote, and Insisted on Equality for All* (New York: Basic Books, 2020).

47. Sherie M. Randolph, *Florynce "Flo" Kennedy: The Life of a Black Feminist Radical* (Chapel Hill: University of North Carolina Press, 2015), 1; *People*, April 14, 1974, 54.

48. Alethia Jones and Virginia Eubanks, eds., with Barbara Smith, *Ain't Gonna Let Nobody Turn Me Around: Forty Years of Movement Building with Barbara Smith* (Albany: SUNY Press, 2014); Amanda Hess, "Forces in Opposition," *New York Times Magazine*, February 12, 2017, 42.

49. James Kirchick, "Stonewall Wasn't the Start of the Gay Rights Struggle," *Wall Street Journal*, June 22–23, 2019; *The Lavender Scare*, directed by Josh Howard, broadcast June 18, 2019, https://www.pbs.org/video/lavender-scare-9ugluo/; George Chauncey, "The Crusader," review of *The Deviant's War: The Homosexual vs. the United States of America* by Eric Cervini, *New York Times Book Review*, June 14, 2020, 15.

50. Charles Kaiser, "He Told America 'Gay Is Good,'" review of *The Deviant's War: Homosexual vs. the United States of America*, by Eric Cervini, *Washington Post*, June 14, 2020, B6; Neel Burton, "When Homosexuality Stopped Being a Mental Disorder," *Psychology Today*, https://www.psychologytoday.com/us/blog/hide-and-seek/201509/when-homosexuality-stopped-being-a-mental-disorder; Peter Kihss, "8 Psychiatrists Are Seeking New Vote on Homosexuality as Mental Illness," *New York Times*, May 26, 1974, 39, https://www.nytimes.com/1974/05/26/archives-psychiatrists-are-seeking-new-vote-on-homosexuality-as-mental.html.

51. Neal Broverman, "Don't Let History Forget About Compton's Cafeteria Riot," www.advocate.com/transgender/2018/8/02/dont-let-history-forget-about-comptons-cafeteria-riot.

52. *Stonewall Uprising*, directed by Kate Davis and David Heilbroner, broadcast April 24, 2011, https://pbs.org/wgbh/americanexperience/films/stonewall/; Joanne Meyerowitz, "Stonewall: 50 Years Later," *The American Historian*, May 2019, 1; Martin B. Duberman, *Stonewall: The Definitive Story of the LGBTQ Rights Uprising That Changed America*, rev. ed. (New York: Penguin Random House, 2019); William Yardley, "Storme DeLarverie, Early Leader in Gay Rights Movement, Dies at 93," *New York Times*, May 29, 2014, www.nytimes.com/2014/05/30/nyregion/storme-delarverie-early-leader-in-the-gay-rights-movement-dies-at-93.html.

53. "Séance at the Palace," *Time*, August 18, 1967, http://content.time.com/time/subscriber/article/0,33009,840977,00.html; William Goldman, "Judy Floats," *Esquire*, January 1969.

54. Michael Gold and Derek M. Norman, "After 50 Years, Police Apology for Stonewall," *New York Times*, June 7, 2019, A1, 22.

55. Kruse, 82; David W. Dunlap, "Franklin Kameny, Gay Rights Pioneer, Dies ay 86," *New York Times*, October 12, 2011, https://www.nytimes.com/2011/10/13/us /franklin-kameny-gay-rights-pioneer-dies-at-86.html.

56. https://www.ourbodiesourselves.org/our-story/history/.

57. Rebecca Traister, "Warning: Abortion's Deadly DIY Past Could Soon Become Its Future," *New York*, January 9–22, 2017, 35.

58. Kate Manning, "The Amateur Abortionists," *New York Times*, April 23, 2017; *Heather Booth: Changing the World*, directed by Lilly Rivlin, released July 27, 2017, https://www.wmm.com/catalog/film/heather-booth-changing-the-world.

59. Jennifer Holland, "Abolishing Abortion: The History of the Pro-Life Movement in America," *The American Historian* (November 2016): 36–40; Lauren MacIvor Thompson, "Women Have Always Had Abortions," *New York Time*, December 15, 2019, SR7.

60. Elisabeth Griffith, *In Her Own Right: The Life of Elizabeth Cady Stanton* (New York: Oxford University Press, 1984), 133, 155.

61. "Massachusetts Passes Repeal of 1845 Abortion Ban," *Time*, July 23, 2018, https ://time.com/5346036/massachusetts-abortion-ban-roe-v-wade/.

62. Traister, "Warning," 32.

63. John Irving, "The Anti-Abortion Crusade's Cruel History," *New York Times*, June 24, 2019, A25.

64. Elaine Tyler May, *Homeward Bound: American Families in the Cold War Era*, rev ed. (New York: Basic Books, 2017), 145.

65. Holland, 38.

66. Holland, 37.

67. Glenn Kessler, "The Fact Checker: False Planned Parenthood Stat: 'Thousands' of Women Died Every Year Pre-Roe," *Washington Post*, June 2, 2019, A4.

68. Traister, "Warning," 35; Cokie Roberts, "The History of U.S. Abortion Laws," *Morning Edition*, June 5, 2019; Katherine Q. Seelye, "Patricia Maginnis, Pioneering Abortion-Rights Activist, Dies at 93," *New York Times*, September 6, 2021, B6.

69. Leslie Friedman Goldstein, *The Constitutional Rights of Women: Cases in Law and Social Change*, rev. ed. (Madison: University of Wisconsin Press, 1988), 334.

70. Clare Cushman, ed., *Supreme Court Decisions and Women's Rights: Milestones to Equality*, 2nd ed. (Washington, DC: CQ Press, 2011), 196–97.

71. Ann Gerhart, "The Revisionist Party," *Washington Post*, August 30, 2012, C1; Linda Napikoski, "Articles in the First Issue of Ms. Magazine," https://www.thoughtco .com/ms-magazine-first-issue-3529076.

72. *Roe v. Wade*, 410 US 113 (1973) and *Doe v. Bolton*, 410 US 179 (1973), in Goldstein, 337–58.

73. Goldstein, 338–41; Cushman, 196–97.

74. Michael S, Rosenwald, "Canon vs. Constitutional Law Can Be a Struggle for Catholics," *Washington Post*, July 10, 2018, B5.

75. Cushman, 197.

76. Emily Langer, "Norma McCorvey, 1947–2017: Jane Roe of Roe v. Wade Decision," *Washington Post*, February 19, 2017, A1, 8; Norma McCorvey with Andy Meisler,

I Am Roe: My Life, Roe v. Wade, and Freedom of Choice (New York: HarperCollins, 1994); Monica Hesse, "The Deathbed Revelation of 'Jane Roe,'" *Washington Post,* May 21, 2020, C1; Margaret Talbot, "The Real Roe," *New Yorker,* September 20, 2021, 68.

77. Goldstein, 337.

78. "Sandra Cano, the "Doe" in Doe v. Bolton Is a Pro-Life Speaker," www.wonderfullymadeministry.com; "Interview with Mary Doe (Sandra Cano) of Doe v. Bolton," https://www.priestsforlife.org/testimonies/1460-interview-with-mary-doe-sandra-cano-of-doe-vs-bolton.

79. Ben Kenigsberg, "How Did Abortion Become Political?" *New York Times,* September 13, 2018.

80. Philip Shabecoff, "Ford-Carter Stands on Abortion Held Similar, With One Exception," *New York Times,* September 21, 1976, https://www.nytimes.com/1976/09/21/archives/fordcarter-stands-on-abortion-held-similar-with-one-exception.html; John E. Jackson and Maris A. Vinovskis, "Public Opinion, Elections, and the 'Single-Issue' Issue," in *The Abortion Dispute and the American System,* ed. Gilbert Y. Steiner (Washington, DC: The Brookings Institution, 1983), 74–75.

81. Maggie Astor, "What Is the Hyde Amendment," *New York Times,* June 8, 2019, A12, https://www.nytimes.com/2019/06/07/us/politics/what-is-the-hyde-amendment.html.

82. Cushman, 198–99.

83. Karen Tumulty, "On Abortion, Biden Is Out of Step with Democrats," *Washington Post,* June 6, 2019, A21.

84. Jackson, 68, 76.

85. Susan Page, *The Matriarch: Barbara Bush and the Making of an American Dynasty* (New York: Hachette Book Group Inc., 2019), 81, 103, 210.

86. Alix Kates Shulman, "'A Marriage Agreement,'—" 1970, *Lilith,* November 29, 2012, https://www.lilith.org/articles/a-marriage-agreement-%E2%80%891970/; Charlotte Templin, "Interview with Alix Kates Shulman," *The Missouri Review,* November 10, 2011, https://www.missourireview.com/article/an-interview-with-alix-kates-shulman/. Textbook was *Basic Contract Law* by Lon Fuller.

87. Douglas Martin, "Phyllis Schlafly, 1924–2016: 'First Lady' of a Movement That Steered U.S. to the Right," *New York Times,* September 6, 2016, A1; Patricia Sullivan, "Phyllis Schlafly, 92: Fierce Anti-Feminist Pushed GOP to Right on Social Issues," *Washington Post,* September 6, 2016, A1.

88. Carol Felsenthal, *The Sweetheart of the Silent Majority: The Biography of Phyllis Schlafly* (Garden City, NY: Doubleday & Co., Inc., 1981), 171; Donald T. Critchlow, *Phyllis Schlafly and Grassroots Conservatism* (Princeton: Princeton University Press, 2006).

89. Lepore, *These Truths,* 556.

90. "2 Trade Charges in Race to Head GOP Women," *New York Times,* May 3, 1967, A22; Warren Weaver, Jr., "GOP Women Split as Parley Opens," *New York Times,* May 6, 1967; Warren Weaver, Jr., "Defeated Faction Considers Forming Separate Group," *New York Times,* May 7, 1967, 33.

91. Warren Weaver, Jr., "Defeated Leader Sets Up a Rival Group for Republican Women," *New York Times,* August 9, 1967.

92. Mansbridge, 110–116; Mary Frances Berry, *Why ERA Failed* (Bloomington: Indiana University Press, 1986), 80–84; author, "Partisan Politics and the Equal Rights

Amendment, 1970–1984," American Historical Association Meeting, Chicago, Illinois, December 29, 1984.

93. Author interview with Phyllis Schlafly, June 9, 1988, Eagle Forum Office, Washington, DC.

94. Lepore, *These Truths*, 655.

95. Felsenthal, 115–16.

96. Sullivan, Schlafly WP obit.

97. Sally Quinn, review of *Phyllis Schlafly: Sweetheart of the Silent Majority* by Carol Felsenthal, *Washington Post*, July 11, 1974.

98. Tanya Melich, *The Republican War Against Women: An Insider's Report from Behind the Lines* (New York: Bantam Books, 1996), 56, 63–68; Amy Shapiro, *Millicent Fenwick: Her Way* (New Brunswick, NJ: Rutgers University Press, 2003), 177; Joseph Lelyveld, "Normally Proper G.O.P. Women Come Out Fighting Over the E.R.A.," *New York Times*, August 17, 1976, www.nytimes.com/1976/08/17/archives/normally-proper-gop -women-come-out-fighting-over-era.html. The author was a member of the NWPC Republican Task Force.

99. ERAmerica papers, Library of Congress, Washington, DC.

100. Author interview with Sheila Greenwald, Executive Director of ERAmerica, June 17, 1988.

101. Kramer, "Road Warrior," 53.

102. Spruill, 118–19, 124–25.

103. Lepore, *Truths*, 660–61; Spruill, 207–08.

104. Spruill, 257.

105. Spruill, 265–67.

106. Spruill, 271–75.

107. "We Have a Lot to Win," NWPC convention program, July 1979, 3, author's records; Greenwald interview; James Lardner and Neil Henry, "Over 40,000 ERA Backers March on Hill," *Washington Post*, July 10, 1978, A1.

108. *Congressional Record*, House J.Res. 638, August 15, 1978; *Congressional Record*, Senate, October 4, 1978.

109. Livingston Taylor, "ERA Rescission Vetoed in Kentucky," *Washington Post*, March 21, 1978, http://www.washingtonpost.com/archives/politics/1978/03/21/era-recission -vetoed-in-kentucky/b6a72232-f433-40b5-b2be-ddd23914e204/; "Mariwyn D. Heath, ERAmerica Political Committee, BPW ERA Coordinator," c. 1979, ERAmerica file 47, Library of Congress Manuscript Collection, Washington, DC.

110. Jo Freeman, "What's in a Name? Does It Matter How the ERA Is Written?" https ://www.jofreeman.com/lawandpolicy/eraname.htm.

111. Matthews, vii–ix.

112. Author telephone interview with Alice Tetelman, of the NWPC Republican Task Force, February 5, 2021; Jo Freeman, "Republican Politics: Let's Make a Deal," July 30, 1980, https://www.jofreeman.com/conventions/RepubPol1980.htm; Melich, 126–40; Douglas Martin, "Mary D. Crisp, 83, Feminist GOP Leader, Dies," *New York Times*, April 17, 2007, https://www.nytimes.com/2007/04/17/17 crisp.html.

113. Martin, Schlafly obit; Meredith Blake, "How Accurate Is 'Mrs. America's' Portrayal of Republican Women? We Investigated," *Los Angeles Times*, May 6, 2020, https

://www.latimes.com/entertainment-arts/tv/story/2020-05-06/mrs-america-fact-check-jill-ruckelshaus-lottie-beth-hobbs.

114. Rebecca Morin, "Trump Honors 'True Patriot' Phyllis Schlafly at her Funeral," Politico, September 10, 2016, https://www.politico.com/story/2016/09/donald-trump-phyllis-schlafly-funeral-227994.

115. Brenda Feigen, *Not One of the Boys: Living Life as a Feminist* (New York: Alfred A. Knopf, 2000), 72; www.aclu.org/about/aclu-history; "Judge Dorothy Kenyon Is Dead; Champion of Social Reform, 83," *New York Times*, February 14, 1972, https://www.nytimes.com/1972/02/14/archives/judge-dorothy-kenyon-is-dead-champion-of-social-reform-83-legul.html.

116. *Hoyt v. Florida (1961)*, Oyez, www.oyez.org/cases/1961/31; Cushman, 30–33.

117. Linda K. Kerber, "Judge Ginsburg's Gift," *Washington Post*, August 1, 1993, https://www.washingtonpost.com/archive/opinions/1993/08/01/judge-ginsburgs-gift/036d8f58-fef8-4af8-8eae-772a8d9dd0a0/; *New York Times* Kenyon obit.

118. Jane Sherron De Hart, *Ruth Bader Ginsburg: A Life* (New York: Alfred A. Knopf, 2018), 133, 139, 144; "Tribute: The Legacy of Ruth Bader Ginsburg and WRP Staff," https://www.wclu.org/other/tribute-legacy-ruth-bader-ginsburg-and-wrp-staff.

119. *Reed v. Reed (1971)*, Oyez, www.oyez.org/cases/1971/70-4; Cushman, 41-44; Feigen, 13.

120. De Hart, 150–51.

121. *Frontiero v. Richardson* (1973), Oyez, www.oyez.org/cases/1972/71-1694; Kerber; De Hart, 154.

122. *Taylor v. Louisiana* (1975), Oyez, www.oyez.org/cases/1974/73-5744; Cushman, 34–36; Warren Weaver, Jr., "High Court Back's Women's Jury Rights," *New York Times*, January 22, 1975, https://www.nytimes.com/1975/01/22/archives/high-court-backs-womens-jury-rights-supreme-court-supports-the.html.

123. *Weinberger v. Wiesenfeld* (1975), Oyez, www.oyez.org/cases/1974/73-1892; Cushman, 70–74; Robert Barnes, "Justice Ginsburg Takes This Former Client's Wedding to Heart," *Washington Post*, May 26, 2014.

124. *Craig v. Boren* (1976), Oyez, www.oyez.org/cases/1976/75-628; Cushman, 49–57.

125. Melena Ryzik, "The Supreme Court's Ninja Warrior," *New York Times*, May 13, 2018, A26; Linda Greenhouse, "Lady Justice," review of *Ruth Bader Ginsburg: A Life*, by Jane Sherron De Hart, *New York Times Book Review*, November 4, 2018, 14; Neil A. Lewis, "Patricia Wald, Broke Barrier on DC Appeals Court, Dies at 90," *New York Times*, January 13, 2019, A21.

126. Kruse, 75; https://www.fbi.gov/news/stories/celebrating-women-special-agents; Harrison Smith, A1; Collins, 344; Sinn Kale, "The Legendary Women's Rights Activist Who Mailed Obama a Coat Hanger," VICE, May 18, 2016, www.vice.com/en/article/kb4myn/the-legendary-womens-rights-activist-who-mailed-obama-a-coat-hanger.

127. https://www.army.mil/article/47238/the_first_women_of_west_point; https://www.americanrhodes.org/assets/attachments; https://www.nobelprize.org/prizes/medicine/1977/yalow/facts; Reagan Upshaw, "Feminist Artist Judy Chicago in Full Bloom," *Washington Post*, July 18, 2021, E!2.

128. Gloria Steinem, "A Great Woman Who Was Everywoman," *New York Times*, July 21, 2001, A15, www.nytimes.com/2001/07/21/opinion/a-great-woman-who-was

-everywoman.html; Peggy McGlone, "Uneasy Pioneer: Exhibit Takes a New Look at Katharine Graham," *Washington Post*, May 9, 2021, E1.

129. Email from Ann Compton to author, March 24, 2020; Harrison Smith, "Cookie Roberts, 1943–2019: Pioneer, Champion of Women in Media," *Washington Post*, September 18, 2019, A1; Amy Argetsinger, "Phyllis George: Miss America Became a Trailblazing Sportcaster," *Washington Post*, May 18, 2020, B3; Emily Langer, "June Bacon-Bercey, "First Female TV Meteorologist in US," *Washington Post*, January 8, 2020, B6.

130. Kruse, 77; Howard Sachar, "Women Rabbis: History of the Struggle for Ordination," https://www.myjewishlearning.com/article/women-rabbis-a-history; Neil Genslinger, "Alison Cheek, Priest Despite Episcopal Ban on Women, Dies at 92," *New York Times*, September 13, 2019, A27; "Dr. Pauli Murray, Episcopal Priest," *New York Times*, July 4, 1985, A12, https://www.nytimes.com/1985/07/04/us/dr -pauli-murray-episcopal-priest.html; Collins, 75; Harrison Smith, "Barbara Harris: Anglican Communion's First Female Bishop Was a Champion for Civil Rights," *Washington Post*, March 17, 2020.

131. Susan Stewart, "Farrah Fawcett Dies of Cancer at 62," *New York Times*, June 25, 2009, https://www.nytimes.com/2009/06/26/arts/television/26fawcett.html; Nekesa Mumbi Moody, "Diahann Carroll, 84, Tony-Winning and Oscar-nominated Actress Won Acclaim as a Pathbreaker," *Washington Post*, October 5, 2019, C1; Maria Reinstein, "The Greatest TV Shows of All Time," *Parade*, September 22, 2019, 8; Kruse, 52, 76, 52.

132. Steve Wulf, "The Incredibly Quirky True Story of the 'Supersisters' Card Set," https://www.espn.com/espnw/news-commentary/article/12426260/the-incredibly -quirky-true-story-supersisters-card-set.

133. W. Bradford Wilcox, "The Evolution of Divorce," *National Affairs*, Fall 2009, https://nationalaffairs.com/publications/detail/the-evolution-of-divorce.

134. "History of the Surgeon General's Report on Smoking," https://www.cdc.gov /tobacco/data_statistics/sgr/index.htm.

135. Karen Harris, "'You've Come a Long Way, Baby': Virginia Slims and the Women's Lib Movement," *History Daily*, March 21, 2019, historydaily.org/youve-come-a-long -way-baby-virginia-slims-and-the-womens-lib-movement; C. R. Kennedy, "'You've Come a Long Way, Baby': What Every Mid-Century Modern Enthusiast Should Know and Love," A Vintage Chick, November 10, 2019, https://avintagechick .com/2019/11/10/youve-come-a-long-way-baby-what-every-mid-century-modern -enthusiast-should-know-and-love/.

136. Joseph E. Hower, "'You've Come a Long Way—Maybe': Working Women, Comparable Worth, and the Transformation of the American Labor Movement, 1964–1989," *Journal of American History* 107, no. 3 (December 2020): 658.

Chapter Seven: Factions & Firsts, 1980–1992

1.   "Fashion: Material World, 1980s," *American Style*, CNN, airdate January 20, 2019.

2.   Jill Lepore, *These Truths: A History of the United States* (New York: W.W. Norton & Co., 2018), 666; Tanya Melich, *The Republican War Against Women* (New York: Bantam Books, 1996), 35; Frances Fitzgerald, "The Triumphs of the New Right," *The New Review of Books* (November 19, 1981): 19–26.

3. "On This Day in History: June 30, 1982: Women's Political Habits Show Sharp Change," *New York Times*, June 30, 2017, A2.

4. https://ropercenter.cornell.edu/how-groups-voted-1980; "The Gender Gap: Voting Choices in Presidential Elections," Center for American Women in Politics [hereafter CAWP], https://cawp.rutgers.edu/facts/voters/gender_gap; Gail Collins, "The Unfinished Business of the Women's Vote," *New York Times*, August 2, 2020, SR2.

5. Melinda Henneberger, "After Years of Convincing, the DNC Acknowledges All Issues Are Women's Issues," *Washington Post*, September 30, 2014, A4; Paul Vitello, "Dotty Lynch, Pollster Who Saw the Gender Gap, Is Dead at 69," *New York Times*, August 11, 2014, https://www.nytimes.com/2014/08/12/us/dotty-lynch-pollster -who-saw-the-gender-gap-is-dead-at-69.html.

6. Author interview with Catherine East, April 1987.

7. Jennifer Steinhauer, "2019 Belongs to Shirley Chisholm," *New York Times*, July 7, 2019, SR2; Douglas Martin, "Geraldine A. Ferraro, Who Ended Men's Club of National Politics, Dies at 75," *New York Times*, March 28, 2011, A22; Monica Hesse, "Biden's Pick Will Have to Lug More Baggage," *Washington Post*, August 8, 2020, C1.

8. https://ropercenter.cornell.edu/how-groups-voted-1984; CAWP, "Gender Gap"; Emily R. Malcolm with Craig Unger, *When Women Win: Emily's List and the Rise of Women in American Politics* (Boston: Houghton Mifflin Harcourt, 2016), 48; Maureen Dowd, "No Wrist Corsages, Please," *New York Times*, August 9, 2020, SR9; Ruth Marcus, "Two Divergent Roads for America," *Washington Post*, August 13, 2020.

9. "Jesse Jackson," History Channel online, February 4, 2021, www.history.com/topics /black-history/jesse-jackson; Steve Kornacki, "Journey to Power: The History of Black Voters, 1976 to 2020," NBC News, July 29, 2019, https://www.nbcnews.com/politics /2020-elections/journey-to-power-history-black-voters-1976-2020-n1029581.

10. Jessica Bennett, "Overlooked No More: Before Kamala Harris, There Was Charlotta Bass," *New York Times*, September 4, 2020, https://www.nytimes.com/2020/09/04 /obituaries/charlotta-bass-vice-president-overlooked.html.

11. Amanda Hess, "Ferraro to Palin to Harris: What Has, and Hasn't Changed," *New York Times*, August 20, 2020, A14; Martin, "Ferraro" obit.

12. "History of Women of Color in U.S. Politics," Center for American Women and Politics, https://cawp.rutgers.edu/history-women-color-us-politics.

13. Malcolm, 24–25, 29–30.

14. Douglas Martin, "Harriet Woods, 79, Women's Political Leader, Dies," *New York Times*, February 10, 2007, https://www.nytimes.com/2007/02/10/obituaries /10woods.html; Malcolm, 36–37.

15. Malcolm, 40, 51.

16. Malcolm, 57–60.

17. Committee on House Administration of the U.S. House of Representatives, "Barbara Mikulski," *Women in Congress, 1917–2006* (Washington, DC: U.S. Government Printing Office, 2006), 876–77; Malcolm, 62.

18. Malcolm, 72–76, 81.

19. Martin, "Woods."

20. Malcolm, 85–86.

21. "Past Candidates and Election Information," Center for American Women and Politics, https://cawp.rutgers.edu/election-watch/past-candidate-and-election

-information; Malcolm, 88; "What's Wrong With This Picture?" The Fund For a
Feminist Majority newsletter, 1987.

22. "Nancy Pelosi," *Women in Congress,* 896–97; Jean Marbella, "Politics and Family:
Speaker Nancy Pelosi and Other Relatives Remember 'Young Tommy' D'Alesandro
at Baltimore Mass," *Baltimore Sun,* October 23, 2019, https://www.baltimoresun
.com/politics/bs-md-ci-dalesandro-funeral-20191023-73fcamwbjfdphghly
5youcwcfm-story.html.

23. "Former Texas Governor Ann Richards Dies at 73," *New York Times,* September 13,
2006, https://www.nytimes.com/2006/09/13/us/14wire-richards.html; Malcolm,
104–05; Deborah G. Felder, *A Century of Women: The Most Influential Events in
Twentieth Century Women's History* (Secaucus, NJ: Carol Publishing Co., 1999), 352.

24. Roberto Suro, "The 1990 Elections: Governor—Texas; Fierce Election for Governor
Is Narrowly Won by Richards," *New York Times,* November 7, 1990, https://www
.nytimes.com/1990/11/07/us/1990-elections-governor-texas-fierce-election-for
-governor-narrowly-won-richards.html.

25. Richards obituary.

26. Malcolm, 119–20; Catherine Decker, "Governor's Race Close at the Wire: Election:
The Feinstein-Wilson Battle Sets a Spending Record," *Los Angeles Times,* November 4,
1990, https://www.latimes.com/archives/la-xpm-1990-11-04-mn-5648-story.html.

27. Denise Lu and Kate Zernike, "The Women Who Could Shatter Glass Ceilings in
Governors' Races This Year," *New York Times,* August 6, 2018, https://www.nytimes
.com/interactive/2018/08/06/us/politics/women-governors-primaries.html.

28. Patricia Sullivan, "Gayle Peters Melich: Advocate for Women, Political Activist,"
Washington Post, July 28, 2005, B6.

29. Evan Thomas, *FIRST: Sandra Day O'Connor* (New York: Random House, 2019);
Linda R. Hirshman, *Sisters in Law: How Sandra Day O'Connor and Ruth Bader
Ginsburg Went to the Supreme Court and Changed the World* (New York: HarperCollins
Publishers, 2015).

30. Linda Greenhouse, "Senate Confirms Judge O'Connor; She Will Join High Court
Friday," *New York Times,* September 22, 1981, A1, www.nytimes.com/1981/09/22
/us/senate-confirms-judge-o-connor-she-will-join-high-court-friday.html.

31. Thomas, 151.

32. Michael Brice-Saddler, "William Proposed; Sandra Said No; They Reunited on the
Court," *Washington Post,* October 31, 2018, https://www.washingtonpost.com
/history/2018/10/31/william-proposed-sandra-said-no-they-reunited-supreme-court.

33. Thomas, 161.

34. John A. Farrell, "What Happened After Nixon Failed to Appoint a Woman to the
Supreme Court," June 21, 2020, https://www.politico.com/news/magazine/2020
/06/21/pat-nixon-woman-supreme-court-311408.

35. Felder, 351.

36. Clare Cushman, ed. *Supreme Court Decisions and Women's Rights: Milestones to
Equality,* 2nd ed. (Washington, DC: CQ Press, 2011), 215–23; *In re Lockwood*
(1894), supreme.justia.com/cases/federal.

37. Howard Cabiao, "Charlotte E. Ray (1850–1911)," BlackPast, November 16, 2010,
https://www.blackpast.org/african-american-history/ray-charlotte-e-1850-1911/;
James Hohmann, "The Legacy of Constance of Constance Baker Motley,"

Washington Post, February 3, 2022, A19; Jennifer Szalai, review of *Civil Eights Queen: Constance Baker Motley and the Struggle for Equality* by Tomiko Brown-Nagin, *New York Times*, January 27, 2022, C2.

38. Emily Bazelon, "Meet the First Women Who Approached the Bench," review of *Rebels at the Bar: The Fascinating Forgotten Stories of America's First Women Lawyers* by Jill Norgren, *Washington Post*, June 30, 2013, B1; "Lucy Terry Prince, Poet, Abolitionist, Orator," African American Registry, https://aaregistry.org/story/lucy -terry-prince-poet-abolitionist-orator-born/; Cushman, 226-30.

39. Cushman, 240–46; Emily Baumgaertner, "Justice Kavanaugh's Law Clerks Are All Women, A First for the Supreme Court," *New York Times*, October 9, 2018, https ://www.nytimes.com/2018/10/09/us/politics/kavanaugh-women-law-clerks.html; Mark Joseph Stern, "The Supreme Court is Terrible at Hiring Diverse Law Clerks, but Neil Gorsuch Is Surprisingly Good at It," *Slate*, April 16, 2018, https://slate .com/news-and-politics/2018/04/the-supreme-court-is-terrible-at-hiring-diverse -law-clerks-but-neil-gorsuch-is-surprisingly-good-at-it.html; Adam Liptak, "The Persistent Gender Gap in Who Argues Before the Supreme Court," *New York Times*, January 18, 2022, A13.

40. Taylor Telford, "She Waited 60 Years To Take This Flight," *Washington Post*, July 2, 2021, A18.

41. Meghan Bartels, "Jerrie Cobb, Record-Breaking Pilot and Advocate for Female Spaceflight, Has Died," Space.com, April 19, 2019, https://www.space.com/jerrie -cobb-died-mercury-13-women-in-space.html.

42. Katharine Q. Seelye, "Geraldyn M. Cobb, 88, Who Found a Glass Ceiling in Space, Dies," *New York Times*, April 19, 2019, https://www.nytimes.com/2019/04/19 /obituaries/geraldyn-m-cobb-dead.html; Margaret A. Weitekamp, *Right Stuff, Wrong Sex: America's First Women in Space Program* (Baltimore: Johns Hopkins University Press, 2004).

43. Felder, 298–99; Denise Grady, "Sally Ride: American Woman Who Shattered Space Ceiling," *New York Times*, July 23, 2012, https://www.nytimes.com/2012/07/24 /science/space/sally-ride-trailblazing-astronaut-dies-at-61.html; Monica Hesse, "Harris Knows Things No Vice President Has Ever Known," *Washington Post*, October 31, 2020, C1.

44. Grady, "Ride."

45. Felder, 300.

46. Denise Grady, "A Deadline Call on Posthumous Privacy," *New York Times*, July 23, 2017, A2.

47. Nola Taylor Tillman, "Mae Jemison: Astronaut Biography," Space.com, October 4, 2018, https://www.space.com/17169-mae-jemison-biography.html.

48. "NASA Astronaut Dr. Ellen Ochoa," Johnson Space Center, 2019, https://www .nasa.gov/centers/johnson/about/people/orgs/bios/ochoa.html; Karen Zraick, "Routine Repair Mission That Was Anything but Ordinary," *New York Times*, October 19, 2019, A11; Felder, 300; Christina Koch and Jessica Meir, "A Small Step and a Giant Leap: Spacesuits That Fit All of Us," *Washington Post*, November 12, 2019.

49. "Affirmative Action," https://hr.cornell.edu/our-workplace/diversity-inclusion /equal-opportunity-and-affirmative-action.

50. Kevin M. Kruse and Julian E. Zelizer, *Fault Lines: A History of the United States Since 1974* (New York: W.W. Norton & Co., 2019), 61.

51. *Regents of the University of California v. Bakke* (1978), Oyez, www.oyez.org/cases /1979/76-811.

52. Thomas, 259.

53. https://constitutioncenter.org/blog/how-martin-luther-king-jr-s-birthday-became -a-holiday-3.

54. Nikole Hannah-Jones, "It Was Never About Busing," *New York Times,* July 14, 2019, SR6.

55. Melich, 157–58.

56. Lepore, *These Truths,* 671.

57. W. Bradford Wilcox, "The Evolution of Divorce," *National Affairs,* 41 (Fall 2009), https://www.nationalaffairs.com/publications/detail/the-evolution-of-divorce #.XcP20PUk1BY; "Historical Divorce Rate Statistics," https://hr.cornell.edu /our-workplace/diversity-inclusion/equal-opportunity-and-affirmative-action.

58. Deirdre Bair, *Calling It Quits: Late Life Divorce and Starting Over* (New York: Random House, 2007), 176–77.

59. William H. Chafe, *The Road to Equality: American Women Since 1962: An Era of Liberation,* Vol. 10 of *The Young Oxford History of Women in the United States,* Nancy F. Cott, ed. (New York: Oxford University Press, 1994), 120, 127.

60. Lepore, *These Truths,* 688–89.

61. *Kirchberg v. Feenstra* (1981), Oyez, www.oyez.org/cases/1980/79-1388; Cushman, 83–84.

62. *County of Washington [OR] v. Gunther* (1981), Oyez, www.oyez.org/cases/1980/80 -429; Cushman, 146–47.

63. *Rostker v. Goldberg* (1981), Oyez, www.oyez.org/cases/1980/80-251; Cushman, 98–102.

64. *Board of Directors, Rotary International v. Rotary Club of Duarte* (1987), Oyez, www .oyez.org/cases/1986/86-421.

65. *Grove City College v. Bell* (1984), Oyez, www.oyez.org/cases/1983/82-792.

66. *Mississippi University for Women v. Hogan* (1982), Oyez, www.oyez.org/cases /1981/81-406; Cushman, 86–91.

67. Jonathan Martin, "An Era of Leaders Who Thought of Duty and Service First," *New York Times,* December 7, 2018, A17; Karen Tumulty, "George H. W. Bush, 41st President of the United States, Dies at 94," *Washington Post,* November 30, 2018, https://www.washingtonpost.com/local/obituaries/george-hw-bush-41st -president-of-the-united-states-dies-at-94/2018/11/30/42fa2ea2-61e2-11e8-99d2 -0d678ec08c2f_story.html.

68. Elaine Tyler May, *Homeward Bound: American Families in the Cold War Era,* rev. ed. (New York: Basic Books, 2017), 217; Steven A. Holmes, "House Backs Bush Veto of Family Leave Bill," *New York Times,* July 26, 1990, https://www.nytimes.com /1990/07/26/us/house-backs-bush-veto-of-family-leave-bill.html.

69. ADA.gov.

70. Nora McGreevy, "The ADA Was a Monumental Achievement 30 Years Ago, but the Fight for Equal Rights Continues," *Smithsonian,* June 24, 2020, https://www. smithsonianmag.com/history/history-30-years-since-signing-americans-disabilities -act-180975409/.

71. Cushman, 200–03.

72. Melich, 237.

73. Joseph Liu, "A History of Key Abortion Rulings of the US Supreme Court," Pew Research Center, January 16, 2013, https://www.pewforum.org/2013/01/16/a -history-of-key-abortion-rulings; Cushman, 204-05.

74. *Planned Parenthood of Southeastern Pennsylvania v. Casey* (1992), Oyez, www.oyez .org/cases/1991/91-744.

75. Cushman, 204–06.

76. https://www.nytimes.com/1999/03/05/us/justice-blackmun-author-of-abortion -right-dies.html.

77. Linda Greenhouse, "The Invisible Hand on Abortion," *New York Times,* July 21, 2019; *Hodgson v. Minnesota* (1990), Oyez, www.oyez.org/cases/1989/88-1125.

78. *Meritor Savings Bank, FSB v. Vinson* (1986), Oyez, www.oyez.org/cases/1985/84 -1979; Cushman, 155–58; DeNeen L. Brown, "Woman's Sexual Harassment Lawsuit Made Legal History Four Decades Ago," *Washington Post,* October 13, 2017, C1.

79. *Price Waterhouse v. Hopkins* (1989), Oyez, www.oyez.org/cases/1988/87-1167; Brooks Barnes, "Ann Hopkins, Who Struck an Early Blow to the Glass Ceiling, Dies at 74," *New York Times,* July 17, 2018, https://www.nytimes.com/2018/07/17/obituaries/ann -hopkins-winner-of-workplace-bias-fight-dies-at-74.html; Ann Braniger Hopkins, *So Ordered: Making Partner the Hard Way* (Amherst: University of Massachusetts Press, 1996).

80. Cushman, 127–33; Marisa Lati, "Gender Cases Recall Supreme Court Ruling 30 Years Ago," *Washington Post,* October 11, 2019, B4; Emily Bazelon, "Ann Hopkins," *New York Times Magazine,* December 30, 2018, 42.

81. Norman Kempster, "What Really Happened at Tailhook Convention: Scandal: The Pentagon Report Graphically Describes How Fraternity-style Hi-jinks Turned into a Hall of Horrors," *Los Angeles Times,* April 24, 1993, https://www.latimes.com /archives/la-xpm-1993-04-24-mn-26672-story.html; Michael Winerip, "Revisiting the Military's Tailhook Scandal," *New York Times,* May 13, 2013, https://www.ny times.com/2013/05/13/booming/revisiting-the-militarys-tailhook-scandal-video.html.

82. Timothy M. Phelps and Helen Winternitz, *Capitol Games: Clarence Thomas, Anita Hill, and the Story of a Supreme Court Nomination* (New York: Hyperion, 1992), 13–14, 33–35.

83. Jane Mayer and Jill Abramson, *Strange Justice: The Selling of Clarence Thomas* (Boston: Houghton Mifflin Co., 1994), 220–23, 231.

84. Mayer, 248.

85. Malcolm, 142; Mayer, 251.

86. Mayer, 261.

87. Nell Irvin Painter, "Hill, Thomas, and the Use of Racial Stereotype," in *Race-ing Justice, En-gendering Power: Essays on Anita Hill, Clarence Thomas, and the Construction of Social Reality,* ed. Toni Morrison (New York: Pantheon Books, 1992), 209–14; Martha S. Jones, *Vanguard: How Black Women Broke Barriers, Won the Votes, and Insisted on Equality for All* (New York: Basic Books, 2020), 268.

88. Mayer, 269; Malcolm, 135.

89. Mayer, 345–46. Hill recalled the number at 70%: Jessica Bennett, "How History Changed Anita Hill," *New York Times,* June 17, 2019, https://www.nytimes.com /2019/06/17/us/anita-hill-women-power.html.

90. Mayer, 278–79.
91. Mayer, 288, 277, 290.
92. Mayer, 292–93.
93. Mayer, 298–99.
94. Mayer, 319–20, 337–44.
95. Mayer, 346.
96. Jo Thomas, "Anita Hill Plans to Leave Teaching Post in Oklahoma," *New York Times,* November 13, 1996, https://www.nytimes.com/1996/11/13/us/anita-hill-plans-to-leave-teaching-post-in-oklahoma.html.
97. Susan Chira, "Hill Reflects: 'Clearly the Tide Has Not Turned,'" *New York Times,* December 7, 2018, A20; Dan Zak, "The Voice Beside the Robe," *Washington Post,* December 31, 20018, C1.
98. R. W. Apple Jr., "The Thomas Confirmation," www.nytimes.com/1991/10/16/us/thomas-confirmation-senate-confirms-thomas-52-48-ending-week-bitter-battle-time.html; Malcolm, 141-43; Mayer, 348. Justice Brett Kavanaugh was confirmed 50-48 on October 6, 2017.
99. Mayer, 349–50.
100. Evan Thomas, 274–75.
101. Mayer, 353–54.
102. Mayer, 337; Matt Stevens, "From Reluctant Regret to Taking 'Responsibility,'" *New York Times,* May 1, 2019; Sheryl Gay Stolberg and Carl Hulse, "Biden's 'Regret" For Hill's Pain Fails to Soothe," *New York Times,* April 26,2019, A1.
103. Lydia Chavez, "Women's Movement, Its Ideals Accepted, Faces Subtler Issues," *New York Times,* July 17, 1987, A10; Susan Blake, "Betty Friedan's Second Stage: Marching Ahead or Going Astray," review of *The Second Sex,* by Betty Freidan, *Second Century Radcliffe News* (April 1982).
104. Phil Gailey, "Whither the Women's Movement?" *New York Times,* December 13, 1985.
105. Barbara Vobejda, "At 25, NOW Still Defining Feminism, Deflecting Critics," *Washington Post,* January 11, 1992, A3; Patricia Ireland, "The State of NOW," *Ms.,* July/August 1992, 24–27.
106. Rebecca Traister, "The End of the Hairy Joyless Feminist," *Washington Post,* May 13, 2012.
107. Richard Aldous, "The Dividing Line," review of *The Age of Entitlement* by Christopher Caldwell, *Wall Street Journal,* May 23–24, 2020, C9.
108. Carol F. Steinbach, "Women's Movement II," *National Journal,* August 29, 1987, 2145–49.
109. Malcolm, 140.
110. Malcolm, 146–47, 153–57.
111. "Women Candidates for Congress 1974–2018," Center for American Women and Politics, https://cawp.rutgers.edu/facts/levels-office/congress/history-women-us-congress.
112. Malcolm, 146, 172.
113. "On This Day in History: July 29, 1992: Black Woman's Senate Race Is Acquiring a Celebrity Aura," *New York Times,* July 29, 2017, A2
114. "Patti Murray," *Women in Congress,* 884–85; Malcolm, 169.
115. Malcolm, 123.

116.   https://cawp.rutgers.edu/facts.

117.   Theodore R. Johnson, "The Loneliness of the Black Senator," *New York Times Magazine,* January 24, 1921, 42–3.

118.   Malcolm, 171.

119.   Melich, 188, 202; "Candace Straight," June 13, 2021, https://www.insidernj.com /candace-straight-new-jersey-trailblazing-advocate-women-died.

120.   "The Decade of Women, 1992–2002," *Women in Congress,* 553–57.

121.   Gail Collins, "The Senate Bathroom Angle," *New York Times,* December 22, 2016, A27.

122.   Kruse, 201.

123.   "The Gender Gap: Three Decades Old, as Wide as Ever," Pew Research Center, March 29, 2012, https://www.people-press.org/2012/03/29/the-gender-gap-three -decade.

124.   Kruse, 199; Lepore, *Truths,* 691.

125.   Whitney Straub, review of *A War for the Soul of America: A History of the Culture Wars* by Andrew Hartman, *Journal of American History* (March 2016): 1271–72.

126.   Lepore, *These Truths,* 696–97; Amanda Fitzsimons, "She Doesn't Believe All Women," *The Atlantic,* October 2019, 16–19.

127.   Hillary Rodham Clinton, *Living History* (New York: Simon & Schuster, 2003), 31–33, 36, 38–39.

128.   Clinton, 40–41.

129.   Clinton, 42–3, 69.

130.   Clinton, 76ff.

131.   Gourley, 115; Clinton, 77.

132.   "Fashion: Material World, 1980s," *American Style,* CNN, airdate January 20, 2019.

133.   Nancy Gibbs, "Who Am I to You?" *Time,* October 26, 2009, 64; David W. Dunlap, "When 'Mrs.' Became 'Ms.,'" *New York Times,* August 21, 2017, A2.

134.   Bonnie J. Morris and D-M Withers, *The Feminist Revolution* (Washington, DC: Smithsonian Books, 2018), 107–11; Roberta Smith, "Right Where She Belongs,' *New York Times,* April 2, 2021, C1.

135.   Emily Langer, "Wilhelmina Cole Holladay, Champion of Women in the Arts, Dies at 98," *Washington Post,* March 8, 2021, www.washingtonpost.com/local /obituaries/wilhelmina-cole-holladay-dead/2021/03/08/cc2c988c-8010-11eb-ac37 -4383f7709abe_story.html.

136.   Isis Davis-Marks, "Sweeping Survey Unites Works of 100 Women Artists of the Past Century," *Smithsonian,* April 16, 2021, www.smithsonianmag.com/smart -news/exhibitionn-bostons-museum-fine-arts-finally-gives-women-artists-their-due -180977515/.

137.   Claire Cain Miller, "'A Cabinet of Firsts': Momentous Yet Fragile," *New York Times,* January 22, 2021, A12.

Chapter Eight: Isolation & Intersectionality, 1993–2008

1.   Lisa Levenstein, *They Didn't See Us Coming: The Hidden History of Feminism in the Nineties* (New York: Basic Books, 2020), 15.

2.   Jane Coaston, "The Intersectionality Wars," *Vox,* May 28, 2019, www.vox.com/the -highlight/2019/5/20/185428343/intersectionality-conservatism-law-race-gender -discrimination.

3. Bill McAllister, "Suffrage Design Splits the Vote," *Washington Post,* August 4, 1995, http://www.washingtonpost.com/archive/lifestyle/1995/08/04/suffrage-design -splits-the-vote/4563e29c-ee34-4e75-bec4-ef94374ce3f5/.

4. Lorraine Boissoneault, "The Suffragist Statue Trapped in a Broom Closet for 75 Years," *Smithsonian,* May 12, 2017, https://www.smithsonianmag.com/history /suffragist-statue-trapped-broom-closet-75-years-180963274/; Kevin Merida, "A Vote Against Suffrage Statue," *Washington Post*, April 14, 1997, www.washington post.com/archive/politics/1997/04/14/a-vote-against-suffrage-statue/00881928 -0cbb-4723-a145-81f5771f4738/; Karen Staser, "From the Crypt to the Capitol Rotunda," *NMWH Magazine*, vol 37, April 2021, 12-15; Jordan Pilant, "The Politics of Representation: The Fight for the Smithsonian Women's History Museum," *The Politic*, May 1, 2020, https://thepolitic.org/the-politics-of-representation-the-fight -for-the-smithsonian-womens-history-museum.

5. Clinton, *My Life*, 462–63. The author was in the audience and among a group of historians invited to the White House to help draft the speech.

6. Jennie Yabroff, "From Barricades to Blogs," *Newsweek*, October 22, 2007, 44.

7. Alice Hines, "Bitch Magazine Turns Twenty," *New Yorker*, May 23, 2016, www .newyorker.com/culture/culture-desk/bitch-magazine-turns-twenty.

8. Madeline Albright, *Madame Secretary: A Memoir* (New York: HarperCollins, 2003); Madeline Albright, *Read My Pins: Stories from a Diplomat's Jewel Box* (New York: HarperCollins, 2009); Megan Gambino, "Madeline Albright on her Life in Pins," *Smithsonian,* June 2010, https://www.smithsonianmag.com/arts-culture/madeline -albright-on-her-life-in-pins-149191/.

9. Carl Hulse, "Janet Reno, First Woman to Serve as US Attorney General, Dies at 78," *New York Times,* November 7, 2016, https://www.nytimes.com/2016/11/08/us /janet-reno-dead.html.

10. Kevin M. Kruse and Julian E. Zelizer, *Fault Lines: A History of the United States Since 1974* (New York: W.W. Norton & Co., 2019), 702.

11. Richard L. Berke, "The Supreme Court: The Overview: Clinton Names Ruth Ginsburg, Advocate for Women, to Court," *New York Times*, June 15, 1993, https ://www.nytimes.com/1993/06/15/us/supreme-court-overview-clinton-names-ruth -ginsburg-advocate-for-women-court.html.

12. Rich Tenorio, "The 8 Jewish Justices Who Made the US Supreme Court Jump," July 31, 2017, https://www.timesofisrael.com/the-8-jewish-justices-who-made -the-us-supreme-court-jump/.

13. Ruth Bader Ginsburg, "A Look At Roe v. Wade v. Ginsburg: The Case Against the Case," *Washington Post*, June 20, 1993, quoting RBG lecture at NYU law school, www.washingtonpost.com/archive/opinions/1993/06/20/a-look-at-roe-v-wade-v -ginsburg-the-case-against-the-case/41596c4e-c489-4809-98ca-85dc39718932/.

14. Linda Greenhouse, "Ruth Bader Ginsburg, Supreme Court's Feminist Icon, Is Dead at 87," *New York Times,* September 18, 2020, A1.

15. Linda Greenhouse, "Senate, 96-3, Easily Confirms Judge Ginsburg as a Justice," *New York Times*, August 4, 1993, *New York Times,* https://www.nytimes.com /1993/08/04/us/senate-96-3-easily-affirms-judge-ginsburg-as-a-justice.html; Michelle Goldberg, "No More Deception on Abortion," *New York Times,* September 22, 2020, A23.

16.   Irin Carmon and Shana Knizhnik, *Notorious RBG: The Life and Times of Ruth Bader Ginsburg* (New York: Dey Street Books, 2015).

17.   Linda R. Hirshman, *Sisters in Law: How Sandra Day O'Connor and Ruth Bader Ginsburg Went to the Supreme Court and Changed the World* (New York: HarperCollins, 2016), 202-03; Richard Wolf, "Justice Ruth Bader Ginsburg's Top Opinions and Dissents, from VMI to Voting Right Act," *USA Today,* September 18, 2020, www.usatoday.com/story/news/politics/2020/09/18/i-dissent-justice-ruth -bader-ginsburgs-most-memorable-opinions/2661426002/.

18.   *Harris v. Forklift Systems* (1993), Oyez, www.oyez.org/cases/1993/92-1168.

19.   *J.E.B. v. Alabama ex rel T.B.* (1994), Oyez, www.oyez.org/cases/1993/92-1239.

20.   Megan A. Sholar, "The History of Family Leave Policies in the United States," *The American Historian,* November 2016, 41–45; US Department of Labor, "US Department of Labor Clarifies FMLA Definition of 'Son and Daughter,'" http ://www.dol.gov/newsroom/releases/whd/whd20100622#:~:text=WASHINGTON %20—%20The%20U.S.%20Department%20of,the%20legal%20or%20biological %20relationship.

21.   Claire Cain Miller and Liz Alderman, "The Flexibility Gap," *New York Times,* December 14, 2014, BU1.

22.   Briana Bierschbach, "This Woman Fought To End Minnesota's 'Marital Rape' Exception, and Won," *Morning Edition,* May 4, 2019.

23.   "History of the Violence Against Women Act," Legal Momentum, https://www .legalmomentum.org/history-vawa.

24.   Jill Lepore, *These Truths: A History of the United States* (New York: W.W. Norton & Co., 2018), 699–70.

25.   Carl Hulse, "What It Took to Pass Assault Weapons Ban, and What It Cost," *New York Times,* September 8, 2019, A21.

26.   *United States v. Morrison* (2000), Oyez, www.oyez.org/cases/1999/99-5.

27.   "Violence Against Women Act," National Network to End Domestic Violence, https://nnedv.org/content/violence-against-women-act; Jay Willis, "Why Can't the Senate Pass the Violence Against Women Act?" *GQ,* December 13, 2019, www .gq.com/story/senate-violence-against-women-act.

28.   Alejandro de la Garza, "'Don't Ask, Don't Tell,' Was a Complicated Turning Point for Gay Rights," *Time,* July 19, 2018," https://time.com/5339634/dont-ask-dont-tell -25-year-anniversary/.

29.   "The First Major Same-Sex Marriage Case: Baehr v. Lewin (Miike)," https://www .findlaw.com/family/marriage/1993-the-hawaii-case-of-baehr-v-lewin.html.

30.   https://www.lambdalegal.org/in-court/cases/baehr-v-miike.

31.   Richard Socarides, "Why Bill Clinton Signed the Defense of Marriage Act," *The New Yorker,* March 8, 2013, https://www.newyorker.com/news/news-desk /why-bill-clinton-signed-the-defense-of-marriage-act.

32.   E. J. Graff, "Inside the Slow, Strategic Battle for Marriage Equality," review of *Awakening: How Gays and Lesbians Brought Marriage Equality to America* by Nathaniel Frank Belknap, *Washington Post,* July 16, 2017, B6.

33.   *Romer v. Evans* (1996), Oyez, www.oyez.org/cases/1995/94-1039.

34.   "New Details Emerge in Matthew Shepard Murder," ABC News, January 6, 2004, https://abcnews.go.com/2020/story?id=277685.

35. Lawrence Van Gelder, "Celebrations as a TV Lesbian Goes Prime Time," *New York Times*, May 1, 1997, https://www.nytimes.com/time/magazine/article /0,9171,137532,00.html; Bruce Handy, "He Called Me Ellen Degenerate?" *Time*, June 24, 2001, content.time.com/time/magazine/article/0,9171,137532,00.html.

36. "Women in Combat Zones," https://www.history.com/news/u-s-military-lifts-ban -on-women-in-combat.

37. Eileen Patten and Kim Parker, "A Snapshot of Active Duty Women," December 22, 2011, https://www.pewresearch.org/social-trends/2011/12/22/a-snapshot-of-active -duty-women/.

38. Russell L. Riley, "Bill Clinton: Domestic Affairs," UVA Miller Center, https ://millercenter.org/president/clinton/domestic-affairs; Kruze, 211.

39. Mary Pilon, "How Bill Clinton's Welfare Reform Changed America," History Channel online, https://www.history.com/news/clinton-1990s-welfare -reform-facts.

40. Kathryn Edin and H. Luke Shaefer, "20 Years Since Welfare 'Reform,'" *The Atlantic*, August 22, 2016, https://www.theatlantic.com/business/archive/2016/08/20-years -welfare-reform/496730/; Barbara Vobejda and Judith Havemann, "2 HHS Officials Quit Over Welfare," *Washington Post*, September 12, 1996, https://www .washingtonpost.com/wp-srv/national/longterm/welfare/quit.htm.

41. Lepore, *These Truths*, 706–12; Hayley Miller, "Hillary Clinton Says Bill Clinton's Affair With Monica Lewinsky Was Not an Abuse of Power," *Huffington Post*, October 14, 2018, https://www.huffpost.com/entry/hillary-clinton-monica -lewinsky-affair_n_5bc39984e4b0bd9ed55b4b82; Jodi Eichler-Levine, "Sex, Politics and American Christians," review of *Moral Combat: How Sex Divided American Christians and Fractured American Politics* by R. Marie Griffith, *Washington Post*, January 28, 2018, B8; Monica Lewinsky, "Emerging from 'The House of Gaslight' in the Age of #MeToo," *Vanity Fair*, February 25, 2018, https://www .vanityfair.com/news/2018/02/monica-lewinsky-in-the-age-of-metoo#.

42. Dan Balz, "Impeachment Drama Isn't Going to Fade in 2020 Race," *Washington Post*, December 8, 2019, A2.

43. Frank Newport, "Presidential Job Approval: Bill Clinton's High Ratings in the Midst of Crisis, 1998," *Gallup*, June 4, 1999, https://news.gallup.com/poll/4609 /presidential-job-approval-bill-clintons-high-ratings-midst.aspx.

44. Guy Gugliotta and Juliet Eilperin, "Gingrich Steps Down in Face of Rebellion," *Washington Post*, November 7, 1998, https://www.washingtonpost.com/wp-srv /politics/govt/leadership/stories/gingrich110798.htm; Alison Mitchell, "The Speaker Steps Down: The Career: The Fall of Gingrich, an Irony in an Odd Year," *New York Times*, November 7, 1998, https://www.nytimes.com /1998/11/07/us/the-speaker-steps-down-the-career-the-fall-of-gingrich-an -irony-in-an-odd-year.html.

45. Adam Liptak, "Trump's Vow vs. the Constitution," *New York Times*, November 26, 2019; Peter Baker and Helen Dewar, "The Senate Acquits President Clinton," *Washington Post*, February 13, 1999, https://www.washingtonpost.com/politics /clinton-impeachment/senate-acquits-president-clinton/.

46. Kruse, 135–36, 138–40; "June 1, 1980, CNN Launches," History Channel online, https://www.history.com/this-day-in-history/cnn-launches.

47.   Dylan Matthews, "Everything You Need to Know About the Fairness Doctrine,"
        Washington Post, August 23, 2011, https://www.washingtonpost.com/blogs/ezra
        -klein/post/everything-you-need-to-know-about-the-fairness-doctrine-in-one-post
        /2011/08/23/glQAN8CXZJ_blog.html.

48.   Lepore, *These Truths*, 703-04.

49.   Matt McKinney, "Mike Pence Radio Show from the 1990s," WRTV, July 20, 2016,
        https://www.wrtv.com/news/local-news/watch-mike-pences-radio-show-from-the-90s.

50.   Katharine Q. Seelye, "Republicans Get a Pep Talk from Rush Limbaugh," *New York
        Times*, December 12, 1994, https://www.nytimes.com/1994/12/12/us/republicans
        -get-a-pep-talk-from-rush-limbaugh.html; Mayer, *Strange Justice*, 357.

51.   Catherine Gourley, *Ms. And the Material Girl: Perceptions of Women from the 1970s to
        the 1990s*, vol. 5 of *Images and Issues of Women in the Twentieth Century* (Minneapolis,
        MN: Twenty-First Century Books, 2008), 115.

52.   Hillary Rodham Clinton, *Living History* (New York: Simon & Schuster, 2003),
        305-06; "World Conferences on Women," UN Women, https://www.unwomen.org
        /how-we-work/intergovernmental-support.

53.   Lisa Levenstein, "A Social Movement for a Global Age: US Feminism and the
        Beijing Women's Conference of 1995," *Journal of American History* 105, no. 2
        (September 2018): 339.

54.   Sumi Cho, Kimberle Williams Crenshaw and Leslie McCall, "Toward Field of
        Intersectionality Studies: Theory, Applications, and Praxis," *Signs*, 38 (Summer
        2013): 786-810; Levenstein, 339, 342, 364, 360.

55.   "Mona Van Duyn," Poetry Foundation, https://www.poetryfoundation.org/poets
        /mona-van-duyn; "Rita Dove," Poetry Foundation, https://www.poetryfoundation
        .org/poets/rita-dove; Margalit Fox, "Toni Morrison, 1931–2019: A Beloved Novelist
        of Black Identity in America," *New York Times*, August 7, 2019, A1.

56.   Elizabeth Weil, "Did Venus Williams Ever Get Her Due?" *New York Times
        Magazine*, August 25, 2019, 43ff.

57.   Amei Wallach, "Fabric of Their Lives," *Smithsonian Magazine*, October 2006, www
        .smithsonianmag.com/arts-culture/an-interview-with-amei-wallach-author-of-fabric
        -of-their-lives-134194216/.

58.   Ann Killion, "'Summer of the Women:' How 1996 Olympics Changes Sports
        Forever," *San Francisco Chronicle*, July 29, 2016, https://www.sfchronicle.com/news
        /article/Summer-of-the-Women-How-1996-Olympics-8636042.php; Allison
        Yarrow, "Nancy Kerrigan Deserves a Moment of Redemption Too," *Washington Post*,
        January 17, 2018, C1.

59.   Kristin Tice Studeman, "See Cool Vintage Nike Women's Ads Through the Ages,"
        The Cut, April 2015, https://www.thecut.com/2015/04/see-vintage-nike-womens
        -ads-through-the-ages.html.

60.   Jere Longman, "The Sports Bra Seen Round the World Has New Meaning 20 Years
        Later," *New York Times*, July 5, 2019, https://nytimes.com/2019/07/05/sports/soccer
        /brandi-chastain-womens-world-cup-image.html; Brandi Chastain, *It's Not About
        the Bra: Play Hard, Play Fair and Put the Fun Back Into Competitive Sports* (New York:
        William Morrow, 2004).

61.   "Mia Hamm, Athlete," Biograhpy.com, April 27, 2017, https://www.biography.com
        /athlete/mia-hamm.

62.   Gourley, 86.

63.   Emily Nussbaum, "Difficult Women," *New Yorker,* July 22, 2013, https://www
      .newyorker.com/magazine/2013/07/29/difficult-women.

64.   Alison Glock, "She Likes to Watch," *New York Times,* February 6, 2005, https://www
      .nytimes.com/2005/02/06/arts/television/she-likes-to-watch.html.

65.   "How Schools Shortchange Girls," AAUW Report, https://wcwonline.org/images
      /pdf/how-schools-shortchange-girls-executive_summary.pdf; Felder, *Century,* 315–18.

66.   Carol Gilligan, *In a Different Voice: Psychological Theory and Women's Development*
      (Cambridge: Harvard University Press, 1982); Mary Pipher, *Reviving Ophelia:*
      Saving the Selves of Adolescent Girls (New York: G.P. Putnam's Sons, 1994); Amisha
      Padnani, "Leslie W. Wolfe, 74, a Feminist with a Multiethnic Approach," *New York*
      Times, December 8, 2017.

67.   "Gender Equality in Education Act of 1993," https://www.congress.gov/bill/103rd
      -congress/house-bill/1793?s=1&r=9.

68.   Deanna Pan, "Shannon Faulkner Says, 'I Do Consider Myself a Citadel Alumni' During
      Historic Return," *Charleston Post and Courier,* March 3, 2018, https://www.postand
      courier.com/news/shannon-faulkner-says-i-do-consider-myself-a-citadel-alumni-during
      -her-historic-return/article_2a51c556-1e47-11e8-beea-4f0b27568b0c.html.

69.   *US v. Virginia* (1996), Oyez, www.oyez.org/cases/1995/94-1941.

70.   Clare Cushman, ed., *Supreme Court Decisions and Women's Rights: Milestones to Equality.*
      2nd ed. (Washington, DC: CQ Press, 2011), 57–63; Laura Vozzella, "Justice Ginsburg
      Visits VMI Campus She Helped Transform," *Washington Post,* February 2, 2017, B1.
      Caitlin Byrd, "Nancy Mace Pushes Back After Shannon Faulkner Claims To Be
      Citadel Grad: 'She Doesn't Wear The Ring,'" *Charleston Post and Courier,* March 5,
      2018, https://www.postandcourier.com/politics/nancy-mace-pushes-back-after
      -shannon-faulkner-claims-to-be-citadel-grad-she-doesnt-wear/article_5f9196a8
      -2093-11e8-8172-c3d50811c29c.html; Richard Fausset, "Three Black Belts and 70
      Push-Ups," *New York Times,* May 4, 2019.

71.   Alice Kessler-Harris, *Women Have Always Worked: A Concise History,* 2nd ed. (Urbana:
      University of Illinois Press, 2018).

72.   E. J. Graff, "The Working Mommy Trap," The Longview Institute, http://www
      .longviewinstitute.org/research/graff/workingmomtrap/view/index.html; Nell
      Henderson, "Whither the Women?" *Washington Post,* July 7, 2006, http://www
      .washingtonpost.com/archive/business/2006/07/07/whither-the-women-span-class
      bankheadafter-decades-on-rise-labor-participation-rate-is-downspan/7758f961-8381
      -4a1e-b1ad-586d9ca49f18/.

73.   Joanne Lipman, "The Mismeasure of Woman," *New York Times,* October 24, 2009,
      http://www.nytimes.com/2009/10/24/opinion/24lipman.html.

74.   "Women's Earnings: The Pay Gap (Quick Take)," July 31, 2019, https://www
      .catalyst.org/research/womens-earnings-the-pay-gap/.

75.   Julie Creswell, "How Suite It Isn't: A Dearth of Female Bosses," *New York Times,*
      December 17, 2006, http://www.nytimes.com/2006/12/17/business/yourmoney
      /17csuite.html; Lisa Belkin, "The Feminine Critique," *New York Times,* November 1,
      2007, http://www.nytimes.com/2007/11/01/fashion/01WORK.html.

76.   Lisa Belkin, "The Opt-Out Revolution," *New York Times Magazine,* October 26,
      2003, https://www.nytimes.com/2003/10/26/magazine/the-opt-out-revolution .html;

E. J. Graff, "The Opt-Out Myth," *Columbia Journalism Review*, March/April 2007, https://archives.cjr.org/essay/the_optout_myth.php; Linda Hirshman, *Get to Work: A Manifesto for Women of the World* (New York: Viking, 2006); Leslie Morgan Steiner, ed., *Mommy Wars: Stay-at-Home and Career Moms Face Off on Their Choices, Their Lives, Their Families* (New York: Random House, 2006).

77.   Tracy Thompson, "A War Inside Your Head," *Washington Post*, February 15, 1998, https://www.washingtonpost.com/archive/lifestyle/magazine/1998/02/15/a-war -inside-your-head/6217ab6d-ca19-4cd0-b3d2-d4e2f1aa70aa/; Jennie Yabroff, "From Barricades to Blogs," *Newsweek*, October 22, 2007, 44.

78.   Patricia Cohen, "Today, Some Feminists Hate the Word 'Choice,'" *New York Times*, January 15, 2006.

79.   Bryce Covert, "Working Women Peaked Two Decades Ago," *New York Times*, September 2, 2019.

80.   Daniel E. Slotnik, "Overlooked No More: Dorothy Bolden, Who Started a Movement for Domestic Workers," *New York Times*, February 20, 2019, https ://www.nytimes.com/2019/02/20/obituaries/dorothy-bolden-overlooked.html.

81.   Lauren Hilgers, "Out of the Shadows," *New York Times Magazine*, February 21, 2019, https://longform.org/posts/out-of-the-shadows.

82.   Gloria Steinem, "Ai-jen Poo, Labor Organizer," *Time*, April 18, 2012.

83.   Lepore, *These Truths*, 673–74; author conversation with Doris Meissner, former head of the INS, now senior policy advisor, Migration Policy Institute, Washington, DC, November 30, 2019.

84.   Eileen Boris and Annelise Orleck, "Feminism and The Labor Movement: A Century of Collaboration and Conflict," New Labor Forum, January 2011, https ://newlaborforum.cuny.edu/2011/01/03/feminism-and-the-labor-movement.

85.   Clive Thompson, "The First Computers Were Human," *Smithsonian Magazine*, June 2019, 12, 14; Dava Sobel, *The Glass Universe: How the Ladies of the Harvard Observatory Took the Measure of the Stars* (New York: Viking, 2017).

86.   Thompson, *Smithsonian*, 83.

87.   Susan Cominus, "Sidelined," *Smithsonian Magazine*, October 2019, 46–47.

88.   Jessica Valenti, *Full Frontal Feminism: A Young Woman's Guide to Why Feminism Matters*, 2nd ed. (Berkeley, CA: Seal Press, 2014), 223–24.

89.   Kruse, 239–42.

90.   *Bush v. Gore* (2000), Oyez, www.oyez.org/cases/2000/00-949.

91.   "4/04/2001: Journalists review recount," UVA Miller Center, https://millercenter.org /president/george-w-bush/key-events; Gail Collins, "The Unfinished Business of the Women's Vote," *New York Times*, August 2, 2020, SR2.

92.   "Women Appointed to Presidential Cabinets," https://cawp.rutgers.edu/sites/default /files/resources/womenapptdtoprescabinets.pdf.

93.   "Condoleezza Rice (1954–)," Biography.com, January 19, 2018, https://www.biography .com/political-figure/condoleezza-rice.

94.   "Elaine L. Chao," https://www.biography.com/political-figure/elaine-l-chao.

95.   Ron Fournier, "Chavez Withdraws As Labor Nominee," Associated Press, January 9, 2001, https://apnews.com/article/9208b09923d88681ad766feb26fa77b6.

96.   "Laura Welch Bush, The White House," https://www.whitehouse.gov/about-the -white-house/first-families/laura-welch-bush.

97.   Joseph Liu, "A History of Key Abortion Rulings of the US Supreme Court," Pew
      Forum, January 16, 2013, https://www.pewforum.org/2013/01/16/a-history
      -of-key-abortion-rulings; Julie Rovner, "'Partial Birth Abortion': Separating Fact
      from Spin," *NPR*, February 21, 2006, www.npr.org/2006/02/21/5168163
      /partial-birth-abortion-separating-fact-from-spin.

98.   Abigail Abrams, "'We Are Grabbing Our Own Microphones': How Advocates of
      Reproductive Justice Stepped into the Spotlight," *Time*, November 21, 2019, https
      ://time.com/5735432/reproductive-justice-groups.

99.   Cameron W. Barr and Elizabeth Williamson, "Women's Rally Draws Vast Crowd,"
      Washington Post, April 26, 2004, A1.

100. "A History of Key Abortion Rulings of the US Supreme Court," https://www
      .pewforum.org/2013/01/16/a-history-of-key-abortion-rulings.

101. *Castle Rock v. Gonzales* (2005), Oyez, www.oyez.org/cases/2004/04-278.

102. *Ledbetter v. Goodyear Tire and Rubber Company* (2007), Oyez, www.oyez.org/cases
      /2006/05-1074.

103. "History of Women in Congress," https://cawp.rutgers.edu/facts/levels-office
      /congress/history-women-us-congress.

104. "Colorado Lawmaker Continues Tradition of Bolo Ties in Capitol," https://www
      .indianz.com/News/2015/017151.asp; Ryan Teague Beckwith, "How Barb Mikulski
      Paved the Way for Hillary Clinton's Pantsuits," *Time*, March 2, 2015, https://time
      .com/3728510/barb-mikulski-hillary-clinton-pantsuits/; Kent Cooper, "The Long and
      Short of Capitol Style," *Roll Call*, June 9, 2005, https://www.rollcall.com/news/-9592-1
      .html; Robin Givhan, "Moseley Braun: Lady in Red," *Chicago Tribune*, January 21, 2004,
      http://www.chicagotribune.com/news/ct-xpm-2004-01-21-0401210033-story.html.

105. Sheryl Gay Stolberg, "'It's About Time' A Baby Comes to the Senate Floor," *New
      York Times*, April 19, 2018, https://www.nytimes.com/2018/04/19/us/politics/baby
      -duckworth-senate-floor.html.

106. Yabroff, *Newsweek*, October 22, 2007.

107. Nancy Pelosi, "Remarks Upon Becoming Speaker of the House, January 4, 2007,"
      Iowa State University Archives of Women's Political Communication, https://awpc
      .cattcenter.iastate.edu/2017/03/21/remarks-upon-becoming-speaker. Author's note:
      The Archive of Women's Political Communication is part of the Carrie Chapman
      Catt Center at her alma mater.

108. William Branigin, "Pelosi Sworn In as First Woman Speaker of the House,"
      Washington Post, January 4, 2007, http://www.washingtonpost.com/archive
      /business/technology/2007/01/04/pelosi-sworn-in-as-first-woman-speaker-of-the
      -house/32917f2c-c075-4d7a-b404-90e8c9fe7cea/.

109. Helena Andrews and Emily Heil, "Pelosi Donates Her Suit, House Speaker's Gavel
      to the Smithsonian," *Washington Post*, March 8, 2018, C2.

110. "History of Women Governors," https://cawp.rutgers.edu/facts/levels-office
      /statewide-elective-executive/history-women-governors.

111. Liette Gidlow, "Taking the Long View of Election 2008," in *Obama, Clinton, Palin:
      Making History in Election 2008*, ed. Liette Gidlow (Urbana: University of Illinois
      Press, 2011), 3–4.

112. "Transcript: *New York Times*, Hillary Clinton Endorses Barack Obama," *New York
      Times*, June 7, 2008, https://www.nytimes.com/elections/2008/president

/conventions/videos/transcripts/20080826_CLINTON_SPEECH.html; Theresa Vargas, "She Coined the Term 'Glass Ceiling.' She Fears It Will Outlive Her," *Washington Post*, March 1, 2018, www.washingtonpost.com/news/retropolis/wp /2018/03/01/she-coined-the-phrase-glass-ceiling-she-didnt-expect-it-to-outlive-her/.

113. Rebecca Traister, *Big Girls Don't Cry: The Election That Changed Everything for American Women* (New York: Free Press/Simon & Schuster, 2010), 66, 179, 28.

114. Christina Bellantoni, "Running (for President) in Heels," *More*, December 2011, 118; Traister, *Big Girls*, 66.

115. Rebecca Traister, review of *The Highest Glass Ceiling: Women's Quest for the American Presidency* by Ellen Fitzpatrick, *New York Times*, March 15, 2016.

116. "Likeable? Enough Already," *The Missouri Review*, January 28, 2008, www .missourireview.com/likeable-enough-already.

117. Bellantoni, 118.

118. Elisabeth Israels Perry, "The Difference that 'Difference' Makes," in Gidlow, *OCP*, 150.

119. Hillary Rodham Clinton, *What Happened* (New York: Simon & Schuster, 2017), 118–19; Katheryn Kish Sklar, "Hillary Rodham Clinton, the Race Question and the 'Masculine Mystique," *OCP*, 23.

120. Melanie Gustafson, "Defining a Maverick: Putting Palin in the Context of Western Women's Political History," *OCP*, 94–101; Rebecca Traister, "Cowgirl Country," *New York Times Magazine*, January 23, 2011, 12.

121. Eugene Scott, "1 in 5 Women Doubt a Woman Can Win the Presidency," *Washington Post*, January 23, 2020, www.washingtonpost.com/politics/2020/01/23 /one-five-women-doubt-that-woman-can-win-presidency/.

122. John G. Geer, ed., *Public Opinion and Polling Around the World: A Historical Encyclopedia*, Vol. 1 (Santa Barbara, CA: ABC-CLIO Publishing, 2004), 378.

123. Traister, *Big Girls*, 91; Catherine E. Rymph, "Political Feminism and the Problem of Sarah Palin," Gidlow, *OCP*, 145–46.

Chapter Nine: Leaning In & Losing, 2009–2016

1. "Barack Obama's Remarks to the Democratic National Convention," *New York Times*, July 27, 2007, https://www.nytimes.com/2004/07/27/politics/campaign /barack-obamas-remarks-to-the-democratic-national.html.

2. Kevin M. Kruse and Julian E. Zelizer, *Fault Lines: A History of the United States Since 1974* (New York: W.W. Norton & Co., 2019), 240–41.

3. David Paul Kuhn, "Exit Polls: How Obama Won," *Politico*, November 5, 2008, https ://www.politico.com/story/2008/11/exit-polls-how-obama-won-015297; Roper Center for Public Opinion, "How Groups Voted in 2008," ropercenter.cornell .edu/how-groups-voted-2008; "Dissecting the 2008 Electorate: Most Diverse in History," https://www.pewresearch.org/hispanic/2009/04/30/dissecting-the-2008 -electorate-most-diverse-in-us-history/.

4. Glenda Elizabeth Gilmore, "The 2008 Election, Black Women's Politics, and the Long Civil Rights Movement," in *Obama, Clinton, Palin: Making History in the 2008 Election*, ed. Liette Gidlow (Urbana: Illinois University Press, 2011), 53–57; Melinda Henneberger, "Five Myths About Women Voters," *Washington Post*, April 22, 2012.

5. Michelle Obama, *Becoming* (New York: Crown, 2018), 264–65.

6. Mike Allen, "Obama Slams New Yorker Portrayal," *Politico*, July 13, 2008, https ://www.politico.com/story/2008/07/obama-slams-new-yorker-portrayal-011719.

7. Mitch Kachun, "Michelle Obama, the Media Circus, and America's Racial Obsession," in *Obama, Clinton, Palin*, 41; Jeffrey Jones, "Michelle Obama Ends Hillary Clinton's Run as Most Admired," *Gallup*, December 27, 2018, https://news .gallup.com/poll/245669/michelle-obama-ends-hillary-clinton-run-admired.aspx.

8. "Fact Sheet on Women Serving in Congress," Center for American Women and Politics, www.cawp.rutgers.edu/fact-sheet-archive-women-congress.

9. Kruse, 295; "Women Appointed to Presidential Cabinets," Center for American Women and Politics, https://cawp.rutgers.edu/sites/default/files/resources /womenapptdtoprescabinets.pdf.

10. Sheryl Gay Stolberg, "Obama Signs Equal-Pay Legislation," *New York Times*, January 29, 2009, https://www.nytimes.com/2009/01/30/us/politics/30ledbetter -web.html; *Ledbetter v. Goodyear Tire and Rubber Company* (2007), Oyez, www.oyez .org/cases/2006/05-1074.

11. Nancy Gibbs, "What Women Want Now: A Time Special Report," *Time*, October 26, 2009, 25–33.

12. "Paycheck Fairness Act (2012)," www.govtrack.us/congress/bills; "The Paycheck Fairness Act," American Bar Association, https://www.americanbar.org/advocacy /governmental_legislative_work/priorities_policy/discrimination/the-paycheck -fairness-act/.

13. "A History of Women in the US Military," Infoplease, February 28, 2017, https://www .infoplease.com/us/military-affairs/history-women-us-military; Annie Groer, "Outgoing Defense Secretary Leon Panetta Lefts Military Ban on Women in Combat," *Washington Post*, January 23, 2013, https://www.washingtonpost.com /blogs/she-the-people/wp/2013/01/23/outgoing-defense-secretary-leon-panetta-lifts -military-ban-on-women-in-combat.

14. J. D. Simkins, "This Sergeant Became the First Woman in the US Army to Earn a Silver Star for Combat Valor," *Military Times*, June 14, 2019, www.militarytimes .com/off-duty/military-culture/2019/06/14/this-sergeant-became-the-first-woman -in-the-us-army-to-earn-a-silver-star-for-combat-valor/.

15. "President Obama's Record on Empowering Women and Girls," https://obama whitehouse.archives.gov/issues/women; "White House Council on Women and Girls," https://obamawhitehouse.archives.gov/administration/eop/cwg.

16. Robert Pear, "Senate Passes Health Care Overhaul on Part-Line Vote," *New York Times*, December 24, 2009, https://www.nytimes.com/2009/12/25/health/policy /25health.html.

17. Alan Silverleib, "House Passes Health Care Bill on 219-212 Vote," *CNNPolitics*, March 22, 2010, www.cnn.com/2010/POLITICS/03/21/health.care.main/index.html.

18. Sheryl Gay Stolberg and Robert Pear, "Obama Signs Health Care Overhaul Bill, With a Flourish," *New York Times*, March 23, 2010, https://www.nytimes.com/2010 /03/24/health/policy/24health.html.

19. Kruse, 297–98, 301.

20. Sarah Jones, "The Tea Party Is Alive and Well," *New York*, August 28, 2019; Kruse, 300, 310; Jill Lepore, *These Truths: A History of the United States* (New York: W.W. Norton & Co., 2018), 255; Aaron Blake, "The Tea Party Is Alive and Well—in

Spirit at Least," *Washington Post*, January 14, 2015, https://www.washingtonpost
.com/news/the-fix/wp/2015/01/14/the-tea-party-is-alive-and-well-in-spirit-at-least/.

21. Nancy McKeon, "Between Votes, A Place for a Pit Stop," *Washington Post*, July 29,
     2011, C1; Karen Tumulty, "Female Candidates Made Gains in the 2012 Election,"
     Washington Post, November 7, 2012, https://www.washingtonpost.com/politics
     /decision2012/female-candidates-made-gains-in-the-2012-election/2012/11/07
     /9b2e6f02-291c-11e2-b4e0-346287b7e56c_story.html.

22. Debbie Walsh and Kathy Kleeman, "Finding Madame President," *Washington Post*,
     April 3, 2011, B1.

23. Mark Meckler and Jenny Beth Martin, *Tea Party Patriots: The Second American
     Revolution* (New York: Henry Holt & Co., 2012), 1–4, 10.

24. Lisa Miller, "Evangelical Women Create Their Own Brand of Feminism,"
     Washington Post, July 30, 2011, B1.

25. *Fire From the Heartland: The Awakening of the Conservative Woman*, directed by Stephen
     K. Bannon (Washington, DC: Citizens United Productions, 2010), DVD; Elizabeth
     Flowers, review of *This Is Our Message: Women's Leadership in the New Christian Right* by
     Emily Suzanne Johnson, *Journal of American History* 107, no. 4 (March 2021): 1048–49.

26. "Bachmann, Michele," https://history.house.gov/People/Detail/10411.

27. Marie Griffith, "The New Evangelical Feminism of Bachmann and Palin,"
     Huffington Post, September 5, 2011, https://www.huffingtonpost.com/marie
     -griffith/evangelical-feminism_b_891579.html; Catherine E. Rymph, "Political
     Feminism and the Problem of Sarah Palin," in *Obama, Clinton, Palin*, 135–47.

28. Christina Bellantoni, "Running (For President) in Heels," *MORE*, December 2011,
     146ff; Amanda Hess, "Ferraro to Palin to Harris: What Has and Hasn't Changed,"
     New York Times, August 20, 2020, A14.

29. Obama, 270–71; Peter Slevin, "Why Michelle Obama's 2008 Convention Speech
     Was a Major Turning Point for Her," *Washington Post*, July 20, 2016, https://wapo
     .st/29NWSkU?tid+ss_mail.

30. Anne-Marie Slaughter, "Why Women Still Can't Have It All," *The Atlantic*, July/
     August 2012, www.theatlantic.com/magazine/archive/2012/07/why-women-still
     -cant-have-it-all/309020/; Rachel Shreir, "Feminism Fizzles," *The Chronicle of Higher
     Education*, January 28, 2013, https://www.chronicle.com/article/feminism-fizzles/.

31. Jennifer Szalai, "Had It All: The Feminist Mantra That Never Was," *New York
     Times Magazine*, January 4, 2015, 9–10.

32. Matt Weinberger and Paige Leskin, "The Rise and Fall of Marissa Mayer," *Business
     Insider*, February 11, 2020, www.businessinsider.com/yahoo-marissa-mayer-rise
     -and-fall-2017-6; Lisa Miller, "Symbolism on Board: Marissa Mayer and the
     Lessons of Sarah Palin," *New York*, July 30, 2012, 9–10.

33. Connie Schultz, "Is Sheryl Sandberg Good for Feminism? It's Complicated," review
     of *Lean In: Women, Work, and the Will to Lead*, by Sheryl Sandberg, *Washington Post*,
     March 3, 2013, B1.

34. Rosa Brooks, "Recline! Why 'Leaning In' Is Killing Us," *Foreign Policy*, February 21,
     2014, foreignpolicy.com/2014/02/21/recline; Ruth Marcus, "A Corporate Titan and
     Single Mom," *Washington Post*, May 8, 2016.

35. Caitlin Gibson, "The Epic Stumble of Lean In," *Washington Post*, December 27,
     2018, C1.

36. Alison Brzenchek and Mari Castenada, "'The Real Housewives,' Gendered Affluence and the Rise of the Docusoap," *Communications Department Faculty Published*, 2017, https://scholarworks.umass.edu/cgi/viewcontent.cgi?article=1050& context=communication_faculty_pubs; Gloria Steinem, interview by Andy Cohen, *After Show*, Bravo TV, December 2, 2015.

37. Tom Geler, "17 Female US Presidents in Movies and TV," November 2, 2020, https://www.thewrap.com/female-us-president-movies-tv-actress-woman/.

38. Marc Fisher, "Over the Past Half-Century, A Strong Shift to the Right," *Washington Post*, August 29, 2012, A1.

39. Roper Center for Public Opinion, "How Groups Voted in 2012," ropercenter.cornell .edu/how-groups-voted-2012; Karen McVeigh and Julian Borger, "Women's Vote Carries Obama to Victory on Historic Election Night," *The Guardian*, November 7, 2012, www.theguardian.com/world/2012/nov/07/womens-vote-obama -victory-election.

40. Sarah Wheaton, "For the First Time on Record, Black Voting Rate Outpaced Rate for Whites in 2012," *New York Times*, May 8, 2013, https://www.nytimes .com/2013/05/09/us/politics/rate-of-black-voters-surpassed-that-for-whites-in-2012 .html; Maya Harris, "Women of Color: A Growing Force in the American Electorate," Center for the American Woman and Progress, October 30, 2014, www .americanprogress.org/article/women-of-color.

41. Liam Donovan, "From the Tea Party to Trump: The GOP in the 2010s," interview by Lulu Garcia-Navarro, *Weekend Edition Sunday*, December 29, 2019; Wylecia Wiggs Harris, "The Power of Black Women Voters," September 27, 2016, https ://www.lwv.org/educating-voters/power-black-women-voters; Ruth Marcus, "Cause for Concern about Voting Rights," *Washington Post*, February 28, 2021, A29.

42. Catalina Camia, "Record Number of Women in Congress Out to Change Tone," *USAToday*, January 3, 2013, www.usatoday.com/story/news/politics/2013/01/03 /women-congress-senate-record/1807657/.

43. "History of Women in the US Congress," Center for American Women and Politics, https://www.lwv.org/educating-voters/power-black-women-vote/.

44. Tumulty, "Female Candidates."

45. Jennifer Steinhauer, "Once Few, Women Hold More Power in Senate," *New York Times*, March 22, 2013, A1; Tumulty.

46. Rachel Weiner, "Barbara Mikulski, First Female Chair of Senate Appropriations, Returns to Minority," *Washington Post*, November 16, 2014, http://wapo.st /11gWxBF?tid+ss; Emily Heil, "More Women, Less Gridlock?" *Washington Post*, December 13, 2012, A28.

47. Gail Collins, "Twenty and Counting," *New York Times*, December 8, 2012.

48. Lizette Alvarez and Cara Buckley, "Zimmerman Acquitted in Trayvon Martin Killing," *New York Times*, July 13, 2013, https://www.nytimes.com/2013/07/14/us /george-zimmerman-verdict-trayvon-martin.html.

49. Richard Luscombe, "Michael Dunn Sentenced to Life Without Parole for Killing Florida Teenager," *The Guardian*, October 17, 2014, www.theguardian.com /us-news/2014/oct/17/michael-dunn-sentenced-life-without-parole-florida.

50. Mcbath.house.gov; Jelani Cobb, "The Crucial Significance of Lucy McBath's Win in Georgia's Sixth Congressional District," *New Yorker*, November 17, 2018, www

.newyorker.com/news/daily-comment/the-crucial-significance-of-lucy-mcbaths
-win-in-georgias-sixth-congressional-district.

51. "Sandy Hook Elementary Shooting: What Happened?" CNN, www.cnn.com
/interactive/2012/12/sandy-hook-timeline/index.html; "President Obama Speaks
Out on the Shooting in Connecticut," https://obamawhitehouse.archives.gov
/blog/2012/12/14/president-obama-speaks-shooting-connecticut.

52. Gregory Korte and Catalina Camia, "Obama on Senate Gun Vote: 'A Shameful
Day," *USAToday,* April 17, 2013, www.usatoday.com/story/news/politics/2013/04/17
/guns-background-checks-manchin-senate/2090105/.

53. Jonathan Weisman, "Senate Blocks Drive for Gun Control," *New York Times,*
April 17, 2013, https://www.nytimes.com/2013/04/18/us/politics/senate-obama
-gun-control.html.

54. "Obama's Remarks After Senate Gun Votes," *New York Times,* April 18, 2013,
https://www.nytimes.com/2013/04/18/us/politics/obamas-remarks-after-senate
-gun-votes.html.

55. "Our Co-Founders," https://blacklivesmatter.com/herstory/.

56. Katie Benner, "Eric Garner's Death Will Not Lead to Federal Charges for NYPD
Officer," *New York Times,* June 16, 2019, https://www.nytimes.com/2019/07/16
/nyregion/eric-garner-daniel-pantaleo.html.

57. "Timeline of Events in Shooting of Michael Brown in Ferguson," https://apnews
.com/article/shootings-police-us-news-st-louis-michael-brown-9aa3203369254769
9a3b61da8fd1fc62; Jada Yuan, "Marching Right into the House," *Washington Post,*
December 23, 2020, C1.

58. James Hohmann, "'Demilitarizing the Police Could Be A More Fruitful Rallying Cry
for Reformers Than 'Defunding,'" *The Daily 202, Washington Post,* June 9, 2020, www
.washingtonpost.com/news/powerpost/paloma/daily-202/2020/06/09/daily-202
-demilitarizing-the-police-could-be-a-more-fruitful-rallying-cry-for-reformers-than
-defunding/5edf0e54602ff12947e87c9e/.

59. Jason Horowitz, Nick Corasaniti and Ashley Southall, "Nine Killed in Shooting at
Black Church in Charleston," *New York Times,* June 17, 2015, https://www.nytimes.
com/2015/06/18/us/church-attacked-in-charleston-south-carolina.html; Kevin
Liptak, "Obama's Charleston Eulogy: 'Amazing Grace'" *CNNPolitics,* June 29, 2015,
www.cnn.com/2015/06/26/politics/obama-charleston-eulogy-pastor/index.html.

60. Emily Shapiro, "Key Moments in Charleston Church Shooting Case as Dylann
Roof Pleads Guilty to State Charges," ABC News, April 10, 2017, http://abcn.ws
/2or2RG1.

61. Ruth Marcus, "End the 'A Few Bad Apples' Fiction," *Washington Post,* June 7, 2020, 29.

62. Homa Khaleeli, "#SayHerName: Why Kimberle Crenshaw Is Fighting for Forgotten
Women," *Guardian,* May 30, 2016, www.theguardian.com/lifeandstyle/2016
/may/30/sayhername-why-kimberle-crenshaw-is-fighting-for-forgotten-women;
Mary Louise Kelly, "Say Her Name: How the Fight for Racial Justice Can Be More
Inclusive of Black Women," *All Things Considered,* July 7, 2020.

63. "Sonia Sotomayor," Oyez, www.oyez.org/justices/sonia_sotomayor; Sonia
Sotomayor, *My Beloved World* (New York: Alfred A. Knopf, 2013).

64. *Citizens United v. Federal Election Commission* (2010), Oyez, www.oyez.org/cases
/2008/08-205.

65. "Elena Kagan," Oyez, www.oyez.org/justices/elena_kagan; Margaret Talbot, "The Pivotal Justice," *New Yorker*, November 18, 2019, 36ff.

66. Gail Collins, "Doing Some Heavy Lifting," *New York Times*, November 29, 2014, A15.

67. "Mrs. Lorena W. Weeks, Appellant, v. Southern Bell Telephone," law.justia.com /cases/federal/appellate-courts.

68. *Cleveland Board of Education v. LaFleur* (1974), Oyez, www.oyez.org/cases/1973/72 -777; www.eeoc.gov/pregnancy-discrimination; Gail Collins, "The Woes of Working Woman," *New York Times*, December 6, 2014, A21.

69. *Young v. United Parcel Service, Inc.* (2015), Oyez, www.oyez.org/cases/2014/12-1226; Robert Barnes, "Supreme Court Weighs UPS Case," *Washington Post*, December 4, 2014.

70. Transcript, "Fighting for Overdue Protections for Pregnant Workers," CBS News, January 12, 2020.

71. Nina Totenberg, "Birth Control at the Supreme Court: Does Free Coverage Violate Religious Freedom?" *Morning Edition*, March 23, 2016.

72. Stephanie Simon, "Hobby Lobby Aims for Obamacare Win, Christian Nation," *Politico*, January 16, 2014, www.politico.com/story/2014/06/hobby-lobby-supreme -court-case-107877.

73. *Burwell v. Hobby Lobby Stores* (2013), Oyez, www.oyez.org/cases/2013/13-354.

74. Jeremy W. Peters and Michel D. Shear, "A Ruling That Both Sides Can Run With," *New York Times*, July 1, 2014, A1.

75. *Zubik v. Burwell* (2016), Oyez, www.oyez.org/cases/2015/14-1418; Robert Barnes, "Divided Justices Offer Compromise on Contraceptives," *Washington Post*, March 30, 2016, A1.

76. Linda Greenhouse, "The Facts About Abortion," *New York Times*, February 27, 2016, SR1.

77. Dahlia Lithwick, "The Women Take Over," *Slate*, March 2, 2016, slate.com/news -and-politics/2016/03/in-oral-arguments-for-the-texas-abortion-case-the-three -female-justices-upend-the-supreme-courts-balance-of-power.html; *Whole Woman's Health v. Hellerstedt* (2016), Oyez, www.oyez.org/cases/2015/15-274.

78. *United States v. Windsor* (2013), Oyez, www.oyez.org/cases/2012/12-307.

79. Michael S. Rosenwald, "How Jim Obergefell Became the Face of the Supreme Court Gay Marriage Case," *Washington Post*, April 6, 2015, http://wapo.st/1y9bAgP?tid=ss _mail.

80. *Obergefell v. Hodges* (2015), Oyez, www.oyez.org/cases/2014/14-556; Tara Law, "9 Landmark Supreme Court Cases That Shaped LGBTQ Rights in America," *Time*, October 8, 2019, https://time.com/5694518/lgbtq-supreme-court-cases/?utm.

81. *Shelby County v. Holder* (2013), Oyez, www.oyez.org/cases/2012/12-96.

82. Vann R. Newkirk II, "How *Shelby County v. Holder* Broke America," *The Atlantic*, July 10, 2018, https://www.theatlantic.com/politics/archive/2018/07/how-shelby -county-broke-america/564707/.

83. "Women Elected to the 114th Congress," Center for American Women and Politics," https://cawp.rutgers.edu/blog/women-114th-congress.

84. Sheryl Gay Stolberg, "More Women Than Ever in Congress, but With Less Power than Before," *New York Times*, February 3, 2015, A10.

85. "Shelley Moore Capito," www.capito.senate.gov/about/about-shelley;"Joni Ernst," www.ernst.senate.gov/about; "Love, Ludmya Bourdeau (Mia)," www.house.gov /People/Detail/15032411201; "Stefanik, Elise," www.house.gov/People/Listing /S/STEFANIK,-Elise-M--(S001196)/; Joni Ernst, *Daughter of the Heartland: My Ode to the Country That Raised Me* (New York: Simon & Schuster, Inc., 2020).

86. Editorial, "Women's Voice Remains Faint in Politics," *New York Times*, September 14, 2017, A22; Sheryl Gay Stolberg, "Women in Both Parties Are Disappointed by Their Modest Election Gains," *New York Times*, November 5, 2014; Celinda Lake and Kellyanne Conway with Catherine Whitney, *What Women Really Want* (New York: Free Press, 2005).

87. Judith Warner, "Glass Ceiling: 104 Women in Congress, Does It Matter?" *Politico*, January/February 2015, www.politico.com/magazine/magazine/story/2015/01/104 -women-in-congress-does-it-matter-113903/.

88. David Von Drehle, "Can Anyone Stop Hillary?" *Time*, January 16, 2014, http ://content.time.com/time/magazine/article/0,9171,2162918,00.html.

89. Amy Chozick, "Hillary Clinton Announces 2016 Presidential Bid," *New York Times*, April 12, 2015, https://www.nytimes.com/2015/04/13/us/politics/hillary-clinton -2016-presidential-campaign.html.

90. Andrew Prokop, "Bernie Sanders 2016: A Primer," *Vox*, July 28, 2015, www.vox.com /2015/7/28/18093566/bernie-sanders-issues-policies.

91. www.nytimes.com/elections/2016/results/primaries/iowa; www.nytimes.com /elections/2016/results/primaries/new-hampshire.

92. Jeff Stein, "Let's Clear Up Some Confusion about the Superdelegates and Bernie Sanders," *Vox*, May 6, 2016, www.vox.com/2016/5/6/11597550/superdelegates -bernie-sanders-clinton; Antonio Moore, "How Democratic Superdelegates Decides the 2016 Election," *Huffington Post*, December 6, 2017, https://www.huffingtonpost .com/entry/how-super-delegates-decid_b_10098414.

93. "Transcript of Hillary Clinton's Address to the Democratic National Convention," *New York Times*, July 28, 2016, https://www.nytimes.com/2016/07/29/us/politics /hillary-clinton-dnc-transcript.html.

94. "Women's Voices: She Is the Nominee," Letter to the Editor, *New York Times*, July 28, 2016.

95. Hillary Rodham Clinton, *What Happened* (New York: Simon & Schuster, 2017), 40–41, 52.

96. Allison Graves, "Did Hillary Call African-American Youth 'Superpredators'?", *Politifact*, August 28, 2016, www.politifact.com/factchecks/2016/aug/28 /reince-priebus/did-hillary-clinton-call-african-american-youth-su/.

97. Heidi M. Przybyla, "On Honesty Issues, Hillary Clinton Fights Own Missteps, Gender Stereotypes," *USAToday*, September 6, 2016, www.usatoday.com/story/news /politics/elections/2016/09/06/hillary-clinton-trust-female-candidates-president -trump/89339494/; Jennifer Weiner, "Taking My Daughter to Vote," *New York Times*, November 9, 2016.

98. Amy Chozick, *Chasing Hillary: Ten Years, Two Presidential Campaigns, and One Intact Glass Ceiling* (New York: HarperCollins, Inc., 2018), 79–87; Clinton, *What Happened*, 220–23.

99. Lauren Gambino and Madhvi Pankhania, "How We Got Here: A Complete Timeline of 2016's Historic US Election," *The Guardian*, November 8, 2016, www

.theguardian.com/us-news/2016/nov/07/us-election-2016-complete-timeline
-clinton-trump-president.

100. Annie Correal, "Pantsuit Nation, a 'Secret' Facebook Hub, Celebrates Clinton,"
New York Times, November 8, 2016, www.nytimes.com/2016/11/09/us/politics
/facebook-pantsuit-nation-clinton.html; Joel Achenbach, "Pantsuit Nation: For
Many Women, Clinton's Bid Inspires Poignant Moments in Voting Booth,"
Washington Post, November 9, 2016.

101. Sarah L. Kaufman, "'Pantsuit Power' Flashmob Video for Hillary Clinton: Two
Women, 170 Dancers and No Police," *Washington Post*, October 7, 2016, www
.washingtonpost.com/news/arts-and-entertainment/wp/2016/10/07/pantsuit-power
-flashmob-video-for-hillary-clinton-two-women-170-dancers-no-police/; "Pantsuit
Flash Mob in NYC for HRC," www.youtube.com/watch?v=EjUOUZZc45Y.

102. www.census.gov/quickfacts/table/US/LFE046218; "Gender Differences in Voter
Turnout," https://cawp.rutgers.edu/facts/voters/gender-differences-voter-turnout.

103. Katie Rogers, "White Women Helped Elect Donald Trump," *New York Times*,
November 9, 2016, www.nytimes.com/2016/12/01/us/politics/white-women
-helped-elect-donald-trump.html; Vanessa Williams, "Black Women—Hillary
Clinton's Most Reliable Voting Bloc—Look Beyond Defeat," *Washington Post*,
November 12, 2016, www.washingtonpost.com//politics/black-women-hillary
-clintons-most-reliable-voting-bloc--look-beyond-defeat/2016/11/12/86d9182a
-a845-11e6-ba59-a7d93165c6d4_story.html; Aamna Mohdin, "American Women
Voted Overwhelmingly for Clinton, Except White Ones," *Quartz*, November 9,
2016, qz.com/833003/election-2016-all-women-voted-overwhelmingly-for
-clinton-except-the-white-ones/.

104. Molly Ball, "Donald Trump Didn't Really Win 52% of White Women in 2016,"
Time, October 18, 2018, time.com/5422644/trump-white-women-2016/; Jay
Newton-Small, "Why Some Women Won't Vote for a Woman for President,"
Washington Post, May 19, 2019, B2; Susan Chira, "What Women Lost," *New York
Times*, January 1, 2017, SR1.

105. Alec Tyson and Shivs Maniam, "Behind Trump's Victory: Divisions by Race,
Gender and Education," Pew Research Center, November 9, 2016, www.pew
research.org/fact-tank/2016/11/09/behind-trumps-victory-divisions-by-race
-gender-education/; "How Groups Voted 2016," ropercenter.cornell.edu/how
-groups-voted-2016; David Brooks, "The Gender War Is On! And Fake," *New York
Times*, July 3, 2018, A21.

106. Jennifer Senior, "Defiance, Dark Humor and Candor," review of *What Happened* by
Hillary Rodham Clinton, *New York Times*, September 12, 2017, C2.

107. "Electoral College Fast Facts," https://history.house.gov/Institution/Electoral
-College/Electoral-College/.

108. Philip Bump, "Donald Trump Will Be President Thanks to 80,000 People in Three
States," *Washington Post*, December 1, 2016, www.washingtonpost.com/news/the
-fix/wp/2016/12/01/donald-trump-will-be-president-thanks-to-80000-people
-in-three-states/; Brooke Seipel, "Trump's Victory Margin Smaller Than Total Stein
Votes in Key Swing States, *The Hill*, December 1, 2016, thehill.com/blogs/blog
-briefing-room/news/308353-trump.

109. Senior review.

110.   Jessica Valenti, "In 2016, the Anti-Clinton Sexism Will Be More Subtle," *Washington Post*, January 26, 2014.

111.   Susan Chira, "Ugly Campaign Descended into a Battle of Two Caricatures," *New York Times*, November 10, 2016, P8; John Sides, Michael Tesler and Lynn Vavreck, "Five Myths: The 2016 Campaign," *Washington Post*, October 7, 2018, B2.

112.   "Transcript of Hillary Clinton's Remarks," *Time*, September 10, 2016, time.com /Hillary-clinton-basket-of-deplorables-transcript.

113.   "Books on the 2016 Presidential Campaign," www.p2016.org/more/bookspost.

114.   Chozick, *Chasing*, 363–65; Clinton, *What Happened*, 385–86.

115.   Clinton, *What Happened*, 18–19; Chozick, *Chasing*, 371.

116.   "Hillary Conceded Defeat," *Time*, November 9, 2016, time.com/read-hillary -clintons-concession-speech-full-transcript; Clinton, *What Happened*, 388–89; Chozick, 371–72.

Chapter Ten: Enraged & Empowered, 2017–2020

1.   Katherine Q. Seelye and Claire Cain Miller, "Female Clinton Supporters Are Left Feeling Gutted," *New York Times*, November 10, 2016, www.nytimes.com /2016/11/11/us/politics/female-clinton-supporters-are-left-feeling-gutted.html; Susan Chira, "What Women Lost," *New York Times*, January 1, 2017, SR1; Elie Mystal, "For Minority and Women Elites, This Is An Utter Repudiation," Above the Law, November 9, 2016, abovethelaw.com/2016/11/for-minority-and-women -elites; Jodi Kantor, "Cheering for the First Female President, Until They Weren't," *New York Times*, November 9, 2016, www.nytimes.com/2016/11/10/us/elections /shock-women-clinton-supporters.html.

2.   Perry Stein and Sandhya Somashekhar, "Inauguration Protest Began as a Vent," *Washington Post*, January 4, 2017; Nina Agrawal, "How the Women's March Came into Being," *Chicago Tribune*, January 21, 2017, https://www.chicagotribune.com /la-na-pol-womens-march-live-how-the-women-s-march-came-into-1484865755 -htmlstory.html.

3.   Amanda Hess, "Forces in Opposition," *New York Times Magazine*, February 12, 2017, 42.

4.   Julia Felsenthal, "These Are the Women Organizing the Women's March on Washington," *Vogue*, January 10, 2017, http://www.vogue.com/article/meet-the -women-of-the-womens-march-on-washington.

5.   Farah Stockman, "Women's March Opens a Raw Dialogue on Race," *New York Times*, January 10, 2017; Sheryl Gay Stolberg, "Views on Abortion Strain Call to Unite At Women's March," *New York Times*, January 19, 2017; Perry Stein, "Who Gets to Decide Who is Feminist?" *Washington Post*, January 19, 2017; Lauren Enriquez, "Pro-Life, But Left Out," *New York Times*, February 27, 2017.

6.   Agrawal, "How the Women's March Came into Being."

7.   Hess, *NYTM*, 38.

8.   Kathryn Rubino, "The Women's March on Washington Is Bringing Back the ERA," Above the Law, January 23, 2017, https://abovethelaw.com/2017/01/the-womens -march-on-washington-is-bringing-back-the-era/; Emily Crockett, "The 'Women's March on Washington,' Explained," *Vox*, January 17, 2017, https://www.vox.com /identities/2016/11/21/13651804/women-march-washington-trump-inauguration.

9.   Gretchen Frazee, "What the Women's March Wants," *PBS Newshour,* January 18, 2017; Tom Toles cartoon, "Impressive Turnout," *Washington Post,* January 18, 2017.

10.   Perry Stein, "200 Buses Have Applied for City Parking…," *Washington Post,* January 12, 2017; Eugene Robinson, "Progressives Use March To Start a Movement," January 24, 2017, https://www.news-daily.com/opinion/eugene-robinson-progressives-use-the -march-to-make-a-movement/article_2c1c8e9b-57c7-522a -89a7-4fcc6549d3c2.html; Luz Lazo and Martine Powers, "March Turnout Pushes Metro to Breaking Point," *Washington Post,* January 22, 2017.

11.   www.pussyhatproject.com; Robin Givhan, "The MAGA Hat Is Not a Statement of Policy; It's an Inflammatory Declaration of Identity," *Washington Post,* January 24, 2019, https://www.washingtonpost.com/lifestyle/style/the-maga-hat-is-not-a -statement-of-policy-its-an-inflammatory-declaration-of-identity/2019/01/23 /9fe84bc0-1f39-11e9-8e21-59a09ff1e2a1_story.html; Danielle Kurtzleben, "With 'Pussyhats' Liberals Get Their Own Version of the Red Trucker Hat," *Weekend Edition Sunday,* January 22, 2017; Petula Dvorak, "The Women's March Needs Passion and Purpose, Not Pink Pussycat Hats," *Washington Post,* January 12, 2017.

12.   *New Yorker,* February 6, 2017; Darcy Adams, email message to author, February 4, 2017.

13.   Noted by author; Samantha Weiner and Emma Jacobs, eds., *Why I March: Images from the Women's March Around the World* (New York: Abrams Image, 2017).

14.   Emily Crockett, "Women's March on Washington Schedule," January 19, 2017, https://www.vox.com/identities/2017/1/19/14323732/womens-march-washington -schedule-route-speakers-performers; "America Ferrera Speaks at Women's March on Washington," *CBS News,* January 21, 2017 (video can be found on youtube.com).

15.   "Trump Offers Scattershot Response to Global Women's March," *NewsHour,* PBS, January 22, 2017, www.pbs.org/newshour/politics/trump-response-womens-march.

16.   David Brooks, "After the March," *New York Times,* January 25, 2017.

17.   Ai-Jen Poo, interview by David Greene and Steve Inskeep, "After Massive Marches, Activists Look to 'Channel Energy' At Local Level," *Morning Edition,* January 26, 2017; Susan Chira and Jonathan Martin, "Marchers Map Out Next Steps," *New York Times,* January 23, 2017; Hahrie Han, "The Secrets of Successful Activism," *New York Times,* December 17, 2019.

18.   "Indivisible: A Practical Guide for Resisting the Trump Agenda," www.indivisible .com; Dayna Evans, "The Indivisible Guide Is Your Resource for Resisting the Trump Agenda," *The Cut,* January 30, 2017, https://www.thecut.com/2017/01 /resistance-surviving-trump-indivisible-guide.html.

19.   Perry Stein, "Women's March Looks to Keep Moving Forward," *Washington Post,* July 20, 2017; Kathleen Parker, "The Year of the Woman," *Washington Post,* March 21, 2018, A21; Scott Clement, Sandhya Somashekhar, and Michael Alison Chandler, "Female Democrats To Step Up Activism, Poll Says," *Washington Post,* February 2, 2017.

20.   Jasmine C. Lee, "Trump's Cabinet So Far Is More White and Male Than Any First Cabinet Since Reagan's," *New York Times,* March 10, 2017, www.nytimes.com /interactive/2017/01/13/us/politics/trump-cabinet-women-minorities.html; Adam Entous, "A Devil's Bargain," *New Yorker,* June 29, 2020, 35.

21.   Susan Chira, "Another Powerful Woman. Same Sexist Attacks." *New York Times,* March 6, 2017, A1.

22.   Emily Heil, "First Lady Melania Trump Says No Politics at the Black Tie Dinner
       for Governors," *Washington Post*, February 26, 2017, https://www.washingtonpost
       .com/news/reliable-source/wp/2017/02/26/first-lady-melania-trump-says-no-politics
       -at-the-black-tie-dinner-for-governors/.

23.   Miriam Valverder, "Here's What Donald Trump Did His First Week as President,"
       Politifact, January 27, 2017, www.politifact.com/article/2017/jan/heres-what-donald
       -trump-did-first-week-president-u/; Carol Morello, "State Dept.: Abortion Policy
       Has Little Effect on Aid," *Washington Post*, August 19, 2020, A2.

24.   Michelle Hackman, "Pence Vows Support at Antiabortion Rally," *Wall Street Journal*,
       January 28-29, 2017, A3; Julie Zauzmer, Steve Hendrix, and Michael E. Ruane,
       "Pence: 'Life Is Winning Again in America,'" *Washington Post*, January 28, 2017;
       Sheryl Gay Stolberg, "Strategist Who Helped Manage Trump's Win Will Speak at a
       Major Anti-Abortion March," *New York Times*, January 13, 2017.

25.   Michael Crowley, "Trump To Be First President to Speak at March for Life," *New
       York Times*, January 23, 2020.

26.   E. J. Dionne, Jr., "Trump's Futile Politics of Outrage," *Washington Post*, April 9,
       2018; Dan Zak, "The Parley in the Park," *Washington Post*, July 24, 2018; Katie
       Rogers,
       "A City Where Dissent Becomes a Lifestyle," *New York Times*, March 16, 2017.

27.   "Women's March, Inc. (National)," https://www.influencewatch.org/non-profit
       /womens-march-national.

28.   Petula Dvorak, "Working Is What Women Do. And Everyone Benefits from Our
       Labor," *Washington Post*, March 9, 2017; Perry Stein and Michael Alison Chandler,
       "Women Protest, Skip Work as Part of 'Day Without a Woman' Strike," March 8, 2017,
       https://wapo.st/2mh6rPP?tid=ss_mail&utm_term=.8bd716c5bc66; Petula Dvorak, "A
       Day Without a Woman? Tough Ask," *Washington Post*, March 10, 2017, B1.

29.   Monica Davey, "At Women's Convention in Detroit, a Test of Momentum and
       Focus," *New York Times*, October 28, 2017, https://www.nytimes.com/2017/10/28
       /us/women-convention-detroit-march.html.

30.   Ausma Zehanat Khan, "A Muslim Activist, Fearless in the Face of Hate," review of
       We Are Not Here To Be Bystanders: A Memoir of Love and Resistance, by Linda Sarsour,
       Washington Post, April 5, 2020, B8; Farah Stockman, "Women's March Roiled
       by Accusations of Anti-Semitism," *New York Times,* December 23, 2018; Marissa
       J. Lang, "Three Years After Taking to the Streets, the Women's March Is at a
       Crossroads," *Washington Post,* January 13, 2020, B1.

31.   Marissa J. Lang, "Three Years After Taking to the Streets, the Women's March is at
       a Crossroads," *Washington Post*, January 13, 2020, B1.

32.   Michael Alison Chandler and Joe Heim, "Women's March Returns," *Washington
       Post,* January 21, 2018.

33.   Marissa J. Lang, "Women's March 3rd Year: Divided and Diminished," *Washington
       Post,* January 19, 2019; Michael Wines and Farah Stockman, "For Third Women's
       March, Smaller Crowds and Some Frayed Edges," *New York Times,* January 20, 2019;
       Dan Merica and Sophie Tatum, "Kirsten Gillibrand Condemns Anti-Semitism at
       Women's March," CNN, January 19, 2019, https://www.cnn.com/2019/01/19
       /politics/kirsten-gillibrand-womens-march/index.html; Wines and Stockman,
       New York Times, January 20, 2019.

34. Marissa J. Lang, "Women's March to Hold Week of Events in DC," *Washington Post,* January 8, 2020, B1; Marissa J. Lang and Samantha Schmidt, "Election Year Brings Feeling of Hope at Women's March," *Washington Post,* January 19, 2020, C1.

35. Dana R. Fisher, *American Resistance: From the Women's March to the Blue Wave* (New York: Columbia University Press, 2019).

36. Petula Dvorak, "Covid Halts Women's March, and Progress," *Washington Post,* January 5, 2021, B1.

37. Todd Gitlin, *The Sixties: Years of Hope, Days of Rage* (New York: Bantam, 1989), xxii; Zeynep Tufekci, *Twitter and Tear Gas: The Power and Fragility of Networked Protest* (New Haven: Yale University Press, 2017); Julie Turkewitz, "A March on History: How Demonstrations Have Shaped America," *New York Times,* January 22, 2017, A10; Glenda Elizabeth Gilmore, "The Myth of the 'Good" Protest," *New York Times,* November 21, 2017.

38. Hahrie Han, "The Secrets of Successful Activism," *New York Times,* December 17, 2019.

39. "Women in the U.S. Congress 2017," www.cawp.rutgers.edu/women-us-congress-2017.

40. Jennifer Steinhauer, "GOP's Female Senators Struggle to Win Influence," *New York Times,* May 10, 2017, A22.

41. Petula Dvorak, "2017: The Unexpected Year of the Woman," *Washington Post,* December 29, 2017, B1.

42. Brittany Bronson, "When Women Legislate," *New York Times,* April 18, 2017.

43. Jess Bidgood, "Alabama Women 'Make a Stand' in First Election of the #MeToo Era," *New York Times,* December 13, 2017, https://www.nytimes.com/2017/12/13 /us/alabama-women-doug-jones-metoo.html.

44. Dana Milbank, "Women Are Speaking. Does Anyone Listen?" *New York Times,* September 20, 2017; Michelle Ruiz, "No, Hillary Clinton, the First Woman to Win a Major-Party Presidential Nomination, Does Not Need to Shut Up About It," *Vogue,* September 11, 2017, www.vogue.com/article/hillary-clinton-what-happened -doesnt-have-to-shut-up.

45. www.metoomvmt.org/about.

46. Ashley May, "Who Are the 'Silence Breakers' Featured as 'Time' Person of the Year?" *USA Today,* December 6, 2017, https://usatoday.com/story/life/nation-now/2017/12/06 /who-silence-breakers-festured-time-person-year-me-too/926243001/.

47. Emily Crockett, "Here Are the Women Who Have Publicly Accused Roger Ailes of Sexual Harassment," *Vox,* August 15, 2016, https://www.vox.com/2016/8/15 /12416662/roger-ailes-fox-sexual-harrassment; Christine Hauser and Maggie Astor, "The Larry Nassar Case: What Happened and How the Fallout Is Spreading," *New York Times,* January 25, 2018, https://www.nytimes.com/2018/01/25/sports/larry -nassar-gymnastics-abuse.html.

48. Megan Garber, "Why Was Bill O'Reilly Really Fired?" *Atlantic,* April 19, 2017, https://www.theatlantic.com/news/archive/2017/04/why-was-bill-oreilly-really -fired/523614/; Graham Bowley and Joe Coscarelli, "Bill Cosby, Once a Model of Fatherhood, Is Sentenced to Prison," *New York Times,* September 25, 2018, https ://www.nytimes.com/2018/09/25/arts/television/bill-cosby-sentencing.html.

49. Jodi Kantor and Megan Twohey, *She Said: Breaking the Sexual Harassment Story That Helped Ignite a Movement* (New York: Penguin Random House, 2019); Ronan

Farrow, *Catch and Kill: Lies, Spires and a Conspiracy to Protect Predators* (New York: Hachette Book Group, Inc., 2019).

50. Maureen Dowd, "Harvey Weinstein, Hollywood's Oldest Horror Story," *New York Times,* October 14, 2017, SR1; Jessica Bennett, "The 'Click' Moment: How the Weinstein Scandal Unleashed a Tsunami," *New York Times,* November 5, 2017, https://www.nytimes.com/2017/11/05/us/sexual-harrasment-weinstein-trump.html.

51. Anna North, "7 Positive Changes That Have Come from the #MeToo Movement," *Vox,* October 4, 2019, www.vox.com/identities/2019/10/4/20852639/me-too -movement-sexual-harassment-law-2019.

52. Karen Zraick, "Former Obama Aide Will Take Over Time's Up," *New York Times,* October 8, 2019, C3; Ellen McCarthy, "Anita Hill Chosen to Lead Commission on Sexual Harassment," *Washington Post,* December 17, 2017; Robin Givhan, "Fashion Made a Statement, Accessorized with Activism," *Washington Post,* January 8, 2018, C1.

53. Robert Barnes, "Kennedy Urged Consideration of Kavanaugh for High Court, Book Says," *Washington Post,* November 22, 2019, A11.

54. Anemona Hartocollis and Dana Goldstein, "Tolerance Wanes on the Hard-Drinking Bros-Will-Be-Bros Culture," *New York Times,* September 30, 2018, A24; Gina Belafonte, "'Risky Business' and Brett Kavanaugh, 35 Years Later," *New York Times,* September 30, 2018, 31.

55. Peter Baker and Carl Hulse, "Echoes of Anita Hill, But in a Different Era for Women," *New York Times,* September 17, 2018, A1; Rebecca Traister, "Fury Is a Political Weapon," *New York Times,* September 30, 2018, SR1; Anita Hill, "Let's Talk About How to End Sexual Violence," *New York Times,* May 9, 2019, https ://www.nytimes.com/2019/05/09/opinion/anita-hill-sexual-violence.html.

56. Haley Sweetland Edwards, "How Christine Blasey Ford's Testimony Changed America," *Time,* October 4, 2018, time.com/5415027/christine-blasey-ford -testimony/; Philip Rucker and Robert Costa, "'The Trauma for a Man': Male Fury and Fear Rises in GOP on Defense of Kavanaugh," *Washington Post,* October 1, 2018, www.washingtonpost.com/politics/the-trauma-for-a-man-male-fury-and -fear-rises-in-gop-in-defense-of-kavanaugh/2018/10/01/f48499a2-c595-11e8-b2b5 -79270f9cce17_story.html.

57. Rebecca Johnson, "All the Rage," *Vogue,* December 2018, 70–76; Elizabeth Dias, "Mormon Women's Group Seeks a Break in the Process," *New York Times,* September 27, 2018.

58. Ruth Marcus, "Two Friends, One Judge—and a Fight for the Senate and Supreme Court," *New York Times,* November 24, 2019, A22.

59. www.murkowski.senate.gov/about-lisa.

60. Marcus, "Friends," A23–24.

61. Heather Caygle, "Record Breaking Number of Women Run for Office," Politico, March 8, 2018, www.politico.com/story/2018/03/08/women-rule-midterms-443267; Dan Balz, "8 Questions for the Midterm Elections," *Washington Post,* September 4, 2018; Elaine Kamarck, "2018: Another Year of the Woman," Brookings, November 7, 2018, www .brookings.edu/blog/fixgov/2018/11/07/2018-another-year.

62. Kate Zernike, "Women Break Barriers, but Feel Shortchanged," *New York Times,* October 31, 2018, A1.

63.   Kate Zernike, "Women's New Political Strategy: Rip Up the Script and Run as You," *New York Times,* July 15, 2018, A1; Caitlin Moscatello, *See Jane Run: The Inspiring Story of the Women Changing American Politics* (Boston: E.P. Dutton, 2019); Joe Pinsker, "The Job of Campaigning Is Extremely Family-Unfriendly," *Atlantic,* July 27, 2019, https://www.theatlantic.com/family/archive/2019/07/campaign-funds -child-care-fec/594943/.

64.   Susan Chira, "Mom Is Running for Office," *New York Times,* April 15, 2018; Kate Zernike, "Jousting With Election Opponents and Wiping Runny Noses," *New York Times,* September 13, 2018, A14.

65.   Fairfight.com/about-stacey-abrams; Melanye Price, "A Win for Black Women," *New York Times,* August 13, 2020, A23.

66.   "Women in the U.S. Congress 2019," www.cawp.rutgers.edu/women-us-congress-2019.

67.   Beatrice Jin, "Congress's Incoming Class Is Younger, Bluer, More Diverse than Ever," *Politico,* November 23, 2018, https://www.politico.com/interactives/2018 /interactive_116th-congress-freshman-younger-bluer-diverse/; fairfight.com/about -stacey-abrams.

68.   Emily Davie, Dine Herbst, and Sandra Sobieraj Westfall, "Women Take the Lead," *People,* December 17, 2018, 124–27; Dan Balz, "A Democratic Freshman Faces the Task of Governing," *Washington Post,* January 6, 2019, A2; "Special Section: The Women of the 116th Congress,'" *New York Times,* January 17, 2019, F; Jennifer Steinhauer, *The Firsts: The Inside Story of the Women Reshaping Congress* (Chapel Hill, NC: Algonquin Books of Chapel Hill, 2020).

69.   Danielle Kurtzleben, "The New Congress Has a Record Number of Women—But Very Few Republican Women," *Morning Edition,* January 3, 2019; Susan Chira, "Banner Year for Female Candidates Doesn't Extend to GOP Women," *New York Times,* November 16, 2018, A12; Nancy L. Cohen, "Why Female G.O.P. Politicians Are Vanishing," *New York Times,* January 1, 2020; Susan Brooks, "Election Watch," Women & Politics Institute, American University, webinar broadcast June 3, 2020.

70.   Catie Edmondson and Jasmine C. Lee, "Meet the New Freshmen in Congress: More Democrats, Diversity and Women," *New York Times,* December 1, 2018, A21; Janet Adamy, "Black Women's Long Struggle for Voting Rights," *Wall Street Journal,* August 1–2, 2020, C3; https://www.rollcall.com/2018/12/18/six-states-will-boast-all -women-senate-delegations-in-2019/; Jonathan Martin and Alexander Burns, "Woman in Congress: A First for Mississippi," *New York Times,* March 22, 2018, A10.

71.   Adam Taylor, "U.S. Gains Female Lawmakers but Trails Other Nations," *Washington Post,* October 10, 2019.

72.   Elahe Izadi and Kayla Epstein, "A Squad Is Born," *Washington Post,* July 29, 2019, C1; Christina Zhao, "Nancy Pelosi Dismisses Ocasio-Cortez, Omar, Tlaib, Pressley as Just 'Four People' After Democrats Split on Border Bill," *Newsweek,* July 6, 2019.

73.   Elise Viebeck, "Historic Gains As 100-Plus Women Sworn in to Congress," *Washington Post,* January 4, 2019, A5.

74.   Adam Nagourney and Sydney Ember, "Red Statehouse Blue Statehouse," *New York Times,* November 8, 2018, F1.

75.   "Women in Elective Office 2019: Statewide," Center for American Women and Politics, https://cawp.rutgers.edu/women-elective-office-2019; Emily

Wax-Thibodeaux, "Where Women Call the Shots," *Washington Post*, May 20, 2019, A1; Karen Tumulty, "In Colorado Politics, Power Has a New Look," *Washington Post*, April 14, 2019, A21; Karen Tumulty, "A Pink Wave Sweeps Michigan," *Washington Post*, August 12, 2018.

76.   Adeel Hassan, "Picture That Was Worth 17 Victories in Texas Judicial Elections," *New York Times*, November 10, 2018.

77.   Amy Chozick, "Down With the Year of the Woman," *New York Times*, October 21, 2018; Karen Tumulty, "In Politics, Women Are the Norm, Not a Novelty," *Washington Post*, November 7, 2018; Monica Hesse, "People, Stop Calling is a 'Pink Wave,'" *Washington Post*, November 8, 2018, C1.

78.   Lisa Lerer, "Gillibrand's Failed Run Show's Feminism's Promise and Limits," *New York Times*, September 2 2019, A1.

79.   Susan Chira, "Last Name Is No Longer Women's First Asset," *New York Times*, March 11, 2019, A8; Karen Tumulty, "2020's True Running Mates," *Washington Post*, March 20, 2019, A21.

80.   Sabrina Siddiqui, "Why the 'Likability' Question Pursues 2020 Female Candidates Even as They Make History," *The Guardian*, February 4, 2019, https://www .theguardian.com/us-news/2019/feb/04/why-the-likability-question-pursues-2020 -female-candidates-even-as-they-make-history; Margaret Carlson, "There's No 'This Woman' Anymore," *Washington Post*, February 11, 2019.

81.   Michelle Cottle, "Maybe Next Time Ladies," *New York Times*, March 5, 2020, A26; Karen Tumulty, "An Online Onslaught Awaits Biden VP Pick," *Washington Post*, August 6, 2020, A23; Editorial Board, "Amy Klobuchar and Elizabeth Warren Are Democrats' Top Choices for President," *New York Times*, January 20, 2020, A24.

82.   Jessica Bennett, "The Political Headwinds for Forceful Women," *New York Times*, August 10, 2020, A13; Maggie Astor, "Those Stubborn Double Standards," *New York Times*, November 8, 2019, A16; Lisa Lerer, "Taking Feminism to Heart, If Not to the Caucuses," *New York Times*, January 18, 2020, A1.

83.   Monica Hesse, "Sexism Doesn't Have a Breezy Answer," *Washington Post*, January 16, 2020, C1.

84.   Timothy Egan, "The Prosecutor Trump Fears Most," *New York Times*, August 14, 2020.

85.   Marc Fisher, "Mask Advocates Push Back, Seeking Mandates, Courtesy," *Washington Post*, August 20, 2020, A4.

86.   Campbell Robertson and Robert Gebeloff, "When It Comes to 'Essential,' It's a Woman's World Today," *New York Times*, April 19, 2020, A1.

87.   Jeremy W. Peters, "A Culture War Is Simmering in Quarantine," *New York Times*, April 21, 2020, A1; David Brooks, "What the Working Class Is Trying to Say," *New York Times*, November 9, 2018, A29; Lola Fadulu, "Rule Will End Food Stamps for 700,000," *New York Times*, December 5, 2019, A1.

88.   Nicholas Kristof, "The Forgotten Americans, Now Under Trump," *New York Times*, February 9, 2020, SR9; Rosa Brook, "For Working Class Americans, Disaster Is a Misstep Away," review of *Tightrope: Americans Reaching for Hope* by Nicholas Kristof and Sheryl Wu Dunn, *Washington Post*, February 2, 2020, B7.

89.   Vanessa Williams, "Report: Black Women Work Hard but Are Undervalued and Underpaid," *Washington Post*, June 9, 2017; "Labor Force Participation: Women," https://fred.stlouisfed.org/series/LNS11300002.

90.   Samantha Schmidt, "Women Hit Hardest by Job Losses," *Washington Post,* May 11,
       2020, A1; Heather Long, "As Schools Remain Closed, Mothers Are Leaving the
       Workforce," *Washington Post,* November 7, 2020, A11; Patricia Cohen, "Recession's
       Toll on Women Point to a Lasting Setback," *New York Times,* November 18, 2020, A1.

91.   Brigid Schulte, interviewed by Terry Gross, *Fresh Air,* May 21, 2020, https://fresh
       airarchive.org/segments/pandemic-makes-evident-grotesque-gender-inequality
       -household-work.

92.   Heather Long, "Lack of Child Care Slowing Recovery," *Washington Post,* July 4,
       2020, A1; Justin Lahart, "School's at Home? So Long, Career," *Wall Street Journal,*
       July 25–26, 2020, B12; Jennifer Medina and Lisa Lerer, "Corner Office? Try a
       Closet Office, With Chores and Day Care," *New York Times,* April 24, 2020, A19;
       Hanna Rosin, *The End of Men and the Rise of Women* (New York: Riverhead
       /Penguin, 2012); Alicia Sasser Modestino, "Child-care Crisis Could Set Women
       Back a Generation," *Washington Post,* August 2, 2020, G1.

93.   Sue Shellenbarger, "The Challenges That Working Mothers Still Face," *Wall Street
       Journal,* January 4–5, 2020, C1; Claire Cain Miller, "How To Close a Gender Gap:
       True Job Flexibility," *New York Times,* February 7, 2017.

94.   Brigid Schulte and Haley Swenson, "An Unexpected Upside to Lockdown: Men
       Have Discovered Housework," *The Guardian,* June 17, 2020, www.theguardian.com
       /us-news/2020/jun/17/gender-roles-parenting-housework-coronavirus-pandemic;
       Bee Wilson, "Feeding a Family Isn't a Job for Mothers Alone," *Wall Street Journal,*
       May 11–12, 2019, C1.

95.   Claire Cain Miller, "Nearly Half of Men Say They Do Most of the Home
       Schooling. 3 Percent of Women Agree," *New York Times,* May 6, 2020, https
       ://www.nytimes.com/2020/05/06/upshot/pandemic-chores-homeschooling
       -gender-html.

96.   Darcy Lockman, "What 'Good' Fathers Get Away With," *New York Times,* May 5,
       2019, SR2; Darcy Lockman, *All the Rage: Mothers, Fathers, and the Myth of Equal
       Partnership* (New York: HarperCollins Publishers, 2019).

97.   Christopher Ingraham, "The Labor Value of Parents At Home," *Washington Post,*
       September 3, 2019; Katha Pollitt, "Day Care for All," *New York Times,* February 10,
       2019, SR1.

98.   Shellenbarger, "Challenges," *WSJ;* Eric Yoder, "'Drafting Error' Means Some
       Federal Workers Excluded from Family Leave Law," *Washington Post,* January 10,
       2020, A4.

99.   Evan Hill et al., "How George Floyd Was Killed in Police Custody," *New York
       Times,* May 31, 2020, https://www.nytimes.com/2020/05/31/us/george-floyd
       -investigation.html; Cherisse Johnson, "Will Smith on Race Relations in America:
       'It Isn't Getting Worse, It's Getting Filmed,'" July 31, 2016, HIPHOPDX, https
       ://hiphopdx.com/news/id.39832/title.will-smith-on-race-relations-in-america-it
       -isnt-getting-worse-its-getting-filmed.

100.   Serio Pecanha, "I Can't Breathe," *Washington Post,* July 7, 2020, A27.

101.   Weiyi Cai, et al., "Special Report: How Black Lives Matter Reached Every Corner
       of the United States," *New York Times,* June 16, 2020, F1; Amy Harmon, "'Utterly
       Different' Scene at Protests as White Faces Turn Out in Droves, Too," *New York
       Times,* June 13, 2020, A19; Michelle Boorstein and Hannah Natanson, "Mitt

Romney, Marching with Evangelicals, Becomes First U.S. Senator to Join George Floyd Protests in DC," *Washington Post*, June 8, 2020, https://www.washingtonpost .com/dc-md-va/2020/06/07/romney-protest-black-lives-matter/.

102. Jose A. Del Real, Robert Samuels, and Tim Craig, "From Slogan to Movement, Embraced by the Masses," *Washington Post*, June 10, 2020, A1; Ruth Marcus, "The Systemic Rot in Our Justice System," *Washington Post*, June 16, 2020, A25.

103. Tiffany Hsu, "Aunt Jemima To Be Renamed, After 131 Years," *New York Times*, June 18, 2020, B1; Zachary Lewis, "Small Bird, With Name Honoring a Confederate General, Gets New Moniker," *Washington Post*, August 13, 2020, A20; Rick Rojas, "Alliance Brings Down Flag in Mississippi," *New York Times*, July 11, 2020, A1; Mihir Zavdri, "Boy Scouts Announce Diversity Merit Badge and Support for Black Lives Matter," *New York Times*, June 17, 2020.

104. Aris Folley, "John Lewis Visits 'Black Lives Matter Plaza,' Calls Protests Very Moving," *The Hill*, June 7, 2020, thehill.com/homenews/house/501591-john-lewis -visits-black-lives-matter-plaza.

105. *June Medical Services, LLC v. Russo*, Oyez, www.oyez.org/cases/2019/18-1323; Linda Greenhouse, "The Fictional Middle Ground on Abortion," *New York Times*, March 13, 2020.

106. Linda Greenhouse, "Chasing Abortion Rights Across the State Line," *New York Times*, November 27, 2016.

107. Ian Millhiser, "The Coming Supreme Court Showdown Over Birth Control," www .vox.com/2020/1/14/21059931/supreme-court-birth-control-religious-liberty -pennsylvania-little-sisters.

108. *Little Sisters of the Poor Saints Peter and Paul Home v. Pennsylvania*, Oyez, www.oyez .org/cases/2019/19-431.

109. Alexander Burns, "Joe Biden's Campaign Announcement Video, Annotated," *New York Times*, April 25, 2019, https://www.nytimes.com/2019/04/25/us/politics /biden-campaign-video-announcement-html.

110. Teo Armus, "Kamala Harris Isn't the First Black Woman to Run for VP. Meet Charlotta Bass," *Washington Post*, August 12, 2020, https://www.washingtonpost .com/nation/2020/08/12/bass-kamala-first-black-vp/.

111. David Ignatius, "Harris's Story Is American As Can Be," *Washington Post*, August 17, 2020, A19; Michele L. Norris, "Trump's Nickname for Harris Is a Punch That Doesn't Land," *Washington Post*, August 14, 2020, A19; Petula Dvorak, "Harris for VP Is Peak Gen X," *Washington Post*, August 14, 2020, B1; Sonia Rao, "Her Ethnicity Takes Discussion Beyond Black and White," *Washington Post*, August 19, 2020, C1.

112. Peter Baker, "Racist Attacks, Conspiracy Theories and War on the Post Office," *New York Times*, August 18, 2020, A19; Katie Rogers, "Trump, Pushing a Racist Proposition, Questions Harris's U.S. Citizenship," *New York Times*, August 14, 2020, A21; Ashley Parker, "As Trump Targets Harris, A Favorite Insult Takes on a Different Connotation," *Washington Post*, August 13, 2020, A7; Katie Rogers, "Trump's View of Women: 'Nasty' Like Harris or Housewives," *New York Times*, August 13, 2020, A16.

113. Sara Burnett and Amanda Seitz, "'We Have Her Back': The War Room Blocking Kamala Harris' Trolls," *Christian Science Monitor*, August 12, 2020, www.csmonitor .com/USA/Politics/2020/0812/We-Have-Her-Back-The-war-room-blocking

-Kamala-Harris-trolls; Annie Linskey and Isaac Stanley-Becker, "Biden Camp Braces for Sexism Over VP Pick," *Washington Post*, August 9, 2020, A1.

114. Ronald G. Shafer, "Sweat, Steak and Style: In 1948, TV Gave Political Conventions a Makeover," *Washington Post*, August 18, 2020, B5; Jeff Greenfield, "The Lost Draw of Conventions: The Drama," *Wall Street Journal*, August 22–23, 2020, C7.

115. Michael M. Grynbaum, "Convention Drew Ratings That Reflect Divide in U.S.," *New York Times*, August 22, 2020, A16; Paul Sonne, "Trumps Use of the Marine Band Prompts Questions," *Washington Post*, October 12, 2020, A2.

116. Kay Nolan and Michael D. Shear, "Insults and Untruths Flow at Trump Campaign Stops," *New York Times*, August 17, 2020; Jonathan Martin, "A Nominee Who Trusted His Message," *New York Times*, August 22, 2020, A1.

117. Michael Barone, "The Normalcy of Trump's Republican Party," *Wall Street Journal*, August 22–23, 2020, A11.

118. Aris Folley, "Kamala Harris Draws Support from Unique Bloc: Sorority Sisters," *The Hill*, August 16, 2020, thehill.com/homenews/campaign/512162-kamala -harris-draws-support.

119. Petula Dvorak, "Trump Uses Old Ideals to Woo Suburban Women," *Washington Post*, October 16, 2020, B1; Lisa Lerer and Jennifer Medina, "Mothers Are Fed Up, and Democrats Aim to Get Their Vote," *New York Times*, August 18, 2020, A18.

120. Amy B. Wang, "Trump Demeans Women, Just as He Needs Their Votes," *Washington Post*, October 31, 2020, A8.

121. Lerer, "Mothers Fed Up"; Yuval Levin, "Putting It All Back Together," review of *The Upswing* by Robert D. Putnam and Shaylyn Romney Garrett, *Wall Street Journal*, October 10-11, 2020, C7.

122. Danielle Kurtzleben, "The Complicated History of Moms as the Face of Protest Movements," *Morning Edition*, July 28, 2020.

123. Dani McClain, *We Live For the We: The Political Power of Black Motherhood* (New York: Bold Type Books/Hachette Inc., 2019).

124. Seyward Darby, *Sisters in Hate: American Women on the Front Lines of White Nationalism* (New York: Little Brown and Co., 2020), 7–12.

125. Kurtzleben, "Complicated."

126. Dani Blum, "'The Moms Are Here': 'Wall of Moms' Groups Mobilize Nationwide," *New York Times*, July 27, 2020, https://www.nytimes.com/2020/07/27/parenting /wall-of-moms-protests.html.

127. Danielle Kurtzleben, "What the 'Wall of Moms' Protests Say About Motherhood, Race in America," *Politics Podcast*, July 28, 2020, NPR; Jennifer Weiner, "'Suburban Housewives' Revolt," *New York Times*, July 28, 2020.

128. Vanessa Friedman, "What Does It Mean to 'Look Like A Mom'?" *New York Times*, July 30, 2020, D2.

129. Robin Givhan, "The Black Lives Matter Movement Hits a Different Kind of Wall," *Washington Post*, August 6, 2020.

130. Henry Goldblatt, "Not All of Them Want to Speak to the Manager," *New York Times*, August 2, 2020, ST2; Petula Dvorak, "We Need a Name for 'Karen' Behavior," *Washington Post*, December 10, 2021, B1.

131. Susan Page and Sarah Elbeshbishi, "Exclusive: The Conventions Over, Joe Biden Leads Donald Trump by a Narrower 50%-43% in USAToday/Suffolk Poll," *USA*

Today, September 2, 2020, usatoday.com/story/nes/poitics/elections/2020/09/02
/biden-leads-trump-narrower-7-points-post-conventions-suffolk-poll/3446536001/.

132. Danya Ruttenberg, "Jewish Tradition Calls on the Rest of Us to Act in Ginsburg's
     Memory," *Washington Post*, September 22, 2020, www.washingtonpost.com/outlook
     /2020/09/22/ginsburg-rosh-hashanah-tzaddik.

133. Nicholas Fandos and Emily Cochrane, "A Historic Tribute for Ginsburg Inside a
     Capitol Divided Over Replacing Her," *New York Times*, September 26, 2020, A16.

134. Linda Greenhouse, "Ruth Bader Ginsburg, Supreme Court's Feminist Icon, Is Dead
     at 87," *New York Times*, September 18, 2020, www.nytimes.com/2020/09/18/us/ruth
     -bader-ginsburg-dead.html; Vanessa Friedman, "Ginsburg's Collar: An Accessory, a
     Symbol and a Gauntlet," *New York Times*, September 21, 2020, A16.

135. www.timesofisrael.com/relative-confirms-ginsburgs-dying-wish-was-to-keep
     -trump-from-filling-her-seat/; Aaron Blake, "The Brazen Claim by Trump and
     Tucker Carlson about Ruth Bader Ginsburg's Dying Wish," *Washington Post*,
     September 22, 2020, www.washingtonpost.com/politics/2020/09/22/tucker-carlson
     -trump-baselessly-suggest-ginsburgs-granddaughter-lied-about-ginsburgs-dying
     -wish/.

136. Thehill.com/homenews/senate/517194-senate-republicans-face-tough-decision-on
     -replacing-ginsburg.

137. Amy Howe, "Profile of a Potential Nominee: Amy Coney Barrett," September 21,
     2020, https://www.scotusblog.com/2020/09/profile-of-a-potential-nominee-amy
     -coney-barrett/; Elizabeth Dias, Rebecca R. Ruiz, and Sharon LaFraniere, "Court
     Nominee Is Conservative Rooted in Faith," *New York Times*, October 12, 2020, A1;
     Matt Keeley, "Who Is Amy Coney Barrett's Family?" *Newsweek*, September 20,
     2020, www.newsweek.com/who-amy-coney-barretts-family-potential-supreme
     -court-nominee-mother-seven-has-six-siblings-1533120.

138. Samantha Lock, "Father of Seven: Who Is Amy Coney Barrett's Husband Jesse M.
     Barrett?" *US Guardian*, September 27, 2020, www.the-sun.com/news/who-amy
     -coney-barretts-husband-jesse/.

139. Ruth Graham and Sharon LaFraniere, "Close-Knit Faith Group Helped Shape
     Barrett," *New York Times*, October 9, 2020, A1.

140. "Religious Group Scrubs All References to Amy Coney Barrett from Its Website,"
     The Guardian, September 30, 2020, www.theguardian.com/us-news/2020/sep/30
     /people-of-praise-amy-coney-barrett-website.

141. Ruth Graham, "Barrett's Life Inspires Conservative Women," *New York Times*,
     September 29, 2020, A21.

142. Ruth Marcus, "A Judicial Record That Should Alarm Liberals," *Washington Post*,
     September 22, 20202, A21.

143. E. J. Dionne, "Amy Coney Barrett and the GOP's Hypocrisy About Religion,"
     Washington Post, September 28, 2020, A21.

144. Linda Greenhouse, "Questions for Amy Coney Barrett," *New York Times*, October 11,
     2020, SR6; Marjorie Cohn, "Barrett Is Poised To Become Most Radical Right-Wing
     Member of Supreme Court," TruthOut, October 16, 2020, www.truthout.org/articles
     /barrett-is-poised-to-become-the-most-radical-right-wing-member-of-supreme-court.

145. Nicholas Fandos, "Democrats, Facing Confirmation Battle, Fear Feinstein Isn't Up
     to the Task," *New York Times*, October 11, 2020, A30.

146. Ruth Marcus, "Barrett's Telling Silences," *Washington Post,* October 16, 2020, A23; Eugene Scott, "Originalism and the People Left Out of the Constitution," *Washington Post,* October 19, 2020, A2; Seung Min Kim and Karoun Demirjian, "Barrett on Swift Course to Supreme Court Confirmation," *Washington Post,* October 16, 2020, A12.

147. Claire Cain Miller and Alisha Haridasani Gupta, "Mothers in Public Office Still Walk a 'Tightrope,'" *New York Times,* October 15, 2020, A1; Melissa Block, "GOP Uses Barrett's Motherhood to Appeal to Suburban Voters, Analysts Say," *Morning Edition,* October 14, 2020.

148. Seung Min Kim, "Abortion Rights Group Calls for Feinstein To Lose Judiciary Committee Post," *Washington Post,* October 17, 2020, A4.

149. Seung Min Kim, "Barrett Confirmed to Supreme Court," *Washington Post,* October 27, 2020, A1.

150. Seung Min Kim, "Rancor in Senate with Barrett Set for Confirmation," *Washington Post,* October 24, 2020, A8; Ruth Marcus, "The Bombshell Consequences of This Pick," *Washington Post,* September 27, 2020, A27; David Cole, "This Is the Supreme Court's Tipping Point," *Washington Post,* September 27, 2020, A27; Robin Givhan, "Trump Revels in Barrett's Moment in the Spotlight," *Washington Post,* October 28, 2020, A2.

151. Shane Goldmacher, "Six Takeaways From the First Presidential Debate," *New York Times,* September 30, 2020, www.nytimes.com/live/2020/09/30/us/politics/debate-takeaways.html.

152. Rachel Treisman, "Kentucky Grand Jury Indicts 1 of 3 Officers in Breonna Taylor Case," *NPR,* September 23, 2020; Petula Dvorak, "Is It Too Late To Hope for a Black Woman on the Supreme Court?" *Washington Post,* October 27, 2020, B1.

153. David Nakamura, "Chorus of 'Dear Leader' Comparisons from Trump Critics," *Washington Post,* October 11, 2020, A7.

154. "Trump Returns Home After Downplaying Disease," *New York Times,* October 7, 2020, www.nytimes.com/live2020/10/05/world/covid-trump.

155. "Harris vs. Pence: 'Never Has Something So Boring Been So Appreciated,'" *New York Times,* October 8, 2020, www.nytimes.com/2020/10/08/opinion/vice-presidential-debate-highlights.html.

156. Michael M. Grynbaum, "This Week's Debate Has Officially Been Cancelled," *New York Times,* October 11, 2020, https://www.nytimes.com/2020/10/11/us/elections/this-weeks-presidential-debate-has-officially-been-canceled.html.

157. Maggie Astor, "Facing a 'Double Bind' of Racism and Sexism," *New York Times,* October 10, 2020, A13; Karen Tumulty, "How Sexist, Racist Attacks on Harris Spread," *Washington Post,* October 11, 2020, A27.

158. Nicholas Bogel-Burroughs, Shaila Dewan, and Kathleen Gray, "Whitmer Said To Be Targeted In Kidnap Plot," *New York Times,* October 9, 2020, A1; Abigail Hauslohner, Matt Zapotosky, Kayla Ruble, and Devlin Barrett, "History of Self-Styled Militia Groups Has Long Vexed Michigan Authorities," *Washington Post,* October 11, 2020, A11.

159. Mike Giglio, "A Pro-Trump Militant Group Has Recruited Thousands of Police, Soldiers and Veterans," *The Atlantic,* January 11, 2021, www.theatlantic.com/magazine/archive/2020/11/right-wing-militias-civil-war/616473/.

160.   William Wan and Jacqueline Dupree, "U.S. Breaks Record for Daily Cases," *Washington Post,* October 24, 2020, A1; "Coronavirus Disease 2020," https://g.co /kgs/pKwe7W; *CBS Evening News,* October 18, 2020.

161.   Debbie Lord, "Election 2020: When Does Early Voting Begin; Which States Do It?" Kiro 7 News, September 3, 2020, www.kiro7.com/news/trending/election-2020 -when-does-early-voting-begin-which-states-do-it/VGLJWCOAV5M5G4Y6M SCDFSTGA/.

162.   Michael McDonald, "Early Vote Analysis for Sunday, Oct. 25: Early Voting Continues at a Record Pace," US Elections Project, https://electproject.github.io /Early-Vote-2020G/index.html.

163.   Mark Berman, "Guns at Voting Sites Emerge as Flash Point in Michigan," *Washington Post,* October 27, 2020, A9; Dave Boucher, "No Ruling Yet from Michigan Supreme Court Likely Means Open Carry Allowed on Election Day," *Detroit Free Press,* November 2, 2020, www.freep.com/story/news/politics/electgions/2020/11/02 /no-word-michigan-court-open-carry-ban-election-day/6121466002/.

164.   "State of the Race," *New York Times,* October 24, 2020, A17.

Epilogue: Not Enough

1.   "National General Election VEP Turnout Rates, 1789-Present," www.electproject .org/national-1789-present; "Gender Differences in Voter Turnout," www.cawp .rutgers.edu/facts/voters/turnout.

2.   Erin Delmore, "This Is How Women Voters Decided the 2020 Election," November 13, 2020, www.nbcnews.com/know-your-value/feature/how-women-voters-decided -2020-election/ncna1247746; Dora Mekouar, "Women Outnumber and Outvote Men, But They Don't Vote Alike," *Voice of America,* May 5, 2021, www.voanews .com/a/usa_all-about-america_women-outnumber-and-outvote-men-they-dont -vote-alike/6205437.html.

3.   Michael W. Ruane. "Similarities Striking at Century Mark," *Washington Post,* November 2, 2020; John M. Barry, "History Tells Us What a Virus Can Do to a President," *Washington Post,* October 6, 2020, A25.

4.   Caitlin Myers, "Restricting Abortion Restricts Women's Lives," *Washington Post,* November 30, 2021, A25.

5.   Katha Pollitt, "What Abortion Rights Supporters Need to Say," *New York Times,* August 5, 2015.

6.   Katha Pollitt, "The Long Fight for Reproductive Rights Is Only Getting Harder," *Washington Post,* May 17, 2020, B7; Frances Robles, "With Flurry of Bills, Republican Legislatures Make Abortions Harder to Get," *New York Times,* May 10, 2015, A1; Linda Greenhouse, "The Fictional Middle Ground on Abortion," *New York Times,* March 13, 2020.

7.   Sabrina Tavernise, "Abortion Rates in U.S. Show a Steady Decline, But Not for Poor Women," *New York Times,* July 11, 2019, A17; Seth Stephens-Davidowitz, "The Return of the D.I.Y. Abortion," *New York Times,* March 6, 2016, SR2.

8.   Ariana Eunjung Cha, "Alabama Governor Signs Nation's Most Restrictive Abortion Law," *Washington Post,* October 30, 2019, A2.

9.   Ariana Eunjung Cha and Scott Clement, "Abortion Rights Support Steady Despite Growing Partisan Divide, Survey Finds," *Washington Post,* August 14, 2019, A3;

Emily Guskin and Scott Clement, "Abortion Support Is the Highest It's Been in Two Decades As Challenges Mount," *Washington Post*, July 10, 2019, www .washingtonpost.com/politics/2019/07/10/abortion-support-is-highest-its-been -two-decades-challenges-roe-mount; Arian Eunjung Cha, "Poll: 59 Percent Back Abortion Rights," *Washington Post*, January 22, 2020, A2.

10.   Alexandra DeSanctis, "How Democrats Purged 'Safe, Legal Rare,' From Their Party," *Washington Post*, November 17, 2019, B3; Robert Costa, "Sen. Hawley Lays Down Strict Antiabortion Marker for High Court Nominees," *Washington Post*, July 27, 2020, A4.

11.   Michael Lewis, "Men vs. Women: Differences in Shopping Habits & Buying," *Money Crashers*, March 1, 2022, www.moneycrashers.com/men-vs-women-shopping -habits-buying-decisions/.

12.   Francesca Donner and Emma Goldberg, "In 25 Years, the Pay Gap Has Shrunk by Just 8 Cents," *New York Times*, March 24, 2021, www.nytimes.com/2021/03/24/us /equal-pay-day-explainer.html.

13.   Monica Hesse, "Why Are We Surprised the Birthrate Is Down?", *Washington Post*, June 6, 2021, B1.

14.   Erin Barry, "25% of US Households Are Either Unbanked or Underbanked," CNBC, March 9, 2021, https://www.cnbc.com/2019/03/08/25percent-of-us -households-are-either-unbanked-or-underbanked.html; "2009 FDIC Survey of Unbanked and Underbanked Households," updated 2021, https://www.fdic.gov /analysis/household-survey/2009/index.html.

15.   "Women in Elective Office 2019," www.cawp.rutgers.edu/women-elective-office-2019.

16.   Chris Murphy, *The Violence Inside Us: A Brief History of an Ongoing American Tragedy* (New York: Random House, 2020).

17.   ncadv.org/statistics; Alisa Roth, "When Home Is the Most Dangerous Place," review of *No Visible Bruises: What We Don't Know About Domestic Violence Can Kill Us* by Rachel Louise Snyder, *New York Times Book Review*, June 9, 2019, 15; Ashley Southall, "Decline in Police Reports About Domestic Violence May Be 'Very Scary' Sign," *New York Times*, April 19, 2020, A17; Linda Hirshman, *Reckoning: The Epic Battle Against Sexual Abuse and Harassment* (New York: Houghton Mifflin Harcourt, 2019).

18.   Laura L. Rogers, "The Violence Against Women Act, An Ongoing Fixture," February 19, 2020, https://www.justice.gov/archives/ovw/blog/violence-against -women-act-ongoing-fixture-nation-s-response-domestic-violence-dating; Jay Willis, "Why Can't the Senate Pass the Violence Against Women Act," *GQ*, December 13, 2019, www.gq.com/story/senate-violence-against-women-act.

19.   "The Sheppard–Towner Maternity and Infancy Act," https://history.house.gov /Historical-Highlights/1901-1950/The-Sheppard%E2%80%93Towner-Maternity -and-Infancy-Act/.

20.   Steven Ross Johnson, "The US Maternal Mortality Rate Surges by Nearly 20% in 2020," *US News & World Report*, February 23, 2022, https://www.usnews.com/news /health-news/articles/2022-02-23/u-s-maternal-mortality-rate-surged-in-2020.

21.   Luis Velarde, "In U.S., A Rising Death Rate in Maternity Wards," *Washington Post*, February 19, 2019, E1; Lindsey Bever, "60 Percent of Women's Pregnancy-related Deaths Are Preventable, CDC Says," *Washington Post*, May 14, 2019; "Maternal Mortality: An American Crisis," transcript, CBS News, August 5, 2018.

22.   Erin Duffin, "Percentage of the U.S. Population with a College Degree by Gender, 1940-2019," March 31, 2020, www.statista.com/statistics/184272/educational -attainment-of-college-diploma-or-higher-education-by-gender; Mark J. Perry, "Women Earned Majority of Doctoral Degrees in 2019 for 11th Straight Year and Outnumber Men in Grad School 141 to 100," https://www.aei.org/carpe-diem /women-earned-majority-of-doctoral-degrees-in-2019-for-11th-straight-year -and-outnumber-men-in-grad-school-141-to-100/#:~:text=Perry&text=The%20 Council%20of%20Graduate%20Schools,at%20US%20universities%20in%202019.

23.   Nikki Katz, "Black Women Are the Most Educated Group in the U.S.," ThoughtCo., June 20, 2020, www.thoughtco.com/black-women-most-educated-group-us-4048763?; Richard V. Reeves and Katherine Guyot, "Black Women Are Earning More College Degrees, But That Alone Won't Close Race Gaps," December 4, 2017, www.brookings .edu/blog/social-mobility-memos/2017/12/04/black-women-are-earning-more-college -degrees-but-that-alone-wont-close-race-gaps/.

24.   Andrew Van Dam, "Once Sidelined, Women and Minorities Are Finally Returning to the Workforce," *Washington Post,* November 11, 2019, A16; Ai-Jen Poo and Palak Shah, "The Future of Work Looks Like This," *New York Times,* July 5, 2020, SR13.

25.   "Women in the Legal Profession," https://www.abalegalprofile.com/women/.

26.   Patrick Boyle, "Nation's Physician Workforce Evolving: More Women, a Bit Older, and Toward Different Specialties," Association of American Medical Colleges, February 2, 2021, https://www.aamc.org/data-reports/workforce/interactive-data /active-physicians-sex-and-specialty-2015; Linda Searing, "The Big Number: Women Now Outnumber Men in Medical Schools," *Washington Post,* December 23, 2019, www.washingtonpost.com/health/the-big-number-women-now-outnumber -men-in-medical-schools/2019/12/20/8b9eddea-2277-11ea-bed5-880264cc91a9 _story.html.

27.   "Society of Women Engineers Research Update: Women in Engineering by the Numbers,"https://alltogether.swe.org/2019/11/swe-research-update-women-in -engineering-by-the-numbers-nov-2019/.

28.   Alia Wong, "The US Teaching Population Is Getting Bigger, and More Female," *The Atlantic,* February 2, 2019, https://www.theatlantic.com/education/archive /2019/02/the-explosion-of-women-teachers/582622/.

29.   Bridget Turner Kelly, "Though More Women Are on College Campuses, Climbing the Professor Ladder Remains Challenge," March 29, 2019, https://www.brookings .edu/blog/brown-center-chalkboard/2019/03/29/though-more-women-are-on -college-campuses-climbing-the-professor-ladder-remains-a-challenge/.

30.   "Women Presidents," American Council of Education, 2017, https://www.aceacps .org/women-presidents/.

31.   Alan Blinder, "The Power Gap in the Power Five," *New York Times,* September 15, 2019, SP1.

32.   Amy Chozick, "Female Ranchers Are Reclaiming the West," *New York Times,* January 13, 2019, BU6.

33.   Arielle Emmett, "What Are U.S. Airlines Missing? Women Pilots," *Smithsonian Magazine,* September 2020, www.smithsonianmag.com/air-space-magazine/what-are -us-airlines-missing-women-180975608.

34. "Only 4% of Professional Firefighters Are Women," transcript, CBS News, June 24, 2020.

35. "Plumber Demographics and Statistics in the US," https://www.zippia.com/plumber-jobs/demographics/.

36. "The Women of NASA," National Women's History Museum, October 2, 2017, https://www.womenshistory.org/exhibits/women-nasa; Christian Davenport, "Astronaut Brings a Record Home," *Washington Post,* February 7, 2020, A17.

37. Christian Davenport, "NASA to Name Building for Trailblazer," *Washington Post,* June 25, 2020, A18; "Planned NASA Space Telescope Renamed After Astronomer Nancy Grace Roman," *Physics World,* May 21, 2020, https://physicsworld.com/a/planned-nasa-space-telescope-renamed-after-astronomer-nancy-grace-roman.

38. "2020 Nobel Prizes Honor Three Women in Science," October 7, 2020, https://publishing.aip.org/about/news/2020-nobel-prizes-honor-three-women-in-science/.

39. Jana Rich, "It's Time for Women to Have Both a Seat and Voice in the Boardroom," *Washington Post,* January 22, 2020; Alex Katsomitros, "Against the Odds, Ursula Burns' Extraordinary Rise to the Top," *World Finance,* April 1, 2019, www.worldfinance.com/markets/against-the-odds-ursula-burns; Emily Flitter and Anupreeta Das, "Citigroup Names Female Chief, Breaching a Wall Street Barrier," *New York Times,* September 11, 2020, A1.

40. Susan E, Reed, "Corporate Boards Are Diversifying. The C-Suite Isn't," *Washington Post,* January 6, 2019, B2; Jana Rich; Emily Bobrow, "Ursula Burns," *Wall Street Journal,* June 12-13, 2021, C6.

41. Denise Lu, Jon Huang, et al., "The Faces of Power in the United States," *New York Times,* September 12, 2020, A14–16.

42. Hillary Hoffower, "Shonda Rhimes Is Worth at Least $35 Million," *Business Insider,* December 29, 2020, www.businessinsider.com/shonda-rhimes-net-worth-fortune-spending-greys-anatomy-2020-9.

43. Missy Ryan, "Share of Women in Military Didn't Grow Much Over 14 Years, Study Funds," *Washington Post,* May 21, 2020, A20.

44. www.army.mil/article/228392/first_female_four_star_general_dunwoody; Eric Schmidt and Helene Cooper, "Promotions for Female Generals Were Delayed Over Fears of Trump's Reaction," *New York Times,* February 17, 2021, www.nytimes.com/2021/02/17/us/politics/women-generals-promotions-trump.html.

45. Missy Ryan, "Army's Tougher Fitness Test Brings Huge Gender Gap," *Washington Post,* September 27, 2020, A7.

46. Frances Stead Sellers and Dan Lamothe, "Sex Assaults Reported by Service Members Spiked Last Year, Pentagon Says," *Washington Post,* May 3, 2019, A9; Helene Cooper et al., "An Outspoken Pilot With One Long-Kept Secret," *New York Times,* March 27, 2019, A1.

47. Franklyn Carter, "Federal Judge Dismisses U.S. Women's Soccer Team's Equal Pay Claim," *All Things Considered,* May 2, 2020.

48. Mary Louise Kelly, "Stewie Gets Her Own Sneaks: WNBA Star Pens First Deal in a Decade," *All Things Considered,* May 12, 2021.

49. Lauren M. Johnson, "Two Female Coaches and a Female Official Make NFL History by Being on the Field at the Same Time," CNN, September 27, 2020, www.cnn.com/2020/09/27/us/browns-washington-game-females-nfl-history-trnd/index.html.

50. Roman Stubbs, "Making Strides for Transgender Rights," *Washington Post*, July 28, 2020, D1; James Dawson, "New Idaho Law Targets Transgender Residents," *Weekend Edition Saturday*, July 4, 2020.

51. "Women in the Workforce: United States (Quick Take)," Catalyst, October 14, 2020, https://www.catalyst.org/research/women-in-the-workforce-united-states/; Cheridan Chrisnacht and Briana Sullivan, "The Choices Working Mothers Make: About Two-Thirds of 23.5 Million Working Women with Children Under 18 Worked Full-Time in 2018," US Census Bureau, May 8, 2020, https://www.census .gov/library/stories/2021/03/moms-work-and-the-pandemic.html; Kathryn A. Edwards, "Women Are Leaving the Labor Force in Records Numbers," TheRANDBlog, November 24, 2020, https://www.rand.org/blog/2020/11/women -are-leaving-the-labor-force-in-record-numbers.html.

52. Claire Cain Miller, "What Women Lost," *New York Times*, May 23, 2021, BU1.

53. "US Minimum Wage Statistics & Facts," *Statista*, August 10, 2021, https ://www.statista.com/topics/5920/minimum-wage-in-the-united-states/.

54. Eli Rosenberg, "Workers Are Fired Up, But Union Participation Is Still on the Decline, New Statistics Show," *Washington Post*, January 23, 2020, www.washingtonpost .com/business/2020/01/22/workers-are-fired-up-union-participation-is-still-decline -new-statistics-show/; "The Union Advantage for Women," statusofwomendata.org /uploads/2015/08.

55. Aaron O'Neill, "Total Fertility Rate of United States, 1800-2020," February 17, 2021, https://www.statista.com/statistics/1033027/fertility-rate-us-1800-2020/.

56. Caitlin Gibson, "The Ride of the Only Child: How America Is Coming Around to the Idea of 'Just One,'" *Washington Post*, June 19, 2019, https://www.washingtonpost.com /lifestyle/on-parenting/the-rise-of-the-only-child-how-america-is-coming-around-to -the-idea-of-just-one/2019/06/19/b4f75480-8eb9-11e9-8f69-a2795fca3343_story.html; Gretchen Livingston, "Family Size Among Mothers," Pew Research Center, May 7, 2015, www.pewsocialtrends.org/2015/05/07/family-size-among-mothers.

57. David Brooks, "The Age of Possibility," *New York Times*, November 15, 2012.

58. Bill Chappell, "U.S. Births Fell to a 32-Year Low in 2018; CDC Says Birthrate Is in Record Slump," May 15, 2019, www.npr.org/2019/05/15/72351879/u-s-births -fell-to-a-32-year-low-in-2018-cdc-says-birthrate-is-at-record-level; Joe Pinsker, "We're Talking About More Than Half a Million People Missing from the U.S. Population," *The Atlantic Daily*, July 23, 2020, https://www.theatlantic.com/family /archive/2020/07/us-coronavirus-deaths-births-population/614503/; Peggy Noonan, "Social Distancing Was a Problem Before Covid," *Wall Street Journal*, November 27–28, 2021, A15.

59. Megan McCardle, "The Lasting Consequences of a Declining U.S. Birthrate," *Washington Post*, June 4, 2021, A21.

60. "U.S. Marriage Rates Hit New Recorded Low," U.S. Congress Joint Economic Committee Report, April 29, 2020, www.jec.senate.gov/public/index.cfm /republicans/2020/4/marriage-rate-blog-test.

61. Rebecca Lake, "What Is the Average Age of Marriage in the US?" *Brides*, https ://www.brides.com/what-is-the-average-age-of-marriage-in-the-u-s-4685727; Fernanda Santos, "I Didn't See the Insidious Ways Women Are Held Back, Until I Became a Widow," *Washington Post*, February 4, 2021, A19.

62. Jean Folger, "Keeping Your Name After Marriage," February 12, 2022, www
.investopedia.com/keeping-your-name-after-marriage-4687593.

63. Wendy Wang, "The U.S. Divorce Rate Has Hit 50-Year Low," *Institute for Family
Studies,* November 10, 2020, https://ifstudies.org/blog/the-us-divorce-rate-has-hit-a
-50-year-low; "Divorce Statistics: Over 115 Studies, Facts and Rates for 2018," www
.wf-lawyers.com/divorce-statistics-and-facts/.

64. Helena Andrews-Dyer, "You're Not Imagining It: This Is Why Celebrity Divorce
Announcements Have Gotten So Aggressively Nice," *Washington Post,* January 21,
2022, www.washingtonpost.com/arts-entertainment/2022/01/21/celebrity-divorces
-jason-momoa-lisa-bonet/.

65. Jo Craven McGinty, "Divorces Are Down, Unless You're 55 or Older," *Wall Street
Journal,* June 22–23, 2019, A2; Johnny Wood, "The United States Divorce Rare Is
Dropping, Thanks to Millennials," *World Economic Forum,* October 5, 2018.

66. Russell Berman, "Ruth Bader Ginsburg Versus the Equal Rights Amendment," *The
Atlantic,* February 15, 2020, www.theatlantic.com/politics/archive/2020/02
/ruth-bader-ginsburg-equal-rights-amendment/606556.

67. Julie C. Suk, "How the ERA Could Become Part of the Constitution," *Washington
Post,* January 26, 2020, B1; Patricia Sullivan, "Too Late To Ratify ERA, Justice
Dept. Says in Opinion," *Washington Post,* January 9, 2020; Glenn Kessler, "The ERA
and the Archivist of the United States: Anatomy of a False Claim," *Washington Post,*
February 13, 2022, A4.

68. Sheryl Gay Stolberg, "House Moves to Revive Equal Rights Amendment," *New York
Times,* February 14, 2020.

69. Denise Grady, "Anatomy Does Not Determine Gender, Experts Say," *New York
Times,* October 23, 2018.

70. German Lopez, "The House Passed a Sweeping LGBTQ Rights Bill," *Vox,* May 17,
2019, https://www.vox.com/policy-and-politics/2019/5/17/18627771/equality
-act-house-congress-lgbtq-rights-discrimination; Chris Cioffi, "These 8 Republicans
Voted for the Equality Act," May 17, 2019, www.rollcall.com/2019/05/17/these
-8-republicans-voted-for-the-equality-act/.

71. *Georgia* (2020), Oyez, www.oyez.org/cases/2019/17-1618; Monic Hesse, "Supreme
Court's LGBTQ Ruling Is an Ode to Aimee Stephens," *Washington Post,* June 7,
2020, C1.

72. Robert Barnes and Moriah Balingit, "Supreme Court Sustains Policy Backing
Transgender Students," *Washington Post,* May 29, 2019, A4.

73. Frank Bruni, "Trump the Troglodyte," *New York Times,* June 21, 2002, SR3; Adam
Liptak, "Supreme Court Revives Transgender Ban for Military Service," *New York
Times,* January 23, 2019, A1.

74. Samantha Schmidt, "1 in 6 Adults in Gen Z Identify as LGBTQ, Survey Finds,"
Washington Post, February 25, 2021, A3.

75. "Women in Elective Office 2020," https://cawp.rutgers.edu/women-elective
-office-2020; Antonio Olivo, "Race for Lieutenant Governor Will Make History in
Virginia," *Washington Post,* June 10, 2021, B1; Sergio Pecanha, "A 100-Year Journey:
Gender Equality in Politics," *Washington Post,* August 23, 2020, A23.

76. James M. Lindsay, "The 2020 Election Numbers," blog post, Council of Foreign
Relations, December 15, 2020, www.cfr.org/blog/2020-election-numbers.

77.   Carrie Elizabeth Blazina and Drew Desilver, "A Record Number of Women Are Serving in the 117th Congress," January 15, 2021, www.pewresearch.org/Gender -&-Leadership; "Women Serving in the 117th Congress 2021-22," www.cawp .rutgers.edu/list-women-currently-serving; Katherine Tully-McManus, "Record Number of House GOP Women Just One of Many 'Firsts' for 117th Congress," *Roll Call*, November 12, 2020, www.rollcall.com/2020/11/12/record-number-of -house-gop-women-just-one-of-many-firsts-for-117th-congress.

78.   Dante Chinni, "GOP Registration Drop After Capitol Attack Is Part of Larger Trend," *NBC News*, February 7, 2021, www.nbcnews.com/politics/meet-the-press /gop-registration-drop-after-capitol-attack-part-of-larger-trend-n1256966.

79.   Adele Logan Alexander, *Princess of the Hither Isles: A Black Suffragist's Story from the Jim Crow South* (New Haven: Yale University, 2019).

80.   Lois Scharf, "'The Forgotten Woman': Working Women, the New Deal and Women's Organizations," in *Decades of Discontent: The Women's Movement, 1920–1940*, Lois Scharf and Joan M. Jensen, eds. (Westport, CT: Greenwood Press, 1983), 243.

81.   Kim Brooks, "On Families: Feminism Has Failed Women," *New York Times*, December 27, 2020, SR5; "Letters: What Has Feminism Achieved?" *New York Times*, January 3, 2021, SR8.

82.   Peter Sokolowski, "Merriam-Webster's Word of the Year Is Feminism," interviewed by Rachel Martin, *Morning Edition*, December 25, 2017; Kristine Phillips, "Merriam-Webster's Word of the Year Largely Has Kellyanne Conway to Thank," *Washington Post*, December 12, 2017.

83.   Julie Lythcott-Haims, "Urgent Look at How Race, Class Divide Women," review of *Hood Feminism: Notes from Women that the Movement Forgot* by Mikki Kendall, *Washington Post*, April 14, 2020, C1.

84.   "Black Women and the Wage Gap," National Partnership for Women & Families, January 2021, https://www.nationalpartnership.org/our-work/resources/economic -justice/fair-pay/african-american-women-wage-gap.pdf.

85.   Juliana Menasce Horowitz, "A Century After Women Gained the Right to Vote, Majority of Americans See Work To Do on Gender Equality," *Pew Research Center*, July 7, 2020, www.pewsocialtrends.org/2020/07/07/a-century-after-women-gained.

86.   Hannah Natanson, "Jane Fonda's '70 Mug Shot Defined Feminist Rebellion for Years," *Washington Post*, November 27, 2019, B5; Cara Buckley, "Jane Fonda's Arresting Development," *New York Times*, November 4, 2019, C1.

87.   Anne Marie Chaker, "Barbie's Running for President, Too," *Wall Street Journal*, July 13, 2016; Amy B. Wang, "Walmart Pulls Cosmopolitan Magazine from Checkout Areas," *Washington Post*, March 29, 2018, C4; "As Natural Hair Goes Mainstream, One High School Hair Ban Sparks Firestorm," transcript, ABC News, September 15, 2016; Linda Holmes, "Amid Backlash, Hallmark Channel To 'Reinstate' Same-Sex Wedding Ad," *Morning Edition*, December 16, 2019.

88.   Lauren Collins, "Contested," review of *Looking for Miss America: A Pageant's 100-Year Quest to Define Womanhood* by Margot Mifflin, *New Yorker*, September 20, 2020, 72; Katharine Seelye, "Jo-Carroll Dennison, Oldest Surviving Former Miss America, Is Dead at 97," *New York Times*, October 31, 2021, A22.

89.   Kimberly A. Hamlin, "Why We Should Say Goodbye to the Miss America Pageant," *Washington Post*, December 19, 2019, www.washingtonpost.com

/outlook/2019/12/19/why-we-should-say-goodbye-miss-america-pageant/; Kathleen
Parker, "Queen Carlson Wins Again," *Washington Post,* January 3, 2018.

90. Emily Yahr, "'Miss America Can Be a Scientist:' Camille Schrier of Virginia Wins
After Onstage Chemistry Experiment," *Washington Post,* December 20, 2019.

91. Collins, 72–75; Laura M. Hilson, "Black Women Reign at Beauty Pageants," *New
York Times,* December 15, 2019; Tariro Mzezewa, "Wearing the Crown of Miss
Juneteenth," *New York Times,* June 17, 2021, D7.

92. "As Miss Navajo Nation, She Helped Her Community Through the Pandemic,"
Weekend Edition Sunday, October 10, 2021.

93. "Women's Suffrage Centennial Commission Agency Report, 2018-2020," http
://www.womensvote100.org/.

94. Kevin Merida, "A Vote Against Suffrage Statue," *Washington Post,* April 14, 1997,
www.washingtonpost.com/archive/politics/1997/04/14/a-vote-against-suffrage
-statue/00881928-0cbb-4723-a145-81f5771f4738/.

95. Alisha Haridasani Gupta, "For Three Suffragists, A Monument Well Past Due,"
New York Times, August 6, 2020, www.nytimes.com/2020/08/06/arts/design
/suffragist-19th-amendment-central-park-html.

96. Helen Stoilas, "Biden Inauguration Is Largely Virtual—But Some Live Art Is
Planned," *The Art Newspaper,* January 19, 2021, www.theartnewspaper
.com/2021/01/19/biden-inauguration-is-largely-virtualbut-some-live-art
-is-planned; "2021 Inauguration Plans," wtop.com/inauguration/2021/01
/faq-what-are-the-current-plans-for-the-2021-inauguration.

97. Chris Richards, "Our National Anthem End With a Question: Lady Gaga
Answered It the Best She Could," *Washington Post,* January 20, 2021, https
://www.washingtonpost.com/entertainment/music/lady-gaga-national-anthem
-inauguration/2021/01/20/a69088d8-5b51-11eb-a976-bad6431e03e2_story
.html; Vanessa Friedman, "Joe Biden and Kamala Harris Make Meaning the Hottest
Inaugural Fashion Trend," *New York Times,* January 20, 2021, www.nytimes.com
/2021/01/20/style/inaugural-fashion-kamala-harris-jill-biden.html; Michael Gold,
"Jennifer Lopez Sang Classic Tributes to America at the Inauguration," *New York
Times,* January 20, 2021, www.nytimes.com/2021/01/20/jennifer-lopez-inauguration
.html.

98. Claire Cain Miller, "'A Cabinet of Firsts': Momentous Yet Fragile," *New York Times,*
January 22, 2021, A12; Yonat Shimron, "If Confirmed by Senate, Biden's Picks
Bring Religious Diversity to Cabinet," *Washington Post,* January 23, 2021, B2.

99. Emilia Petrarca, "Bask in the Brilliance of Amanda Gorman," *The Cut,* January 20,
2021, www.thecut.com/2021/01/amanda-gorman-inauguration-poem-prada.html.

100. Alexander Alter, "Amanda Gorman Captures the Moment, In Verse," *New York
Times,* January 21, 2021, www.nytimes.com/2021/01/19/books/amanda-gorman-
inauguration-hill-we-climb.html; "Imagining How We 'Can Still Heal,' in Verse,"
New York Times, January 21, 2021, A22.

SELECTED BIBLIOGRAPHY

INTERVIEWS
Carol Burris
Flora Crater
Catherine East
Marian Wright Edelman
Patricia Goldman
Sheila Greenwald
Mariwyn Heath
Mildred Jeffrey
Edith Mayo
Jane Pierson
Phyllis Schlafly
Alice Tetelman

MANUSCRIPT COLLECTIONS
John F. Kennedy Presidential Library and Museum, Boston, MA
    Robert Kennedy Papers
Library of Congress Manuscript Collection, Washington, DC
    Anna Kelton Wiley Papers
    ERAmerica Papers
Library of Congress Prints and Photographs
Schlesinger Library, Radcliffe College, Cambridge, MA
    Katherine Ellickson Papers
    Esther Peterson Papers
Sophia Smith Collection, Smith College, Northampton, MA
    Equal Rights Amendment Campaign Archives
    Women's Rights Collection
Walter R. Reuther Library, Wayne State University, Detroit, MI

WEBSITES

National Park Service: nps.gov

National Women's History Museum: nwhm.org

Women and Social Movements in the United States: proquest.libguides.com/wass

SECONDARY SOURCES

Alexander, Adele Logan. *Princess of the Hither Isles: A Black Suffragist's Story in the Jim Crow South*. New Haven: Yale University Press, 2019.

Anderson, Carol. *One Person, No Vote: How Voter Suppression Is Destroying Our Democracy*. New York: Bloomsbury Publishing, 2019.

Anderson, Karen. *Wartime Women: Sex Roles, Family Relations, and the Status of Women During World War II*. Westport, CT: Greenwood Press, 1981.

Baker, Jean H. *Margaret Sanger: A Life of Passion*. New York: Hill and Wang, 2011.

Barber, Lucy G. *Marching on Washington: The Forging of An American Political Tradition*. Berkeley: University of California Press, 2002.

Becker, Susan D. *The Origins of the Equal Rights Amendment: American Feminism Between the Wars*. Westport, CT: Greenwood Press, 1981.

Bell, Janet Dewart. *Lighting the Fires of Freedom: African American Women in the Civil Rights Movement*. New York: The New Press, 2018.

Bell-Scott, Patricia. *The Firebrand and the First Lady: Portrait of a Friendship: Pauli Murray, Eleanor Roosevelt, and the Struggle for Social Justice*. New York: Alfred A. Knopf, 2016.

Berry, Mary Frances. *Why ERA Failed: Politics, Women's Rights, and the Amending Process of the Constitution*. Bloomington: Indiana University Press, 1986.

Bingham, Clara. *Witness to the Revolution: Radicals, Resisters, Vets, Hippies, and the Year America Lost Its Mind and Found Its Soul*. New York: Random House, 2016.

Blackwell, Maylei. *Chicana Power! Contested Histories of Feminism in the Chicano Movement*. Austin: University of Texas Press, 2011.

Blair, Melissa Estes. *Revolutionizing Expectations: Women's Organizations, Feminism, and American Politics, 1965-1980*. Athens: University of Georgia Press, 2014.

Blight, David W. *Frederick Douglass: Prophet of Freedom*. New York: Simon & Schuster, 2018.

Boggs, Lindy, with Katherine Hatch. *Washington Through a Purple Veil: Memoirs of a Southern Woman*. New York: Harcourt Brace & Co., 1994.

Brown, Dorothy M. *Setting a Course: American Women in the 1920s*. Boston: G.K. Hall & Co., 1987.

Cahill, Cathleen D. *Recasting the Vote: How Women of Color Transformed the Suffrage Movement*. Chapel Hill: University of North Carolina Press, 2020.

Carroll, Susan J., and Richard L. Fox. *Gender and Elections: Shaping the Future of American Politics*. 4th ed. New York: Cambridge University Press, 2018.

Chafe, William H. *The American Woman: Her Changing Social, Economic, and Political Role, 1920-1970*. New York: Oxford University Press, 1972.

———. *The Road to Equality: American Women Since 1962: An Era of Liberation*, Vol. 10 of *The Young Oxford History of Women in the United States*, Nancy F. Cott, ed. New York: Oxford University Press, 1994.

Charron, Katherine Mellen. *Freedom's Teacher: The Life of Septima Clark*. Chapel Hill: University of North Carolina Press, 2009.

Chesler, Ellen. *Woman of Valor: Margaret Sanger and the Birth Control Movement in America*. New York: Simon & Schuster, 1992.

Chozick, Amy. *Chasing Hillary: Ten Years, Two Presidential Campaigns, and One Intact Glass Ceiling.* New York: Harper Collins Publishers, 2018.

Clinton, Hillary Rodham. *Living History.* New York: Simon & Schuster, 2003.

———. *What Happened.* New York: Simon & Schuster, 2017.

Cobble, Dorothy Sue, Linda Gordon and Astrid Henry. *Feminism Unfinished: A Short, Surprising History of American Women's Movements.* New York: Liveright Publishing, 2014.

Collier-Thomas, Bettye, and V.P. Franklin, eds. *Sisters in the Struggle: African American Women in the Civil Rights-Black Power Movement.* New York: New York University Press, 2001.

Collins, Gail. *When Everything Changed: The Amazing Journey of American Women from 1960 to the Present.* New York: Little, Brown and Co., 2009.

Committee on House Administration of the U.S. House of Representatives. *Women in Congress, 1917–2006.* Washington, DC: U.S. Government Printing Office, 2006.

Cook, Blanche Wiesen. *Eleanor Roosevelt, 1884-1933.* Vol. 1. New York: Viking, 1992.

———. *Eleanor Roosevelt: 1933-1938.* Vol. 2. New York: Viking, 1999.

———. *Eleanor Roosevelt: The War Years and After, 1939-1962.* Vol. 3. New York: Viking, 2016.

Coontz, Stephanie. *A Strange Stirring: The Feminine Mystique and American Women at the Dawn of the 1960s.* New York: Basic Books, 2011.

———. *The Way We Never Were: American Families and the Nostalgia Trip.* New York: Basic Books, 1992.

Cooper, John Milton, Jr. *Woodrow Wilson: A Biography.* New York: Alfred A. Knopf, 2009.

Corder, J. Kevin, and Christina Wolbrecht. *Counting Women's Ballots: Female Voters from Suffrage through the New Deal.* New York: Cambridge University Press, 2016.

Critchlow, Donald T. *Phyllis Schlafly and Grassroots Conservatism: A Woman's Crusade.* Princeton: Princeton University Press, 2005.

Cushman, Clare, ed. *Supreme Court Decisions and Women's Rights: Milestones to Equality.* 2d ed. Washington, DC: CQ Press, 2011.

Darby, Seyward. *Sisters in Hate: American Women on the Front Lines of White Nationalism.* New York: Little Brown and Co./Hachette Book Group, 2020.

De Hart, Jane Sherron. *Ruth Bader Ginsburg: A Life.* New York: Alfred P. Knopf, 2018.

Deutsch, Sarah Jane. *From Ballots to Breadlines: American Women 1920-1940, From the Roaring Twenties to the Great Depression.* Vol. 8 of *The Young Oxford History of Women in the United States,* Nancy F. Cott, ed. New York: Oxford University Press, 1994.

Dodson, Angela P. *"Remember the Ladies": Celebrating Those Who Fought for Freedom at the Ballot Box.* New York: Center Street/Hachette Books, 2017.

Downey, Kirstin. *The Woman Behind the New Deal: The Life of Frances Perkins, FDR's Secretary of Labor and His Moral Conscience.* New York: Doubleday, 2009.

Duberman, Martin B. *Stonewall: The Definitive History of the LGBTQ Rights Uprising That Changed America.* Rev. ed. New York: Penguin Random House, 2019.

DuBois, Ellen Carol. *Suffrage: Women's Long Battle for the Vote.* New York: Simon & Schuster, 2020.

East, Catherine. *American Women: 1963, 1983, 2003.* Washington, DC: The National Federation of Business and Professional Women's Clubs, Inc., 1983.

Eig, Jonathan. *The Birth of the Pill: How Four Crusaders Reinvented Sex and Launched a Revolution.* New York: W.W. Norton & Co., 2014.

Eric-Udorie, June, ed. *Can We All Be Feminists? New Writing . . . on Intersectionality, Identity and the Way Forward for Feminism.* New York: Penguin Press, 2018.

Faderman, Lillian. *To Believe in Women: What Lesbians Have Done for America, A History.* Boston: Houghton Mifflin Co., 1999.

———. *The Gay Revolution: The Story of the Struggle.* New York: Simon & Schuster Paperbacks, 2015.

Fairclough, Adam. *To Redeem the Soul of America: The Southern Christian Leadership Council and Martin Luther King, Jr.* Athens: University of Georgia Press, 2001.

Farmer, Ashley D. *Remaking Black Power: How Black Women Transformed an Era.* Chapel Hill: University of North Carolina Press, 2017.

Feigen, Brenda. *Not One of the Boys: Living Life as a Feminist.* New York: Alfred A. Knopf, 2000.

Felder, Deborah G. *A Century of Women: The Most Influential Events in Twentieth Century Women's History.* Secaucus, NJ: Carol Publishing Co., 1999.

Felsenthal, Carol. *The Sweetheart of the Silent Majority: The Biography of Phyllis Schlafly.* New York: Doubleday and Co., 1981.

Fisher, Dana R. *American Resistance: From the Women's March to the Blue Wave.* New York: Columbia University Press, 2019.

Fitzpatrick, Ellen. *The Highest Glass Ceiling: Women's Quest for the American Presidency.* Cambridge: Harvard University Press, 2016.

Flexner, Eleanor. *Century of Struggle: The Woman's Rights Movement in the United States.* Rev. ed. Cambridge: Belknap Press of Harvard University Press, 1975.

Foerstel, Karen, and Herbert N. Foerstel. *Climbing the Hill: Gender Conflict in Congress.* Westport, CT: Praeger, 1996.

Forsythe, Clarke D. *Abuse of Discretion: The Inside Story of Roe v Wade.* New York: Encounter Books, 2013.

Fowler, Robert Booth. *Carrie Catt: Feminist Politician.* Boston: Northeastern University Press, 1986.

Frederickson, Caroline. *Under the Bus: How Working Women Are Being Run Over.* New York: New Press, 2015.

Freeman, Jo. *A Room at a Time: How Women Entered Party Politics.* Lanham, MD: Rowman & Littlefield Publishing, Inc., 2002.

———. *We Will Be Heard: Women's Struggles for Political Power in the United States.* Lanham, MD: Rowman & Littlefield Publishing, Inc., 2008.

Friedan, Betty. *The Feminine Mystique.* Rev. ed. New York: W.W. Norton & Co., 1963, 1997.

———. *The Second Stage.* New York: Summit Books, 1981.

Gardner, Michael R. *Harry Truman and Civil Rights: Moral Courage and Political Risks.* Carbondale: Southern Illinois University Press, 2002.

Gates, Henry Louis, Jr. *The Black Church: This Is Our Story, This Is Our Song.* New York: Penguin Press, 2021.

George, Emily. *Martha W. Griffiths.* Lanham, MD: University Press of America, 1982.

Gerber, Robin. *Barbie and Ruth: The Story of the World's Most Famous Doll and the Woman Who Created Her.* New York: HarperCollins, 20009.

Giddings, Paula J. *Ida: A Sword Among Lions: Ida B. Wells and the Campaign Against Lynching.* New York: Armistad/HarperCollins, 2008.

———. *When and Where I Enter: The Impact of Black Women on Race and Sex in America.* New York: William Morrow, 1984.

Gilmore, Glenda Elizabeth. *Gender and Jim Crow: Women and the Politics of White Supremacy in North Carolina, 1986-1920.* Chapel Hill: University of North Carolina Press, 1996.

Gitlin, Todd. *The Sixties: Years of Hope, Days of Rage.* Rev. ed. New York: Bantam, 1989.

Goldstein, Leslie Friedman. *The Constitutional Rights of Women: Cases in Law and Social Change.* Rev. ed. Madison: University of Wisconsin Press, 1988.

Gordon, Ann D., and Bettye Collier-Thomas, et al., eds. *African American Women and the Vote, 1837-1965.* Amherst: University of Massachusetts Press, 1997.

Gordon, Linda. *The Second Coming of the KKK: The Ku Klux Klan of the 1920s and the American Political Tradition.* New York: Liveright, 2017.

Greenhouse, Steven. *Beaten Down, Worked Up: The Past, Present and Future of American Labor.* New York: Alfred A. Knopf, 2019.

Griffith, Elisabeth. *In Her Own Right: The Life of Elizabeth Cady Stanton.* New York: Oxford University Press, 1984.

Griffith, R. Marie. *Moral Combat: How Sex Divided American Christians & Fractured American Politics.* New York: Basic Books, 2017.

Halberstam, David. *The Fifties.* New York: Villard/Random House, 1993.

Hall, Gloria T., Patricia Bell-Scott and Barbara Smith, eds. *All the Women Are White, All the Blacks Are Men, But Some of Us Are Brave.* New York: Feminist Press at CUNY, 1981.

Hall, Jacquelyn Dowd. *Revolt Against Chivalry: Jessie Daniel Ames and the Women's Campaign Against Lynching.* Rev. ed. New York: Columbia University Press, 1993.

Hamlin, Kimberly A. *Darwin, Science, and Women's Rights in Gilded Age America.* Chicago: University of Chicago Press, 2014.

Hanson, Joyce A. *Mary McLeod Bethune: Black Women's Political Activism.* Columbia: University of Missouri Press, 2013.

Hanson, Katherine, Vivian Guilfoy and Sarita Pillai. *More Than Title IX: How Equity in Education Has Shaped the Nation.* Lanham, MD: Rowman and Littlefield Publishers, Inc., 2009.

Harley, Sharon, and Rosalyn Terborg-Penn, eds. *The Afro-American Woman: Struggles and Images.* Baltimore, MD: Classic Black Press, 1978.

Harrison, Cynthia E. *On Account of Sex: The Politics of Women's Issues, 1945-1968.* Berkeley: University of California Press, 1988.

Hartmann, Susan M. *The Home Front and Beyond: American Women in the 1940s.* Boston: Twayne Publishers, 1982.

Harvey, Anna L. *Votes Without Leverage: Women in American Electoral Politics, 1920-1970.* Cambridge, UK: Cambridge University Press, 1998.

Heilbrun, Carolyn G. *The Education of a Woman: Gloria Steinem.* New York: Dial Press, 1995.

Hirshman, Linda R. *Get to Work: A Manifesto for Women of the World.* New York: Viking, 2006.

———. *Reckoning: The Epic Battle Against Sexual Abuse and Harassment.* New York: Houghton Mifflin Harcourt, 2019.

———. *Sisters in Law: How Sandra Day O'Connor and Ruth Bader Ginsburg Went to the Supreme Court and Changed the World.* New York: HarperCollins Publishers, 2015.

Hochschild, Arlie Russell, with Anne Macburg. *The Second Shift: Working Families and the Revolution at Home.* New York: Viking Penguin, Inc., 1989.

Hull, N.E.H., and Peter Charles Hoffer. *Roe v. Wade: The Abortion Rights Controversy in American History.* 2d. ed. rev. Lawrence: University Press of Kansas, 2010.

Jones, Martha S. *All Bound Up Together: The Woman Question in African American Public Culture, 1830- 1900.* Raleigh: University of North Carolina Press, 2007.

———. *Vanguard: How Black Women Broke Barriers, Won the Vote, and Insisted on Equality for All.* New York: BasicBooks, 2020.

Kabaservice, Geoffrey. *Rule and Run: The Downfall of Moderation and the Destruction of the Republican Party, from Eisenhower to the Tea Party.* New York: Oxford University Press, 2012.

Kantor, Jodi, and Megan Twohey. *She Said: Breaking the Sexual Harassment Story that Helped Ignite a Movement.* New York: Penguin Random House, 2019.

Kennedy, David M. *Freedom from Fear: The American People in Depression and War, 1929-1945.* New York: Oxford University Press, 1999.

———. *Over There: The First World War and American Society.* New York: Oxford University Press, 1979; 2004.

Kessler-Harris, Alice. *Women Have Always Worked: A Concise History.* 2d ed. Urbana: University of Illinois Press, 2018.

King, Mary. *Freedom Song: A Personal Story of the 1960s Civil Rights Movement.* New York: William Morrow & Co., 1987.

Klapper, Melissa R. *Ballots, Babies and Banners for Peace: American Jewish Activism, 1890-1940.* New York: New York University Press, 2013.

Kray, Christine L., Tamar W. Carroll and Hinda Mandell, eds. *Nasty Women and Bad Hombres: Gender and Race in the 2016 US Presidential Election.* Rochester, NY: University of Rochester Press, 2018.

Kristof, Nicholas, and Sheryl WuDunn. *Tightrope: Americans Reaching for Hope.* New York: Knopf, 2020.

Kruse, Kevin M., and Julian E. Zelizer. *Fault Lines: A History of the United States Since 1974.* New York: W.W. Norton & Co., 2019.

Lake, Celinda, and Kellyanne Conway with Catherine Whitney. *What Women Really Want.* New York: Free Press, 2005.

Lane, Ann J. *To Herland and Beyond: The Life and Work of Charlotte Perkins Gilman.* New York: Pantheon Books, 1990.

Lee, Chana Kai. *For Freedom's Sake: The Life of Fannie Lou Hamer.* Urbana: University of Illinois Press, 1999.

Lemert, Charles, and Esme Bhan. *The Voice of Anna Julia Cooper.* Lanham, MD: Rowman & Littlefield Publishers, Inc., 1998.

Lemons, J. Stanley. *The Woman Citizen: Social Feminism in the 1920s.* Urbana: University of Illinois Press, 1975.

Lepore, Jill. *The Secret History of Wonder Woman.* New York: Alfred A. Knopf, 2014.

———. *These Truths: A History of the United States.* New York: W.W. Norton & Co., 2018.

Levenstein, Lisa. *They Didn't See Us Coming: The Hidden History of Feminism in the Nineties.* New York: Hatchette/BasicBooks, 2020.

Lockman, Darcy. *All the Rage: Mothers, Fathers, and the Myth of Equal Partnership.* New York: HarperCollins Publishers, 2019.

Loevy, Robert D. *To End All Segregation: The Politics of the Passage of the Civil Rights Act of 1964.* Lanham, MD: University Press of America, 1990.

Lunardini, Christine A. *From Equal Suffrage to Equal Rights: Alice Paul and The National Woman's Party, 1910-1928.* New York: New York University Press, 1986.

Malcolm, Ellen R., with Craig Unger. *When Women Win: Emily's List and the Rise of Women in American Politics.* Boston: Houghton Mifflin Harcourt, 2016.

Marcus, Ruth. *Supreme Ambition: Brett Kavanagh and the Conservative Takeover.* New York: Simon & Schuster, 2019.

Margolick, David, and Hilton Als. *Strange Fruit: The Biography of a Song.* New York: Ecco Press Harper Collins Pub., 2001.

Marks, Susan. *Finding Betty Crocker: The Secret Life of America's First Lady of Food.* Minneapolis: University of Minnesota Press, 2005.

Matthews, Donald G., and Jane Sherron DeHart. *Sex, Gender, and the Politics of ERA: A State and A Nation.* New York: Oxford University Press, 1990.

May, Elaine Tyler. *Homeward Bound: American Families in the Cold War Era.* Rev. ed. New York: Basic Books, 2017.

———. *Pushing the Limits: American Women 1940-1961, From Rosie the Riveter to the Baby Boom and Beyond.* Vol. 9 of *The Young Oxford History of Women in the United States,* Nancy F. Cott, ed. New York: Oxford University Press, 1994.

Mayer, Jane, and Jill Abramson. *Strange Justice: The Selling of Clarence Thomas.* Boston: Houghton Mifflin Co., 1994.

McCabe, Katie, and Dovey Johnson Roundtree. *Justice Older Than the Law: The Life of Dovey Johnson Roundtree.* Jackson: University Press of Mississippi, 2009.

McCammon, Holly J., and Lee Ann Banaszak, eds. *100 Years of the Nineteenth Amendment: An Appraisal of Women's Political Activism.* New York: Oxford University Press, 2018.

McCorvey, Norma, with Andy Meisler. *I Am Roe: My Life, Roe v Wade, and Freedom of Choice.* New York: HarperCollins, 1994.

McMillen, Sally G. *Lucy Stone: An Unapologetic Life.* New York: Oxford University Press, 2015.

Meckler, Mark, and Jenny Beth Martin. *Tea Party Patriots: The Second American Revolution.* New York: Henry Holt & Co., 2012.

Melich, Tanya. *The Republican War Against Women: An Insider's Report from Behind the Lines.* New York: Bantam Books, 1996.

Mifflin, Margot. *Looking for Miss America: A Pageant's 100-Year Quest to Define Womanhood.* Berkeley, CA: Counterpoint, 2020.

Morrison, Toni, ed. *Race-ing Justice, En-gendering Power: Essays on Anita Hill, Clarence Thomas, and the Construction of Social Reality.* New York: Pantheon Books, 1992.

Muncy, Robyn. *Creating a Female Dominion in American Reform, 1890-1935.* New York: Oxford University Press, 1991.

Murray, Pauli. *Song in a Weary Throat: An American Pilgrimage.* New York: Harper & Row, 1987.

New York Times. *The Women of the 116th Congress: Portraits of Power.* New York: Abrams Image, 2019.

New York Times Editors. *The Roaring '20s: Flappers/Bootleggers/Gangsters/Suffragists.* New York: Meredith Corp., 2020.

Obama, Michelle. *Becoming.* New York: Crown, 2018.

O'Farrell, Brigid, and Joyce L. Kornbluh, eds. *Rocking the Boat: Union Women's Voices, 1915-1975.* New Brunswick, NJ: Rutgers University Press, 1996.

Okrent, Daniel. *The Guarded Gate: Bigotry, Eugenics and the Law That Kept Two Generations of Jews, Italians and Other European Immigrants Out of America.* New York: Scribner, 2019.

Olson, Lynne. *Freedom's Daughters: The Unsung Heroines of the Civil Rights Movement from 1830 to 1970.* New York: Scribner, 2001.

Painter, Nell Irwin. *Creating Black American: African-American History and Its Meanings, 1619 to the Present.* New York: Oxford University Press, 2006.

———. *The History of White People*. New York: W.W. Norton & Co., 2011.

Parker, Alison M. *Unceasing Militant: The Life of Mary Church Terrell*. Chapel Hill: University of North Carolina Press, 2020.

Paterson, Judith. *Be Somebody: A Biography of Marguerite Rawalt*. Austin, TX: Eakin Press, 1986.

Patterson, James T. *Grand Expectations: The United States, 1945-1974*. New York: Oxford University Press, 1996.

Phelps, Timothy M., and Helen Winternitz. *Capitol Games: Clarence Thomas, Anita Hill, and the Story of a Supreme Court Nomination*. New York: Hyperion, 1992.

Purdum, Todd S. *An Idea Whose Time Has Come: Two Presidents, Two Parties, and the Battle for the Civil Rights Act of 1964*. New York: Henry Holt and Co., 2014.

Randolph, Sherie M. *Florynce "Flo" Kennedy: The Life of a Black Feminist Radical*. Chapel Hill: University of North Carolina Press, 2015.

Ransby, Barbara. *Ella Baker and the Black Freedom Movement: A Radical Democratic Vision*. Chapel Hill: University of North Carolina Press, 2003.

———. *Making All Black Lives Matter: Reimagining Freedom in the 21st Century*. Oakland: University of California Press, 2018.

Roberts, Rebecca Boggs. *Suffragists in Washington, D.C.: The 1913 Parade and the Fight for the Vote*. Charleston, S.C.: The History Press, 2017.

Robinson, Jo Ann Gibson. *The Montgomery Bus Boycott and the Women Who Started It: The Memoir of Jo Ann Gibson Robinson*. Knoxville: University of Tennessee Press, 1987.

Rosen, Ruth. *The World Split Open: How the Modern Women's Movement Changed America*. New York: Viking, 2000.

Rosenberg, Rosalind. *Jane Crow: The Life of Pauli Murray*. New York: Oxford University Press, 2017.

Roth, Benita. *Separate Roads to Feminism: Black, Chicana, and White Feminist Movements in America's Second Wave*. New York: Cambridge University Press, 2004.

Rouse, Jacqueline Anne. *Lugenia Burns Hope: Black Social Reformer*. Athens: University of Georgia Press, 1992.

Ruiz, Vicki L. *Cannery Women, Cannery Lives: Mexican Women, Unionization, and the California Food Processing Industry, 1930-1950*. Albuquerque: University of New Mexico Press, 1987.

Rupp, Leila J., and Verta Taylor. *Survival in the Doldrums: The American Women's Rights Movement, 1945 to the 1960s*. New York: Oxford University Press, 1987.

Rymph, Catherine E. *Republican Women: Feminism and Conservatism from Suffrage Through the Rise of the New Right*. Chapel Hill: University of North Carolina Press, 2006.

Scharf, Lois, and Joan M. Jensen, eds. *Decades of Discontent: The Women's Movement, 1920-1940*. Westport, CT: Greenwood Press, 1983.

Schlafly, Phyllis. *The Power of the Positive Woman*. New York: Jove Publications, Inc., 1977.

Schulte, Brigid. *Overwhelmed: Work, Love, and Play When No One Has the Time*. New York: Farrar, Strauss and Giroux, 2014.

Scutts, Joanna. *The Extra Woman: How Marjorie Hillis Led a Generation of Women to Live Alone and Like It*. New York: Liveright Publishing, 2017.

Sklar, Kathryn Kish. *Florence Kelley & the Nation's Work: The Rise of Women's Political Culture, 1830-1900*. New Haven: Yale University Press, 1995.

Snyder, Rachel Louise. *No Visible Bruises: What We Don't Know About Domestic Violence Can Kill Us*. New York: Bloomsbury Publishers, 2019.

Spruill, Marjorie J. *Divided We Stand: The Battle Over Women's Rights and Family Values That Polarized American Politics*. New York: Bloomsbury, 2017.

Steinem, Gloria. *My Life on the Road.* New York: Random House, 2016.

Steiner, Leslie Morgan, ed. *Mommy Wars: Stay-at-Home and Career Moms Face Off on Their Choices, Their Lives, Their Families.* New York: Random House, 2006.

Swinth, Kirsten. *Feminism's Forgotten Fight: The Unfinished Struggle for Work and Family.* Cambridge: Harvard University Press, 2018.

Taranto, Stacie, and Leandra Zarnow, eds. *Suffrage at 100: Women in American Politics Since 1920.* Baltimore: Johns Hopkins University Press, 2020.

Terborg-Penn, Rosalyn. *African American Women in the Struggle for the Vote, 1850-1920.* Bloomington: University of Indiana Press, 1998.

Thomas, Evan. *FIRST: Sandra Day O'Connor.* New York: Random House, 2019.

Traister, Rebecca. *Big Girls Don't Cry: The Election that Changed Everything for American Women.* New York: Free Press/Simon & Schuster, 2010.

———. *Good and Mad: The Revolutionary Power of Women's Anger.* New York: Simon & Schuster, 2018.

Tufekci, Zeynep. *Twitter and Tear Gas: The Power and Fragility of Networked Protest.* New Haven: Yale University Press, 2017.

Tyson, Timothy B. *The Blood of Emmett Till.* New York: Simon & Schuster, 2017.

Valenti, Jessica. *Full Frontal Feminism: A Young Woman's Guide to Why Feminism Matters.* 2d. ed. Berkeley, CA: Seal Press, 2014.

Valk, Anne M. *Radical Sisters: Second-Wave Feminism and Black Liberation in Washington, DC.* Urbana: University of Illinois Press, 2008.

Van Voris, Jacqueline. *Carrie Chapman Catt: A Public Life.* New York: CUNY Feminist Press, 1987.

Walker-Williams, Marcia. *Reverend Addie Wyatt: Faith and the Fight for Labor, Gender, and Racial Equality.* Urbana: University of Illinois Press, 2016.

Ware, Susan. *American Women's Suffrage: Voices from the Long Struggle for the Vote, 1776-1965.* New York: Literary Classics of the United States, Inc., 2020.

———. *Beyond Suffrage: Women in the New Deal.* Cambridge: Harvard University Press, 1981.

———. *Partner and I: Molly Dewson, Feminism, and New Deal Politics.* New Haven: Yale University Press, 1987.

———. *Why They Marched: Untold Stories of the Women Who Fought for the Right to Vote.* Cambridge: Belknap/Harvard University Press, 2019.

Watts, Jill. *The Black Cabinet: The Untold Story of African Americans and Politics During the Age of Roosevelt.* New York: Grove Press, 2020..

Weber, Sandra. *The Woman Suffrage Statue: A History of Adelaide Johnson's "Portrait Monument" at the United States Capitol.* Jefferson, NC: McFarland & Co., Inc., 2016.

Weiss, Elaine F. *The Woman's Hour: The Great Fight to Win the Vote.* New York: Viking, 2018.

Weitekamp, Margaret A. *Right Stuff, Wrong Sex: America's First Women in Space Program.* Rev. ed. Baltimore: Johns Hopkins University Press, 2004.

Wheeler, Marjorie Spruill. *New Women of the New South: The Leaders of the Woman Suffrage Movement in the Southern States.* New York: Oxford University Press, 1993.

Wilkerson, Isabel. *The Warmth of Other Suns: The Epic Story of America's Great Migration.* New York: Random House, 2010.

Willenz, June A. *Women Veterans: America's Forgotten Heroines.* New York: Continuum, 1983.

Williams, Keira V. *Amazons in America: Matriarchs, Utopians, and Wonder Women in U.S. Popular Culture.* Baton Rouge: Louisiana University Press, 2019.

Winslow, Barbara. *Shirley Chisholm: Catalyst for Change*. Boulder, CO: Westview Press, 2014.

Yellin, Carol Lynn, and Janann Sherman. *The Perfect 36: Tennessee Delivers Woman Suffrage*. Oakridge, TN: The Iris Press, 1998.

Zahniser, J. D., and Amelia R. Fry. *Alice Paul: Claiming Power*. New York: Oxford University Press, 2014.

INDEX